MW00979454

不
以
文
害
辭,

不
以
辭
害
意,

以
意
逆
志,

是
爲
得
志.
之.

Mencius, V. Pt. I. iv. 2.

THE CHINESE CLASSICS VOLUME 1

Works of Chinese Classics Printed by
St. George Press:

Chinese Classics Volume 1: Confucius
Chinese Classics Volume 2: Mencius
Chinese Classics Volume 4: The Book
of Poetry Part 1 and 2

THE CHINESE CLASSICS VOLUME 2:

With

Translation, Critical and Exegetical Notes, Prolegomena, and Copious Indexes.

By James Legge, D.D.,

In Seven Volumes

Volume II.,

The Works of Mencius

St. George Press

ISBN:9798852656025

This St. George Press edition, published in 2023 is a full and faithful republication of second edition of 1893 Volume 2 "The Chinese Classics" Series

CONTENTS.

— ·· —

THE PROLEGOMENA.

CHAPTER I.

OF THE WORKS OF MENCIUS.

CHAPTER II.

MENCIUS AND HIS DISCIPLES.

CHAPTER III.

OF YANG CHÛ AND MO TÎ.

CHAPTER IV.

WORKS CONSULTED IN PREPARING THE VOLUME.

THE BODY OF THE VOLUME.

THE WORKS OF MENCIUS.

INDEXES.

PROLEGOMENA

CHAPTER I.

OF THE WORKS OF MENCIUS.

SECTION I.

1. In the third of the catalogues of Liû Hsin[1], containing a list of the Works of Scholars[2] which had been collected up to his time (about A.D. 1), and in the first subdivision, devoted to authors of the classical or orthodox School, we have the entry—'The Works of Mencius, in eleven Books[3].' At that date, therefore, Mencius's writings were known and registered as a part of the literature of China.

2. A hundred years before Hsin, we have the testimony of the historian Sze-mâ Ch'ien. In the seventy-fourth Book of his 'Historical Records,' there is a brief memoir of Mencius[4], where he says that the philosopher, having withdrawn into private life, 'along with the disciples of Wan Chang, prefaced the *Shih* and the *Shû*, unfolded the views of Confucius, and made "The Works of Mencius, in seven Books[5]."'

The discrepancy that appears between these testimonies, in regard to the number of the Books which went by the common name of Mencius, will be considered in the sequel. In the meanwhile it is shown that the writings of Mencius were recognised by scholars a hundred years before the Christian era, which takes us back to little more than a century and a half from the date assigned to his death.

---

[1] See vol. i. proleg. pp. 4, 5. [2] 諸子略. [3] 孟子十一篇. [4] 史記,
七十四, 列傳, 第十四. [5] 與萬章之徒, 序詩書, 述仲尼
之意, 作孟子七篇.

B

3. Among writers of the Han dynasty earlier than Sze-mâ Ch'ien, there were Han Ying[1] and Tung Chung-shû[2], contemporaries, in the reigns of the emperors Wăn, Ching, and Wû[3] (B.C. 179–87). Portions of their Works remain, and in them are found quotations from Mencius[4].

4. But we find references to Mencius and his Works anterior to the dynasty of Han. In the literary remains of K'ung Fû, to whose concealment of many of the classical Works on the issuing of the edict for their destruction posterity is so much indebted[5], there are accounts of Mencius, and many details of his history[6].

Between Mencius and the rise of the Ch'in dynasty flourished the philosopher Hsün Ch'ing[7], of whose writings enough is still preserved to form a large volume. By many he is regarded as the ablest of all the followers of Confucius. He several times makes mention of Mencius, and one of his most important chapters, 'That Human Nature is Evil[8], seems to have been written expressly against Mencius's doctrine of its goodness. He quotes his arguments, and endeavours to set them aside.

5. I have used the term *recognition* in the heading of this section, because the scholars of the Han dynasty do not seem to have had any trouble in forming or settling the text of Mencius such as we have seen they had with the Confucian Analects.

And here a statement made by Châo Ch'î, whose labours upon our philosopher I shall notice in the next section, deserves to be considered. He says :—'When Ch'in sought by its fires to destroy the Classical Books, and put the scholars to death in pits, there was an end of the School of Mencius. His Works, however, were included under the common name of "Philosophical," and so the tablets containing them escaped destruction[9].' Mâ Twan-lin does not hesitate to say that the statement is incorrect[10]; and it seems strange that Mencius should have been exempted from the sweep of a measure intended to extinguish the memory of the most ancient and illustrious

---

[1] 韓嬰. [2] 董仲舒. [3] 太宗孝文皇帝; 孝景皇帝; 世宗孝武皇帝. [4] See 四書拓餘說, 孟子, art. 1. and 焦孝廉 孟子正義, notes to Châo Ch'î's preface. [5] See vol. i. proleg. p. 36. [6] I have not been able to refer to the writings of K'ung Fû themselves, but extracts from them are given in the notes to Chû Hsî's preface to Mencius in the 四書經註集證. [7] 荀卿. [8] 荀子, 性惡篇. [9] 其書號爲諸子, 故篇籍得不泯絕; see Châo Ch'î's preface to Mencius. [10] 文獻通考, Bk. clxxxiv, upon Mencius.

sovereigns of China and of their principles. But the same thing is affirmed in regard to the writings of at least one other author of antiquity. the philosopher Yü[1]; and the frequent quotations of Mencius by Han Ying and Tung Chung-shû, indicating that his Works were a complete collection in their times, give some confirmation to Ch'î's account.

On the whole, the evidence seems rather to preponderate in its favour. Mencius did not obtain his place as 'a classic' till long after the time of the Ch'in dynasty ; and though the infuriate emperor would doubtless have given special orders to destroy his writings, if his attention had been called to them, we can easily conceive their being overlooked, and escaping with a mass of others which were not considered dangerous to the new rule.

6. Another statement of Châo Ch'î shows that the Works of Mencius, once recognised under the Han dynasty, were for a time at least kept with a watchful care. He says that, in the reign of the emperor Hsiâo-wăn (B.C. 178-155), 'the Lun-yü, the Hsiâo-ching, Mencius, and the R-yâ were all put under the care of a Board of "Great Scholars," which was subsequently done away with, only "The Five Ching" being left under such guardianship[2].' Chû Hsî has observed that the Books of the Han dynasty supply no evidence of such a Board ; but its existence may be inferred from a letter of Liû Hsin, complaining of the supineness with which the scholars seconded his quest for the scattered monuments of literature. He says :—'Under the emperor Hsiâo-wăn, the Shû-ching reappeared, and the Shih-ching began to sprout and bud afresh. Throughout the empire, a multitude of books were continually making their appearance, and among them the Records and Sayings of all the Philosophers, which likewise had their place assigned to them in the Courts of Learning, and a Board of Great Scholars appointed to their charge[3].'

As the Board of Great Scholars in charge of the Five Ching was instituted B.C. 135, we may suppose that the previous arrangement hardly lasted half a century. That it did exist for a time, however,

[1] 逢行珪註鬺子叙云,遭秦暴亂,書紀略盡,鬺子不與焚燒; see 焦孝廉孟子正義, notes on Châo Ch'î's preface. [2] 孝文皇帝欲廣遊學之路,論語,孝經,孟子,爾雅,皆置博士,後罷傳記博士,獨立五經而已. [3] See the 文獻通考, Bk. clxxiv. pp. 9, 10.

shows the value set upon the writings of Mencius, and confirms the point which I have sought to set forth in this section,—that there were Works of Mencius current in China before the Han dynasty, and which were eagerly recognised and cherished by the scholars under it, who had it in charge to collect the ancient literary productions of their country.

SECTION II.

CHÂO CH'Î AND HIS LABOURS UPON MENCIUS.

1. It has been shown that the Works of Mencius were sufficiently well known from nearly the beginning of the Han dynasty; but its more distinguished scholars do not seem to have devoted themselves to their study and elucidation. The Classics claimed their first attention. There was much labour to be done in collecting and collating the fragments of them, and to unfold their meaning was the chief duty of every one who thought himself equal to the task. Mencius was but one of the literati, a scholar like themselves. He could wait. We must come down to the second century of the Christian era to find the first commentary on his writings.

In the prolegomena to the Confucian Analects, Section i. 7, I have spoken of Chăng Hsüan or Chăng K'ang-ch'ăng, who died at the age of seventy-four, some time between A.D. 190–220, after having commented on every ancient classical book. It is said by some [1] that he embraced the Works of Mencius in his labours. If he did so, which to me is very doubtful, the result has not come down to posterity. To give to our philosopher such a treatment as he deserved, and compose a commentary that should descend to the latest posterity, was the work of Châo Ch'î, of whom we have a memoir in the fifty-fourth chapter of the Biographies in the Books of the second Han dynasty.

2. Ch'î was born A.D. 108. His father was a censor about the

---

[1] In the 'Books of the Sûi dynasty' (A.D. 589-617), Bk. xxxix, 經籍志, 二, we find that there were then in the national Repositories three Works on Mencius,—Châo Ch'î's, one by Chăng Hsüan, and one by Liû Hsî (劉熙), also a scholar of Han, but probably not earlier than Châo Ch'î. The same Works were existing under the T'ang dynasty (618-907);—see the 'Books of T'ang,' Bk. xlix, 藝文志, 三. By the rise of the Sung dynasty (A.D. 975 or 960), however, the two last were both lost. The entries in the Records of Sûi and T'ang would seem to prove that Chăng Hsüan had written on Mencius, but in the sketches of his life which I have consulted,—and that in the 'Books of the After Han dynasty,' 列傳第二十五, must be the basis of all the rest,—there is no mention made of his having done so.

court of the emperor Hsiâo-ân [1], and gave him the name of Chiâ, which he afterwards changed into Ch'î for the purpose of concealment, changing also his original designation of T'âi-ch'ing into Pin-ch'ing [2]. It was his boast that he could trace his descent from the ancient sovereign Chwan-hsü [3], B.C. 2510.

In his youth Ch'î was distinguished for his intelligence and diligent study of the Classics. He married a niece of the celebrated scholar and statesman Mâ Yung [4], but bore himself proudly towards him and her other relatives. A stern independence and hatred of the sycophancy of the times were from the first characteristic of him, and proved the source of many troubles.

When he was over thirty, Ch'î was attacked with some severe and lingering illness, in consequence of which he lay upon his bed for seven years. At one time, thinking he was near his end, he addressed a nephew who was with him in the following terms :—
'Born a man into the world, in retirement I have not displayed the principles exemplified on Mount Chî [5], nor in office achieved the merit of Î and Lü [6]. Heaven has not granted me such distinction. What more shall I say? Set up a round stone before my grave, and engrave on it the inscription,—" Here lies a recluse of Han, by surname Châo and by name Chiâ. He had the will, but not the opportunity. Such was his fate. Alas!"'

Contrary to expectation, Ch'î recovered, and in A.D. 154 we find him again engaged in public life, but in four years he is flying into obscurity under a feigned name, to escape the resentment of T'ang Hăng [7], one of the principal ministers, and his partisans. He saved his life, but his family and relatives fell victims to the vengeance of his enemies, and for some time he wandered about the country of the Chiang and Hwâi, or among the mountains and by the sea-coast on the north of the present Shan-tung. One day as he was selling cakes in a market-place, his noble presence attracted the attention of Sun Ch'ung [8], a young gentleman of Ân-ch'iû, who was passing by in a carriage, and to him on being questioned he made known his

---

[1] 孝安皇帝. [2] 趙歧, 字邠卿, 初名嘉, 字臺卿, 後避難, 故自改名字. [3] 顓頊. [4] 馬融. [5] 箕山之操. It was to Mount Chî that 巢父 and 許由, two ancient worthies, are said to have withdrawn, when Yâo wished to promote them to honour. [6] These are the well-known Î Yin (伊尹) and T'âi-kung Wang (太公望). [7] 唐衡. [8] 安邱, 孫崇. The name Ân-ch'iû still remains in the district so called of the department of Ch'ing-châu (青州)

history. This proved a fortunate rencontre for him. Sun Ch'ung
took him home, and kept him for several years concealed somewhere
'in the centre of a double wall [1].' And now it was that he solaced
his hard lot with literary studies. He wooed the muse in twenty-
three poetical compositions, which he called 'Songs of Adversity [2],'
and achieved his commentary on Mencius

On the fall of the T'ang faction, when a political amnesty was
proclaimed, Ch'î emerged from his friendly confinement, but only to
fall a victim again to the intrigues of the time. The first year of the
emperor Ling, A.D. 168, was the commencement of an imprisonment
which lasted more than ten years; but nothing could crush his
elasticity, or daunt his perseverance. In 185, when he had nearly
reached fourscore, he was active as ever in the field of political strife,
and wrought loyally to sustain the fortunes of the falling dynasty.
He died at last in A.D. 201, when he was over ninety, in Ching-châu,
whither he had gone on a mission in behalf of his imperial master.
Before his death he had a tomb prepared for himself, which
was long shown, or pretended to be shown, in what is now the
district city of Chiang-ling in the department of Ching-châu in
Hû-pei [3].

3. From the above account of Châo Ch'î, it will be seen that his
commentary on Mencius was prepared under great disadvantages.
That he, a fugitive and in such close hiding, should have been able
to produce a work such as it is, shows the extent of his reading and
acquirements in early days. I have said so much about him, because
his name should be added to the long roll of illustrious men who
have found comfort in sore adversity from the pursuits of literature
and philosophy. As to his mode of dealing with his subject, it will
be sufficient to give his own account:—

'I wished to set my mind on some literary work, by which I might
be assisted to the government of my thoughts, and forget the
approach of old age. But the six classics had all been explained
and carefully elucidated by previous scholars. Of all the orthodox
school there was only Mencius, wide and deep, minute and exquisite,
yet obscure at times and hard to see through, who seemed to me to
deserve to be properly ordered and digested. Upon this I brought
forth whatever I had learned, collected testimonies from the Classics

'復壁中.   '尾屯歌,二十三章.   '湖北,荊州府,
江陵縣.

and other books, and divided my author into chapters and sentences. My annotations are given along with the original text, and of every chapter I have separately indicated the scope. The Books I have divided into two Parts, the first and second, making in all fourteen sections.

'On the whole, with regard to my labour, I do not venture to think that it speaks the man of mark, but as a gift to the learner, it may dispel some doubts and resolve perplexities. It is not for me, however, to pronounce on its excellencies or defects. Let men of discernment who come after me observe its errors and omissions and correct them ;—that will be a good service[1].'

SECTION III.

OTHER COMMENTATORS.

1. All the commentaries on Mencius made prior to the Sung dynasty (A.D. 960[2]) having perished, excepting that of Châo Ch'î, I will not therefore make an attempt to enumerate them particularly. Only three names deserve to be mentioned, as frequent reference is made to them in Critical Introductions to our philosopher. They were all of the T'ang dynasty, extending, if we embrace in it what is called 'The After T'ang,' from A.D. 618 to 936. The first is that of Lû Shan-ching[3], who declined to adopt Châo Ch'î's division of the whole into fourteen sections or parts, and many of whose interpretations, differing from those of the older authority, have been received into the now standard commentary of Chû Hsî. The other two names are those of Chang Yî[4] and Ting Kung-chû[5], whose principal object was to determine the sounds and tones of characters about which there could be dispute. All that we know of their views is from the works of Sun Shih and Chû Hsî, who have many references to them in their notes.

2. During the Sung dynasty, the commentators on Mencius were a multitude, but it is only necessary that I speak of two.

The most distinguished scholar of the early reigns was Sun Shih[6], who is now generally alluded to by his posthumous or honorary epithet of 'The Illustrious Duke[7].' We find him high in favour and

---

[1] See the 孟子題辭.   [2] Some date the commencement of the Sung dynasty in A.D. 960.   [3] 陸善經.   [4] 張鎰.   [5] 丁公著.   [6] 孫奭.   [7] 宣公.

reputation in the time of T'âi-tsung (976–998), Chăn-tsung (998-1022), and Zăn-tsung (1023–1063)[1]. By imperial command, in association with several other officers, he prepared a work in two Parts, under the title of 'The Sounds and Meaning of Mencius,' and presented it to the court[2]. Occasion was taken from this for a strange imposture. In the edition of 'The Thirteen Ching,' Mencius always appears with 'The Commentary of Châo Ch'î' and 'The Correct Meaning of Shun Shih[3].' Under the Sung dynasty, what were called 'correct meanings' were made for most of the Classics. They are commentaries and annotations on the principal commentator who is considered as the expounder of the Classic, the author not hesitating, however, to indicate any peculiar views of his own. The genuineness of Shih's 'Correct Meaning of Mencius' is questioned by few, but there seems to be no doubt of its being really a forgery, at the same time that it contains the substance of the true work of 'The Illustrious Duke,' so far as that embraced the meaning of Mencius and of Châo Ch'î. The account of it given in the preface to 'An Examination of the Text in the Commentary and Annotations on Mencius,' by Yüan Yüan of the present dynasty, is—'Sun Shih himself made no "Correct Meaning;" but some one—I know not who—supposing that his Work was really of that character, and that there were many things in the commentary which were not explained, and passages also of an unsatisfactory nature, he transcribed the whole of Shih's Work on "The Sounds and Meaning," and having interpolated some words of his own, published it under the title of "The Annotations of Sun Shih." He was the same person who is styled by Chû Hsî "a scholar of Shâo-wû[4]."'

In the twelfth century Chû Hsî appeared upon the stage, and entered into the labours of all his predecessors. He published one Work separately upon Mencius[5], and two upon Mencius and the Confucian Analects[6]. The second of these, 'Collected Comments on the Analects and Mencius,' is now the standard authority on the

---

[1] 太宗,真宗,仁宗. [2] 孟子音義,二卷.—In or about the year 1008, a book was found, at one of the palace gates, with the title of 'The Book of Heaven' (天書). The emperor at first was inclined to go in state and accept it, but he thought of consulting Shih. Shih replied according to a sentiment of Mencius (V. Pt. I. v. 3) that 'Heaven does not speak,' and asked how then there could be any Book of Heaven. Was this Book of Heaven, thus rejected on Shih's counsel, a copy of our Sacred Scriptures, which some Nestorian Christian was endeavouring in the manner indicated to bring before the court of China? [3] 漢趙氏註,宋孫奭疏. [4] 阮云孟子註疏校勘記序. [5] 孟子指要. [6] 論孟集義; 論孟集註.

subject, and has been the test of orthodoxy and scholarship in the literary examinations since A. D. 1315.

3. Under the present dynasty two important contributions have been made to the study of Mencius. They are both published in the 'Explanations of the Classics under the Imperial Dynasty of Ch'ing[1].' The former, bearing the title of 'An Examination of the Text in the Commentary and Annotations of Mencius,' forms the sections from 1039 to 1054. It is by Yüan Yüan, the Governor-General under whose auspices that compilation was published. Its simple aim is to establish the true reading by a collation of the oldest and best manuscripts and editions, and of the remains of a series of stone tablets containing the text of Mencius, which were prepared in the reign of Kâo-tsung (A.D. 1128–1162), and are now existing in the Examination Hall of Hăng-châu. The second Work, which is still more important, is embraced in the sections 1117–1146. Its title is—'The Correct Meaning of Mencius, by Chiâo Hsün, a Chü-zăn of Chiang-tû[2].' It is intended to be such a Work as Sun Shih would-have produced, had he really made what has been so long current in the world under his name. I must regret that I was not earlier acquainted with it.

SECTION IV.

INTEGRITY; AUTHORSHIP; AND RECEPTION AMONG THE CLASSICAL BOOKS.

1. We have seen how the Works of Mencius were catalogued by Liû Hsin as being in 'eleven Books,' while a century earlier Sze-mâ Ch'ien referred to them as consisting only of 'seven.' The question has very much vexed Chinese scholars whether there ever really were four additional Books of Mencius which have been lost.

2. Châo Ch'î says in his preface :—'There likewise are four additional Books, entitled "A Discussion of the Goodness of Man's Nature," "An Explanation of Terms," "The Classic of Filial Piety," and "The Practice of Government." But neither breadth nor depth marks their composition. It is not like that of the seven acknowledged Books. It may be judged they are not really the production of Mencius, but have been palmed upon the world by some subsequent imitator of him[3].' As the four Books in question are lost, and only

[1] See vol. i. proleg. p. 133.   [2] 孟子正義, 江都焦孝廉循著.
[3] 又有外書四篇, 性善辯, 文說, 孝經, 爲政, 其文不能

a very few quotations from Mencius, that are not found in his Works which we have, can be fished up from ancient authors, our best plan is to acquiesce in the conclusion of Châo Ch'î. The specification of ' Seven Books ' by Sze-mâ Ch'ien is an important corroboration of it. In the two centuries preceding our era, we may conceive that the four Books whose titles are given by him were made and published under the name of Mencius, and Hsin would only do his duty in including them in his catalogue, unless their falsehood was generally acknowledged. Ch'î devoting himself to the study of our author, and satisfied from internal evidence that they were not his, only did his duty in rejecting them. There is no evidence that his decision was called in question by any scholar of the Han or the dynasties immediately following, when we may suppose that the Books were still in existence.

The author of ' Supplemental Observations on the Four Books[1],' says upon this subject :—' " It would be better to be without books than to give entire credit to them[2];"—this is the rule for reading ancient books laid down by Mencius himself, and the rule for us after-men in reading about what purport to be lost books of his The seven Books which we have " comprehend *the doctrine of* heaven and earth, examine and set forth ten thousand topics, discuss the subjects of benevolence and righteousness, reason and virtue, the nature *of man* and the decrees *of Heaven*, misery and happiness[3]." Brilliantly are these things treated of, in a way far beyond what any disciple of Kung-sun Ch'âu or Wan Chang could have attained to. What is the use of disputing about other matters? Ho Sheh has his " Expurgated Mencius[4]," but Mencius cannot be expurgated. Lin Chin-sze has his "Continuation of Mencius," but Mencius needs no continuation.   I venture to say—" *Besides the Seven Books there were no other Works of Mencius*." '

3. I have said, in the note at the end of this volume, that Châo Ch'î gives the total of the characters in Mencius as 34,685, while they are now found actually to amount to 35,226. This difference has been ingeniously accounted for by supposing that the continually recurring

宏深, 不與內篇相似, 似非孟子本眞, 後世依放而託
也.   [1] See vol. i. prolog. p. 131.   [2] Mencius, VII. Pt. II. iii.   [3] This is the language of Châo Ch'î.   [4] Ma Twan-lin mentions two authors who had taken in hand to expurgate Mencius, but neither of them is called 何涉. He mentions Lin Chin-sze. calling him Lin Shân-sze (林愼思), and his Work.

'Mencius' and 'Mencius said' were not in his copies. There would be no use for them on his view that the whole was composed by Mencius himself. If they were added subsequently, they would about make up the actual excess of the number of characters above his computation. The point is not one of importance, and I have touched on it simply because it leads us to the question of the *authorship* of the Works.

4. On this point Sze-mâ Ch'ien and Châo Ch'î are agreed. They say that Mencius composed the seven Books himself, and yet that he did so along with certain of his disciples. The words of the latter are:—'He withdrew from public life, collected and digested the conversations which he had had with his distinguished disciples, Kung-sun Ch'âu, Wan Chang, and others, on the difficulties and doubts which they had expressed, and also compiled himself his deliverances as *ex cathedrâ;*—and so published the seven Books of his writings.'

This view of the authorship seems to have been first called in question by Han Yü[1], commonly referred to as 'Han, the duke of Literature[2],' a famous scholar in the eighth and ninth centuries, under the Tang dynasty, who expressed himself in the following terms:— 'The Books of Mencius were not published by himself. After his death, his disciples, Wan Chang and Kung-sun Ch'âu, in communication with each other, recorded the words of Mencius[3].'

5. If we wish to adjudicate in the matter, we find that we have a difficult task in hand. One thing is plain—the book is not the work of many hands like the Confucian Analects. 'If we look at the style of the composition,' says Chû Hsî, 'it is as if the whole were melted together, and not composed by joining piece to piece[4].' This language is too strong, but there is a degree of truth and force in it. No principle of chronology guided the arrangement of the different parts, and a foreigner may be pardoned if now and then the 'pearls' seem to him 'at random strung;' yet the collection is characterised by a uniformity of style, and an endeavour in the separate Books to preserve a unity of matter. This consideration, however, is not

---

[1] 韓愈,字退之. [2] 韓文公. [3] 孟軻之書,非軻自著, 軻既沒,其徒萬章公孫丑,相與記軻所言焉耳; see note by Chû Hsî in his prefatory notice to Mencius. [4] 觀其筆勢,如鎔鑄而成, 非綴緝所就者; quoted in 四書拓餘說,孟子, art. I.

enough to decide the question. Such as the work is, we can conceive it proceeding either from Mencius himself, or from the labours of *a few of his disciples engaged on it in concert.*

The author of the 'Topography of the Four Books[1]' has this argument to show that the Works of Mencius are by Mencius himself:—'The Confucian Analects,' he says, 'were made by the disciples, and therefore they record minutely the appearance and manners of the sage. But the seven Books were made by Mencius himself, and therefore we have nothing in them excepting the words and public movements of the philosopher[2].' This peculiarity is certainly consonant with the hypothesis of Mencius's own authorship, and so far may dispose us to adopt it.

On the other hand, as the princes of Mencius's time to whom any reference is made are always mentioned by the honorary epithets conferred on them after their death, it is argued that those at least must have been introduced by his disciples. There are many passages, again, which savour more of a disciple or other narrator than of the philosopher himself. There is, for instance, the commencing sentences of Book III. Pt. I :—'When the duke Wăn of T'ăng was crown-prince, having to go to Ch'û, he went by way of Sung, and visited Mencius (lit. *the philosopher Măng*). Mencius discoursed to him how the nature of man is good, and when speaking, always made laudatory reference to Yâo and Shun. When the crown-prince was returning from Ch'û, he again visited Mencius. Mencius said to him " Prince, do you doubt my words ? The path is one, and only one."'

6. Perhaps the truth after all is as the thing is stated by Sze-mâ Ch'ien,—that Mencius, *along with some of his disciples,* compiled and composed the Work. It would be in their hands and under their guardianship after his death, and they may have made some slight alterations, to prepare it, as we should say, for the press. Yet allowing this, there is nothing to prevent us from accepting the sayings and doings as those of Mencius, guaranteed by himself.

7. It now only remains here that I refer to the reception of Mencius's Works among the Classics. We have seen how they were not admitted by Liû Hsin into his catalogue of classical works. Mencius

---

[1] See vol. i. proleg. p. 131.

[2] 論語成于門人之手,故記聖人容貌甚悉,七篇成于已手,故但記言語或出處; see 皇清經解, Sect. xxiv, at the end.

was then only one of the many scholars or philosophers of the orthodox school. The same classification obtains in the Books of the Sùi
and T'ang dynasties ; and in fact it was only under the dynasty of
Sung that the Works of Mencius and the Confucian Analects were
authoritatively ranked together. The first explicitly to proclaim
this honour as due to our philosopher was Ch'ǎn Chih-châi [1], whose
words are—'Since the time when Han, the duke of Literature,
delivered his eulogium, " Confucius handed *the scheme of doctrine* to
Mencius, on whose death the line of transmission was interrupted [2],"
the scholars of the empire have all associated Confucius and Mencius
together. The Books of Mencius are certainly superior to those of
Hsün and Yang, and others who have followed them. Their productions are not to be spoken of in the same day with his.' Chû
Hsî adopted the same estimate of Mencius, and by his 'Collected
Comments' on him and the Analects bound the two sages together
in a union which the government of China, in the several dynasties
which have succeeded, has with one temporary exception approved
and.confirmed.

[1] 陳直齋. The name and the account I take from the 'Supplemental Observations on the Four Books,' art. I, on Mencius. 直, I apprehend, is a misprint for 止, the
individual referred to being probably 陳傅良, a great scholar and officer of the twelfth
century, known also by the designations of 君擧 and 止齋.   [2] This eulogy of Han
Yü is to be found subjoined to the brief introduction in the common editions of Mencius. The
whole of the passage there quoted is :—' Yâo handed *the scheme of doctrine* down to Shun ; Shun
handed it to Yü ; Yü to T'ang ; T'ang to Wăn, Wû, and the duke of Châu ; Wăn. Wû, and the
duke of Châu to Confucius ; and Confucius to Mencius, on whose death there was no further
transmission of it. In Hsün and Yang there are snatches of it, but without a nice discrimination ; they talk about it, but without a definite particularity.'

CHAPTER II.

MENCIUS AND HIS DISCIPLES.

SECTION I.

LIFE OF MENCIUS.

1. The materials for a Memoir of Mencius are very scanty. The birth and principal incidents of Confucius's life are duly chronicled in the various annotated editions of the Ch'un Ch'iŭ, and in Sze-mâ Ch'ien. It is not so in the case of Mencius. Ch'ien's account of him is contained in half a dozen columns which are without a single date. That in the 'Cyclopædia of Surnames' only covers half a page. Châo Ch'í is more particular' in regard to the early years of his subject, but he is equally indefinite. Our chief informants are K'ung Fû, and Liû Hsiang in his 'Record of Noteworthy Women[1],' but what we find in them has more the character of legend than history.

Paucity and uncertainty of materials.

It is not till we come to the pages of Mencius himself that we are treading on any certain ground. They give the principal incidents of his public life, extending over about twenty-four years. We learn from them that in the course of that time he was in such and such places, and gave expression to such and such opinions; but where he went first and where he went last, it is next to impossible to determine. I have carefully examined three attempts, made by competent scholars of the present dynasty, to construct a Harmony that shall reconcile the statements of the 'Seven Books' with the current chronologies of the time, and do not see my way to adopt entirely the conclusions of any one of them[2]. The value of the Books lies in the record

---

[1] 劉向列女傳.

[2] The three attempts are—one by the author of 'Supplemental Observations on the Four Books,' an outline of which is given in his Notes on Mencius, art. III; one by the author of the 'Topography of the Four Books,' and forming the twenty-fourth section of the 'Explanations of the Classics under the Ch'ing Dynasty;' and one prefixed to the Works of Mencius, in 'The Four Books, with the Relish of the Radical Meaning' (vol. i. proleg. p. 130). These three critics display much ingenuity and research, but their conclusions are conflicting.—I may be pardoned in saying that their learned labours have affected me just as those of the Harmonisers of the Gospel Narratives used to do in former years,—bewildering more than edifying. Most cordially do I agree with Dean Alford (New Testament, vol. i. preleg. I. vii. 5):—'If the Evangelists have delivered to us truly and faithfully the Apostolic Narratives, and if the Apostles spoke as the Holy Spirit enabled them, and brought events and sayings to their recollection, then we may be sure that *if we knew the real process of the transactions*

which they furnish of Mencius's sentiments, and the lessons which these supply for the regulation of individual conduct and national policy. It is of little importance that we should be able to lay them down in the strict order of time.

With Mencius's withdrawal from public life, all traces of him disappear. All that is said of him is that he spent his later years along with his disciples in the preparation and publication of his Works.

From this paragraph it will be seen that there is not much to be said in this section. I shall relate, first, what is reported of the early years and training of our philosopher, and then look at him as he comes before us in his own pages, in the full maturity of his character and powers.

2. Mencius is the latinized form of Măng-tsze[1], 'The philosopher Măng.' His surname thus connects him with the Măng or Măng-sun

His surname; birth-place; parents; the year of his birth, B.C. 371.

family, one of the three great Houses of Lû, whose usurpations were such an offence to Confucius in his time. Their power was broken in the reign of duke Âi (B.C. 494-468), and they thenceforth dwindle into comparative insignificance. Some branches remained in obscurity in Lû, and others went forth to the neighbouring States.

The branch from which Mencius sprang found a home in the small adjacent principality of Tsâu[2], which in former times had been known by the name of Chû[3]. It was afterwards absorbed by Lû, and its name is said to be still retained in one of the districts of the department of Yen-châu in Shan-tung[4]. There I visited his temple in 1873, saw his image, and drank of a spring which supplied a well of bright, clear water close by. Confucius was a native of a district of Lû having the same name, which many contend was also the birthplace of Mencius, making him a native of Lû and not of the State of Tsâu. To my mind the evidence is decidedly against such a view[5].

themselves, that knowledge would enable us to give an account of the diversities of narration and arrangement which the Gospels now present to us. But without such knowledge, all attempts to accomplish this analysis in minute detail must be merely conjectural, and must tend to weaken the Evangelic testimony rather than to strengthen it.'

[1] 孟子. [2] 騶 (written also 鄒) 國. [3] 邾. [4] 山東, 兗州府, 鄒縣. [5] 閻若璩 and 曹之升 stoutly maintain the different sides of this question, the latter giving five arguments to show that the Tsâu of Mencius was the Tsâu of Lû. As Mencius went from Ch'î on the death of his mother to bury her in Lû (Bk. II. Pt. II. vii), this appears to prove that he was a native of that State. But the conclusion is not

Mencius's name was K'o[1]. His designation does not appear in his Works, nor is any given to him by Sze-mâ Ch'ien or Châo Ch'î. The latter says that he did not know how he had been styled; but the legends tell that he was called Tsze-chü[2], and Tsze-yü[3]. The same authorities—if we can call them such—say that his father's name was Chî[4], and that he was styled Kung-î[5]. They say also that his mother's maiden surname was Chang[6]. Nothing is related of the former but that he died when his son was quite young, but the latter must have a paragraph to herself. 'The mother of Mencius' is famous in China, and held up to the present time as a model of what a mother should be.

The year of Mencius's birth was probably the fourth of the sovereign Lieh, B.C. 372[7]. He lived to the age of 84, dying in the year B.C. 289, the 26th of the sovereign Nan[8], with whom terminated the long sovereignty of the Châu dynasty. The first twenty-three years of his life thus synchronized with the last twenty-three of Plato's. Aristotle, Zeno, Epicurus, Demosthenes, and other great men of the West, were also his contemporaries. When we place Mencius among them, he can look them in the face. He does not need to hide a diminished head.

3. It was his misfortune, according to Châo Ch'î, 'to lose his father at an early period[9]; but in his youthful years he enjoyed the lessons of his kind mother, who thrice changed her residence on his account.'

Mencius's mother.

necessary. Lû had been for several generations the State of his family, and on that account he might wish to inter his parent there, according to the custom of the Châu dynasty (see the Lî Chî, Bk. II. Sect. I. i. 27). The way in which Tsâu always appears as the residence of Mencius, when he is what we should say 'at home,' appears to me decisive of the question, though neither of the disputants presses it into his service. Compare Bk. III. Pt. I. ii ; Bk. VI. Pt. II. i and v. The point is really of no importance, for the States of Tsâu and Lû adjoined. 'The rattle of the watchman in the one was heard in the other.'

[1] 軻. [2] 子車 and 子居, the one character taking the place of the other from the similarity of the sound. [3] 子輿. [4] 激. [5] 公宜. I find 宜 sometimes instead of 宜. [6] 仉氏. [7] 烈王,四年,己酉. [8] 赧王二十六年,壬申.—The 'Genealogical Register of the Mäng Family' says that Mencius was born in the year 己酉, the 37th of the sovereign Ting (定), on the 2nd day of the 4th month, and died in the year 壬申, the 26th of the sovereign Nan, on the 15th day of the 1st month. (See 四書拓餘說,孟子, art. III.) The last of these dates is to be embraced on many grounds, but the first is evidently a mistake. Ting only reigned 28 years, and there is no 己酉 year among them. Reckoning back 84 years from the 26th of Nan, we come to a 己酉 year, the 4th of Lieh, which is now generally acquiesced in as the year of Mencius's birth. [9] Ch'î's words are—夙喪其父. The legend-writers are more

At first they lived near a cemetery, and Mencius amused himself with acting the various scenes which he witnessed at the tombs. 'This,' said the lady, 'is no place for my son;'—and she removed to a house in the market-place. But the change was no improvement. The boy took to playing the part of a salesman, vaunting his wares, and chaffering with customers. His mother sought a new house, and found one at last close by a public school. There her child's attention was taken with the various exercises of politeness which the scholars were taught, and he endeavoured to imitate them. The mother was satisfied. 'This,' she said, 'is the proper place for my son.'

Han Ying relates another story of this period. Near their house was a pig-butcher's. One day Mencius asked his mother what they were killing the pigs for, and was told that it was to feed him. Her conscience immediately reproved her for the answer. She said to herself, 'While I was carrying this boy in my womb, I would not sit down if the mat was not placed square, and I ate no meat which was not cut properly;—so I taught him when he was yet unborn[1]. And now when his intelligence is opening, I am deceiving him;—this is to teach him untruthfulness!' With this she went and bought a piece of pork in order to make good her words.

As Mencius grew up, he was sent to school. When he returned home one day, his mother looked up from the web which she was weaving, and asked him how far he had got on. He answered her with an air of indifference that he was doing well enough, on which she took a knife and cut through the thread of her shuttle. The idler was alarmed, and asked what she meant, when she gave him a long lecture, showing that she had done what he was doing,—that her cutting through her thread was like his neglecting his learning. The admonition, it is said, had its proper effect; the lecture did not need to be repeated.

There are two other narratives in which Chang-shih figures, and though they belong to a later part of Mencius's life, it may be as well to embrace them in the present paragraph.

His wife was squatting down one day in her own room, when

precise, and say that Mencius was only three years old when his father died. This statement, and Ch'î's as well, are difficult to reconcile with what we read in Bk. I. Pt. II. xvi, about the style in which Mencius buried his parents. If we accept the legend, we are reduced there to great straits.

[1] See Chû Hsî's 小學 內篇, 立教, 第一, which begins with the educational duties of the mother, while the child is yet unborn.

Mencius went in.   He was so much offended at finding her in that position, that he told his mother, and expressed his intention to put her away, because of 'her want of propriety.'   'It is you who have no propriety,' said his mother, 'and not your wife.   Do not "The Rules of Propriety" say, "When you are about to ascend a hall, raise your voice; when you enter a door, keep your eyes low?"   The reason of the rules is that people may not be taken unprepared; but you entered the door of your private apartment without raising your voice, and so caused your wife to be caught squatting on the ground The impropriety is with you and not with her.'   On this Mencius fell to reproving himself, and did not dare to put away his wife.

One day, when he was living with his mother in Ch'î, she was struck with the sorrowfulness of his aspect as he stood leaning against a pillar, and asked him the cause of it.   He replied, 'I have heard that the superior man occupies the place for which he is adapted, accepting no reward to which he does not feel entitled, and not covetous of honour and emolument.   Now my doctrines are not practised in Ch'î:—I wish to leave it, but I think of your old age, and am anxious.'   His mother said, 'It does not belong to a woman to determine anything of herself, but she is subject to the rule of the three obediences.   When young, she has to obey her parents; when married, she has to obey her husband; when a widow, she has to obey her son.   You are a man in your full maturity, and I am old. Do you act as your conviction of righteousness tells you you ought to do, and I will act according to the rule which belongs to me.   Why should you be anxious about me?'

Such are the accounts which I have found of the mother of Mencius.   Possibly some of them are inventions, but they are devoutly believed by the people of China;—and it must be to their profit. *We* may well believe that she was a woman of very superior character, and that her son's subsequent distinction was in a great degree owing to her influence and training[1].

4. From parents we advance to be under tutors and governors. The moulding hand that has wrought upon us in the pliant years of

Mencius's in-structors; and early life.

youth always leaves ineffaceable traces upon the character.   Can anything be ascertained of the in-structor or instructors of Mencius?   The reply to this inquiry must be substantially in the negative, though many

---

[1] All these stories are given in the notes to the preface to Mencius in the 四書經註集證.

have affirmed that he sat as a pupil at the feet of Tsze-sze, the grandson of Confucius. We are told this by Châo Ch'î, whose words are :—'As he grew up, he studied under Tsze-sze, acquired all the knowledge taught by "The Learned," and became thoroughly acquainted with "The Five Ching," being more especially distinguished for his mastery of the *Shih* and the *Shû*[1].' A reference to dates, however, shows that this must be incorrect. From the death of Confucius to the birth of Mencius there were 108 years, and supposing—what is by no means probable—that Tsze-sze was born in the year his father died, he must have been 112 years old when Mencius was born. The supposition of their having stood to each other in the relation of master and scholar is inconsistent, moreover, with the style in which Mencius refers to Tsze-sze. He mentions him six or seven times, showing an intimate acquaintance with his history, but never once in a manner which indicates that he had personal intercourse with him [2].

Sze-mâ Ch'ien's account is that 'Mencius studied under the disciples of Tsze-sze[3].' This may have been the case. There is nothing on the score of time to make it impossible, or even improbable ; but this is all that can be said about it. No famous names out of the school of Tsze-sze have been transmitted to posterity, and Mencius nowhere speaks as if he felt under special obligation to any instructor.

One short sentence contains all that he has said bearing on the point before us :—'Although I could not be a disciple of Confucius myself, I have endeavoured to cultivate *my character and knowledge* by means of others *who were*[4].' The chapter to which this belongs is rather enigmatical. The other member of it says :—'The influence of a sovereign sage terminates with the fifth generation. The influence of an unsceptred sage does the same.' By 'an unsceptred sage' Mencius is understood to mean Confucius ; and by extending his influence all over five generations, he shows how it was possible for him to place himself under it by means of others who had been in direct communication with the Master.

We must leave the subject of Mencius's early instructors in the obscurity which rests upon it. The first forty years of his life are

[1] 長師孔子之孫子思, 治儒術之道, 通五經, 尤長於詩書.   [2] See the Index of Proper Names.   [3] 受業子思之門人.
[4] See Book IV. Pt. II. xxii.

little more than a blank to us. Many of them, we may be sure, were spent in diligent study. He made himself familiar during them with all the literature of his country. Its classics, its histories, its great men, had received his careful attention. Confucius especially became to him the chief of mortal men, the object of his untiring admiration; and in his principles and doctrines he recognised the truth for want of an appreciation of which the bonds of society all round him were being relaxed, and the kingdom hastening to a general anarchy.

How he supported himself in Tsâu, we cannot tell. Perhaps he was possessed of some patrimony; but when he first comes forth from his native State, we find him accompanied by his most eminent disciples. He probably imitated Confucius by assuming the office of a teacher,—not that of a schoolmaster in our acceptation of the word, but that of a professor of morals and learning, encouraging the resort of inquiring minds, in order to resolve their doubts and inform them on the true principles of virtue and society. These disciples would minister to his wants, though we may presume that he sternly maintained his dignity among them, as he afterwards did towards the princes of the time, when he appeared among them as a *lecturer* in another sense of the term. Two instances of this are recorded, though we cannot be sure that they belonged to the earlier period of his life.

'When Kăng of T'ăng made his appearance in your school,' said the disciple Kung-tû, 'it seemed proper that a polite consideration should be paid to him, and yet you did not answer him;—why was that?' Mencius replied, 'I do not answer him who questions me presuming on his ability, nor him who presumes on his talents, nor him who presumes on his age, nor him who presumes on services performed to me, nor him who presumes on old acquaintance. Two of those things were chargeable on Kăng of T'ăng[1].'

The other instance is that of Chiâo of Ts'âo, who said to Mencius, 'I shall be having an interview with the prince of Tsâu, and can ask him to let me have a house to lodge in. I wish to remain here, and receive instruction at your gate.' 'The way of truth,' replied the philosopher, 'is like a great road. It is not difficult to know it. The evil is only that men will not seek it. Do you go home

---

[1] See Bk. VII. Pt. I. xliii.

and search for it, and you will have abundance of teachers[1].' This was firmly said, yet not unkindly. It agrees with his observation:— 'There are many arts in teaching. I refuse, as inconsistent with my character, to teach a man, but I am only thereby still teaching him[2].'

5. The state of China had waxed worse and worse during the interval that elapsed between Confucius and Mencius. The elements

State of China in Mencius's time. of disorganization which were rife in the times of the earlier sage had gone on to produce their natural results. One feeble sovereign had followed another on the throne, and the dynasty of Châu was ready to vanish away. Men were persuaded of its approaching extinction. The feeling of loyalty to it was no longer a cherished sentiment; and the anxiety and expectation was about what new rule would take its place.

Many of the smaller fiefs or principalities had been reduced to a helpless dependence on, or been absorbed by, the larger ones. Of Lû, Chǎng, Wei, Wû, Ch'ǎn, and Sung[3], conspicuous in the Analects, we read but little in Mencius. Tsin[4] had been dismembered, and its fragments formed the nuclei of three new and vigorous kingdoms, —Wei, Châo, and Han[5]. Ch'î still maintained its ground, but was barely able to make head against the State of Ch'in[6] in the West, and Ch'û in the South[7]. The struggle for supremacy was between these two; the former, as it was ultimately successful, being the more ambitious and incessant in its aggressions on its neighbours.

The princes were thus at constant warfare with one another. Now two or more would form a league to resist the encroaching Ch'in, and hardly would that object be accomplished before they were at war among themselves. Ambitious statesmen were continually inflaming their quarrels. The recluses of Confucius's days, who withdrew in disgust from the world and its turmoil, had given place to a class of men who came forth from their retirements provided with arts of war or schemes of policy which they recommended to the contending chiefs. They made no scruple of changing their allegiance, as they were moved by whim or interest. Kung-sun Yen and Chang Î may be mentioned as specimens of those characters. 'Are they not really great men?' it was once asked of Mencius.

---

[1] Bk. VI. Pt. II. ii. 6.　　[2] Bk. VI. Pt. II. xvi.　　[3] 魯, 鄭, 衞, 吳, 陳, 宋.
[4] 晉.　　[5] 魏, 趙, 韓.　　[6] 秦.　　[7] 楚.

'Let them once be angry, and all the princes are afraid. Let them live quietly, and the flames of trouble are extinguished throughout the kingdom[1].'

It is not wonderful that in such times the minds of men should have doubted of the soundness of the ancient principles of the acknowledged sages of the nation. Doctrines, strange and portentous in the view of Mencius, were openly professed. The authority of Confucius was disowned. The foundations of government were overthrown; the foundations of truth were assailed. Two or three paragraphs from our philosopher will verify and illustrate this representation of the character of his times:—

'A host marches *in attendance on the ruler*, and stores of provisions are consumed. The hungry are deprived of their food, and there is no rest for those who are called to toil. Maledictions are uttered by one to another with eyes askance, and the people proceed to the commission of wickedness. Thus the royal ordinances are violated, and the people are oppressed, and the supplies of food and drink flow away like water. The rulers yield themselves to the *bad* current, or they urge their *evil* way *against a good one;* they are wild; they are utterly lost[2].'

'The five chiefs of the princes were sinners against the three kings. The princes of the present day are sinners against the five chiefs. The great officers of the present day are sinners against the princes. . . . The crime of him who connives at and aids the wickedness of his prince is small, but the crime of him who anticipates and excites that wickedness is great. The officers of the present day all go to meet their sovereigns' wickedness, and therefore I say that they are sinners against them[3].'

'Sage sovereigns cease to arise, and the princes of the States give the reins to their lusts. Unemployed scholars indulge in unreasonable discussions. The words of Yang Chû and Mo Tî fill the kingdom. If you listen to people's discourses, you will find that they have adopted the views either of Yang or of Mo. *Now,* Yang's principle is—"each one for himself," which does not acknowledge *the claims of* the sovereign. Mo's principle is—"to love all equally," which does not acknowledge *the peculiar affection due to* a father. But to acknowledge neither king nor father is to be in the state of a beast. Kung-ming Î said, "In their kitchens there is fat meat. In their

---

[1] Bk. III. Pt. II. i.   [2] Bk. I. Pt. II. iv. 6. 8.   [3] Bk. VII. Pt. II. vii. 1, 4.

stables there are fat horses. But their people have the look of
hunger, and on the wilds there are those who have died of famine.
This is leading on beasts to devour men." If the principles of Yang
and Mo are not stopped, and the principles of Confucius not set
forth, those perverse speakings will delude the people and stop up
the path of benevolence and righteousness. When benevolence and
righteousness are stopped up, beasts will be led on to devour men,
and men will devour one another [1].'

6. It is in Ch'í that we first meet with Mencius as a counsellor of
the princes [2], and it was in this State that he spent much the greater

Mencius the first time in Ch'í; some time between B.C. 332 and 323. part of his public life. His residence in it, however,
appears to have been divided into two portions, and
we know not to which of them to refer many of the
chapters which describe his intercourse with the
prince (or king, as he claimed to be) and his ministers ; but, as
I have already observed, this is to us of little moment. Our interest
is in what he did and said. It matters little that we cannot assign
to each saying and doing its particular date.

That he left Ch'í the first time before B. C. 323 is plausibly inferred
from Bk. II. Pt. II. xiv. 3 [3]; and assuming that the conversation in
the same Book, Pt. I. ii, took place immediately before or after his
arrival [4], we can determine that he did not enter the State before B. C.
331, for he speaks of himself as having attained at forty years of age
to 'an unperturbed mind.' The two chapters contain the most
remarkable expressions indicative of Mencius's estimate of himself.
In the first, while he glorifies Confucius as far before all other men
who had ever lived, he declines having comparisons drawn between
himself and any of the sage's most distinguished disciples. In the

---

[1] Bk. III. Pt. II. ix. 9.   [2] In the 'Annals of the Nation' (vol. i. proleg. p. 134),
Mencius's visit to king Hûi of Liang is set down as having occurred in B.C. 335, and under
B.C. 318 it is said—'Mencius goes from Liang to Ch'í.' The visit to Liang is placed too early,
and that to Ch'í too late. The disasters of king Hûi, mentioned in Bk. I. Pt. I. v. 1, had not
all taken place in B.C. 318 ; and if Mencius remained seventeen years in Liang, it is strange
we have only five conversations between him and king Hûi. So far from his not going to
Ch'í till B.C. 318, it will be seen from the next note that he was leaving Ch'í before B.C. 323.
[3] Mencius's words are—'From the commencement of the Châu dynasty till now more than
700 years have elapsed.' It was to the purpose of his argument to make the time appear as
long as possible. Had 800 years elapsed, he would surely have said so. But as the Châu
dynasty commenced in B.C. 1121, the year B.C. 322 would be its 800th anniversary, and
Mencius's departure from Ch'í did not take place later than the year before B.C. 323.
[4] This chapter and the one before it have very much the appearance of having taken place on
the way from Tsâu to Ch'í. Mencius has been invited to a powerful court. He is emerging
from his obscurity. His disciples expect great things for him. Kung-sun Ch'âu sees him
invested with the government of Ch'í. and in the elation of his heart makes his inquiries.

second, when going away sorrowful because he had not wrought the good which he desired, he observes:—'Heaven does not yet wish that the kingdom should enjoy tranquillity and good order. If it wished this, who is there besides me to bring it about?'

We may be certain that Mencius did not go to Ch'î uninvited. His approach was waited for with curious expectation, and the king, spoken of always by his honorary epithet of Hsüan, 'The Illustrious,' sent persons to spy out whether he was like other men[1]. They had their first interview at a place called Ch'ung, which was so little satisfactory to the philosopher that he resolved to make only a short stay in the State. Circumstances occurred to change this resolution, but though he remained, and even accepted office, yet it was only honorary;—he declined receiving any salary[2].

From Ch'ung he appears to have retired to P'ing-lû, where Ch'û, the prime minister, sent him a present, wishing, no doubt, to get into his good graces. I call attention to the circumstance, though trifling in itself, because it illustrates the way in which Mencius carried himself to the great men. He took the gift, but subsequently, when he went to the capital, he did not visit the minister to acknowledge it. His opinion was that Ch'û might have come in person to P'ing-lû to see him. 'There was a gift, but no corresponding respect[3].'

With the governor of P'ing-lû, called K'ung Chü-hsin, Mencius spoke freely, and found him a man open to conviction. 'If one of your spearmen,' said Mencius to him, 'were to lose his place in the ranks three times in one day, would you put him to death or not?' 'I would not wait for three times to do so,' replied Chü-hsin. Mencius then charged home upon him the sufferings of the people, saying they were equivalent to his losing his place in the ranks. The governor defended himself on the ground that those sufferings were a consequence of the general policy of the State. To this the other replied, 'Here is a man who receives charge of the sheep and cattle of another, undertaking to feed them for him;—of course he must search for pasture-ground and grass. If, after searching for those, he cannot find them, will he return his charge to the owner? or will he stand by and see them die?' The governor's reply was, 'Herein I am guilty[4].'

When Mencius presented himself at the capital of the State, he

[1] Bk. IV. Pt. II. xxxii.   [2] Bk. II. Pt. II. xiv   [3] Bk. II. Pt. II. v.   [4] Bk. II. Pt. II. iv.

was honourably received by the king. Many of the conversations with the sovereign and officers which are scattered through the seven Books, though the first and second are richest in them, must be referred to this period. The one which is first in place[1], and which contains the fullest exposition of the philosopher's views on government, was probably first likewise in time[2]. It sets forth the grand essential to the exercise of royal government,—a heart on the part of the sovereign impatient of the sufferings of the people, and eager to protect them and make them happy; it brings home to king Hsüan the conviction that he was not without such a heart, and presses on him the truth that his not exercising it was from a want of will and not from any lack of ability; it exposes unsparingly the errors of the course he was pursuing; and concludes by an exhibition of the outlines and happy issues of a true royal sway.

Of this nature were all Mencius's communications with the sovereign; but he lays himself open in one thing to severe censure. Afraid apparently of repelling the prince from him by the severity of his lessons, he tries to lead him on by his very passions. 'I am fond of beauty,' says the king, 'and that is in the way of my attaining to the royal government which you celebrate.' 'Not at all,' replies the philosopher. 'Gratify yourself, only do not let your doing so interfere with the people's getting similar enjoyment for themselves[3].' So the love of money, the love of war, and the love of music are dealt with. Mencius thought that if he could only get the good of the people to be recognised by Hsüan as the great aim which he was to pursue, his tone of mind would be so elevated, that the selfish passions and gratifications of which he was the slave would be purified or altogether displaced. And so it would have been. Where he fails, is in putting his points as if benevolence and selfishness, covetousness and generosity might exist together. Chinese moralists rightly find fault with him in this respect, and say that Confucius never condescended to such a style of argument.

Notwithstanding the apparent cordiality of the king's reception of him, and the freedom with which Mencius spoke his mind at their interviews, a certain suspiciousness appears to have been maintained between them. Neither of them would bend to the other.

[1] Bk. I. Pt. I. vii.   [2] I judge that this was the first set conversation between king Hsüan and Mencius, because of the inquiry with which the king opens it,—'May I be informed by you of the transactions of Hwan of Ch'î, and Wǎn of Tsin?' A very brief acquaintance with our philosopher would have taught him that he was the last person to apply to about those characters.   [3] Bk. I. Pt. II. i. iii. v; et al.

Mencius would not bow to the royal state; Hsüan would not vail bonnet to the philosopher's cloak. We have one amusing instance of the struggles to which this sometimes gave rise. One day Mencius was preparing to go to court of his own free will, when a messenger arrived from the king, saying he had intended to come and see him, but was prevented by a cold, and asking whether Mencius would not appear at the audience next morning. Mencius saw that this was a device on the part of the king to avoid stooping to visit him, and though he had been about to go to court, he replied at once that he was unwell. He did not hesitate to meet the king's falsehood with one of his own.

He did not wish, however, that the king should be ignorant of the truth, and went out next morning to pay a visit of condolence. He supposed that messengers would be sent from the court to inquire about his health, and that, when they took back word that he had gone out visiting, the king would understand how his sickness of the day before was only feigned.

It happened as he expected. The king sent a messenger, and his physician besides. Mencius being out, they were received by Măng Chung, either his son or cousin, who complicated the affair by an invention of his own. 'To-day,' he said, ' he was a little better, and hastened to go to court. I don't know whether he has reached it by this time or not.' No sooner were the visitors gone with this story, than he sent several persons to look for the philosopher, and urge him to go to the court before he returned home.

It was now necessary that a full account of the matter should reach the royal ears; and to accomplish this, Mencius neither went home nor to court, but spent the night at the house of one of the high officers. They had an animated discussion. The officer accused Mencius of showing disrespect to the king. The philosopher replied that no man in Ch'î showed so much respect for the sovereign as he did, for it was only he who brought high and truly royal subjects under his notice.

'That,' said the officer, ' is not my meaning. The rule is—" When the prince's order calls, the carriage must not be waited for." You were going to the court, but when you heard the king's message. you did not do so. This seems not in accordance with that rule.' Mencius explained :—' There are three things universally acknowledged to be honourable,—nobility, age, and virtue. In courts, nobility holds the first place; in villages, age; and for helping one's generation and presiding over the people, the other two are not equal to virtue. The possession of one of the three does not authorise the despising of one who has the other two.

'A prince who is to accomplish great deeds will have ministers whom he does not call to go to see him. When he wishes to consult with them, he goes to them. The prince who does not honour the virtuous, and delight in their ways of doing, to this extent, is not worth having to do with.

'There was T'ang with Î Yin :—he first learned of him, and then made him his minister; and so without difficulty he became sovereign. There was the duke Hwan with Kwan Chung:—he first learned of him, and then made him his minister; and so without difficulty he became chief of all the princes.

'So did T'ang behave to Î Yin, and the duke Hwan to Kwan Chung, that they would not venture to call them to go to them. If Kwan Chung might not be called to him by his prince, how much less may I be called, who would not play the part of Kwan Chung[1]!'

We are to suppose that these sentiments were conveyed to the king by the officer with whom Mencius spent the night. It is a pity that the exposition of them could only be effected in such a round-about manner, and was preceded by such acts of prevarication. But where the two parties were so suspicious of each other, we need not wonder that they separated before long. Mencius resigned his honorary appointment, and prepared to return to Tsâu. On this occasion king Hsüan visited him, and after some complimentary expressions asked whether he might expect to see him again. 'I dare not request permission to visit you *at any particular time*,' replied Mencius, 'but, indeed, it is what I desire[2].'

The king made another attempt to detain him, and sent an officer, called Shih, to propose to him to remain in the State, on the understanding that he should have a house large enough to accommodate his disciples, and an allowance of ten thousand measures of grain to support them. All Mencius's efforts had not sufficed to make king Hsüan and his ministers understand him. They thought he was really actuated like themselves by a desire for wealth. He indignantly rejected the proposal, and pointed out the folly of

---

[1] Bk. II. Pt. II. ii.   [2] Bk. II. Pt. II. x.   I consider that this chapter, and others here referred to, belong to Mencius's first departure from Ch'î. I do so because we can hardly suppose that the king and his officers would not have understood him better by the end of his second residence. Moreover, while Mencius retires, his language in x. 2 and xi. 5. 6 is of such a nature that it leaves an opening for him to return again.

it, considering that he had already declined a hundred thousand measures in holding only an honorary appointment[1].

So Mencius turned his back on Ch'î; but he withdrew with a slow and lingering step, stopping three nights in one place, to afford the king an opportunity to recall him on a proper understanding. Some reproached him with his hesitancy, but he sufficiently explained himself. 'The king,' he said, 'is, after all, one who may be made to do good. If he were to use me, would it be for the happiness of Ch'î only? It would be for the happiness of the people of the whole kingdom. I am hoping that the king will change; I am daily hoping for this.

'Am I like one of your little-minded people? They will remonstrate with their prince, and on their remonstrance not being accepted, they get angry, and, with their passion displayed in their countenance, they take their leave, and travel with all their strength for a whole day, before they will rest[2].'

7. After he left Ch'î, Mencius found a home for some time in the small principality of T'ăng, on the south of Ch'î, in the ruler of

Mencius in T'ăng;—from his leaving Ch'î to B.C. 318.

which he had a sincere admirer and docile pupil. He did not proceed thither immediately, however, but seems to have taken his way to Sung, which consisted mostly of the present department of Kwei-tei in Ho-nan[3]. There he was visited by the crown-prince of T'ăng, who made a long detour, while on a journey to Ch'û, for the purpose of seeing him. The philosopher discoursed on the goodness of human nature, and the excellent ways of Yâo and Shun. His hearer admired, but doubted. He could not forget, however, and the lessons which he received produced fruit before long.

---

[1] I have said in a note, Bk. II. Pt. II. x. 5, that 100,000 *chung* was the fixed allowance of a 卿, which Mencius had declined to receive. When we look narrowly into the matter, however, we see that this could hardly be the case. It is known that four measures were used in Ch'î,—the 豆, 區, 釜, and 鍾, and that a *chung* was=ten *fû*, or six 石 and four *tôu*. 10,000 *chung* would thus=64,000 stone, and Mencius declined 640,000 stone of grain. No officer of Ch'î could have an income so much as that. The measures of the Han dynasty are ascertained to have been only one-fifth the capacity of the present. Assuming that those of Châu and Han agreed, and bringing the above computations to the present standard, Mencius was offered an annual amount of 12,800 stone of grain for his disciples, and he had himself refused in all 128,000 stone. With this reduction, and taking any grain we please as the standard of valuation, the amount is still much beyond what we can suppose to have been a 卿's salary.— 閻若璩 supposes that Mencius intends by 100,000 *chung* the sum of the income during all the years he had held his honorary office.   [2] Bk. II. Pt. II. xii.   [3] This is gathered from Bk. III. Pt. I. i. 1, where the crown-prince of T'ăng visits Mencius, and from Bk. II. Pt. II. iii. where his accepting a gift in Sung appears to have been subsequent to his refusing one in Ch'î.

From Sung Mencius returned to Tsâu, by way of Hsieh. In both Sung and Hsieh he accepted large gifts from the rulers, which help us in some measure to understand how he could maintain an expenditure which must have been great, and which gave occasion also for an ingenious exposition of the principles on which he guided his course among the princes. 'When you were in Ch'î,' said one of his disciples, 'you refused a hundred *yi* of fine gold, which the king sent, while in Sung you accepted seventy *yi*, and in Hsieh fifty[1]. If you were right in refusing the gift in the first case, you did wrong in accepting it in the other two. If you were right in accepting it in those two cases, you were wrong in refusing it in Ch'î. You must accept one of these alternatives.' 'I did right in all the cases,' replied Mencius. 'When I was in Sung, I was about to undertake a long journey. Travellers must be provided with what is necessary for their expenses. The prince's message was—" a present against travelling expenses ;" why should I have declined the gift? In Hsieh I was under apprehensions for my safety, and taking measures for my protection. The message was—" I have heard you are taking measures to protect yourself, and send this to help you in procuring arms." Why should I have declined the gift? But when I was in Ch'î, I had no occasion for money. To send a man a gift when he has no occasion for it is to bribe him. How is it possible that a superior man should be taken with a bribe[2]?'

Before Mencius had been long in Tsâu, the crown-prince of T'ǎng succeeded to the rule of the principality, and calling to mind the lessons which he had heard in Sung, sent an officer to consult the philosopher on the manner in which he should perform the funeral and mourning services for his father[3]. Mencius of course advised him to carry out in the strictest manner the ancient regulations. The new prince's relatives and the officers of the State opposed, but

---

[1] I have supposed in the translation, Bk. II. Pt. II. iii. 1, that the metal of these gifts was silver and not gold. 閻若璩, however, seems to make it clear that we ought to understand that it was gold. (See 皇清經解, 孟子生卒年月考, p. 6.) Pressed with the objection that 2,400 ounces of gold seems too large a sum, he goes on to make it appear that under the Ch'in dynasty, a yi or twenty-four ounces of gold was only equal to 15,000 cash, or fifteen taels of silver of the present day! This is a point on which I do not know that we can attain any positive certainty.   [2] Bk. II. Pt. II. iii.   [3] Bk. III. Pt. I. ii. The note of time which is relied on as enabling us to follow Mencius here is the intimation, Bk. I. Pt. II. xiv, that 'Ch'î was about to fortify Hsieh.' This is referred to B.C. 320, when king Hsüan appointed his brother 田嬰 over the dependency of Hsieh, and took measures to fortify it.

ineffectually.   Mencius's counsel was followed, and the effect was great.   Duke Wăn became an object of general admiration.

By and by Mencius proceeded himself to T'ăng.   We may suppose that he was invited thither by the prince as soon as the rules of mourning would allow his holding free communication with him. The chapters which give an account of their conversations are really interesting.   Mencius recommended that attention should be chiefly directed to the encouragement of agriculture and education.   He would have nourishment secured both for the body and the mind of every subject[1].   When the duke was lamenting the danger to which he was exposed from his powerful and encroaching neighbours, Mencius told him he might adopt one of two courses ;—either leave his State, and like king T'âi go and find a settlement elsewhere, or be prepared to die for his patrimony.   'If you do good,' said he, 'among your descendants in after generations there will be one who shall attain to the royal dignity.   But results are with Heaven.   What is Ch'î to you, O prince ?   Be strong to do good. That is all your business[2].'

After all, nothing came of Mencius's residence in T'ăng.   We should like to know what made him leave it.   Confucius said that, if any of the princes were to employ him, he should achieve something considerable in twelve months, and in the course of three years, the government would be perfected[3].   Mencius taught that, in his time, with half the merit of former days double the result might be accomplished[4].   Here in T'ăng a fair field seemed to be afforded him, but he was not able to make his promise good. Possibly the good purposes and docility of duke Wăn may not have held out, or Mencius may have found that it was easier to theorise about government, than actually to carry it on.   Whatever may have been the cause, we find him in B.C. 319 at the court of king Hûi of Liang.

Before he left T'ăng, Mencius had his rencounter with the disciples of the 'shrike-tongued barbarian of the South,' one Hsü Hsing, who came to T'ăng on hearing of the reforms which were being made at Mencius's advice by the duke Wăn   This was one of the dreamy speculators of the time, to whom I have already alluded.   He pretended to follow the lessons of Shăn-năng, one of the reputed founders of the kingdom and the father of husbandry, and came to T'ăng with

---

[1] Bk. III. Pt. I. iii.   [2] Bk. I. Pt. II. xiii. xiv. xv.   [3] Confucian Analects, XIII. x.
[4] Bk. II. Pt. I. i. 13.

his plough upon his shoulder, followed by scores of followers, all wearing the coarsest clothes, and supporting themselves by making mats and sandals. It was one of his maxims that 'the magistrates should be labouring-men.' He would have the sovereign grow his own rice, and cook his own meals. Not a few of 'The Learned' were led away by his doctrines, but Mencius girt up his loins to oppose the heresy, and ably vindicated the propriety of a division of labour, and of a lettered class conducting the government. It is just possible that the appearance of Hsü Hsing, and the countenance shown to him, may have had something to do with Mencius's leaving the State.

8. Liang was another name for Wei, one of the States into which Tsin had been divided. King Hûi, early in his reign, B.C. 364, had

Mencius in Liang;—B.C. 319, 318.

made the city of Tâ-iiang, in the present department of K'âi-fâng, his capital, and given its name to his whole principality. It was the year before his death, when Mencius visited him [1]. A long, stormy, and disastrous rule was about to terminate, but the king was as full of activity and warlike enterprise as ever he had been. At his first interview with Mencius, he addressed him in the well-known words, 'Venerable Sir, since you have not counted it far to come here, a distance of a thousand *lî*, may I presume that you are likewise provided with counsels to profit my kingdom?' Mencius in reply starts from the word *profit*, and expatiates eloquently on the evil consequences that must ensue from making a regard to profit the ground of conduct or the rule of policy. As for himself, his theme must be benevolence and righteousness. On these he would discourse, but on nothing else, and in following them a prince would obtain true and sure advantages.

Only five conversations are related between king Hûi and the philosopher. They are all in the spirit of the first which has just been described, and of those which he had with king Hsüan of Ch'î.

---

[1] There are various difficulties about the reign of king Hûi of Liang. Sze-mâ Ch'ien makes it commence in 369 and terminate in 334. He is then succeeded by Hsiang (襄), whose reign ends in 318; and he is followed by Âi (哀) till 295. What are called 'The Bamboo Books' (竹書) extend Hûi's reign to B.C. 318, and the next twenty years are assigned to king Âi. 'The Annals of the Nation' (which are compiled from 'The General Mirror of History' [通鑑]) follow the Bamboo Books in the length of king Hûi's reign, but make him followed by Hsiang; and take no note of a king Âi.—From Mencius we may be assured that Hûi was succeeded by Hsiang, and the view of his Life. which I have followed in this sketch, leads to the longer period assigned to his reign.

There is the same freedom of expostulation, or, rather, boldness of reproof, and the same unhesitating assurance of the success that would follow the adoption of his principles. The most remarkable is the third, where we have a sounder doctrine than where he tells king Hsüan that his love of beauty and money and valour need not interfere with his administration of royal government. Hûi is boasting of his diligence in the government of his State, and sympathy with the sufferings of his people, as far beyond those of any of the neighbouring rulers, and wondering how he was not more prosperous than they. Mencius replies, 'Your Majesty is fond of war;—let me take an illustration from it. The drums sound, and the weapons are crossed, when suddenly the soldiers on one side throw away their coats of mail, trail their weapons behind them, and run. Some of them run a hundred paces, and some run only fifty. What would you think if those who run fifty paces were to laugh at those who run a hundred paces?' 'They may not do so,' said the king; 'they only did not run a hundred paces, but they also ran.' 'Since your Majesty knows this,' was the reply, 'you need not hope that your people will become more numerous than those of the neighbouring kingdoms.' The king was thus taught that half-measures would not do. Royal government, to be effectual, must be carried out faithfully and in its spirit.

King Hûi died in B.C. 319, and was succeeded by his son, the king Hsiang. Mencius appears to have had but one interview with him. When he came out from it, he observed to some of his friends: —'When I looked at him from a distance, he did not appear like a sovereign; when I drew near to him, I saw nothing venerable about him [1].'

It was of no use to remain any longer in Liang; he left it, and we meet with him again in Ch'î.

9. Whether he returned immediately to Ch'î we cannot tell, but the probability is that he did, and remained in it till the year

Mencius the second time in Ch'î;—to B.C. 311.

B.C. 311 [2]. When he left it about seven years before, he had made provision for his return in case of a change of mind in king Hsüan. The philosopher, I

---

[1] Bk. I. Pt. I. vi.　[2] This conclusion is adopted because it was in 311 that Yen rebelled, when the king said that he was very much ashamed when he thought of Mencius, who had strongly condemned his policy towards the State of Yen.—This is another case in which the chronology is differently laid down by the authorities, Sze-mâ Ch'ien saying that Yen was taken by king Min (湣 王), the son and successor of Hsüan.

apprehend, was content with an insufficient assurance of such an alteration. Be that as it may, he went back, and took an appointment again as a high noble.

If he was contented with a smaller reformation on the part of the king than he must have desired, Mencius was not himself different from what he had been. In the court and among the high officers his deportment was equally unbending ; he was the same stern mentor.

Among the officers was one Wang Hwan, called also Tsze-âo, a favourite with the king, insolent and presuming. Him Mencius treated with an indifference and even contempt which must have been very provoking. A large party were met one time at the house of an officer who had lost a son, for the purpose of expressing their condolences. Mencius was among them, when suddenly Wang Hwan made his appearance. One and another moved to do him honour and win from him a smile,—all indeed but Mencius, who paid no regard to him. The other complained of the rudeness, but the philosopher could show that his conduct was only in accordance with the rules of Propriety [1].

Another time, Mencius was sent as the chief of a mission of condolence to the court of Tǎng, Wang Hwan being the assistant commissioner. Every morning and evening he waited upon Mencius, who never once exchanged a word with him on the business of their mission [2].

Now and then he became the object of unpleasant remark and censure. At his instigation, an officer, Ch'i Wâ, remonstrated with the king on some abuse, and had in consequence to resign his office. The people were not pleased with Mencius, thus advising others to their harm, and yet continuing to retain his own position undisturbed. 'In the course which he marked out for Ch'i Wâ,' they said, 'he did well, but we do not know as to the course which he pursues for himself.' The philosopher, however, was never at a loss in rendering a reason. He declared that, as his office was honorary, he could act 'freely and without restraint either in going forward or retiring [3].' In this matter we have more sympathy with the condemnation than with the defence.

Some time during these years there occurred the death of Mencius's excellent mother. She had been with him in Ch'i, and

[1] Bk. IV. Pt. II. xxvii.　　　[2] Bk. II. Pt. II. vi.　　　[3] Bk. II. Pt. II. v.

VOL. II.　　　　　　　　　　D

he carried the coffin to Lû, to bury it near the dust of his father
and ancestors. The funeral was a splendid one. Mencius perhaps
erred in having it so from his dislike to the Mohists, who advocated
a spare simplicity in all funeral matters[1]. His arrangements certainly
excited the astonishment of some of his own disciples[2], and were the
occasion of general remark[3]. He defended himself on the ground
that 'the superior man will not for all the world be niggardly to his
parents,' and that, as he had the means, there was no reason why he
should not give all the expression in his power to his natural feelings.

Having paid this last tribute of filial duty, Mencius returned to
Ch'î, but he could not appear at court till the three years of his
mourning were accomplished[4]. It could not be long after this when
trouble and confusion arose in Yen, a large State to the north-west
of Ch'î, in the present Chih-lî. Its prince, who was a poor weakling,
wished to go through the sham of resigning his throne to his prime
minister, understanding that he would decline it, and that thus he
would have the credit of playing the part of the ancient Yâo, while
at the same time he retained his kingdom. The minister, however,
accepted the tender, and, as he proved a tyrannical ruler, great
dissatisfaction arose. Ch'ăn T'ung, an officer of Ch'î, asked Mencius
whether Yen might be smitten. He replied that it might, for its
prince had no right to resign it to his minister, and the minister
no right to receive it. 'Suppose,' said he, 'there were an officer
here with whom you were pleased, and that, without informing the
king, you were privately to give him your salary and rank ; and suppose that this officer, also without the king's orders, were privately to
receive them from you :—would such a transaction be allowable?
And where is the difference between the case of Yen and this[5]?'

Whether these sentiments were reported to king Hsüan or not, he
proceeded to attack Yen, and found it an easy prey. Mencius was
charged with having advised the measure, but he ingeniously re-
pudiated the accusation. 'I answered Ch'ăn T'ung that Yen might
be smitten. If he had asked me—"Who may smite it?" I would
have answered him—"He who is the minister of Heaven may smite
it." Suppose the case of a murderer, and that one asks me—"May
this man be put to death?" I will answer him—"He may." If he

---

[1] Bk. III. Pt. I. v. 2.   [2] Bk. II. Pt. II. vii.   [3] Bk. I. Pt. II. xvi.   [4] Some are
of opinion that Mencius stopped all the period of mourning in Lû, but the more natural conclusion, Bk. II. Pt. II. vii. 1, seems to me that he returned to Ch'î, and stayed at Ying,
without going to court.   [5] Bk. II. Pt. II. viii.

ask me—"Who may put him to death?" I will answer him—"The
chief criminal judge may put him to death." But now with one
Yen to smite another Yen:—how should I have advised this?' This
reference to 'The minister of Heaven' strikingly illustrates what
was said about the state of China in Mencius's time. He tells us in
one place that hostile States do not correct one another, and that
only the supreme authority can punish its subjects by force of
arms[1]. But there was now no supreme authority in China. He
saw in the sovereign but 'the shadow of an empty name.' His
conception of a minister of Heaven was not unworthy. He was one
who, by the distinction which he gave to talents and virtue, and by
his encouragement of agriculture and commerce, attracted all people
to him as a parent. He would have no enemy under heaven, and
could not help attaining to the royal dignity[2].

King Hsüan, after conquering and appropriating Yen, tried to
get Mencius's sanction of the proceeding, alleging the ease and
rapidity with which he had effected the conquest as an evidence
of the favour of Heaven. But the philosopher was true to himself.
The people of Yen, he said, had submitted, because they expected
to find in the king a deliverer from the evils under which they
groaned. If they were pleased, he might retain the State. but if he
tried to keep it by force, there would simply be another revolution[3].

The king's love of power prevailed. He determined to keep his
prey, and ere long a combination was formed among the neighbouring princes to wrest Yen from him. Full of alarm he again
consulted Mencius, but got no comfort from him. 'Let him restore
his captives and spoils, consult with the people of Yen, and appoint
them a ruler;—so he might be able to avert the threatened attack[4].'

The result was as Mencius had predicted. The people of Yen
rebelled. The king felt ashamed before the philosopher, whose second
residence in Ch'î was thus brought to an unpleasant termination.

10. We do not know that Mencius visited any of the princes after
this. On leaving Ch'î, he took his way again to Sung, the duke of
Mencius in Lû; which had taken the title of king in B.C. 318. A
—B.C. 309. report also had gone abroad that he was setting
about to practise the true royal government, but Mencius soon
satisfied himself of its incorrectness[5].

The last court at which we find him is that of Lû, B.C. 309. The

[1] Bk. VII. Pt. II. ii.   [2] Bk. II. Pt. I. v.   [3] Bk. I. Pt. II. x.   [4] Bk. I. Pt. II. xi.
[5] See Bk. III. Pt. II. v. vi.

duke P'ing had there called Yo-chăng, one of the philosopher's disciples, to his councils, and indeed committed to him the administration of the government. When Mencius heard of it, he was so overjoyed that he could not sleep[1].

The first appearance (in point of time) of this Yo-chăng in the seven Books is not much to his credit. He comes to Ch'i in the train of Wang Hwan, the favourite who was an offence to the philosopher, and is very sharply reproved for joining himself to such a character ' for the sake of the loaves and fishes[2].' Other references to him are more favourable. Mencius declares him to be ' a good man,' ' a real man[3].' He allows that ' he is not a man of vigour,' nor ' a man wise in council,' nor ' a man of much information,' but he says—' he is a man that loves what is good,' and ' the love of what is good is more than a sufficient qualification for the government of the kingdom ;—how much more is it so for the State of Lû[4]?'

Either on his own impulse or by Yo-chăng's invitation, Mencius went himself also to Lû, hoping that the prince who had committed his government to the disciple might be willing to listen to the counsels of the master. The duke was informed of his arrival by Yo-chăng, and also of the deference which he exacted. He resolved to go and visit him and invite him to the court. The horses were put to the carriage, and the duke was ready to start, when the intervention of his favourite, a worthless creature called Tsang Ts'ang, diverted him from his good purpose. When told by the duke that he was going to visit the scholar Măng, Ts'ang said, ' That you demean yourself to pay the honour of the first visit to a common man, is, I apprehend, because you think that he is a man of talents and virtue. From such men the rules of ceremonial proprieties and right proceed ; but on the occasion of this Măng's second mourning, his observances exceeded those of the former. Do not go to see him, my prince.' The duke said, ' I will not ;'—and carriage and horses were ordered back to their places.

As soon as Yo-chăng had an audience of the duke, he explained the charge of impropriety which had been brought against Mencius; but the evil was done. The duke had taken his course. ' I told him ' said Yo-chăng, ' about you, and he was coming to see you, when Tsang Ts'ang stopped him.' Mencius replied to him, ' A man's

[1] Bk. VI. Pt. II. xiii.   [2] Bk. IV. Pt. I. xxv.   [3] Bk. VII. Pt. II. xxv.   [4] Bk. VI. Pt. II. xlii.

advancement is effected, it may be, by others, and the stopping him
is, it may be, from the efforts of others. But to advance a man or
to stop his advance is.really beyond the power of other men; my not
finding in the prince of Lû a ruler who would confide in me, and put
my counsels into practice, is from Heaven. How could that scion
of the Tsang family cause me not to find the ruler that would suit
me¹?'

Mencius appears to have accepted this intimation of the will of
Heaven as final. He has a remarkable saying, that Heaven controls
the development of a man's faculties and affections, but as there is
an adaptation in his nature for these, the superior man does not
say—' It is the appointment of Heaven².' In accordance with this
principle he had striven long against the adverse circumstances
which threw his hopes of influencing the rulers of his time again
and again in the dust. On his first leaving Lû we saw how he
said:—' Heaven does not yet wish that the country should enjoy
tranquillity and good order.' For about fifteen years, however, he
persevered, if peradventure there might be a change in the Heavenly
councils. Now at last he bowed in submission. The year after and
he would reach his grand climacteric. We lose sight of him. He
retired from courts and great officers. We can but think and con-
jecture of him, according to tradition, passing the last twenty years
of his life amid the more congenial society of his disciples, discoursing
to them, and compiling the Works which have survived as his
memorial to the present day.

11. I have endeavoured in the preceding paragraphs to put together the principal incidents of Mencius's history as they may be
gathered from his Writings. There is no other source of information about him, and we must regret that they tell us nothing of his
domestic life and habits. In one of the stories about his mother
there is an allusion to his wife, from which we may conclude that
his marriage was not without its bitternesses. It is probable that
the Măng Chung, mentioned in Bk. II. Pt. II. ii, was his son, though
this is not easily reconcileable with what we read in Bk. VI. Pt. I. v.
of a Măng Ch'î, who was, according to Châo Ch'î, a brother of Măng
Chung. We must believe that he left a family, for his descendants
form a large clan at the present day. Hsî-wăn, the fifty-sixth in
descent from Mencius, was, in the reign of Chiâ-ching (A.D. 1522-

¹ Bk. I. Pt. II. xvi.   ² Bk. III. Pt. II. i. ii.

1566), constituted a member of the Han-lin college, and of the Board in charge of the Five Ching, which honour was to be hereditary in the family, and the holder of it to preside at the sacrifices to his ancestor[1]. China's appreciation of our philosopher could not be more strikingly shown. Honours flow back in this empire. The descendant ennobles his ancestors. But in the case of Mencius, as in that of Confucius, this order is reversed. No excellence of descendants can extend to them ; and the nation acknowledges its obligations to them by nobility and distinction conferred through all generations upon their posterity.

SECTION II.

HIS INFLUENCE AND OPINIONS.

1. Confucius had hardly passed off the stage of life before his merits began to be acknowledged. The duke Âi, who had neglected his counsels when he was alive, was the first to pronounce his eulogy, and to order that public sacrifices should be offered to him. His disciples proclaimed their estimation of him as superior to all the sages whom China had ever seen. Before long this view of him took possession of the empire ; and since the Han dynasty, he has been the man whom sovereign and people have delighted to honour.

The memory of Mencius was not so distinguished. We have seen that many centuries elapsed before his Writings were received among

Acknowledgement of Mencius's merits by the government. the Classics of the empire. It was natural that under the same dynasty when this was done the man himself should be admitted to share in the sacrifices presented to Confucius.

The emperor Shăn Tsung[2], in A.D. 1083, issued a patent, constituting Mencius 'Duke of the kingdom of Tsâu[3],' and ordering a temple to be built to him in the district of Tsâu, at the spot where the philosopher had been interred. In the following year it was enacted that he should have a place in the temple of Confucius, next to that of Yen Yüan, the favourite disciple of the sage.

In A.D. 1330, the emperor Wăn Tsung[4], of the Yüan dynasty, made an addition to Mencius's title, and styled him 'Duke of the

---

[1] See Morrison's Dictionary, on Mencius, character 孟.   [2] 神宗, A.D. 1068-1085.   [3] 鄒國公.   [4] 文宗, A.D. 1330-1333.

State of Tsâu, Inferior Sage[1].' This continued till the rise of the
Ming dynasty, the founder of which, Hung-wû, had his indignation
excited in 1372 by one of Mencius's conversations with king Hsüan.
The philosopher had said :—' When the prince regards his ministers
as his hands and feet, the ministers regard their prince as their belly
and heart ; when he regards them as his dogs and horses, they regard
him as any other man ; when he regards them as ground or grass,
they regard him as a robber and an enemy[2].' To apply such names
as *robber* and *enemy* in any case to sovereigns seemed to the imperial
reader an unpardonable outrage, and he ordered Mencius to be
degraded from his place in the temples of Confucius, declaring also
that if any one remonstrated on the proceeding he should be dealt
with as guilty of ' Contempt of Majesty.'

The scholars of China have never been slow to vindicate the
memory of its sages and worthies. Undeterred by the imperial
threat, Ch'ien T'ang[3], a president of the Board of Punishments,
appeared with a remonstrance, saying,—' I will die for Mencius,
and my death will be crowned with glory.' The emperor was moved
by his earnestness, and allowed him to go scathless. In the following
year, moreover, examination and reflection produced a change of
mind. He issued a second proclamation to the effect that Mencius,
by exposing heretical doctrines and overthrowing perverse speakings,
had set forth clearly the principles of Confucius, and ought to be
restored to his place as one of his assessors[4].

[1] 鄒國亞聖公. The 亞 has been translated ' second-rate,' but it is by no
means so depreciating a term as that, simply indicating that Mencius was second to Confucius.
The title 亞聖 was first applied to him by Châo Ch'î.   [2] Bk. IV. Pt. II. iii.   [3] 錢唐.
[4] I have taken this account from 'The Sacrificial Canon of the Sage's Temples' (vol. i.
proleg. p. 132). Dr. Morrison in his Dictionary. under the character 亞, adds that the
change in the emperor's mind was produced by his reading the remarkable passage in Bk. VI.
Pt. II. xv, about trials and hardships as the way by which Heaven prepares men for great
services. He thought it was descriptive of himself, and that he could argue from it a good
title to the crown ;—and so he was mollified to the philosopher. It may be worth while to
give here the concluding remarks in 'The Paraphrase for Daily Lessons, Explaining the
Meaning of the Four Books' (vol. i. proleg. p. 130), on the chapter of Mencius which was
deemed by the imperial reader so objectionable :—' Mencius wished that sovereigns should
treat their ministers according to propriety, and nourish them with kindness, and therefore
he used these perilous words in order to alarm and rouse them. As to the other side, the
part of ministers, though the sovereign regard them as his hands and feet, they ought
notwithstanding to discharge most earnestly their duties of loyalty and love. Yea, though
he regard them as dogs and horses, or as the ground and grass, they ought still more to
perform their part in spite of all difficulties, and oblivious of their persons. They may on no
account make the manner in which they are regarded, whether it be of appreciation or
contempt, the standard by which they regulate the measure of their grateful service. The
words of Confucius, that *the ruler should behave to his ministers according to propriety, and the ministers*

In 1530, the ninth year of the reign of Chiâ-ching, a general revision was made of the sacrificial canon for the sage's temple, and the title of Mencius was changed into—'The philosopher Măng, Inferior Sage.' So it continues to the present day. His place is the second on the west, next to that of the philosopher Tsăng. Originally, we have seen, he followed Yen Hûi, but Hûi, Tsze-sze, Tsăng, and Măng were appointed the sage's four assessors, and had their relative positions fixed, in 1267.

2. The second edict of Hung-wû, restoring Mencius to his place in the temples of Confucius, states fairly enough the services which

Estimate of Mencius by himself and by scholars. he is held to have rendered to his country. The philosopher's own estimate of himself has partly appeared in the sketch of his Life [1]. He seemed to start with astonishment when his disciple Kung-sun Ch'âu was disposed to rank him as a sage [2]; but he also said on one occasion—'When sages shall rise up again, they will not change my words [3].' Evidently, he was of opinion that the mantle of Confucius had fallen upon him. A work was to be done in his generation, and he felt himself able to undertake it. After describing what had been accomplished by the great Yü, by Châu-kung, and Confucius, he adds:—'I also wish to rectify men's hearts, and to put an end to those perverse doctrines, to oppose their one-sided actions, and banish away their licentious expressions; and thus to carry on the work of the three sages [4].'

The place which Mencius occupies in the estimation of the literati of China may be seen by the following testimonies, selected from those appended by Chû Hsî to the prefatory notice of his Life in the 'Collected Comments.'

Han Yü [5] says, 'If we wish to study the doctrines of the sages, we must begin with Mencius.' He also quotes the opinion of Yang Tsze-yün [6], 'Yang and Mo were stopping up the way *of truth*, when Mencius refuted them, and scattered their delusions without difficulty ;' and then remarks upon it :—'When Yang and Mo walked abroad, the true doctrine had nearly come to nought. Though

serve their sovereign with faithfulness, contain the unchanging rule for all ages.' The authors of the 'Daily Lessons' did their work by imperial order, and evidently had the fear of the court before their eyes. Their language implies a censure of our philosopher. There wil' ever be a grudge against him in the minds of despots, and their creatures will be ready to depreciate him.

[1] See above, pp. 23, 24.   [2] Bk. II. Pt. I. ii. 18, 19.   [3] Bk. III. Pt. II. ix. 10.
[4] Bk. III. Pt. II. ix. 13.   [5] See above, pp. 11, 12.   [6] 楊子雲 ;—died A. D. 18.

Mencius possessed talents and virtue, even those of a sage, he did not occupy the throne. He could only speak and not act. With all his earnestness, what could he do? It is owing, however, to his words, that learners now-a-days still know how to revere Confucius, to honour benevolence and righteousness, to esteem the true sovereign and despise the mere pretender. But the grand rules and laws of the sage and sage-sovereigns had been lost beyond the power of redemption ; only one in a hundred of them was preserved. Can it be said in those circumstances that Mencius had an easy task? Yet had it not been for him, we should have been buttoning the lappets of our coats on the left side, and our discourse would have been all confused and indistinct ;—it is on this account that I have honoured Mencius, and consider his merit not inferior to that of Yü.'

One asked the philosopher Ch'ang [1] whether Mencius might be pronounced to be a sage. He replied, 'I do not dare to say altogether that he was a sage, but his learning had reached the extremest point.' The same great scholar also said :—'The merit of Mencius in regard to the doctrine of the sages is more than can be told. Confucius only spoke of *benevolence*, but as soon as Mencius opens his mouth, we hear of *benevolence* and *righteousness*. Confucius only spoke of the *will* or *mind*, but Mencius enlarged also on *the nourishment of the passion-nature*. In these two respects his merit was great.' 'Mencius did great service to the world by his teaching the goodness of man's nature.' 'Mencius had a certain amount of the heroical spirit, and to that there always belong some jutting corners, the effect of which is very injurious. Yen Yüan, all round and complete, was different from this. He was but a hair's-breadth removed from a sage, while Mencius must be placed in a lower rank, a great worthy, an inferior sage.' Ch'ang was asked where what he called the heroical spirit of Mencius could be seen. 'We have only to compare his words with those of Confucius,' he said, 'and we shall perceive it. It is like the comparison of ice or crystal with a precious jade-stone. The ice is bright enough, but the precious stone, without so much brilliancy, has a softness and richness all its own [2].' The scholar

---

[1] 程子; see vol. i. proleg. p. 24.

[2] This is probably the original of what appears in the 'Mémoires concernant les Chinois,' in the notice of Mencius, vol. iii, and which Thornton (vol. ii. pp. 216, 217) has faithfully translated therefrom in the following terms :—'Confucius, through prudence or modesty, often dissimulated ; he did not always say what he might have said : Mâng-tsze, on the contrary, was incapable of constraining himself ; he spoke what he thought, and without the

Yang [1] says :—'The great object of Mencius in his writings is to rectify men's hearts, teaching them to preserve their heart and nourish their nature, and to recover their lost heart. When he discourses of benevolence, righteousness, propriety, and knowledge, he refers to the principles of these in the heart commiserating, feeling shame and dislike, affected with modesty and complaisance, approving and disapproving. When he speaks of the evils springing from perverted speakings, he says—"Growing first in the mind, they prove injurious to government." When he shows how a prince should be served, he says—"Correct what is wrong in his mind. Once rectify the prince, and the kingdom will be settled." With him the thousand changes and ten thousand operations of men all come from the mind or heart. If a man once rectify his heart, little else will remain for him to do. In "The Great Learning," the cultivation of the person, the regulation of the family, the government of the State, and the tranquillisation of the empire, all have their root in rectifying the heart and making the thoughts sincere. If the heart be rectified, we recognise at once the goodness of the nature. On this account, whenever Mencius came into contact with people, he testified that man's nature is good. When Âu-yang Yung-shû [2] says, that in the lessons of the sages, man's nature does not occupy the first place, he is wrong. There is nothing to be put before this. Yâo and Shun are the models for ten thousand ages simply because they followed their nature. And to follow our nature is just to accord with Heavenly principle. To use plans and arts, away from this, though they may be successful in great achievement, is the selfishness of human desires, and as far removed from the mode of action of the sage, as earth is from heaven.' I shall close these testimonies with a sentence from Chû Hsî himself. He says :—'Mencius, when compared with Confucius, always appears to speak in too lofty a style ; but when we hear him proclaiming the goodness of man's

---

least fear or reserve. He resembles ice of the purest water, through which we can see all its defects as well as its beauties : Confucius, on the other hand, is like a precious gem, which, though not so pellucid as ice, has more strength and solidity.' The former of these sentences is quite alien from the style of Chinese thinking and expression.

[1] 楊氏. This is 楊時, styled 中立, but more commonly referred to as 楊龜山. He was one of the great scholars of the Sung dynasty, a friend of the two Ch'ǎng. He has a place in the temples of Confucius.　[2] 歐陽永叔. This was one of China's greatest scholars. He has now a place in the temples of Confucius.

nature, and celebrating Yâo and Shun, then we likewise perceive
the solidity of his discourses[1].'

3. The judgment concerning our philosopher contained in the
above quotations will approve itself to every one who has carefully

Correctness of
the above testi-
monies. Men-
cius's own pecu-
liarities appear
in his expositions
of doctrine.

perused his Works.　The long passage from Yang
Kwei-shan is especially valuable, and puts the principal characteristic of Mencius's teachings in a clear
light.　Whether those teachings have the intrinsic
value which is ascribed to them is another question,
which I will endeavour to discuss in the present section without
prejudice.　But Mencius's position with reference to 'the doctrines
of the sages' is correctly assigned.　We are not to look for new
truths in him.　And this does not lead his countrymen to think less
highly of him.　I ventured to lay it down as one grand cause of
the position and influence of Confucius, that he was simply the
preserver of the monuments of antiquity, and the exemplifier and
expounder of the maxims of the golden age of China.　In this
Mencius must share with him.

But while we are not to look to Mencius for new truths, the
peculiarities of his natural character were more striking than those
of his master.　There was an element of 'the heroical' about him.
He was a dialectician, moreover.　If he did not like disputing, as
he protested that he did not, yet, when forced to it, he showed
himself a master of the art.　An ingenuity and subtlety, which we
cannot but enjoy, often mark his reasonings.　We have more
sympathy with him than with Confucius.　He comes closer to us.
He is not so awe-ful, but he is more admirable.　The doctrines of
the sages take a tinge from his mind in passing through it, and it
is with that Mencian character about them that they are now held
by the cultivated classes and by readers generally.

I will now call attention to a few passages illustrative of these
remarks.　Some might prefer to search them out for themselves in
the body of the volume, and I am far from intending to exhaust the
subject.　There will be many readers, however, pleased to have the
means of forming an idea of the man for themselves brought within
small compass.　My next object will be to review his doctrine con
cerning man's mental constitution and the nourishment of the
passion-nature, in which he is said to have rendered special service

[1] See 朱子全書, 卷二十.

to the cause of truth. That done, I will conclude by pointing out what I conceive to be his chief defects as a moral and political teacher. To the opinions of Yang Chû and Mo, which he took credit to himself for assailing and exposing, it will be necessary to devote another chapter.

4. It was pointed out in treating of the opinions of Confucius, that he allowed no 'right divine' to a sovereign, independent of his

Specimens of Mencius's opinions, and manner of advocating them.

exercising a benevolent rule. This was one of the topics, however, of which he was shy. With Mencius, on the contrary, it was a favourite theme. The degeneracy of the times and the ardour of his disposition prompted him equally to the free expression of his convictions about it.

'The people,' he said, 'are the most important element *in a nation*; the spirits of the land and grain are the next; the sovereign

On government.—The people more important than the sovereign.

is the lightest. When a prince endangers the altars of the spirits of the land and grain, he is changed, and another appointed in his place. When the sacrificial victims have been perfect, the millet in its vessels all pure, and the sacrifices offered at their proper seasons, if yet there ensue drought, or the waters overflow, the spirits of the land and grain are changed, and others appointed in their place[1].'

'*The people are the most important element in a nation, and the sovereign is the lightest*;'—that is certainly a bold and ringing

An unworthy sovereign may be dethroned or put to death.

affirmation. Mencius was not afraid to follow it to the conclusion that the sovereign who was exercising an injurious rule should be dethroned. His existence is not to be allowed to interfere with the general good. Killing in such a case is no murder. King Hsüan once asked, 'Was it so that T'ang banished Chieh, and that king Wû smote Châu?' Mencius replied, ' It is so in the records.' The king asked, ' May a minister then put his sovereign to death?' Our philosopher's reply was :— 'He who outrages the benevolence proper to his nature is called a robber ; he who outrages righteousness is called a ruffian. The robber and ruffian we call a mere fellow. I have heard of the cutting off of the fellow Châu, but I have not heard in his case of the putting a sovereign to death[2].'

With regard to the ground of the relation between ruler and

---

[1] Bk. VII. Pt. II. xiv.   [2] Bk. I. Pt. II. viii.

people, Mencius refers it very clearly to the will of God. In one
The ground of the relation between ruler and people. place he adapts for his own purpose the language of king Wû in the Shû-ching :—'Heaven having produced the inferior people, appointed for them rulers and teachers, with the purpose that they should be assisting to God, and therefore distinguished them throughout the four quarters of the kingdom[1].' But the question arises—How can this will of Heaven be known? Mencius has endeavoured to answer it. He says:—'Heaven gives the throne, but its appointment is not conferred with specific injunctions. Heaven does not speak. It shows its will by a man's personal conduct and his conduct of affairs.' The conclusion of the whole matter is :—'Heaven sees according as the people see ; Heaven hears according as the people hear[2].'

It may not be easy to dispute these principles. I for one have no hesitation in admitting them. Their application, however, must *An unworthy ruler may be dethroned by his relatives.* always be attended with difficulty. Here is a sovereign who is the very reverse of a minister of God for good. He ought to be removed, but who is to remove him? Mencius teaches in one passage that the duty is to be performed by his relatives who are also ministers. The king Hsüan asked him about the office of chief ministers. Mencius said, 'Which chief ministers is your Majesty asking about?' 'Are there differences among them,' inquired the king. 'There are,' was the reply ; 'there are the chief ministers who are noble and relatives of the prince, and there are those who are of a different surname.' The king said, 'I beg to ask about the chief ministers who are noble and relatives of the prince.' Mencius answered, 'If the prince have great faults, they ought to remonstrate with him, and if he do not listen to them after they have done so again and again, they ought to dethrone him.' The king on this looked moved, and changed countenance. Mencius said, 'Let not your Majesty be offended. You asked me, and I dare not answer but according to truth[3].'

This plan for disposing of an unworthy sovereign has been acted on in China and in other countries. It is the best that can be *Virtuous ministers, and the minister of Heaven, may dethrone a ruler.* adopted to secure the throne in the ruling House. But where there are no relatives that have the virtue and power to play such a part, what is to be done? Mencius has two ways of meeting this difficulty. Contrary

[1] Bk. I. Pt. II. iii. 7.   [2] Bk. V. Pt. I. v.   [3] Bk. V. Pt. II. ix.

to his general rule[1] for the conduct of ministers who are not relatives, he allows that even they may, under certain conditions, take summary measures with their sovereign. His disciple Kung-sun Ch'âu said to him, 'Î Yin said, "I cannot be near and see him so disobedient to reason," and therewith he banished T'âi-chiâ to T'ung. The people were much pleased. When T'âi-chiâ became virtuous, he brought him back, and the people were again much pleased. When worthies are ministers, may they indeed banish their sovereigns in this way when they are not virtuous?' Mencius replied, 'If they have the same purpose as Î Yin, they may. If they have not the same purpose, it would be usurpation[2].' His grand device, however, is what he calls 'the minister of Heaven.' When the sovereign has become worthless and useless, his hope is that Heaven will raise up some one for the help of the people;—some one who shall so occupy in his original subordinate position as to draw all eyes and hearts to himself[3]. Let him then raise the standard, not of rebellion, but of righteousness[4], and he cannot help attaining to the highest dignity. So it was with the great T'ang; so it was with the kings Wǎn and Wû. Of the last Mencius says :—'There was one man'—i.e. the tyrant Châu—'pursuing a violent and disorderly course in the kingdom, and king Wû was ashamed of it. By one display of his anger, he gave repose to all the people[5].' He would have been glad if any one of the princes of his own time had been able to vault in a similar way to the sovereign throne, and he went about counselling them to the attempt. 'Let your Majesty,' said he to king Hsüan, 'in like manner, by one burst of anger, give repose to all the people of the nation.' This was in fact advising to rebellion, but the philosopher would have recked little of such a charge. The house of Châu had forfeited in his view its title to the kingdom. Alas! among all the princes he had to do with, he did not find one who could be stirred to so honourable an action.

We need not wonder that Mencius, putting forth the above views so boldly and broadly, should not be a favourite with the rulers of China. His sentiments, professed by the literati, and known and read by all the people, have operated powerfully to compel the good behaviour of 'the powers that be.' It may be said that they encourage the aims of selfish ambition, and the lawlessness of the

---

[1] Bk. V. Pt. II. ix. 1.   [2] Bk. VII. Pt. I. xxxi.   [3] Bk. II. Pt. I. v. 6.   [4] 起義兵, 'a raising of righteous soldiers;'—this is what all rebel leaders in China profess to do.   [5] Bk. I. Pt. II. iii. 7.

licentious mob. I grant it. They are lessons for the virtuous, and not for the lawless and disobedient, but the government of China would have been more of a grinding despotism, if it had not been for them.

On the readiness of the people to be governed Mencius only differs from Confucius in the more vehement style in which he expresses his views. He does not dwell so much on the influence of personal virtue, and I pointed out, in the sketch of his Life, how he all but compromised his character in his communications with king Hsüan, telling him that his love of women, of war, and of wealth might be so regulated as not to interfere with his exercise of true royal government. Still he speaks at times correctly and emphatically on this subject. He quotes Confucius's language on the influence generally of superiors on inferiors, —that 'the relation between them is like that between the wind and grass; the grass must bend when the wind blows upon it[1],' and he says himself:—'It is not enough to remonstrate with a sovereign on account of the mal-employment of ministers, nor to blame errors of government. It is only the great man who can rectify what is wrong in the sovereign's mind. Let the prince be benevolent, and all his acts will be benevolent. Let the prince be righteous, and all his acts will be righteous. Let the prince be correct, and all his acts will be correct. Once rectify the prince, and the kingdom will be firmly settled[2].'

The influence of personal character in a ruler.

But the misery which he saw around him, in consequence of the prevailing anarchy and constant wars between State and State, led Mencius to insist on the necessity of what he called 'a benevolent government.' The king Hsiang asked him, 'Who can unite the kingdom under one sway?' and his reply was, 'He who has no pleasure in killing men can so unite it[3].' His being so possessed with the sad condition of his time likewise gave occasion, we may suppose, to the utterance of another sentiment sufficiently remarkable. 'Never,' said he, 'has he who would by his excellence subdue men been able to subdue them. Let a prince seek by his excellence to nourish men, and he will be able to subdue the whole kingdom. It is impossible that any one should become ruler of the kingdom to whom it has not yielded the subjection of the heart[4].' The highest style of excellence will of course

Benevolent government, and its effects.

[1] Bk. III. Pt. I. ii. 4.   [2] Bk. IV. Pt. I. xx.   [3] Bk. I. Pt. I. vi.   [4] Bk. IV. Pt. II xvi.

have its outgoings in benevolence. Apart from that, it will be powerless, as Mencius says. His words are akin to those of Paul:—'Scarcely for a righteous man will one die: yet peradventure for a good man some would even dare to die.'

On the effects of a benevolent rule he says:—'Chieh and Châu's losing the throne arose from their losing the people; and to lose the people means to lose their hearts. There is a way to get the throne:—get the people, and the throne is got. There is a way to get the people:—get their hearts, and the people are got. There is a way to get their hearts:—it is simply to collect for them what they like, and not to lay on them what they dislike. The people turn to a benevolent rule as water flows downwards, and as wild beasts fly to the wilderness. As the otter aids the deep waters, driving the fish into them, and as the hawk aids the thickets, driving the little birds to them, so Chieh and Châu aided T'ang and Wû, driving the people to them. If among the present sovereigns of the kingdom there were one who loved benevolence, all the other princes would aid him by driving the people to him. Although he wished not to become sovereign, he could not avoid becoming so[1].'

Two principal elements of this benevolent rule, much insisted on by Mencius, deserve to be made prominent. They are to be found indicated in the Analects, and in the older Classics also, but it was reserved for our philosopher to set them forth, sharply defined in his own style, and to show the connexion between them. They are:—that the people be made well off, and that they be educated; and the former is necessary in order to the efficiency of the other.

To make the people prosperous, and to educate them, are important elements in a benevolent rule.

Once, when Confucius was passing through Wei in company with Yen Yû, he was struck with the populousness of the State. The disciple said, 'Since the people are thus numerous, what more shall be done for them?' Confucius answered, 'Enrich them.' 'And when they have been enriched, what more shall be done for them?' The reply was—'Teach them[2].' This brief conversation contains the germs of the ideas on which Mencius delighted to dwell.

We read in one place:—'Let it be seen to that their fields of grain and hemp are well cultivated, and make the taxes on them light:—so the people may be made rich.

[1] Bk. IV. Pt. I. ix.   [2] Confucian Analects, XIII. ix.

'Let it be seen to that they use their resources of food seasonably, and expend their wealth only on the prescribed ceremonies:—so their wealth will be more than can be consumed.

'The people cannot live without water and fire; yet if you knock at a man's door in the dusk of the evening, and ask for water and fire, there is no man who will not give them, such is the abundance of these things. A sage governs the kingdom so as to cause pulse and grain to be as abundant as water and fire. When pulse and grain are as abundant as water and fire, how shall the people be other than virtuous[1]?'

Again he says:—'In good years the youth of a country are most of them good, while in bad years they abandon themselves to evil[2].'

It is in his conversations, however, with king Hsüan of Ch'î and duke Wăn of Tăng, that we find the fullest exposition of the points in hand. 'It is only scholars'—officers, men of a superior order—'who, without a certain livelihood, are able to maintain a fixed heart. As to the people, if they have not a certain livelihood, it follows that they will not have a fixed heart. And if they have not a fixed heart, there is nothing which they will not do in the way of self-abandonment, of moral deflection, of depravity, and of wild license. When they have thus been involved in crime, to follow them up and punish them:—this is to entrap the people. Therefore an intelligent ruler will regulate the livelihood of the people, so as to make sure that, above, they shall have sufficient wherewith to serve their parents, and, below, sufficient wherewith to support their wives and children; that in good years they shall always be abundantly satisfied, and that in bad years they shall escape the danger of perishing. After this he may urge them, and they will proceed to what is good, for in this case the people will follow after that with ease[3].'

It is not necessary to remark here on the measures which Mencius recommends in order to secure a certain livelihood for the people. They embrace the regulation both of agriculture and commerce[4]. And education would be directed simply to illustrate the human relations[5]. What he says on these subjects is not without shrewdness, though many of his recommendations are inappropriate to the present state of society in China itself as well as in other countries. But his principle, that good government should contemplate, and

[1] Bk. VII. Pt. I. xxiii.　　[2] Bk. VI. Pt. I. vii.　　[3] Bk. I. Pt. I. vii. 20, 21; Bk. III. Pt. I. iii. 3.　　[4] Bk. III. Pt. I. iii; Bk. I. Pt. II. iv; Bk. II. Pt. I. v, et al.　　[5] Bk. III. Pt. I. iii. 10.

will be seen in, the material wellbeing of the people, is worthy of all honour. Whether government should interfere to secure the education of the people is questioned by not a few. The religious denomination to which I have the honour to belong has distinguished itself by opposing such a doctrine in England,—more zealously perhaps than wisely. But when Mencius teaches that with the mass of men education will have little success where the life is embittered by a miserable poverty, he shows himself well acquainted with human nature. Educationists now seem generally to recognise it, but I think it is only within a century that it has assumed in Europe the definiteness and importance with which it appeared to Mencius here in China two thousand years ago.

We saw how Mencius, when he was residing in T'ǎng, came into contact with a class of enthusiasts, who advocated a return to the primitive state of society,

'When Adam delved and Eve span.'

They said that wise and able princes should cultivate the ground equally and along with their people, and eat the fruit of their labour,

Necessity for a division of labour, and that government be conducted by a lettered class.

—that 'to have granaries, arsenals, and treasuries was an oppressing of the people.' Mencius exposed these errors very happily, showing the necessity to society of a division of labour, and that the conduct of government should be in the hands of a lettered class. 'I suppose,' he said to a follower of the strange doctrines, 'that Hsü Hsing sows grain and eats the produce. Is it not so?' 'It is so,' was the answer. 'I suppose that he also weaves cloth, and wears his own manufacture. Is it not so?' 'No; Hsü wears clothes of hair-cloth.' 'Does he wear a cap?' 'He wears a cap.' 'What kind of cap?' 'A plain cap.' 'Is it woven by himself?' 'No; he gets it in exchange for grain.' 'Why does Hsü not weave it himself?' 'That would injure his husbandry.' 'Does Hsü cook his food in boilers and earthenware pans, and does he plough with an iron share?' 'Yes.' 'Does he make those articles himself?' 'No; he gets them in exchange for grain.' On these admissions Mencius proceeds :—'The getting those various articles in exchange for grain is not oppressive to the potter and the founder, and the potter and the founder in their turn, in exchanging their various articles for grain, are not oppressive to the husbandman. How should such a thing be supposed? But why does not Hsü, *on his principles*,

act the potter and founder, supplying himself with the articles
which he uses solely from his own establishment? Why does he
go confusedly dealing and exchanging with the handicraftsmen?
Why does he not spare himself so much trouble?' His opponent
attempted a reply :—'The business of the handicraftsman can by
no means be carried on along with the business of husbandry.'
Mencius resumed :—'Then, is it the government of the kingdom
which alone can be carried on along with the practice of husbandry?
Great men have their proper business, and little men have their
proper business. Moreover, in the case of any single individual,
whatever articles he can require are ready to his hand, being
produced by the various handicraftsmen ;—if he must first make
them for his own use, this way of doing would keep all the people
running about upon the roads. Hence there is the saying:—" Some
men labour with their minds, and some with their strength. Those
who labour with their minds govern others; those who labour with
their strength are governed by others. Those who are governed
by others support them; those who govern others are supported by
them." This is a principle universally recognised[1].'

Sir John Davis has observed that this is exactly Pope's line,

'And those who think still govern those who toil[2].'

Mencius goes on to illustrate it very clearly by referring to the
labours of Yâo and Shun. His opponent makes a feeble attempt
at the end to say a word in favour of the new doctrines he had
embraced :—'If Hsü's doctrines were followed there would not be
two prices in the market, nor any deceit in the kingdom. If a boy
were sent to the market, no one would impose on him ; linen and
silk of the same length would be of the same price. So it would
be with bundles of hemp and silk, being of the same weight; with
the different kinds of grain, being the same in quantity ; and with
shoes which were the same in size.' Mencius meets this with
a decisive reply :—'It is the nature of things to be of unequal
quality ; some are twice, some five times, some ten times, some
a hundred times, some a thousand times, some ten thousand times
as valuable as others. If you reduce them all to the same standard,
that must throw the world into confusion. If large shoes were of
the same price with small shoes, who would make them? For

---

[1] Bk. III. Pt. I. iv.   [2] The Chinese, vol. ii. p. 56.

people to follow the doctrines of Hsü would be for them to lead one
another on to practise deceit.   How can they avail for the government of a State?'

There is only one other subject which I shall here notice, with
Mencius's opinions upon it,—the position, namely, which he occupied

Mencius's
position as
'a Teacher.'

himself with reference to the princes of his time.   He
calls it that of 'a Teacher,' but that term in our
language very inadequately represents it.   He wished
to meet with some ruler who would look to him as 'guide,
philosopher, and friend,' regulating himself by his counsels, and
thereafter committing to him the entire administration of his
government.   Such men, he insisted, there had been in China
from the earliest ages.   Shun had been such to Yâo; Yü and
Kâo-yâo had been such to Shun; Î Yin had been such to T'ang;
T'âi-kung Wang had been such to king Wăn; Châu-kung had
been such to the kings Wû and Ch'ăng; Confucius might have
been such to any prince who knew his merit; Tsze-sze was such,
in a degree, to the dukes Hûi of Pî and Mû of Lû[1].   The wandering scholars of his own day, who went from court to court, sometimes with good intentions and sometimes with bad, pretended to
this character; but Mencius held them in abhorrence.   They disgraced the character and prostituted it, and he stood forth as its
vindicator and true exemplifier.

Never did Christian priest lift up his mitred front, or show his
shaven crown, or wear his Geneva gown, more loftily in courts and
palaces than Mencius, the Teacher, demeaned himself.   We have
seen what struggles sometimes arose between him and the princes
who would fain have had him bend to their power and place.   'Those,'
said he, 'who give counsel to the great should despise them, and
not look at their pomp and display.   Halls several fathoms high,
with beams projecting several cubits:—these, if my wishes were to
be realised, I would not have.   Food spread before me over ten
cubits square, and attendant women to the amount of hundreds:—
these, though my wishes were realised, I would not have.   Pleasure
and wine, and the dash of hunting, with thousands of chariots
following after me:—these, though my wishes were realised, I would
not have.   What they esteem are what I would have nothing to do
with; what I esteem are the rules of the ancients.—Why should

[1] See Bk. V. Pt. II. iii. vii, et al.

I stand in awe of them[1]?' Before we bring a charge of pride
against Mencius on account of this language and his conduct in
accordance with it, we must bear in mind that the literati in China
do in reality occupy the place of priests and ministers in Christian
kingdoms. Sovereign and people have to seek the law at their lips.
The ground on which they stand,—'the rules of the ancients,'—
affords but poor footing compared with the Word of God; still it
is to them the truth, the unalterable law of right and duty, and, as
the expounders of it, they have to maintain a dignity which will
not compromise its claims. That 'scholars are the first and head
of the four classes of the people' is a maxim universally admitted.
I do desiderate in Mencius any approach to humility of soul, but
I would not draw my illustrations of the defect from the boldness
of his speech and deportment as 'a Teacher.'

But in one respect I am not sure but that our philosopher failed
to act worthy of the character which he thus assumed. The great
men to whom he was in the habit of referring as his
patterns nearly all rose from deep poverty to their
subsequent eminence. 'Shun came from among the
channelled fields; Fû Yüeh was called to office from the midst of
his building-frames; Kâo Ko from his fish and salt[2].' 'Î Yin was a
farmer in Hsin. When T'ang sent persons with presents of silk, to
entreat him to enter his service, he said, with an air of indifference
and self-satisfaction, "What can I do with those silks with which
T'ang invites me? Is it not best for me to abide in the channelled
fields, and there delight myself with the principles of Yâo and
Shun[3]?"' It does not appear that any of those worthies accepted
favours while they were not in office, or from men whom they
disapproved. With Mencius it was very different: he took largely
from the princes whom he lectured and denounced. Possibly he
might plead in justification the example of Confucius, but he carried
the practice to a greater extent than that sage had ever done,—to
an extent which staggered even his own disciples and elicited their
frequent inquiries. For instance, 'P'ang Kăng asked him, saying,
"Is it not an extravagant procedure to go from one prince to another
and live upon them, followed by several tens of carriages, and
attended by several hundred men?"' Mencius replied, 'If there be

The charge against him of living on the princes.

not a proper ground for taking it, a single bamboo-cup of rice may
not be received from a man. If there be such a proper ground, then
Shun's receiving the empire from Yâo is not to be considered excessive. Do you think it was excessive?' 'No,' said the other, 'but
for a scholar performing no service to receive his support notwithstanding is improper.' Mencius answered, 'If you do not have an
intercommunication of the productions of labour, and an interchange
of men's services, so that one from his overplus may supply the
deficiency of another, then husbandmen will have a superfluity of
grain, and women will have a superfluity of cloth. If you have
such an interchange, carpenters and carriage-wrights may all get
their food from you. Here now is a man who, at home, is filial,
and, abroad, respectful to his elders, and who watches over the
principles of the ancient kings, awaiting the rise of future learners,—
and yet you will refuse to support him. How is it that you give
honour to the carpenter and carriage-wright, and slight him who
practises benevolence and righteousness?' P'ang Käng said, 'The
aim of the carpenter and carriage-wright is by their trades to seek
for a living. Is it also the aim of the superior man in his practice
of principles to seek for a living?' 'What have you to do,' returned
Mencius, 'with his purpose? He is of service to you. He deserves
to be supported, and should be supported. And let me ask—Do
you remunerate a man's intention, or do you remunerate his service?'
To this Käng replied, 'I remunerate his intention.' Mencius said,
'There is a man here who breaks your tiles and draws unsightly
figures on your walls;—his purpose may be thereby to seek for his
living, but will you indeed remunerate him?' 'No,' said Käng;
and Mencius then concluded, 'That being the case, it is not the
purpose which you remunerate, but the work done[1].'

The ingenuity of Mencius in the above conversation will not be
questioned. The position from which he starts in his defence, that
society is based on a division of labour and an interchange of services,
is sound, and he fairly hits and overthrows his disciples on the point
that we remunerate a man not for his aim but for his work done. But
he does not quite meet the charge against himself. This will better
appear from another brief conversation with Kung-sun Ch'âu on the
same subject. 'It is said, in the Book of Poetry,' observed Châu,

'"He will not eat the bread of idleness."

[1] Bk. III. Pt. II. iv.

How is it that we see superior men eating without labouring?'
Mencius replied, 'When a superior man resides in a country, if the
sovereign employ his counsels, he comes to tranquillity, wealth,
honour, and glory; if the young in it follow his instructions, they
become filial, obedient to their elders, true-hearted, and faithful.—
What greater example can there be than this of not eating the
bread of idleness[1]?'

The argument here is based on the supposition that the superior
man has free course, is appreciated by the sovereign, and venerated
and obeyed by the people. But this never was the case with Mencius.
Only once, the short time that he was in T'ăng, did a ruler listen
favourably to his counsels. His lessons, it may be granted, were
calculated to be of the greatest benefit to the communities where
he was, but it is difficult to see the 'work done,' for which he could
claim the remuneration. His reasoning might very well be applied
to vindicate a government's extending its patronage to literary men,
where it recognised in a general way the advantages to be derived
from their pursuits. Still more does it accord with that employed
in western nations where ecclesiastical establishments form one of
the institutions of a country. The members belonging to them
must have their maintenance, independently of the personal character
of the rulers. But Mencius's position was more that of a reformer.
His claims were of those of his personal merit. It seems to me
that P'ang Kăng had reason to doubt the propriety of his course,
and characterise it as extravagant.

Another disciple, Wan Chang, pressed him very closely with the
inconsistency of his taking freely the gifts of the princes on whom
he was wont to pass sentence so roundly. Mencius had insisted
that, where the donor offered his gift on a ground of reason and in
a manner accordant with propriety, even Confucius would have
received it. 'Here now,' said Chang, 'is one who stops and robs
people outside the city gates. He offers his gift on a ground of
reason and in a proper manner;—would it be right to receive it so
acquired by robbery?' The philosopher of course said it would
not, and the other pursued:—'The princes of the present day take
from their people just as a robber despoils his victim. Yet if they
put a good face of propriety on their gifts, the superior man receives
them. I venture to ask you to explain this.' Mencius answered:—

[1] Bk. VII. Pt I. xxxii.

' Do you think that, if there should arise a truly imperial sovereign, he would collect the princes of the present day and put them all to death ? Or would he admonish them, and then, on their not changing their ways, put them to death ? Indeed to call every one who takes what does not properly belong to him a robber, is pushing a point of resemblance to the utmost, and insisting on the most refined idea of righteousness[1].'

Here again we must admire the ingenuity of Mencius ; but it amuses us more than it satisfies. It was very well for him to maintain his dignity as 'a Teacher,' and not go to the princes when they called him, but his refusal would have had more weight, if he had kept his hands clean from all their offerings. I have said above that if less awe-ful than Confucius, he is more admirable. Perhaps it would be better to say he is more brilliant. There is some truth in the saying of the scholar Ch'ǎng, that the one is the glass that glitters, and the other the jade that is truly valuable.

Without dwelling on other characteristics of Mencius, or culling from him other striking sayings,—of which there are many,—I proceed to exhibit and discuss his doctrine of the goodness of human nature.

5. If the remarks which I have just made on the intercourse of Mencius with the princes of his day have lowered him somewhat

Mencius's view of human nature; its identity with that of Bishop Butler. in the estimation of my readers, his doctrine of human nature, and the force with which he advocates it, will not fail to produce a high appreciation of him as a moralist and thinker. In concluding my exhibition of the opinions of Confucius in the former volume, I have observed that 'he threw no light on any of the questions which have a world-wide interest.' This Mencius did. The constitution of man's nature, and how far it supplies to him a rule of conduct and a law of duty, are inquiries than which there can hardly be any others of more importance. They were largely discussed in the Schools of Greece. A hundred vigorous and acute minds of modern Europe have occupied themselves with them. It will hardly be questioned in England that the palm for clear and just thinking on the subject belongs to Bishop Butler, but it will presently be seen that his views and those of Mencius are, as nearly as possible, identical. There is a difference of nomenclature and a combination

[1] Bk. V. Pt. II. iv.

of parts, in which the advantage is with the Christian prelate. Felicity of illustration and charm of style belong to the Chinese philosopher. The doctrine in both is the same.

The utterances of Confucius on the subject of our nature were few and brief. The most remarkable is where he says:—'Man is

View of Confucius.
born for uprightness. If a man be without uprightness and yet live, his escape *from death* is the effect of mere good fortune[1].' This is in entire accordance with Mencius's view, and as he appeals to the sage in his own support[2], though we cannot elsewhere find the words which he quotes, we may believe that Confucius would have approved of the sentiments of his follower, and frowned on those who have employed some of his sayings in confirmation of other conclusions[3]. I am satisfied in my own mind on this point. His repeated enunciation of 'the golden rule,' though only in a negative form, is sufficient evidence of it.

The opening sentence of 'The Doctrine of the Mean,'—'What Heaven has conferred is called THE NATURE; an accordance with

View of Tsze-sze.
this nature is called THE PATH; the regulation of the path is called INSTRUCTION,'—finds a much better illustration from Mencius than from Tsze-sze himself. The germ of his doctrine lies in it. We saw reason to discard the notion that he was a pupil of Tsze-sze; but he was acquainted with his treatise just named, and as he has used some other parts of it, we may be surprised that in his discussions on human nature he has made no reference to the above passage.

What gave occasion to his dwelling largely on the theme was the prevalence of wild and injurious speculations about it. In

Prevalent view of man's nature in Mencius's time.
nothing did the disorder of the age more appear. Kung-tû, one of his disciples, once went to him and said, 'The philosopher Kâo says:—"Man's nature is neither good nor bad." Some say:—"Man's nature may be made to practise good, and it may be made to practise evil; and accordingly, under Wăn and Wû, the people loved what was good, while, under Yû and Lî, they loved what was cruel." Others say:—"The nature of some is good, and the nature of others is bad. Hence it was that under such a sovereign as Yâo there yet appeared Hsiang; that with such a father as Kû-sâu there yet appeared Shun; and that

---

[1] Analects, VI. xvii.   [2] Bk. VI. Pt. I. vi. 8; viii. 4.   [3] See the annotations of the editor of Yang-tsze's (楊 子, the 楊 is often written 揚) Work, 脩 身 篇, in the 十 子 全 書 (vol. i. proleg. p. 132).

with Châu for their sovereign, and the son of their elder brother
besides, there were found Ch'i, the viscount of Wei, and the prince
Pi-kan." And now you say :—"The nature is good." Then are all
those opinions wrong [1] ?'

'The nature of man is good,'—this was Mencius's doctrine. By
many writers it has been represented as entirely antagonistic to
Christianity ; and, as thus broadly and briefly enunciated, it sounds
startling enough. As fully explained by himself, however, it is not
so very terrible. Butler's scheme has been designated ' the system
of Zeno baptised into Christ [2].' That of Mencius, identifying closely
with the master of the Porch, is yet more susceptible of a similar
transformation.

But before endeavouring to make this statement good, it will be
well to make some observations on the opinion of the philosopher
View of the Kâo. He was a contemporary of Mencius, and they
philosopher Kâo. came into argumentative collision. One does not see
immediately the difference between his opinion, as stated by Kung-tû,
and the next. Might not man's nature, though neither good nor
bad, be made to practise the one or the other ? Kâo's view went
to deny any essential distinction between good and evil,—virtue
and vice. A man might be made to act in a way commonly called
virtue and in a way commonly called evil, but in the one action
there was really nothing more approvable than in the other. ' Life,'
he said, ' was what was meant by nature [3].' The phenomena of
benevolence and righteousness were akin to those of walking and
sleeping, eating and seeing. This extravagance afforded scope for
Mencius's favourite mode of argument, the *reductio ad absurdum*.
He showed, on Kâo's principles, that ' the nature of a dog was
like the nature of an ox, and the nature of an ox like the nature
of a man.'

The two first conversations [4] between them are more particularly
worthy of attention, because, while they are a confutation of his
Mencius's ex- opponent, they indicate clearly our philosopher's own
posure of Kâo's theory. Kâo compared man's nature to a willow tree,
errors, and state-
ment of his own and benevolence and righteousness to the cups and
doctrine. bowls that might be fashioned from its wood. Mencius replied that it was not the nature of the willow to produce cups
and bowls ; they might be made from it indeed, by bending and

[1] Bk. VI. Pt. I. vi. 1-4.   [2] Wardlaw's Christian Ethics, edition of 1833. p. 119.
[3] Bk. VI. Pt. I. iii   [4] Bk. VI. Pt. I. i ii.

cutting and otherwise injuring it; but must humanity be done
such violence to in order to fashion the virtues from it? Kâo
again compared the nature to water whirling round in a corner;—
open a passage for it in any direction, and it will flow forth
accordingly. 'Man's nature,' said he, 'is indifferent to good and
evil, just as the water is indifferent to the east and west.' Mencius answered him:—'Water indeed will flow indifferently to the
east or west, but will it flow indifferently up or down? The
tendency of man's nature to good is like the tendency of water
to flow downwards. There are none but have this tendency to good,
just as all water flows downwards. By striking water and causing
it to leap up, you may make it go over your forehead, and, by
damming and leading it, you may force it up a hill; but are such
movements according to the nature of water? It is the force
applied which causes them. When men are made to do what is
not good, their nature is dealt with in this way.'

Mencius has no stronger language than this, as indeed it would
be difficult to find any stronger, to declare his belief in the goodness
of human nature. To many Christian readers it proves a stumbling-
block and offence. But I venture to think that this is without
sufficient reason. He is speaking of our nature in its ideal, and not
as it actually is,—as we may ascertain from the study of it that it
ought to be, and not as it is made to become. My rendering of the
sentences last quoted may be objected to, because of my introduction
of the term *tendency*; but I have Mencius's express sanction for
the representation I give of his meaning. Replying to Kung-tû's
question, whether all the other opinions prevalent about man's
nature were wrong, and his own, that it is good, correct, he said:—
'From the feelings proper to it, we see that it is constituted for
the practice of what is good. *This is what I mean in saying that
the nature is good.* If men do what is not good, the blame cannot
be imputed to their natural powers[1].' Those who find the most
fault with him, will hardly question the truth of this last declaration. When a man does wrong, whose is the blame,—the sin?
He might be glad to roll the guilt on his Maker, or upon his
nature,—which is only an indirect charging of his Maker with
it;—but it is his own burden, which he must bear himself.

The proof by which Mencius supports his view of human nature as formed only for virtue is twofold. First, he maintains that there

Proofs that human nature is formed for virtue —First, from its moral constituents.

are in man a natural principle of benevolence, a natural principle of righteousness, a natural principle of propriety, and a natural principle of apprehending moral truth. 'These,' he says, 'are not infused into us from without. We are certainly possessed of them; and a different view is simply from want of reflection[1].' In further illustration of this he argued thus:—'All men have a mind which cannot bear to see the sufferings of others;—my meaning may be illustrated thus;—Even now-a-days,' i.e. in these degenerate times, 'if men suddenly see a child about to fall into a well, they will without exception experience a feeling of alarm and distress. They will feel so, not as a ground on which they may gain the favour of the child's parents, nor as a ground on which they may seek the praise of their neighbours and friends, nor from a dislike to the reputation of having been unmoved by such a thing. From this case we may see that the feeling of commiseration is essential to man, that the feeling of shame and dislike is essential to man, that the feeling of modesty and complaisance is essential to man, and that the feeling of approval and disapproval is essential to man. These feelings are the principles respectively of benevolence, righteousness, propriety, and the knowledge *of good and evil*. Men have these four principles just as they have their four limbs[2].'

Let all this be compared with the language of Butler in his three famous *Sermons upon Human Nature*. He shows in the first of these:—'First, that there is a natural principle of benevolence in man; secondly, that the several *passions* and *affections*, which are distinct both from benevolence and self-love, do in general contribute and lead us to *public* good as really as to private; and thirdly, that there is a principle of reflection in men, by which they distinguish between, approve and disapprove their own actions[3].'

<hr>

[1] Bk. VI. Pt. I. vi. 7.   [2] Bk. II. Pt. I. vi. 3, 4, 5, 6.

[3] I am indebted to Butler for fully understanding Mencius's fourth feeling, that of approving and disapproving, which he calls 'the principle of knowledge,' or wisdom. In the notes, Bk. II. Pt. I. vi. 5, I have said that he gives to this term 'a moral sense.' It is the same with Butler's principle of reflection, by which men distinguish between, and approve or disapprove, their own actions.—I have heard gentlemen speak contemptuously of Mencius's case in point, to prove the existence of a feeling of benevolence in man. 'This,' they have said, 'is Mencius's idea of virtue, to save a child from falling into a well. A mighty display of virtue, truly!' Such language arises from misconceiving Mencius's object in putting the case. 'If there be,' says Butler, 'any affection in human nature, the object and end of which is the good of another, this is itself benevolence. Be it ever so short, be it in ever so low a degree, or ever so unhappily confined, it proves the assertion and points out what we were designed for, as

Is there anything more in this than was apprehended and expressed by Mencius? Butler says in the conclusion of his first discourse that 'Men follow their nature to a certain degree but not entirely; their actions do not come up to the whole of what their nature leads them to; and they often violate their nature.' This also Mencius declares in his own forceful manner:—'When men having these four principles, yet say of themselves that they cannot develop them, they play the thief with themselves, and he who says of his prince that he cannot develop them, plays the thief with his prince[1].' 'Men differ from one another in regard to the principles of their nature;—some as much again as others, some five times as much, and some to an incalculable amount:—it is because they cannot carry out fully their natural powers[2].'

So much for the first or preliminary view of human nature insisted on by Mencius, that it contains principles which are disinterested and virtuous. But there wants something

Second proof that human nature is formed for virtue: —that it is a constitution, where the higher principles should serve the lower.

more to make good the position that virtue ought to be supreme, and that it is for it, in opposition to vice, that our nature is formed. To use some of the 'licentious talk' which Butler puts into the mouth of an opponent:—'Virtue and religion require not only that we do good to others, when we are led this way, by benevolence and reflection happening to be stronger than other principles, passions, or appetites; but likewise that the *whole character* be formed upon thought and reflection; that *every* action be directed by some determinate rule, some other rule than the strength or prevalence of any principle or passion. What sign is there in our nature (for the inquiry is only about what is to be collected from thence) that this was intended by its Author? Or how does so various and fickle a temper as that of man appear adapted thereto? . . . As brutes have various instincts, by which they are carried on to the end the Author of their nature intended them for, is not man in the same condition, with this difference

really as though it were in a higher degree and more extensive.' 'It is sufficient that the seeds of it be implanted in our nature.' The illustration from a child falling into a well must be pronounced a happy one. How much lower Mencius could go may be seen from his conversation with king Hsüan, Bk. I. Pt. I. vii, whom he leads to a consciousness of his commiserating mind from the fact that he had not been able to bear the frightened appearance of an ox which was being led by to be killed, and ordered it to be spared. The kindly heart that was moved by the suffering of an animal had only to be carried out, to suffice for the love and protection of all within the four seas.

[1] Bk. II. Pt. I. vi. 6.　　　　[2] Bk. VI. Pt. I. vi. 7.

only, that to his instincts (i.e. appetites and passions) is added the
principle of reflection or conscience? And as brutes act agreeably
to their nature in following that principle or particular instinct
which for the present is strongest in them; does not man likewise
act agreeably to his nature, or obey the law of his creation, by following that principle, be it passion or conscience, which for the
present happens to be strongest in him? . . . Let every one then
quietly follow his nature; as passion, reflection, appetite, the several
parts of it, happen to be the strongest; but let not the man of
virtue take it upon him to blame the ambitious, the covetous, the
dissolute; since these, equally with him, obey and follow their
nature [1].'

To all this Butler replies by showing that the principle of reflection or conscience is 'not to be considered merely as a principle in
the heart, which is to have some influence as well as others, but as
a faculty, in kind and in nature, supreme over all others, and which
bears its own authority of being so;' that the difference between
this and the other constituents of human nature is not 'a difference
in strength or degree,' but 'a difference *in nature* and *in kind;*'
that 'it was placed within to be our proper governor; to direct and
regulate all under principles, passions, and motives of action:—this
is its right and office; thus sacred is its authority.' It follows from
the view of human nature thus established, that 'the inward frame
of man is *a system or constitution;* whose several parts are united,
not by a physical principle of individuation, but by the respects
they have to each other, the chief of which is the subjection which
the appetites, passions, and particular affections have to the one
supreme principle of reflection or conscience [2].'

Now, the *substance* of this reasoning is to be found in Mencius.
Human nature—the inward frame of man—is with him *a system or
constitution* as much as with Butler. He says, for instance :—
'There is no part of himself which a man does not love; and as he
loves all, so he must nourish all. There is not an inch of skin which
he does not love, and so there is not an inch of skin which he will
not nourish. FOR EXAMINING WHETHER HIS WAY OF NOURISHING BE
GOOD OR NOT, WHAT OTHER RULE IS THERE BUT THIS, THAT HE DETER-
MINE BY REFLECTING ON HIMSELF WHERE IT SHOULD BE APPLIED?

'Some parts of the body are noble and some ignoble; some great

[1] See Sermon Second.   [2] See note to Sermon Third.

and some small. The great must not be injured for the small, nor
the noble for the ignoble. He who nourishes the little belonging
to him is a little man, and he who nourishes the great is a great
man[1].'

Again :—' Those who follow that part of themselves which is
great are great men ; those who follow that part which is little are
little men[2].'

The great part of ourselves is the moral elements of our constitution ; the lower part is the appetites and passions that centre in
self. He says finely :—' There is a nobility of Heaven, and there is
a nobility of man. Benevolence, righteousness, self-consecration,
and fidelity, with unwearied joy in what is good ;—these constitute
the nobility of Heaven. To be a duke, a noble, or a great officer ;—
this constitutes the nobility of man[3].'

There is one passage very striking :—' For the mouth to desire
sweet tastes, the eye to desire *beautiful* colours, the ear to desire
pleasant sounds, the nose to desire *fragrant* odours, and the four
limbs to desire ease and rest ;—these things are natural. But there
is the appointment *of Heaven* in connexion with them ; and the
superior man does not say *of his pursuit of them*, " It is my nature."
The exercise of love between father and son, *the observance of*
righteousness between sovereign and minister, the rules of ceremony
between host and guest, *the display of* knowledge in recognising
the worthy, and *the fulfilling* the heavenly course by the sage ;—
these are the appointment *of Heaven*. But there is *an adaptation
of our* nature for them ; and the superior man does not say, in
reference to them, " It is the appointment *of Heaven*[4]." '

From these paragraphs it is quite clear that what Mencius considered as deserving properly to be called the nature of man, was
not that by which he is a creature of appetites and passions, but
that by which he is lifted up into the higher circle of intelligence
and virtue. By the phrase, ' the appointment of Heaven,' most
Chinese scholars understand the will of Heaven, limiting in the first
case the gratification of the appetites, and in the second the exercise
of the virtues. To such limitation Mencius teaches there ought to
be a cheerful submission so far as the appetites are concerned, but
where the virtues are in question, we are to be striving after them
notwithstanding adverse and opposing circumstances. THEY ARE

[1] Bk. VI. Pt. I. xiv.   [2] Bk. VI. Pt. I. xv.   [3] Bk. VI. Pt. I. xvi.   [4] Bk. VII.
Pt. II. xxiv.

OUR NATURE, what we were made for, what we have to do. I will
refer but to one other specimen of his teaching on this subject.
'The will,' he said, using that term for the higher moral nature in
activity,—' the will is the leader of the passion-nature. The passion-
nature pervades and animates the body. The will is first and chief,
and the passion-nature is subordinate to it [1].'

My readers can now judge for themselves whether I exaggerated
at all in saying that Mencius's doctrine of human nature was, as
nearly as possible, identical with that of Bishop Butler. Sir James
Mackintosh has said of the sermons to which I have made reference,
and his other cognate discourses, that in them Butler ' taught truths
more capable of being exactly distinguished from the doctrines of
his predecessors, more satisfactorily established by him, more com-
prehensively applied to particulars, more rationally connected with
each other, and therefore more worthy of the name of *discovery*,
than any with which we are acquainted; if we ought not, with some
hesitation, to except the first steps of the Grecian philosophers
towards a Theory of Morals [2].' It is to be wished that the attention of this great scholar had been called to the writings of our
philosopher. Mencius was senior to Zeno, though a portion of their
lives synchronised. Butler certainly was not indebted to him for
the views which he advocated; but it seems to me that Mencius
had left him nothing to *discover*.

But the question now arises—' Is the view of human nature
propounded by Mencius correct?' So far as yet appears, I see not
The proper use of Mencius's views thus far considered. how the question can be answered otherwise than in
the affirmative. Man was formed for virtue. Be it
that his conduct is very far from being conformed to
virtue, that simply fastens on him the shame of guilt. Fallen as
he may be,—fallen as I believe and know he is,—his nature still
bears its testimony, when properly interrogated, against all unrighteousness. Man, heathen man, *a Gentile without the law, is still
a law to himself.* So the apostle Paul affirms; and to no moral
teacher of Greece or Rome can we appeal for so grand an illustration of the averment as we find in Mencius. I would ask those
whom his sayings offend, whether it would have been better for
his countrymen if he had taught a contrary doctrine, and told them
that man's nature is bad, and that the more they obeyed all its

[1] Bk. II. Pt. I. li. 9.   [2] Encyclopædia Britannica (8th edition), Second Preliminary
Dissertation ; on Butler.

lusts and passions, the more would they be in accordance with it, and the more pursuing the right path? Such a question does not need a reply. The proper use of Mencius's principles is to reprove the Chinese—and ourselves as well—of the thousand acts of sin of which they and we are guilty, that come within their sweep and under their condemnation.

From the ideal of man to his actualism there is a vast descent. Between what he ought to be and what he is, the contrast is melancholy. *Benevolence*, said our philosopher, 'is the characteristic of man[1].' It is 'the wide house in which the world should dwell,' while *propriety* is 'the correct position in which the world should ever be found,' and *righteousness* is 'the great path which men should ever be pursuing[2].' In opposition to this, however, hatred, improprieties, unrighteousness are constant phenomena of human life. We find men hateful and hating one another, quenching the light that is in them, and walking in darkness to perform all deeds of shame. 'There is none that doeth good; no, not one.' Mencius would have denied this last sentence, claiming that the sages should be excepted from it; but he is ready enough to admit the fact that men in general do evil and violate the law of their nature. They sacrifice the noble portion of themselves for the gratification of the ignoble; they follow that part which is little, and not that which is great. He can say nothing further in explanation of the fact. He points out indeed the effect of injurious circumstances, and the power of evil example; and he has said several things on these subjects worthy of notice:—'It is not to be wondered at that the king is not wise! Suppose the case of the most easily growing thing in the world;—if you let it have one day's genial heat, and then expose it for ten days to cold, it will not be able to grow. It is but seldom that I have an audience of the king, and when I retire, there come all those who act upon him like the cold. Though I succeed in bringing out some buds of goodness, of what avail is it[3]?' 'In good years the children of the people are most of them good, while in bad years the most of them abandon themselves to evil. It is not owing to their natural powers conferred on them by Heaven that they are thus different: the abandonment is owing to the circumstances through which they allow their minds to be

Marginal note: How Mencius admitted much actual evil, and how he accounted for it.

---

[1] Bk. VII. Pt. II. xvi.   [2] Bk. III. Pt. II. ii. 3.   [3] Bk. VI. Pt. I. ix.

ensnared and drowned in evil. There now is barley: let it be sown and covered up; the ground being the same, and the time of sowing likewise the same, it grows rapidly up, and when the full time is come, it is all found to be ripe. Any inequalities *of produce* will be owing to *the difference of* the soil as rich or poor, the unequal nourishment afforded by the rains and dews, and to the different ways in which man has performed his business[1].'

The inconsistencies in human conduct did not escape his observation. After showing that there is that in human nature which will sometimes make men part with life sooner than with righteousness, he goes on:—'And yet a man will accept ten thousand *chung* without any consideration of propriety and righteousness. What can they add to him? · When he takes them, is it not that he may obtain beautiful mansions, that he may secure the services of wives and concubines, or that the poor and needy may be helped by him?' The scalpel is used here with a bold and skilful hand. The lust of the flesh, and the lust of the eyes, and the pride of life are laid bare, nor does our author stop, till he has exposed the subtle workings of the delusion that the end may sanctify the means, that evil may be wrought that good may come. He pursues:—'In the former case the offered bounty was not received, though it would have saved from death, and now the emolument is taken for the sake of beautiful mansions. The bounty that would have preserved from death was not received, and the emolument is taken to get the services of wives and concubines. The bounty that would have saved from death was not received, and the emolument is taken that one's poor and needy acquaintance may be helped. Was it then not possible likewise to decline this? This is a case of what is called—"Losing the proper nature of one's mind[2]."'

To the principle implied in the concluding sentences of this quotation Mencius most pertinaciously adheres. He will not allow Original badness cannot be predicated from actual evil. that original badness can be predicated of human nature from any amount of actual wickedness. 'The trees,' said he, 'of the Niû Mountain were once beautiful. Being situated, however, in the borders of a large State, they were hewn down with axes and bills;—and could they retain their beauty? Still, through the activity of the vegetative life day and night, and the nourishing influence of the

rain and dew, they were not without buds and sprouts springing
forth;—but then came the cattle and goats, and browsed upon them.
To these things is owing the bare and stripped appearance of the
mountain, which when people see, they think it was never finely
wooded. But is this the proper nature of the mountain? And so also
of what properly belongs to man:—shall it be said that the mind
of any man was without benevolence and righteousness? The way
in which a man loses his proper goodness of mind is like the way in
which the trees are denuded by axes and bills. Hewn down day
after day, can the mind retain its beauty? But there is a development of its life day and night; and in the calm air of the morning,
just between night and day, the mind feels in a degree the desires
and aversions which are proper to humanity; but the feeling is not
strong, and it is fettered and destroyed by what takes place during
the day. This fettering takes place again and again; the restorative
influence of the night is not sufficient to preserve *the proper goodness of the mind;* and when this proves insufficient for that purpose,
the nature becomes not much different from that of the irrational
animals, which when people see, they think that it never had those
powers *which I assert.* But does this condition represent the
feelings proper to humanity[1]?'

Up to this point I fail to perceive anything in Mencius's view of
human nature that is contrary to the teachings of our Christian

The actual per-
fection of the
sages, and pos-
sible perfection
of all.

scriptures, and that may not be employed with advantage by the missionary in preaching the Gospel
to the Chinese. It is far from covering what we
know to be the whole duty of man, yet it is defective
rather than erroneous. Deferring any consideration of this for
a brief space, I now inquire whether Mencius, having an ideal of
the goodness of human nature, held also that it had been and could
be realised? The answer is that he did. The actual realisation
he found in the sages, and he contended that it was within the
reach of every individual. 'All things which are the same in kind,'
he says, 'are like one another;—why should we doubt in regard to
man, as if he were a solitary exception to this? The sage and we
are the same in kind[2].' The feet, the mouths, the eyes of the sages
were not different from those of other people, neither were their
minds. 'Is it so,' he was once asked, 'that all men may be Yâos

and Shuns?' and he answered, 'It is,' adding by way of explanation:—'To walk slowly, keeping behind his elders, is to perform
the part of a younger brother, and to walk quickly and precede his
elders is to violate that duty.   Now, is it what a man cannot do,—
to walk slowly?   IT IS WHAT HE DOES NOT DO.   The course of Yâo
and Shun was simply that of filial piety and fraternal duty.   Wear
the clothes of Yâo, repeat the words of Yâo, and do the actions of
Yâo;—and you will just be a Yâo[1].'

Among the sages, however, Mencius made a distinction.   Yâo
and Shun exceeded all the rest, unless it might be Confucius. Those
three never came short of, never went beyond, the law of their
nature.   The ideal and the actual were in them always one and the
same.   The others had only attained to perfection by vigorous effort
and culture.   Twice at least he has told us this.   'Yâo and Shun
were what they were by nature; T'ang and Wû were so by returning
to natural virtue[2].'   The actual result, however, was the same, and
therefore he could hold them all up as models to his countrymen of
the style of man which they all ought to be and might be.   What
the compass and square were in the hands of the workman,
enabling him to form perfect circles and squares, the sages, 'perfectly exhibiting the human relations,' might be to every earnest
individual, enabling him to perfect himself as they were perfect[3].

Here we feel that the doctrine of Mencius wants an element which
Revelation supplies.   He knows nothing of the fact that 'by one
man sin entered into the world, and death by sin;
and so death passed' (passed on, extended, διῆλθεν)
'to all men, because all sinned.'   We have our ideal
as well as he; but for the living reality of it we must
go back to Adam, as he was made by God in His own
image, after His likeness.   In him the model is soon
shattered, and we do not discover it again, till God's own Son
appears in the world, made in the likeness of sinful flesh, yet without sin.   While He died for our transgressions, He left us also an
example, that we should walk in His steps; and as we do so, we
are carried on to glory and virtue.   At the same time we find a law
in our members warring against the law in our minds, and bringing
us into captivity to sin.   However we may strive after our ideal,
we do not succeed in reaching it.   The more we grow in the know-

*Mencius's doc-
trine contains no
acknowledgment
of the universal
proneness to evil.
His ideal has
been realised by
sages, and may be
realised by all.*

---

[1] Bk. VI. Pt. II. ii. 1, 4, 5.   [2] Bk. VII. Pt. I. xxx. 1; Pt. II. xxxiii. 1.   [3] Bk. IV.
Pt. I. ii. 1.

ledge of Christ, and see in Him the glory of humanity in its true
estate, the greater do we feel our own distance to be from it, and
that of ourselves we cannot attain to it. There is something wrong
about us ; we need help from without in order to become even what
our nature, apart from Revelation, tells us we ought to be.

When Mencius therefore points us to Yâo, Shun, and Confucius,
and says that they were perfect, we cannot accept his statement.
Understanding that he is speaking of them only in the sphere of
human relations, we must yet believe that in many things they came
short. One of them, the greatest of the three in Mencius's estimation, Confucius, again and again confesses so of himself. He was
seventy years old, he says, before he could follow what his heart
desired without transgressing what was right [1]. It might have been
possible to convince the sage that he was under a delusion in this
important matter even at that advanced age ; but what his language
allows is sufficient to upset Mencius's appeal to him. The image of
sagely perfection is broken by it. It proves to be but a brilliant
and unsubstantial phantasm of our philosopher's own imagining.

When he insists again, that every individual may become what
he fancies that the sages were,—i. e. perfect, living in love, walking
in righteousness, observant of propriety, approving whatsoever is
good, and disapproving whatever is evil,—he is pushing his doctrine
beyond its proper limits ; he is making a use of it of which it is not
capable. It supplies a law of conduct, and I have set it forth as
entitled to our highest admiration for the manner in which it does
so ; but law gives only the knowledge of what we are required to
do ; it does not give the power to do it. We have seen how when
it was necessary to explain accurately his statement that the nature
of man is good, Mencius defined it as meaning that ' it is constituted
for the practice of that which is good.' Because it is so constituted,
it follows that every man ought to practise what is good. But some
disorganisation may have happened to the nature ; some sad change
may have come over it. The very fact that man has, in Mencius's
own words, to recover his ' lost mind [2],' shows that the object of the
constitution of the nature has not been realised. Whether he can
recover it or not, therefore, is a question altogether different from
that of its proper design.

In one place, indeed, Mencius has said that ' the great man is he

---

[1] Confucian Analects, II. iv. 6.   [2] Bk. VI. Pt. I. xi. 4.

who does not lose his child's-heart [1].' I can only suppose that, by that expression—'the child's-heart,' he intends the ideal goodness which he affirms of our nature. But to attribute that to the child as actually existing in it is absurd. It has neither done good nor evil. It possesses the capacity for either. It will by-and-by awake to the consciousness that it ought to follow after the one and eschew the other; but when it does so,—I should rather say when *he* does so for the child has now emerged from a mere creature existence, and assumed the functions of a moral being, he will find that he has already given himself to inordinate affection for the objects of sense; and in the pursuit of gratification he is reckless of what must be acknowledged to be the better and nobler part, reckless also of the interest and claims of others, and glows, whenever thwarted, into passion and fury. The youth is more pliant than the man in whom the dominion of self-seeking has become ingrained as a habit; but no sooner does he become a subject of law, than he is aware of the fact that when he would do good, evil is present with him. The boy has to go in search of his 'lost heart,' as truly as the man of fourscore. Even in him there is an 'old man, corrupt according to the deceitful lusts,' which he has to put off.

Butler had an immense advantage over Mencius, arising from his knowledge of the truths of Revelation. Many, admiring his

Butler's advantage over Mencius, and that he does not make the same application of their common principles.

sermons, have yet expressed a measure of dissatisfaction, because he does not in them make explicit reference to the condition of man as fallen and depraved. That he fully admitted the fact we know.

He says elsewhere:—'Mankind are represented in scripture to be in a state of ruin.' 'If mankind are corrupted and depraved in their moral character, and so are unfit for that state which Christ is gone to prepare for His disciples; and if the assistance of God's Spirit be necessary to renew their nature, in the degree requisite to their being qualified for that state; all which is implied in the express, though figurative declaration, *Except a man be born of the Spirit, he cannot see the kingdom of God* [2.]' . . . How is it, then, that there is no mention of this in the sermons? Dissatisfaction, I have said, has been expressed on account of this silence, and it would have taken the form of more pointed utterance, and more decided condemnation, but for the awe of his great

[1] Bk. IV. Pt. II. xii.   [2] The Analogy of Religion, Part II. chap. i.

name, and the general appreciation of the service he rendered to Christianity in his work on 'The Analogy of Religion.' But, in truth, dissatisfaction at all is out of place. Butler wrote his sermons as he wrote his Analogy, in consequence of the peculiar necessity of his times. More particularly against Hobbes, denying all moral sentiments and social affections, and making a regard to personal advantage the only motive of human action, it was his business to prove that man's nature is of a very different constitution, comprehending disinterested affections, and above all the supreme element of conscience, which, 'had it strength as it has right, would govern the world.' He proves this, and so accomplishes his work. He had merely to do with the ideal of humanity. It did not belong to him to dwell on the actual feebleness of man to perform what is good. He might have added a few paragraphs to this effect; but it was not the character of his mind to go beyond the task which he had set himself. What is of importance to be observed here is, that he does not make the application of their common principles which Mencius does. He knows of no perfect men; he does not tell his readers that they have merely to set about following their nature, and that, without any aid from without, they will surely and easily go on to perfection.

Mencius is not to be blamed for his ignorance of what is to us the *Doctrine of the Fall*. He had no means of becoming acquainted with it. We have to regret, however, that his study of human nature produced in him no deep *feeling* on account of men's proneness to go astray. He never betrays any consciousness of his own weakness. In this respect he is again inferior to Confucius, and is far from being, as I have said of him in another aspect of his character, 'more admirable' than he. In the former volume I have shown that we may sometimes recognise in what the sage says of himself the expressions of a genuine humility. He acknowledges that he comes short of what he knows he ought to be. We do not meet with this in Mencius. His merit is that of the speculative thinker. His glance is searching and his penetration deep; but there is wanting that moral sensibility which would draw us to him, in our best moments, as a man of like passions with ourselves. The absence of humility is naturally accompanied with a lack of *sympathy*. There is a hardness about his teachings. He is the professor, performing an operation in the class-room, amid a throng of pupils who are admiring his science

Marginal note: Mencius's lacking in humility, and sympathy with human error.

and dexterity, and who forgets in the triumph of his skill the
suffering of the patient. The transgressors of their nature are to
Mencius 'the tyrants of themselves,' or 'the self-abandoned.' The
utmost stretch of his commiseration is a contemptuous 'Alas for
them[1]!' The radical defect of the orthodox moral school of China,
that there only needs a knowledge of duty to insure its performance,
is in him exceedingly apparent. Confucius, Tsze-sze, and Mencius,
most strangely never thought of calling this principle in question.
It is always as in the formula of Tsze-sze :—' Given the sincerity,
and there shall be the intelligence; given the intelligence, and there
shall be the sincerity.'

I said above that Mencius's doctrine of human nature was
defective, inasmuch as even his ideal does not cover the whole
field of duty. He says very little of what we owe
to God. There is no glow of natural piety in his
pages. Instead of the name *God*, containing in
itself a recognition of the divine personality and
supremacy, we hear from him more commonly, as from Confucius,
of *Heaven*. Butler has said:—'By the love of God, I would
understand all those regards, all those affections of mind, which
are due immediately to Him from such a creature as man, and
which rest in Him as their end[2].' Of such affections Mencius
knows nothing. In one place he speaks of 'delighting in Heaven[3],'
but he is speaking, when he does so, of the sovereign who with
a great State serves a small one, and the delight is seen in certain
condescensions to the weak and unworthy. Never once, where he
is treating of the nature of man, does he make mention of any
exercise of the mind as due directly to God. The services of
religion come in China under the principle of propriety, and are
only a cold formalism; but even here, other things come with
Mencius before them. We are told:—'The richest fruit of love is
this,—the service of one's parents; the richest fruit of righteousness is this,—the obeying one's elder brothers; the richest fruit of
wisdom is this,—the knowing those two things, and not departing
from them; the richest fruit of propriety is this,—the ordering
and adorning those two things[4].' How different is this from the

Mencius's ideal of human nature does not embrace duty to God.

[1] Bk. IV. Pt. I. x.   [2] First Sermon *Upon the Love of God*.   [3] Bk. I. Pt. II. ii. 3.
[4] Bk. IV. Pt. I. xxvii. My friend, the Rev. Mr. Moule, (now Bishop) of Ningpo, has supplied
me with the following interesting coincidence with the sentiments of Mencius in this passage,
from one of the letters of Charles Lamb to Coleridge, dated November 14, 1796:—'Oh, my friend,
cultivate the filial feelings; and let no one think himself relieved from the kind charities of

reiterated declaration of the Scriptures, that 'the fear of the Lord is the beginning of wisdom!' The first and great commandment, 'Thou shalt *love* the Lord thy God, with all thy heart and soul and mind and strength,' was never thought of, much less delivered, by any Chinese philosopher or sage. Had Mencius apprehended this, and seen how all our duties to our fellow-men are to be performed as to God, he could not have thought so highly as he did of man's powers; a suspicion might have grown up that there is a shadow on the light which he has in himself.

This absence from Mencius's ideal of our nature of the recognition of man's highest obligations is itself a striking illustration of man's estrangement from God. His usage of the term Heaven has combined with the similar practice of his Master to prepare the way for the grosser conceptions of the modern literati, who would often seem to deny the divine personality altogether, and substitute for both God and Heaven a mere principle of order or fitness of things. It has done more: it has left the people in the mass to become an easy prey to the idolatrous fooleries of Buddhism. Yea, the *unreligiousness* of the teachers has helped to deprave still more the religion of the nation, such as it is, and has made of its services a miserable pageant of irreverent forms.

It is time to have done with this portion of my theme. It may be thought that I have done Mencius more than justice in the first part of my remarks, and less than justice at the last; but I hope it is not so. A very important use is to be made both of what he succeeds in, and where he fails, in his discoursing upon human nature. His principles may be, and, I conceive, ought to be, turned against himself. They should be pressed to produce the conviction of sin. There is enough in them, if the conscience be but quickened by the Spirit of God, to make the haughtiest scholar cry out, 'O wretched man that I am! who shall deliver me from this body of death?' Then may it be said to him with effect, ' Behold the Lamb of God, who taketh away the sin of the world!' Then may Christ, as a new and true exemplar of all that man should be, be displayed, 'altogether lovely,' to the trembling mind! Then may a *new heart* be received from Him, that shall thrill in the acknowledgment of the claims both of men and God, and girding up the loins of the mind, address itself to walk in all His commandments and ordinances

relationship : these shall give him peace at the last ; *these are the best foundation for every species of benevolence.*'

blameless! One thing should be plain. In Mencius's lessons on
human duty there is no hope for his countrymen. If they serve as
a schoolmaster to bring them to Christ, they will have done their
part; but it is from Christ alone that the help of the Chinese can
come.

6. Besides giving more explicit expression to the doctrine of the
goodness of man's nature than had been done before him, Mencius
has the credit also of calling attention to *the nourishment of the
passion-nature*. It may be questioned whether I translate his
language exactly by this phrase. What I render *the passion-nature*,
Julien renders by *'vitalis spiritus.'* The philosopher says himself
that it is difficult to describe what he intends. Attempting such
a description, he says:—'This is it:—It is exceedingly great and
exceedingly strong. Being nourished by rectitude, and sustaining
no injury, it fills up all between heaven and earth. This is it:—It
is the mate and assistant of righteousness and reason. Without it
man is in a state of starvation. It is produced by the accumulation
of righteous deeds; it is not to be taken, as by surprise, by incidental
acts of righteousness. If the mind does not feel complacency in the
conduct, *this* is starved[1].' From such predicates we may be sure that
it is not anything merely or entirely *physical* of which he is speaking. 'The righteous,' said Solomon, 'are bold as a lion.' The
Hebrew saying is very much in Mencius's style. That boldness is
the result of the *nourishment* for which he thought he had a peculiar
aptitude. Strong in it and in a knowledge of words, a faculty of
discovering the moral aberrations of others from their forms of
speech, he was able to boast of possessing 'an unperturbed mind;'
he could 'sit in the centre' of his being, 'and enjoy bright day,
whatever clouds and storms gathered around him.

The nourishment, therefore, of 'the passion-nature,' 'the vital
spirit,' or whatever name we choose to give to the subject, is only
an effect of general good-doing. This is the practical lesson from
all Mencius's high-sounding words. He has illustrated it amusingly:
—'There was a man of Sung, who was grieved that his growing corn
was not longer, and pulled it up. Having done this, he returned
home, looking very wearied, and said to his people, "I am tired
to-day. I have been helping the corn to grow long." His son ran
to look at it, and found the corn all withered. There are few in the

[1] Bk. II. Pt. I. ii. 13-15.

world, who do not assist the corn *of their passion-nature* to grow long. Some consider it of no benefit to them, and let it alone:—they do not weed their corn. Those who assist it to grow long, pull out their corn. What they do is not only of no benefit to the nature, but it also injures it[1].'

This portion of Mencius's teaching need not detain us. He has put a simple truth in a striking way. That is his merit. It hardly seems of sufficient importance to justify the use which has been made of it in vindicating for him a place among the sages of his country.

7. I said I should end the discussion of Mencius's opinions by pointing out what I conceive to be his chief defects as a moral and political teacher. His defects, however, in the former respect have been already not lightly touched on. So far as they were the consequence of his ignorance, without the light which Revelation sheds on the whole field of human duty, and the sanctions which it discloses of a future state of retribution, I do not advance any charge against his character. That he never indicates any wish to penetrate futurity, and ascertain what comes after death; that he never indicates any consciousness of human weakness, nor moves his mind Godward, longing for more light:—these are things which exhibit strongly the contrast between the mind of the East and the West. His self-sufficiency is his great fault. To know ourselves is commonly supposed to be an important step to humility; but it is not so with him. He has spoken remarkably about the effects of calamity and difficulties. He says:—'When Heaven is about to confer a great office on a man, it first exercises his mind with suffering, and his sinews and bones with toil; it exposes his body to hunger, and subjects him to extreme poverty; it confounds his undertakings. By all these methods it stimulates his mind, hardens his nature, and supplies his incompetencies[2].' Such have been the effects of Heaven's exercising some men with calamities; but if the issue has been a fitting for the *highest offices*, there has been a softening of the nature rather than a hardening of it. Mencius was a stranger to the humbling of the lofty looks of man, and the bowing down of his haughtiness, that the Lord alone may be exalted.

His faults as a political teacher are substantially the same as those of Confucius. More than was the case with his sayings of

---

[1] Bk. II. Pt. I. ii. 16.   [2] Bk. VI. Pt. II. xv.

a political character, the utterances of Mencius have reference to the
condition and needs of his own age.   They were for the time then
being, and not for all time.   He knew as little as Confucius of any
other great and independent nation besides his own; and he has
left one maxim which is deeply treasured by the rulers and the
people of China at the present day, and feeds the supercilious idea
which they are so unwilling to give up of their own superiority
to foreigners.   'I have heard,' said he, 'of men using *the doctrines*
of our great land to change barbarians, but I have never yet heard
of any being changed by barbarians.'   'I have heard of birds leaving
dark valleys to remove to lofty trees, but I have not heard of their
descending from lofty trees to enter into dark valleys[1].'   Mongol
and Tartar sway have not broken the charm of this dangerous
flattery, because only in warlike energy were the Mongols and
Tartars superior to the Chinese, and when they conquered the
country they did homage to its sages.   During the last five-and-
twenty years, Christian Powers have come to ask admission into
China, and to claim to be received as her equals.   They do not wish
to conquer her territory, though they have battered and broken her
defences.   With fear and trembling their advances are contemplated.
The feeling of dislike to them arises from the dread of their power,
and suspicion of their faith.   It is feared that they come to subdue;
it is known that they come to change.   The idol of Chinese
superiority is about to be broken.   Broken it must be ere long,
and a new generation of thinkers will arise, to whom Mencius will
be a study but not a guide.

SECTION III.

HIS IMMEDIATE DISCIPLES.

The disciples of Mencius were much fewer in number, and of less
distinction than those of Confucius.   The longest list does not make
them amount to twenty-five; and it is only to complete my plan
that I devote a page or two here to their names and surnames.

The chief authority in reference to them is Châo Ch'î.   In A.D.
115, the then emperor of the Sung dynasty conferred titles on all
mentioned by Ch'î as disciples or pupils of Mencius, and enacted

[1] Bk. III. Pt. I. iv. 12, 15.

that they should share in the sacrifices offered to their master in his temple in the district of Tsâu. Chû Hsî gives his verdict in the 'Collected Comments' against two of them, and no subsequent scholar has ventured to restore them to their place in the Mencian school. Other names, however, have been found by different writers to supply their room. It is not worth our while to take notice of their discussions.

1. Yo-chăng K'o, styled Tsze-âo (樂正克, 字子敖), a native of Lû. He was titled in 1115 as the 'State-advantaging Marquis' (利國侯). Under the present dynasty, in 1724, he had a place assigned him in the temples of Confucius, the 35th on the west, in the outer court, with the common title of 'The Ancient Worthy, the Philosopher Yo-chăng.'

2. Wan Chang (萬章). He was titled in 1115 as the 'Baron of Extensive Arousing' (博興伯). He has now the next place to the preceding in the Confucian temples.

3. Kung-sun Ch'âu (公孫丑), a native of Ch'î. He was also elevated to the temple of Confucius, and has now the place, east, corresponding to that of Wan Chang, on the west. His title conferred in 1115 was—'Baron of Longevity and Glory' (壽光伯).

4. Kung-tû (公都), immediately precedes Kung-sun Ch'âu in the temples. In the temple of Mencius he was the 'Baron of Tranquillity and Shadiness' (平陰伯).

The above four are the only disciples of Mencius who have places assigned to them in the temples of Confucius.

5. Ch'ăn Tsin (陳臻). 6. Ch'ung Yü (充虞). 7. Chî-sun (季孫). 8. Tsze-shû Î (子叔疑).

These two last are held by Chû Hsî not to have been disciples of Mencius.

9. Kâo (高子). This is to be distinguished from another scholar of the same name, referred to in Bk. VI. Pt. II. iii.

10. Hsü Pî (徐辟). 11. Hsien-ch'iû Măng (咸丘蒙).

12. Ch'ăn Tâi (陳代). 13. P'ăng Kăng (彭更). 14. Û-lû Lien (屋盧連). 15. T'âo Ying (桃應).

These fifteen are said by Châo Ch'î to have been disciples of Mencius. The four that follow are said to have studied under him, or to have been his pupils.

16. Măng Chung (孟仲子). 17. Kâo (告子). This Kâo

can hardly be said to have studied under Mencius ; he only argued with him.   18. Tăng Kăng, or Kăng of Tăng (滕更).   19. Păn-ch'ăng Kwo (盆成括).

These nineteen rest on the authority of Châo Ch'î.   Others have added to them—20. Kung-ming Kâo (公明高).   21. K'wang Chang (匡章).   22. Ch'ăn Chung (陳仲).   23. Lî Lâu (離婁).

APPENDIX.

I have thought it would be interesting to many readers to append here the Essays of two distinguished scholars of China on the subject of Human Nature.   The one is in direct opposition to Mencius's doctrine ; according to the other, his doctrine is insufficient to explain the phenomena.   The author of the first, Hsün K'wang (荀 [al. 孫] 況), more commonly called Hsün Ch'ing (卿), was not very much posterior to Mencius.   He is said to have borne office both in Ch'î and Ch'û, and to have had at one time Lî Sze (李斯), the prime minister of Shih Hwang-tî, as a pupil.   His Works which still remain form a considerable volume.   The second essay is from the work of Han Yü, mentioned above, Chap. I. Sect. IV. 4.   I shall not occupy any space with criticisms on the style or sentiments of the writers.   If the translation appear at times to be inelegant or obscure, the fault is perhaps as much in the original as in myself. A comprehensive and able sketch of 'The Ethics of the Chinese, with special reference to the Doctrines of Human Nature and Sin,' by the Rev. Griffith John, was read before the North China Branch of the Royal Asiatic Society, in November, 1859, and has been published separately.   The essays of Hsün and Han are both reviewed in it.

I. THAT THE NATURE IS EVIL.—By the PHILOSOPHER HSÜN

The nature of man is evil; the good which it shows is factitious. There belongs to it, even at his birth, the love of gain, and as actions are in accordance with this, contentions and robberies grow up, and self-denial and yielding to others are not to be found; there belong to it envy and dislike, and as actions are in accordance with these, violence and injuries spring up, and self-devotedness and faith are not to be found; there belong to it the desires of the ears and the eyes, leading to the love of sounds and beauty, and as the actions are in accordance with these, lewdness and disorder spring up, and righteousness and propriety, with their various orderly displays, are not to be found. It thus appears, that to follow man's nature and yield obedience to its feelings will assuredly conduct to contentions and robberies, to the violation of the duties belonging to every one's lot, and the confounding of all distinctions, till the issue will be in a state of savagism; and that there must be the influence of teachers and laws, and the guidance of propriety and righteousness, from which will spring self-denial, yielding to others, and an observance of the well-ordered regulations of conduct, till the issue will be a state of good government.—From all this it is plain that the nature of man is evil; the good which it shows is factitious.

To illustrate.—A crooked stick must be submitted to the pressing-frame to soften and bend it, and then it becomes straight; a blunt knife must be submitted to the grindstone and whetstone, and then it becomes sharp: so, the nature of man, being evil, must be submitted to teachers and laws, and then it becomes correct; it must be submitted to propriety and righteousness, and then it comes under government. If men were without teachers and laws, their condition would be one of deflection and insecurity, entirely incorrect; if they were without propriety and righteousness, their condition would be one of rebellious disorder, rejecting all government. The sage kings of antiquity, understanding that the nature of man was thus evil, in a state of hazardous deflection, and incorrect, rebellious and disorderly, and refusing to be governed, set up the principles of righteousness and propriety, and framed laws and regulations to straighten and ornament the feelings of that nature and correct them,

荀子性惡篇

人之性惡其善者偽也。今人之性、生而有好利焉、順是故爭奪生而辭讓亡焉、生而有疾惡焉、順是故殘賊生、而忠信亡焉、生而有耳目之欲、有好聲色焉、順是故淫亂生、而禮義文理亡焉、然則從人之性、順人之情、必出於爭奪合於犯分亂理而歸於暴、故必將有師法之化、禮義之道、然後出於辭讓、合於文理、而歸於治、用此觀之、然則人之性惡明矣、其善者偽也。

故枸木必將待檃栝烝矯、然後直、鈍金必將待礱厲、然後利、今人之性惡、必將待師法然後正、得禮義然後治、今人無師法、則偏險而不正、無禮義則悖亂而不治、古者聖王以人之性惡、以爲偏險而不正、悖亂而不治、是以爲之起禮義制法度、以矯飾人之情性而正之、以擾化人之情性而導之也、使皆出於治、合於道者也。今之人化師法積文學道禮義

to tame and change those same feelings and guide them, so that they might all go forth in the way of moral government and in agreement with reason. Now, the man who is transformed by teachers and laws, gathers on himself the ornament of learning, and proceeds in the path of propriety and righteousness is a superior man; and he who gives the reins to his nature and its feelings, indulges its resentments, and walks contrary to propriety and righteousness is a mean man. Looking at the subject in this way, we see clearly that the nature of man is evil; the good which it shows is factitious.

Mencius said, 'Man has only to learn, and his nature appears to be good;' but I reply,—It is not so. To say so shows that he had not attained to the knowledge of man's nature, nor examined into the difference between what is natural in man and what is factitious. The natural is what the constitution spontaneously moves to:—it needs not to be learned, it needs not to be followed hard after; propriety and righteousness are what the sages have given birth to:—it is by learning that men become capable of them, it is by hard practice that they achieve them. That which is in man, not needing to be learned and striven after, is what I call natural; that in man which is attained to by learning, and achieved by hard striving, is what I call factitious. This is the distinction between those two. By the nature of man, the eyes are capable of seeing, and the ears are capable of hearing. But the power of seeing is inseparable from the eyes, and the power of hearing is inseparable from the ears;—it is plain that the faculties of seeing and hearing do not need to be learned. Mencius says, 'The nature of man is good, but all lose and ruin their nature, and therefore it becomes bad;' but I say that this representation is erroneous. Man being born with his nature, when he thereafter departs from its simple constituent elements, he must lose it. From this consideration we may see clearly that man's nature is evil. What might be called the nature's being good, would be if there were no departing from its simplicity to beautify it, no departing from its elementary dispositions to sharpen it. Suppose that those simple elements no more needed beautifying, and the mind's thoughts no more needed to be turned to good, than the power of vision which is inseparable from the eyes, and the power of hearing which is inseparable from the ears, need to be learned, *then we might say that the nature is good, just as* we say that the eyes see and the ears hear. It is the nature of man, when hungry, to desire to be filled; when cold, to desire to be warmed; when tired, to desire rest:—these are the feelings and nature of man. But now, a man is hungry, and in the presence of an elder he does not dare to eat before him:—he is yielding to that elder; he is tired with labour, and he does not dare to ask for rest:—he is working for some one. A son's yielding to his father and a younger

不離耳故曰目明而耳聰也今人之性飢而
於善若夫可以見之明不離目可以聽之聰
離其資而利之也使夫資朴之於美心意之
性惡明矣所謂性善者不離其朴而美之不
朴雖其資必失而喪之用此觀之然則人之
性故也曰若是則過矣今人之性善將皆失喪其
可學明矣孟子曰今人之性善將皆失喪其
不離目可以聽之聰不離耳目明而耳聰不
人之性目可以見耳可以聽夫可以見之明
事而成之在人者謂之僞是性僞之分也今
可學不可事而在人者謂之性可學而能可
之所生也人之所學而能所事而成者也不
性者天之就也不可學不可事禮義者聖人
知人之性而不察乎人之性僞之分者也凡
孟子曰人之學者其性善曰是不然是不及
也
人用此觀之然則人之性惡明矣其善者僞
者爲君子縱性情安恣睢而違禮義者爲小

brother to his elder, a son's labouring for his father and a younger brother for his elder:—these two instances of conduct are contrary to the nature and against the feelings; but they are according to the course laid down for a filial son, and to the refined distinctions of propriety and righteousness. It appears that if there were an accordance with the feelings and the nature, there would be no self-denial and yielding to others. Self-denial and yielding to others are contrary to the feelings and the nature. In this way we come to see how clear it is that the nature of man is evil; the good which it shows is factitious.

An inquirer will ask, 'If man's nature be evil, whence do propriety and righteousness arise?' I reply:—All propriety and righteousness are the artificial production of the sages, and are not to be considered as growing out of the nature of man. It is just as when a potter makes a vessel from the clay;—the vessel is the product of the workman's art, and is not to be considered as growing out of his nature. Or it is as when another workman cuts and hews a vessel out of wood;—it is the product of his art, and is not to be considered as growing out of his nature. The sages pondered long in thought and gave themselves to practice, and so they succeeded in producing propriety and righteousness, and setting up laws and regulations. Thus it is that propriety and righteousness, laws and regulations, are the artificial product of the sages, and are not to be considered as growing properly from the nature of man.

If we speak of the fondness of the eyes for beauty, or of the mouth for pleasant flavours, or of the mind for gain, or of the bones and skin for the enjoyment of ease;—all these grow out of the natural feelings of man. The object is presented and the desire is felt; there needs no effort to produce it. But when the object is presented, and the affection does not move till after hard effort, I say that this effect is factitious. Those cases prove the difference between what is produced by nature and what is produced by art.

Thus the sages transformed their nature, and commenced their artificial work. Having commenced this work with their nature, they produced propriety and righteousness. When propriety and righteousness were produced, they proceeded to frame laws and regulations. It appears, therefore, that propriety and righteousness, laws and regulations, are given birth

是聖人之所生也故聖人之所以同於衆其不異於衆
起於性而生禮義禮義生而制法度然則禮義法度者
是性偽之所生其不同之徵也故聖人化性而起偽偽
者也夫感而不能然必且待事而後然者謂之生於偽
是皆生於人之情性者也感而自然不待事而後生之
若夫目好色耳好聲口好味心好利骨體膚理好愉佚
度者是生於聖人之偽非故生於人之性也
聖人積思慮習偽故以生禮義而起法度然則禮義法
木而成器然則器生於工人之偽非故生於人之性也
然則器生於工人之偽非故生於人之性也故工人斲
於聖人之偽非故生於人之性也故陶人埏埴而為器
問者曰人之性惡則禮義惡生應之曰凡禮義者是生
性矣用此觀之然則人之性惡明矣其善者偽也
禮義之文理也故順情性則不辭讓矣辭讓則悖於情
乎兄此二行者皆反於性而悖於情也然而孝子之道
代也夫子之讓乎父弟之讓乎兄子之代乎父弟之代
而不敢先食者將有所讓也勞而不敢求息者將有所
欲飽寒而欲煖勞而欲休此人之情性也今人飢見長

to by the sages. Wherein they agree with all other men and do not differ from them, is their nature ; wherein they differ from and exceed other men, is this artificial work.

Now to love gain and desire to get ;—this is the natural feeling of men. Suppose the case that there is an amount of property or money to be divided among brothers, and let this natural feeling to love gain and to desire to get come into play ;—why, then the brothers will be opposing, and snatching from, one another. But where the changing influence of propriety and righteousness, with their refined distinctions, has taken effect, a man will give up to any other man. Thus it is that if they act in accordance with their natural feelings, brothers will quarrel together ; and if they have come under the transforming influence of propriety and righteousness, men will give up to other men, to say nothing of brothers. Again, the fact that men wish to do what is good, is because their nature is bad. The thin wishes to be thick ; the ugly wish to be beautiful ; the narrow wishes to be wide ; the poor wish to be rich ; the mean wish to be noble :—when anything is not possessed in one's self, he seeks for it outside himself. But the rich do not wish for wealth ; the noble do not wish for position :—when anything is possessed by one's self, he does not need to go beyond himself for it. When we look at things in this way, we perceive that the fact of men's wishing to do what is good is because their nature is evil. It is the case indeed, that man's nature is without propriety and benevolence :— he therefore studies them with vigorous effort and seeks to have them. It is the case that by nature he does not know propriety and righteousness :—he therefore thinks and reflects and seeks to know them. Speaking of man, therefore, as he is by birth simply, he is without propriety and righteousness, without the knowledge of propriety and righteousness. Without propriety and righteousness, man must be all confusion and disorder ; without the knowledge of propriety and righteousness, there must ensue all the manifestations of disorder. Man, as he is born, therefore, has in him nothing but the elements of disorder, passive and active. It is plain from this view of the subject that the nature of man is evil ; the good which it shows is factitious.

When Mencius says that 'Man's nature is good,' I affirm that it is not so. In ancient times and now, throughout the kingdom, what is meant by good is a condition of correctness, regulation, and happy government ; and what is meant by evil, is a condition of deflection, insecurity, and refusing to be under government :—in this lies the distinction between being good and being evil. And now, if man's nature be really so correct, regulated, and happily governed in

則有惡用聖王惡用禮義矣哉雖有聖王禮義
善惡之分也已今誠以人之性固正理平治邪
謂善者正理平治也所謂惡者偏險悖亂也是
孟子曰人之性善曰是不然凡古今天下之所
之性惡明矣其善者偽也
義則悖然則生而已則悖亂在己用此觀之人
則人無禮義不知禮義人無禮義則亂不知禮
性不知禮義故思慮而求知之也然則生而已
惡也今人之性固無禮義故彊學而求有之也
者必不及於外用此觀之人之欲爲善者爲性
求於外故富而不願財貴而不願勢苟有之中
惡顯美狹願廣貧願富賤願貴苟無之中者必
國人矣凡人之欲爲善者爲性惡也夫薄願厚
兄弟相拂奪矣且化禮義之文理若是則讓乎
國人矣故順情性則弟兄爭矣化禮義則讓乎
夫好利而欲得者且順情性好利而欲得若是則
者性也所以異而過衆者僞也假之人有弟

itself, where would be the use for sage kings? where would be the use for propriety and righteousness? Although there were the sage kings, propriety, and righteousness, what could they add to the nature so correct, regulated, and happily ruled in itself? But it is not so; the nature of man is bad. It was on this account, that anciently the sage kings, understanding that man's nature was bad, in a state of deflection and insecurity, instead of being correct; in a state of rebellious disorder, instead of one of happy rule, set up therefore the majesty of princes and governors to awe it; and set forth propriety and righteousness to change it; and framed laws and statutes of correctness to rule it; and devised severe punishments to restrain it: so that its outgoings might be under the dominion of rule, and in accordance with what is good. This is *the true account of* the governance of the sage kings, and the transforming power of propriety and righteousness. Let us suppose a state of things in which there shall be no majesty of rulers and governors, no influence of propriety and righteousness, no rule of laws and statutes, no restraints of punishment:—what would be the relations of men with one another, all under heaven? The strong would be injuring the weak, and spoiling them; the many would be tyrannizing over the few, and hooting them; a universal disorder and mutual destruction would speedily ensue. When we look at the subject in this way, we see clearly that the nature of man is evil; the good which it shows is factitious.

He who would speak well of ancient times must have undoubted references in the present; he who would speak well of Heaven must substantiate what he says from *the state of man*. In discourse and argument it is an excellent quality when the divisions which are made can be brought together like the halves of a token. When it is so, the arguer may sit down, and discourse of his principles; and he has only to rise up, and they may be set forth and displayed and carried into action. When Mencius says that the nature of man is good, there is no bringing together in the above manner of his divisions. He sits down and talks, but there is no getting up to display and set forth his principles, and put them in operation:—is not his error very gross? To say that the nature is good does away with the sage kings, and makes an end of propriety and righteousness; to say that the nature is bad exalts the sage kings, and dignifies propriety and righteousness. As the origin of the pressing-boards is to be found in the crooked wood, and the origin of the carpenter's marking-line is to be found in things not being straight; so the rise of princes and governors, and the illustration of propriety and righteousness, are to be traced to the badness of the nature. It is clear from this view of the subject that the nature of man is bad; the good which it shows is factitious.

將曷加於正理平治也哉、今不然、人之性惡、故
古者聖人以人之性惡以爲偏險而不正、悖亂
而不治、故爲之立君上之勢以臨之、明禮義以
化之、起法正以治之、重刑罰以禁之、使天下皆
出於治合於善也、是聖王之治而禮義之化也、
今當試去君上之勢無禮義之化法正之治、
無刑罰之禁倚而觀天下民人之相與也、若是
則夫彊者害弱而奪之、衆者暴寡而譁之、天下
之悖亂而相亡不待頃矣、用此觀之、然則人之
性惡明矣、其善者僞也。

故善言古者、必有節於今、善言天者、必有徵於
人、凡論者貴其有辨、合有符驗、故坐而言之、起
而可設張、而可施行、今孟子曰、人之性善、無辨
合符驗、坐而言之、起而不可設張、而不可施行、
豈不過甚矣哉、故性善則去聖王、息禮義矣、性
惡則與聖王、貴禮義矣、故檃栝之生、爲枸木
也、繩墨之起、爲不直也、立君上、明禮義、爲性惡
也、用此觀之、然則人之性惡明矣、其善者僞
也。

A straight piece of wood does not need the pressing-boards to make it straight;—it is so by its nature. A crooked piece of wood must be submitted to the pressing-boards to soften and straighten it, and then it is straight; it is not straight by its nature. So it is that the nature of man, being evil, must be submitted to the rule of the sage kings, and to the transforming influence of propriety and righteousness, and then its outgoings are under the dominion of rule, and in accordance with what is good. This shows clearly that the nature of man is bad; the good which it shows is factitious.

An inquirer may say *again*, 'Propriety and righteousness, though seen in an accumulation of factitious deeds, do yet belong to the nature of man; and thus it was that the sages were able to produce them.' I reply:—It is not so. A potter takes a piece of clay, and produces an earthen dish from it; but are that dish and clay the nature of the potter? A carpenter plies his tools upon a piece of wood, and produces a vessel; but are that vessel and wood the nature of the carpenter? So it is with the sages and propriety and righteousness; they produced them, just as the potter works with the clay. It is plain that there is no reason for saying that propriety and righteousness, and the accumulation of their factitious actions, belong to the proper nature of man. Speaking of the nature of man, it is the same in all,—the same in Yâo and Shun and in Chieh and the robber Chih, the same in the superior man and in the mean man. If you say that propriety and righteousness, with the factitious actions accumulated from them, are the nature of man, on what ground do you proceed to ennoble Yâo and Yü, to ennoble *generally* the superior man? The ground on which we ennoble Yâo, Yü, and the superior man, is their ability to change the nature, and to produce factitious conduct. That factitious conduct being produced, out of it there are brought propriety and righteousness. The sages stand indeed in the same relation to propriety and righteousness, and the factitious conduct resulting from them, as the potter does to his clay:—we have a product in either case. This representation makes it clear that propriety and righteousness, with their factitious results, do not properly belong to the nature of man. *On the other hand*, that which we consider mean in Chieh, the robber Chih, and the mean man generally, is that they follow their nature, act in accordance with its feelings, and indulge its resentments, till all its outgoings are a greed of gain, contentions, and rapine.—It is plain that the nature of man is bad; the good which it shows is factitious.

直木不待檃栝而直者、其性直也、枸木必將待檃栝烝矯、然後直者、以其性不直也、今人之性惡、必將待聖王之治、禮義之化、然後皆出於治、合於善也、用此觀之、然則人之性惡明矣、其善者僞也。

問者曰、禮義積僞者、是人之性、故聖人能生之也。應之曰、是不然、夫陶人埏埴而生瓦、然則瓦埴豈陶人之性也哉、工人斲木而生器、然則器木豈工人之性也哉、夫聖人之於禮義也、辟則陶埏而生之也、然則禮義積僞者、豈人之本性也哉、凡人之性者、堯舜之與桀跖、其性一也、君子之與小人、其性一也、今將以禮義積僞、爲人之性邪、然則有曷貴堯禹、曷貴君子矣哉、凡所貴堯禹君子者、能化性、能起僞、僞起而生禮義、然則聖人之於禮義積僞也、亦陶埏而生之也。用此觀之、然則禮義積僞者、豈人之性也哉、所賤於桀跖小人者、從其性、順其情、安恣睢、以出乎貪利爭奪、故人之性惡明矣、其善者僞也。

Heaven did not make favourites of Tsăng Shăn, Min Tsze-ch'ien, and Hsiâo-chi, and deal unkindly with the rest of men. How then was it that they alone were distinguished by the greatness of their filial deeds, that all which the name of filial piety implies was complete in them? The reason was that they were entirely subject to the restraints of propriety and righteousness.

Heaven did not make favourites of the people of Ch'î and Lû, and deal unkindly with the people of Ch'in. How then was it that the latter were not equal to the former in the rich manifestation of the filial piety belonging to the righteousness of the relation between father and son, and the respectful observance of the proprieties belonging to the separate functions of husband and wife? The reason was that the people of Ch'in followed the feelings of their nature, indulged its resentments, and contemned propriety and righteousness. We are not to suppose that they were different in their nature.

What is the meaning of the saying, that 'Any traveller on the road may become like Yü?' I answer:—All that made Yü what he was, was his practice of benevolence, righteousness, and his observance of laws and rectitude. But benevolence, righteousness, laws, and rectitude are all capable of being known and being practised. Moreover, any traveller on the road has the capacity of knowing these, and the ability to practise them:—it is plain that he may become like Yü. If you say that benevolence, righteousness, laws, and rectitude are not capable of being known and practised, then Yü himself could not have known, could not have practised them. If you will have it that any traveller on the road is really without the capacity of knowing these things, and the ability to practise them, then, in his home, it will not be competent for him to know the righteousness that should rule between father and son; and, abroad, it will not be competent for him to know the rectitude that should rule between sovereign and minister. But it is not so. There is no one who travels along the road, but may know both that righteousness and that rectitude:—it is plain that the capacity to know and the ability to practise belong to every traveller on the way. Let him, therefore, with his capacity of knowing and ability to practise, take his ground on the knowableness and practicableness of benevolence and righteousness;—and it is clear that he may become like Yü. Yea, let any traveller on the way addict himself to the art of learning with all his heart and

天非私曾騫孝已而外眾人也然而曾騫孝已獨厚於孝之實而全於孝之名者何也以綦於禮義故也。

天非私齊魯之民而外秦人也然而於父子之義夫婦之別不如齊魯之孝其敬父者何也以秦人之從情性安恣睢慢於禮義故也豈其性異矣哉塗之人可以為禹曷謂也曰凡禹之所以為禹者以其為仁義法正也然則仁義法正有可知可能之理然而塗之人也皆有可以知仁義法正之質皆有可以能仁義法正之具然則其可以為禹明矣今以仁義法正為固無可知可能之理邪然則唯禹不知仁義法正不能仁義法正也將使塗之人固無可以知仁義法正之質而固無可以能仁義法正之具邪然則塗之人也且內不可以知父子之義外不可以知君臣之正不然今塗之人者皆內可以知父子之義外可以知君臣之正然則其可以知之質可以能之具其在塗之人明矣今使塗之人者以其可以知之質可以能之具本夫

the entire bent of his will, thinking, searching, and closely examining ;—let him do this day after day, through a long space of time, accumulating what is good, and he will penetrate as far as a spiritual Intelligence, he will become a ternion with Heaven and Earth. It follows that *the characters of* the sages were what any man may reach by accumulation.

It may be said :—'To be sage may thus be reached by accumulation ;—why is it that all men cannot accumulate *to this extent?*' I reply :—They may do so, but they cannot be made to do so. The mean man might become a superior man, but he is not willing to be a superior man. The superior man might become a mean man, but he is not willing to be a mean man. It is not that the mean man and the superior man may not become the one the other; their not becoming the one the other is because it is a thing which may be, but cannot be made to be. Any traveller on the road may become like Yü :—the case is so ; that any traveller on the road can really become like Yü :—this is not a necessary conclusion. Though any one, however, cannot really become like Yü, that is not contrary at all to the truth that he may become so. One's feet might travel all over the world, but there never was one who was really able to travel all over the world. There is nothing to prevent the mechanic, the farmer, and the merchant from practising each the business of the others, but there has never been a case when it has really been done. Looking at the subject in this way, we see that what may be need not really be ; and although it shall not really be, that is not contrary to the truth that it might be. It thus appears that the difference is wide between what is really done or not really done, and what may be or may not be. It is plain that these two cases may not become the one the other.

Yáo asked Shun what was the character of the feelings proper to man. Shun replied, 'The feelings proper to man are very unlovely ; why need you ask about them ? When a man has got a wife and children, his filial piety withers away ; under the influence of lust and gratified desires, his good faith to his friends withers away ; when he is full of dignities and emoluments, his loyalty to his sovereign withers away. The natural feelings of man ! The natural feelings of man ! They are very unlovely. Why need you ask about them ? It is only in the case of men of the highest worth that it is not so.'

仁義之可知之理可能之具然則其可以爲禹明矣今使塗之人伏術爲學專心一志思索孰察加日縣久積善而不息則通於神明參於天地矣故聖人者人之所積而致矣。

曰聖可積而致然而皆不可積何也曰可以而不可使也故小人可以爲君子而不肯爲君子可以爲小人而不肯爲小人小人君子者未嘗不可以相爲也然而不相爲者可以而不可使也故塗之人可以爲禹然則塗之人能爲禹未必然也雖不能爲禹無害可以爲禹足可以徧行天下然而未嘗有能徧行天下者也夫工匠農賈未嘗不可以相爲事也然而未嘗能相爲事也用此觀之然則可以爲未必能也雖不能無害可以爲然則能不能之與可不可其不可以相爲明矣。

堯問於舜曰人情何如舜對曰人情甚不美又何問焉妻子具而孝衰於親嗜欲得而信衰於友爵祿盈而忠衰於君人之情乎人之情乎甚不美又何問焉唯賢者爲不然。

There is a knowledge characteristic of the sage; a knowledge characteristic of the scholar and superior man; a knowledge characteristic of the mean man; and a knowledge characteristic of the mere servant. In much speech to show his cultivation and maintain consistency, and though he may discuss for a whole day the reasons of a subject, to have a unity pervading the ten thousand changes of discourse:—this is the knowledge of the sage. To speak seldom, and in a brief and sparing manner, and to be orderly in his reasoning, as if its parts were connected with a string:—this is the knowledge of the scholar and superior man. Flattering words and disorderly conduct, with undertakings often followed by regrets:—these mark the knowledge of the mean man. Hasty, officious, smart, and swift, but without consistency; versatile, able, of extensive capabilities, but without use; decisive in discourse, rapid, exact, but the subject unimportant; regardless of right and wrong, taking no account of crooked and straight, to get the victory over others the guiding object:—this is the knowledge of the mere servant.

There is bravery of the highest order; bravery of the middle order; bravery of the lowest order. Boldly to take up his position in the place of the universally acknowledged Mean; boldly to carry into practice his views of the doctrines of the ancient kings; in a high situation, not to defer to a bad sovereign, and in a low situation not to follow the current of a bad people; to consider that there is no poverty where there is virtue, and no wealth or honour where virtue is not; when appreciated by the world, to desire to share in all men's joys and sorrows; when unknown by the world, to stand up grandly alone between heaven and earth, and have no fears:—this is the bravery of the highest order. To be reverently observant of propriety, and sober-minded; to attach importance to adherence to fidelity, and set little store by material wealth; to have the boldness to push forward men of worth and exalt them, to hold back undeserving men, and get them deposed:—this is the bravery of the middle order. To be devoid of self-respect and set a great value on wealth; to feel complacent in calamity, and always have plenty to say for himself; saving himself in any way, without regard to right and wrong; whatever be the real state of a case, making it his object to get the victory over others:—this is the bravery of the lowest order.

The *fan-zo* and the *ch'ü-sh'* were the best bows of antiquity; but without their regulators, they could not adjust themselves. The *tsang* of duke Hwan, the *ch'üeh* of T'ai-kung, the *hi* of

有聖人之知者、有士君子之知者、有小人之知者、
有役夫之知者。多言則文而類、終日議其所以言、
之千舉萬變、其統類一也、是聖人之知也。少言則
徑而省、論而法、若佚之以繩、是士君子之知也。其
言也諂、其行也悖、其舉事多悔、是小人之知也。齊
給便敏而無類、雜能旁魄而無用、折速粹孰而不
急、不恤是非、不論曲直、以期勝人為意、是役夫之
知也。

有上勇者、有中勇者、有下勇者。天下有中、敢直其
身、先王有道、敢行其意、上不循於亂世之君、下不
俗於亂世之民、仁之所在、無貧窮、仁之所亡、無富
貴天下知之、則欲與天下同苦樂之、天下不知之、
則傀然獨立天地之閒、而不畏、是上勇也。禮恭而
意儉、大齊信焉、而輕貨財、賢者敢推而尚之、不肖
者敢援而廢之、是中勇也。輕身而重貨、恬禍而廣
解、苟免不恤是非、然不然之情、以期勝人為意、是
下勇也。

繁弱鉅黍、古之良弓也、然而不得排檠、則不能自

king Wăn, the *hú* of prince Chwang, the *kan-tsiang, mŏ-yĕ, chü-chüeh* and *p'i-lü* of Ho-lü—these were the best swords of antiquity; but without the grindstone and whetstone they would not have been sharp; without the strength of the arms that wielded them they would not have cut anything.

The *hwui-liü*, the *li-ch'i*, the *hsien-li*, and the *lü-r*—these were the best horses of antiquity; but there were still necessary for them the restraints in front of bit and bridle, the stimulants behind of whip and cane, and the skilful driving of a Tsáo-fú, and then they could accomplish a thousand *li* in one day.

So it is with man:—granted to him an excellent capacity of nature and the faculty of intellect, he must still seek for good teachers under whom to place himself, and make choice of friends with whom he may be intimate. Having got good masters and placed himself under them, what he will hear will be the doctrines of Yáo, Shun, Yü, and Tang; having got good friends and become intimate with them, what he will see will be deeds of self-consecration, fidelity, reverence, and complaisance:—he will go on from day to day to benevolence and righteousness, without being conscious of it: a natural following of them will make him do so. On the other hand, if he live with bad men, what he will hear will be the language of deceit, calumny, imposture, and hypocrisy; what he will see will be conduct of filthiness, insolence, lewdness, corruptness, and greed:—he will be going on from day to day to punishment and disgrace, without being conscious of it; a natural following of them will make him do so.

The Record says, 'If you do not know your son, look at his friends; if you do not know your prince, look at his confidants.' All is the influence of association! All is the influence of association!

右離而已矣離而已矣
傳曰不知其子視其友不知其君視其左
者離使然也
邪食利之行也身且加於刑戮而不自知
處則所聞者欺誣詐偽也所見者汙漫淫
義而不自知也者離使然也今與不善人
則所見者忠信敬讓之行也身日進於仁
所聞者堯舜禹湯之道也得良友而友之
而事之擇良友而友之得賢師而事之則
以造父之馭然後一日而致千里也夫人雖有性質美而心辯知必將求賢師
驊騮騹驥纖離綠耳此皆古之良馬也然
而前必有銜轡之制後有鞭策之威加之
力則不能斷
良劍也然而不加砥厲則不能利不得人
賢闔閭之干將莫邪鉅闕辟閭此皆古之
正桓公之蔥太公之闕文王之錄莊君之

II. AN EXAMINATION OF THE NATURE OF MAN.—By HAN WĂN-KUNG.

The NATURE dates from the date of the life ; the FEELINGS date from contact with external things. There are three GRADES of the nature, and it has five CHARACTERISTICS. There are also three GRADES of the feelings, and they have seven CHARACTERISTICS. To explain myself:—The three grades of the nature are—the Superior, the Middle, and the Inferior. The superior grade is good, and good only ; the middle grade is capable of being led : it may rise to the superior, or sink to the inferior ; the inferior is evil, and evil only. The five characteristics of the nature are—Benevolence, Righteousness, Propriety, Sincerity, and Knowledge. In the Superior Grade, the first of these characteristics is supreme, and the other four are practised. In the Middle Grade, the first of these characteristics is not wanting : it exists, but with a little tendency to its opposite ; the other four are in an ill-assorted state. In the Inferior Grade there is the opposite of the first characteristic, and constant rebelliousness against the other four. The grade of the nature regulates the manifestation of the feelings in it. Again:—The three grades of the feelings are the Superior, the Middle, and the Inferior ; and their seven characteristics are—Joy, Anger, Sorrow, Fear, Love, Hatred, and Desire. In the Superior Grade, these seven all move, and each in its due place and degree. In the Middle Grade, some of the characteristics are in excess, and some in defect ; but there is a seeking to give them their due place and degree. In the Inferior Grade, whether they are in excess or defect, there is a reckless acting according to the one in immediate predominance. The grade of the feelings regulates the influence of the nature in reference to them.

Speaking of the nature, Mencius said :—'Man's nature is good ;' the philosopher Hsün said :—'Man's nature is bad ;' the philosopher Yang said :—'In the nature of man good and evil are mixed together.' Now, to say that the nature, good at first, subsequently becomes

韓文公原性篇

性也者、與生俱生也、情也者、接於物而生也。

性之品有三而其所以爲情者七曰何也曰性之品有

三、而其所以爲性者五、情之品有

上中下三、上焉者善焉而已矣、中焉者可導

而上下也、下焉者惡焉而已矣、其所以爲性

者五、曰仁曰義曰禮曰信曰智、上焉者之於

五也、主於一而行於四、中焉者之於五也、一

也不少、有焉則少焉、其於四也混、下焉者

之於五也、反於一而悖於四、性之於情、視其

品。情之品有上中下三、其所以爲情者七曰

喜曰怒曰哀曰懼曰愛曰惡曰欲、上焉者之

於七也、動而處其中、中焉者之於七也、有所

甚、有所亡、然而求合其中者也、下焉者之於

七也、亡與甚、直情而行者也、情之於性、視其

品。

孟子之言性曰、人之性善、荀子之言性曰、人

之性惡、楊子之言性曰、人之性善惡混、夫始

bad ; or that, bad at first, it subsequently becomes good ; or that, mixed at first, it subsequently becomes, it may be, good, it may be, bad :—in each of these cases only the nature of the middle grade is dealt with, and the superior and inferior grades are neglected. Those philosophers are right about one grade, and wrong about the other two.

When Shû-yü was born, his mother knew, as soon as she looked at him, that he would fall a victim to his love of bribes. When Yang Sze-wo was born, the mother of Shû-hsiang knew, as soon as she heard him cry, that he would cause the destruction of all his kindred. When Yûeh-taiâo was born, Tsze-wăn considered it was a great calamity, knowing that through him the ghosts of the Zo-âo family would all be famished.—With such cases before us, can it be said that the nature of man (i. e. all men) is good ?

When How-chi was born, his mother had no suffering ; and as soon as he began to creep, he displayed all elegance and intelligence. When king Wăn was in his mother's womb, she experienced no distress ; after his birth, those who tended him had no trouble ; when he began to learn, his teachers had no vexation.—With such cases before us, can it be said that the nature of man (i. e. all men) is evil ?

Chû was the son of Yâo, and Chûn the son of Shun ; Kwan and Ts'âi were sons of king Wăn. They were instructed to practise nothing but what was good, and yet they turned out villains. Shun was the son of Kû-sâu, and Yü the son of K'wăn. They were instructed to practise nothing but what was bad, and yet they turned out sages.—With such cases before us, can it be said that in the nature of man (i. e. all men) good and evil are blended together ?

Having these things in view, I say that the three philosophers, to whom I have referred, dealt with the middle grade of the nature, and neglected the superior and the inferior ; that they were right about the one grade, and wrong about the other two.

It may be asked, 'Is it so, then, that the superior and inferior grades of the nature can never be changed?' I reply:—The nature of the superior grade, by application to learning, becomes more intelligent, and the nature of the inferior grade, through awe of power, comes to have few faults. The superior nature, therefore, may be taught, and the inferior nature may be restrained ; but the grades have been pronounced by Confucius to be unchangeable.

善而進惡歟、始惡而進善歟、始也混而今也善惡歟、皆舉其中而遺其上下者也、得其一而失其二者也。

叔魚之生也、其母親之、知其必以賄死、楊食我之生也、叔向之母聞其號也、知必滅其宗、越椒之生也、子文以爲大戚、知若敖氏之鬼不食也、人之性果善乎。

后稷之生也、其母無災、其始匍匐也、則岐岐然、嶷嶷然、文王之在母也、母不憂、既生也、傅不勤、旣學也、師不煩、人之性果惡乎。

堯之朱、舜之均、文王之管蔡、習非不善也、而卒爲姦、瞽叟之舜、鯀之禹、習非不惡也、而卒爲聖人、人之性善惡果混乎。

故曰、三子之言性也、舉其中而遺其上下者也、得其一而失其二者也。

曰、然則性之上下者、其終不可移乎、曰、上之性、就學而愈明、下之性、畏威而寡罪、是故、上者可學、而下者可制也、其品則孔子謂不移也。

It may be asked, 'How is it that those who nowadays speak about the nature do so differently from this?' I reply:—Those who nowadays speak about the nature blend with their other views those of Buddhism and Lâo-tsze; and doing so, how could they speak otherwise than differently from me?

異。而奚言老雜言老雜言今也。此，異性之曰，
不言者，而佛也，而佛者，之曰，何於者，言今

CHAPTER III.

OF YANG CHÙ AND MO TÏ.

SECTION I.

THE OPINIONS OF YANG CHÙ.

1. 'The words of Yang Chù and Mo Tï,' said Mencius, 'fill the world. If you listen to people's discourses throughout it, you will find that they have adopted the views of the one or of the other. Now, Yang's principle is—"Each one for himself," which does not acknowledge the claims of the sovereign. Mo's principle is—"To love all equally," which does not acknowledge the peculiar affection due to a father. To acknowledge neither king nor father is to be in the state of a beast. If their principles are not stopped, and the principles of Confucius set forth, their perverse speakings will delude the people, and stop up the path of benevolence and righteousness.

'I am alarmed by these things, and address myself to the defence of the doctrines of the former sages, and to oppose Yang and Mo. I drive away their licentious expressions, so that such perverse speakers may not be able to show themselves. When sages shall rise up again, they will not change my words[1].'

His opposition to Yang and Mo was thus one of the great labours of Mencius's life, and what he deemed the success of it one of his great achievements. His countrymen generally accede to the justice of his claim ; though there have not been wanting some to say — justly, as I think and will endeavour to show in the next section — that Mo need not have incurred from him such heavy censure. For Yang no one has a word to say. His leading principle as stated by Mencius is certainly detestable, and so far as we can judge from the slight accounts of him that are to be gathered from other quarters, he seems to have been about 'the least erected spirit,' who ever professed to reason concerning the life and duties of man.

2. The generally received opinion is that Yang belonged to the

[1] Bk. III. Pt. II. ix. 9, 10.

period of 'The Warring States,' the same era of Chinese history as
Mencius.　He was named Chû, and styled Tsze-chü [1].　In a note on
Bk. III. Pt. II. ix. 9, I have supposed that he was of the times of
Confucius and Lâo-tsze, having then before me a passage of the Tâoist
philosopher Chwang, in which he gives an account of an interview
between Lâo-tsze and Yang Chû [2].　That interview, however, must
be an invention of Chwang.　The natural impression which we receive from all the references of Mencius is that Yang must have been
posterior to Confucius, and that his opinions had come into vogue
only in the times of our philosopher himself.　This view would be
placed beyond doubt if we could receive as genuine the chapter on
Yang, which is contained in the writings of the philosopher Lieh.
And so far we may accept it, as to believe that it gives the sentiments
which were attributed to him in the first century before our era [3].
The leading principle ascribed to him by Mencius nowhere appears
in it in so many words, but the general tenour of his language is
entirely in accordance with it.　This will appear from the following
specimens, which are all to be found in the seventh chapter of the
Books of Lieh.　The corresponding English and Chinese paragraphs
are indicated by the same letters prefixed to them :—

ª 'Yang Chû said, "A hundred years are the extreme limit of longevity ; and not one man in
a thousand enjoys such a period of life.　Suppose the case of one who does so :—infancy borne
in the arms, and doting old age, will nearly occupy the half ; what is forgotten in sleep, and
what is lost in the waking day, will nearly occupy the half ; pain and sickness, sorrow and
bitterness, losses, anxieties, and fears, will nearly occupy the half.　There may remain ten years
or so ; but I reckon that not even in them will be found an hour of smiling self-abandonment,
without the shadow of solicitude.—What is the life of man then to be made of ?　What
pleasure is in it ?

ᵇ '"Is it to be prized for the pleasure of food and dress ? or for the enjoyments of music and
beauty ?　But one cannot be always satisfied with these pleasures ; one cannot be always
toying with beauty and listening to music.　And then there are the restraints of punishments
and the stimulants of rewards ; the urgings and the repressings of fame and laws :—these
make one strive restlessly for the vain praise of an hour, and calculate on the residuary glory
after death ; they keep him, as with body bent, on the watch against what his ears hear and his
eyes see, and attending to the right and the wrong of his conduct and thoughts.　In this way

[1] 楊朱字子居.　[2] See 莊子, 雜篇, 第五, the 寓言, at the end.
[3] Dr. Morrison says of Lieh (Dictionary, character 子) :—'Lieh-tsze, an eminent writer
of the Tâo sect ; lived about the same time as Lâo-tsze, the founder of the sect (B.C. 585).'
Lieh's Works are published, with the preface of Liû Hsiang written B.C. 13.　Hsiang says Lieh
was a native of Châng (鄭), and a contemporary of duke Mû (繆 or 穆).　But Mû's reign
extended from B.C. 627 to 604.　There is evidently an anachronism somewhere.　Hsiang
goes on to speak of Lieh's writings, specifying the chapter on Yang Chû, in which there are
references to Confucius and his acknowledged fame.　Another of Lieh's chapters is all devoted
to Confucius's sayings and doings.—This is not the place to attempt an adjustment of the
difficulties.　The chapter about Yang Chû was current in Liû Hsiang's time, and we may cull
from it to illustrate the character of the man.

he loses the real pleasure of his years, and cannot allow himself for a moment.—In what does he differ from an individual manacled and fettered in an inner prison? The people of high antiquity knew both the shortness of life, and how suddenly and completely it might be closed by death, and therefore they obeyed the movements of their hearts, refusing not what it was natural for them to like, nor seeking to avoid any pleasure that occurred to them. They paid no heed to the incitements of fame; they enjoyed themselves according to their nature; they did not resist the common tendency of all things to self-enjoyment; they cared not to be famous after death. They managed to keep clear of punishment; as to fame and praise, being first or last, long life or short life,—these things did not come into their calculations." [a]

[b] 'Yang Chŭ said, "Wherein people differ is the matter of life; wherein they agree is death. While they are alive, we have the distinctions of intelligence and stupidity, honourableness and meanness; when they are dead, we have so much stinking rottenness decaying away:—this is the common lot. Yet intelligence and stupidity, honourableness and meanness, are not in one's power; neither is that condition of putridity, decay, and utter disappearance. A man's life is not in his own hands, nor is his death; his intelligence is not his own, nor is his stupidity, nor his honourableness, nor his meanness. All are born and all die;—the intelligent and the stupid, the honourable and the mean. At ten years old some die; at a hundred years old some die. The virtuous and the sage die; the ruffian and the fool also die. Alive, they were Yâo and Shun; dead, they were so much rotten bone. Alive, they were Chieh and Châu; dead, they were so much rotten bone. Who could know any difference between their rotten bones? While alive, therefore, let us hasten to make the best of life; what leisure have we to be thinking of anything after death?"'

[a] 楊朱曰百年壽之大齊得百年者千無一焉設有一者孩抱以逮昏老幾居其半矣夜眠之所弭晝覺之所遺又幾居其半矣痛疾哀苦亡失憂懼又幾居其半矣量十數年之中迺然而自得亡介焉之慮者亦亡一時之中爾則人之生也奚為哉奚為樂哉為美厚爾為聲色爾而美厚復不可常饜足聲色不可常翫聞乃復為刑賞之所進退違禮之所禁勸名法之所進退遑遑競一時之虛譽規死後之餘榮偊偊爾慎耳目之觀聽惜身意之是非徒失當年之至樂不能自肆於一時重囚纍梏何以异哉太古之人知生之暫來知死之暫往故從心而動不違自然所好當身之娛非所去也故不為名所勸從性而游不逆萬物所好死後之名非所取也故不為刑所及名譽先後年命多少非所量也

[b] 楊朱曰萬物所異者生也所同者死也生則有賢愚貴賤是所異也死則有臭腐消滅是所同也雖然賢愚貴賤非所能也臭腐消滅亦非所能也故生非所生死非所死賢非所賢愚非所愚貴非所貴賤非所賤然而萬物齊生齊死齊賢齊愚齊貴齊賤十年亦死百年亦死仁聖亦死凶愚亦死生則堯舜死則腐骨生則桀紂死則腐骨腐骨一矣孰知其異且趣當生奚遑死後

c 'Măng-sun Yang asked Yang-tsze, saying, "Here is a man who sets a high value on his life, and takes loving care of his body, hoping that he will not die:—does he do right?" "There is no such thing as not dying," was the reply. "But if he does so, hoping for long life, is he right?" Yang-tsze answered, "One cannot be assured of long life. Setting value upon life will not preserve it; taking care of the body will not make it greatly better. And, in fact, why should long life be made much of? There are the five feelings with their likings and dislikings,—now as in old time; there are the four limbs, now at ease, now in danger,—now as in old time; there are the various experiences of joy and sorrow,—now as in old time; there are the various changes from order to disorder, and from disorder to order,—now as in old time:—all these things I have heard of, and seen, and gone through. A hundred years of them would be more than enough, and shall I wish the pain protracted through a longer life?" Măng-sun said, "If it be so, early death is better than long life. Let a man go to trample on the pointed steel, or throw himself into the caldron or flames, to get what he desires." Yang-tsze answered, "No. Being once born, take your life as it comes, and endure it; and seeking to enjoy yourself as you desire, so await the approach of death. When you are about to die, treat the thing with indifference and endure it; and seeking to accomplish your departure, so abandon yourself to annihilation. Both death and life should be treated with indifference; they should both be endured:—why trouble one's self about earliness or lateness in connexion with them?"'

d 'Ch'in-tsze asked Yang Chû, saying, "If you could benefit the world by parting with one hair of your body, would you do it?" "The world is not to be benefited by a hair," replied Yang. The other urged, "But suppose it could be, what would you do?" To this Yang gave no answer, and Ch'in went out, and reported what had passed to Măng-sun Yang. Măng-sun said, "You do not understand our Master's mind:—let me explain it to you. If by enduring a slight wound in the flesh, you could get ten thousand pieces of gold, would you endure it?" "I would." "If by cutting off one of your limbs, you could get a kingdom, would you do it?" Ch'in was silent; and after a little, Măng-sun Yang resumed, "To part with a hair is a slighter matter than to receive a wound in the flesh, and that again is a slighter matter than to lose a limb:—that you can discern. But consider:—A hair may be

c 孟孫陽問楊子曰、有人於此、貴生愛身、以蘄不死、可乎、曰、理無不死、以蘄久生、可乎、曰、理無久生、生非貴之所能存、身非愛之所能厚、且久生奚爲、五情好惡、古猶今也、四體安危、古猶今也、世事苦樂、古猶今也、變易治亂、古猶今也、旣聞之矣、旣見之矣、旣更之矣、百年猶厭其多、況久生之苦也乎、孟孫陽曰、若然速亡、愈於久生、則踐鋒刃、入湯火、得所志矣、楊子曰、不然、旣生則廢而任之、究其所欲以俟於死、將死則廢而任之、究其所之以放於盡、無不廢、無不任、何遽遲速於其間乎、

d 禽子問楊朱曰、去子體之一毛、以濟一世、汝爲之乎、楊子曰、世固非一毛之所濟、禽子曰、假濟、爲之乎、楊子弗應、禽子出語孟孫陽、孟孫陽曰、子不達夫子之心、吾請言之、有侵若肌膚獲萬金者、若爲之乎、曰、爲之、孟孫陽曰、有斷若一節、得一國、子爲之乎、禽子默然有閒、孟孫陽曰、一毛微於肌膚、肌膚微於一節省矣、然則積一毛以成肌膚、積肌膚以成一節、一毛固一體萬分中之一物、奈何輕

multiplied till it becomes as important as the p'ece of flesh, and the piece of flesh may be multiplied till it becomes as important as a limb. A single hair is just one of the ten thousand portions of the body;—why should you make light of it?" Ch'in-tsze replied, "I cannot answer you. If I could refer your words to Lâo Tan or Kwan Yin, they would say that you were right; but if I could refer my words to the great Yü or Mo Tî, they would say that I was right." Măng-sun Yang, on this, turned round, and entered into conversation with his disciples on another subject.'

" 'Yang Chû said, "All agree in considering Shun, Yü, Châu-kung, and Confucius to have been the most admirable of men, and in considering Chieh and Châu to have been the most wicked.

' " Now, Shun had to plough the ground on the south of the Ho, and to play the potter by the Lêi lake. His four limbs had not even a temporary rest; for his mouth and belly he could not find pleasant food and warm clothing. No love of his parents rested upon him; no affection of his brothers and sisters. When he was thirty years old, he had not been able to get the permission of his parents to marry. When Yâo at length resigned to him the throne, he was advanced in age; his wisdom was decayed; his son Shang-chün proved without ability; and he had finally to resign the throne to Yü. Sorrowfully came he to his death. Of all mortals never was one whose life was so worn out and empoisoned as his. K'wăn was required to reduce the deluged land to order; and when his labours were ineffectual, he was put to death on mount Yü, and Yü, his son, had to undertake the task, and serve his enemy. All his energies were spent on his labours with the land; a child was born to him, but he could not foster it; he passed his door without entering; his body became bent and withered; the skin of his hands and feet became thick and callous. When at length Shun resigned to him the throne, he lived in a low, mean house, while his sacrificial apron and cap were elegant. Sorrowfully came he to his death. Of all mortals never was one whose life was so saddened and embittered as his. On the death of king Wû, his son, king Ch'ăng was young and weak. Châu-kung had to undertake all the royal duties. The duke of Shâo was displeased, and evil reports spread through the kingdom. Châu-kung had to reside three years in the east; he slew his elder brother, and banished his younger; scarcely did he escape with his life. Sorrowfully came he to his death. Of all mortals never was one whose life was so full of hazards and terrors as his. Confucius understood the ways of the ancient sovereigns and kings. He responded to the invitations of the princes of his time. The tree was cut down over him in Sung; the traces of his footsteps were removed in Wei; he was reduced to

事。

。楊朱曰、天下之美、歸之舜、禹、周、孔、天下之

惡、歸之桀、紂。然而舜耕於河陽、陶於雷澤、四

體不得暫安、口腹不得美厚、父母之所不愛、

弟妹之所不親、行年三十、不告而娶、及受堯

之禪、年已長、智已衰、商鈞不才、禪位於禹、戚

戚然以至於死、此天人窮毒者也。鮌治水土、

績用不就、殛諸羽山、禹纂業事讐、惟荒土功、

子産不字、過門不入、身體偏枯、手足胼胝、及

受舜禪、卑宮室、美紱冕、戚戚然以至於死、此

天人之憂苦者也。武王既終、成王幼弱、周公

攝天子之政、邵公不悅、四國流言、居東三年、

誅兄放弟、僅免其身、戚戚然以至於死、此天

人之危懼者也。孔子明帝王之道、應時君之

聘、伐樹於宋、削迹於衞、窮於商周、圍於陳蔡、

之乎。禽子曰、吾不能所以荅子。然則以子之

言、問老聃關尹、則子言當矣。以吾言問大禹

墨翟、則吾言當矣。孟孫陽因顧與其徒說他

extremity in Shang and Châu; he was surrounded in Ch'ăn and Ts'âi; he had to bend to the head of the Chi family; he was disgraced by Yang Hû. Sorrowfully came he to his death. Of all mortals never was one whose life was so agitated and hurried as his.

' "Those four sages, during their life, had not a single day's joy. Since their death they have had a *grand* fame that will last through myriads of ages. But that fame is what no one who cares for what is real would choose. Celebrate them;—they do not know it. Reward them;—they do not know it. Their fame is no more to them than to the trunk of a tree or a clod of earth.

' " *On the other hand*, Chieh came into the accumulated wealth of many generations; to him belonged the honour of the royal seat; his wisdom was enough to enable him to set at defiance all below; his power was enough to shake the world. He indulged the pleasures to which his eyes and ears prompted him; he carried out whatever it came into his thoughts to do. Brightly came he to his death. Of all mortals never was one whose life was so luxurious and dissipated as his. *Similarly*, Châu came into the accumulated wealth of many generations; to him belonged the honour of the royal seat; his power enabled him to do whatever he would; his will was everywhere obeyed; he indulged his feelings in all his palaces; he gave the reins to his lusts through the long night; he never made himself bitter by the thought of propriety and righteousness. Brightly came he to his destruction. Of all mortals never was one whose life was so abandoned as his.

' "These two villains, during their life, had the joy of gratifying their desires. Since their death, they have had the *evil* fame of folly and tyranny. But the reality *of enjoyment* is what no fame can give. Reproach them;—they do not know it. Praise them;—they do not know it. Their *ill* fame is no more to them than to the trunk of a tree, or to a clod of earth.

' "To the four sages all admiration is given; yet were their lives bitter to the end, and their common lot was death. To the two villains all condemnation is given; yet their lives were pleasant to the last, and their common lot was likewise death."'

3. The above passages are sufficient to show the character of Yang Chû's mind and of his teachings. It would be doing injustice to Epicurus to compare Yang with him, for though the Grecian philosopher made happiness the chief end of human pursuit, he taught also that 'we cannot live pleasurably without living virtuously and justly.' The Epicurean system is, indeed, unequal

以至終亦同歸於死矣
同歸於死矣彼二凶雖惡之所歸樂
異矣彼四聖雖美之所歸苦以至終
之不知雖稱之弗知此與株塊奚以
暴之名彼二實者固非名之所與也雖毀譽
也彼二凶也生有從欲之歡死被愚
熙熙然以至於誅此天民之放縱者
於傾官縱欲於長夜不以禮義自苦
南面之尊威無不行志無不從肆情
民之逸蕩者也熙熙然以至於死此天
意慮之所爲熙熙然以至於死此天
下威足以震海內恣耳目之所娛窮
累世之資居南面之尊智足以距羣
雖賞之不知與株塊無以異矣樂籍
名者固非實之所取也雖稱之弗知
聖者生無一日之歡死有萬世之名
至於死此天民之遑遽者也凡彼四
受屈於季氏見辱於陽虎戚戚然以

to the capacity, and far below the highest complacencies of human nature; but it is widely different from the reckless contempt of all which is esteemed good and great that defiles the pages where Yang is made to tell his views.

We are sometimes reminded by him of fragmentary utterances in the Book of Ecclesiastes.—'In much wisdom is much grief; and he that increaseth knowledge increaseth sorrow.' 'As it happeneth to the fool, so it happeneth even to me; and why was I then more wise? Then I said in my heart, that this also is vanity. For there is no remembrance of the wise more than of the fool for ever; seeing that which now is in the days to come shall all be forgotten. And how dieth the wise man? As the fool. Therefore I hated life; because the work that is wrought under the sun is grievous to me: for all is vanity and vexation of spirit.' 'There is a man whose labour is in wisdom, and in knowledge, and in equity....All his days are sorrows, and his travail grief; yea, his heart taketh not rest in the night:—this is also vanity. There is nothing better for a man than that he should eat and drink, and that he should make his soul enjoy good in his labour.' 'That which befalleth the sons of men befalleth beasts; even one thing befalleth them: as the one dieth, so dieth the other; yea, they have all one breath; so that a man hath no pre-eminence above a beast: for all is vanity. All go to one place; all are of the dust, and all turn to dust again.... Wherefore I perceive that there is nothing better than that a man should rejoice in his own works; for that is his portion: for who shall bring him to see what shall be after him?'

But those thoughts were suggestions of evil from which the Hebrew Preacher recoiled in his own mind; and he put them on record only that he might give their antidote along with them. He vanquished them by his faith in God; and so he ends by saying, 'Let us hear the conclusion of the whole matter:—Fear God, and keep His commandments: for this is the whole duty of man. For God shall bring every work into judgment, with every secret thing, whether it be good, or whether it be evil.' Yang Chû has no redeeming qualities. His reasonings contain no elements to counteract the poison that is in them. He never rises to the thought of God. There are, he allows, such ideas as those of propriety and righteousness, but the effect of them is merely to embitter and mar the enjoyment of life. Fame is but a phantom which only the fool will pursue. It is the same with all at death.

There their being ends. After that there is but so much putridity
and rottenness. With him therefore the conclusion of the whole
matter is :—'Let us eat and drink ; let us live in pleasure ; gratify
the ears and eyes ; get servants and maidens, music, beauty, wine ;
when the day is insufficient, carry it on through the night ; EACH
ONE FOR HIMSELF.'

Mencius might well say that if such 'licentious talk' were not
arrested, the path of benevolence and righteousness would be stopped
up. If Yang's principles had been entertained by the nation, every
bond of society would have been dissolved. All the foundations of
order would have been destroyed. Vice would have become rampant,
and virtue would have been named only to be scorned. There
would have remained for the entire State only what Yang saw in
store for the individual man—'putridity and rottenness.' Doubtless
it was owing to Mencius's opposition that the foul and dangerous
current was stayed. He raised up against it the bulwark of human
nature formed for virtue. He insisted on benevolence, righteousness,
propriety, fidelity, as the noblest attributes of man's conduct. More
was needed, but more he could not supply. If he had had a living
faith in God, and had been in possession of His revealed will, the
present state of China might have been very different. He was able
to warn his countrymen of the gulf into which Yang Chû would
have plunged them ; but he could direct them in the way of truth
and duty only imperfectly. He sent them into the dark cave of
their own souls, and back to the vague lessons and imperfect
examples of their sages ; and China has staggered on, waxing
feebler and feebler, to the present time. Her people need to be
directed above themselves and beyond the present. When stars
shine out to them in heaven and from eternity, the nation will perhaps renew its youth, and go forward from strength to strength.

SECTION II.

THE OPINIONS OF MO TÎ.

1. Very different from Yang Chû was Mo Tî. They stood at
the opposite poles of human thought and sentiment; and we may
wonder that Mencius should have offered the same stern opposition
to the opinions of each of them. He did well to oppose the doctrine
whose watchword was—'Each one for himself;' was he right in
denouncing, as equally injurious, that which taught that the root of
all social evils is to be traced to the want of mutual love?

It is allowed that Mo was a native and officer of the State of
Sung; but the time when he lived is a matter of dispute. Sze-mâ
Ch'ien says that some made him to be a contemporary of Confucius,
and that others placed him later[1]. He was certainly later than
Confucius, to whom he makes many references, not always complimentary, in his writings. In one of his Treatises, moreover, mention
is made of Wăn-tsze[2], an acknowledged disciple of Tsze-hsiâ, so
that he must have been very little anterior to Mencius. This is
the impression also which I receive from the references to him in
our philosopher.

In Liû Hsin's third catalogue the Mohist writers form a subdivision. Six of them are mentioned, including Mo himself to whom
seventy-one p'ien, or Books, are attributed. So many were then
current under his name; but eighteen of them have since been lost.
He was an original thinker. He exercised a bolder, though not
a more correct, judgment on things than Confucius or his followers.
Antiquity was not so sacred to him, and he did not hesitate to
condemn the literati—the orthodox—for several of their doctrines
and practices.

Two of his peculiar views are adverted to by Mencius, and
vehemently condemned. The one is about the regulation of
funerals, where Mo contended that a spare simplicity should be
the rule[3]. On that I need not dwell. The other is the doctrine

[1] 史記, 七十四卷; 孟子, 荀卿, 列傳第十四, at the end.
[2] 文子.   [3] Bk. III. Pt. I. v.

of 'Universal Love¹.' A lengthy exposition of this remains in the Writings which go by Mo's name, though it is not from his own pen, but that of a disciple. Such as it is, with all its repetitions, I give a translation of it. My readers will be able, after perusing it, to go on with me to consider the treatment which the doctrine received at the hands of Mencius.

UNIVERSAL LOVE¹. PART I.

It is the business of the sages to effect the good government of the world. They must know, therefore, whence disorder and confusion arise, for without this knowledge their object cannot be effected. We may compare them to a physician who undertakes to cure men's diseases :—he must ascertain whence a disease has arisen, and then he can assail it with effect, while, without such knowledge, his endeavours will be in vain. Why should we except the case of those who have to regulate disorder from this rule? They must know whence it has arisen, and then they can regulate it.

It is the business of the sages to effect the good government of the world. They must examine therefore into the cause of disorder ; and when they do so they will find that it arises from the want of mutual love. When a minister and a son are not filial to their sovereign and their father, this is what is called disorder. A son loves himself, and does not love his father ;—he therefore wrongs his father, and seeks his own advantage : a younger brother loves himself, and does not love his elder brother ;—he therefore wrongs his elder brother, and seeks his own advantage : a minister loves himself, and does not love his sovereign ;—he therefore wrongs his sovereign, and seeks his own advantage :—all these are cases of what is called disorder. Though it be the father who is not kind to his son, or the elder brother who is not kind to his younger brother, or the sovereign who is not gracious to his minister :—the case comes equally under the general name of disorder. The father loves himself, and does not love his son ;—he therefore wrongs his son, and seeks his own advantage : the elder brother loves himself, and does not love his

愛也不愛子故虧子而自利兄
臣此亦天下之不慈弟君之不慈父自
不慈子兄之不慈弟君之不慈父自
君而自利此所謂亂也雖父之
兄而自利弟自愛不愛兄故虧
父而自利弟自愛不愛父故虧
所謂亂也子自愛不愛父故虧
起起不相愛臣子之不孝君父
不察亂之所自起富察亂何自
聖人以治天下為事者也不可
知亂之所自起則弗能治
必知亂之所自起焉能治之不
起則弗能攻治亂者何獨不然
自起焉能攻之不知疾之所自
之攻人之疾者然必知疾之所
亂之所自起則不能治譬之如醫
亂之所自起焉能治之不知亂
聖人以治天下為事者也必知

¹ 兼愛,—兼 represents *a hand grasping two stalks of grain.* 兼愛 is 'a love that grasps or unites many in its embrace.' I do not know how to render it better than by 'universal love.' Mencius and the literati generally find the idea of equality in it also, and 兼愛 is with them = 'To love all equally.'

younger brother ;—he therefore wrongs his younger brother, and seeks his own advantage : the sovereign loves himself, and does not love his minister ;—he therefore wrongs his minister, and seeks his own advantage. How do these things come to pass? They all arise from the want of mutual love. Take the case of any thief or robber :—it is just the same with him. The thief loves his own house, and does not love his neighbour's house ;—he therefore steals from his neighbour's house to benefit his own : the robber loves his own person, and does not love his neighbour ;—he therefore does violence to his neighbour to benefit himself. How is this? It all arises from the want of mutual love. Come to the case of great officers throwing each other's Families into confusion, and of princes attacking one another's States :—it is just the same with them. The great officer loves his own Family, and does not love his neighbour's ;—he therefore throws his neighbour's Family into disorder to benefit his own : the prince loves his own State, and does not love his neighbour's ;—he therefore attacks his neighbour's State to benefit his own. All disorder in the kingdom has the same explanation. When we examine into the cause of it, it is found to be the want of mutual love.

Suppose that universal, mutual love prevailed throughout the kingdom ;—if men loved others as they love themselves, disliking to exhibit what was unfilial . . . .[1] And moreover would there be those who were unkind? Looking on their sons, younger brothers, and ministers as themselves, and disliking to exhibit what was unkind . . . . the want of filial duty would disappear. And would there be thieves and robbers? When every man regarded his neighbour's house as his own, who would be found to steal? When every one regarded his neighbour's person as his own, who would be found to rob? Thieves and robbers would disappear. And would there be great officers throwing one another's Families into confusion, and princes attacking one another's States? When officers regarded the Families of others as their own, what one would make confusion? When princes regarded other States as their own, what one would begin an attack? Great officers throwing one another's Families into confusion, and princes attacking one another's States, would disappear.

If, indeed, universal, mutual love prevailed throughout the kingdom ; one State not attacking another, and one Family not throwing another into confusion ; thieves and robbers nowhere existing ; rulers and ministers, fathers and sons, all being filial and kind :—in such a condition

自愛也不愛弟故虧弟而自利君自愛也不愛臣故虧臣而自利是何也皆起不相愛雖至天下之為盜賊者亦然盜愛其室不愛異室故竊異室以利其室賊愛其身不愛人故賊人以利其身此何也皆起不相愛雖至大夫之相亂家諸侯之相攻國者亦然大夫各愛其家不愛異家故亂異家以利其家諸侯各愛其國不愛異國故攻異國以利其國天下之亂物具此而已矣察此何自起皆起不相愛

若使天下兼相愛人若愛其身惡施不孝猶有不慈者乎視子弟與臣若其身惡施不慈不孝亡有猶有盜賊乎故視人之室若其室誰竊視人身若其身誰賊故盜賊亡有猶有大夫之相亂家諸侯之相攻國者乎視人家若其家誰亂視人國若其國誰攻故大夫之相亂家諸侯之相攻國者亡有若使天下兼相愛國與國不相攻家與家不相亂盜賊無有君臣父子皆能孝慈若此則天下

the nation would be well governed. On this account, how may sages, whose business it is to effect the good government of the kingdom, do but prohibit hatred and advise to love? On this account it is affirmed that universal mutual love throughout the country will lead to its happy order, and that mutual hatred leads to confusion. This was what our master, the philosopher Mo, meant, when he said, 'We must above all inculcate the love of others.'

也人不不墨亂相愛下愛惡得事天人治
者勤可子故惡則兼故而不者下以故
此愛以曰子則治相天勤禁惡爲治當

UNIVERSAL LOVE. PART II.

Our Master, the philosopher Mo, said, 'That which benevolent men consider to be incumbent on them as their business, is to stimulate and promote all that will be advantageous to the nation, and to take away all that is injurious to it. This is what they consider to be their business.'

And what are the things advantageous to the nation, and the things injurious to it? Our master said, 'The mutual attacks of State on State; the mutual usurpations of Family on Family; the mutual robberies of man on man; the want of kindness on the part of the ruler and of loyalty on the part of the minister; the want of tenderness and filial duty between father and son and of harmony between brothers:—these, and such as these, are the things injurious to the kingdom.'

And from what do we find, on examination, that these injurious things are produced[1]? Is it not from the want of mutual love?

Our Master said, 'Yes, they are produced by the want of mutual love. Here is a prince who only knows to love his own State, and does not love his neighbour's;—he therefore does not shrink from raising all the power of his State to attack his neighbour. Here is the chief of a Family who only knows to love it, and does not love his neighbour's;—he therefore does not shrink from raising all his powers to seize on that other Family. Here is a man who only knows to love his own person, and does not love his neighbour's;—he therefore does not shrink from using all his resources to rob his neighbour. Thus it happens, that the princes, not loving one another, have their battle-fields; and the chiefs of Families, not loving one another, have their mutual

人不相愛則必相賊君臣不相愛
野戰家主不相愛則必相篡人與
賊人之身是故諸侯不相愛則必
不愛人之身是以不憚舉其身以
家而不愛人之家是以不憚舉其
家以篡人之家今人獨知愛其
國以攻人之國今家主獨知愛其
其國不愛人之國是以不憚舉其
子言以不相愛生今諸侯獨知愛
何用生哉以不相愛生耶〇于墨
則天下之害也〇然則崇此害亦
惠忠父子不慈孝兄弟不和調此
之相篡人之相賊君臣不
今若國之與國之相攻家之與家
也天下之害何也〇子墨子言曰
此爲事者也〇然則天下之利何
必與天下之利除去天下之害以
子墨子言曰仁人之所以爲事者

¹ Here I would read, in the Chinese text, 察 for 崇 and 由 for 用.—然則察此害亦何由生哉. The translation is accordingly.

usurpations; and men, not loving one another, have their mutual robberies; and rulers and ministers, not loving one another, become unkind and disloyal; and fathers and sons, not loving one another, lose their affection and filial duty; and brothers, not loving one another, contract irreconcileable enmities. Yea, men in general not loving one another, the strong make prey of the weak; the rich do despite to the poor; the noble are insolent to the mean; and the deceitful impose upon the stupid. All the miseries, usurpations, enmities, and hatreds in the world, when traced to their origin, will be found to arise from the want of mutual love. On this account, the benevolent condemn it.'

They may condemn it; but how shall they change it?

Our Master said, 'They may change it by the law of universal mutual love and by the interchange of mutual benefits.'

How will this law of universal mutual love and the interchange of mutual benefits accomplish this?

Our Master said, '*It would lead* to the regarding another's kingdom as one's own: another's family as one's own: another's person as one's own. That being the case, the princes, loving one another, would have no battle-fields; the chiefs of families, loving one another, would attempt no usurpations; men, loving one another, would commit no robberies[1]; rulers and ministers, loving one another, would be gracious and loyal; fathers and sons, loving one another, would be kind and filial; brothers, loving one another, would be harmonious and easily reconciled. Yea, men in general loving one another, the strong would not make prey of the weak; the many would not plunder the few; the rich would not insult the poor; the noble would not be insolent to the mean; and the deceitful would not impose upon the simple. The way in which all the miseries,

雖不下父之天相則不既兼愛愛視相家視不則則愛不強愚凡則
然侮之子然下愛不野交相交人視人野戰相惠慈弱人相然交強
天貧人相而之則野戰相愛相之之家相不惠慈弱不惠慈弱不惠慈弱惠忠
下富皆愛今士不相賊利愛之惡家相利愛國若相身是故諸侯相愛

[1] The Chinese text is here very confused for several sentences. There are evidently transpositions, omissions, and additions. I have ventured to correct and arrange it as follows:—

After 不相賊. I read, 君臣相愛. 則惠忠. 父子相愛. 則慈孝. 兄弟相愛. 則和調. 天下之人 皆相愛強不執弱. 眾不刦寡 富不侮貧. 貴不敖賤 詐不欺愚 凡天下禍篡怨恨 可使毋之起者 以兼相愛生也. 是以仁者譽之. ○然而今天下之士. 君子. 曰. 然乃若兼. 則善矣. 雖然. 天下之難物也. ○子墨子言曰. 天下之士. 君子. 特不識其利辯之故也. 今若云云.

usurpations, enmities, and hatreds in the world, may be made not to arise, is universal mutual love. On this account, the benevolent value and praise it.'

Yes; but the scholars of the kingdom and superior men say, 'True; if there were this universal love, it would be good. It is, however, the most difficult thing in the world.'

Our Master said, 'This is because the scholars and superior men simply do not understand the advantageousness *of the law*, and to conduct their reasonings upon that. Take the case of assaulting a city, or of a battle-field, or of the sacrificing one's life for the sake of fame :—this is felt by the people everywhere to be a difficult thing. Yet, if the ruler be pleased with it, both officers and people are able to do it :—how much more might they attain to universal mutual love, and the interchange of mutual benefits, which is different from this! When a man loves others, they respond to and love him ; when a man benefits others, they respond to and benefit him ; when a man injures others, they respond to and injure him ; when a man hates others, they respond to and hate him :—what difficulty is there in the matter? It is only that rulers will not carry on the government on this principle, and so officers do not carry it out in their practice.

'Formerly, the duke Wăn of Tsin liked his officers to be coarsely dressed, and, therefore, they all wore rams' furs, a leathern swordbelt, and a cap of bleached cotton. Thus attired, they went in to the prince's levee, and came out and walked through the court. Why did they do this? The sovereign liked it, and therefore the ministers did it. The duke Ling of Ch'ù liked his officers to have small waists, and, therefore, they all limited themselves to a single meal. They held in their breath in putting on their belts, and had to help themselves up by means of the wall. In the course of a year, they looked black, and as if they would die of starvation. Why did they do this¹? The sovereign liked it, and, therefore, the ministers were able to do it. Kâu-chi'en, the king of Yüeh, liked his ministers to be brave, and taught them to be accustomed to be so. At a general assembly of them, he set on fire the ship where they were, and to try them, said, "All the precious things of Yüeh are here." He then with his own hands beat a drum, and urged them on. When they heard the drum thundering, they rushed confusedly about, and trampled in the fire, till more than a hundred of them perished, when he struck the gong, and called them back².

其臣和合之焚舟失火試其士曰越
能之也昔越王句踐好士之勇教馴
息然後帶扶牆然後起比期年朝有
士細要靈王之臣皆以一飯為節脇
君說之故臣為之也昔者楚靈王好
入以見於君出以踐朝是其故何也
臣皆牂羊之裘韋以帶劍練帛之冠
昔者晉文公好士之惡衣故文公之
不以為行故也
害之此何難之有特上弗以為政士
者人必從而惡之害人者人必從而
而愛之利人者人必從而利之惡人
交相利則與此異夫愛人者人必從
君說之則士眾能為之況於兼相愛
身為名此天下百姓之所皆難也苟
其利辯其故也今若夫攻城野戰殺
子墨子言曰天下之士君子特不識

¹ In 是其故是也, the second 是 is plainly a misprint for 何. ² Here a sentence or two are wanting, to complete the paragraph in harmony with the two which precede. The characters which follow—長故子墨子言曰—should also be expunged. I have omitted them in the translation.

'Now, little food, bad clothes, and the sacrifice of life for the sake of fame ;—these are what it is difficult for people to approve of. Yet, when the sovereign was pleased with it, they were all able, *in those cases*, to bring themselves to them. How much more could they attain to universal mutual love, and the interchange of mutual benefits, which is different from such things! When a man loves others, they respond to and love him ; when a man benefits others, they respond to and benefit him ; when a man hates others, they respond to and hate him ; when a man injures others, they respond to and injure him. It is only that rulers will not carry on their government on this principle, and, so, officers do not carry it out in their practice.'

Yes ; but now the officers and superior men say, 'Granted ; the universal practice of mutual love would be good ; but it is an impracticable thing. It is like taking up the T'âi mountain, and leaping with it over the Ho or the Chî.'

Our Master said, 'That is not the proper comparison for it. To take up the T'âi mountain, and leap with it over the Ho or the Chî, may be called an exercise of most extraordinary strength ; it is, in fact, what no one, *from* antiquity to the present time, has ever been able to do. But how widely different from this is the practice of universal mutual love, and the interchange of mutual benefits !

'Anciently, the sage kings practised this. How do we know that they did so ? When Yü reduced all the country to order :—in the west, he made the western Ho and the Yü-tâu, to carry off the waters of Ch'û-sun-wang ; in the north, he made the Fang-yüan, the Pâi-chû, Hâu-chih-ti, and the Tâu of Fû-t'o ; setting up also the Ti-ch'û, and chiselling out the Lung-mân, to benefit Yen, Tâi, Hû, Mo, and the people of the western Ho ; in the east, he drained the waters to Lû-fang and the marsh of Mâng-chû, reducing them to nine channels, to limit the waters of the eastern country, and benefit the people of Ch'î-châu ; and in the south, he made the Chiang, the Han, the Hwâi, the Zû, the course of the eastern current, and the five lakes, to benefit Ching, Ch'û, and Yüeh, the people of the wild south. These were the doings of Yü ; and I am now for practising the *same* universal *mutual love*.

'When king Wân brought the western country to good order, his light spread, like the sun

國之寶盡在此,越王親自鼓其士而進之,士聞鼓音
破碎亂行蹈火,而死者,左右百人有餘,越王擊金而
退之,是故子墨子言曰,乃若夫少食惡衣殺身而爲
名,此天下百姓之所皆難也,若苟君說之,則衆能爲
之,況兼相愛交相利與此異矣,夫愛人者人亦從而
愛之,利人者人亦從而利之,惡人者人亦從而惡之,
害人者人亦從而害之,此何難之有焉,特上不以爲
政而士不以爲行故也.

然而今天下之士君子曰,然,乃若兼則善矣,雖然,不
可行之物也,譬若挈太山越河濟也.○子墨子言是
非其譬也,夫挈太山而越河濟,可謂畢刦有力矣,自
古及今,未有能行之者也,況乎兼相愛交相利,則與
此異古者聖王行之,何以知其然,古者禹治天下,西
爲西河漁竇,以洩渠孫皇之水,北爲防原泒注后之
邸嘑池之竇灑爲底柱鑿爲龍門,以利燕代胡貉與
西河之民,東方漏之陸防孟諸之澤灑爲九澮以楗
東土之水,以利冀州之民,南爲江漢淮汝東流之注,
五湖之處,以利荊楚于越南夷之民,此言禹之事吾

or the moon, over its four quarters. He did not permit great States to insult small ones ; he did not permit the multitude to oppress the fatherless and the widow; he did not permit violence and power to take from the husbandmen their millet, pannicled millet, dogs, and swine. Heaven, as if constrained, visited king Wăn with blessing. The old and childless were enabled to complete their years ; the solitary and brotherless could yet mingle among the living; the young and parentless found those on whom they could depend, and grew up. These were the doings of king Wăn ; and I am now for practising the same universal mutual love.

'King Wû tunneled through the T'âi mountain. The Record says, "There is a way through the mountain, made by me, the descendant of the kings of Châu :—I have accomplished this great work. I have got my virtuous men, and rise up full of reverence for Shang, Hsiâ, and the tribes of the south, the east, and the north. Though he has his multitudes of relatives, they are not equal to my virtuous men. If guilt attach to the people anywhere throughout the kingdom, it is to be required of me, the One man."' This describes the doings of king Wû, and I am now for practising the same universal mutual love[1].

If, now, the rulers of the kingdom truly and sincerely wish all in it to be rich, and dislike any being poor ; if they desire its good government, and dislike disorder ; they ought to practise universal mutual love, and the interchange of mutual benefits. This was the law of the sage kings ; it is the way to effect the good government of the nation; it may not but be striven after.

可不務爲也。
利此聖王之法天下之治道也不
下之治而惡其亂富兼相愛交相
忠實欲天下之富而惡其貧欲天
是故子墨子言曰今天下之君子
一人此言武王之事吾今行兼矣
仁人尚作以祇商夏蠻夷醜貉雖
有周親不若仁人萬方有罪維予
山有道曾孫周王有事大事旣獲
矣昔者武王將事泰山隧傳曰泰
依而長此文王之事則吾今行兼
生人之間少失其父母者有所放
終其壽連獨無兄弟者有所雜於
文王慈是以老而無子者有所得
爲暴勢尊稿人黍稷狗彘天屑臨
大國侮小國不爲衆庶侮鰥寡不
日若月乍光于四方于西土不爲
今行兼矣昔者文王之治西土若

[1] I do not recollect to have read elsewhere of king Wû's tunneling through the T'âi mountain. In what Mo quotes from some Record, we have sentences from different parts of the Shû-ching brought together. The account of the labours of Yü contains names also not elsewhere found. There are, no doubt, many errors in the text.—I omit the 是故子墨子言曰, which follow 行兼矣.

UNIVERSAL LOVE. PART III.

Our Master, the philosopher Mo, said, 'The business of benevolent men requires that they should strive to stimulate and promote what is advantageous to the kingdom, and to take away what is injurious to it.'

Speaking, now, of the present time, what are to be accounted the most injurious things to the kingdom[1]? They are such as the attacking of small States by great ones; the inroads on small Families by great ones; the plunder of the weak by the strong; the oppression of the few by the many; the scheming of the crafty against the simple; the insolence of the noble to the mean. To the same class belong the ungraciousness of rulers[2], and the disloyalty of ministers; the unkindness of fathers, and the want of filial duty on the part of sons. Yea, there is to be added to these the conduct of the mean men[2], who employ their edged weapons and poisoned stuff, water and fire, to rob and injure one another.

Pushing on the inquiry now, let us ask whence all these injurious things arise. Is it from loving others and advantaging others? It must be answered 'No;' and it must likewise be said, They arise clearly[3] from hating others and doing violence to others.' If it be further asked whether those who hate and do violence to others hold the principle of loving all, or that of making distinctions, it must be replied, 'They make distinctions.' So then, it is this principle of making distinctions between man and man, which gives rise to all that is most injurious in the kingdom. On this account we conclude that that principle is wrong.

Our Master said, 'He who condemns others must have whereby to change them.' To condemn men, and have no means of changing them, is like saving them from fire by plunging them in water. A man's language in such a case must be improper. On this account our Master said, 'There is the principle of loving all, to take the place of that which makes distinctions.'

將必無可焉○是故子墨子曰兼以易

而無以易之譬之猶以水救火也其說

子墨子曰非人者必有以易之若非人

別非也。

之交別者果生天下之大害者與是故

而賊人者兼與別與即曰別也。然即

必曰從惡人賊人生分名乎天下惡人

生此自愛人利人生與即必曰非也。

害也姑嘗本原若衆害之所自此胡自

刃毒藥水火以交相虧賊此又天下之

天下之害也又與今人之賤人執其兵

也父母之不慈也子者之不孝也此又

人與爲人君者之不惠也臣者之不忠

寡詐之謀愚貴之敖賤此天下之害也

也大家之亂小家也強之劫弱衆之暴

下之害孰爲大○曰若大國之攻小國

子墨子言曰仁人之事者必務求與天

下之利除天下之害○然當今之時天

' I suppose that the compiler—the disciple of Mo—begins to speak here. Throughout this part, however, the changes in the argument are indistinctly marked.   ' 人與 should here be expunged from the Chinese text.   ' 又與 should here be expunged. ' I translate 分名 by 'clearly.' 名 is probably a misprint for 明.

If, now, we ask, 'And how is it that universal love can change *the consequences of* that other principle which makes distinctions?' the answer is, 'If princes were as much for the States of others as for their own, what one among them would raise the forces of his State to attack that of another?—he is for that other as much as for himself. If they were for the capitals of others as much as for their own, what one would raise the forces of his capital to attack that of another?—he is for that as much as for his own. If chiefs regarded the Families of others as their own, what one would lead the power of his Family to throw that of another into confusion?—he is for that other as much as for himself. If, now, States did not attack, nor holders of capitals smite, one another, and if Families were guilty of no mutual aggressions, would this be injurious to the kingdom, or its benefit?' It must be replied, 'This would be advantageous to the kingdom.' Pushing on the inquiry, now, let us ask whence all these benefits arise. Is it from hating others and doing violence to others? It must be answered, 'No;' and it must likewise be said, 'They arise clearly from loving others and doing good to others.' *If it be further asked* whether those who love others and do good to others hold the principle of making distinctions between man and man, or that of loving all, it must be replied, 'They love all.' So then it is this principle of universal mutual love which really gives rise to all that is most beneficial to the nation. On this account we conclude that that principle is right[1].

Our Master said, a little while ago, 'The business of benevolent men requires that they should strive to stimulate and promote what is advantageous to the kingdom, and to take away what is injurious to it.' We have now traced the subject up, and found that it is the principle of universal love which produces all that is most beneficial to the kingdom, and the principle of making distinctions which produces all that is injurious to it. On this account what our

別。〇然即兼之可以易別之故。何也。〇

曰藉爲人之國若爲其國夫誰獨舉其

國以攻人之國者哉爲彼猶爲己也。

爲人之都若爲其都夫誰獨舉其都以

伐人之都者哉爲彼猶爲己也爲人之

家若爲其家夫誰獨舉其家以亂人之

家者爲其家猶爲己也然即國都不相

攻伐人家不相亂此天下之害與天

下之利與即必曰天下之利也姑嘗本

原若衆利之所自生此胡自生此自惡

人賊人生與即必曰非然也必曰從愛

人利人生分名乎天下愛人而利人者。

別與兼與即必曰兼也然即之交兼者。

果生天下之大利者與是故子墨子曰

兼是也

且鄉吾本言曰仁人之事者必務求與

天下之利除天下之害〇今吾本原兼

之所生天下之大利者吾本原別之所

[1] I here transpose 子墨子曰, and put it after 兼是也. This is required by the preceding argument, which ends simply with 是故別非也. With this transposition, however, some other liberties must still be taken with the next paragraph. In 仁人之是者,是 should evidently be 事. In the concluding phrase—出乎 若方—the adoption of an old gloss, that 乎 should be 平, enables us to make sense of it. What follows, from 今吾將 down to 即若其利, is confused and difficult. 與, in 與天下之利, is a misprint for 興; but there must be other corruptions and omissions as well. One can see the author's drift: and I have tried to translate accordingly.

Master said, 'The principle of making distinctions between man and man is wrong, and the principle of universal love is right,' turns out to be correct as the sides of a square

If, now, we just desire to promote the benefit of the kingdom, and select for that purpose the principle of universal love, then the acute ears and piercing eyes of people will hear and see for one another; and the strong limbs of people will move and be ruled for one another; and men of principle will instruct one another. It will come about that the old, who have neither wife nor children, will get supporters who will enable them to complete their years; and the young and weak, who have no parents. will yet find helpers that shall bring them up. On the contrary, if this principle of universal love is held not to be correct, what benefits will arise from such a view? What can be the reason that the scholars of the kingdom, whenever they hear of this principle of universal love. go on to condemn it? Plain as the case is, their words in condemnation of this principle do not stop;—they say, 'It may be good, but how can it be carried into practice?'

Our Master said, 'Supposing that it could not be practised, it seems hard to go on likewise to condemn it. But how can it be good, and yet incapable of being put into practice?'

Let us bring forward two instances to test the matter:—Let any one suppose the case of two individuals, the one of whom shall hold the principle of making distinctions, and the other shall hold the principle of universal love. The former of these will say, 'How can I be for the person of my friend as much as for my own person? how can I be for the parents of my friend as much as for my own parents?' Reasoning in this way, he may see his friend hungry, but he will not feed him; cold, but he will not clothe him; sick, but he will not nurse him; dead, but he will not bury him. Such will be the language of the individual holding the principle of distinction, and such will be his conduct. The language of the other, holding the principle of universality, will be different, and also his conduct. He will say, 'I have heard that he who wishes to play a lofty part among men, will be for the person of his friend as much as for his own person, and for the parents of his friend as much as for his own parents. It is only thus that he can attain his distinction?' Reasoning in this way, when he sees his friend hungry, he will feed him; cold, he will clothe him; sick, he will nurse him; dead, he will bury him. Such will be the language of him who holds the principle of universal love, and such will be his conduct.

生天下之大害者也。是故子墨子曰、別非而兼是

者出乎若方也今吾將正求與天下之利而取之

以兼爲正是故以聰耳明目相爲視聽乎是以股

肱畢強相爲動宰乎而有道肆相教誨是以老而

無妻子者有所侍養以終其壽幼弱孤童之無父

母者有所放依以長其身今唯毋以兼爲正即若

其利也不識天下之士所以皆聞兼而非者其故

何也○然而天下之士非兼者之言猶未止也曰、

即善矣雖然豈可用哉

子墨子曰用而不可雖我亦將非之且焉有善而

不可用者○姑嘗兩而進之誰以爲二士使其一

士者執別使其一士者執兼是故別士之言曰吾

豈能爲吾友之身若爲吾身爲吾友之親若爲吾

親是故退睹其友飢即不食寒即不衣疾病不侍

養死喪不葬埋別士之言若此行若此兼士之言

不然行亦不然曰吾聞爲高士於天下者必爲其

友之身若爲其身爲其友之親若爲其親然後可

以爲高士天下是故退睹其友飢則食之寒則衣

The words of the one of these individuals are a condemnation of those of the other, and their conduct is directly contrary. Suppose now that their words are perfectly sincere, and that their conduct will be carried out,—that their words and actions will correspond like the parts of a token, every word being carried into effect; and let us proceed to put the following questions on the case :—Here is a plain in the open country, and an officer, with coat of mail, gorget, and helmet is about to take part in a battle to be fought in it, where the issue, whether for life or death, cannot be foreknown ; or here is an officer about to be dispatched on a distant commission from Pâ to Yüeh, or from Ch'î to Ching, where the issue of the journey, going and coming, is quite uncertain :—on either of these suppositions, to whom will the officer entrust the charge of his house, the support of his parents, and the care of his wife and children ?—to one who holds the principle of universal love? or to one who holds that which makes distinctions? I apprehend there is no one under heaven, man or woman, however stupid, though he may condemn the principle of universal love, but would at such a time make one who holds it the subject of his trust. This is in words to condemn the principle, and when there is occasion to choose between it and the opposite, to approve it ;—words and conduct are here in contradiction. I do not know how it is that throughout the kingdom scholars condemn the principle of universal love, whenever they hear it [1].

Plain as the case is, their words in condemnation of it do not cease, but they say, 'This principle may suffice perhaps to guide in the choice of an officer, but it will not guide in the choice of a sovereign [2].'

Let us test this by taking two illustrations :—Let any one suppose the case of two sovereigns, the one of whom shall hold the principle of mutual love, and the other shall hold the principle which makes distinctions. In this case, the latter of them will say, 'How can I be as much for the persons of all my people as for my own? This is much opposed to human feelings. The life of man upon the earth is but a very brief space ; it may be compared to the rapid

[1] From 子墨子曰,用而不可 down to this, the general meaning is plain enough. But there must be several corruptions in the text. 哉, for instance, after 別 之有是乎, is, plainly, for 我.   [2] Here there should follow, 'Our Master said,' and some observations introductory to the two illustrations of the sovereigns. This has been lost, however, and all that remains of it is the solitary 子, in 子姑嘗云云.

movement of a team of horses whirling past a small chink.' Reasoning in this way, he may see his people hungry, but he will not feed them; cold, but he will not clothe them; sick, but he will not nurse them; dead, but he will not bury them. Such will be the language of the sovereign who holds the principle of distinctions, and such will be his conduct. Different will be the language and conduct of the other who holds the principle of universal love. He will say, 'I have heard that he who would show himself a *virtuous and* intelligent sovereign, ought to make his people the first consideration, and think of himself only after them.' Reasoning in this way, when he sees any of the people hungry, he will feed them; cold, he will clothe them; sick, he will nurse them; dead, he will bury them. Such will be the language of the sovereign who holds the principle of universal love, and such his conduct. If we compare the two sovereigns, the words of the one are condemnatory of those of the other, and their actions are opposite. Let us suppose that their words are equally sincere, and that their actions will make them good,—that their words and actions will correspond like the parts of a token, every word being carried into effect; and let us proceed to put the following questions on the case:—Here is a year when a pestilence walks abroad among the people; many of them suffer from cold and famine; multitudes die in the ditches and water-channels. If at such a time they might make an election between the two sovereigns whom we have supposed, which would they prefer? I apprehend there is no one under heaven, however stupid, though he may condemn the principle of universal love, but would at such a time prefer to be under the sovereign who holds it. This is in words to condemn the principle, and, when there is occasion to choose between it and the opposite, to approve it;—words and conduct are here in contradiction. I do not know how it is that throughout the kingdom scholars condemn the principle of universal love, whenever they hear it.

Plain as the case is, their words in condemnation of it do not cease; but they say, 'This universal *mutual love* is benevolent and righteous. That we grant, but how can it be practised? The impracticability of it is like that of taking up the T'âi mountain, and leaping with it over the Chiang or the Ho. We do, indeed, desire this universal love, but it is an impracticable thing!'

Our Master said, 'To take up the T'âi mountain, and leap with it over the Chiang or the

子墨子曰夫挈泰山以超江河自古之及今生民而

未有也今若夫兼相愛交相利此自先聖六王者親行之何知先聖六王之親行之也

夫挈泰山以超江河也故兼者聖王之道也王公大人之所以安也萬民衣食之所以足也故君子莫若審兼而務行之為人君必惠為人臣必忠為人父必慈為人子必孝為人兄必友為人弟必悌

行相反與膚使若二君者言必信行必果使言行之合猶合符節也無言而不行也然即敢問今歲有癘疫萬民多有勤苦凍餒轉死溝壑中者既已眾矣不識將擇之二君者將何從也我以為當其於此也天下無愚夫愚婦雖非兼君必從兼君是也言而非兼擇即取兼此言行拂也不識天下所以皆聞兼而非兼之者其故何也○然而天下之士非兼者之言也猶未止也曰兼即仁矣義矣雖然豈可為哉吾譬兼之不可為也猶挈泰山以超江河也故兼者直願之也

夫豈可為之物哉

民飢即不食寒即不衣疾病不侍養死喪不葬埋別君之言若此行若此君之言曰吾聞為明君於天下者必先萬民之身然後為其身然後可以為明君於天下是故退睹其萬民飢即食之寒即衣之疾病侍養之死喪葬埋之兼君之言若此行若此然即交若之二君者言相非而

死喪不葬埋別君之言若此行若此兼君之言曰吾聞為高士於天下者必先萬民之身然後為其身然後可以為高士於天下是故退睹其

人之生乎地上之無幾何也譬之猶馳駟而過隙也是故退睹其萬民飢即不食寒即不衣疾病不侍養

Ho, is a thing which never has been done, from the highest antiquity to the present time, since men were ; but the exercise of mutual love and the interchange of mutual benefits,—this was practised by the ancient sages and six kings.'

How do you know that the ancient sages and the six kings practised this?

Our Master said, ' I was not of the same age and time with them, so that I could myself have heard their voices, or seen their faces; but I know what I say from what they have transmitted to posterity, written on bamboo or cloth, cut in metal or stone, or engraven on their vessels.'

'It is said in "The Great Declaration,"—"King Wăn was like the sun or like the moon ; suddenly did his brightness shine through the four quarters of the western region [1]."

'According to these words, king Wăn exercised the principle of universal love on a vast scale. He is compared to the sun or moon which shines on all, without partial favour to any spot under the heavens ;—such was the universal love of king Wăn.' What our Master insisted on was thus exemplified in him.

Again, not only does "The Great Declaration " speak thus ;—we find the same thing in "The Declaration of Yü." Yü said, " Ye multitudes, listen all to my words. It is not only I who dare say a word in favour of war ;—against this stupid prince of Miâo we must execute the punishment appointed by Heaven. I am therefore leading your hosts, and go before you all to punish the prince of Miâo [1]."

'Thus Yü punished the prince of Miâo, not to increase his own riches and nobility, nor to obtain happiness and emolument, nor to gratify his ears and eyes ;—he did it, seeking to promote what was advantageous to the kingdom, and to take away what was injurious to it. It appears from this, that Yü held the principle of universal love.' What our Master insisted on may be found in him.

'And not only may Yü thus be appealed to ;—we have "The words of Tang" to the same effect. Tang said, "I, the child Lî, presume to use a dark-coloured victim, and announce to Thee, O supreme Heavenly Sovereign :—Now there is a great drought, and it is right I should

敢蔽有罪不敢赦簡在帝心萬方有罪即當朕

湯曰惟予小子履敢用元牡告於上天后曰今

天大旱即當朕身履未知得罪于上下有善不

求焉○且不惟禹誓爲然雖湯說即亦猶是也

害○即此禹兼也雖子墨子之所謂兼者於禹

千福祿樂耳目也以求與天下之利除天下之

靈以征有苗禹之征有苗也非以求以重富貴

稱亂蠢茲有苗用天之罰若予旣率爾羣對諸

是也禹曰濟濟有衆咸聽朕言非惟小子敢行

王取法焉○且不惟泰誓爲然雖禹誓即亦猶

○即此文王兼也雖子墨子之所謂兼者於文

下之博大也譬之日月兼照天下之無有私也

○照光於四方於西土即此言文王之兼愛天

傳遺後世子孫者知之泰誓曰文王若日若月

其色也以其所書於竹帛鏤於金石琢於槃盂

○子墨子曰吾非與之並世同時親聞其聲見

六王者親行之○何知先聖六王之親行之也

來未嘗有也今若夫兼相愛交相利此自先聖

[1] See 'The Great Declaration,' III. 6. The language is somewhat different from the citation.
[1] 'The Declaration of Yü' is what is called 'The Counsels of Yü.' In the twentieth paragraph we find the passage here quoted, or rather we find something like it.

be held responsible for it. I do not know but that I have offended against the Powers above and below. But the good I dare not keep in obscurity, and the sinner I dare not pardon. The examination of this is with Thy mind, O God. If the people throughout the kingdom commit offences it is to be required of me. If I commit offences, it does not concern the people[1]." From these words we perceive that T'ang, possessing the dignity of sovereign, and the wealth of the kingdom, did not shrink from offering himself as a sacrifice which might be acceptable to God and *other* spiritual beings.' It appears from this that T'ang held the principle of universal love. What our Master insisted on was exemplified in T'ang.

And not only may we appeal in this way to the 'Declarations,' 'Charges,' and 'Words of T'ang,'—we find the same thing in 'The Poems of Châu[2].' One of those poems says,

'Wide and long is the Royal way,   It is straight as an arrow.
Without deflection, without injustice.   It is smooth as a whetstone.
The Royal way is plain and level,   The officers tread it ;
Without injustice, without deflection.   The lower people see it.'

In not this speaking of the *Royal* way in accordance with our style[3]? Anciently, Wän and Wû, acting with exact justice and impartiality, rewarded the worthy and punished the oppressive, allowing no favouritism to influence them towards their own relatives. It appears from this that Wän and Wû held the principle of universal love. What our Master insisted on was exemplified in them.—How is it that the scholars throughout the kingdom condemn this universal love, whenever they hear of it? Plain as the case is, the words of those who condemn the principle of universal love do not cease. They say, 'It is not advantageous to the entire devotion to parents which is required ;—it is injurious to filial piety[4].' Our Master said, ' Let us bring this objection to the test :—A filial son, having *the happiness of* his parents at heart, considers how it is to be secured. Now, does he, so considering, wish men to love and benefit his parents? or does he wish them to hate and injure his parents?' On this view of the question, it must be evident that he wishes men to love and benefit his parents. And what

人愛利其親與意欲人之惡賊其親
度者吾不識孝子之為親度者亦欲
于墨子曰姑嘗本原之孝子之為親
止曰意不忠親之利而害為孝乎〇
何也然而天下之非兼者之言猶未
下之人所以皆聞兼而非之者其故
之所謂兼者於文武取法焉不識天
為正均分賞罰暴勿有親戚兄弟
視若吾言非語道之謂也古者文武
矢其易若底君子之所履小人之所
偏不黨亦猶是也周詩曰王道蕩蕩不
詩即亦惟誓命與湯說為然周
法焉〇且不惟誓命與湯說為然周
兼也雖子墨子之所謂兼者於湯取
犧牲以祠說于上帝鬼神〇即此湯
為天子富有天下然且不憚以身為
身朕身有罪無及萬方卽此言湯貴

[1] See 'The Announcement of T'ang' (湯告) in various places. Compare also more particularly the Analects, XX. i. 3.   [2] In the quotation which is immediately subjoined, the first four lines are from a rhythmical passage of the Shû-ching, V. iv. 13. The remaining four are in the Shih-ching, II. v. Ode ix. st. 1.   [3] Such I suppose to be the meaning of 若吾言非語道之謂也, if it were amended.   [4] The sentence is not clear,—意不忠親之利而害為孝乎. I have done what I could with it. The scope of the whole paragraph is sufficiently plain. The 遇, farther on, is supposed to be for 偶.

must he himself first do in order to gain this object? If I first address myself to love and benefit men's parents, will they for that return love and benefit to my parents? or if I first address myself to hate men's parents, will they for that return love and benefit to my parents? It is clear that I must first address myself to love and benefit men's parents, and they will return to me love and benefit to my parents. The conclusion is that a filial son has no alternative.—He must address himself in the first place to love and do good to the parents of others. If it be supposed that this is an accidental course, to be followed on emergency by a filial son, and not sufficient to be regarded as a general rule, let us bring it to the test of what we find in the Books of the ancient kings.—It is said in the Tă Yă,

> 'Every word finds its answer; He threw me a peach;
> Every action its recompense. I returned him a plum.'

These words show that he who loves others will be loved, and that he who hates others will be hated. How is it that the scholars throughout the kingdom condemn this principle of universal love, when they hear it?

Is it that they deem it so difficult as to be impracticable? But there have been more difficult things, which yet have been done. *For instance*, king Ling of Ching was fond of small waists. In his time, the officers of Ching restricted themselves to a handful of rice, till they required a stick to raise themselves, and in walking had to hold themselves up by the wall. Now, it is a difficult thing to restrict one's self in food, but they were able to do it, because it would please king Ling.—It needs not more than a generation to change the manners of the people, such is their desire to move after the pattern of their superiors.

Again, Kâu-chien, the king of Yüeh, was fond of bravery. He spent three years in training his officers to be brave; and then, not knowing fully whether they were so, he set fire to the ship where they were, and urged them forward by a drum into the flames. They advanced, one rank over the bodies of another, till an immense number perished in the water or the flames; and it was not till he ceased to beat the drum, that they retired. Those officers of Yüeh might be pronounced to be full of reverence. To sacrifice one's life in the flames is a difficult thing, but they were able to do it, because it would please their king.—It needed not

與以說觀之、即欲人之愛利其親也、然即吾惡先從
事即得此、若我先從事乎愛利人之親然後人報我
愛利吾親乎、意我先從事乎惡人之親然後人報我
以愛利吾親乎、即必吾先從事乎愛利人之親然後
人報我以愛利吾親也、然即之交孝子者果不得已
乎、毋先從事愛利人之親者與、意以天下之孝子爲
所道曰、無言而不讐、無德而不報、投我以桃報之以
李、即此言愛人者必見愛也、而惡人者必見惡也、不
識天下之士所以皆聞愛而非之者其故何也、
意以爲難而不可爲耶、嘗有難此而可爲者、昔荊靈
王好小要靈王之身、荊國之士飯不踰乎一固據
而後與扶垣而後行、故約食爲其難爲也、然後爲之而
靈王說之、未踰於世而民可移也、即求以鄉其上也、
昔者越王勾踐好勇教其士臣三年、以其知未足
以知之也、焚舟失火鼓而進之、其士偃前列伏水火
而死、有不可勝數也、當此之時、不鼓而退也、越國之
士、可謂顫矣、故焚身爲其難爲也、然後爲之、越王說之

I 2

more than a generation to change the manners of the people, such is their desire to move after the pattern of their superiors. *Once more,* duke Wăn of Tsin was fond of garments of coarse flax. In his time, the officers of Tsin wore wide clothes of that fabric, with rams' furs, leathern swordbelts, and coarse canvas sandals. Thus attired, they went in to the duke's levee, and went out and walked through the court. It is a difficult thing to wear such clothes, but they were able to do it, because it would please duke Wăn.—It needs but a generation to change the manners of the people, such is their desire to move after the pattern of their superiors.

Now, little food, a burning ship, and coarse clothes,—these are among the most difficult things to endure; but because the sovereign would be pleased with the enduring them, they were able *in those cases* to do it. It needed no more than a generation to change the manners of the people. Why? Because such is their desire to move after the pattern of their superiors. And now, as to universal mutual love[1], it is an advantageous thing and easily practised,—beyond all calculation. The only reason why it is not practised is, in my opinion, because superiors do not take pleasure in it. If superiors were to take pleasure in it, stimulating men to it by rewards and praise, and awing them from opposition to it by punishments and fines, they would, in my opinion, move to it,—the practice of universal mutual love, and the interchange of mutual benefits,—as fire rises upwards, and as water flows downwards:—nothing would be able to check them. This universal love was the way of the sage kings; it is the principle to secure peace for kings, dukes, and great men; it is the means to secure plenty of food and clothes for the myriads of the people. The best course for the superior man is to well understand the principle of universal love, and to exert himself to practise it. It requires the sovereign to be gracious, and the minister to be loyal; the father to be kind, and the son to be filial; the elder brother to be friendly, and the younger to be obedient. Therefore the superior man,—with whom the chief desire is to see gracious sovereigns and loyal ministers; kind fathers and filial sons; friendly elder brothers and obedient younger ones,—ought to insist on the indispensableness of the practice of universal love. It was the way of the sage kings; it would be the most advantageous thing for the myriads of the people.

之、未踰於世、而民可移也、即求以鄉上也、昔者
晉文公好苴服當文公之時晉國之士大布之
衣牂羊之裘練帛之冠且苴之屨入見文公出
以踐之朝故苴服爲其難爲也、然後爲也、即
說之、未踰於世而民可移也、即求以鄉其上也。
是故約食焚舟苴服、此天下之至難爲也、然後
爲而上說之、未踰於世而民可移也、何故也、即
求以鄉其上也。今若夫兼相利此其有利且易
爲也。不可勝計也、我以爲則無有上說之者而
已矣。苟有上說之者、勸之以賞譽威之以刑罰、
我以爲人之於就兼相愛交相利也、譬之猶火
之就上水之就下也、不可防止於天下、故兼者
聖王之道也王公大人之所以安也萬民衣食
之所以足也、故君子莫若審兼而務行之、爲人
君必惠爲人臣必忠爲人父必慈爲人子必孝、
爲人兄必友爲人弟必悌、故君子莫若欲爲惠
君忠臣慈父孝子友兄悌弟、當若兼之不可不
行也、此聖王之道而萬民之大利也。

[1] For 兼相利 we should read 兼相愛.

2. Notwithstanding the mutilations and corruptions in the text of the preceding Essay, its general scope is clearly discernible, and we obtain from it a sufficient account of Mo's doctrine on the subject of 'Universal Love.' We have now to consider the opposition offered to this doctrine by Mencius. He was not the first, however, to be startled and offended by it. The Essay shows that it was resented as an outrage on the system of orthodox belief during all the lifetime of Mo and his immediate disciples. Men of learning did not cease to be clamorous against it. From the allusions made by Mencius to its prevalence in his days, it would appear that it had overcome much of the hostility which it at first encountered. He stepped forward to do battle with it, and though he had no new arguments to ply, such was the effect of his onset. that ' Universal Love ' has ever since been considered save by some eccentric thinkers, as belonging to the Limbo of Chinese vanities, among other things 'abortive, monstrous, or unkindly mixed.'

We may approach the question conveniently by observing that Mo's attempts to defend his principle were in several points far from the best that could be made. His references to the examples of Yü, T'aug, and the kings Wăn and Wû, are of this nature. Those worthies well performed the work of their generation. They punished the oppressor, and delivered the oppressed. Earnest sentiments of justice and benevolence animated their breasts and directed their course. But they never laid down the doctrine of ' Universal Love,' as the rule for themselves or others.

When he insists, again, that the people might easily be brought to appreciate and practise his doctrine, if their rulers would only set them the example, he shows the same overweening idea of the influence of superiors, and the same ignorance of human nature, which I have had occasion to point out in both Confucius and Mencius. His references to duke Wăn of Tsin, duke Ling of Ch'û, and Kâu-chien of Yüeh, and his argument from what they are said to have effected, only move us to smile. And when he teaches that men are to be *awed* to love one another '*by punishments and fines,*' we feel that he is not understanding fully what he says nor whereof he affirms.

Still, he has broadly and distinctly laid it down, that if men would only universally love one another, the evils which disturb and embitter human society would disappear. I do not say that he has taught the *duty* of universal love. His argument is conducted

on the ground *of expediency*[1]. Whether he had in his own mind
a truer, nobler foundation for his principle, does not immediately
appear. Be that as it may, his doctrine was that men were to be
exhorted to love one another,—to love one another as themselves.
According to him, 'princes should be as much for the States of
others as for their own. One prince should be for every other as for
himself.' So it ought to be also with the Heads of clans, with
ministers, with parents, and with men generally.

Here it was that Mencius joined issue with him. He affirmed
that 'to love all equally did not acknowledge the peculiar affection
due to a parent.' It is to be observed that Mo himself nowhere
says that his principle was that of loving all EQUALLY.. His disciples
drew this conclusion from it. In the third Book of Mencius's Works,
we find one of them, Î Chih, contending that the expression in the
Shû-ching, about the ancient kings acting towards the people, 'as if
they were watching over an infant,' sounded to him as if love were
to be *without difference of degree*, the manifestation of it simply
commencing with our parents[2]. To this Mencius replied conclusively
by asking, 'Does Î really think that a man's affection for the child
of his brother is merely like his affection for the child of his neighbour?' With still more force might he have asked, 'Is a man's
affection for his father merely like his affection for the father of his
neighbour?' Such a question, and the necessary reply to it, are
implied in his condemnation of Mo's system, as being 'without
father,' that is, denying the peculiar affection due to a father. If
Mo had really maintained that a man's father was to be no more
to him than the father of any other body, or if his system had
necessitated such a consequence, Mencius would only have done his
duty to his country in denouncing him, and exposing the fallacy of
his reasonings. As the case is, he would have done better if he had
shown that no such conclusion necessarily flows from the doctrine
of 'Universal Love,' or its preceptive form that we are to love our
neighbour as ourselves.

Of course it belonged to Mo himself to defend his views from the
imputation. But what he has said on the point is not satisfactory.
In reply to the charge that his principle was injurious to filial piety,
he endeavoured to show, that, by acting on it, a man would best

---

[1] This and several other points are well put by the Rev. Dr. Edkins, in his Essay, referred
to on p. 133. See Journal of the North-China Branch of the Royal Asiatic Society, No. II,
May, 1859.   [2] See Bk. III. Pt. I. v. 3.

secure the happiness of his parents :—as he addressed himself in the
first place to love, and do good to, the parents of others, they would
recompense to him the love of, and good-doing to, his parents.   It
might be so, or it might not.   The reply exhibits strikingly in what
manner Mo was conducted to the inculcation of universal love, and
that really it had in his mind no deeper basis than its expediency.
This is his weak point; and if Mencius, whose view of the constitution
of human nature, and the binding force of the virtues, apart from
all consideration of consequences, was more comprehensive and
correct than that of Mo, had founded his opposition on this ground,
we could in a measure have sympathised with him.   But while Mo
appeared to lose sight of the other sentiments of the human mind
too much, in his exclusive contemplation of the power of love, he
did not doubt but his principle would make sons more filial, and
ministers more devoted, and subjects more loyal.   The passage
which I have just referred to, moreover, does not contain the
admission that the love was to be *without any difference of degree*.
The fact is, that he hardly seems to have realised the objection with
which Mencius afterwards pressed the advocacy of it by his followers.
If he did do so, he blinked the difficulty, not seeing his way to give
a full and precise reply to it.

This seems to be the exact state of the case between the two
philosophers.   Mo stumbled on a truth, which, based on a right
foundation, is one of the noblest which can animate the human
breast, and affords the surest remedy for the ills of society.   There
is that in it, however, which is startling, and liable to misrepresenta-
tion and abuse.   Mencius saw the difficulty attaching to it, and
unable to sympathise with the generosity of it, set himself to meet
it with a most vehement opposition.   Nothing, certainly, could be
more absurd than his classing Yang Chu and Mo Ti together, as
equally the enemies of benevolence and righteousness.   When he
tries to ridicule Mo, and talks contemptuously about him, how, if
he could have benefited the kingdom, by toiling till he rubbed off
every hair of his body, he would have done it[1],—this only raises up
a barrier between himself and us.   It reminds us of the *hardness* of
nature which I have elsewhere charged against him.

3. Confucius, I think, might have dealt more fairly and generously
with Mo.   In writing of him, I called attention to his repeated

---

[1] Bk. VII. Pt I. xxvi.

enunciation of 'the golden rule' in a negative form,—'What you do not wish done to yourself, do not do to others[1].' In one place, indeed, he rises for a moment to the full apprehension of it, and recognises the duty of taking the initiative,—of behaving to others in the first instance as he would that they should behave to him[2]. Now, what is this but the practical exercise of the principle of universal love? 'All things whatsoever ye would that men should do to you, do ye even so to them:'—this is simply the manifestation of the requirement, 'Thou shalt love thy neighbour as thyself.' Confucius might have conceded, therefore, to Mo, that the rule of conduct which he laid down was the very best that could be propounded. If he had gone on to remove it from the basis of expediency, and place it on a better foundation, he would have done the greatest service to his countrymen, and entitled himself to a place among the sages of the world.

On this matter I am happy to find myself in agreement with the 'Prince of Literature,' Han Yü[3]. 'Our literati,' says he, 'find fault with Mo because of what he has said on "The Estimation to be attached to Concord[4]," on "Universal Love," on "The Estimation to be given to Men of Worth[5]," on "The Acknowledging of Spiritual Beings[6]," and on "The Awe in which Confucius stood of Great Men,

---

[1] Vol. i. proleg. p. 109.   [2] See proleg. on the 'Doctrine of the Mean,' pp. 48, 49, vol. i.

[3] See the Works of Han Wăn-kung, 十一卷, 讀墨子篇.

[4] This is the title of one of Mo's Essays, the 尚同, forming the third Book of his Works. Generalising after his fashion, he traces all evils up to a want of concord, or agreement of opinion; and goes on to assert that the sovereign must be recognised as the 'Infallible Head,' to lay down the rule of truth and right, saying 天子之所是, 皆是之, 天子 之所非, 皆非之. 'What the sovereign approves, all must approve; what the sovereign condemns, all must condemn.' It is an unguarded utterance; and taken absolutely, apart from its connexion, may be represented very much to Mo's disadvantage. See 'Supplemental Observations on the Four Books,' on Mencius, Book I. art. lix. The coincidence between this saying and the language of Hobbes is remarkable.—'Quod legislator praeceperit, id pro bono, quod vetuerit, id pro malo habendum esse.' (De Cive, cap. xii. 1.)

[5] This is another of Mo's pieces,—尚賢, the second Book of his Works. He finds a cure for the ills of the nation in princes' honouring and employing only men of worth, without paying regard to their relatives. This is contrary to the third of Confucius's nine standard rules for the government of the nation, set forth in his conversation with duke Âi, as related in the 'Doctrine of the Mean,' ch. xx. But Mo would only discountenance nepotism, where it ought to be discountenanced.

[6] This is found in the eighth Book of Mo. The first and second parts of the essay, however, are unfortunately lost. In the third he tells several queer ghost stories, and adduces other proofs, to show the real existence of spiritual beings, and that they take account of men's actions to reward or to punish them. He found another panacea for the ills of the kingdom in this truth. His doctrine here, however, is held to be inconsistent with Confucius's reply to

and, when he resided in any State, did blame its Great Officers[1]"
But when the Ch'un Ch'iû finds fault with arrogant ministers, is not
this attaching a similar value to concord? When Confucius speaks
of "overflowing in love to all, and cultivating the friendship of the
good," and of how "the extensive conferring of benefits constitutes
a sage," does he not teach universal love? When he advises "the
esteem of the worthy;" when he arranged his disciples into "the
four classes," so stimulating and commending them; when he says
that "the superior man dislikes the thought of his name not being
mentioned after death:"—does not this show the estimation he
gave to men of worth? When "he sacrificed as if the spiritual
beings were present," and condemned "those who sacrificed as if
they were not really sacrificing[2];" when he said, "When I sacrifice,
I shall receive blessing:"—was not this acknowledging spiritual
beings? The literati and Mo equally approve of Yâo and Shun,
and equally condemn Chieh and Châu; they equally teach the
cultivation of the person, and the rectifying of the heart, reaching
on to the good government of the nation, with all its States and
Families:—why should they be so hostile to each other? In my
opinion, the discussions which we hear are the work of their
followers, vaunting on each side the sayings of their Teacher; there
is no such contrariety between the real doctrines of the two
Teachers. Confucius would have made use of Mo's views; and
Mo would have made use of those of Confucius. If they would
not have made use of each other's sentiments, they could not have
been K'ung and Mo.'

4. It seems proper, in closing this discussion of Mo's views, to
notice the manner in which the subject of 'universal love' appears
in Christianity. Its whole law is comprehended in the one word—
Love; but how wide is the scope of the term compared with all
which it ever entered into the mind of Chinese sage or philosopher
to conceive!

Fan Ch'ih, Analects, VI. xx, that wisdom consists in respecting spiritual beings, but at the
same time keeping aloof from them. But as between Confucius and Mo, on this point we
would agree rather with the latter. He holds an important truth, mingled with superstition;
the sage would seem to be sceptical.

[1] Han avoids saying anything on this point. The author of 'Supplemental Observations'
is equally silent.

[2] Han is here quoting Analects, III. xii. 2, 吾不與祭如不祭, which he
points and interprets after a way of his own. He does not read 與 but 與, in the sense of
許, 'to grant to,' 'to approve of.'

It is most authoritative where the teachers of China are altogether silent, and commands:—'Thou shalt love the Lord, thy God, with all thy heart, and with all thy soul, and with all thy strength, and with all thy mind.' For the Divine Being Christianity thus demands from all men supreme love ;—the love of all that is majestic, awing the soul ; the love of all that is beautiful, wooing the heart ; the love of all that is good, possessing and mastering the entire nature. Such a love, existing, would necessitate obedience to every law, natural or revealed. Christianity, however, goes on to specify the duties which every man owes, as the complement of love to God, to his fellow-men :—'Owe no man anything, but to love one another, for he that loveth another hath fulfilled the law. For this—"Thou shalt not commit adultery," "Thou shalt not kill," "Thou shalt not steal," "Thou shalt not bear false witness," "Thou shalt not covet ;" and if there be any other commandment :—the whole is briefly comprehended in this saying, "Thou shalt love thy neighbour as thyself."' This commandment is 'like to' the other, differing from it only in not requiring the *supreme* love which is due to God alone. The rule which it prescribes,—such love to others as we feel for ourselves,—is much more definitely and intelligibly expressed than anything we find in Mo, and is not liable to the cavils with which his doctrine was assailed. Such a love to men, existing, would necessitate the performance of every relative and social duty ; we could not help doing to others as we would that they should do to us.

Mo's universal love was to find its scope and consummation in the good government of China. He had not the idea of man as man, any more than Confucius or Mencius. How can that idea be fully realised, indeed, where there is not the right knowledge of one living and true God, the creator and common parent of all ? The love which Christianity inculcates is a law of humanity ; paramount to all selfish, personal feelings ; paramount to all relative, local, national attachments ; paramount to all distinctions of race or of religion. Apprehended in the spirit of Christ, it will go forth even to the love of enemies ; it will energize in a determination to be always increasing the sum of others' happiness, limited only by the means of doing so.

But I stop. These prolegomena are not the place for disquisition ; but I deemed it right to say thus much here of that true, universal love, which at once gives glory to God and effects peace on earth.

CHAPTER IV.

WORKS WHICH HAVE BEEN CONSULTED IN THE PREPARATION OF THIS VOLUME.

The Works which have been consulted are mostly the same as those used in the preparation of the first volume, of which a list is there given. I have only to add to that :—

I.—OF CHINESE WORKS.

墨子十五卷,目一卷. 'The Philosopher Mo, in fifteen Books, with one Book on the Titles of his Essays.' This Work was edited and annotated in the forty-eighth year of Ch'ien-lung (A.D. 1784), by Pi Yüan (畢沅), lieutenant-governor of Shen-hsî. From the notes appended to Mo's Essay on 'Universal Love' in the last chapter, it will be seen that the task of editing has been very imperfectly executed. I suppose it is vain to express a wish that some foreign scholar would take it in hand.

五百家註音辯韓昌黎先生全集, 'The Collected Writings of Han Ch'ang-lî, with the Verbal and Critical Notes of five hundred Scholars.' Ch'ang-lî is a local designation for Han Yü, styled T'ûi-chih (退之), and canonized as Wăn-kung (文公), or 'Prince of Literature.' I have said, p. 12, that he was a scholar of the eighth century, but he extended on into the ninth, dying A.D. 824. He stands out as perhaps the most distinguished scholar of the long space between the Han and Sung dynasties. The edition of his Works which I have, with such a collation of commentators, was first published by a Hsü Tâo-chî (許道基), in the twenty-eighth year of Ch'ien-lung (A.D. 1761).

II.—OF TRANSLATIONS AND OTHER WORKS.

MENG TSEU, vel MENCIUM, inter Sinenses Philosophos, Ingenio, Doctrina, Nominisque Claritate, CONFUCIO PROXIMUM, edidit, Latina interpretatione, ad interpretationem Tartaricam utramque recensita, instruxit, et perpetuo commentario, e Sinicis deprompto, illustravit Stanislaus Julien. Paris, 1824–1829.

THE WORKS OF MENCIUS.

BOOK I.

KING HÛI OF LIANG. PART I.

利吾國乎。 亦將有以 千里而來 曰叟不遠 梁惠王。 孟子見 章句上 梁惠王

CHAPTER I. 1. Mencius *went to* see king Hûi of Liang.

2. The king said, 'Venerable sir, since you have not counted it far to come here, a distance of a thousand *lî*, may I presume that you are provided with counsels to profit my kingdom?'

TITLE OF THE WORK.—孟子, 'The philosopher Mǎng.' The Work thus simply bears the name, or surname rather, of him whose conversations and opinions it relates, and is said to have been compiled in its present form by the author himself. On the use of 子, after the surname, see on Analects, I. i. The surname and this 子 were combined by the Romish missionaries, and latinized into Mencius, which it is well to adopt throughout the translation, and thereby avoid the constant repetition of the word 'philosopher,' Mǎng not being distinguished, like K'ung (Confucius), by the crowning epithet of 'The Master.'

TITLE OF THIS BOOK.—梁惠王章句 上, 'King Hûi of Liang, in chapters and sentences. Part I.' Like the Books of the Confucian Analects, those of this Work are headed by two or three characters at or near their commencement. Each Book is divided into two parts, called 上 下, 'Upper and Lower.' This arrangement was made by Châo Ch'î (趙歧), a scholar of the eastern Han dynasty (died A.D. 201), by whom the chapters and sentences were also divided, and the 章句上 章句下 remain to the present day, a memorial of his work.

1. BENEVOLENCE AND RIGHTEOUSNESS MENCIUS'S ONLY TOPICS WITH THE PRINCES OF HIS TIME; AND THE ONLY PRINCIPLES WHICH CAN MAKE A

COUNTRY PROSPEROUS. 1. 'King Hûi of Liang.' —In the time of Confucius, Tsin (晉) was one of the great States of the nation, but the power of it was usurped by six great families. By B.C. 452, three of those were absorbed by the other three, viz. Wei, Châo, and Han (魏, 趙, and 韓), which continued to encroach on the small remaining power of their prince, until at last they extinguished the ruling house, and divided the whole territory among themselves. The sovereign Wei Lieh (威烈), in his 23rd year, B.C. 402, conferred on the chief of each family the title of Marquis (侯). Wei, called likewise, from the name of its capital, Liang, occupied the south-eastern part of Tsin, Han and Châo lying to the west and north-west of it. The Liang, where Mencius visited king Hûi, is said to have been in the present department of K'âi-fǎng. Hûi, 'The Kindly,' is the posthumous epithet of the king, whose name was Yung (罃). The title of *king* had been usurped by Ying, at some time before Mencius first visited him, which, it is said, he did in the 35th year of his government, B.C. 336. Mencius visited him on invitation, it must be supposed, and the simple 見—被招往見. 2. Mencius was a native of Tsâu (鄒), in Lû, the name of which is still retained in the Tsâu district of the department of Yen-châu (兗州), in Shan-

孟子對曰、王何必曰、利
亦有仁義而已矣、王曰、何
何以利吾國、大夫曰、何
以利吾家、士庶人曰、
以利吾身上下交征利、
而國危矣、萬乘之國、弒
其君者必千乘之家、
乘之國弒其君者必百
乘之家、萬取千焉、千取
百焉不為不多矣、苟為

3. Mencius replied, 'Why must your Majesty use that word "profit?" What I am provided with, are *counsels to* benevolence and righteousness, and these are my only topics.

4. 'If your Majesty say, "What is to be done to profit my kingdom?" the great officers will say, "What is to be done to profit our families?" and the inferior officers and the common people will say, "What is to be done to profit our persons?" Superiors and inferiors will try to snatch this profit the one from the other, and the kingdom will be endangered. In the kingdom of ten thousand chariots, the murderer of his sovereign shall be *the chief of* a family of a thousand chariots. In a kingdom of a thousand chariots, the murderer of his prince shall be *the chief of* a family of a hundred chariots. To have a thousand in ten thousand, and a hundred in a thousand, cannot be said not to be a large allotment, but if righteousness be put last, and profit be put first, they will not be satisfied without snatching *all.*

tung. The king, in complimentary style, calls the distance from Tsâu to Liang a thousand *lî*. It is difficult to say what was the exact length of the ancient *lî*. At present it is a little more than one-third of an English mile. The 亦, 'also,' occasions some difficulty.—With reference to what is it spoken? Some compare the 亦 . . . 乎 with 不亦乎, Analects, I. i. Others say that the king refers to the many scholars who at the time made it their business to wander from country to country, as advisers to the princes :—' You *also*, like other scholars,' &c. Then, when Mencius, in par. 3. replies— 亦有仁義, they say that he refers to Yâo, Shun, &c., as his models :—' I, like them,' &c.

But this is too far-fetched. Wang Yin-chih inclines to consider 亦 as for the most part merely a helping particle; especially does he regard it so after 不 in an interrogative clause. Observe the force of 將, delicately and suggestively putting the question. 3. 對,—marking the answer of an inferior, used from respect to the king. 曰 is 'to say,' followed directly by the words spoken. It is not ' to speak of.' 而已矣 mark very decidedly Mencius's purpose to converse only of 仁 and 義. 4. 征,—here = 取, 'to take.' 交征, 'mutually

樂此不賢者雖有此
孟子對曰賢者而後
鹿曰賢者亦樂此乎。
立於沼上顧鴻鴈麋
孟子見梁惠王王
而已矣何必曰利。
君者也王亦曰仁義
者也未有義而後其
饜未有仁而遺其親
後義而先利不奪不

5. 'There never has been a benevolent man who neglected his parents. There never has . been a righteous man who made his sovereign an after consideration.

6. 'Let your Majesty also say, "Benevolence and righteousness, and let these be your only themes." Why must you use that word—"profit?"'

CHAP. II. 1. Mencius, *another day*, saw king Hûi of Liang. The king *went and* stood *with him* by a pond, and, looking round at the large geese and deer, said, 'Do wise and good *princes* also find pleasure in these things?'

2. Mencius replied, 'Being wise and good, they have pleasure in these things. If they are not wise and good, though they have these things, they do not find pleasure.

to take;' i. e. superiors from inferiors, and inferiors from superiors. 乘, in 4th tone, 'a carriage or chariot.' The sovereign's domain, = 1,000 li square, produced 10,000 war chariots. A kingdom producing 1,000 chariots was that of a Âdu, or marquis. He is here called 百乘 之家, instead of 百乘之君, because the sovereign has just been denominated by that term. 後 and 先 are verbs. See Analects, VI. xx. 5. The 仁 and 義 here are supposed to result from the sovereign's example.

2. RULERS MUST SHARE THEIR PLEASURES WITH THE PEOPLE. THEY CAN ONLY BE HAPPY WHEN THEY RULE OVER HAPPY SUBJECTS. 1. 王立,— 'The king stood;' and the meaning is not that Mencius found him by the pond. The king seems to have received him graciously, and to have led him into the park. 於沼上,—

compare Analects, VI. vii. but for which passage I should translate here—'over a pond,' i. e. in some building over the water, such as is still very common in China. 鴻 means 'large geese,' and 麋 is the name for a large kind of deer, but they are joined here, as adjectives, to 鴈 and 鹿. 賢者=賢者之君, 'worthy princes.' It does not refer to Mencius, as some make it out. The reply makes this plain. The king's inquiry is prompted by a sudden dissatisfaction with himself, for being occupied so much with such material gratifications, and = 'Amid all their cares of government do these pleasures find a place with good princes?' 3. See the Shih-ching, III. i. Ode VIII. st. 1, 2. The ode tells how his people delighted in king Wân. For 鶴 the Shih-ching reads 喜. 於 is read wû, an interjection. 古之人 referring to king Wân, but

不樂也詩云經始靈臺經之
營之庶民攻之不日成之經
始勿亟庶民子來王在靈囿
麀鹿攸伏麀鹿濯濯白鳥鶴
鶴王在靈沼於牣魚躍文王
以民力為臺為沼而民歡樂
之謂其臺曰靈臺謂其沼曰
靈沼樂其有麋鹿魚鼈古之
人與民偕樂故能樂也湯誓
曰時日害喪予及女偕亡民

3. 'It is said in the Book of Poetry,
  "He measured out and commenced his marvellous tower ;
  He measured it out and planned it.
  The people addressed themselves to it,
  And in less than a day completed it.
  When he measured and began it, *he said to them*—Be not so
      earnest :
  But the multitudes came as if they had been his children.
  The king was in his marvellous park ;
  The does reposed about,
  The does so sleek and fat :
  And the white birds shone glistening.
  The king was by his marvellous pond ;
  How full was it of fishes leaping about!"

'King Wăn used the strength of the people to make his tower
and his pond, and yet the people rejoiced to do the work, calling
the tower "the marvellous tower," calling the pond "the marvellous
pond," and rejoicing that he had his large deer, his fishes, and
turtles. The ancients caused the people to have pleasure as well
as themselves, and therefore they could enjoy it.

4. 'In the Declaration of T'ang it is said, "O sun, when wilt thou

put generally. 4. See the Shû-ching, IV. Bk. 1. | had pointed to the sun, saying that, as surely
i. 3;—T'ang's announcement of his reasons for | as the sun was in heaven, so firm was he on his
proceeding against the tyrant Chieh. The | throne. The people took up his words, and
words quoted are those of the people. Chieh | pointing to the sun, thus expressed their hatred

欲與之偕亡雖有臺池

鳥獸豈能獨樂哉。

梁惠王曰寡人之於

國也盡心焉耳矣河內

凶則移其民於河東、

其粟於河內河東凶亦

然察鄰國之政無如寡

人之用心者鄰國之民

不加少寡人之民不加

多何也。孟子對曰王好

expire? We will die together with thee." The people wished *for Chieh's death*, though they should die with him. Although he had towers, ponds, birds, and animals, how could he have pleasure alone?'

CHAP. III. 1. King Hûi of Liang said, 'Small as my virtue is, in the government of my kingdom, I do indeed exert my mind to the utmost. If the year be bad on the inside of the river, I remove *as many of* the people *as I can* to the east of the river, and convey grain to the country in the inside. When the year is bad on the east of the river, I act on the same plan. On examining the government of the neighbouring kingdoms, I do not find that there is any prince who exerts his mind as I do. And yet the people of the neighbouring kingdoms do not decrease, nor do my people increase. How is this?'

2. Mencius replied, 'Your Majesty is fond of war;—let me take

of the tyrant, preferring death with him to life under him. 時-是; 害 is read *ho*; 喪, in 4th tone. Châo Ch'i gives quite another turn to the quotation, making the words an address of the people to Tang :—'This day he (Chieh) must die. We will go with you to kill him.' Chû Hsî's view is to be preferred. I do not think that the last two clauses are to be understood generally :—'When the people wish to die with a prince,' &c. They must specially refer to Chieh.

3. HALF MEASURES ARE OF LITTLE USE. THE GREAT PRINCIPLES OF ROYAL GOVERNMENT MUST BE FAITHFULLY AND IN THEIR SPIRIT CARRIED OUT. 1. The combination of particles—焉耳矣 —gives emphasis to the king's profession of his own devotedness to his kingdom. 寡人 was the designation of themselves used by the princes in speaking to their people, 寡德之人 'I, the man of small virtue.' I shall hereafter simply render it by 'I.' Liang was on the south of the river, i.e. the *Ho*, or Yellow river, but portions of the Wei territory lay on the other side, or north of the river. This was called the inside of the river, because the ancient royal capitals had mostly been there, in the province of Ch'î (冀州), comprehending the present Shan-hsî; and the country north of the Ho, looked at from them, was of course 'within,' or on this side of it. 粟,— now used commonly for millet and maize, but here for grain generally. 加少,加多, literally, 'add few, add many.' To explain the 加, it is said the expressions = 分外少,

食也斧斤以時入山林材
罟不入洿池魚鼈不可勝
違農時穀不可勝食也數
無望民之多於鄰國也。不
是亦走也曰王如知此則
何如曰不可直不百步耳、
後止以五十步笑百步則
百步而後止或五十步而
刃既接棄甲曳兵而走或
戰請以戰喻填然鼓之兵

an illustration from war.—*The soldiers move forward to* the sound of the drums; and after their weapons have been crossed, *on one side* they throw away their coats of mail, trail their arms behind them, and run. Some run a hundred paces and stop; some run fifty paces and stop. What would you think if those who run fifty paces were to laugh at those who run a hundred paces?' The king said, 'They should not do so. Though they did not run a hundred paces, yet they also ran away.' 'Since your Majesty knows this,' replied Mencius, 'you need not hope that your people will become more numerous than those of the neighbouring kingdoms.

3. 'If the seasons of husbandry be not interfered with, the grain will be more than can be eaten. If close nets are not allowed to enter the pools and ponds, the fishes and turtles will be more than can be consumed. If the axes and bills enter the hills and forests *only* at the proper time, the wood will be more than can be used.

牙外多, 'not fewer, nor larger, than they should for such States be.' 2. 填然 is said to express the sound of the drum. In 鼓之 鼓 is used as a verb, and 之 refers to 戰 士, or soldiers. It was the rule of war to advance at the sound of the drum, and retreat at the sound of the gong. 是亦走也,—literally, 'this also,' i.e. the fifty paces, 'was running away.' 3. Here we have an outline of the first principles of royal government, in contrast with the measures on which the king plumes himself in the 1st par. The 不 is

not imperative—'do not.' The first clauses of the various sentences are conditional. In spring there was the sowing; in summer, the weeding; and in autumn, the harvesting:—those were the seasons and works of husbandry, from which the people might not be called off. 勝, 1st tone. The dictionary explains it by 'to bear,' 'to be adequate to.' 穀不可勝 食—'there is no eating-power adequate to eat the grain.' 數, here read *tsü*, 'close-meshed.' The meshes of a net were anciently required to be large, of the size of four inches. People might only eat fish a foot long. 山=

飢矣謹庠序之教申之以
奪其時數口之家可以無
可以食肉矣百畝之田勿
彘之畜無失其時七十者
十者可以衣帛矣雞豚狗
也五畝之宅樹之以桑五
養生喪死無憾王道之始
是使民養生喪死無憾也
不可勝食材木不可勝用
木不可勝用也穀與魚鼈

When the grain and fish and turtles are more than can be eaten, and there is more wood than can be used, this enables the people to nourish their living and mourn for their dead, without any feeling against any. This condition, in which the people nourish their living and bury their dead without any feeling against any, is the first step of royal government.

4. 'Let mulberry trees be planted about the homesteads with their five *mâu*, and persons of fifty years may be clothed with silk. In keeping fowls, pigs, dogs, and swine, let not their times of *breeding* be neglected, and persons of seventy years may eat flesh. Let there not be taken away the time that is proper for the cultivation of the farm with its hundred *mâu*, and the family of several mouths that is supported by it shall not suffer from hunger. Let careful attention be paid to education in schools, inculcating in it especially the filial and fraternal duties, and grey-haired men will

wooded hills. 林 =forests in the plains. The time to work in the forests was, according to Chû Hsî, in the autumn, when the growth of the trees for the year was stopped. But in the Châu-lî, we find various rules about cutting down trees,—those on the south of the hill, for instance, in midwinter, those on the north, in summer, &c., which may be alluded to. 無 憾 I have translated, 'without any feeling against any,' the ruler being specially intended. 4. The higher principles which complete royal government. We can hardly translate 畝 by 'an acre,' it consisting, at present at least, only of 240 square paces, or 1200 square cubits, and anciently it was much smaller, 100 square paces, of six cubits each, making a *mâu*. The ancient theory for allotting the land was to mark it off in squares of 900 *mâu*, the middle square being called the 公田 or 'government fields.' The other eight were assigned to eight husbandmen and their families, who cultivated the public field in common. But from this twenty *mâu* were cut off, and, in portions of two-and-a-half *mâu*, assigned to the farmers to build on, who had also the same amount of ground in their towns or villages, making five *mâu* in all for their houses. And to have the ground all for growing grain, they were required to plant mulberry

孝悌之義頒白者不負戴
於道路矣七十者衣帛食
肉黎民不飢不寒然而不
王者未之有也狗彘食人
食而不知檢塗有餓莩而
不知發人死則曰非我也
歲也是何異於刺人而殺
之曰非我也兵也王無罪
歲斯天下之民至焉。
梁惠王曰寡人願安承

not be seen upon the roads, carrying burdens on their backs or on their heads. It never has been that the ruler of a State, where such results were seen,—persons of seventy wearing silk and eating flesh, and the black-haired people suffering neither from hunger nor cold,—did not attain to the royal dignity.

5. 'Your dogs and swine eat the food of men, and you do not make any restrictive arrangements. There are people dying from famine on the roads, and you do not issue the stores *of your granaries* for them. When people die, you say, "It is not owing to me; it is owing to the year." In what does this differ from stabbing a man and killing him, and then saying—"It was not I; it was the weapon?" Let your Majesty cease to lay the blame on the year, and instantly from all the nation the people will come to you.'

CHAP. IV. 1. King Hûi of Liang said, 'I wish quietly to receive your instructions.'

trees about their houses, for the nourishment of silkworms. 雞豚 (a young pig) 狗 (the grain-fed, or edible dog) 彘 (the sow) 之畜,—literally, 'as to the nourishing of the fowl,' &c. 數口之家—the ground was distinguished into three kinds;—best, medium, and inferior, feeding a varying number of mouths. To this the expression alludes. 庠 序 See on Bk. III. Pt. I. iii. 10. 王, 4th tone, 'to come to reign,' 'to become regnant

sovereign.'' 5. Mencius now boldly applies the subject, and presses home his faults upon the king. 食人食;—the second 食 is read *tsze*, 4th tone. 檢=制, 'to regulate.' The phrase 不知檢 is not easy;—the translation given accords with the views of most of the commentators.

4. A CONTINUATION OF THE FORMER CHAPTER, CARRYING ON THE APPEAL, IN THE LAST PARAGRAPH, ON THE CHARACTER OF KING HÛI's OWN GOVERNMENT. 1. 安, 'quietly,' i.e. sincerely and

教孟子對曰、殺人以梃與
刃、有以異乎。曰、無以異也。
以刃與政、有以異乎。曰、無
以異也。曰、庖有肥肉、廄有
肥馬、民有飢色、野有餓莩、
此率獸而食人也。獸相食、
且人惡之為民父母、行政、
不免於率獸而食人、惡在
其為民父母也。仲尼曰、始
作俑者、其無後乎。為其象

2. Mencius replied, 'Is there any difference between killing a man with a stick and with a sword?' *The king* said, 'There is no difference.'

3. 'Is there any difference between doing it with a sword and with *the style of* government?' 'There is no difference,' was the reply.

4. *Mencius then* said, 'In your kitchen there is fat meat; in your stables there are fat horses. *But* your people have the look of hunger, and on the wilds there are those who have died of famine. This is leading on beasts to devour men.

5. 'Beasts devour one another, and men hate them *for doing so.* When *a prince,* being the parent of his people, administers his government so as to be chargeable with leading on beasts to devour men, where is his parental relation to the people?'

6. Chung-ni said, 'Was he not without posterity who first made wooden images *to bury with the dead?* *So he said,* because

without constraint. It is said 安對勉强看見其出于誠意. 2, 3. 有以異乎-有所以異乎,—literally, 'Is there whereby they are different?' 4. 野,—outside a town were the 郊 (*chiáo*), *suburbs,* but without buildings; outside the *chiáo* were the 牧 (*mú*), *pasture-grounds;* and outside the *mú* were the 野 (*yě*), *wilds.* 5. 且 has the force of 'and yet,' i.e. though they are beasts. So that a 'how much more' is carried on, in effect, to the rest of the paragraph. 人惡之,—

惡, 4th tone, the verb. 惡在-惡, 1st tone, = 何. 'Being the parent of the people,' i.e. this is his designation, and what he ought to be. 6. 俑,—in ancient times, bundles of straw were made, to represent men imperfectly, called 芻靈, and carried to the grave, and buried with the dead, as attendants upon them. In middle antiquity, i.e. after the rise of the Cháu dynasty, for those bundles of straw, wooden figures of men were used, having springs in them, by which they could move. Hence they were called 俑, as if 俑-踊.

則可孟子對曰、地方
死者一洒之、如之何
於楚寡人恥之、願比
地於秦七百里、南辱
於齊長子死焉西喪
也、及寡人之身東敗
下莫強焉叟之所知
〔五章〕梁惠王曰晉國天
其使斯民飢而死也。
人而用之也、如之何

that man made the semblances of men, and used them *for that
purpose :*—what shall be thought of him who causes his people to
die of hunger ?'

CHAP. V. 1. King Hûi of Liang said, 'There was not in the
nation a stronger State than Tsin, as you, venerable Sir, know.
But since it descended to me, on the east we have been defeated by
Ch'î, and then my eldest son perished; on the west we have lost
seven hundred *lî* of territory to Ch'in; and on the south we have
sustained disgrace at the hands of Ch'û. I have brought shame on
my departed predecessors, and wish on their account to wipe it away,
once for all. What course is to be pursued to accomplish this ?'

2. Mencius replied, 'With a territory which is only a hundred *lî*
square, it is possible to attain to the royal dignity.

By and by, came the practice of burying living persons with the dead, which Confucius thought was an effect of this invention, and therefore be branded the inventor as in the text. 其 無後乎.—the 乎 is partly interrogative, and partly an exclamation = *nonne*. 為, 3rd tone, = *because*. 如之何 is by some taken as = 'what would he (viz. Confucius) have thought,' &c.? I prefer taking it as in the translation. The designation of Confucius by *Chung-ni* is to be observed. See Doctrine of the Mean, ii. 1.

5. HOW A RULER MAY BEST TAKE SATISFACTION FOR LOSSES WHICH HE HAS SUSTAINED. THAT BENEVOLENT GOVERNMENT WILL RAISE HIM HIGH ABOVE HIS ENEMIES. 1. After the partition of the State of Tsin by the three families of Wei, Châo, and Han (note, chap.i), they were known as the three Tsin, but king Hûi would here seem to appropriate to his own principality the name of the whole State. He does not, however, refer to the strength of Tsin before its partition, but under his two predecessors in the State of Wei. It was in the thirtieth year of his reign, and B.C. 340, that the defeat was received from Ch'î, when his eldest son was taken captive, and afterwards died. That from Ch'in was in the year B.C. 361, when the old capital of the State was taken, and afterwards peace had to be secured by various surrenders of territory. The disgrace from Ch'û was also attended with the loss of territory;—some say seven, some say eight, towns or districts. The nominative to the verbs 敗 喪, and 辱 does not appear to be 寡 人 so much as 晉. 寡人恥之 may be translated—'I am ashamed of these things,' but most commentators make 之 refer to 先人, Hûi's predecessors when Tsin was strong; as in the translation. The same reference they also give to 死者, as not said generally of 'the dead,'—those who had died in the various wars. This view is on the whole preferable to the other, and it gives a better antecedent for the 之 in 洒之. 一 = by one blow, one great

民甲梃事以脩易刑如百
時利以其事其易薄施里
使兵撻長其孝者税仁而
不矣秦上父弟以歛政可
得彼楚可兄忠暇深於以
耕奪之使出信日耕民王
耨其堅制以入　　省王

3. 'If your Majesty will *indeed* dispense a benevolent government to the people, being sparing in the use of punishments and fines, and making the taxes and levies light, so causing that the fields shall be ploughed deep, and the weeding of them be carefully attended to, and that the strong-bodied, during their days of leisure, shall cultivate their filial piety, fraternal respectfulness, sincerity, and truthfulness, serving thereby, at home, their fathers and elder brothers, and, abroad, their elders and superiors,—you will then have a people who can be employed, with sticks which they have prepared, to oppose the strong mail and sharp weapons of the troops of Ch'in and Ch'û.

4. 'The *rulers of those States* rob their people of their time, so that they cannot plough and weed their fields, in order to support

movement. 洒=洗. 比, the 4th tone, = 焉, 'for.' 2. See Part II. ii. 1; but it seems necessary to take the 方 in this and similar cases as in the translation. There is a pause at 地:—'with territory, which is,' &c. This is the reply to the king's wish for counsel to wipe away his disgraces. He may not only avenge himself on Ch'î, Ch'in, and Ch'û, but he may make himself chief of the whole nation. How, is shown in the next paragraph. 3. 省刑罰,薄稅斂 are the two great elements of benevolent government, out of which grow the other things specified. 刑罰 can hardly be separated. The dictionary says that 刑 is the general name of 罰. If we make a distinction, it must be as in the translation; 罰 is the redemption-fine for certain crimes.' So 稅斂 together represent all taxes. Great differences of opinion obtain as to the significance of the individual terms. Some make 稅 to be the proportion of the land-produce paid to the government, and 斂 all other contributions. By some this explanation is just reversed. A third party makes 稅 to be the tax of produce, and 斂 the graduated *collection* thereof. This last view suits the connexion here. 易 read i, the 3rd tone, = 治. 壯者,—at 30, a man is said to be 壯. Translators have rendered it here by 'the young,' but the meaning is the strong-bodied,—those who could be employed to take the field against the enemy. 可使 does not appear to be—'you can make or employ,' but to be passive with special reference to the 壯者 above. 省, read *shǎng*. 撻—'to strike,' 'to smite'—here = 'to oppose.' 4. 彼, 'they' or 'those,' i.e. the rulers of Ch'in and Ch'û. 奪, the 4th tone. It is so toned in the case of children supporting their parents, and inferiors their superiors. See in Analects, II. vii. 5. 夫, the 2nd tone, here = 則.

以養其父母父母凍餓兄
弟妻子離散彼陷溺其民
王往而征之夫誰與王敵
故曰仁者無敵王請勿疑
孟子見梁襄王出語人
曰望之不似人君就之而
不見所畏焉卒然問曰天
下惡乎定吾對曰定于一
孰能一之對曰不嗜殺人
者能一之孰能與之對曰

their parents. Their parents suffer from cold and hunger. Brothers, wives, and children are separated and scattered abroad.

5. 'Those *rulers, as it were,* drive their people into pit-falls, or drown them. Your Majesty will go to punish them. In such a case, who will oppose your Majesty?

6. 'In accordance with this is the saying,—"The benevolent has no enemy." I beg your Majesty not to doubt *what I say.*'

CHAP. VI. 1. Mencius went to see the king Hsiang of Liang.

2. On coming out *from the interview,* he said to some persons, 'When I looked at him from a distance, he did not appear like a sovereign; when I drew near to him, I saw nothing venerable about him. Abruptly he asked me, "How can the kingdom be settled?" I replied, "It will be settled by being united under one *sway.*"

3. '"Who can so unite it?"

4. 'I replied, "He who has no pleasure in killing men can so unite it."

5. '"Who can give it to him?"

6. 'I replied, "All the people of the nation will unanimously

6. 故, not 'therefore;' it may indicate a de-duction from what precedes, or be simply an illustration of it. 勿疑. 'Do not doubt.' It is strange that Julien, in his generally accurate version, should translate this by '*ne cuncteris.*' Hesitancy would, indeed, be an effect of doubt-ing Mencius's words, not the proverb just quoted, but specially the affirmation in par. 2. But the words may not be so rendered.

6. DISAPPOINTMENT OF MENCIUS WITH THE KING HSIANG. BY WHOM THE TORN NATION MAY BE UNITED UNDER ONE SWAY. 1. On the death of king Hûi, he was succeeded by his son Ho (赫), called here by his honorary epithet, Hsiang, = 'The land-enlarger and virtuous.' The interview here recorded seems to have taken place immediately after Ho's accession, and Mencius, it is said, was so disappointed by it that he soon left the country. 2. 語, the 4th tone. The 人 probably refers to some friends of the philosopher, and is not to be taken gener-

天下莫不與也王知夫苗乎
七八月之閒旱則苗槁矣天
油然作雲沛然下雨則苗浡
然興之矣其如是孰能禦之
今夫天下之人牧未有不嗜
殺人者也如有不嗜殺人者
則天下之民皆引領而望之
矣誠如是也民歸之由水之
就下沛然誰能禦之。
齊宣王問曰齊桓晉文之

give it to him. Does your Majesty understand the way of the growing grain? During the seventh and eighth months, when drought prevails, the plants become dry. Then the clouds collect densely iu the heavens, they send down torrents of rain, and the grain erects itself, as if by a shoot. When it does so, who can keep it back? Now among the shepherds of men throughout the nation, there is not one who does not find pleasure in killing men. If there were one who did not find pleasure in killing men, all the people in the nation would look towards him with outstretched necks. Such being indeed the case, the people would flock to him, as water flows downwards with a rush, which no one can repress."'

CHAP. VII. 1. The king Hsüan of Ch'î asked, saying, 'May

ally. 卒 read *tsʻ*û. 卒然,—compare 率
爾, Analects, XI. xxiv. 4. On 望之 就之,
compare Analects, XIX. ix. Châo Ch'î makes
定于 —— to = 'It will be settled by him who
makes benevolent government his one object.'
But this is surely going beyond the text. 5. The
與 is here explained, by Chû Hsî and others,
as equivalent to 歸, founding, no doubt, on the
民歸之 in the end. But in Bk. V. Pt. I. v,
we have a plain instance of 與, used in connexion with the bestowment of the throne, as
in the translation which I have ventured to give,
which seems to me, moreover, to accord equally
well, if not better, with the rest of the chapter.

6. The 7th and 8th months of Châu were the
5th and 6th of the Hsiâ dynasty, with which the
months of the present dynasty agree. 今夫,
一夫, the 1st tone, is used as in the Analects,
XI. ix. 3. The 之 at the end is to be referred
to 水, the whole, from 由 (=猶), being an
illustration of the people's turning with resist-
less energy to a benevolent ruler.

7. LOVING AND PROTECTING THE PEOPLE IS THE
CHARACTERISTIC OF ROYAL GOVERNMENT, AND THE
SURE PATH TO THE ROYAL DIGNITY. This long
and interesting chapter has been arranged in
five parts. In the first part, paras. 1-5, Mencius unfolds the principle of royal government,
and tells the king of Ch'î that he possesses

禦也。曰、若寡人 民而王莫之能 可以王矣。曰、保 乎曰、德何如、則 聞也。無以、則王 無傳焉臣未之 事者、是以後世 徒無道桓文之 子對曰、仲尼之 事、可得聞乎孟

I be informed by you of the transactions of Hwan of Ch'i, and Wǎn of Tsin?'

2 Mencius replied, 'There were none of the disciples of Chung-ni who spoke about the affairs of Hwan and Wǎn, and therefore they have not been transmitted to these after-ages;—your servant has not heard them. If you will have me speak, let it be about royal government.'

3. The king said, 'What virtue must there be in order to attain to royal sway?' Mencius answered, 'The love and protection of the people; with this there is no power which can prevent a ruler from attaining to it.'

4. *The king* asked again, 'Is such an one as I competent to

it. In the second part, paras. 6-8, he leads the king on to understand his own mind, and apprehend how he might exercise a royal government. In the third, paras. 9-12, he unfolds how the king may and ought to carry out the kindly heart which he possessed. In the fourth part, paras. 13-17, he shows the absurdity of the king's expecting to gain his end by the course he was pursuing, and how rapid would be the response to an opposite one. In the last part, he shows the government that loves and protects the people in full development, and crowned with royal sway. 1. The king Hsüan ('The Distinguished,' 聖善周聞曰宣), the second of his family, who governed in Ch'i, by surname T'ien (田), and named P'i-chiang (辟疆), began his reign B.C. 332. By some the date of this event is placed nine years earlier. The time of Mencius's visit to him is also matter of dispute;—see 'Life of Mencius,' in the Prolegomena. The ruler of Ch'i was properly only a duke (公 in posthumous title), or a marquis (while alive, 侯); the title of *king* was a usurpation. Hwan and Wǎn,—see Analects, XIV. xvi. They were the greatest of the five leaders of the princes, who played so conspicuous a part in the middle time of the Chau dynasty, but to whom Confucius and Mencius so positively refused their approval. 2. 道 is a verb, = 'to speak of,' in which sense it had formerly a tone different from its usage as a noun. 無以、則王乎,—以 is taken by Chu Hsi as = 已, which it is as well to acquiesce in. See Chao Ch'i's commentary for the all but impossibility of making any sense of the passage in any other way. 王, the 4th tone, and so generally throughout the chapter. As the royal title, it is in the 2nd tone, the simple name of dignity; as implying the attainment or exercise of that dignity, it is the 4th tone. By translating it by 'royal government,' 'royal sway,' we come nearer to giving Mencius's meaning than if we were to use any other term. 3. Here the nominatives of 'king' and 'Mencius' are dropped before 曰, as frequently afterwards. The 曰 just serves the purpose of our points of quotation. 保, 'to preserve,' 'to protect.' I translate it, according to Chu Hsi's account, as = 愛護. A pause is to be made at 民, and 而王 joined to the remainder of the sentence. 4. The hall, or 堂, here mentioned, was probably that where the king was giving audience, and attending to the affairs of government. 牛何之,—the 之 is the verb, = 往. 舍,—also a verb, in 3rd tone. 諸-

者、可以保民乎哉曰、可曰、何由
知吾可也曰臣聞之胡齕曰、王
坐於堂上有牽牛而過堂下者、
王見之曰牛何之對曰、將以釁
鐘。王曰、舍之吾不忍其觳觫若
無罪而就死地對曰然則廢釁
鐘與。曰、何可廢也以羊易之。不
識有諸曰有之。曰、是心足以王
矣、百姓皆以王爲愛也臣固知

love and protect the people?' *Mencius* said, 'Yes.' 'How do you know that I am competent for that?' 'I heard the following incident from Hû Ho:—"The king," said he, "was sitting aloft in the hall, when a man appeared, leading an ox past the lower part of it. The king saw him, and asked, Where is the ox going? The man replied, We are going to consecrate a bell with its blood. The king said, Let it go. I cannot bear its frightened appearance, as if it were an innocent person going to the place of death. The man answered, Shall we then omit the consecration of the bell? *The king* said, How can that be omitted? Change it for a sheep." I do not know whether this incident really occurred.'

5. *The king* replied, 'It did,' and *then Mencius* said, 'The heart seen in this is sufficient to carry you to the royal sway. The people all supposed that your Majesty grudged *the animal*, but your servant knows surely, that it was your Majesty's not being able to bear *the sight, which made you do as you did.*'

之, and at the same time with an indirect interrogative force. Chû Hsî explains 釁 from the meaning of 釁 as 'a crack,' 'a crevice,' saying:—'After the casting of a bell, they killed an animal, took its blood, and smeared over the crevices.' But the first meaning of 釁 is—'a sacrifice by blood,' and anciently 'almost all things,' connected with their religious worship, were among the Chinese purified with blood;—their temples, and the vessels in them. See the Lî Chî, Bk. XXII. The reference here is to the religious rite. The only thing is that, in using an ox to consecrate his bell, the prince of Ch'î was usurping a royal privilege. 5. 愛 may be taken as the finite verb, = 'you loved, i.e. grudged the animal,' or

無傷也是乃仁術也見牛未見
羊也宜乎百姓之謂我愛也曰
何心哉我非愛其財而易之以
地則牛羊何擇焉王笑曰是誠
惡知之王若隱其無罪而就死
姓之以王爲愛也以小易大彼
故以羊易之也曰王無異於百
不忍其轂觫若無罪而就死地
者齊國雖褊小吾何愛一牛卽
王之不忍也王曰然誠有百姓

6. *The king* said, 'You are right. And yet there really was an
appearance of what the people condemned. But though Ch'i be
a small and narrow State, how should I grudge one ox? Indeed
it was because I could not bear its frightened appearance, as if it
were an innocent person going to the place of death, that therefore
I changed it for a sheep.'

7. *Mencius* pursued, 'Let not your Majesty deem it strange that
the people should think you were grudging *the animal*. When you
changed a large one for a small, how should they know *the true reason*?
If you felt pained by its being led without guilt to the place of
death, what was there to choose between an ox and a sheep?' The
king laughed and said, 'What really was my mind in the matter?
I did not grudge the expense of it, and changed it for a sheep!—
There was reason in the people's saying that I grudged it.'

8. 'There is no harm *in their saying so*,' said *Mencius*. 'Your
conduct was an artifice of benevolence. You saw the ox, and had not

as = 'to be niggardly,'—'you were parsimoni-
ous.' 6. It is better to make a pause after 然,
and give the meaning as in the translation.
Châo Ch'î runs it on to the next clause. 誠
有百姓者 is elliptical, and the particle
者 denotes this, requiring the supplement

which I have given. 卽 acknowledges the
truth of Mencius's explanation. 7. 隱 = 痛,
是誠何心哉 expresses the king's quan-
dary. He is now quite perplexed by the way
in which Mencius has put the case. 8. 仁術
—compare Analects, VI. xxviii. 3, 仁之方.

羊也君子之於禽獸也見其生、
不忍見其死聞其聲不忍食其
肉是以君子遠庖廚也。王說曰、
詩云、他人有心予忖度之。夫子
之謂也。夫我乃行之反而求之、
不得吾心夫子言之、於我心有
戚戚焉。此心之所以合於王者
何也。曰有復於王者曰、吾力足
以舉百鈞、而不足以舉一羽、明
足以察秋毫之末、而不見輿薪、

seen the sheep. So is the superior man affected towards animals, that, having seen them alive, he cannot bear to see them die; having heard their dying cries, he cannot bear to eat their flesh. Therefore he keeps away from his slaughter-house and cook-room.'

9. The king was pleased, and said, 'It is said in the Book of Poetry, "The minds of others, I am able by reflection to measure;"—this is verified, my Master, in your discovery of my motive. I indeed did the thing, but when I turned my thoughts inward, and examined into it, I could not discover my own mind. When you, Master, spoke those words, the movements of compassion began to work in my mind. How is it that this heart has in it what is equal to the royal sway?'

10. *Mencius* replied, 'Suppose a man were to make this statement to your Majesty:—" My strength is sufficient to lift three thousand catties, but it is not sufficient to lift one feather;—my eyesight is sharp enough to examine the point of an autumn hair,

We must take the two words 庖廚 together as indicating the kitchen, where the victims were both killed and cooked. 9. 說=悅。 For the ode, see the Book of Poetry, II. v. Ode IV st. 4, where the 他人 has a special reference. 夫子之謂也.—literally, '(This was) a speaking about you, my Master.' 10. 復, read *fû*, the 4th tone, often meaning to report the execution of a mission, as in the phrase—復命. Here it is='to inform.' 獨可與,—in order to bring out the force of the 獨, 'only, it is necessary to make two sentences of this in

則王許之乎曰否今恩足以
及禽獸而功不至於百姓者、
獨何與然則一羽之不舉爲
不用力焉輿薪之不見爲不
用明焉百姓之不見保爲不
用恩焉故王之不王不爲也
非不能也。曰不爲者與不能
者之形何以異曰挾太山以
超北海語人曰我不能是誠
不能也爲長者折枝語人曰、

but I do not see a waggon-load of faggots ;"—would your Majesty allow what he said?' 'No,' *was the answer, on which Mencius proceeded*, 'Now here is kindness sufficient to reach to animals, and no benefits are extended from it to the people.—How is this? Is an exception to be made here? The truth is, the feather is not lifted, because strength is not used ; the waggon-load of firewood is not seen, because the eyesight is not used ; and the people are not loved and protected, because kindness is not employed. Therefore your Majesty's not exercising the royal sway, is because you do not do it, not because you are not able to do it.'

11. *The king* asked, 'How may the difference between the not doing a thing, and the not being able to do it, be represented?' *Mencius* replied, 'In such a thing as taking the T'âi mountain under your arm, and leaping over the north sea with it, if you say to people—"I am not able to do it," that is a real case of not being able. In such a matter as breaking off a branch from a tree at the order of a superior, if you say to people—"I am not able to do it," that is a case of not doing it, it is not a case of not being able to do

English. 不爲也, it is said,—不肯 爲, 'not willing to do it,' but it is better to add nothing to the simple text. We have here, indeed, the famous distinction of 'moral' and 'physical' ability. 11. 形,—'the form,' 'or figure ;'—literally ' How may the figure . . . . be differenced ?' 語人,—語, in 4th tone,— 告. 12. Châo Ch'î makes the opening here = 'Treat as their age requires your own old (English idiom seems to require the and person), and treat the old of others in the same way,' but there seems to be a kind of *constructio præegnans*, conveying all that appears in the translation.

古之人所以大過人者、無他
保四海不推恩無以保妻子、
心加諸彼而已故推恩足以
于兄弟以御于家邦言舉斯
可運於掌詩云、刑于寡妻至
老幼吾幼、以及人之幼、天下
枝之類也。老吾老、以及人之
北海之類也王之不王是折
故王之不王、非挾太山以超
我不能是不爲也非不能也、

it. Therefore your Majesty's not exercising the royal sway, is not such a case as that of taking the T'ái mountain under your arm, and leaping over the north sea with it. Your Majesty's not exercising the royal sway is a case like that of breaking off a branch from a tree.

12. 'Treat with the reverence due to age the elders in your own family, so that the elders in the families of others shall be similarly treated; treat with the kindness due to youth the young in your own family, so that the young in the families of others shall be similarly treated:—do this, and the kingdom may be made to go round in your palm. It is said in the Book of Poetry, "His example affected his wife. It reached to his brothers, and his family of the State was governed by it."—The language shows how *king Wăn* simply took his *kindly* heart, and exercised it towards those parties. Therefore the carrying out his kindness of heart *by a prince* will suffice for the love and protection of all within the four seas, and if he do not carry it out, he will not be able to protect his wife and children. The way in which the ancients came

天下可運於掌 is made by most commentators to mean—'you may pervade the kingdom with your kindness so easily.' But I must believe that it is the *effect*, and not the *means*, which is thus represented. For the ode, see the Shih-ching, III. i. Ode VI. st. 2. The original celebrates the virtue of king Wăn, and we must translate in the third person, and not

in the first. 御=迓, but the meaning is disputed. Here Chû Hsí explains it by 治 The philosopher now introduces a new element into his discourse. It is no longer the 不忍 之心, 'the heart that cannot bear,' i. e. the humane heart, which is necessary to raise to

可得聞與王笑而不言曰
所大欲也曰王之所大欲
否吾何快於是將以求吾
諸侯然後快於心與王曰
王興甲兵危士臣構怨於
皆然心爲甚王請度之抑
知輕重度然後知長短物
於百姓者獨何與權然後
恩足以及禽獸而功不至
爲善惟其所爲而已矣今

greatly to surpass other men, was no other but this :—simply that they knew well how to carry out, so as to affect others, what they themselves did. Now your kindness is sufficient to reach to animals, and no benefits are extended from it to reach the people.—How is this? Is an exception to be made here?

13. 'By weighing, we know what things are light, and what heavy. By measuring, we know what things are long, and what short. The relations of all things may be thus determined, and it is of the greatest importance to estimate *the motions of* the mind. I beg your Majesty to measure it.

14. 'You collect your equipments of war, endanger your soldiers and officers, and excite the resentment of the other princes;—do these things cause you pleasure in your mind?'

15. The king replied, 'No. How should I derive pleasure from these things? My object in them is to seek for what I greatly desire.'

16. *Mencius* said, 'May I hear from you what it is that you greatly desire?' The king laughed and did not speak. *Mencius*

the royal sway, but it is 推此心, 'the carrying out of this heart.' All may have the heart, but all may not be gifted, so to carry it out that it shall affect all others. We cannot wonder that the princes whom Mencius lectured should have thought his talk 迂濶, *transcendental*. 13. The first 度 is 4th tone, *tù*, 'a measure,' the instrument for measuring. But both it and 權 are equivalent to active verbs. 心爲甚 means, that the mind, as affected from without, and going forth to affect, may be light or heavy, long or short, i. e. may be right or wrong, and that in different degrees;—and that it is more important to estimate the character of its action, than to weigh or measure other things. 14. Here Mencius helps the king to measure his mind. 抑—about the same as our 'come now,' or 'well then.' Further on, its equally accepted meaning of 'or' suits the connexion better. 16. The 與 are all interrogative, in the 2nd tone, and the 爲 are all in the

爲肥甘不足於口與輕煖不足
於體與抑爲采色不足視於目
與聲音不足聽於耳與便嬖不
足使令於前與王之諸臣皆足
以供之而王豈爲是哉。曰否吾
不爲是也。然則王之所大欲
可知已欲辟土地朝秦楚莅中
國而撫四夷也以若所爲求若
所欲猶緣木而求魚也王曰若
是其甚與曰殆有甚焉緣木求

resumed, '*Are you led to desire it*, because you have not enough of rich and sweet food for your mouth? Or because you have not enough of light and warm *clothing* for your body? Or because you have not enough of beautifully coloured objects to delight your eyes? Or because you have not voices and tones enough to please your ears? Or because you have not enough of attendants and favourites to stand before you and receive your orders? Your Majesty's various officers are sufficient to supply you with those things. How can your Majesty be led to entertain such a desire on account of them?' 'No,' said *the king*; 'my desire is not on account of them.' *Mencius* added, 'Then, what your Majesty greatly desires may be known. You wish to enlarge your territories, to have Ch'in and Ch'ǔ wait at your court, to rule the Middle Kingdom, and to attract to you the barbarous tribes that surround it. But doing what you do to seek for what you desire is like climbing a tree to seek for fish.'

¹7. *The king* said, 'Is it so bad as that?' 'It is even worse,' was the reply. 'If you climb a tree to seek for fish, although you do

4th tone. 便, read *p'ien*, the 2nd tone, joined with the next character. 可知已 —已 gives a positiveness to the assertion. 辟 read as, and = 闢 綠木, from the use of the phrase here, has come to be used for 'to climb a tree,' but it simply is—'from a tree.' 17. The 殆, an introductory part, = 'yes, and.' 蓋亦反其本 is spoken with reference to the king's object of ambition :—'By the course you are pursuing you cannot succeed, for,

立於王之朝耕者皆欲耕於王之
今王發政施仁使天下仕者皆欲
以異於鄒敵楚哉蓋亦反其本矣。
里者九齊集有其一以一服八何
弱固不可以敵彊海內之地方千
固不可以敵大寡固不可以敵眾
王以爲孰勝。曰楚人勝曰然則小
曰可得聞與。曰鄒人與楚人戰則
若所欲盡心力而爲之後必有災。
魚雖不得魚無後災以若所爲求

not get the fish, you will not suffer any subsequent calamity. But doing what you do to seek for what you desire, doing it moreover with all your heart, you will assuredly afterwards meet with calamities.' *The king* asked, 'May I hear *from you the proof of that?*' *Mencius* said, 'If the people of Tsâu should fight with the people of Ch'û, which of them does your Majesty think would conquer?' 'The people of Ch'û would conquer.' 'Yes;—and so it is certain that a small country cannot contend with a great, that few cannot contend with many, that the weak cannot contend with the strong. The territory within the *four* seas embraces nine divisions, each of a thousand *lî* square. All Ch'î together is but one of them. If with one part you try to subdue the other eight, what is the difference between that and Tsâu's contending with Ch'û? For, *with such a desire,* you must turn back to the proper course *for its attainment.*

18. 'Now, if your Majesty will institute a government whose action shall be benevolent, this will cause all the officers in the kingdom to wish to stand in your Majesty's court, and all the farmers

if you wish to do so, you must also turn back | not 'wilds' 出於,—'to come forth in,' i. e. to the root of success.' 18. 野,—'fields,' here; | to pass from their own States into yours. 欲

野、商賈皆欲藏於王之市、行
旅皆欲出於王之塗、天下之
欲疾其君者、皆欲赴愬於王、
其若是孰能禦之、王曰、吾惛
不能進於是矣、願夫子輔吾
志、明以教我、我雖不敏、請嘗
試之曰、無恆產、而有恆心者、
惟士爲能、若民、則無恆產、因
無恆心、苟無恆心、放辟邪侈、
無不爲已、及陷於罪、然後從

to wish to plough in your Majesty's fields, and all the merchants, both travelling and stationary, to wish to store their goods in your Majesty's market-places, and all travelling strangers to wish to make their tours on your Majesty's roads, and all throughout the kingdom who feel aggrieved by their rulers to wish to come and complain to your Majesty. And when they are so bent, who will be able to keep them back?'

19. The king said, 'I am stupid, and not able to advance to this. I wish you, my Master, to assist my intentions. Teach me clearly; although I am deficient in intelligence and vigour, I will essay and try to carry your instructions into effect.'

20. *Mencius* replied, 'They are only men of education, who, without a certain livelihood, are able to maintain a fixed heart. As to the people, if they have not a certain livelihood, it follows that they will not have a fixed heart. And if they have not a fixed heart, there is nothing which they will not do, in the way of self-abandonment, of moral deflection, of depravity, and of wild license. When they thus have been involved in crime, to follow them up and

疾,—'feeling aggrieved, but must restrain their feelings.' 20. 辟, read as, and = 僻 用,—'en-net,' i.e. to entrap. 無所不 爲已,—已, see on par. 16. 21. 終身 generally means 'the whole life.' Perhaps we should translate, If some years be good, they will all their lives have plenty,' i.e. they will in those years lay by a sufficient provision for bad years. This supposes that the people have felt the power of the instruction and moral

救死而恐不贍奚暇治禮義
身苦凶年不免於死亡此惟
母俯不足以畜妻子樂歲終
也制民之產仰不足以事父
而之善故民之從之也輕。今
身飽凶年免於死亡然後驅
父母俯足以畜妻子樂歲終
君制民之產必使仰足以事
在位罔民而可爲也。是故明
而刑之是罔民也焉有仁人

punish them ;—this is to entrap the people. How can such a thing as entrapping the people be done under the rule of a benevolent man?

21. 'Therefore an intelligent ruler will regulate the livelihood of the people, so as to make sure that, for those above them, they shall have sufficient wherewith to serve their parents, and, for those below them, sufficient wherewith to support their wives and children; that in good years they shall always be abundantly satisfied, and that in bad years they shall escape the danger of perishing. After this he may urge them, and they will proceed to what is good, for in this case the people will follow after it with ease.

22. 'Now, the livelihood of the people is so regulated, that, above, they have not sufficient wherewith to serve their parents, and, below, they have not sufficient wherewith to support their wives and children. *Notwithstanding* good years, their lives are continually embittered, and, in bad years, they do not escape perishing. In such circumstances they only try to save themselves from death, and are afraid they will not succeed. What leisure have they to cultivate propriety and righteousness?

training that is a part of royal government, which, however, is set forth as consequent on the regulation of the livelihood. Similarly, below. 之善,—之 is the verb, = 往. 民 之從之也輕,—Julian censures Noel here for rendering 從之 by 'ipsi (principi)

obsequentur,' and rightly. But I am not sure that the error is not rather in the rendering of 從 than in that of 之. The prince is supposed to exemplify, as well as to urge to, the good course, and the well-off people have no difficulty in following him. 23. 反其

哉○王欲行之則盍反其本矣。

五畝之宅樹之以桑五十者

可以衣帛矣雞豚狗彘之畜

無失其時七十者可以食肉

矣百畝之田勿奪其時八口

之家可以無飢矣謹庠序之

教申之以孝悌之義頒白者

不負戴於道路矣老者衣帛

食肉黎民不飢不寒然而不

王者未之有也。

23. 'If your Majesty wishes to effect this *regulation of the livelihood of the people*, why not turn to that which is the essential step to it?

24. 'Let mulberry-trees be planted about the homesteads with their five *mâu*, and persons of fifty years may be clothed with silk. In keeping fowls, pigs, dogs, and swine, let not their times of breeding be neglected, and persons of seventy years may eat flesh. Let there not be taken away the time that is proper for the cultivation of the farm with its hundred *mâu*, and the family of eight mouths that is supported by it shall not suffer from hunger. Let careful attention be paid to education in schools,—the inculcation in it especially of the filial and fraternal duties, and grey-haired men will not be seen upon the roads, carrying burdens on their backs or on their heads. It never has been that the ruler of a State where such results were seen,—the old wearing silk and eating flesh, and the black-haired people suffering neither from hunger nor cold,—did not attain to the royal dignity.'

本, as in par. 17, but with reference to the immediate subject. 24. See ch. iii, the only difference being that, for 數口之家 there, we have 八口之家, eight mouths being the number which 100 mâu of medium land were computed to feed.

KING HÛI OF LIANG. PART II.

樂也直好世俗之樂耳。
曰寡人非能好先王之
以好樂有諸王變乎色、
見於王曰王嘗語莊子
則齊國其庶幾乎他日
如孟子曰王之好樂甚、
未有以對也曰好樂何
於王王語暴以好樂暴
二莊暴見孟子曰暴見
梁惠王章句下

CHAPTER I. 1. Chwang Pâo, seeing Mencius, said to him,
'I had an interview with the king. His Majesty told me that he
loved music, and I was not prepared with anything to reply to him.
What do you pronounce about that love of music?' Mencius
replied, 'If the king's love of music were very great, the kingdom
of Ch'î would be near to *a state of good government!*'

2. Another day, *Mencius*, having an interview with the king, said,
'Your Majesty, *I have heard*, told the officer Chwang, that you love
music;—was it so?' The king changed colour, and said, 'I am
unable to love the music of the ancient sovereigns; I only love the
music that suits the manners of the *present* age.'

1. HOW THE LOVE OF MUSIC MAY BE MADE
SUBSERVIENT TO GOOD GOVERNMENT, AND TO A
PRINCE'S OWN ADVANCEMENT. The chapter is a
good specimen of Mencius's manner,—how he
slips from the point in hand to introduce his
own notions, and would win princes over to
benevolent government by their very vices.
He was no stern moralist, and the Chinese
have done well in refusing to rank him with
Confucius. 1. Chwang Pâo appears to have
been a minister at the court of Ch'î. The 曰
preceding 好樂如何 is unnecessary.
If we translate it, we must render—'He then
said.' But the paraphrasts all neglect it.
庶幾 (the 1st tone) is a phrase signifying

'near to;' sometimes we find 庶 alone, as in
Analects XI. xviii. 1. The subject, nearness
to which is indicated, is often left to be
gathered from the context, as here. The 王
之好樂甚 is a platitude. It should be
the text of the chapter, but Mencius proceeds
to substitute 樂 *lo* for 樂 *yo*, in his own
manner. 2. 直, as in last Pt. ch. iii. 2;
observe how the final 耳 adds to the force
of 'only.' 'Ancient sovereigns' (i.e. Yâo, Shun,
Yü, T'ang, Wăn, and Wû) is a better translation of 先王 than 'former kings.' 3. 由-

曰王之好樂甚、則齊其庶幾
乎今之樂由古之樂也、曰可
得聞與、曰獨樂樂與人樂樂、
孰樂曰不若與人曰與少樂
樂與眾樂樂孰樂曰不若與
眾臣請爲王言樂今王鼓樂
於此百姓聞王鐘鼓之聲管
簫之音舉疾首蹙頞而相告
曰吾王之好鼓樂夫何使我
至於此極也父子不相見兄

3. *Mencius* said, 'If your Majesty's love of music were very great, Ch'î would be near to *a state of good government!* The music of the present day is just like the music of antiquity, *as regards effecting that.*'

4. *The king* said, 'May I hear from you the proof of that?' *Mencius* asked, 'Which is the more pleasant,—to enjoy music by yourself alone, or to enjoy it with others?' 'To enjoy it with others,' was the reply. 'And which is the more pleasant,—to enjoy music with a few, or to enjoy it with many?' 'To enjoy it with many.'

5. *Mencius proceeded*, 'Your servant begs to explain *what I have said about* music to your Majesty.

6. 'Now, your Majesty is having music here.—The people hear the noise of your bells and drums, and the notes of your fifes and pipes, and they all, with aching heads, knit their brows, and say to one another, "That's how our king likes his music! But why does he reduce us to this extremity *of distress?*—Fathers and sons cannot see one another. Elder brothers and younger brothers, wives and

猶. 4. 可得聞與, as in the preceding chapter. 獨樂樂—the second 樂 is to, 'joy,' 'delight.' So, in the next clause, and after 孰. 5. 爲 (the 4th tone) 王, 'for the sake of your Majesty.' 6. 鼓樂,—鼓 is a verb = 作. The ancient dictionary, the 說文, makes a difference between this, and the same word for 'drum,' saying this is formed from 支, named *p'ú*, while the other is formed from 支. The difference of form is not regarded

弟妻子離散今王田獵於此百
姓聞王車馬之音見羽旄之美
舉疾首蹙頞而相告曰吾王之
好田獵夫何使我至於此極也
父子不相見兄弟妻子離散此
無他不與民同樂也今王鼓樂
於此百姓聞王鐘鼓之聲管籥
之音舉欣欣然有喜色而相告
曰吾王庶幾無疾病與何以能
鼓樂也今王田獵於此百姓聞

children, are separated and scattered abroad." Now, your Majesty is hunting here.—The people hear the noise of your carriages and horses, and see the beauty of your plumes and streamers, and they all, with aching heads, knit their brows, and say to one another, "That's how our king likes his hunting! But why does he reduce us to this extremity *of distress*?—Fathers and sons cannot see one another. Elder brothers and younger brothers, wives and children, are separated and scattered abroad." Their feeling thus is from no other reason but that you do not allow the people to have pleasure as well as yourself.

7. 'Now, your Majesty is having music here. The people hear the noise of your bells and drums, and the notes of your fifes and pipes, and they all, delighted, and with joyful looks, say to one another, "That sounds as if our king were free from all sickness! If he were not, how could he enjoy this music?" Now, your Majesty is hunting here.—The people hear the noise of your carriages and

now. 於此, 'here,' used as we use *here* in English, putting a case with little local reference. 舉=俱 or 皆, 'all.' 蹙頞 expresses anguish, not anger. 夫 is here the introductory particle, and is better rendered by *but* than *now*. It will be seen that the pre-ceding 吾王之好鼓樂 is incomplete. The paraphrasts add, to complete it, 固然 已. 7. 田 is used synonymously with 畋, 'to hunt.' 聲 and 音 are to each other much as our sound or noise and tone or note. 音

王車馬之音見羽旄之美、
舉欣欣然有喜色而相告
曰吾王庶幾無疾病與何
以能田獵也此無他與民
同樂也今王與百姓同樂、
則王矣。
齊宣王問曰文王之囿
方七十里有諸孟子對曰
於傳有之曰若是其大乎。
曰民猶以爲小也曰寡人

horses, and see the beauty of your plumes and streamers, and they all, delighted, and with joyful looks, say to one another, "That looks as if our king were free from all sickness! If he were not, how could he enjoy this hunting?" Their feeling thus is from no other reason but that you cause them to have their pleasure as you have yours.

8. 'If your Majesty now will make pleasure a thing common to the people and yourself, the royal sway awaits you.'

CHAP. II. 1. The king Hsüan of Ch'î asked, 'Was it so, that the park of king Wăn contained seventy square *lî*?' Mencius replied, 'It is so in the records.'

2. 'Was it so large as that?' exclaimed *the king*. 'The people,' said *Mencius*, 'still looked on it as small.' *The king* added, 'My

is applied appropriately to the fifes and pipes, and also to the carriages and horses, having reference to the music of the *bells* with which these were adorned. Of 羽旄 Chû Hsî simply says that they were 旌旗, 'belonging to the banners.' The 羽 were feathers adorning the top of the flag-staff; the 旄, a number of ox-tails suspended on a rope, one after another, from the top. 與民同樂, compare Pt. I. ii. 3.

2. How A RULER MUST NOT INDULGE HIS LOVE FOR PARKS AND HUNTING TO THE DISCOMFORT OF THE PEOPLE. 1. 傳, the 4th tone, 'a record,' an historical narration handing down events to futurity (傳於後人) 方七十

里 must be understood—'containing seventy square li,' not 'seventy li square.' In the 日講, the meaning of 方 here (not similarly, however, in Pt. I. v. 2; vii. 17) is given by 四圍, 'in circumference.' The glossarist on Châo Ch'î explains it by 方潤, which, I think, confirms the meaning I have given. The book or books giving account of this park of king Wăn are now lost. 2. 芻者蕘者 are distinguished thus:—'gatherers of grass to feed animals, and gatherers of grass for fuel.' Observe how these nouns, and 雉 and 兔 that follow, get a verbal force from the 者;— the fodderers, the pheasanters, &c. 3. 郊 is

之圍方四十里民猶以爲大何
也曰文王之圍方七十里芻蕘
者往焉雉兎者往焉與民同之
民以爲小不亦宜乎臣始至於
境問國之大禁然後敢入臣聞
郊關之內有圍方四十里殺其
麋鹿者如殺人之罪則是方四
十里爲阱於國中民以爲大不
亦宜乎。
齊宣王問曰交鄰國有道乎、

park contains *only* forty square *lī*, and the people still look on it as large. How is this?' 'The park of king Wăn,' was the reply, 'contained seventy square *lī*, but the grass-cutters and fuel-gatherers had the privilege of entrance into it; so also had the catchers of pheasants and hares. He shared it with the people, and was it not with reason that they looked on it as small?

3. 'When I first arrived at the borders *of your kingdom*, I inquired about the great prohibitory regulations, before I would venture to enter it; and I heard, that inside the barrier-gates there was a park of forty square *lī*, and that he who killed a deer in it, was held guilty of the same crime as if he had killed a man.—Thus those forty square *lī* are a pitfall in the middle of the kingdom. Is it not with reason that the people look upon them as large?'

CHAP. III. 1. The king Hsüan of Ch'ī asked, saying, 'Is there any way *to regulate one's maintenance of* intercourse with

used here in the sense simply of 'borders,' and on the borders of the various States there were 'passes' or 'gates,' for the taxation of merchandize, the examination of strangers, &c. 麋 鹿. see Pt. L. ii. 1. These forest laws of Ch'ī were hardly worse than those enacted by the first Norman sovereigns of England, when whoever killed a deer, a boar, or even a hare, was punished with the loss of his eyes, and with death if the statutes were repeatedly violated.

3. HOW FRIENDLY INTERCOURSE WITH NEIGHBOURING KINGDOMS MAY BE MAINTAINED, AND THE LOVE OF VALOUR MADE SUBSERVIENT TO THE GOOD OF THE PEOPLE, AND THE GLORY OF THE PRINCE. 1. The two first 事 differ in meaning considerably from the two last, and they are explained

國詩云畏天之威于
保天下畏天者保其
者畏天者也樂天者
樂天者也以小事大
踐事吳以大事小者
大故太王事獯鬻句
惟智者爲能以小事
湯事葛文王事昆夷
爲能以大事小是故
孟子對曰有惟仁者

neighbouring kingdoms?' Mencius replied, 'There is. But it requires a perfectly virtuous *prince* to be able, with a great *country*, to serve a small one,—as, for instance, T'ang served Ko, and king Wăn served the Kwăn barbarians. And it requires a wise *prince* to be able, with a small *country*, to serve a large one,—as the king T'âi served the Hsün-yü, and Kâu-ch'ien served Wû.

2. 'He who with a great *State* serves a small one, delights in Heaven. He who with a small *State* serves a large one, stands in awe of Heaven. He who delights in Heaven, will affect with his love and protection the whole kingdom. He who stands in awe of Heaven, will affect with his love and protection his own kingdom.

3. 'It is said in the Book of Poetry, "I fear the Majesty of Heaven, and will thus preserve its favouring decree."'

by 撫字周恤 and 聽從服役 i.e. 'cherishing,' and 'obeying,' respectively, but the translation need not be varied. For the affairs of T'ang with Ko, see III. Pt. II. v. Of those of king Wăn with the Kwăn tribes we have nowhere an account which satisfies Mencius's reference to them. Both Châo Ch'î and Chû Hsî make reference to the Shih-ching, III. i. Ode III. st. 8; but what is there said would seem to be of things antecedent to king Wăn. Of king T'âi and the Hsün-yü, see below, chap. xv. A very readable, though romanced account of Kâu-ch'ien's service of Wû is in the Lieh Kwo Chih (列國志), Bk. lxxx. 是 故 and 故, 'therefore,' introducing illustrations of what has been said, are = our 'as.' 2. 天, says Chû Hsî, 理而已矣, 'Heaven is just principle, and nothing more.' It is a good instance of the way in which he and others often try to expunge the idea of a governing Power and a personal God from their classics. Heaven is here evidently the super-intending, loving Power of the universe. Châo Ch'î says on the whole paragraph :—'The sage delights to pursue the way of Heaven, just as Heaven overspreads everything;—as was evidenced in T'ang and Wăn's protecting the whole kingdom. The wise measure the time and revere Heaven, and so preserve their States;—as was evidenced in king T'âi and Kâu-ch'ien.' This view gives to 天 a positive, substantial meaning, though the personality of the Power is not sufficiently prominent. The commentator 王觀濤 says :—'The Heaven here is indeed the Supreme Heaven, but after all it is equivalent to principle and nothing more!' 保, as in Pt. I. vii. 3. See the Shih-ching, IV. i. Bk. I. Ode VII. st. 3. 保, 'to preserve,' 'to keep.' 時 is here taken = 是; not so in the ode. The final 之 refers to the decree or favour of Heaven. 5. Observe the verbal meaning of 大. 6. See the Shih-ching, III. i. Ode

寵之四方有罪無罪惟我在天
作之君作之師惟曰其助上帝
而安天下之民。書曰天降下民、
天下此文王之勇也文王一怒。
旅以遏徂莒以篤周祜以對于
請大之詩云、王赫斯怒爰整其
哉此匹夫之勇敵一人者也王
勇夫撫劍疾視曰彼惡敢當我
疾寡人好勇對曰王請無好小
時保之王曰、大哉言矣寡人有

4. The king said, 'A great saying! But I have an infirmity;— I love valour.'

5. 'I beg your Majesty,' was the reply, 'not to love small valour. If a man brandishes his sword, looks fiercely, and says, "How dare he withstand me?"—this is the valour of a common man, who can be the opponent only of a single individual. I beg your Majesty to greaten it.

6. 'It is said in the Book of Poetry,

"The king blazed with anger,
And he marshalled his hosts,
To stop the march to Chü,
To consolidate the prosperity of Châu,
To meet the expectations of the nation."

This was the valour of king Wăn. King Wăn, in one burst of his anger, gave repose to all the people of the kingdom.

7. 'In the Book of History it is said, "Heaven having produced the inferior people, made for them rulers and teachers, with the purpose that they should be assisting to God, and therefore distinguished them throughout the four quarters of the land. Whoever

VII. st. 5, where we have 按 for 遏, and 旅 | the same probably that in the ode is called for 莒. 莒 is the name of a State or place, | 共. 以遏徂莒, to stop the march to

下曷敢有越厥志一人衡
行於天下武王恥之此武
王之勇也而武王亦一怒
而安天下之民今王亦一
怒而安天下之民民惟恐
王之不好勇也。
齊宣王見孟子於雪宮、
王曰賢者亦有此樂乎孟
子對曰有人不得則非其
上矣。不得而非其上者非

are offenders, and whoever are innocent, here am I *to deal with them.*
How dare any under heaven give indulgence to their refractory
wills?" There was one man pursuing a violent and disorderly
course in the kingdom, and king Wû was ashamed of it. This was
the valour of king Wû. He also, by one display of his anger, gave
repose to all the people of the kingdom.

8. 'Let now your Majesty also, in one burst of anger, give repose
to all the people of the kingdom. The people are only afraid that
your Majesty does not love valour.'

CHAP. IV. 1. The king Hsüan of Ch'î had an interview with
Mencius in the Snow palace, and said to him, 'Do men of talents
and worth likewise find pleasure in these things?' Mencius replied,
'They do; and if people *generally* are not able *to enjoy themselves,*
they condemn their superiors.'

2. 'For them, when they cannot enjoy themselves, to condemn
their superiors is wrong, but when the superiors of the people do

Chû,' unless we take, with some, 徂 also to be
the name of a place.　7. See the Shû ching, V. i.
Sect. I. 7, but the passage as quoted by Mencius
is rather different from the original text.
惟曰其助上帝,—literally, 'just say-
ing, They shall be aiding to God.' The sentiment
is that of Paul, in Rom. xiii. 1–4, 'The powers
ordained of God are the ministers of God.' In
天下曷敢有越厥志 there is an
allusion to the tyrant Chieh, who is the — 人
in Mencius's subjoined explanation.　8. 惟

恐 is, by some, taken—'The people would only
be afraid,' the preceding clause being = 'If your
Majesty,' &c. I think the present tense is
preferable.

4. A RULER'S PROSPERITY DEPENDS ON HIS
EXERCISING A RESTRAINT UPON HIMSELF, AND
SYMPATHIZING WITH THE PEOPLE IN THEIR JOYS
AND SORROWS.　1. 'The Snow palace' was a
pleasure-palace of the prince of Ch'î. Most commentators say that the king had lodged Mencius
there, and went to see him, but it may not have
been so. Perhaps they only had their interview there. 賢者亦有此樂乎 is

子對曰善哉問也天子適
而可以比於先王觀也晏
海而南放于琅邪吾何脩
曰吾欲觀於轉附朝儛遵
也昔者齊景公問於晏子
天下然而不王者未之有
亦樂其樂憂民之憂者民
者亦非也樂民之樂者民
也為民上而不與民同樂

not make enjoyment a thing common to the people and themselves, they also do wrong.

3. 'When a ruler rejoices in the joy of his people, they also rejoice in his joy; when he grieves at the sorrow of his people, they also grieve at his sorrow. A sympathy of joy will pervade the kingdom; a sympathy of sorrow will do the same :—in such a state of things, it cannot be but that the ruler attain to the royal dignity.

4. 'Formerly, the duke Ching of Ch'î asked the minister Yen, saying, "I wish to pay a visit of inspection to Chwan-fû, and Châo-wû, and then to bend my course southward along the shore, till I come to Lang-yê. What shall I do that my tour may be fit to be compared with the visits of inspection made by the ancient sovereigns ?"

5. 'The minister Yen replied, "An excellent inquiry! When the Son of Heaven visited the princes, it was called a tour of inspec-

different from the question, in nearly the same words, in Pt. I. ii, 賢者 being there 'worthy princes,' and here 'scholars,' men of worth generally, with a reference to Mencius himself. 人不得一人 is to be taken as 民, 'the people,' men generally, and 不得, it is said, 是不得安居之樂, 非指雪宮, is = 'do not get the pleasure of quiet living and enjoyment, not referring to the Snow palace.' 非其上,—非 is used as a verb, = 'to blame,' 'to condemn.' So in the next paragraph. 3. I have given the meaning of the phrases 樂以

天下, 憂以天下, which sum up the preceding part of the paragraph, and are not to be understood as spoken of the ruler only. The 合講 says :—'These two sentences are to be explained from the four previous sentences. The phrase 天下 is only a forcible way of saying what is said by 民. The 以 is to be explained as if we read—不以一身, 乃以天下耳, 'the joy and sorrow is not with (i. e. from) one individual, but from the whole kingdom.' 王, the 4th tone. 4. 晏子, see Confucian Analects, V. xvi. The duke Ching

諸侯曰巡狩巡狩者巡
所守也諸侯朝于天子
曰述職述職者述所職
也無非事者春省耕而
補不足秋省斂而助不
給夏諺曰吾王不遊吾
何以休吾王不豫吾何
以助一遊一豫爲諸侯
度今也不然師行而糧
食飢者弗食勞者弗息

tion, that is, he surveyed the *States* under their care. When the
princes attended at the court of the Son of Heaven, it was called
a report of office, that is, they reported their administration of their
offices. Thus, neither of the proceedings was without a purpose.
And moreover, in the spring they examined the ploughing, and
supplied any deficiency *of seed;* in the autumn they examined the
reaping, and supplied any deficiency of yield. There is the saying
of the Hsiâ dynasty,—If our king do not take his ramble, what will
become of our happiness? If our king do not make his excursion,
what will become of our help? That ramble, and that excursion,
were a pattern to the princes.

6. '"Now, the state of things is different.—A host marches *in
attendance on the ruler*, and stores of provisions are consumed. The
hungry are deprived of their food, and there is no rest for those
who are called to toil. Maledictions are uttered by one to another

occupied the throne for 58 years, from B.C.
546-488. Chwan-fû and Châo-wû were two
hills, which must have been in the north of
Ch'î, and looking on the waters now called the
Gulf of Pei-chih-lî. Lang-yé was the name
both of a mountain and an adjacent city,
referred to the present department of Chû-
ahâng, in Ch'ing-châu. 修=作爲, 'to do.'
5 狩巡, see the Shû-ching, II. i. 8, 9. 狩
is used as =守. It does not seem necessary
to repeat the 巡狩 and 述職 in the translation. This tour of inspection appears to have
been made, under the Châu dynasty, once in
twelve years, while the princes had to present
themselves at court (朝, read ch'ào) once in

six years. From 春, 'in the spring,' the
practices appropriate to the various princes, as
well as the sovereign, are described, though,
as appears from the last clause, with special
reference to the latter. 豫 or 預~遊 By
一遊一預 the spring and autumn visita-
tions are intended, each called ——. 6. 師,
properly a body of 2,500 men, but here generally
=a host, a multitude. 睊睊胥讒.民
乃作慝 are referred to the people, and
the next two clauses to the princes. Yet the
乃 after 民 would rather indicate a different
subject for the clause before. 諸侯憂,—

臣相說之樂蓋徵招角招是
補不足召太師曰爲我作君
於國出舍於郊於是始興發
行惟君所行也景公說大戒
亡先王無流連之樂荒亡之
無厭謂之荒樂酒無厭謂之
從流上而忘反謂之連從流
侯憂從流下而忘反謂之流
民飲食若流流連荒亡爲諸
睊睊胥讒民乃作慝方命虐

with eyes askance, and the people proceed to the commission of wickedness. Thus the *royal* ordinances are violated, and the people are oppressed, and *the supplies of* food and drink flow away like water. *The rulers* yield themselves to the current, or they urge their way against it; they are wild; they are utterly lost :—these things proceed to the grief of the inferior princes.

7. ' " Descending along with the current, and forgetting to return, is what I call yielding to it. Pressing up against it, and forgetting to return, is what I call urging their way against it. Pursuing the chase without satiety is what I call being wild. Delighting in wine without satiety is what I call being lost.

8. ' "The ancient sovereigns had no pleasures to which they gave themselves as on the flowing stream; no doings which might be so characterized as wild and lost.

9. ' " It is for you, my prince, to pursue your course." '

10. ' The duke Ching was pleased. He issued a proclamation throughout his State, and went out and occupied a shed in the borders. From that time he began to open his granaries to supply the wants of the people, and calling the Grand music-master, he said to him—" Make for me music to suit a prince and his minister pleased

諸 侯, by Chû Hsî and others, is explained as in the translation, though this view seems rather forced. Châo Ch I makes them refer to the princes proper; but how can it be said that these things in which they delighted were a 'grief' to them? 10. 太 師, see Analects, VIII. xv. 徵 (read *chî*, the 3rd tone) and 角 are the

也、其詩曰、畜君何
尤、畜君者、好君也。
齊宣王問曰、人
皆謂我毀明堂、毀
諸已乎、孟子對曰、
夫明堂者、王者之
堂也、王欲行王政、
則勿毀之矣。王曰、
王政可得聞與。對
曰、昔者文王之治

with each other." And it was then that the Chî-shâo and Chio-shâo were made, in the words to which it was said, "Is it a fault to restrain one's prince?" He who restrains his prince loves his prince.'

CHAP. V. 1. The king Hsüan of Ch'î said, 'People all tell me to pull down and remove the Hall of Distinction. Shall I pull it down, or stop *the movement for that object?*'

2. Mencius replied, 'The Hall of Distinction is a Hall appropriate to the sovereigns. If your Majesty wishes to practise the true royal government, then do not pull it down.'

3. The king said, 'May I hear from you what the true royal government is?' 'Formerly,' was the reply, 'king Wăn's govern-

names of two of the five notes in the Chinese scale, the fourth and third. 招 is used for 韶, the name given to the music of Shun. This was said to be preserved in Ch'î, and the same name was given to all Ch'î music. The Chî-shâo and Chio-shâo were, I suppose, two tunes or pieces of music, starting with the notes 徵 and 角 respectively.

5. TRUE ROYAL GOVERNMENT WILL ASSUREDLY RAISE TO THE SUPREME DIGNITY, AND NEITHER GREED OF WEALTH, NOR LOVE OF WOMAN, NEED INTERFERE WITH ITS EXERCISE. However his admirers may try to defend him, here, and in other chapters, Mencius, if he does not counsel to, yet suggests, rebellion. In his days, the Châu dynasty was nearly a century distant from its extinction. And then his accepting the princes, with all their confirmed habits of vice and luxury, and telling them those need not interfere with the benevolence of their government, shows very little knowledge of man, or of men's affairs. 1. 明堂,—not 'the Ming or Brilliant Hall.' It was the name given to the palaces occupied in different parts of the country by the sovereigns in their tours of inspection mentioned in the last chapter. See the Book of Rites, Bk. XII. The name Ming was given to them, because royal government,

&c., were 'displayed' by means of them. The one in the text was at the foot of the T'ai mountain in Ch'î, and as the Son of Heaven no longer made use of it, the suggestion on which he consulted Mencius was made to king Hsüan. In 毀諸已乎 we have two questions,—'Shall I destroy it (諸, the interrogative of hesitancy, so common in Mencius), or, Shall I stop?' 2. The first and third 王 here might have the 4th tone; they quite differ from the second, which is merely the style of king Hsüan. I may give here a note from the 集證 (Pt. I. i. 1) on the force of the terms 君 and 王:—'He who is followed by the people till they form a *flock* (羣), is a *chün*. He to whom they turn and go (往之) is a *wang*. Thus the title *wang* expresses the idea of the people's turning and resorting to him who holds it, but the possessor of a State can barely be called a *chün*. It is only the possessor of the whole kingdom who can be styled *wang*.' 3. Ch'î was a double-peaked hill, giving its name to the adjoining country, the old State of Ch'î. Its name is still retained in the district of Ch'î-shan, in Făng-hsiang, the most western department of Shen-hsî, bordering on Kan-sû. 耕者九

岐也耕者九一仕者世祿

關市譏而不征澤梁無禁

罪人不孥老而無妻曰鰥

老而無夫曰寡老而無子

曰獨幼而無父曰孤此四

者天下之窮民而無告者

文王發政施仁必先斯四

者詩云哿矣富人哀此煢

獨王曰善哉言乎曰王如

善之則何爲不行王曰寡

ment of Ch'î was as follows:—The husbandmen *cultivated for the government* one-ninth of the land; the descendants of officers were salaried; at the passes and in the markets, *strangers* were inspected, but *goods* were not taxed: there were no prohibitions respecting the ponds and weirs; the wives and children of criminals were not involved in their guilt. There were the old and wifeless, or widowers; the old and husbandless. or widows; the old and childless, or solitaries; the young and fatherless, or orphans:—these four classes are the most destitute of the people, and have none to whom they can tell their wants, and king Wăn, in the institution of his government with its benevolent action, made them the first objects of his regard, as it is said in the Book of Poetry,

> "The rich may get through *life well*;
> But alas! for the miserable and solitary!"'

4. The king said, 'O excellent words!' *Mencius* said, 'Since your Majesty deems them excellent, why do you not practise them?' 'I have an infirmity,' said the king; 'I am fond of wealth.' The

—, a square 5 was divided into nine parts, each containing 100 món; eight farming families were located upon them, one part being reserved for government. which was cultivated by the joint labours of the husbandmen;—see III. Pt. 1. iii. 仕者世祿,—'officers, hereditary emolument; that is, descendants of meritorious officers, if men of ability, received office, and, even if they were not, they had pensions, in reward of the merit of their fathers. 'Ponds and weirs,'—it is not to be understood that the ponds were artificial. 先斯四. 一先 is the verb. For the ode, see the Shih-ching, II. iv. Ode VIII. st. 13, where for 勞 we find 惸. + 公劉 'The duke Liû,' was the great grandson of Hâu-chî, the high ancestor of the Châu family. By him the waning fortunes of his house were revived, and he founded a settlement in 豳 (*Pin*), the present Pin-châu (邠州), in Shen-hsî. The account of his doing so is found in the ode quoted, Shih-ching, III. ii.

人有疾寡人好貨對曰、昔者。
公劉好貨詩云乃積乃倉乃
裹餱糧于橐于囊思戢用光、
弓矢斯張干戈戚揚爰方啟
行故居者有積倉行者有裹
糧也然後可以爰方啟行王
如好貨與百姓同之於王何
有王曰寡人有疾寡人好色。
對曰昔者大王好色愛厥妃。
詩云古公亶父來朝走馬率

reply was, 'Formerly, Kung-liû was fond of wealth. It is said in the Book of Poetry,

> "He reared his ricks, and filled his granaries,
> He tied up dried provisions and grain,
> In bottomless bags, and sacks,
> That he might gather his people together, and glorify *his State*.
> With bows and arrows all-displayed,
> With shields, and spears, and battle-axes, large and small,
> He commenced his march."

In this way those who remained in their old seat had their ricks and granaries, and those who marched had their bags of provisions. It was not till after this that he thought he could begin his march. If your Majesty loves wealth, give the people power to gratify the same feeling, and what difficulty will there be in your attaining the royal sway?'

5. The king said, 'I have an infirmity; I am fond of beauty.' The reply was, 'Formerly, king T'âi was fond of beauty, and loved his wife. It is said in the Book of Poetry,

> "Kû-kung T'an-fû
> Came in the morning, galloping his horse,
> By the banks of the western waters,

Ode IV. st. 1. For 乃 we have in the Shih-ching 迺, and for 戢輯 積, read *ts'in*, in 4th tone, 'to store up,' 'stores.' Chû Hsî explains:—'stores in the open air.' 5. The king T'âi (see the Doctrine of the Mean, chap. xviii) was the ninth in descent from Kung Liû, by name T'an-fû (in 3rd tone). He removed from

西水滸至于岐下爰及姜
女聿來胥宇當是時也內
無怨女外無曠夫王如好
色與百姓同之於王何有。
孟子謂齊宣王曰王之
臣有託其妻子於其友而
之楚遊者比其反也則凍
餒其妻子則如之何。王曰
棄之曰士師不能治士則
如之何。王曰已之曰四境

As far as the foot of Ch'î hill,
Along with the lady of Chiang;
They came and together chose the site for their settlement."
At that time, in the seclusion of the house, there were no dissatisfied women, and abroad, there were no unmarried men. If your Majesty loves-beauty, let the people be able to gratify the same feeling, and what difficulty will there be in your attaining the royal sway?'

CHAP. VI. 1. Mencius said to the king Hsüan of Ch'î, 'Suppose that one of your Majesty's ministers were to entrust his wife and children to the care of his friend, while he himself went into Ch'û to travel, and that, on his return, *he should find that* the friend had let his wife and children suffer from cold and hunger;—how ought he to deal with him?' The king said, 'He should cast him off.'

2. *Mencius* proceeded, 'Suppose that the chief criminal judge could not regulate the officers *under him*, how would you deal with him?' The king said, 'Dismiss him.'

3. *Mencius again* said, 'If within the four borders *of your*

Pin to Ch'î, as is celebrated in the ode, Shih-ching, III. i. Ode III. st. 2. 古公＝先公 'the ancient duke,' T'an-fû's title, before it was changed into 大王, 'the king, or sovereign, T'âi.'

6. BRINGING HOME HIS BAD GOVERNMENT TO THE KING OF CH'Î. 1. 之楚,—之 is the verb = 往. 比, in 4th tone,—及, as in Analects, XI. xxv. 4, 5. 凍 and 餒 = active, *hiphil*

verbs. It is better to prefix 'suppose that,' or 'if,' to the whole sentence, in the translation, as the cases in the remaining paragraph cannot well be put directly, as this might be. The replies suggest the renderings of 如之何 which I have given. 2. 士師, see on Analects, XVIII. ii. 治 is the 2nd tone. In the next paragraph, it is in the 4th. The two instances well illustrate the difference of signification, which the tone makes.

喻戚可不慎與左右皆曰
如不得已將使卑喻尊疏
不才而舍之曰國君進賢
其亡也王曰吾何以識其
臣矣昔者所進今日不知
也有世臣之謂也王無親
故國者非謂有喬木之謂
孟子見齊宣王曰所謂
左右而言他。
之內不治則如之何王顧

kingdom there is not good government, what is to be done?' The king looked to the right and left, and spoke of other matters.

CHAP. VII. 1. Mencius, having an interview with the king Hsüan of Ch'î, said to him, 'When men speak of "an ancient kingdom," it is not meant thereby that it has lofty trees in it, but that it has ministers *sprung from families which have been noted in it* for generations. Your Majesty has no intimate ministers *even.* Those whom you advanced yesterday are gone to-day, and you do not know it.'

2. The king said, 'How shall I know that they have not ability, and so avoid employing them at all?'

3. The reply was, 'The ruler of a State advances to office men of talents and virtue only as a matter of necessity. Since he will thereby cause the low to overstep the honourable, and distant to overstep his near relatives, ought he to do so but with caution?

4. 'When all those about you say,—"This is a man of talents

7. THE CARE TO BE EMPLOYED BY A PRINCE IN THE EMPLOYMENT OF MINISTERS; AND THEIR RELATION TO HIMSELF AND THE STABILITY OF HIS KINGDOM. 1. On the idiom 之謂, see Prémare, on character 之; but the examples which he adduces are not quite similar to those in this passage. Literally, the opening sentence would be :—'That which is called an ancient kingdom, is not the saying (之謂) of saying it has lofty trees; it is the saying of—it has heredi-

tary ministers.' The 謂 in 非謂 might be omitted, and yet it adds something in the turn of the sentence. As opposed to 今日, 昔者 = 'yesterday.' Châo Ch'î strangely mistakes the meaning of the last clause, which he makes to be :—'Those whom you advanced on the past day, do evil to-day, and you do not know to cut them off!' 2. 舍=捨, the 3rd tone, 'to let go,' 'to dismiss.' 3. 如不得已,—literally, 'as a thing in which he cannot stop.'

賢、未可也諸大夫皆曰賢未可也、
國人皆曰賢然後察之見賢焉然
後用之、左右皆曰不可、勿聽諸大
夫皆曰不可、勿聽國人皆曰不
然後察之見不可焉然後去之、左〇五章
右皆曰可殺勿聽諸大夫皆曰可
殺、勿聽國人皆曰可殺然後察之
見可殺焉然後殺之、故曰國人殺
之也。如此然後可以為民父母。〇六章

and worth," you may not therefore believe it. When your great officers all say,—"This is a man of talents and virtue," neither may you for that believe it. When all the people say,—"This is a man of talents and virtue," then examine into the case, and when you find that the man is such, employ him. When all those about you say,—"This man won't do," don't listen to them. When all your great officers say,—"This man won't do," don't listen to them. When the people all say,—"This man won't do," then examine into the case, and when you find that the man won't do, send him away.

5. 'When all those about you say,—"This man deserves death," don't listen to them. When all your great officers say,—"This man deserves death," don't listen to them. When the people all say,—"This man deserves death," then inquire into the case, and when you see that the man deserves death, put him to death. In accordance with this we have the saying, "The people killed him."

6. 'You must act in this way in order to be the parent of the people.'

Compare the Chung Yung, xx. 13. 4. 未可, 'you may not yet believe that the man is so and so.' See on Analects, XIII. xxiv. 6. Compare the Great Learning, Commentary x. 3. We may use the second person in translating or, more indefinitely, the third.

齊宣王問曰、湯放桀、武
王伐紂、有諸孟子對曰、於
傳有之曰臣弒其君可乎。
曰賊仁者謂之賊賊義者、
謂之殘殘賊之人謂之一
夫聞誅一夫紂矣、未聞弒
君也。

孟子見齊宣王曰、爲巨
室則必使工師求大木、工
師得大木、則王喜以爲能

CHAP. VIII. 1. The king Hsüan of Ch'î asked, saying, 'Was it so, that T'ang banished Chieh, and that king Wû smote Châu?' Mencius replied, 'It is so in the records.'

2. *The king* said, 'May a minister *then* put his sovereign to death?'

3. *Mencius* said, 'He who outrages the benevolence *proper to his nature*, is called a robber; he who outrages righteousness, is called a ruffian. The robber and ruffian we call a mere fellow. I have heard of the cutting off of the fellow Châu, but I have not heard of the putting a sovereign to death, *in his case.*'

CHAP. IX. 1. Mencius, having an interview with the king Hsüan of Ch'î, said to him, 'If you are going to build a large mansion, you will surely cause the Master of the workmen to look out for large trees, and when he has found such large trees, you will

8. KILLING A SOVEREIGN IS NOT NECESSARILY REBELLION NOR MURDER. 1. Of T'ang's banishment of Chieh, see the Shû-ching, IV. ii, iii; and of the smiting of Châu, see the same, V. i. 2. 弒 is the word appropriated to regicide, which Mencius in his reply exchanges for 誅. 臣.—'a minister,' i.e. here, a subject. 3. 賊, as a verb,＝傷害, 'to nurt and injure,' as in the Analects, several times. 'To outrage' answers well for it here. In the use of 夫, Mencius seems to refer to the expression 獨夫紂 Shû-ching, V. I. Sect. III. 4.

9 THE ABSURDITY OF A RULER'S NOT ACTING

ACCORDING TO THE COUNSEL OF THE MEN OF TALENTS AND VIRTUE, WHOM HE CALLS TO AID IN HIS GOVERNMENT, BUT REQUIRING THEM TO FOLLOW HIS WAYS. In one important point Mencius's illustrations fail. A prince is not supposed to understand either house-building or stone-cutting; he must delegate those matters to the men who do. But government he ought to understand, and he may not delegate it to any scholars or officers.

1. The 工師 was a special officer having charge of all the artisans, &c.;—see the Lî Chî, IV. Sect. I. iii 13, and Sect. IV. i. 17. 勝, the 1st tone,—see Pt. I. iii. 3. 其任 (the 4th tone),—'its use,' i.e. the building of the

勝其任矣、匠人斲而小之、
則王怒以爲不勝其任矣、
夫人幼而學之壯而欲行
之、王曰、姑舍女所學而從
我則何如今有璞玉於此、
雖萬鎰必使玉人彫琢之、
至於治國家則曰、姑舍女
所學而從我則何以異於
教玉人彫琢玉哉。

be glad, thinking that they will answer for the intended object. Should the workmen hew them so as to make them too small, then your Majesty will be angry, thinking that they will not answer for the purpose. Now, a man spends his youth in learning *the principles of right government*, and, being grown up to vigour, he wishes to put them in practice;—if your Majesty says to him, "For the present put aside what you have learned, and follow me," what shall we say?

2. 'Here now you have a gem unwrought, *in the stone.* Although it may be worth 240,000 *taels*, you will surely employ a lapidary to cut and polish it. But when you come to the government of the State, then you say,—"For the present put aside what you have learned, and follow me." How is it that you herein act so differently from your conduct in calling in the lapidary to cut the gem?'

house. The 之 after 學 and 行 are to be understood as referring to 仁 and 義, or as in the translation. 壯 denotes the maturity of thirty years, when one was supposed to be fit for office. 2. The 鎰 was twenty-four Chinese ounces or *taels* (of gold). Chû Hsî, after Châo Ch'î, erroneously makes it twenty ounces. The gem in question, worth so much, would be very dear to the king, *and yet* he would certainly confide to another the polishing of it;—why would he not do so with the State? 國家,— the kingdom, embracing the families and possessions of the nobles. 女=汝. 教, the 1st tone,—使 or 令, 'to make,' not 'to teach.' From 至於, however, was explained by Châo Ch'î (and many still follow him) thus :—'But in the matter of the government of your State, you say,—For the present put aside what you have learned, and follow me. In what does this differ from your teaching—i.e. wishing to teach—the lapidary to cut the gem?' This is the interpretation which Julien adopts in his translation. The other upon the whole appears to me the better. The first 則 is a difficulty in Châo Ch'î's view; the second, in the other. But the final 哉 turns the balance in its favour, and accordingly I have adopted it.

齊人伐燕勝之宣王問
曰或謂寡人勿取或謂寡
人取之以萬乘之國伐萬
乘之國五旬而舉之人力
不至於此不取必有天殃
取之何如孟子對曰取之
而燕民悅則取之古之人
有行之者武王是也取之
而燕民不悅則勿取古之
人有行之者文王是也以

CHAP. X. 1. The people of Ch'î attacked Yen, and conquered it.

2. The king Hsüan asked, saying, 'Some tell me not to take possession of it for myself, and some tell me to take possession of it. For a kingdom of ten thousand chariots, attacking another of ten thousand chariots, to complete the conquest of it in fifty days, is an achievement beyond *mere* human strength. If I do not take possession of it, calamities from Heaven will surely come upon me. What do you say to my taking possession of it?'

3. Mencius replied, 'If the people of Yen will be pleased with your taking possession of it, then do so.—Among the ancients there was *one* who acted on this principle, namely king Wû. If the people of Yen will not be pleased with your taking possession of it, then do not do so.—Among the ancients there was *one* who acted on this principle, namely king Wăn.

4. 'When, with *all the strength of* your country of ten thousand

10. THE DISPOSAL OF KINGDOMS RESTS WITH THE MINDS OF THE PEOPLE. VOX POPULI VOX DEI. We shall find this doctrine often put forth very forcibly by Mencius. Here the king of Ch'î insinuates that it was the will of Heaven that he should take Yen, and Mencius sends him to the will of the people, by which only the other could be ascertained. 1. The State of Yen (the 1st tone) lay north-west from Ch'î, forming part of the present province of Chih-lî. Its prince, a poor weakling, had resigned his throne to his prime minister, and great confusion ensued, so that the people welcomed the appearance of the troops of Ch'î, and made

no resistance to them. 2. 舉之 is explained as = 勝之, 'to conquer it;' but 舉 has not this signification. Literally, we might render 'and up with it.' 3. The common saying is that king Wăn 三分天下有其二, 'had possession of two of the three parts of the kingdom.' Still he did not think that the people were prepared for the entire extinction of the Yin dynasty, and left the completion of the fortunes of his house to his son, king Wû. 4. 食, read *tsze*, 4th tone, 'rice.' 漿 is

萬乘之國伐萬乘之國、簞
食壺漿以迎王師、豈有他
哉避水火也、如水益深、如
火益熱亦運而已矣。
齊人伐燕取之、諸侯將
謀救燕宣王曰、諸侯多謀
伐寡人者、何以待之孟子
對曰臣聞七十里爲政於
天下者湯是也、未聞以千
里畏人者也書曰、湯一
征

chariots, you attacked another country of ten thousand chariots, and *the people brought* baskets of rice and vessels of congee, to meet your Majesty's host, was there any other reason for this but that they hoped to escape out of fire and water? If you make the water more deep and the fire more fierce, they will in like manner make *another* revolution.'

CHAP. XI. 1. The people of Ch'î, having smitten Yen, took possession of it, *and upon this*, the princes of the various States deliberated together, and resolved to deliver Yen *from their power.* The king Hsüan said *to Mencius*, 'The princes have formed many plans to attack me:—how shall I prepare myself for them?' Mencius replied, 'I have heard of one who with seventy *lî* exercised all the functions of government throughout the kingdom. That was T'ang. I have never heard of a *prince* with a thousand *lî* standing in fear of others.'

2. 'It is said in the Book of History, As soon as T'ang began

properly congee, but here used generally for beverages; some say wine. 壺, 'a goblet,' 'a jug,' 'a vase,' a vessel for liquids generally.— The first paragraph, it is said, is constructed according to the rules of composition attributed to Confucius in his 'Spring and Autumn,' the 人 refusing honour to the king of Ch'î. 伐 expresses the ill deserts of Yen. And 勝之 intimates that the conquest was from the disinclination of Yen to fight, not from the power of Ch'î.

11. AMBITION AND AVARICE ONLY MAKE ENEMIES AND BRING DISASTERS. SAFETY AND PROSPERITY LIE IN A BENEVOLENT GOVERNMENT. 1. 將 before 謀救 indicates the execution of the plans to be still in the future. 者 in 諸侯…者 makes the clause like one in English beginning with a nominative absolute. 待之,—literally, 'await them.' 2. See the Shû-ching, IV. ii. 6. Mencius has introduced the clause 天

自葛始天下信之東面而
征西夷怨南面而征北狄
怨曰奚爲後我民望之若
大旱之望雲霓也歸市者
不止耕者不變誅其君而
弔其民若時雨降民大悦
書曰徯我后后來其蘇今
燕虐其民王往而征之民
以爲將拯己於水火之中
也簞食壺漿以迎王師若

his work of executing justice, he commenced with Ko. The whole kingdom had confidence in him. When he pursued his work in the east, the rude tribes on the west murmured. So did those on the north, when he was engaged in the south. Their cry was—'' Why does he put us last ?'' *Thus*, the people looked to him, as we look in a time of great drought to the clouds and rainbows. The frequenters of the markets stopped not. The husbandmen made no change *in their operations*. While he punished their rulers, he consoled the people. *His progress* was like the falling of opportune rain, and the people were delighted. It is said *again* in the Book of History, " We have waited for our prince *long ;* the prince's coming will be our reviving !"

3. 'Now *the ruler of* Yen was tyrannizing over his people, and your Majesty went and punished him. The people supposed that you were going to deliver them out of the water and the fire, and brought baskets of rice and vessels of congee, to meet your Majesty's host. But you have slain their fathers and elder brothers, and put

下信之, and there are some other differ-ences from the original text. Ko was a small territory, which is referred to the present district of Ning-ling (寧陵) in Kwei-teh (歸.德), in Honan. 望雲霓,—the modern commentators ingeniously interpret :— 'The people look for rain in drought, and murmur at his not coming, as they dread the appearance of a rainbow, on which the rain will stop.' This is perhaps over-refining, and making too much of the 望. Châo Ch'î says :—

'The rainbow appears when it rains, so people, in time of drought, long to see it.' The second quotation is from the same paragraph of the Shû-ching, where we have 子 for 我. Compare last chapter. 若, in 若殺云 云, is not our 'if,' but rather 'since.' The critics say 是指數之詞 不作設詞 看, 'it is demonstrative, not conditional.' 父 兄, 一父 is not *fathers* only, but *uncles* as well.

殺其父兄、係累其子弟毀其

宗廟遷其重器如之何其可

也天下固畏齊之彊也今又

倍地而不行仁政、是動天下

之兵也。王速出令反其旄倪、

止其重器謀於燕衆置君而

後去之則猶可及止也。

鄒與魯鬨穆公問曰吾有

司死者三十三人而民莫之

死也誅之則不可勝誅不誅

their sons and younger brothers in confinement. You have pulled down the ancestral temple *of the State,* and are removing *to Ch'i* its precious vessels. How can such a course be deemed proper? *The rest of* the kingdom is indeed *jealously* afraid of the strength of Ch'i; and now, when with a doubled territory you do not put in practice a benevolent government;—it is this which sets the arms of the kingdom in motion.

4. 'If your Majesty will make haste to issue an ordinance, restoring *your captives,* old and young, stopping *the removal of* the precious vessels, *and saying that, after* consulting with the people of Yen, you will appoint them a ruler, and withdraw from the country;—in this way you may still be able to stop *the threatened attack.*'

CHAP. XII. 1. There had been a brush between Tsâu and Lû, when the duke Mû asked *Mencius,* saying, 'Of my officers there were killed thirty-three men, and none of the people would die in their defence. Though I sentenced them to death *for their conduct,* it is impossible to put such a multitude to death. If I do not put them

其宗廟, 其宗器,—其 = 'its or his,' i.e. the kingdom's or the prince's, not their, the people's. 4. 旄, 4th tone, used for 耄, 'people of eighty and ninety.' The clauses after the first are to be understood as the substance of the order or ordinance, which Mencius advised the king to issue.

12. THE AFFECTIONS OF THE PEOPLE CAN ONLY

HE SECURED THROUGH A BENEVOLENT GOVERNMENT. AS THEY ARE DEALT WITH BY THEIR SUPERIORS, SO WILL THEY DEAL BY THEM. 1. Tsâu, the native State of Mencius, was a small territory, whose name is still retained, in the district of Tsâu-hsien, in Yen-châu of Shan-tung. 鬨 is explained—'the noise of a struggle.' It is a brush, a skirmish. Tsâu could not stand long against the forces of Lû. Mû,—'the Dis-

之也君無尤焉君行仁政
爾者也夫民今而後得反
戒之戒之出乎爾者反乎
是上慢而殘下也曾子曰
廩實府庫充有司莫以告
方者幾千人矣而君之倉
轉乎溝壑壯者散而之四
曰凶年饑歲君之民老弱
救如之何則可也孟子對
則疾視其長上之死而不

to death, then there is *the crime unpunished of* their looking angrily on at the death of their officers, and not saving them. How is the exigency of the case to be met?'

2. Mencius replied, 'In calamitous years and years of famine, the old and weak of your people, who have been found lying in the ditches and water-channels, and the able-bodied who have been scattered about to the four quarters, have amounted to several thousands. All the while, your granaries, O prince, have been stored with grain, and your treasuries and arsenals have been full, and not one of your officers has told you *of the distress*. Thus negligent have the superiors *in your State* been, and cruel to their inferiors. The philosopher Tsăng said, "Beware, beware. What proceeds from you, will return to you again." Now at length the people have paid back the conduct of their officers to them. Do not you, O prince, blame them.

3. 'If you will put in practice a benevolent government, this

penser of virtue, and Maintainer of righteousness, outwardly showing inward feeling,'—is the posthumous epithet of the duke. 有司 are to be taken together,—'officers;'—see Analects, VIII. iv. 莫之死 is to be completed 莫(or 莫肯)爲之死; compare Analects, XIV. xvii. 則疾視云云 is not to be translated,—'they will hereafter look angrily on, &c.;' the reference is to the crime that had taken place. 2. 凶年=years of

pestilence, and other calamities, such as are immediately described. 夫, 1st tone, indicates the application of the saying. 今而後= 'now at last.'—They had long been wishing to show their feeling, but only now had they found the opportunity. 反之,-之 refers to the 有司. 3. 其上,—embracing the prince and officers generally; 其長 (the 3rd tone), the officers only. 死其長,—to be supplemented, as in par. 1.

斯民親其上、死其長矣。

滕文公問曰、滕小國也、間於
齊楚事齊乎事楚乎孟子對曰、
是謀非吾所能及也無已則有
一焉鑿斯池也築斯城也與民
守之效死而民弗去則是可爲
也。

滕文公問曰、齊人將築薛、吾
甚恐如之何則可孟子對曰、昔
者、大王居邠狄人侵之去之岐

people will love you and all above them, and will die for their officers.'

CHAP. XIII. 1. The duke Wăn of Tăng asked *Mencius*, saying, 'Tăng is a small kingdom, and lies between Ch'î and Ch'û. Shall I serve Ch'î? Or shall I serve Ch'û?'

2. Mencius replied, 'This plan *which you propose* is beyond me. If you will have me counsel you, there is one thing *I can suggest.* Dig deeper your moats; build higher your walls; guard them as well as your people. *In case of attack*, be prepared to die *in your defence*, and have the people so that they will not leave you;—this is a proper course.'

CHAP. XIV. 1. The duke Wăn of Tăng asked *Mencius*, saying, 'The people of Ch'î are going to fortify Hsieh. *The movement* occasions me great alarm. What is the proper course for me to take in the case?'

2. Mencius replied, 'Formerly, when king T'âi dwelt in Pin, the barbarians of the north were *continually* making incursions upon it. He *therefore* left it, went to the foot of mount Ch'î, and there took

13. A PRINCE SHOULD DEFEND ON HIMSELF, AND NOT RELY ON, OR TRY TO PROPITIATE, OTHER POWERS.
1. Tăng still gives its name to a district of Yen-châu in the south of Shan-tung. North of it was Ch'î, and, in the time of Mencius, Ch'û was threatening it from the south. 間, 4th tone, 'to occupy a space between.' 2. 無已, 則有一焉,—compare Pt. I. vii. 2,—無以.

子對曰、昔者太王居邠、
得免焉、如之何則可。孟
也、竭力以事大國、則不
臺　滕文公問曰、滕小國
彼何哉。彊爲善而已矣。
若夫成功、則天也。君如
子創業垂統爲可繼也。
世子孫必有王者矣。君
之不得已也。苟爲善後
山之下居焉、非擇而取

up his residence. He did not take that situation, as having selected it. It was a matter of necessity with him.

3. 'If you do good, among your descendants, in after generations, there shall be one who will attain to the royal dignity. A prince lays the foundation of the inheritance, and hands down the beginning *which he has made*, doing what may be continued *by his successors*. As to the accomplishment of the great result, that is with Heaven. What is that Ch'î to you, O prince? Be strong to do good. That is all your business.'

CHAP. XV. 1. The duke Wăn of T'ăng asked Mencius, saying, 'T'ăng is a small State. Though I do my utmost to serve those large kingdoms *on either side of it*, we cannot escape *suffering from them*. What course shall I take that we may do so?' Mencius

則王乎 斯 池—'these,'='your'moats.' 效死—效=致, as that is used in Analects, I. vii, *et al.* A good deal must be supplied here in the translation, to bring out Mencius's counsel.

14. A PRINCE, THREATENED BY HIS NEIGHBOURS, WILL FIND HIS BEST DEFENCE AND CONSOLATION IN DOING WHAT IS GOOD AND RIGHT. Mencius was at his wit's end, I suppose, to give duke Wăn an answer. It was all very well to tell him to do good, but the promise of a royal descendant would hardly be much comfort to him. The reward to be realised in this world in the person of another, and the reference to Heaven, as to a fate more than to a personal God,—are melancholy. Contrast Psalm xxxvii. 3,—'Trust in the Lord and do good; so shalt thou dwell in the land, and verily thou shalt be fed.' 1. 薛 was the name of an ancient principality, adjoining T'ăng. It had long been incorporated with

Ch'î, which now resumed an old design of fortifying it,—that is, I suppose, of repairing the wall of its principal town, as a basis of operations against T'ăng. 2. See chap. iii, and also the next. 去之岐山下,—It is best to take 之 here as the verb,=往 3. 君子,—generally, 'a prince.' 垂統—統, 'the end of a cocoon, or clue,' 'a beginning.' 若夫, the 夫 is not a mere expletive, but is used as in Analects, XI. ix. 3, *et al.*, 'as to this,'—the accomplishing,' &c. 彊, the 3rd tone, is the verb.

15. TWO COURSES OPEN TO A PRINCE PRESSED BY HIS ENEMIES;—FLIGHT OR DEATH. 1. Compare chap. iii. 屬,—read *chû*, the 4th tone, 'to assemble,' 'meet with.' 耆,—'a sexagenarian.' 二三子,—see Analects, VII. xxiii, *et al.*

狄人侵之事之以皮幣不得免
焉事之以犬馬不得免焉事之
以珠玉不得免焉乃屬其耆老
而告之曰狄人之所欲者吾土
地也吾聞之也君子不以其所
以養人者害人二三子何患乎
無君我將去之去邠踰梁山邑
於岐山之下居焉邠人曰仁人
也不可失也從之者如歸市或
曰世守也非身之所能爲也效

replied, 'Formerly, when king T'âi dwelt in Pin, the barbarians of the north were *constantly* making incursions upon it. He served them with skins and silks, and still he suffered from them. He served them with dogs and horses, and still he suffered from them. He served them with pearls and gems, and still he suffered from them. Seeing this, he assembled the old men, and announced to them, saying, "What the barbarians want is my territory. I have heard this,—that a ruler does not injure his people with that wherewith he nourishes them. My children, why should you be troubled about having no prince? I will leave this." *Accordingly*, he left Pin, crossed the mountain Liang, *built* a town at the foot of mount Ch'î, and dwelt there. The people of Pin said, "He is a benevolent man. We must not lose him." Those who followed him looked like crowds hastening to market.

2. *On the other hand*, some say, "*The kingdom* is a thing to be kept from generation to generation. One individual cannot under-

何患乎無君 seems to mean :—'If I remain here, I am sure to die from the barbarians. I will go and preserve your ruler for you.' So the paraphrast in the 備旨. The 日講, however, says :—'My children, why need you be troubled about having no prince? When I am gone, whoever can secure your repose, will be your prince and chief. I will leave this, and go elsewhere.' 歸市 is different rather from the same phrase in chap. vii. There it means traders, here market-goers generally. 2. This paragraph is to be understood as spoken to a ruler, in his own person. Compare

死勿去君請擇於斯二者。

夫魯平公將出嬖人臧倉

者請曰他日君出則必命

有司所之今乘輿已駕矣

有司未知所之敢請公曰

將見孟子曰何哉君所爲

輕身以先於匹夫者以爲

賢乎禮義由賢者出而孟

子之後喪踰前喪君無見

焉公曰諾樂正子入見曰

take to dispose of it in his own person. Let him be prepared to die for it. Let him not quit it."

3. 'I ask you, prince, to make your election between these two courses.'

CHAP. XVI. 1. The duke P'ing of Lû was about to leave *his palace*, when his favourite, one Tsang Ts'ang, made a request to him, saying, 'On other days, when you have gone out, you have given instructions to the officers as to where you were going. But now, the horses have been put to the carriage, and the officers do not yet know where you are going. I venture to ask.' The duke said, 'I am going to see the scholar Măng.' 'How is this?' said the other. 'That you demean yourself, prince, in paying the honour of the first visit to a common man, is, I suppose, because you think that he is a man of talents and virtue. By such men the rules of ceremonial proprieties and right are observed. But on the occasion of this Măng's second mourning, his observances exceeded those of the former. Do not go to see him, my prince.' The duke said, 'I will not.'

2. The officer Yo-chăng entered *the court*, and had an audience.

chap. vii. 爲=專, 'to take the whole disposal of,' 'to deal with.' It is not to be referred to the 守. The paraphrasts make the whole spoken by the ruler;—thus:—'The territory of the State was handed down by my ancestors to their descendants, that they should keep it from generation to generation. It is not what I can assume in my person the disposal of. If calami-ties and difficulties come, my course is to fight to the death to keep it. I may not abandon it, and go elsewhere.' The meaning comes to the same. But the 勿 is against this construction.

16. A MAN'S WAY IN LIFE IS ORDERED BY HEAVEN. THE INSTRUMENTALITY OF OTHER MEN IS ONLY SUBORDINATE. 1. The duke P'ing (i.e. 'The Pacificator') had been informed of Men-cius's worth, it appears, by Yo-chăng, and was

克告於君君爲來見也
同也樂正子見孟子曰
曰非所謂踰也貧富不
否謂棺椁衣衾之美也
三鼎而後以五鼎與曰
前以士後以大夫前以
也曰何哉君所謂踰者
喪踰前喪是以不往見
或告寡人曰孟子之後
君奚爲不見孟軻也曰

He said, 'Prince, why have you not gone to see Măng K'o?' *The duke* said, 'One told me that, on the occasion of the scholar Măng's second mourning, his observances exceeded those of the former. It is on that account that I have not gone to see him.' 'How is this!' answered Yo-chăng. 'By what you call "exceeding," you mean, I suppose, that, on the first occasion, he used the rites appropriate to a scholar, and, on the second, those appropriate to a great officer; that he first used three tripods, and afterwards five tripods.' *The duke* said, 'No; I refer to the greater excellence of the coffin, the shell, the grave-clothes, and the shroud.' Yo-chăng said, 'That cannot be called "exceeding." That was the difference between being poor and being rich.'

3. *After this*, Yo-chăng saw Mencius, and said to him, 'I told

going out, half-ashamed at the same time to do so, to offer the due respect to him as a professor of moral and political science, by visiting him and asking his services. The author of the 四書拓餘說 approves of the view that the incident in this chapter is to be referred to the 4th year of the sovereign 赧, B.C. 311, but the chronology of the duke Ping is very confused. 所之,-之=往. 何哉 is an exclamation of surprise, extending back to 前喪. In 以爲賢乎, the 乎 is hardly so much as an interrogation. I have given its force by —'I suppose.' 出 does not indicate the origin of rites and right, but only their exhibition. The first occasion of Mencius's mourning referred to was that, it is said, for his father.

But his father died, according to the received accounts, when he was only a child of three years old. We must suppose that the favourite invented the story. I have retained the surname Măng here, as suiting the paragraph better than Mencius. 2. 樂正 is a double surname. This individual, whose name was K'o (克;—see par. 3), was a disciple of Mencius. The surname probably arose from one of his ancestors having been the music-master of some State, and the name of his office passing over to become the designation of his descendants. The tripods contained the offerings of meat used in sacrifice. The sovereign used nine, the prince of a State seven, a great officer five, and a scholar three. To each tripod belonged its appropriate kind of flesh. 3. 君爲來.-爲, 4th tone, = 'therefore,' i. e. in consequence of what Yo-chăng had said, the duke was going to visit

使子不遇哉。
氏之子、焉能
魯侯天也、臧
也吾之不遇
止非人所能
止或尼之行
曰行或使之、
以不果來也。
者沮君、君是
嬖人有臧倉

the prince about you, and he was consequently coming to see you, when one of his favourites, named Tsang Ts'ang, stopped him, and therefore he did not come according to his purpose.' *Mencius* said, 'A man's advancement is effected, it may be, by others, and the stopping him is, it may be, from the efforts of others. *But* to advance a man or to stop his advance is *really* beyond the power of other men. My not finding *in* the prince of Lû *a ruler who would confide in me, and put my counsels into practice,* is from Heaven. How could that scion of the Tsang family cause me not to find *the ruler that would suit me?*'

Mencius. 尼 is read in the 3rd and 4th tones, both with the same meaning, = 止, 'to stop.' 不遇魯君 is not spoken merely with reference to the duke's not coming, as he had purposed, to meet him. The phrase 不遇 really conveys all the meaning in the translation, however periphrastic that may seem. With this reference of Mencius to Heaven, compare the language of Confucius. Analects, VII. xxii; IX. v; XIV. xxxviii.

則　先　就　會　子　功　路　公
吾　子　賢　西　誠　可　於　孫
子　之　曾　曰、　齊　復　齊、　丑
與　所　西　吾　人　許　管　問
管　畏　蹵　子　也、　乎。　仲　曰、
仲　也。　然　與　知　孟　晏　夫
孰　曰、　曰、　子　管　子　子　子

公孫丑章句上

CHAPTER I. 1. Kung-sun Ch'âu asked Mencius, saying, 'Master, if you were to obtain the ordering of the government in Ch'î, could you promise yourself to accomplish anew such results as those realized by Kwan Chung and Yen?'

2. Mencius said. 'You are indeed a *true* man of Ch'î. You know about Kwan Chung and Yen, and nothing more.

3. 'Some one asked Tsäng Hsî, saying, "Sir, to which do you give the superiority,—to yourself or to Tsze-lû?" Tsäng Hsî looked uneasy, and said, "He was an object of veneration to my grandfather."

TITLE OF THE BOOK.—The name of Kung-sun Ch'âu, a disciple of Mencius, heading the first chapter, the Book is named from him accordingly. On the 章句上, see note on the title of the first Book.

1. WHILE MENCIUS WISHED TO SEE A TRUE MORAL GOVERNMENT AND SWAY IN THE KINGDOM, AND COULD EASILY HAVE REALIZED IT, FROM THE PECULIAR CIRCUMSTANCES OF THE TIME, HE WOULD NOT, TO DO SO, HAVE HAD RECOURSE TO ANY WAYS INCONSISTENT WITH ITS IDEAL. 1. Kung-sun Ch'âu, one of Mencius's disciples, belonged to Ch'î, and was probably a cadet of the ducal family. The sons of the princes were generally 公子; their sons again, 公孫, 'ducal grandsons,' and these two characters became the surnames of their descendants, who mingled with the undistinguished classes of the people. 當路

literally, 'in a way,' Châo Ch'î says—當仕路也 'in an official way,' and Chû Hsî 居要地 'to occupy an important position.' The gloss in the 備旨 says:—'當路, 操政柄, to grasp the handle of government.' The analogous phrase—當道 is used now to describe an officer's appointment. 管仲, see Confucian Analects, III. xxii; XIV. x, xvii, xviii. 晏子,—see Analects, V. xvi. Men-cius, I. B. II. iv. 2. Tsäng Hsî was the grandson, according to Châo Ch'î and Chû Hsî, of Tsäng Shin, the famous disciple of Confucius. Otherwise he was 曾參's son. This most point—就賢 曾西—compare Analects, XI. xv. 蹵然

賢曾西艴然不悅曰爾何
曾比子於管仲管仲得君
如彼其專也行乎國政如
彼其久也功烈如彼其卑
也爾何曾比子於管
仲曾西之所不爲也而子
爲我願之乎曰管仲以其
君霸晏子以其君顯管仲
晏子猶不足爲與曰以齊
王由反手也曰若是則弟

"Then," pursued the other, "Do you give the superiority to yourself or to Kwan Chung?" Tsăng Hsî, flushed with anger and displeased, said, "How dare you compare me with Kwan Chung? Considering how entirely Kwan Chung possessed *the confidence of* his prince, how long he enjoyed the direction of the government of the State, and how low, *after all*, was what he accomplished,—how is it that you liken me to him?"

4. 'Thus,' concluded *Mencius*, 'Tsăng Hsî would not play Kwan Chung, and is it what you desire for me that I should do so?'

5. *Kung-sun Ch'âu* said, 'Kwan Chung raised his prince to be the leader of all the other princes, and Yen made his prince illustrious, and do you still think it would not be enough for you to do what they did?'

6. *Mencius* answered, 'To raise Ch'î to the royal dignity would be as easy as it is to turn round the hand.'

7. 'So!' returned the other. 'The perplexity of your disciple

according to Chû, is 不安貌 as in the translation. The dictionary gives it, 敬貌 'the appearance of reverence.' 先子,—we see what a wide application this character 子 has. 何曾,—曾 is not to be taken as if it were the sign of the present complete tense, though in the dictionary this passage is quoted under that signification of the character. It is here = 則 or 乃. For more than forty years Kwan Chung possessed the entire confidence of

the duke Hwan. 4. 爲我 = 爲, 4th tone, 'on my behalf.' Sun Shih (孫奭), the paraphrast of Châo Ch'î, takes it as = 以爲:— 'Do you think that I desire to do so?' This does not appear to be Ch'î's own interpretation.

5. 管仲晏子猶不足爲與 — literally, 'and are Kwan Chung and Yen still not sufficient to be played?' 7. 若是 = 'in this case;' but by using our exclamatory *So!* the spirit of the remark is brought out. 且

家遺俗流風善政猶有存者
也紂之去武丁未久也其故
丁朝諸侯有天下猶運之掌
下歸殷久矣久則難變也武
於武丁賢聖之君六七作天
與曰文王何可當也由湯至
言王若易然則文王不足法
武王周公繼之然後大行今
百年而後崩猶未洽於天下
子之惑滋甚且以文王之德

is hereby very much increased. There was king Wăn, moreover,
with all the virtue which belonged to him ; and who did not die
till he had reached a hundred years :—and still *his influence* had not
penetrated throughout the kingdom. It required king Wû and the
duke of Châu to continue his course, before that influence greatly
prevailed. Now you say that the royal dignity might be so easily
obtained :—is king Wăn then not a sufficient object for imitation?'

8. *Mencius* said, 'How can king Wăn be matched? From T'ang
to Wû-ting there had appeared six or seven worthy and sage
sovereigns. The kingdom had been attached to Yin for a long time,
and this length of time made a change difficult. Wû-ting had all the
princes coming to his court, and possessed the kingdom as if it had
been a thing which he moved round in his palm. *Then,* Châu was
removed from Wû-ting by no great interval of time. There were
still remaining some of the ancient families and of the old manners,
of the influence also which had emanated *from the earlier sovereigns,*
and of their good government. Moreover, there were the viscount of

introduces a new subject, and a stronger one for
the point in hand. King Wăn died at 97.—
Ch'ǎu uses the round number. 今言王
若易然。~今言王齊若是之易
然, 'Now you say that Ch'î might be raised to
the royal sway thus easily.' 8. From T'ang to
Wû-ting (B.C. 1765-1323) there were altogether

eighteen sovereigns, exclusive of themselves,
and from Wû-ting to Châu (1323-1153) seven.
朝 (*ch'ǎo*), and tone, used as in Bk. I. Pt. I. vii.
16, *et al.* 微子, 比干, 箕子,—see Ana-
lects, XVIII. i. The latter two are 王子,
as being uncles of Châu, 'royal sons.' 徽仲

又有微子微仲王子比干箕
子膠鬲皆賢人也相與輔相
之故久而後失之也尺地莫
非其有也一民莫非其臣也
然而文王猶方百里起是以
難也齊人有言曰雖有智慧
不如乘勢雖有鎡基不如待
時今時則易然也夏后殷周
之盛地未有過千里者也而
齊有其地矣雞鳴狗吠相聞

Wei and his second son, their Royal Highnesses Pî-kan and the
viscount of Ch'î, and Kâo-ko, all men of ability and virtue, who gave
their joint assistance to Châu *in his government*. In consequence
of these things, it took a long time for him to lose *the throne*. There
was not a foot of ground which he did not possess. There was not
one of all the people who was not his subject. So it was on *his
side*, and king Wǎn at his beginning had only a territory of one
hundred square *lî*. On all these accounts, it was difficult for him
immediately to attain to the royal dignity.

9. 'The people of Ch'î have a saying—"A man may have wisdom
and discernment, but that is not like embracing the favourable
opportunity. A man may have instruments of husbandry, but that
is not like waiting for the *farming* seasons." The present time is
one in which *the royal dignity* may be easily attained.

10. 'In the flourishing periods of the Hsiâ, Yin, and Châu
dynasties, *the royal* domain did not exceed a thousand *lî*, and
Ch'î embraces so much territory. Cocks crow and dogs bark to

was the second son (some say brother) of 微子
Kâo-ko was a distinguished man and minister
of the time,—whose worth was first discovered
by king Wǎn, but who continued loyal to the
House of Yin. 輔相,—相, 4th tone. 失
之,-之 refers to the throne. 文王猶

方云云,—猶, the opp. of former cases,
takes the place of 由. 9. 鎡基,—written
variously, 兹基 鎡錤,—was the name
for a hoe. 10. 夏后, 殷, 周, see Analects,
III. xxi. 辟=闢. The last sentence, as in

而達乎四境而齊有其民矣
地不改辟矣民不改聚矣行
仁政而王莫之能禦也且王
者之不作未有疏於此時者
也民之憔悴於虐政未有甚
於此時者也饑者易為食渴
者易為飲孔子曰德之流行
速於置郵而傳命當今之時
萬乘之國行仁政民之悅之
猶解倒懸也故事半古之人

one another, all the way to the four borders of the State:—so Ch'î possesses the people. No change is needed for the enlarging of its territory: no change is needed for the collecting of a population. If its ruler will put in practice a benevolent government, no power will be able to prevent his becoming sovereign.

11. 'Moreover, never was there a time farther removed than the present from the rise of a true sovereign: never was there a time when the sufferings of the people from tyrannical government were more intense than the present. The hungry readily partake of any food, and the thirsty of any drink.

12. 'Confucius said, "The flowing progress of virtue is more rapid than the transmission of *royal* orders by stages and couriers."

13. 'At the present time, in a country of ten thousand chariots, let benevolent government be put in practice, and the people will be delighted with it, as if they were relieved from hanging by the heels. With half the merit of the ancients, double their achievements

Bk. I. Pt. I. vii. 3. 11. The 爲 in 易爲 食, 易爲飲 is perplexing. We might put it in the 3rd tone, and 食 and 飮 in the same. But in Bk. VII. Pt. I. xxvii, we have the expressions 飢者甘食, 渴者甘 飮, where 食 and 飮 must have their ordinary tones. Stress therefore is not to be laid on the 爲. Perhaps the expressions = 'easily do eating, easily do drinking. 12. The distinction between 置 and 郵 is much disputed. Some make the former a foot-post, but that is unlikely. It denotes the slower conveyance of despatches, and the other the more rapid. So much seems plain. See the 集證, *in loc.* 13. 猶解倒懸.—Chû Hsî simply

孟賁遠矣。曰是不
曰若是、則夫子過
否、我四十不動心。
動心否乎。孟子曰、
王不異矣。如此、則
行道焉、雖由此霸
子加齊之卿相、得
二公孫丑問曰、夫
爲然。
功必倍之、惟此時

is sure to be realized. It is only at this time that such could be the case.'

CHAP. II. 1. Kung-sun Ch'âu asked *Mencius*, saying, 'Master, if you were to be appointed a high noble and the prime minister of Ch'î, so as to be able to carry *your* principles into practice, though you should thereupon raise the ruler to the headship of all the other princes, or *even* to the royal dignity, it would not be to be wondered at.—In such a position would your mind be perturbed or not?' Mencius replied, 'No. At forty, I attained to an unperturbed mind.'

2. *Ch'âu* said, 'Since it is so with you, my Master, you are far beyond Măng Păn.' 'The *mere* attainment,' said *Mencius*, 'is not

says:—倒懸喻困苦。'倒懸' expresses bitter suffering.' Literally, it is 'as if they were loosed from being turned upside down and suspended.'

2. THAT MENCIUS HAD ATTAINED TO AN UNPERTURBED MIND; THAT THE MEANS BY WHICH HE HAD DONE SO WAS HIS KNOWLEDGE OF WORDS AND THE NOURISHMENT OF HIS PASSION-NATURE; AND THAT IN THIS HE WAS A FOLLOWER OF CONFUCIUS. The chapter is divided into four parts:—the first, pars. 1–8, showing generally that there are various ways to attain an unperturbed mind; the second, pars. 9, 10, exposing the error of the way taken by the philosopher Kâo; the third, pars. 11–17, unfolding Mencius's own way; and the fourth, pars. 18–28, showing that Mencius followed Confucius, and praising that Sage as the first of mortals. It is chiefly owing to what Mencius says in this chapter about the nourishment of the passion-nature, that a place has been accorded to him among the sages of China, or in immediate proximity to them. His views are substantially these:—Man's nature is composite; he possesses moral and intellectual powers (comprehended by Mencius under the term 心 'heart,' 'mind,' interchanged with 志, 'the will'), and active powers (summed up under the term 氣, and embracing generally the emotions, desires, appetites). The moral and intellectual powers ought to be supreme and govern, but there is a close connexion between them and the others which give effect to them. The active powers may not be stunted, for then the whole character will be feeble. But on the other hand, they must not be allowed to take the lead. They must get their tone from the mind, and the way to develop them in all their completeness is to do good. Let them be vigorous, and the mind clear and pure, and we shall have the man, whom nothing external to himself can perturb,—Horace's *justum et tenacem propositi virum*. In brief, if we take the *sanum corpus* of the Roman adage, as not expressing the mere physical *body*, but the emotional and physical nature, what Mencius exhibits here, may be said to be '*mens sana in corpore sano.*' The attentive reader will, I think, find the above thoughts dispersed through this chapter, and be able to separate them from the irrelevant matter (that especially relating to Confucius), with which they are put forth. 1. 加, 'to add,' and generally 'to confer upon,' is here to be taken passively,—'If on you were conferred the dignity of, &c. 相, 4th tone.

難告子先我不動心。

曰不動心有道乎曰。

有北宮黝之養勇也。

不膚撓不目逃思以

一毫挫於人若撻之

於市朝不受於褐寬

博亦不受於萬乘之

君視刺萬乘之君若

刺褐夫無嚴諸侯惡

聲至必反之孟施舍

difficult. The scholar Kâo had attained to an unperturbed mind at an earlier period of life than I did.'

3. *Ch'âu* asked, 'Is there any way to an unperturbed mind?' The answer was, 'Yes.

4. 'Pî-kung Yû had this way of nourishing his valour:—He did not flinch from any strokes at his body. He did not turn his eyes aside from any thrusts at them. He considered that the slightest push from any one was the same as if he were beaten *before the crowds* in the market-place, and that what he would not receive from *a common man* in his loose large garments of hair, neither should he receive from a prince of ten thousand chariots. He viewed stabbing a prince of ten thousand chariots just as stabbing a fellow dressed in cloth of hair. He feared not any of all the princes. A bad word addressed to him he always returned.

5. 'Măng Shih-shê had this way of nourishing his valour:—

卿相 are not to be separated by an *or*, as 霸王 must be; see on 公卿, Analects, IX. xv. Ch'âu's meaning is that, with so great an office and heavy a charge, the mind might well be perturbed:—would it be so with his master? With Mencius's reply, compare Confucius's account of himself, Analects, II. iv. 3. 2. Măng Pân was a celebrated bravo, who could pull the horn from an ox's head, and feared no man. Kâo is the same who gives the name to the 6th Book of Mencius. 是不難 is not to be understood so much with reference to the case of Măng Pân, as to the attainment of an unperturbed mind, without reference to the way of attaining to it. 3. 道 here = 方法,'way,' or 'method.' 4. Pî-kung Yû was a bravo, belonging probably to Wei (衞), and con-

nected with its ruling family. 不膚撓 (and tone), 不目逃, literally, 'not akin bend, not eye avoid.' The meaning is not that he had first been wounded in those parts, and still was indifferent to the pain, but that he would press forward, careless of all risks. 思 covers down to 視. 一毫挫, = 'the least push,' = disgrace. 市朝 (*ch'áo*, and tone) are not to be separated, and made—'the market-place or the court.' The latter character is used, because anciently the different parties in the markets were arranged in their respective ranks and places, as the officers in the court. But compare Analects, XIV. xxxviii. L 褐 寬博 = 褐寬博之夫 (or 賤) 5. There is a difficulty with the 施 in 孟施

也曰視不勝猶勝
俊進慮勝而後會
否也舍豈能為必
懼而已矣孟施舍
昔黝似子夏夫二
知其孰賢然而孟
也昔者曾子謂子
男乎吾嘗聞大勇
自反而不縮雖褐
自反而縮雖

He said, "I look upon not conquering and conquering in the same way. To measure the enemy and then advance; to calculate the chances of victory and then engage:—this is to stand in awe of the opposing force. How can I make certain of conquering? I can only rise superior to all fear."

6. 'Măng Shih-shĕ resembled the philosopher Tsăng. Pi-kung Yŭ resembled Tsze-hsiă. I do not know to the valour of which of the two the superiority should be ascribed, but yet Măng Shih-shĕ attended to what was of the greater importance.

7. 'Formerly, the philosopher Tsăng said to Tsze-hsiang, "Do you love valour? I heard an account of great valour from the Master. It speaks thus:—'If, on self-examination, I find that I am not upright, shall I not be in fear even of a poor man in his loose garments of hair-cloth? If, on self-examination, I find that I am upright, I will go forward against thousands and tens of thousands.'"

舍,—this gentleman in the end of the paragraph simply calls himself 舍. Hence the 施 is taken like our 'Mr.';—Măng Hsien-shĕ. The usage of *A* before the name, especially in the south of China, is analogous to this. Notwithstanding the 所 in the first clause of this paragraph, we need not translate differently from the first clause of the preceding. 三軍,—see Ana-lects, VII. x. u; used here simply for 'the enemy.' 就賢,—as in last chapter.

Pi-kung Yŭ thought of others,—of conquering; Măng Shih-shĕ of himself,—of not being afraid. The basis of the reference to the two disciples is the commonly received idea of their several characters. Tsăng Shĕn was reflective, and dealt with himself. Tsze-hsiă was ambitious, and would not willingly be inferior to others. 7. Tsze-hsiang was a disciple of Tsăng. 縮,—properly, the straight seams from the top to the edge, with which an ancient cap was made, metaphorically used for 'straight,' 'upright.' 吾不縮焉 否者不惴

千萬人吾往矣孟施舍之
守氣又不如曾子之守約
也曰敢問夫子之不動心
與告子之不動心可得聞
與告子曰不得於言勿求
於心不得於心勿求於氣
不得於言勿求於心不可
得於言勿求於心不可夫
志氣之帥也氣體之充也
夫志至焉氣次焉故曰持

8. 'Yet, what Măng Shih-shê maintained, being *merely* his physical energy, was after all inferior to what the philosopher Tsăng maintained, which was *indeed* of the most importance.'

9. *Kung-sun Ch'âu* said, 'May I venture to ask an explanation from you, Master, of how you maintain an unperturbed mind, and how the philosopher Kâo does the same?' *Mencius answered*, 'Kâo says,—"What is not attained in words is not to be sought for in the mind; what produces dissatisfaction in the mind, is not to be helped by passion-effort." *This last*,—when there is unrest in the mind, not to seek for relief from passion-effort, may be conceded. But not to seek in the mind for what is not attained in words cannot be conceded. The will is the leader of the passion-nature. The passion-nature pervades and animates the body. The will is *first and* chief, and the passion-nature is subordinate to it. Therefore *I* say,—Maintain firm the will, and do no violence to the passion-nature.'

焉, the interrogation being denoted by the tone of the voice. Still the 焉 is the final particle, and not the initial 'how,' with a different tone, as Julien supposes. 8. Here we first meet the character 氣, so important in this chapter. Its different meanings may be seen in Morrison and Medhurst. Originally it was the same as 气, 'cloudy vapour.' With the addition of 米, 'rice,' or 火, 'fire,' which was an old form, it should indicate 'steam of rice,' or 'steam' generally. The sense in which Mencius uses it is indicated in the translation and in the preliminary note. The sense springs from its being used as correlate to 心, 'the mind,' taken in connexion with the idea of 'energy' inherent in it, from its composition. Thus it signifies the lower portion of man's constitution; and here, that lower part in its lowest sense,—animal vigour or courage. The 又 refers to what had been conceded to Shê in par. 6. I translate as if there were a comma or pause after the two 守. 9. Kâo's principle seems to have been this,—utter indifference to everything external, and entire passivity of mind. Modern writers say that in his words is to be found the essence of Buddhism,—that

問何謂浩然之氣曰
善養吾浩然之氣敢
惡乎長曰我知言我
反動其心敢問夫子
蹶者趨者是氣也而
氣壹則動志也今夫
何也曰志壹則動氣
持其志無暴其氣者
志至焉氣次焉又曰、
其志無暴其氣既曰、

10. *Ch'âu observed*, 'Since you say—" The will is chief, and the passion-nature is subordinate," how do you also say, "Maintain firm the will, and do no violence to the passion-nature?"' *Mencius* replied, 'When it is the will alone which is active, it moves the passion-nature. When it is the passion-nature alone which is active, it moves the will. For instance now, in the case of a man falling or running, that is from the passion-nature, and yet it moves the mind.'

11. 'I venture to ask,' *said Ch'âu again*, 'wherein you, Master, surpass *Kâo*.' *Mencius* told him, 'I understand words; I am skilful in nourishing my vast, flowing passion-nature.'

12. *Ch'âu* pursued, 'I venture to ask what you mean by your vast, flowing passion-nature!' The reply was, 'It is difficult to describe it.

the object of his attainment was the Buddhistic *nirvâna*, and perhaps this helps us to a glimpse of his meaning. Commentators take sides on 不得於言, whether the 'words' are Kâo's own words, or those of others. To me it is hardly doubtful that they must be taken as the words of others. Mencius's account of himself below, as 'knowing words,' seems to require this. At the same time, a reference to Kâo's arguments with Mencius, in Bk. VI, where he changes the form of his assertions, without seeming to be aware of their refutation, gives some plausibility to the other view. Châo Ch'î understands the expression thus :—'If men's words are bad, I will not inquire about their hearts ; if their hearts are bad, I will not inquire about their words!' The 可 is not an approval of Kâo's second proposition, but a concession of it simply as not so bad as his first. Mencius goes on to show wherein he considered it as defective. From his language here, and in the next paragraph, we see that he uses 志 and 心 synonymously. 氣=體之充.— 'the 氣 is the filling up of the body.' 氣 might seem here to be little more than the 'breath,' but that meaning would come altogether short of the term throughout the chapter. 10. Ch'âu did not understand what his master had said about the relation between the mind and the passion-nature, and as the latter was subordinate, would have had it disregarded altogether :—hence his question. Mencius shows that the passion-nature is really a part of our constitution, acts upon the mind, and is acted on by it, and may not be disregarded. 壹—專—. The 反 meets Châu's disregard of the passion-nature, as not worth attending to. 11. The illustration here is not a very happy one, leading us to think of 氣 in its merely material signification, as in the last paragraph. On 知言, see par. 17. On 浩然之氣 there is much vain babbling in the commentaries, to show how the 氣 of heaven and earth

然宋人有閔其苗之不長
勿忘勿助長也無若宋人
之也必有事焉而勿正心
曰告子未嘗知義以其外
有不慊於心則餒矣我故
生者非義襲而取之也行
與道無是餒也是集義所
天地之間其爲氣也配義
剛以直養而無害則塞于
難言也其爲氣也至大至

13. 'This is the passion-nature:—It is exceedingly great, and exceedingly strong. Being nourished by rectitude, and sustaining no injury, it fills up all between heaven and earth.

14. 'This is the passion-nature:—It is the mate and assistant of righteousness and reason. Without it, *man* is in a state of starvation.

15. 'It is produced by the accumulation of righteous deeds; it is not to be obtained by incidental acts of righteousness. If the mind does not feel complacency in the conduct, *the nature* becomes starved. I therefore said, "Kâo has never understood righteousness, because he makes it something external."

16. 'There must be the *constant* practice *of this righteousness*, but without the object *of thereby nourishing the passion-nature*. Let not the mind forget *its work*, but let there be no assisting the growth *of that nature*. Let us not be like the man of Sung. There was a man of Sung, who was grieved that his growing corn was not

is the 氣 also of man. Mencius, it seems to me, has before his mind the ideal of a perfect man, complete in all the parts of his constitution. It is this which gives its elevation to his language. 13. 以直養,—as in parr. 7, 15; 無害,—as in the latter part of par. 15. 塞 is here in the sense of 'to fill up,' not 'to stop up.' Still the 塞乎天地之間 is one of those hæsic expressions, which fill the ear, but do not inform the mind. 14. A pause must be made after the 是, which refers to the 浩然之氣. 餒 refers to 體, in 體之充, in

par. 9. It is better, however, in the translation, to supply 'man,' than 'body.' 15. 襲, 'to take an enemy by surprise;' and 義襲 = 'incidental acts of righteousness.' 餒 refers to the passion-nature itself. The analysis of conduct and feeling here is very good. Mencius's sentiment is just, *The conscience makes cowards of us all*. On the latter sentence, see Bk. VI. v. *et al*. 16. I have given the meaning of the text—必有事焉 而勿正心 勿忘 勿助長 after Châo Ch'î, to whom Chû Hsî also inclines. But for their help, we

窮生於其心害於其政發於
邪辭知其所離遁辭知其所
辭知其所蔽淫辭知其所陷
益而又害之何謂知言曰詖
助之長者揠苗者也非徒無
無益而舍之者不耘苗者也
下之不助苗長者寡矣以爲
子趨而往視之苗則槁矣天
曰今日病矣予助苗長矣其
而揠之者芒芒然歸謂其人

longer, and so he pulled it up. *Having done this*, he returned home, looking very stupid, and said to his people, "I am tired to-day. I have been helping the corn to grow long." His son ran to look at it, and found the corn all withered. There are few in the world, *who do not deal with their passion-nature, as if* they were assisting the corn to grow long. Some indeed consider it of no benefit to them, and let it alone:—they do not weed their corn. They who assist it to grow long, pull out their corn. *What they do is* not only of no benefit *to the nature*, but it also injures it.'

17. *Kung-sun Ch'âu further asked*, 'What do you mean by saying that you understand *whatever* words *you hear?' Mencius* replied, 'When words are one-sided, I know how *the mind of the speaker* is clouded over. When words are extravagant, I know how *the mind* is fallen and sunk. When words are all-depraved, I know how *the mind* has departed *from principle*. When words are evasive, I know how *the mind* is at its wit's end. *These evils* growing in the mind,

should hardly know what to make of it. 正 is taken in the sense of 預期, 'to do with anticipation of, or a view to, an ulterior object.' This meaning of the term is supported by an example from the 春秋傳. 病 = 'tired.' 17. Here, as sometimes before, we miss the preliminary 曰, noting a question by Mencius's interlocutor, and the same omission is frequent in all the rest of the chapter. I have supplied the lacunae after Chû Hsî, who himself follows Lin Chih-ch'î (林之奇), a scholar, who died A.D. 1176. Châo Ch'î sometimes errs egregiously in the last part, through not distinguishing the speakers. With regard to the first ground of Mencius's superiority over Kâo, —his 'knowledge of words,' as he is briefer than on the other, so he is still less satisfactory, —to my mind at least. Perhaps he means to

其政害於其事聖人復
起必從吾言矣宰我子
貢善爲說辭冉牛閔子
顏淵善言德行孔子兼
之曰我於辭命則不能
也然則夫子既聖矣乎
曰惡是何言也昔者子
貢問於孔子曰夫子聖
矣乎孔子曰聖則吾不
能我學不厭而教不倦

do injury to government, and, displayed in the government, are hurtful to the conduct of affairs. When a Sage shall again arise, he will certainly follow my words.'

18. *On this Ch'âu observed*, 'Tsâi Wo and Tsze-kung were skilful in speaking. Zan Niû, the disciple Min, and Yen Yüan, while their words were good, were distinguished for their virtuous conduct. Confucius united the qualities of the disciples in himself, *but still* he said, "In the matter of speeches, I am not competent."—Then, Master, have you attained to be a Sage?'

19. *Mencius* said, 'Oh! what words are these? Formerly Tszekung asked Confucius, saying, "Master, are you a Sage?" Confucius answered him, "A Sage is what I cannot rise to. I learn without satiety, and teach without being tired." Tsze-kung said, "You learn without satiety:—that shows your wisdom. You teach without

say, that however great the dignity to which he might be raised, his knowledge of words, and ability in referring incorrect and injurious speeches to the mental defects from which they sprang, would keep him from being deluded, and preserve his mind unperturbed. One of the scholars Ch'êng uses this illustration:—'Mencius with his knowledge of words was like a man seated aloft on the dais, who can distinguish all the movements of the people below the hall, which he could not do, if it were necessary for him to descend and mingle with the crowd.' The concluding remark gives rise to the rest of the chapter, it seeming to Ch'âu that Mencius placed himself by it on the platform of sages. 18. Compare Analects, XI. ii. 2, to the enumeration in which of the excellences of several of Confucius's disciples there seems to be here a reference. There, however, it is said that Zan Niû, Min, and Yen Yüan were distinguished for

德行, and here we have the addition of 善言, which give a good deal of trouble. Some take 言 as a verb,—'were skilful to speak of virtuous conduct.' So the Tartar version, according to Julien. Sun Shih makes it a noun, as I do. The references to the disciples are quite inept. The point of Châu's inquiry lies in Confucius's remark, found nowhere else, and obscure enough. He thinks Mencius is taking more to himself than Confucius did. Châo Ch'î, however, takes 我於辭云云 as a remark of Mencius, but it is quite unnatural to do so. Observe the force of the 既,—*you have come to be.* 19. 惡, in 1st tone; an exclamation, not interrogative. This conversation with Tszekung is not found in the Analects. Compare

何不不姑淵有夫倦也
事使同舍則聖聖仁子
非治道是具人孔也貢
君則非曰體之子子曰
何進其伯而一不且學
使亂君夷微體居智不
非則不伊敢冉是夫厭
民退事尹問牛何子智
治伯非何所閔言既也
亦夷其如安子也聖教
進也民曰顏昔矣不

窃聞之子夏子游子張皆
者聖人之一體

being tired :—that shows your benevolence. Benevolent and wise :
—Master, you ARE a Sage." Now, since Confucius would not allow
himself to be regarded as a Sage, what words were those?'

20. *Ch'âu said*, 'Formerly, I once heard this :—Tsze-hsiâ, Tsze-yû,
and Tsze-chang had each one member of the Sage. Zan Niû, the
disciple Min, and Yen Yüan had all the members, but in small
proportions. I venture to ask,—With which of these are you pleased
to rank yourself?'

21. *Mencius* replied, ' Let us drop speaking about these, if you
please.'

22. *Ch'âu then* asked, ' What do you say of Po-î and Î Yin?'
' Their ways were different *from mine,*' said *Mencius.* ' Not to serve
a prince whom he did not esteem, nor command a people whom he
did not approve; in a time of good government to take office, and
on the occurrence of confusion to retire :—this was *the way of* Po-î.
To say—" Whom may I not serve? My serving him makes him my
ruler. What people may I not command? My commanding them

Analects, VII. ii, xxviii, which latter chapter
may possibly be another version of what Mencius says here. 20. 竊 is used with other
verbs to give a deferential tone to what they say.
21. Compare Bk. I. Pt. II. xxi. Does Mencius
here indicate that he thought himself superior
to all the worthies referred to—even to Yen
Yüan? Hardly so much as that; but that he
could not be content with them for his model.

22. Po-î.—see Analects, V. xxii. Î Yin,— see
Analects, XII. xxii. 非其君,非其民,—
the emphatic *his,* i. e. as paraphrased in the
translation. 何事非君何使非民
-得君 則事,何所事而非
我 君,得民則使,何所使而

亂亦進伊尹也、可以仕則仕、
可以止則止可以久則久、可
以速則速孔子也皆古聖人
也吾未能有行焉乃所願則
學孔子也伯夷伊尹於孔子
若是班乎曰否自有生民以
來未有孔子也曰然則有同
與曰有得百里之地而君之、
皆能以朝諸侯有天下行一
不義殺一不辜而得天下皆

makes them my people." In a time of good government to take office, and when disorder prevailed, also to take office :—that was *the way of* Î Yin. When it was proper to go into office, then to go into it; when it was proper to keep retired from office. then to keep retired from it ; when it was proper to continue in it long, then to continue in it long ; when it was proper to withdraw from it quickly, then to withdraw quickly :—that was *the way of* Confucius. These were all sages of antiquity, and I have not attained to do what they did. But what I wish to do is to learn to be like Confucius.'

23. *Ch'âu said*, 'Comparing Po-î and Î Yin with Confucius, are they to be placed in the same rank ?' *Mencius* replied, 'No. Since there were living men until now, there never was *another* Confucius.'

24. *Ch'âu* said, 'Then, did they have *any points of* agreement *with him?*' The reply was,—'Yes. If they had been sovereigns over a hundred *lî* of territory, they would, all of them, have brought all the princes to attend in their court, and have obtained the throne. And none of them, in order to obtain the throne. would have committed one act of unrighteousness, or put to death one innocent person. In those things they agreed with him.'

非我民. I have given the meaning, but the conciseness of the text makes it difficult to a learner. The different ways of Po-î, Î Yin, and Confucius are thus expressed :—'The principle of the first was purity—以清爲其 道; that of the second was office—以任爲 其道; that of the third was what the time required—以時爲其道.' 23. The meaning of this paragraph is expressed rightly in the

之於走獸鳳凰之於飛鳥泰
子也有若曰豈惟民哉麒麟
能違也自生民以來未有夫
百世之後等百世之王莫之
知其政聞其樂而知其德由
堯舜遠矣子貢曰見其禮而
宰我曰以予觀於夫子賢於
以知聖人汙不至阿其所好
以異曰宰我子貢有若智足
不爲也是則同曰敢問其所

25. *Ch'âu* said, 'I venture to ask wherein he differed from them.' *Mencius* replied, 'Tsâi Wo, Tsze-kung, and Yû Zo had wisdom sufficient to know the sage. *Even had they been ranking themselves* low, they would not have demeaned themselves to flatter their favourite.

26. '*Now*, Tsâi Wo said, "According to my view of our Master, he was far superior to Yâo and Shun."

27. 'Tsze-kung said, "By viewing the ceremonial ordinances *of a prince*, we know *the character of* his government. By hearing his music, we know *the character of* his virtue. After the lapse of a hundred ages I can arrange, according to their merits, the kings of a hundred ages;—not one of them can escape me. From the birth of mankind till now, there has never been *another* like our Master."

28. 'Yû Zo said, "Is it only among men that it is so? There is the Ch'î-lin among quadrupeds, the Fǎng-hwang among birds, the

translation. If we understand a 之 before the 於, then the idiom is like that of 之 於, in Bk. I. Pt. I. iii. 1. 25. 汙,—*wû*, or *wâ*, 'low-lying water,' used here simply for 'low,' with reference to the wisdom of Tsâi Wo and Tsze-kung, in their own estimation. 阿 in the sense of 'partial,' = 'to flatter.' 26. With this and the two next paragraphs, compare the eulogium of Confucius, in the *Chung Yung*, chaps. 30-32, and Analects, XIX. xxiii-xxv. 鳳凰 — see Analects, XI. ix. 28. The *ch'î is* properly the male, and the *lin*, the female of the animal referred to;—a monster, with a deer's body, an ox's tail, and a horse's feet, which appears to greet the birth of a sage, or the reign of a sage sovereign. Both in 麒麟 and 鳳凰, the names of the male and female are put together,

力服人者非心服也力
七十里文王以百里。
仁者王文王不待大湯以
霸霸必有大國以德行
孟子曰以力假仁者
盛於孔子也。
其萃自生民以來未有
亦類也出於其類拔乎
行潦類也聖人之於民、
山之於丘垤河海之於

Tâi mountain among mounds and ant-hills, and rivers and seas among rain-pools. *Though different in degree, they are* the same in kind. So the sages among mankind are also the same in kind. But they stand out from their fellows, and rise above the level, and from the birth of mankind till now, there never has been one so complete as Confucius."'

CHAP. III. 1. Mencius said, 'He who, using force, makes a pretence to benevolence is the leader of the princes. A leader *of the* princes requires a large kingdom. He who, using virtue, practises benevolence is the sovereign of the kingdom. To become the sovereign of the kingdom, *a prince* need not wait for a large *kingdom*. T'ang did it with *only* seventy *li*, and king Wăn with *only* a hundred.

2. 'When one by force subdues men, they do not submit to him in heart. *They submit, because* their strength is not adequate *to resist*

to indicate one individual of either sex. The image in 拔乎其萃 is that of stalks of grass or grain, shooting high above the level of the waving field. 未有盛於孔子,—'there has not been one more complete than Confucius.' But this would be no more than putting Confucius on a level with other sages. I have therefore translated after the example of Chû Hsî, who says—自古聖人,固 皆異於眾人,然未有如孔子 之盛者也. That 於＝如 is one of the explanations of the character given by 王 引之, in his Treatise on the Particles.

3. THE DIFFERENCE BETWEEN A CHIEFTAIN OF

THE PRINCES AND A SOVEREIGN OF THE KINGDOM ; AND BETWEEN SUBMISSION SECURED BY FORCE AND THAT PRODUCED BY VIRTUE. 1. 霸 and 王 are here the recognised titles and not＝'to acquire the chieftaincy,' 'to acquire the sovereignty.' In the 集證, we find much said on the meaning of the two characters. 王 is from three strokes (三), denoting heaven, earth, and man, with a fourth stroke, ── or unity, going through them, grasping and uniting them together, thus affording the highest possible conception of power or ability. 霸 is synonymous with 伯, and of kindred meaning with the words, of nearly the same sound, 把, 'to

不贍也、以德服人者、中
心悅而誠服也、如七十
子之服孔子也、詩云、自
西自東、自南自北、無思
不服、此之謂也。
孟子曰、仁則榮、不仁
則辱、今惡辱而居不仁
是猶惡溼而居下也。如
惡之莫如貴德而尊士、
賢者在位、能者在職、國

When one subdues men by virtue, in their hearts' core they are pleased, and sincerely submit, as was the case with the seventy disciples in their submission to Confucius. What is said in the Book of Poetry,

"From the west, from the east,
From the south, from the north,
There was not one who thought of refusing submission,"
is an illustration of this.'

CHAP. IV. 1. Mencius said, 'Benevolence brings glory *to a prince*, and the opposite of it brings disgrace. For *the princes of* the present day to hate disgrace and yet to live complacently doing what is not benevolent, is like hating moisture and yet living in a low situation.

2. 'If *a prince* hates disgrace, the best course for him to pursue, is to esteem virtue and honour *virtuous* scholars, giving the worthiest among them places *of dignity*, and the able offices *of trust*. When throughout his kingdom there is leisure and rest *from external*

grasp with the hand,' and 迫, 'to urge,' 'to press.' 2. 力不贍 is translated by Julien, —'*quia nempe vires* (i. e. *vis armorum*) *ad id obtinendum non sufficiunt.*' Possibly some Chinese commentators may have sanctioned such an interpretation, but it has nowhere come under my notice. The 'seventy disciples' is giving a round number, the enumeration of them differing in different works. We find them reckoned at 73, 76, &c. See in the prolegomena to vol. i, p. 112. For the ode see the Shih-ching, III. i. Ode X. st. 6, celebrating the influence of the kings Wǎn and Wǔ. The four quarters are to be viewed from Hâo (鎬), king Wǔ's capital. 思 is not to be taken as an abstract noun, = 'thought.'

鄒浩, a statesman and scholar of the eleventh century, says on this chapter:—'He who subdues men by force, has the intention of subduing them, and they dare not but submit. He who subdues men by virtue, has no intention to subdue them, and they cannot but submit. From antiquity downwards there have been many dissertations on the leaders of the princes, and the true sovereign, but none so deep, incisive, and perspicuous as this chapter.'

4. GLORY IS THE SURE RESULT OF BENEVOLENT GOVERNMENT. CALAMITY AND HAPPINESS ARE MEN'S OWN SEEKING. 1. 居不仁, literally, 'to dwell in not-benevolence,' i. e. complacently to go on in the practice of what is not benevolent. 2. 莫如 covers as far as to 政刑,

無樂之道予緆天雖家
不怠今平孔繆之大閒
自敖國能子尸未國暇
己是家治曰今陰必及
求自閒其爲此雨畏是
之求暇國此下徹之時
者禍及家詩民彼矣明
詩也是誰者或桑詩其
云○福時敢其敢土云政
永○五般侮知侮綢迨刑○三

troubles, let him, taking advantage of such a season, clearly *digest* the
principles of his government with its legal sanctions, and then even
great kingdoms will be constrained to stand in awe of him.

3. 'It is said in the Book of Poetry,
  " Before the heavens were dark with rain,
  I gathered the bark from the roots of the mulberry trees,
  And wove it closely to form the window and door *of my nest;*
  Now, *I thought,* ye people below,
  Perhaps ye will not dare to insult me."
Confucius said, " Did not he who made this ode understand the way
of governing?" If a prince is able rightly to govern his kingdom,
who will dare to insult him?

4. ' But now *the princes* take advantage of the time when throughout their kingdoms there is leisure and rest *from external troubles,*
to abandon themselves to pleasure and indolent indifference ;—they
in fact seek for calamities for themselves.

5. ' Calamity and happiness in all cases are men's own seeking.

and 賢者在位 and the next clause are
to be taken as in apposition simply with the
one preceding See the Doctrine of the Mean,
chap. xx. The 賢者在位 here corresponds to the 尊賢 there, and the 能者
在職 may embrace both the 敬大臣 and
the 體羣臣. 刑,—not punishments, but
penal laws. 3. See the Shih-ching, I. xv. Ode II.

st. 2, where for 今此下民 we have 今
女下民, the difference not affecting the
sense. The ode is an appeal by some small bird
to an owl not to destroy its nest, which bird, in
Mencius's application of the words, is made to
represent a wise prince taking all precautionary
measures. 4. 般,—read *p'an,* and tone, nearly
synonymous with the next character,—樂 (*lo*).
6. For the ode see the Shih-ching, III. i. Ode I.

皆　而　朝　士　俊　圖　謂
悅　不　矣　皆　傑　孟　也。
而　廛　市　悅　在　子
願　則　廛　而　位　曰、
藏　天　而　願　則　尊
於　下　不　立　天　賢
其　之　征　於　下　使
市　商　法　其　之　能、

言
配
命、
自
求
多
福、
太
甲
曰、
天
作
孽
猶
可
違、
自
作
孽
不
可
活
此
之

6. 'This is illustrated by what is said in the Book of Poetry,—

  "Be always studious to be in harmony with the ordinances
    of God,

  So you will certainly get for yourself much happiness;"

and by the passage of the Tâi Chiah,—" When Heaven sends down
calamities, it is still possible to escape from them; when we occasion
the calamities ourselves, it is not possible any longer to live.'''

CHAP. V. 1. Mencius said, 'If *a ruler* give honour to men of
talents and virtue and employ the able, so that offices shall all be
filled by individuals of distinction and mark;—then all the scholars
of the kingdom will be pleased, and wish to stand in his court.

2. 'If, in the market-place *of his capital,* he levy a ground-rent
on the shops but do not tax the goods, or enforce the proper regulations without levying a ground-rent;—then all the traders of the
kingdom will be pleased, and wish to store their goods in his
market-place.

at. 6. 言 念, 'to think of.' For the other
quotation, see the Shû-ching, IV. v. Sect. II. 3,
where we have 逭, 'to escape,' for 活, but
the meaning is the same.

5. VARIOUS POINTS OF TRUE ROYAL GOVERNMENT
NEGLECTED BY THE PRINCES OF MENCIUS'S TIME,
ATTENTION TO WHICH WOULD SURELY CARRY ANY
ONE OF THEM TO THE ROYAL THRONE. 1. Compare
last chapter, par. 2. The wisest among 1,000 men
is called 俊; the wisest among ten is called 傑.
Numbers, however, do not enter into the signification of the terms here. 天下之士
云云.—compare Bk. I. Pt. I. vii. 18. 2. 廛,
'a shop, or market-stance,' is used here as a verb,
'to levy ground-rent for such a shop.' Accord-

ing to Chû Hsî, in the 語類, we are to
understand the market-place here as that in
the capital, which was built on the plan of the
division of the land, after the figure of the
character 井. The middle square behind was
the 市; the centre one was occupied by the
palace; the front one by the ancestral and other
temples, government treasuries, arsenals, &c.;
and the three squares on each side were occupied by the people. He adds that, when traders
became too many, a ground-rent was levied;
when they were few, it was remitted, and only
a surveillance was exercised of the markets by
the proper officers. That surveillance extended
to the inspection of weights and measures, regulation of the price, &c. See its duties detailed

矣。關譏而不征、則天
下之旅皆悅而願出
於其路矣。耕者助而
不稅、則天下之農、皆
悅而願耕於其野矣。
廛無夫里之布、則天
下之民皆悅而願爲
之氓矣。信能行此五
者、則鄰國之民仰之
若父母矣、率其子弟

3. 'If, at his frontier-passes, there be an inspection of persons, but no taxes charged *on goods or other articles*, then all the travellers of the kingdom will be pleased, and wish to make their tours on his roads.

4. 'If he require that the husbandmen give their mutual aid *to cultivate the public field*, and exact no *other* taxes from them ;— then all the husbandmen of the kingdom will be pleased, and wish to plough in his fields.

5. 'If from the occupiers of the shops in his market-place he do not exact the fine of the individual idler, or of the hamlet's quota of cloth, then all the people of the kingdom will be pleased, and wish to come and be his people.

6. 'If *a ruler* can truly practise these five things, then the people in the neighbouring kingdoms will look up to him as a parent. From the first birth of mankind till now, never has any one led

in the Châu-lî, XIV. vii. 3. Compare Bk. I. Pt. II. v. 3; Pt. I. vii. 18. All critics refer for the illustration of this rule to the account of the duties of the 司關, in the Châu-lî, XV. xi. But from that it would appear that the levying no duties at the passes was only in bad years, and hence some have argued that Mencius's lesson was only for the emergency of the time. To avoid that conclusion, the author of 四書拓餘說 contends that the Châu-lî has been interpolated in the place,—rightly, as it seems to me. 4. The rule of 助而不稅 is the same as that of 耕者九一, Bk. I. Pt. II. v. 3. 5. It is acknowledged by commentators that it is only a vague notion which we can obtain of the meaning of this paragraph. Is 廛 to be taken as in the translation, or verbally as in the second paragraph? What was

the 夫布? And what the 里布? It appears from the Châu-lî, that there was a fine, exacted from idlers or loafers in the towns, called 夫布, and it is said that the family which did not plant mulberry trees and flax according to the rules, was condemned to pay one hamlet, or twenty-five families', quota of cloth. But 布 may be taken in the sense of money, simply = 錢, which is a signification attaching to it. We must leave the passage in the obscurity which has always rested on it. Mencius is evidently protesting against some injurious exactions of the time. 氓=民, but the addition of the character 亡 seems intended to convey the idea of the people of other States coming to put themselves under a new rule. 6. 信=實, 'truly.' Observe

治天下可運之掌上所以
忍人之心行不忍人之政
斯有不忍人之政矣以不
之心先王有不忍人之心
六孟子曰人皆有不忍人
也。
吏也然而不王者未之有
於天下無敵於天下者天
有能濟者也如此則無敵
攻其父母自生民以來未

children to attack their parent, and succeeded in his design. Thus, such a ruler will not have an enemy in all the kingdom, and he who has no enemy in the kingdom is the minister of Heaven. Never has there been a ruler in such a case who did not attain to the royal dignity.'

CHAP. VI. 1. Mencius said, 'All men have a mind which cannot bear *to see the sufferings of* others.

2. 'The ancient kings had this commiserating mind, and they, as a matter of course, had likewise a commiserating government. When with a commiserating mind was practised a commiserating government, to rule the kingdom was *as easy a matter* as to make anything go round in the palm.

the reciprocal influence of 其 in 牽其子 弟 ('sons and younger brothers'=children) and 攻其父母. 天吏,—'The minister or officer of Heaven.' On this designation the commentator 饒氏雙峰 observes:—'An officer is one commissioned by his sovereign; the officer of Heaven is he who is commissioned by Heaven. He who bears his sovereign's commission can punish men and put them to death. He may deal so with all criminals. He who bears the commission of Heaven, can execute judgment on men, and smite them. With all who are oppressing and misgoverning their kingdoms, he can deal so.'

6. THAT BENEVOLENCE, PRO-PRIETY, RIGHTEOUSNESS, AND KNOWLEDGE BELONG TO MAN AS NATURALLY AS HIS FOUR LIMBS, AND MAY AS EASILY BE EXERCISED. The assertions made in this chapter are universally true, but they are to be understood as spoken here with special reference to the oppressive ways and government of the princes of Mencius's time. 1. 不 忍 人 alone is used in Bk. I. Pt. I. vii. 4, 5, 6. is added here, because the discourse is entirely of a man's feelings, as exercised towards other men. 心,—'the mind,' embracing the whole mental constitution. The 備旨, after Châo Ch'î, says that 不忍人 means—'cannot bear to injure others.' But it is not only cannot bear to inflict suffering, but also cannot bear to see suffering. The examples in Bk. I. Pt. I. vii, make this plain. 2. 斯,—used adverbially, as in Analects, X. x. 1. 運之,—

心非人也。惻隱之心仁之
讓之心非人也無是非之
無羞惡之心非人也無辭
觀之無惻隱之心非人也、
也非惡其聲而然也。由是
非所以要譽於鄉黨朋友
以內交於孺子之父母也、
皆有怵惕惻隱之心非所
今人乍見孺子將入於井、
謂人皆有不忍人之心者、

3. 'When I say that all men have a mind which cannot bear *to see the sufferings of* others, my meaning may be illustrated thus :— even now-a-days, if men suddenly see a child about to fall into a well, they will without exception experience a feeling of alarm and distress. *They will feel so,* not as a ground on which they may gain the favour of the child's parents, nor as a ground on which they may seek the praise of their neighbours and friends, nor from a dislike to the reputation of *having been unmoved by* such a thing.

4. ' From this case we may perceive that the feeling of commiseration is essential to man, that the feeling of shame and dislike is essential to man, that the feeling of modesty and complaisance is essential to man, and that the feeling of approving and disapproving is essential to man.

5. ' The feeling of commiseration is the principle of benevolence.

之 must be taken generally, = 'a thing,' or as giving a passive signification to the verb.—'The government of the kingdom could be made to go round,' &c. Perhaps the latter construction is to be preferred. The whole is to be translated in the past sense, being descriptive of the ancient kings. 3. 孺, 'an infant at the breast,' here = 'a very young child.' 內 read as 納. 內交,—'to form a friendship with,' 'to get the favour of.' 要,—the 1st tone, = 求. 鄉黨,—compare Analects, VI. iii. 4. 今 is to be joined to 人,—'men of the present time,' in opposition 'to the former kings.'

4. The two negatives 無—非 in the different clauses make the strongest possible affirmation. Literally, 'Without the feeling of commiseration there would not be man,' &c., or ' If a person be without this, he is not a man,' &c. 惻隱 'pain and distress,' but as it is in illustration of the 不忍之心 we may render it by ' commiseration.' 'Shame and dislike,'—the *shame* is for one's own want of goodness, and the *dislike* is of the want of it in other man. 'Modesty and complaisance,'—*modesty* is the unloosing and separating from one's self, and *complaisance* is out-giving to others. 'Approving and disapproving,'—*approving* is the knowledge of goodness, and the approbation of it accordingly, and *disapproving* is the knowledge of what

端也羞惡之心義之端也
辭讓之心禮之端也是非
之心智之端也人之有是
四端也猶其有四體也有
是四端而自謂不能者自
賊者也謂其君不能者賊
其君者也凡有四端於我
者知皆擴而充之矣若火
之始然泉之始達苟能充
之足以保四海苟不充之

The feeling of shame and dislike is the principle of righteousness.
The feeling of modesty and complaisance is the principle of propriety. The feeling of approving and disapproving is the principle
of knowledge.

6. 'Men have these four principles just as they have their four
limbs. When men, having these four principles, yet say of themselves
that they cannot *develop them*, they play the thief with themselves,
and he who says of his prince that he cannot *develop them* plays
the thief with his prince.

7. 'Since all men have these four principles in themselves, let
them know to give them all their development and completion, and
the issue will be like that of fire which has begun to burn, or that
of a spring which has begun to find vent. Let them have their
complete development, and they will suffice to love and protect all

is evil, and disapprobation of it accordingly.
Such is the account of the terms in the text,
given by Chû Hsî and others. The feelings
described make up, he says, the mind of man,
and Mencius 'discoursing about commiseration
goes on to enumerate them all.' This seems to
be the true account of the introduction of the
various principles. They lie together, merely
in apposition. In the 或 問 and 語 類,
however, Chû Hsî labours to develop the other
three from the first.—Observe that 'the feeling
of shame and dislike,' &c., in the original, is—
'the mind that feels and dislikes,' &c. 5. 端
is explained by 端緒, 'the end of a clue,'
that point outside, which may be laid hold of,
and will guide us to all within. From the

feelings which he has specified, Mencius reasons
to the moral elements of our nature. It will
be seen how to 智, 'knowledge,' 'wisdom,' he
gives a moral sense. Compare Gen. ii. 17, iii.
5, 6; Job xxxviii. 36. 6. 賊,—compare Bk.
I. Pt. II. viii. 3, but we can retain its primitive
meaning in the translation. 7. 凡有四
端於我者, not 'all who have,' &c., but
'all having,' &c., 於我, *quasi dicat*, 'in their
ego-ity.' 知皆, 皆 belongs to the 擴
below, and refers to the 四端.—The 備音
says :—知字重看, 'the character 知 is

也不仁不智無禮無義
莫之禦而不仁是不智
之尊爵也人之安宅也
不處仁焉得智夫仁天
也孔子曰里仁爲美擇
匠亦然故術不可不慎
傷人函人惟恐傷人巫
於函人哉矢人惟恐
孟子曰矢人豈不仁
不足以事父母。

within the four seas. Let them be denied that development, and they will not suffice for a man to serve his parents with.'

CHAP. VII. 1. Mencius said, 'Is the arrow-maker less benevolent than the maker of armour of defence? *And yet*, the arrow-maker's only fear is lest men should not be hurt, and the armour-maker's only fear is lest men should be hurt. So it is with the priest and the coffin-maker. *The choice of* a profession, therefore, is a thing in which great caution is required.

2. 'Confucius said, "It is virtuous manners which constitute the excellence of a neighbourhood. If a man, in selecting a residence, do not fix on one where such prevail, how can he be wise?" Now, benevolence is the most honourable dignity conferred by Heaven. and the quiet home in which man should dwell. Since no one can hinder us from being so, if yet we are not benevolent;—this is being not wise.

3. 'From the want of benevolence and the want of wisdom will

to have weight attached to it.' This is true. Mencius may well say—'Let men know,' or 'If men know.' How is it that after all his analyses of our nature to prove its goodness, the application of his principles must begin with an IF?

7. AN EXHORTATION TO BENEVOLENCE FROM THE DISGRACE WHICH MUST ATTEND THE WANT OF IT, LIKE THE DISGRACE OF A MAN WHO DOES NOT KNOW HIS PROFESSION. 1. 矢人豈不仁於,— the 不 belongs not to the 豈, but to the 仁. If we might construe it with the 豈, we should have an instance parallel to 盛於 in ii. 28,—'benevolent as,' the 於 being =

如. 函 has the meaning of 'all armour of defence.' 巫,—see Analects, XIII. xxii, where I have translated it 'wizard.' As opposed to 匠 (here = 'a coffin-maker'), one who makes provision for the death of men, it indicates one who prays for men's life and prosperity. But Mencius pursues his illustration too far An arrow maker need not be inhumane. 2. See Analects, IV. i. The commentators begin to bring in the idea of a profession at 擇不 處仁, but the whole quotation must be taken first in its proper sense. The 不智 at the end refer to the same characters in the quotation. 3. 無 succeeding 不 shows that the

人役也人役而恥爲役由
弓人而恥爲弓矢人而恥
爲矢也。如恥之莫如爲仁。
仁者如射、射者正己而後
發發而不中、不怨勝己者、
反求諸己而已矣。
孟子曰、子路人告之以
有過則喜禹聞善言則拜。
大舜有大焉善與人同、舍
己從人樂取於人以爲善。

ensue the entire absence of propriety and righteousness;—he who is in such a case must be the servant of other men. To be the servant of men and yet ashamed of such servitude, is like a bow-maker's being ashamed to make bows, or an arrow-maker's being ashamed to make arrows.

4. 'If he be ashamed of his case, his best course is to practise benevolence.

5. 'The man who would be benevolent is like the archer. The archer adjusts himself and then shoots. If he misses, he does not murmur against those who surpass himself. He simply turns round and seeks *the cause of his failure* in himself.'

CHAP. VIII. 1. Mencius said, 'When any one told Tsze-lû that he had a fault, he rejoiced.

2. 'When Yü heard good words, he bowed *to the speaker*.

3. 'The great Shun had a still greater *delight in what was good. He regarded* virtue as the common property of himself and others, giving up his own way to follow that of others, and delighting to learn from others to practise what was good.

second clause ensues from the first. 由.— used for 猶. 5 仁者=欲爲仁之人. Compare Analects, III. vii and xvi.

8. How sages and worthies delighted in what is good. 1. Tsze-lû's ardour in pursuing his self-improvement appears in the Analects, V. xiii; XI. xxi. But the particular point mentioned in the text is nowhere else related of him. 2. In the Shû-ching, II. iii. 1, we have an example of this in Yü. It is said,—禹拜昌言,' Yü bowed at these excellent words.' 3. 與人同 is explained by Chû Hsî 公天下之善而不爲私也, 'He considered as public—common—the good of the whole world, and did not think it private to any.' Shun's distinction was that he did not think of himself, as Tsze-lû did, nor of others, as Yü did, but only of what was good, and un-

THE WORKS OF MENCIUS.

惡之心思與鄉人立其冠
朝衣朝冠坐於塗炭推惡
惡人之朝與惡人言、如以
人之朝不與惡人言、立於
事、非其友不友、不立於惡
孟子曰、伯夷非其君不
子莫大乎與人爲善。
善是與人爲善者也。故君
非取於人者。取諸人以爲
自耕稼陶漁以至爲帝無

4. 'From the time when he ploughed and sowed, exercised the potter's art, and was a fisherman, to the time when he became emperor, he was continually learning from others.

5. 'To take example from others to practise virtue, is to help them in the same practice. Therefore, there is no attribute of the superior man greater than his helping men to practise virtue.'

CHAP. IX. 1. Mencius said, 'Po-î would not serve a prince whom he did not approve, nor associate with a friend whom he did not esteem. He would not stand in a bad prince's court, nor speak with a bad man. To stand in a bad prince's court, or to speak with a bad man, would have been to him the same as to sit with his court robes and court cap amid mire and ashes. Pursuing the examination of his dislike to what was evil, we find that he thought it necessary, if he happened to be standing with a villager whose cap was not

consciously was carried to it, where-ver he saw it. 4. Of Shun in his early days it is related in the 'Historical Records,' that 'he ploughed at the Lì (歷) mountain, did potter's work on the banks of the Yellow River, fished in the Lêi lake (雷澤), and made various implements on the Shâu hill (壽丘), and often resided at Fù-hsiâ (負夏).' There will be occasion to consider where these places were, in connexion with some of Mencius's future references to Shun. Dr. Medhurst supposes them to have been in Shan-hsî. See his Translation of the Shû-ching, p. 332. 5. 與 is here in the sense of 助, 'to help.' The meaning is that others, seeing their virtue so imitated, would be stimulated to greater diligence in the doing of it.

9. PICTURES OF PO-î AND HÛi OF LIÛ-HHIÀ, AND MENCIUS'S JUDGMENT CONCERNING THEM. 1. Compare chap. ii. 22. In 惡人之朝、人 refers to the preceding 君, and may be translated prince, but in 與惡人立、人 refers to the preceding 友, and must be translated man. 塗炭, 'mire and charcoal.' 推惡 惡之心、一推 is Mencius's speaking in his

不正望望然去之若將浼焉是
故諸侯雖有善其辭命而至者是
不受也不受也者是亦不屑就
已。柳下惠不羞汙君不卑小官
進不隱賢必以其道遺佚而不
怨阨窮而不憫故曰爾爲爾我
爲我雖袒裼裸裎於我側爾焉
能浼我哉故由由然與之偕而
不自失焉援而止之而止援而
止之而止者是亦不屑去已孟

rightly adjusted, to leave him with a high air, as if he were going to be defiled. Therefore, although some of the princes made application to him with very proper messages, he would not receive their gifts.—He would not receive their gifts, counting it inconsistent with his purity to go to them.

2. 'Hûi of Liû-hsiâ was not ashamed to *serve* an impure prince, nor did he think it low to be an inferior officer. When advanced to employment, he did not conceal his virtue, but made it a point to carry out his principles. When neglected and left without office, he did not murmur. When straitened by poverty, he did not grieve. Accordingly, he had a saying, "You are you, and I am I. Although you stand by my side with breast and arms bare, or with your body naked, how can you defile me?" Therefore, self-possessed, he companied with men indifferently, at the same time not losing himself. *When he wished to leave,* if pressed to remain in office, he would remain.—He would remain in office, when pressed to do so, not counting it required by his purity to go away.'

own person. 思 is the 'thought' of Po-î. 望 望然, according to Chû Hsî, is 'the appearance of going away without looking round.' Châo Ch'î makes it 'the appearance of being ashamed;'—not so well.' The final 已 gives positiveness to the affirmation of the preceding clause. 2. Hûi of Liû-hsiâ,—see Analects, XV. xiii; XVIII. ii, viii. 與之偕.—the 之 properly refers to the party addressed, 'you are you.' 3. Compare chap. ii. 22. 君子.—by this

也。不君不隘不下隘伯子
由子恭與恭惠柳夷曰、

3. Mencius said, 'Po-î was narrow-minded, and Hûi of Liû-hsiâ was wanting in self-respect. The superior man will not manifest either narrow-mindedness, or the want of self-respect.'

term we must suppose that Mencius makes a tacit reference to himself, as having proposed Confucius as his model. The writer 韓元少 says :—'Elsewhere Mencius advises men to imitate Î and Hûi, but he is there speaking to the weak and the mean. When here he advises not to follow Î and Hûi, he is speaking for those who wish to do the right thing at the right time.'

KUNG-SUN CH'ÂU. PART II.

而環七三不地天□□
不而里里如利時孟二章公
勝攻之之人地不子 句孫
夫之郭城和。利如曰、下丑

CHAPTER I. 1. Mencius said, 'Opportunities of time *vouchsafed by* Heaven are not equal to advantages of situation *afforded by* the Earth, and advantages of situation afforded by the Earth are not equal to *the union arising from* the accord of Men.

2. ' *There is a city*, with an inner wall of three *lî* in circumference, and an outer wall of seven.—*The enemy* surround and attack it, but they are not able to take it. Now, to surround and attack it, there

1. NO ADVANTAGES WHICH A RULER CAN OBTAIN TO EXALT HIM OVER OTHERS ARE TO BE COMPARED WITH HIS GETTING THE HEARTS OF MEN. Because of this chapter Mencius has got a place in China among the writers on the art of war, which surely he would not have wished to claim for himself, his design evidently being to supersede the necessity of war and the recourse to arms altogether. 1. In the 天, 地, 人, we have the doctrine of the 三才, or 'Three Powers,' which is brought out so distinctly in the fourth part of the *Chung Yung*, and to show this in a translation requires it to be diffuse. As to what is said at much length in Chinese commentaries about ascertaining the 'time of Heaven' by divination and astrology, it is to be set aside, as foreign to the mind of Mencius in the text, though many examples of the resort to it may be adduced from the records of antiquity. 2. The city here supposed, with its double circle of fortification, is a small one, the better to illustrate the superiority of advantage of situation, just as the next is a large one, to bring out the still greater superiority of the union of men. As to the evidence that a city of the specified dimensions must be the capital of a baronial State (子男之城), see the 集

環而攻之必有得天時
者矣然而不勝者是天
時不如地利也。城非不
高也池非不深也兵革
非不堅利也米粟非不
多也委而去之是地利
不如人和也。故曰域民
不以封疆之界固國不
以山谿之險威天下不
以兵革之利得道者多

must have been vouchsafed to them by Heaven the opportunity of time, and in such case their not taking it is because opportunities of time vouchsafed by Heaven are not equal to advantages of situation afforded by the Earth.

3. '*There is a city, whose* walls are distinguished for their height, and whose moats are distinguished for their depth, where the arms *of its defenders*, offensive and defensive, are distinguished for their strength and sharpness, and the stores of rice and other grain are very large. *Yet it is obliged to* be given up and abandoned. This is because advantages of situation afforded by the Earth are not equal to the union arising from the accord of Men.

4. 'In accordance with these principles it is said, "A people is bounded in, not by the limits of dykes and borders; a State is secured, not by the strengths of mountains and rivers; the kingdom is overawed, not by the sharpness *and strength* of arms." He who finds the proper course has many to assist him. He who loses the proper course has few to assist him. When this,—the being assisted by few,—reaches its extreme point, his own relations revolt from *the*

證, *in loc.* 3. 非不, the repeated negation, not only affirms, but with emphasis:—城非不高, 'the wall is not but high,' i.e. is high indeed. 兵,—sharp weapons of offence. 革,—'leather,' intending, principally, the buff-coat, but including all other armour of defence. 米,—'rice,' without the husk; 粟,—'grain,' generally in the husk. 4. 城, 'a boundary,' 'a border,' is used verbally. 城民, —'to bound a people,' i.e. to separate them from other States. 封 is 'a dyke,' or 'mound.' The commentator 金仁山 says:—'Anciently, in every State, they made a dyke of earth to show its boundary (封土爲疆). 谿, —'a valley with a stream in it;' here, in opposition to 山, = rivers or streams. The 道, or 'proper course,' intended is that style of govern-

於王前故齊人莫如我敬王
是我非堯舜之道不敢以陳
仁義也云爾則不敬莫大乎
不美也其心曰是何足與言
仁義與王言者豈以仁義為
也曰惡是何言也齊人無以
王之敬子也未見所以敬王
也父子主恩君臣主敬丑見
則父子外則君臣人之大倫
而之景丑氏宿焉景子曰內

and there stop the night. Mr. Ching said to him, 'In the family, there is *the relation of* father and son; abroad, there is *the relation of* prince and minister. These are the two great relations among men. Between father and son the ruling principle is kindness. Between prince and minister the ruling principle is respect. I have seen the respect of the king to you, Sir, but I have not seen in what way you show respect to him.' *Mencius* replied, 'Oh! what words are these? Among the people of Ch'î there is no one who speaks to the king about benevolence and righteousness. Are they thus silent because they do not think that benevolence and righteousness are admirable? *No, but* in their hearts they say, "This man is not fit to be spoken with about benevolence and righteousness." Thus they manifest a disrespect than which there can be none greater. I do not dare to set forth before the king any but the ways of Yâo and Shun. There is therefore no man of Ch'î who respects the king so much as I do.'

of humility.' 要, the 1st tone, = 求. Mâng Chung, having committed himself to a falsehood, in order to make his words good, was anxious that Mencius should go to court. 4. What compelled Mencius to go to Ching Ch'âu was his earnest wish that the king should know that his sickness was merely feigned, and that he had not gone to court, only because he would not be CALLED to do so. As Mâng Chung's falsehood interfered with his first plan, he wished that his motive should get to the king through

Ching Ch'âu, who was an officer of Ch'î. After 宿焉, Châo Ch'î appends a note,—' when he told him all the previous incidents.' No doubt, he did so. 惡, the 1st tone, 'oh!' as in Pt. I. ii. 19. 齊人 .... 者, observe the force of the 者, carrying on the clause to those following for an explanation of it, as if there were a 所以 after 人 云爾.—

也景子曰否非此之謂也
禮曰父召無諾君命召不
俟駕固將朝也聞王命而
遂不果宜與夫禮若不相
似然曰豈謂是與曾子曰
晋楚之富不可及也彼以
其富我以吾仁彼以其爵
我以吾義吾何慊乎哉夫
豈不義而曾子言之是或
一道也天下有達尊三爵

5. Mr. Ching said, ‘Not so. That was not what I meant. In the *Book of* Rites it is said, “When a father calls, the answer must be without a moment's hesitation. When the prince's order calls, the carriage must not be waited for.” You were certainly going to the court, but when you heard the king's order, then you did not carry your purpose out. This does seem as if it were not in accordance with that rule of propriety.’

6. *Mencius* answered him, ‘How can you give that meaning to my conduct? The philosopher Tsǎng said, “The wealth of Tsin and Ch’ü cannot be equalled. Let *their rulers* have their wealth :— I have my benevolence. Let them have their nobility :—I have my righteousness. Wherein should I be dissatisfied *as inferior to them*?” Now shall we say that these sentiments are not right? Seeing that the philosopher Tsǎng spoke them, there is in them, I apprehend, a *real* principle.—In the kingdom there are three things universally acknowledged to be honourable. Nobility is one of them; age is

see Analects, VII. xviii. 5. Different passages are here quoted together from the Book of Rites. 父召無諾,—see Bk. I. Sect. I. iii. 3, 14, ‘A son must cry 唯 to his father, and not 諾, which latter is a lingering response. 君命召不俟駕 is found substantially in Bk. XI. Sect. iii. 2. 夫, in 1st tone, = 斯, as in Analects, XI. ix. 3, *et al*. 6. 豈謂是與 (the 2nd tone).—literally, ‘how means (it)

this?’ 慊 has two opposite meanings, either ‘dissatisfied,’ or ‘satisfied,’ in which latter sense it is also *Anrieh*. Chû Hsî explains this by making it the same as 陳, ‘something held in the mouth,’ according to the nature of which will be the internal feeling. In the text, the idea is that of dissatisfaction. 夫豈不義,—義 is here 當然之理, = ‘what is proper and right,’ the subject being the remarks of Tsǎng. 而曾子言之云云 is

學爲而後臣之故不勞而
不勞而王桓公之於管仲
於伊尹學焉而後臣之故
是不足與有爲也故湯之
則就之其尊德樂道不如
有所不召之臣欲有謀焉
二哉故將大有爲之君必
如德惡得有其一以慢其
鄉黨莫如齒輔世長民莫
一齒一德一朝廷莫如爵

one of them; virtue is one of them. In courts, nobility holds the
first place of the three; in villages, age holds the first place; and
for helping one's generation and presiding over the people, the other
two are not equal to virtue. How can the possession of *only* one of
these *be presumed on* to despise one who possesses the other two?

7. 'Therefore a prince who is to accomplish great deeds will
certainly have ministers whom he does not call to go to him. When
he wishes to consult with them, he goes to them. The prince who
does not honour the virtuous, and delight in their ways of doing, to
this extent, is not worth having to do with.

8. 'Accordingly, there was the behaviour of T'ang to Î Yin :—he
first learned of him, and then employed him as his minister; and
so without difficulty he became sovereign. There was the behaviour
of the duke Hwan to Kwan Chung :—he first learned of him, and
then employed him as his minister; and so without difficulty he
became chief of all the princes.

expanded thus in the 備旨:—'And, Tsäng-
tszé speaking them, they contain' perhaps
another principle different from the vulgar
view.' 鄉黨, Analects, X. i. 齒, 'teeth,'
=age. 7. 不足與有爲 is by some inter-
preted—'is not fit to have to do with them,' i.e.
the virtuous, but I prefer the meaning adopted
in the translation.   8, In the 'Historical
Records,' 殷本記, one of the accounts of
Î Yin's becoming minister to T'ang is, that it

was only after being five times solicited by
special messengers that he went to the prince's
presence;—see the 集證, on Analects, XII.
xxii. The confidence reposed by the duke Hwan
in Kwan Chung appears in Pt. I. i, 3. Kwan
was brought to Ch'í originally as a prisoner to
be put to death, but the duke, knowing his
ability and worth, had determined to employ
him, and therefore, having first caused him to
be relieved of his fetters, and otherwise honourably treated, he drove himself out of his capital
to meet and receive him with all distinction,
listening to a long discourse on government;

受前日之不受是則今日之
十鎰而受於薛餽五十鎰而
兼金一百而不受於宋餽七
三陳臻問曰前日於齊王餽
者乎。
且猶不可召而況不爲管仲
公之於管仲則不敢召管
臣其所受教湯之於伊尹桓
尚無他好臣其所教而不好
霸今天下地醜德齊莫能相

9. 'Now throughout the kingdom, the territories *of the princes* are of equal extent, and in their achievements they are on a level. Not one of them is able to exceed the others. This is from no other reason, but that they love to make ministers of those whom they teach, and do not love to make ministers of those by whom they might be taught.

10. 'So did T'ang behave to Î Yin, and the duke Hwan to Kwan Chung, that they would not venture to call them to go to them. If Kwan Chung might not be called to him by his prince, how much less may he be called, who would not play the part of Kwan Chung?

CHAP. III. 1. Ch'än Tsin asked *Mencius*, saying, 'Formerly, when you were in Ch'î, the king sent you a present of 2,400 taels of fine silver, and you refused to accept it. When you were in Sung, 1,680 taels were sent to you, which you accepted; and when you were in Hsieh, 1,200 taels were sent, which you *likewise* accepted. If your declining to accept the gift in the first case was right, your accepting

see the 集證, on Analects, III. xxii. 9. 臣 —used as a verb. 10. Compare Pt. I. i.

3. BY WHAT PRINCIPLES MENCIUS WAS GUIDED IN DECLINING OR ACCEPTING THE GIFTS OF PRINCES. 1. Ch'än Tsin was one of Mencius's disciples, but this is all that is known of him. 餽,—'to present an offering of food;' here, more generally, 'to send a gift,'=送. 兼金,—'double

metal' (I suppose 白金, or silver), called 'double, as being worth twice as much as the ordinary;'—see Analects, XI. xxi. 一百, i. e. 100 yi (鎰), which, as in Bk. I. Pt. II. ix. 2, I estimate at 24 taels. Sung,—the present Kwei-teh in Ho-nan. Hsieh,—see Bk. I. Pt. II. xiv. The reference here, however, is inconsistent with what is stated in the note there, that Hsieh had long been incorporated with

之也焉有君子而可以貨
有處也無處而餽之是貨
子何爲不受若於齊則未
心辭曰聞戒故爲兵餽之
爲不受當在薛也予有戒
者必以贐辭曰餽贐予何
當在宋也予將有遠行行
一於此矣孟子曰皆是也
日之不受非也夫子必居
受非也今日之受是則前

it in the latter cases was wrong. If your accepting it in the latter cases was right, your declining to do so in the first case was wrong. You must accept, Master, one of these alternatives.'

2. Mencius said, 'I did right in all the cases.

3. 'When I was in Sung, I was about to take a long journey. Travellers must be provided with what is necessary for their expenses. The prince's message was, "A present against travelling-expenses." Why should I have declined the gift?

4. 'When I was in Hsieh, I was apprehensive for my safety, and taking measures for my protection. The message was, "I have heard that you are taking measures to protect yourself, and send this to help you in procuring arms." Why should I have declined the gift?

5. 'But when I was in Ch'i, I had no occasion for money. To send a man a gift when he has no occasion for it, is to bribe him. How is it possible that a superior man should be taken with a bribe?'

Ch'1. 前日今日, mark the relation of time between the cases simply. 今日 is not to be taken as = 'to-day.' 必居一於此, literally, 'must occupy (dwell in) one of these (places).' The meaning is that on either of the suppositions he would be judged to have done wrong. 3. 贐 or 賮, 'a gift to a traveller against the expenses of his journey.' 必以贐,—it is difficult to assign its precise force to the 以. I consider the whole clause to be written as from the point of view of the prince of Sung:—in regard to travellers, he considered it was requisite to use the ceremony of 贐. 4. We must paraphrase 戒心 considerably to bring out the meaning. 爲, in 4th tone. 兵, 'a weapon of war,' or the character may be taken here for 'a weapon-bearer,' 'a soldier.' 5 未有處也,—Julien says,—'sicut nos Gallice; il n'y a pas lieu a,' but if it were so 處 would be the noun, in the 4th tone, whereas it

取乎。

四 孟子之平陸謂其大夫

曰子之持戟之士一日而

三失伍則去之否乎曰不

待三然則子之失伍也亦

多矣凶年饑歲子之民老

嬴轉於溝壑壯者散而之

四方者幾千人矣曰此非

距心之所得爲也曰今有

受人之牛羊而爲之牧之

CHAP. IV. 1. Mencius having gone to P'ing-lù, addressed the governor of it, saying, 'If *one of* your spearmen should lose his place in the ranks three times in one day, would you, Sir, put him to death or not?' 'I would not wait for three times *to do so*,' was the reply.

2. *Mencius* said, 'Well then, you, Sir, have likewise lost your place in the ranks many times. In bad calamitous years, and years of famine, the old and feeble of your people, who have been found lying in the ditches and water-channels, and the able-bodied, who have been scattered about to the four quarters, have amounted to several thousand.' *The* governor replied, 'That is a state of things in which it does not belong to me Chü-hsin to act.'

3. 'Here,' said *Mencius*, 'is a man who receives charge of the cattle and sheep of another, and undertakes to feed them for him;—

is the verb in the 3rd, = 'to manage,' 'to dispose of.' 未有處＝未有所遂.

4. How Mencius brought conviction of their faults home to the king and an officer of Ch'i. 1. 之 is the verb＝往. P'ing-lù was a city on the southern border of Ch'i;—in the present department of Yen-châu in Shan-tung. The officer's name, as we learn from the last paragraph, was K'ung Chü-hsin. 大夫 here＝宰, 'Governor' or 'Commandant.' The 戟 is variously described. Some say it had three points; others that it had a branch or blade on one side. No doubt, its form varied. 去, the

3rd tone, 'to away with.' Commentators concur in the meaning given in the translation. 2. 凶年云云.—compare Bk. I. Pt. II. xii. 2. Julien finds a difficulty in the 'several thousand,' as not applicable to the population of P'ing-lù. But it was Mencius's way to talk roundly. To make 千人 'one thousand,' we must read 幾, in 1st tone, and suppose the preposition 乎 suppressed. The meaning of the officer's reply is—that to provide for such a state of things, by opening the granaries and other measures, devolved on the supreme authority of the State, and not on him. 3. Compare 非身之所能爲 Bk. I. Pt. II. xv. 2.

靈丘而請士師似也爲其
則寡人之罪也。孟子謂蚳䵷曰子之辭
孔距心爲王誦之。王曰此
臣知五人焉知其罪者。惟
曰見於王曰王之爲都者。他
與曰此則距心之罪也。凶年
其人乎抑亦立而視其死
求牧與芻而不得則反諸
者、則必爲之求牧與芻矣、

of course he must search for pasture-ground and grass for them. If, after searching for those, he cannot find them, will he return *his charge to* the owner? or will he stand by and see them die?' 'Herein,' said the officer, 'I am guilty.'

4. Another day, *Mencius* had an audience of the king, and said to him, 'Of the governors of your Majesty's cities I am acquainted with five, but the only one of them who knows his faults is K'ung Chü-hsin.' He then repeated the conversation to the king, who said, 'In this matter, I am the guilty one.'

CHAP. V. 1. Mencius said to Ch'î Wâ, 'There seemed to be reason in your declining the governorship of Ling-ch'iû, and requesting to be appointed chief criminal judge, because *the latter office* would afford you the opportunity of speaking *your views.* Now

The first 牧 is the verb; the second a noun, = pasture-grounds. 諸=於　其人.— 'the man,' i.e. their owner. 抑亦,—the force of the 亦 is—'or—here is another supposition—will be, &c.?' Mencius means that Chü-hsin should not hold office in such circumstances. 4. 見 in 4th tone. 爲都者.—爲 has the sense of 'to administer,' 'to govern;' compare Analects, IV. xiii. 都.— properly 'a capital city,' but also used more generally. In the dictionary we find:—(1) Where the sovereign has his palace is called 都. (2) The cities conferred on the sons and younger brothers of the princes were called 都; in fact, every city with an ancestral temple containing the tablets of former rulers. (3) The cities from which nobles and great officers derived their support were called 都　爲王,—爲 in 4th tone.

5. THE FREEDOM BELONGING TO MENCIUS IN RELATION TO THE MEASURES OF THE KING OF CH'Î FROM HIS PECULIAR POSITION, AS UNSALARIED. 1. Of Ch'î Wâ we only know what is stated here. Ling-ch'iû is supposed to have been a city on the borders of Ch'î, remote from the court, Ch'î Wâ having declined the governorship of it, that he might be near the king. 士師,—see Bk. I. Pt. II. vi. 2. 爲其可以言,—

可
以
言
也、
今
既
數
月
矣、
未
可

以
言
與、
蚳
鼃
諫
於
王
而
不
用、

致
為
臣
而
去
齊
人
曰、
所
以
為

蚳
鼃
則
善
矣、
所
以
自
為、
則
吾

不
知
也、
公
都
子
以
告
曰
吾
聞

之
也、
有
官
守
者
不
得
其
職
則

去、
有
言
責
者
不
得
其
言
則
去

我
無
官
守
我
無
言
責
也、
則
吾

進
退
豈
不
綽
綽
然
有
餘
裕
哉。

六
孟
子
為
卿
於
齊、
出
弔
於
滕

several months have elapsed, and have you yet found nothing of which you might speak?'

2. *On this*, Ch'î Wâ remonstrated *on some matter* with the king, and, his counsel not being taken, resigned his office and went away.

3. The people of Ch'î said, 'In the course which he marked out for Ch'î Wâ he did well, but we do not know as to the course which he pursues for himself.'

4. His disciple Kung-tû told him *these remarks*.

5. *Mencius* said, 'I have heard that he who is in charge of an office, when he is prevented from fulfilling its duties, ought to take his departure, and that he on whom is the responsibility of giving his opinion, when he finds his words unattended to, ought to do the same. But I am in charge of no office; on me devolves no duty of speaking out my opinion:—may not I therefore act freely and without any constraint, either in going forward or in retiring?'

CHAP. VI. 1. Mencius, occupying the position of a high dignitary in Ch'î, went on a mission of condolence to Tăng. The king

literally, 'because of the possibility to speak.' As criminal judge, Ch'î Wâ would be often in communication with the king, and could remonstrate on any failures in the administration of justice that came under his notice. 2. 致 'to resign,' 'give up,' as in Analects, I. vii, *et al.* 3. 所以為 (in 3rd tone), literally, 'whereby for,'—所以為之道, as in the transla-

tion. 4. Kung-tû was a disciple of Mencius. See Bk. III. Pt. II. ix. 1; *et al.* 5. We find the phrase 綽綽有裕, with the same meaning as the more enlarged form in the text.

6. MENCIUS'S BEHAVIOUR WITH AN UNWORTHY ASSOCIATE. 1. 'Occupied the position of a high dignitary:'—so I translate here 為卿. Mencius's situation appears to have been only

不知虞之不肖使虞敦匠

齊止於嬴充虞請曰前日、

𡩋孟子自齊葬於魯反於

夫既或治之予何言哉。

而未嘗與言行事何也。曰。

齊滕之路不爲近矣反之。

丑曰齊卿之位不爲小矣

未嘗與之言行事也。公孫

王驩朝暮見反齊滕之路、

王使蓋大夫王驩爲輔行、

also sent Wang Hwan, the governor of Kâ, as assistant-commissioner. Wang Hwan, morning and evening, waited upon Mencius, who, during all the way to T'ăng and back, never spoke to him about the business of their mission.

2. Kung-sun Ch'âu said to Mencius, 'The position of a high dignitary of Ch'î is not a small one; the road from Ch'î to Tăng is not short. How was it that during all the way there and back, you never spoke to Hwan about the matters of your mission?' Mencius replied, 'There were the proper officers who attended to them. What occasion had I to speak to him about them?'

CHAP. VII. 1. Mencius *went* from Ch'î to Lû to bury *his mother*. On his return to Ch'î, he stopped at Ying, where Ch'ung Yü begged to put a question to him, and said, 'Formerly, in ignorance of my incompetency, you employed me to superintend the making of the coffin. As *you were then pressed by* the urgency *of the business*,

honorary, without emolument, and the king employed him on this occasion to give weight by his character to the mission. The officer of 蓋 (read *kâ*) was an unworthy favourite of the king. 輔行, not 'to assist him on the journey,' but with reference to what was the business (所行) of it. 見,—4th tone. 反 implies the 往, or 'going,' as well as 'returning.'

2 齊卿之位 refers to Wang Hwan, who had been temporarily raised to that dignity for the occasion. 夫 (in 2nd tone) 既或,—

'Now there were some'—i.e. the proper officers —治之,'who attended to them.' The glossarist of Châo Ch'î understands this as spoken of Wang:—'He perhaps attended to them,' i.e. he thought that he knew all about them, and never put any questions to me; but the view adopted is more natural, and gives more point to Mencius's explanation of his conduct.

7. THAT ONE OUGHT TO DO HIS UTMOST IN THE BURIAL OF HIS PARENTS;—ILLUSTRATED BY MENCIUS'S BURIAL OF HIS MOTHER. Compare Bk. I. Pt. II. xvi. 1. The tradition is that Mencius had his mother with him in Ch'î, and that he carried her body to the family sepulchre in Lû.

人皆用之吾何爲獨
悅得之爲有財古之
爲悅無財不可以爲
於人心不得不可以
直爲觀美也、然後盡
自天子達於庶人、非
中古棺七寸、槨稱之、
然曰古者棺槨無度、
竊有請也。木若以美
事、嚴、虞不敢請。今願

I did not venture to put any question to you. Now, however, I wish to take the liberty to submit the matter. The wood *of the coffin*, it appeared to me, was too good.'

2. *Mencius* replied, 'Anciently, there was no rule for the size of either the inner or the outer coffin. In middle antiquity, the inner coffin was made seven inches thick, and the outer one the same. This was *done by all*, from the sovereign to the common people, and not simply for the beauty of the appearance, but because they thus satisfied *the natural feelings of* their hearts.

3. 'If prevented *by statutory regulations from making their coffins in this way*, men cannot have the feeling of pleasure. If they have not the money *to make them in this way*, they cannot have the feeling of pleasure. When they were not prevented, and had the money, the ancients all used this style. Why should I alone not do so?

How long he remained in Lû is uncertain ;—perhaps the whole three years proper to the mourning for a parent. Whether his stopping at Ying was for a night merely, or a longer period, is also disputed. Ch'ung Yü was one of his disciples. It has appeared strange that Yü should have cherished the matter so long, and submitted it to his master after a lapse of three years. (This is on the supposition that Mencius's return to Ch'l was after the completion of the three years' mourning.) But it is replied in the 四書釋地, that this only illustrates how fond Mencius's disciples were of applying to him for a solution of their doubts, and the instance of Ch'ǎn Tsin, chap. iii, is another case in point of the length of time they would keep things in mind. 請,—as in Bk. I. Pt. II. xvi. 1, ' to beg to put a question.' 敦 = 董治, 'to attend to.' 匠, as in Pt. I. vii. 1.

不肯,—see Chung Yung, chap. iv. 嚴 is explained as in the translation. But for the critics, I should render,—' In the gravity of your sorrow.' 竊,—see Pt. I. ii. 20. 2. 'Middle antiquity' commences with the Châu dynasty. 稱, the 4th tone, 'to correspond, or be equal, to.' 盡於人心,一於 is not what they call an 'empty character,' merely completing the rhythm of the sentence. The whole = ' they felt complete (that they had done their utmost) in their human hearts.' Mencius's account of the equal dimensions of the outer and inner coffin does not agree with what we find in the Lî Chî, XIX. ii. 31. It must be borne in mind also, that the seven inches of the Châu dynasty were only = rather more than four inches of the present day. 3. 不得, being opposed to 無財, requires to be supplemented, as in the

之祿爵夫士也亦無王命
不告於王而私與之吾子
子噲有仕於此而子悅之
與人燕子之不得受燕於
伐與孟子曰可子噲不得
〔六章〕沈同以其私問曰燕可
親。之也君子不以天下儉其
膚於人心獨無恔乎吾聞
不然。且比化者無使土親

4. 'And moreover, is there no satisfaction to the natural feelings of a man, in preventing the earth from getting near to the bodies of his dead?

5. 'I have heard that the superior man will not for all the world be niggardly to his parents.'

CHAP. VIII. 1. Shăn T'ung, on his own impulse, asked *Mencius*, saying, 'May Yen be smitten?' Mencius replied, 'It may. Tsze-k'wâi had no right to give Yen to another man, and Tsze-chih had no right to receive Yen from Tsze-k'wâi. *Suppose* there were an officer here, with whom you, Sir, were pleased, and that, without informing the king, you were privately to give to him your salary and rank; and suppose that this officer, also without the king's orders, were privately to receive them from you:—would *such a transaction* be allowable? And where is the difference between *the case of Yen and* this?'

translation. For 為有財, some would give 而有財. The 而 reads better, but the meaning is the same. 4. 比 (the 4th tone) 化者,—the same as 比死者 in Bk. I. Pt. I. v. 1. 化 is used appropriately with reference to the dissolution of the bodies of the dead. 膚, 'skin'＝the bodies. 恔, the 4th tone, *hsiáo*. 獨無恔乎,—the meaning is —'shall this thing *alone* give no satisfaction to

a son's feelings?' 5. 不以天下云云 —Châo Ch'î interprets this:—'will not deny anything in all the world which he can command to his parents.' So, substantially, the modern paraphrasts.

8. DESERVED PUNISHMENT MAY NOT BE INFLICTED BUT BY PROPER AUTHORITY. A STATE OR NATION MAY ONLY BE SMITTEN BY THE MINISTER OF HEAVEN The incidents in the history of Yen referred to are briefly these:—Tsze-k'wâi, a weak silly man, was wrought upon to resign his throne to his prime minister Tsze-chih, in the expectation that Tsze-chih would decline the honour, and

之今以燕伐燕何爲勸之哉。
則將應之曰爲士師則可以殺
應之曰可彼如曰孰可以殺之
人者或問之曰人可殺與則將
曰爲天吏則可以伐之今有殺
彼如曰孰可以伐之則將應之
與吾應之曰可彼然而伐之也
燕有諸曰未也沈同問燕可伐
於是齊人伐燕或問曰勸齊伐
而私受之於子則可乎何以異

2. The people of Ch'i smote Yen. Some one asked Mencius, saying, 'Is it really the case that you advised Ch'i to smite Yen?' He replied, 'No. Shǎn T'ung asked me whether Yen might be smitten, and I answered him, "It may." They accordingly went and smote it. If he had asked me—"Who may smite it? I would have answered him, "He who is the minister of Heaven may smite it." Suppose the case of a murderer, and that one asks me—"May this man be put to death?" I will answer him—"He may." If he ask me—"Who may put him to death?" I will answer him,— "The chief criminal judge may put him to death." But now with *one* Yen to smite *another* Yen:—how should I have advised this?'

that thus he would be praised as acting the part of the ancient Yáo, while he retained his kingdom. Tsze-chih, however, accepted the tender, and Tsze-k'wái was laid upon the shelf. By-and-by, his son endeavoured to wrest back the throne, and great confusion and suffering to the people ensued. Compare Bk. I. Pt. II. x, xi. I. Shǎn (so read, as a surname) T'ung appears to have been a high minister of the State. It is difficult to find a word by which to translate 伐, which implies the idea of Yen's deserving to be punished. 吾子,—referring to Shǎn

T'ung, but we cannot translate it literally in English. 夫士也夫, in the 2nd tone. -斯;士 is the same person as 仕 above, 'a scholar seeking official employment.' 2. 應, the 4th tone. 彼然,—彼 refers to the king and people of Ch'i. 彼如曰,—彼 refers only to Sh'ǎn T'ung. 天吏, see Pt. I. v. 6. The one Yen is of course Ch'i, as oppressive as Yen itself.

燕人畔、王曰吾甚慙於
孟子陳賈曰王無患焉王
自以爲與周公孰仁且智。
王曰惡是何言也。曰周公
使管叔監殷管叔以殷畔、
知而使之是不仁也。不知
而使之是不智也。仁智周
公未之盡也。而況於王乎、
賈請見而解之見孟子問
曰周公何人也。曰古聖人

Chap. IX. 1. The people of Yen having rebelled, the king *of Ch'î* said, 'I feel very much ashamed *when I think* of Mencius.'

2. Ch'ăn Chiâ said to him, 'Let not your Majesty be grieved. Whether does your Majesty consider yourself or Châu-kung the more benevolent and wise?' The king replied, 'Oh! what words are those?' 'The duke of Châu,' said *Chiâ*, 'appointed Kwan-shû to oversee *the heir of* Yin, but Kwan-shû with the power of the Yin State rebelled. If knowing that this would happen he appointed Kwan-shû, he was deficient in benevolence. If he appointed him, not knowing that it would happen, he was deficient in knowledge. If the duke of Châu was not completely benevolent and wise, how much less can your Majesty be expected to be so! I beg to go and see Mencius, and relieve your Majesty from that feeling.'

3. *Ch'ăn Chiâ* accordingly saw Mencius, and asked him, saying, 'What kind of man was the duke of Châu?' 'An ancient sage,'

9. How Mencius beat down the attempt to argue in excuse of errors and misconduct. 1. The people of Yen set up the son of Tsze-k'wâi as king, and rebelled against the yoke which Ch'î had attempted to impose on them. 'Ashamed when I think of Mencius,'—i. e. because of the advice of Mencius in regard to Yen which he had neglected. See Bk. I. Pt. II. x, xi. 2. Ch'ăn Chiâ was an officer of Ch'î. Châu-kung,—see Analects, VII. v, *et al.* The case Chiâ refers to was this:—On king Wû's extinction of the Yin dynasty, sparing the life of Châu's son, he conferred on him the small State of Yin from which the dynasty had taken its name, but placed him under the surveillance of his own two brothers, *Hsien* (鮮) and *Tû* (度), one of them older, and the other younger, than his brother Tan (旦), who was Châu-kung. Hsien has come down to us under the title of Kwan-shû, Kwan being the name of the principality which he received for himself. After Wû's death, and the succession of his son, Hsien and Tû rebelled, when Châu-kung took action against them, put the former to death, and banished the other. 監 (the 1st tone) 殷, —the 殷 here is the son of the sovereign Châu. That below is the name of the State. 解之. —I take 解 in the sense of 'to loose,' 'to free

也。使管叔監殷管叔以殷畔
也有諸曰然曰周公知其將畔
而使之與曰不知也然則聖人
且有過與曰周公弟也管叔兄
也周公之過不亦宜乎且古之
君子過則改之今之君子過則
順之古之君子其過也如日月
之食民皆見之及其更也民皆
仰之今之君子豈徒順之又從
爲之辭。

was the reply. 'Is it the fact, that he appointed Kwan-shû to oversee *the heir* of Yin, and that Kwan-shû with the State of Yin rebelled?' 'It is.' 'Did the duke of Châu know that he would rebel, and *purposely* appoint him to that office?' *Mencius* said, 'He did not know.' 'Then, though a sage, he still fell into error?' 'The duke of Châu,' answered *Mencius*, 'was the younger brother. Kwan-shû was his elder brother. Was not the error of Châu-kung in accordance with what is right?

4. 'Moreover, when the superior men of old had errors, they reformed them. The superior men of the present time, when they have errors, persist in them. The errors of the superior men of old were like eclipses of the sun and moon. All the people witnessed them, and when they had reformed them, all the people looked up to them *with their former admiration*. But do the superior men of the present day only persist in their errors? They go on to apologize for them likewise.'

from,' with reference to the feeling of shame, not 'to explain.' 3. Before 然則 there should be a 曰, as it is the retort of Ch'ân Chiâ. 聖人且有過與—且 implies a succeeding clause—'how much more may one inferior to him!'—況下于公者乎

What Mencius means in conclusion is, that brother ought not to be suspicious of brother: that it is better to be deceived than to impute evil. 4. In 今之君子, the 君子 must be taken vaguely. 更, the 1st tone,—改. Shall we refer it to the sun and moon, or to the ancient worthies? Primarily, its application is

為我言之時子因陳子而
夫國人皆有所矜式子盍
室養弟子以萬鍾使諸大
子曰我欲中國而授孟子
耳固所願也他日王謂時
此而得見乎對曰不敢請
棄寡人而歸不識可以繼
可得得侍同朝甚喜今又
見孟子曰前日願見而不
王孟子致為臣而歸王就

CHAP. X. 1. Mencius gave up his office, and *made arrangements for* returning *to his native State*.

2. The king came to visit him, and said, 'Formerly, I wished to see you, but in vain. Then, I got the opportunity of being by your side, and all my court joyed exceedingly along with me. Now again you abandon me, and are returning home. I do not know if hereafter I may expect to have another opportunity of seeing you.' Mencius replied, 'I dare not request permission to visit you *at any particular time*, but, indeed, it is what I desire.'

3. Another day, the king said to the officer Shih, 'I wish to give Mencius a house, somewhere in the middle of the kingdom, and to support his disciples with *an allowance of* 10,000 *chung*, that all the officers and the people may have *such an example* to reverence and imitate. Had you not better tell him this for me?'

4. Shih took advantage to convey this message by means of the disciple Ch'ên, who reported his words to Mencius.

to the heavenly bodies. 為之辭, the double object after 為. The remark was a severe thrust at Ch'ên Chiá's own conduct.

10. MENCIUS IN LEAVING A COUNTRY OR REMAINING IN IT WAS NOT INFLUENCED BY PECUNIARY CONSIDERATIONS, BUT BY THE OPPORTUNITY DENIED OR ACCORDED TO HIM OF CARRYING HIS PRINCIPLES INTO PRACTICE. 1. 致為臣,—致 as in chap. v. 2, only it is here simply 'resignation,' with little of the idea of sacrifice. 而歸, 'and returned.' —Châo Ch'î says 'to his house,' and in accordance with this, he interprets 不敢請耳

below, 'I do not venture to ask you to come in person to see me,' which is surely absurd enough. The meaning must be what I have given. 2. 前日,—referring to the time before Mencius first came to Ch'î. 同朝 (ch'áo, 2nd tone)=同朝之臣, 'all the officers of the court with himself.' 繼此 = 繼此見, 'in continuation of this seeing.' Mencius sees that the king with his complimentary expressions is really bidding him adieu, and answers, accordingly, in as complimentary a way, intimating his purpose to be

市者以其所有易其所無
之中有私龍斷焉○七節古之為
孰不欲富貴而獨於富貴
矣又使其子弟為卿人亦
疑使已為政不用則亦已
欲富乎季孫曰異哉子叔
欲富辭十萬而受萬○六節是為
子惡知其不可也如使子
言告孟子孟子曰○五節然夫時
以告孟子陳子以時子之

5. Mencius said, 'Yes; but how should the officer Shih know that the thing could not be? Suppose that I wanted to be rich, having formerly declined 100,000 *chung*, would my now accepting 10,000 be the conduct of one desiring riches?

6. 'Chî-sun said, "A strange man was Tsze-shû Î. He pushed himself into the service of government. *His prince* declining to employ him, he had to retire indeed, but he again schemed that his son or younger brother should be made a high officer. Who indeed is there of men but wishes for riches and honour? But he only, among the seekers of these, tried to monopolize the conspicuous mound.

7. '"Of old time, the market-dealers exchanged the articles which they had for others which they had not, and simply had certain officers to keep order among them. It happened that there was

gone. 3. The king after all does not like the idea of Mencius's going, and thinks of this plan to retain him, which was in reality what Mencius, in chap. iii, calls 'bribing' him. 為 the 4th tone. 4. Ch'ân here is the Ch'ân Tsin of chap. iii. 因 is explained by 依託 'entrusted to.' But it is more, and = to take advantage of,' with reference to Ch'ân's being a disciple of Mencius. 5. Mencius does not find it convenient to state plainly his real reason for going,—that he was not permitted to see his principles carried into practice, and therefore repels simply the idea of his being accessible to pecuniary considerations. 100,000 *chung* was the fixed allowance of a 鄉, which Mencius had declined to receive. 6. Of Chî-sun and

Tsze-shû Î we know only what is mentioned here. Châo Ch'î says that they were disciples of Mencius, and that Chî-sun made his remark with a view to induce Mencius to push forward his disciples into the employment which he could not get for himself. But such a view is inadmissible. 使已 使其子弟—the first 使, it is said, merely refers to the prince's employment of him, and the second to his contriving and bringing about the employment of his son or younger brother; but why should we not give the character the same force in both cases? 龍, the 3rd tone, read as and = 壟, 'a mound.' 斷, 4th tone, 'cut,' 'abrupt,' 'well defined.' 7. 治, 2nd tone. Observe

Q 2

者、有司者治之耳、有賤丈
夫焉、必求龍斷而登之、以
左右望而罔市利、人皆以
爲賤、故從而征之、征商
此賤丈夫始矣。
十一 孟子去齊宿於晝、有欲
爲王留行者、坐而言、不應、
隱几而臥。客不悅曰、弟子
齊宿而後敢言、夫子臥而
不聽請勿復敢見矣。曰、坐、

a mean fellow, who made it a point to look out for a conspicuous mound, and get up upon it. Thence he looked right and left, to catch in his net the whole gain of the market. The people all thought his conduct mean, and therefore they proceeded to lay a tax upon his wares. The taxing of traders took its rise from this mean fellow."'

CHAP. XI. 1. Mencius, having taken his leave of Ch'î, was passing the night in Châu.

2. A person who wished to detain him on behalf of the king, *came and* sat down, and began to speak to him. *Mencius* gave him no answer, but leant upon his stool and slept.

3. The visitor was displeased, and said, 'I passed the night in careful vigil, before I would venture to speak to you, and you, Master, sleep and do not listen to me. Allow me to request that I may not again presume to see you.' *Mencius* replied, 'Sit down,

the force of 耳, 'only,' which also belongs to it in par. 2, weakening the 不敢請 征之,—the 之 should be referred to the mean individual spoken of.

11. HOW MENCIUS REPELLED A MAN, WHO, OFFICIOUSLY AND ON HIS OWN IMPULSE, TRIED TO DETAIN HIM IN CH'Î. 1. 晝 was a city on the southern border of Ch'î. Some think it should be written 畫, and refer it to a place in the present district of 臨淄, but this would place it north from Lû, whither Mencius was retiring.

Mencius withdrew leisurely, hoping that the king would recall him and pledge himself to follow his counsels. 2. 爲 (4th tone) 王,—'for the king,' i.e. knowing it would please the king. 應,—4th tone. 隱,—the 3rd tone, 'to lean upon.' The 几 was a stool or bench, on which individuals might lean forward, or otherwise, as they sat upon their mats. It could be carried in the hand. See the Li Chî, Bk. I. Sect. I. ii. 1, 一謀於長者、必操几杖以從之. 3. 齊 (châi), the 1st tone, = 齋, 'to keep a vigil,' 'to fast.' 齊宿,—'fasted and passed

我明語子昔者魯繆公

無人乎子思之側則不

能安子思泄柳申詳無

人乎繆公之側則不能

安其身子爲長者慮而

不及子思子絕長者乎

長者絕子乎。

孟子去齊尹士語人

曰不識王之不可以爲

湯武則是不明也識其

and I will explain the case clearly to you. Formerly, if the duke Mû had not kept a person by the side of Tsze-sze, he could not have induced Tsze-sze to remain with him. If Hsieh Liû and Shǎn Hsiang had not had a *remembrancer* by the side of the duke Mû, he would not have been able to make them feel at home and remain with him.

4. 'You anxiously form plans with reference to me, but you do not treat me as Tsze-sze was treated. Is it you, Sir, who cut me? Or is it I who cut you?'

CHAP. XII. 1. When Mencius had left Ch'î, Yin Shih spoke about him to others, saying, 'If he did not know that the king could not be made a T'ang or a Wû, that showed his want of intelligence. If he knew that he could not be made such, and came

the night.' 請勿復 (in 4th tone) 敢見 is merely the complimentary way of complaining of what the guest considered the rudeness of his reception. 語, the 4th tone,=告. 繆, here read *Mú*, was the honorary epithet of the duke Hsien (顯), B.C. 409-375. Tsze-sze,—the grandson of Confucius. Shǎn Hsiang,—the son of Tsze-chang (子張), one of Confucius's disciples. Hsieh Liû was a native of Lû, a disciple of the Confucian school. See the Lî Chî, Bk. II. Sect. I. ii. 34, and Bk. XVIII. Sect. II. ii. 11. In this last passage Liû should be Hsieh Liû. 平 = 在 or 在乎. 安 is said to = 留, simply 'to detain,' but its force is more than that, and = 'to make contented, and so induce to remain.' Great respect, it seems, was shown to Tsze-sze, and he had an attendant from the duke to assure him continually of the respect with which he

was cherished. Hsieh Liû and Shǎn Hsiang had not such attendants, but they knew that there were one or more officers by the duke's side, to admonish him not to forget them and other worthies. The visitor calls himself 弟子, 'your disciple.' 4. 爲, 4th tone. Mencius calls himself 長 (the 3rd tone) 者, 'the elder.' 子爲長者云云,—the stranger was anxious for (慮) Mencius to remain in Chî, but the thing was entirely from himself, not from the king; and his thinking that he could detain him by such a visit showed the little store he set by him;—was, in fact, a *cutting* him.

12. HOW MENCIUS EXPLAINED HIS SEEMING TO LINGER IN CH'Î, AFTER HE HAD RESIGNED HIS OFFICE, AND LEFT THE COURT. 1. All that we know of Yin Shih is that he was a man of Ch'î.

王如改諸則必反予夫出
心猶以爲速王庶幾改之、
也予三宿而後出晝於予
去豈予所欲哉予不得已
見王是予所欲也不遇故
夫尹士惡知予哉千里而
士、則茲不悅高子以告。曰、
宿而後出晝是何濡滯也
千里而見王不遇故去三
不可、然且至、則是干澤也、

notwithstanding, that shows he was seeking his own benefit. He came a thousand *lî* to wait on the king; because he did not find in him a ruler to suit him, he took his leave, but how dilatory and lingering was his departure, stopping three nights before he quitted Châu! I am dissatisfied on account of this.'

2. The disciple Kâo informed Mencius *of these remarks.*

3 *Mencius* said, 'How should Yin Shih know me! When I came a thousand *lî* to wait on the king, it was what I desired to do. When I went away because I did not find in him a ruler to suit me, was that what I desired to do? I felt myself constrained to do it.

4. 'When I stopped three nights before I quitted Châu, in my own mind I still considered my departure speedy. I was hoping that the king might change. If the king had changed, he would certainly have recalled me.

5. 'When I quitted Châu, and the king had not sent after me,

Julien properly blames Noel for translating 尹士 by '*literatus cognomine Yin*,' as if 士 were here the noun—'a scholar.' But when he adds that it is here to be pronounced *cái*, to mark that it is a name, this is what neither the dictionary nor any commentary mentions. 語, the 4th tone,= 告. 干澤, 'to seek for favours,' i. e. his own benefit;—see Analects, II. xviii. 不 遇,—see Bk. I. Pt. II. xvi. 3. 茲 = 此, 'this.' What Shih chiefly means to charge against Mencius is the lingering character of his departure. 3 Mencius was constrained to leave by the conviction forced on him that he could not in Ch'î carry his principles into practice. 王庶幾 (the 1st tone) 改之, literally, 'The king fortunately near to change it.' This was the thought at the time in Mencius's mind, and 庶幾 = 'I hoped,' 'I was looking for.' 諸之 + 諸 = 然後, 'then, and not till then.' 浩然. —see Pt. I. ii. 11. 舍=捨, the 3rd tone. 猶. 用 is by many taken as simply = 以;

畫而王不子追也子然後浩然
有歸志子雖然豈舍王哉王由
足用爲善王如用予則豈徒齊
民安天下之民舉安王庶幾改
之子曰望之子豈若是小丈夫
然哉諫於其君而不受則怒悻
悻然見於其面去則窮日之力
而後宿哉尹士聞之曰士誠小
人也。
孟子去齊充虞路問曰夫子

then, and not till then, was my mind resolutely bent on returning
to Tsâu. But, notwithstanding that, how can *it be said that* I give
up the king? The king, after all, is one who may be made to do
what is good. If he were to use me, would it be for the happiness
of the people of Ch'î only? It would be for the happiness of the
people of the whole kingdom. I am hoping that the king will change.
I am daily hoping for this.

6. 'Am I like one of your little-minded people? They will
remonstrate with their prince, and on *their remonstrance not* being
accepted, they get angry; and, with their passion displayed in their
countenance, they take their leave, and travel with all their strength
for a whole day, before they will stop for the night.'

7. When Yin Shih heard this explanation, he said, 'I am indeed
a small man.'

CHAP. XIII. 1. When Mencius left Ch'î, Ch'ung Yü questioned
him upon the way, saying, 'Master, you look like one who carries

—'the king is, after all, competent to do good,'
but 用 expresses more than that. 予曰望
之 conveys in itself no more than the translation, but the king's change of course involved
Mencius's recall to Ch'î. Perhaps we have in the
words an amplification of Mencius's thoughts
before he quitted Châu. 5. Compare with this

paragraph Confucius's defence of Kwan Chung,
Analects. XIV. xviii.

13. MENCIUS'S GRIEF AT NOT FINDING AN OPPOR-
TUNITY TO DO THE GOOD WHICH HE COULD. 1.
Ch'ung Yü,—the same mentioned in chap. vii.
Though Ch'ung Yü attributes the maxim 不
怨天不尤人 to his master, we find it

若有不豫色然前日虞聞諸夫
子曰君子不怨天不尤人曰彼
一時此一時也五百年必有王
者興其閒必有名世者由周而
來七百有餘歲矣以其數則過
矣以其時考之則可矣夫天未
欲平治天下也如欲平治天下
當今之世舍我其誰也吾何爲
不豫哉。

an air of dissatisfaction in his countenance. But formerly I heard you say—"The superior man does not murmur against Heaven, nor grudge against men."'

2. *Mencius* said, 'That was one time, and this is another.

3. 'It is a rule that a true royal sovereign should arise in the course of five hundred years, and that during that time there should be men illustrious in their generation.

4. 'From the commencement of the Châu dynasty till now, more than seven hundred years have elapsed. Judging numerically, the date is past. Examining the *character of the present* time, we might *expect the rise of such individuals in it.*

5. 'But Heaven does not yet wish that the kingdom should enjoy tranquillity and good order. If it wished this, who is there besides me to bring it about? How should I be otherwise than dissatisfied?'

in Confucius, see Analects, XIV. xxxvii. 3. ' 500 years,'—this is speaking in very round and loose numbers, even if we judge from the history of China prior to Mencius. 其間 ' during them,' but the meaning is—at the same time with the sovereign shall arise men able to assist him. 名世 = 有 or 著名于世 4. The Châu dynasty lasted altogether 867 years, and Mencius died, according to some accounts, at the age of 102, in the second year of the last century, little more than fifty years removed from the extinction of the dynasty. 以其時考之則可矣, literally, ' By the time examining it, then may,' i.e. such things may be. 5. 舍我其誰, literally, ' Letting me go, then who?' Compare last chapter, par. 4, and many other places, where Mencius speaks of what he could accomplish. On the reference to the will of Heaven, compare Analects, IX. v. 3.

孟子去齊居
休公孫丑問曰
仕而不受祿古
之道乎曰非也
於崇吾得見王
退而有去志不
欲變故不受也
繼而有師命不
可以請久於齊
非我志也。

CHAP. XIV. 1. When Mencius left Ch'î, he dwelt in Hsiû. *There* Kung-sun Ch'âu asked him, saying, 'Was it the way of the ancients to hold office without receiving salary?'

2. *Mencius replied,* 'No; when I first saw the king in Ch'ung, it was my intention, on retiring from the interview, to go away. Because I did not wish to change this intention, I declined to receive any salary.

3. 'Immediately after, there came orders for the collection of troops, when it would have been improper for me to beg permission to leave. But to remain *so* long in Ch'î was not my purpose.'

14. THE REASON OF MENCIUS'S HOLDING AN HONORARY OFFICE IN CH'Î WITHOUT SALARY, THAT HE WISHED TO BE FREE IN HIS MOVEMENTS. 1. Hsiû was in the present district of T'âng (滕) in the department of Yen-châu. Kung-sun Châu's inquiry was simply for information. This appears from the 非 with which it is answered. 2. Ch'ung must be the name of a place in Ch'î, which cannot be more exactly determined. It is not to be confounded with the ancient principality or barony of the same name. 得見 is evidently = 始見. 3. 師命 may be as in the translation, or—'the appointment to the position of a Tutor,' i.e. honorary adviser to the king. This is the interpretation of the glossarist of Châo Ch'î, and is perhaps preferable to the former.

BOOK III.

TĂNG WĂN KUNG. PART I.

滕文公章句上
二 滕文公為世子、
將之楚過宋而見
孟子孟子道性善
言必稱堯舜世子
自楚反復見孟子
孟子曰世子疑吾
言乎夫道一而已
矣成覵謂齊景公
曰彼丈夫也我丈

CHAPTER I. 1. When the prince, afterwards duke Wăn of Tăng, had to go to Ch'û, he went by way of Sung, and visited Mencius.

2. Mencius discoursed to him how the nature *of man* is good, and when speaking, always made laudatory reference to Yâo and Shun.

3. When the prince was returning from Ch'û, he again visited Mencius. Mencius said to him, 'Prince, do you doubt my words? The path is one, and only one.

4. 'Ch'ăng Ch'ien said to duke King of Ch'î, "They were men. I am a man. Why should I stand in awe of them?" Yen Yüan said,

TITLE OF THIS BOOK.—滕文公, 'The duke Wăn of Tăng.' The Book is so named from the duke Wăn, who is prominent in the first three chapters. Châo Ch'î compares this with the title of the Fifteenth Book of the Analects.

1. HOW ALL MEN BY DEVELOPING THEIR NATURAL GOODNESS MAY BECOME EQUAL TO THE ANCIENT SAGES. 1. The duke Wăn of Tăng,—see Bk. I. Pt. II. xiii. Wăn is the posthumous title. The crown-prince's name appears to have been Hung (宏). Previous to the Han dynasty, the heirs-apparent of the sovereigns and the princes of States were called indifferently 世子 and 太子. Since then, 太子 has been confined to the imperial heir. The title of 世子 was given, it is said, 欲其世世不絕, 'to indicate the wish that the succession should be unbroken *from generation to generation*.' Ch'û and Tăng bordering on each other, the prince must have gone out of his way to visit Mencius. In the 'Topography of the Four Books, continued,' it is said :— 'Since Tăng and Ch'û adjoined, so that one had only to lift his feet and pass into Ch'û, why must the crown-prince go round about, a distance of more than 350 *lî*, to pass by the capital of Sung? The reason was that Mencius was there, and the prince's putting himself to so much trouble, in going and returning, shows his worthiness.' 2. 道=言, a verb, 'to speak or discourse about.' 必, not 'necessarily,' but 'he made it a point.' 稱 is taken by Chû Hsî and others in the sense of 'to appeal to.' This is supported by par. 3, but the word itself has only the meaning in the translation, with which, moreover, Châo Ch'î agrees. 3. 道一而已—道

夫也吾何畏彼哉顏淵曰舜

何人也予何人也有爲者亦

若是。公明儀曰文王我師也。

周公豈欺我哉今滕絕長補

短將五十里也猶可以爲善

國書曰若藥不瞑眩厥疾不

瘳。〔二〕滕定公薨世子謂然友曰

昔者孟子嘗與我言於宋於

心終不忘今也不幸至於大

"What kind of man was Shun? What kind of man am I? He who exerts himself will also become such as he was." Kung-ming Î said, "King Wăn is my teacher. How should the duke of Châu deceive me *by those words?*"

5. 'Now, T'ăng, taking its length with its breadth, will amount, I suppose, to fifty *lî*. *It is small, but* still sufficient to make a good State. It is said in the Book of History, "If medicine do not raise a commotion in the patient, his disease will not be cured by it."'

CHAP. II. 1. When the duke Ting of T'ăng died, the prince said to Yen Yû, 'Formerly, Mencius spoke with me in Sung, and in my mind I have never forgotten *his words.* Now, alas!

seems here to be used as in the Chung Yung, i. 1,—'an accordance with this nature is called the Path,' but viewed here more in the consummation of high sageship and distinction to which it leads, which may be reached by treading it, and which can be reached in no other way. We have here for the first time the statement of Mencius's doctrine, which he subsequently dwells so much on, that 'the nature of man is good.' 4. Of Ch'ăng Chi'ĕn we only know what is here said. 彼丈夫,—彼 referring to the sages. 丈夫,—used for 'man' or 'man,' with the idea of vigour and capability. Kung-ming Î was a disciple first of Tsze-chang, and then of Tsăng Shăn. 文王我師 would appear to have been a remark originally of Châu-kung, which Î appropriates and vindi-

cates on that high authority. 5. 絕長補短.—cutting the long to supplement the short.' Observe the force of 將, as in the translation. 猶 implying—'It is small, but still.' 善國, compare chap. iii :—'a good kingdom' is such an one as is there described. 若藥云云,—see the Shû-ching, IV. viii. Sect. I. 8. 瞑 read *miĕn*, the 4th tone.

2. HOW MENCIUS ADVISED THE DUKE OF T'ANG TO CONDUCT THE MOURNING FOR HIS FATHER. 1. 薨 is the proper term to express the death of any of the feudal princes of the kingdom. Yen Yû had been the prince's Grand tutor (太

故、吾欲使子問於孟子、然
後行事然友之鄒問於孟
子孟子曰、不亦善乎、親喪
固所自盡也曾子曰生事
之以禮死葬之以禮祭之
以禮可謂孝矣。諸侯之禮
吾未之學也雖然吾嘗聞
之矣三年之喪齊疏之服、
飦粥之食自天子達於庶
人三代共之然友反命定

this great duty to my father devolves upon me ; I wish to send you to ask the advice of Mencius, and then to proceed to its *various* services.'

2. Zan Yŭ *accordingly* proceeded to Tsâu, and consulted Mencius. Mencius said, ' Is this not good ? In discharging the funeral duties to parents, men indeed feel constrained to do their utmost. The philosopher Tsăng said, " When parents are alive, they should be served according to propriety ; when they are dead, they should be buried according to propriety ; and they should be sacrificed to according to propriety :—this may be called filial piety." The ceremonies to be observed by the princes I have not learned, but I have heard *these points :*—that the three years' mourning, the garment of coarse cloth with its lower edge even, and the eating of congee, were equally prescribed by the three dynasties, and binding on all, from the sovereign to the mass of the people.'

3. Zan Yŭ reported the execution of his commission, and *the*

傳); I suppose that 然 is the surname. 大故 is a phrase applied to the funeral of, and mourning for, parents ;—'the great cause, or matter.' 2. 之鄒,—之 is the verb, = 往. 不亦善乎,—spoken with reference to the prince's sending to consult him on such a subject. 親喪固所自盡,—compare Analects, XIX. xvii. The words attributed to Tsăng Shăn were originally spoken by Confucius. see Analects, II. v. Tsăng may have appropriated them, and spoken them, so as to make them be regarded as his own, or, what is more likely, Mencius here makes a slip of memory. 齊, 1st tone, read *tsze*; see Analects, IX. ix. 飦, as used in the text, read like and = 饘, denotes congee, like 鬻, but made thicker. 3. 反命, 'returned the commission,' i.e. reported his execution of it and the reply. 世子 must be understood as the subject of 定. 父兄, 'his fathers and brethren,' i.e.

爲我問孟子然友復之鄒。也恐其不能盡於大事子劍今也父兄百官不我足他日未嘗學問好馳馬試有所受之也。謂然友曰吾且志曰喪祭從先祖曰吾至於子之身而反之不可、之行吾先君亦莫之行也、不欲曰吾宗國魯先君莫爲三年之喪父兄百官皆

prince determined that the three years' mourning should be observed. His aged relatives, and the body of the officers, did not wish that it should be so, and said, 'The former princes of Lû, that kingdom which we honour, have, none of them, observed this practice, neither have any of our own former princes observed it. For you to act contrary to their example is not proper. Moreover, the History says,—"In the observances of mourning and sacrifice, ancestors are to be followed," meaning that they received those things from a *proper* source *to hand them down*.'

4. *The prince said again* to Zan Yû, 'Hitherto, I have not given myself to the pursuit of learning, but have found my pleasure in horsemanship and sword-exercise, and now I don't come up to the wishes of my aged relatives and the officers. I am afraid I may not be able to discharge my duty in the great business *that I have entered on*; do you *again* consult Mencius for me.' *On this*, Zan Yû

his uncles and elderly ministers of the ducal family. The phrase is commonly applied by Chinese to the elders of their own surname, whatever be the degrees of their relationship. 吾宗國,—the ducal house of T'ang was descended from one of the sons of king Wǎn (Shû-hsiù, 叔繡), but by an inferior wife, while Châu-kung, the ancestor of Lû, was in the true sovereign line, the author of all the civil institutions of the dynasty, and hence all the other States ruled by descendants of king Wǎn were supposed to look up to Lû. That Châu-kung and the first rulers of T'ang had not observed the three years' mourning is not to be supposed. The crown-prince's remonstrants are wrong in attributing to them the neglect of later dukes. 志,—what particular 'history' they refer to is not known. 吾有所受之,—吾 is to be understood as spoken in the person of the ancestors, and I have therefore rendered it by 'they.' Châo Ch'î, however, says that some made this a reply of the prince:— 'The prince said, *I have one* (i. e. *Mencius*) *from whom I received it*.' 4. 不我足=不以我足滿其意, as in the translation. 恐其不能, —'I am afraid of the not being able, &c.' It is the sentiment of the prince

問孟子孟子曰、然不可以
他求者也孔子曰、君薨聽
於冢宰歠粥面深墨、卽位
而哭百官有司、莫敢不哀、
先之也上有好者下必有
甚焉者矣君子之德風也、
小人之德草也草尚之風
必偃是在世子然友反命。
世子曰、然是誠在我五月
居廬未有命戒百官族人、

went again to Tsâu, and consulted Mencius. Mencius said, 'It is
so, but he may not seek *a remedy* in others, *but only in himself.*
Confucius said, " When a prince dies, his successor entrusts the administration to the prime minister. He sips the congee. His face
is of a deep black. He approaches the place *of mourning*, and weeps.
Of all the officers and inferior ministers there is not one who will
presume not to join in the lamentation, he setting them this example.
What the superior loves, his inferiors will be found to love exceedingly. The relation between superiors and inferiors is like that
between the wind and grass. The grass must bend when the wind
blows upon it." The business depends on the prince.'

5. Zan Yû returned with this answer to his commission, and
the prince said, 'It is so. The matter does indeed depend on me.'
So for five months he dwelt in the shed, without issuing an order or
a caution. All the officers and his relatives said, 'He may be said
to understand *the ceremonies.*' When the time of interment arrived,

himself, and 恐 must be translated in the
first person, and not in the third, as Julien
does. In the 其 there is a reference to his
antecedents, as occasioning the present difficulty. 不可以他求 is taken by Ch'ào
Ch'î, 'You may not seek (to overcome their
opposition) by any other way (but carrying
out what you have begun).' Chû Hsî's view,
as in the translation, is better. In the quotations from Confucius, Mencius has blended
different places of the Analects together, and
enlarged them to suit his own purpose, or, it

may be, the text of the Analects was different in
his time. See Analects, XII. xxi, *et al.* 卽位
而哭,—the 位 is the place where the coffin
lay, during the five months that elapsed between
the death and interment. 5. The 廬 was a
shed, built of boards and straw, outside the
centre door of the palace, against the surrounding wall, which the mourning prince tenanted
till the interment ; see the Lî Chî, XVIII. Sect.
I. i. 7. 可謂曰知? is supposed by Chû
Hsî, with reason, to be corrupted or defective.

民之爲道也、有恆　乘屋、其始播百穀。　茅、宵爾索綯亟其　緩也詩云、晝爾于　孟子曰民事不可　滕文公問爲國。　者大悦。　之戚、哭泣之哀、弔　四方來觀之顔色　可謂曰知、及至葬、

they came from all quarters of the State to witness it.   Those who had come *from other States* to condole with him, were greatly pleased with the deep dejection of his countenance and the mournfulness of his wailing and weeping.

CHAP. III. 1. The duke Wăn of T'ăng asked *Mencius* about *the proper way of* governing a kingdom.

2. Mencius said, ' The business of the people may not be remissly attended to.   It is said in the Book of Poetry,

> " In the day-light go and gather the grass,
> And at night twist your ropes ;
> Then get up quickly on the roofs ;—
> *Soon* must we begin sowing *again* the grain."

3. ' The way of the people is this :—If they have a certain

I have translated as if it were 日可謂知知 —Chû Hsî introduces here the following remarks from the commentator Lin (林) :— ' In the time of Mencius, although the rites to the dead had fallen into neglect, yet the three years' mourning, with the sorrowing heart and afflictive grief, being the expression of what really belongs to man's mind, had not quite perished.   Only, sunk in the slough of manners becoming more and more corrupt, men were losing all their moral nature without being conscious of it.   When duke Wăn saw Mencius, and heard him speak of the goodness of man's nature, and of Yâo and Shun, that was the occasion of moving and bringing forth his better heart, and on this occasion — of the death of his father—he felt sincerely all the stirrings of sorrow and grief.   Then, moreover, when his older relatives and his officers wished not to act as he desired, he turned inwards to reprove himself, and lamented his former conduct which made him not be believed in his present course, not presuming to blame his officers and relatives :—although we must concede an extraordinary natural excellence and ability to him, yet his energy in learning may

not be impeached.   Finally, when we consider how with what decision he finally acted, and how all, near and far, who saw and heard him, were delighted to acknowledge and admire his conduct, we have an instance of how, when that which belongs to all men's minds is in the first place exhibited by one, others are brought, without any previous purpose, to the pleased acknowledgment and approval of it :—is not this a proof that it is indeed true that *the nature of man is good ?'*

3. MENCIUS'S COUNSELS TO THE DUKE OF T'ĂNG FOR THE GOVERNMENT OF HIS KINGDOM.   AGRICULTURE AND EDUCATION ARE THE CHIEF THINGS TO BE ATTENDED TO, AND THE FIRST AS AN ESSENTIAL PREPARATION FOR THE SECOND. 1. 爲, in the sense of 治, ' to govern.' 2. By 民事, ' the business of the people,' is intended husbandry.   For the ode, see the Shih-ching, I. xv. Ode I. st. 7, written, it is said, by Châu-kung, to impress the sovereign Ch'ăng with a sense of the importance and toils of husbandry. 3. Compare Bk. I. Pt. I. vii. 19.   In 民之爲道, the 道 is to be taken lightly, as if the expression

產者、有恆心、無恆產者、
無恆心、苟無恆心、放辟
邪侈、無不爲已、及陷乎
罪、然後從而刑之、是罔
民也、焉有仁人在位、罔
民而可爲也。是故賢君
必恭儉禮下、取於民、有
制、陽虎曰、爲富不仁矣、
爲仁不富矣。夏后氏五
十而貢、殷人七十而助、

livelihood, they will have a fixed heart; if they have not a certain livelihood, they have not a fixed heart. And if they have not a fixed heart, there is nothing which they will not do in the way of self-abandonment, of moral deflection, of depravity, and of wild license. When they have thus been involved in crime, to follow them up and punish them:—this is to entrap the people. How can such a thing as entrapping the people be done under the rule of a benevolent man?

4. 'Therefore, a ruler who is endowed with talents and virtue will be gravely complaisant and economical, showing a respectful politeness to his ministers, and taking from the people only in accordance with regulated limits.

5. 'Yang Hû said, "He who seeks to be rich will not be benevolent. He who wishes to be benevolent will not be rich."

6. 'The sovereign of the Hsiâ dynasty enacted the fifty *mâu* allotment, and the payment of a tax. The founder of the Yin enacted the seventy *mâu* allotment, and the system of mutual aid. The

were 民之爲民也,—'As to the people's being the people,' i.e. the character of the people is as follows. One commentator expounds the passage thus:—民之爲道, 道字只如云民之所以爲民. 此節只言恆產所係之重. 4. 必,—not 'must be,' which would be inconsistent with the 賢, but 'will be,' i.e. will be sure to be. The last two clauses are exegetical of 恭 and 儉. 下 must be understood of 臣, 'ministers,' in contradistinction from the 民, 'people,'

in the next clause, though all are of course 'beneath' the ruler. 5. This Yang Hû is the Yang Ho of the Analects, XVII. i. To accord with his unworthy character, the observation is taken in a bad sense, as a dissuasive against the practice of benevolence, while Mancius quotes it to show the incompatibility of the two aims. Great stress is laid on the 爲. 爲富,爲仁,—'He who makes riches—benevolence—his business.' This force of the character would be well brought out by putting it in 3rd tone, but that would give the observation a good meaning. 6. 夏后氏, 殷人. 周人,—see Analects, III. xxi. By

以養其父母又稱貸而益
盻盻然將終歲勤動不得
必取盈焉爲民父母使民
之凶年糞其田而不足則
多取之而不爲虐則寡取
中以爲常樂歲粒米狼戾
不善於貢貢者校數歲之
龍子曰治地莫善於助莫
一也徹者徹也助者藉也。
周人百畝而徹其實皆什

founder of the Châu enacted the hundred *máu* allotment, and the share system. In reality, *what was paid* in all these was a tithe. The share system means mutual division. The aid system means mutual dependence.

7. 'Lung said, "For regulating the lands, there is no better system than that of mutual aid, and none which is not better than that of taxing. By the tax system, the regular amount was fixed by taking the average of several years. In good years, when the grain lies about in abundance, much might be taken without its being oppressive, and the actual exaction would be small. But in bad years, the produce being not sufficient to repay the manuring of the fields, this system still requires the taking of the full amount. When the parent of the people causes the people to wear looks of distress, and, after the whole year's toil, yet not to be able to nourish their parents, so

the Hsiâ statutes, every husbandman—head of a family—received fifty *máu*, and paid the produce of five of them to the government. This payment was the 貢. By those of Yin, 630 *máu* were divided into nine equal allotments of seventy *máu* each, the central one being reserved for the government, and eight families on the other allotments uniting in its cultivation. By those of Châu, to one family 100 *máu* were assigned, and ten families cultivated 1,000 acres in common, dividing the produce, and paying a tenth to the government. Such is the account here given by Mencius, but it is very general, and not to be taken, especially as relates to the system of the Châu dynasty, as an accurate exposition of it. More in accordance with the accounts in the Châu Lî is his own system recommended below to Pî Chan. 7. Of the Lung quoted here, all that Châo Ch'î and Chû Hsî say, is that he was 'an ancient worthy.' 狼戾 is said to be synonymous with 狼藉, meaning 'abundant.' That this is the signification is plain enough, but how the characters come to indicate it is not clear. 狼 means 'a wolf,' and 藉 is given in connexion with that character as meaning 'the appearance of things scattered about in confusion.' I cannot find any signification of 戾, 'crooked, perverse, &c.,' from which, as joined to 狼, we can well bring out the

三代共之皆所以明人
校殷曰序周曰庠學則
者教也序者射也夏曰
校以教之庠者養也校
周亦助也。設爲庠序學
爲有公田、設爲庠序學
我公田、遂及我私。惟助
祿滕固行之矣。詩云、雨
在其爲民父母也夫世
之使老稚轉乎溝壑惡

that they proceed to borrowing to increase their means, till the old people and children are found lying in the ditches and water-channels:—where, *in such a case*, is his parental relation to the people?"

8. 'As to the system of hereditary salaries, that is already observed in T'ăng.

9. 'It is said in the Book of Poetry,

"May the rain come down on our public field,
And then upon our private fields!"

It is only in the system of mutual aid that there is a public field, and from this passage we perceive that even in the Châu dynasty this system has been recognised.

10. 'Establish *hsiang, hsü, hsio,* and *hsiáo,—all those educational institutions,—*for the instruction of *the people.* The name *hsiang* indicates nourishing *as its object; hsiáo* indicates teaching; and *hsü* indicates archery. By the Hsiâ dynasty the name *hsiáo* was used; by the Yin, that of *hsü;* and by the Châu, that of *hsiang.* As to the *hsio,* they belonged to the three dynasties, *and by that name.* The object of them all is to illustrate the human relations. When

meaning. 聭聭然 is taken by Châo Ch'î as in the translation, and by Chû Hsî as = 'an angry-looking appearance,' which does not suit so well. 稱＝舉, 'to lift up,'＝'to proceed to.' 惡 (the 1st tone) 在其爲民父母,—see Bk. I. Pt. I. iv. 5. 8. 夫, and tone. 世祿,—see Bk. I. Pt. II. v. 3. 9. See the Shih-ching, II. vi. Ode VIII. st. 3, a description of husbandry under the Châu dynasty. 雨, —the verb, 4th tone. The object of the quota-tion is to show that the system of mutual aid obtained under the Châu as well as under the Yin dynasty, and the way is prepared for the instructions given to Pî Chan below. 10. After the due regulation of husbandry, and provision for the 'certain livelihood' of the people, must come the business of education. The *hsio* mentioned were schools of a higher order in the capital of the kingdom and other chief cities of the various States. The others (校, *hsiáo,* 4th tone) were schools in the villages and smaller towns. In the Lî Chî, III. Sect. v. 10, we find the *hsiang* mentioned in connexion with

經界始經界不正井地
子必勉之夫仁政必自
將行仁政選擇而使子
問井地孟子曰子之君
亦以新子之國使畢戰
文王之謂也子力行之
云周雖舊邦其命維新
取法是為王者師也詩
親於下有王者起必來
倫也人倫明於上小民

those are *thus* illustrated by superiors, kindly feeling will prevail among the inferior people below.

11. 'Should a real sovereign arise, he will certainly come and take an example *from you;* and thus you will be the teacher of the true sovereign.

12. 'It is said in the Book of Poetry,

"Although Châu was an old country,
It received a new destiny."

That is said with reference to king Wăn. Do you practise those things with vigour, and you also will by them make new your kingdom.'

13. *The duke afterwards* sent Pî Chan to consult *Mencius* about the nine-squares system of dividing the land. Mencius said to him, 'Since your prince, wishing to put in practice a benevolent government, has made choice of you and put you into this employment, you must exert yourself to the utmost. Now, the first thing towards a benevolent government must be to lay down the boundaries. If the boundaries be not defined correctly, the division of the land into

the time of Shun; And in connexion with the Hsiâ dynasty; Hsio in connexion with the Yin; and Chiâo (膠) in connexion with the Châu. There is thus some want of harmony between that passage and the account in the text. Entertainments were given to the aged at different times, and in the schools, as an example to the young of the reverence accorded by the government to age. So the schools were selected for the practice of archery, as a trial of virtue and skill.

人論明於上,—this can hardly mean, 'when the human relations have been illustrated by the example of superiors.' but must

have reference to the inculcation of those relations by the institution of schools. The pith of Mencius's advice is—'Provide 'the means of education for all, the poor as well as the rich.' 12. See the Shih-ching, III. i. Ode L. st. 1. 其命, 'the appointment,' i.e. which lighted on it from Heaven. 13. To understand the 'nine-squares division of the land,' the form of the character 井 needs only to be looked at. If we draw lines to enclose it—thus, 田—we have a square portion of ground divided into nine equal and smaller squares. But can

不均、穀祿不平、是故
暴君汙吏必慢其經
界。經界既正、分田制
祿、可坐而定也。夫滕
壤地褊小、將爲君子
焉、將爲野人焉。無君
子莫治野人、無野人
莫養君子。請野九一
而助、國中什一使自
賦。卿以下必有圭田、

squares will not be equal, and the produce *available for* salaries will not be evenly distributed. On this account, oppressive rulers and impure ministers are sure to neglect this defining of the boundaries. When the boundaries have been defined correctly, the division of the fields and the regulation of allowances may be determined by you, sitting at your ease.

14. 'Although the territory of T'ǎng is narrow and small, yet there must be in it men of a superior grade, and there must be in it country-men. If there were not men of a superior grade, there would be none to rule the country-men. If there were not country-men, there would be none to support the men of superior grade.

15. 'I would ask you, in the remoter districts, observing the nine-squares division, to reserve one division to be cultivated on the system of mutual aid, and in the more central parts of the kingdom, to make the people pay for themselves a tenth part of their produce.

16. 'From the highest officers down to the lowest, each one must have his holy field, consisting of fifty *mâu*.

we suppose it possible to divide a territory in this way? The natural irregularities of the surface would be one great obstacle. And we find below the 'holy field,' and other assignments, which must continually have been requiring new arrangement of the boundaries. 14. 君子,—here, generally, for officers, men not earning their bread by the sweat of their brow, and the toil of their hands; see next chapter. 野人, 'country-men,'—by their toil self-supporting people generally. 將=殆; 將爲=殆必有. 15. Here the systems of all the three dynasties would seem to be employed, as the nature of the country permitted, or made advisable, their application. 野 as opposed to 國中 must be understood, as in the translation,—'the country,' 'the remoter districts.' The 九 refers to 公田 in par. 13, and the 一 to 制祿. The former would be the best way in such positions of supporting the 野人, and the latter of supporting the 君子. Similarly, the other clause. 16. 圭 is explained by Châo Ch'î by 潔, and Chû Hsî follows him, though we do not find this meaning of the term in the dictionary. The 圭田 then is 'the clean field,' and as its produce was

子矣。　也若夫潤澤之則在君與　所以別野人也。此其大略　田公事畢然後敢治私事。　田八家皆私百畝同養公　而井井九百畝其中爲公　相扶持則百姓親睦方里　出入相友守望相助疾病　畝死徙無出鄉鄉田同井。　圭田、五十畝。餘夫、二十五

17. 'Let the supernumerary males have their twenty-five *mâu*.

18. 'On occasions of death, or removal from one dwelling to another, there will be no quitting the district. In the fields of a district, those who belong to the same nine squares render all friendly offices to one another in their going out and coming in, aid one another in keeping watch and ward, and sustain one another in sickness. Thus the people are brought to live in affection and harmony.

19. 'A square *lî* covers nine squares of land, which nine squares contain nine hundred *mâu*. The central square is the public field, and eight families, each having its private hundred *mâu*, cultivate in common the public field. And not till the public work is finished, may they presume to attend to their private affairs. This is the way by which the country-men are distinguished *from those of a superior grade*.

20. Those are the great outlines of the system. Happily to modify and adapt it depends on the prince and you.'

intended to supply the means of sacrifice, I translate it by 'the holy field.' It was in addition to the hereditary salary mentioned in par. 8. 17. A family was supposed to embrace the grandfather and grandmother, the husband, wife, and children, the husband being the grandparents' eldest son. The extra fields were for other sons whom they might have, and were given to them when they were sixteen. When they married and became heads of families themselves, they received the regular allotment for a family. This is Chû Hsî's account of this paragraph. 18. The social benefits flowing from the nine-square division of the land. 'On occasions of death,' i.e. in burying. 19. Under the Châu dynasty, a hundred *pû* or 'paces' made a *mâu's* length, but the exact amount of the pace can hardly be ascertained. Many contend that the fifty *mâu* of Hsiâ, the seventy of Yin, and the hundred of Châu, were actually of the same dimensions. 養,—the 4th tone, so spoken always, when the subject is the support of a superior by an inferior. 20. 若 夫 (the 2nd tone), = 至 於. 潤 澤, 'the softening and moistening,' i.e. the modifying and adapting.

以其弟辛負耒耜 食陳良之徒陳相 褐捆屨織席以爲 其徒數十人皆衣 爲氓。文公與之處 仁政、願受一廛而 遠方之人聞君行 踵門而告文公曰、 者、許行、自楚之滕 有爲神農之言

CHAP. IV. 1. There came from Ch'û to T'ǎng one Hsü·Hsing, who gave out that he acted according to the words of Shăn-năng. Coming right to his gate, he addressed the duke Wăn, saying, 'A man of a distant region, I have heard that you, Prince, are practising a benevolent government, and I wish to receive a site for a house, and to become one of your people.' The duke Wăn gave him a dwelling-place. His disciples, amounting to several tens, all wore clothes of haircloth, and made sandals of hemp and wove mats for a living.

2. *At the same time*, Ch'ăn Hsiang, a disciple of Ch'ăn Liang, and his younger brother, Hsin, with their plough-handles and shares on

4. MENCIUS'S REFUTATION OF THE DOCTRINE THAT THE RULER OUGHT TO LABOUR AT HUSBANDRY WITH HIS OWN HANDS. HE VINDICATES THE PROPRIETY OF THE DIVISION OF LABOUR, AND OF A LETTERED CLASS CONDUCTING GOVERNMENT. The first three paragraphs, it is said, relate how Hsing, the heresiarch, and Hsiang, his follower, wished secretly to destroy the arrangements advised by Mencius for the division of the land. The next eight paragraphs expose the great error of Hsing, that the ruler must labour at the toils of husbandry as well as the people. From the twelfth paragraph to the sixteenth, Hsiang is rebuked for forsaking his master, and taking up with Hsing's heresy. In the last two paragraphs, Mencius proceeds, from the evasive replies of Hsiang, to give the coup de grâce to the new pernicious teachings. 1. 爲 is explained, by Châo Ch'î, by 治爲, and 言 as = 道, so that 爲 ... 言者 = 'one who cultivated the doctrines. Most others take 爲 = 假託, 'making a false pretence of.' Shăn-năng, 'Won-derful husbandman,' is the style of the second of the five famous 帝, or early 'sovereigns,' of Chinese history. He is also called Yen (炎) Ti, 'the Blazing Sovereign.' He is placed between Fû-hsî and Hwang Ti, though separ-ated from the latter by an intervention of seven

reigns, extending with his own over 515 years. If any faith could be reposed in this chronology, it would place him B.C. 3212. In the appendix to the Yî-ching, he is celebrated as the Father of Husbandry. Other traditions make him the Father of Medicine also. 之滕, — 之 is the verb, = 往. 踵, in the dictionary, after Châo Ch'î is explained by 至, 'came to.' Chû Hsî says that 踵門 = 足至門. 廛 and 氓, see Bk. II. Pt. I. v. 5, but the meaning of 廛 here is different, denoting the ground assigned for the dwelling of a husbandman. 衣 (4th tone) 褐, — it would appear from par. 4 that this 'haircloth' was a very inartificial struc-ture, not woven at least with much art. 屨, — 'sandals of hemp,' opposed to 扉, which were made of grass, and 履, which were made of leather. 捆 is explained by 扣椓 'to beat and hammer. 席 properly denotes single mats made of rushes (莞蒲). This manu-facture of sandals and mats is supposed in the 備旨 to have been only a temporary employ-ment of Hsing's followers till lands should be

而自宋之滕、聞君行聖
人之政、是亦聖人也。願為
聖人氓。陳相見許行而大
悅、盡棄其學而學焉。陳相
見孟子、道許行之言曰、滕
君、則誠賢君也、雖然未聞
道也。賢者與民並耕而食、
饔飧而治。今也滕有倉廩
府庫、則是厲民而以自養
也、惡得賢。孟子曰、許子必

their backs, came from Sung to T‘ăng, saying, 'We have heard that you, Prince, are putting into practice the government of the *ancient sages, showing that* you are likewise a sage. We wish to become the subjects of a sage.'

3. When Ch‘ăn Hsiang saw Hsü Hsing, he was greatly pleased with him, and, abandoning entirely whatever he had learned, became his disciple. Having an interview with Mencius, he related to him *with approbation* the words of Hsü Hsing to the following effect :— 'The prince of T‘ăng is indeed a worthy prince. He has not yet heard, however, the *real* doctrines *of antiquity*. Now, wise and able princes should cultivate the ground equally and along with their people, and eat *the fruit of their labour*. They should prepare their own meals, morning and evening, while at the same time they carry on their government. But now, *the prince of* T‘ăng has his granaries, treasuries, and arsenals, which is an oppressing of the people to nourish himself. How can he be deemed a *real* worthy prince?'

4. Mencius said, 'I suppose that Hsü Hsing sows grain and eats

assigned them. a. Of the individuals mentioned here, we know nothing more than can be gathered from this chapter. The 耕, or share, as originally made by Shǎn-năng, was of wood. In Mencius's time, it had come to be made of iron; see par. 4. 之滕,—之 as above. 3. 道許行之言,—道 is the verb,—稱述. 賢者,—as in Bk. I. Pt I. ii. 1. 饔飧 denote the morning and evening

meals, but must be taken here as verbs, signifying the preparation of those meals. If 倉 and 廩 are to be distinguished, the latter is a granary for rice, the former for other grain. 養, in 4th tone. The object of Hsü Hsing in these remarks would be to invalidate Mencius's doctrine given in the last chapter, par. 14, that the ruler must be supported by the country-men. 4. Observe the force of 必 ... 乎, as in the

種粟而後食乎。曰、然。許子必
織布而後衣乎。曰、否、許子衣
褐。曰、許子冠乎。曰、冠。曰、奚
冠。曰、冠素。曰、自織之與。曰、否、以
粟易之。曰、許子奚爲不自織。
曰、害於耕。曰、許子以釜甑爨
以鐵耕乎。曰、然。自爲之與。曰、
否、以粟易之。以粟易械器者、
不爲厲陶冶。陶冶亦以其械
器易粟者豈爲厲農夫哉且

the produce. Is it not so?' 'It is so,' was the answer. 'I suppose *also* he weaves cloth, and wears his own manufacture. Is it not so?' 'No. Hsü wears clothes of haircloth.' 'Does he wear a cap?' 'He wears a cap.' 'What kind of cap?' 'A plain cap.' 'Is it woven by himself?' 'No. He gets it in exchange for grain.' 'Why does Hsü not weave it himself?' 'That would injure his husbandry.' 'Does Hsü cook his food in boilers and earthenware pans, and does he plough with an iron share?' 'Yes.' 'Does he make those articles himself?' 'No. He gets them in exchange for grain.'

5. *Mencius then said*, 'The getting those various articles in exchange for grain, is not oppressive to the potter and the founder, and the potter and the founder in their turn, in exchanging their various articles for grain, are not oppressive to the husbandman. How should

translation. 粟, 'millet,' but here = grain generally. 衣, 4th tone. 冠素, 'His cap is plain,' i.e. undyed and unadorned. The distinction given by Chû Hsî between 釜 and 甑 is, that the former was used for boiling, and the latter for steaming. Their composition indicates that they were made of iron and clay respectively. The 釜 was distinguished from other iron boilers by having no feet. 5. 以 者 = 'he who gets,' or, as in the translation, 'the getting.' 械,—properly 'stocks,'

but also used synonymously with 器. I have added a sentence to bring out the force of 豈 in 豈爲厲云云. Chû Hsî puts a point at 冶, and taking 舍 (in 3rd tone) in the sense of 止, 'only,' construes it with what follows. This is better than to join it, in the sense of house or shop, with 陶冶. Hsiang is here forced to make an admission, fatal to his new master's doctrine, that every man should do everything for himself. The only difficulty is with the 且, which here = 'but.' The two

許子何不爲陶冶舍皆取諸
其宮中而用之何爲紛紛然
與百工交易何許子之不憚
煩。曰百工之事固不可耕且
爲也然則治天下獨可耕且
爲與有大人之事有小人之
事且一人之身而百工之所
爲備如必自爲而後用之是
率天下而路也故曰或勞心
或勞力勞心者治人勞力者

such a thing be supposed? And moreover, why does not Hsü act the potter and founder, supplying himself with the articles which he uses solely from his own establishment? Why does he go confusedly dealing and exchanging with the handicraftsmen? Why does he not spare himself so much trouble?' *Ch'an Hsiang replied,* 'The business of the handicraftsman can by no means be carried on along with the business of husbandry.'

6. *Mencius resumed,* 'Then, is it the government of the kingdom which alone can be carried on along with the practice of husbandry? Great men have their proper business, and little men have their proper business. Moreover, in the case of any single individual, *whatever articles he can require* are ready to his hand, being produced by the various handicraftsmen:—if he must first make them for his own use, this way of doing would keep all the people running about upon the roads. Hence, there is the saying, "Some labour with their minds, and some labour with their strength. Those who labour with their minds govern others; those who labour with their strength

preceding sentences are Mencius's affirmations, and he proceeds—'But Hsü Haing denies this. Why then does he not himself play the potter and founder, &c.?' 6. In 一人之身 而 百工之所爲備 the construction is not easy. The correct meaning seems to be that given in the translation. Some take 備 in the sense of 'are all required,' which would make the construction simpler:—'for a single person even, all the productions of the handi-craftsmen are necessary.' So, in the paraphrase of the 日講:—'Reckoning in the case of a single individual, his clothes, his food, and his dwelling-place, the productions of the various workers must all be completed in suf-

治於人治於人者食人治
人者食於人天下之通義
也。當堯之時天下猶未平
洪水橫流氾濫於天下草
木暢茂禽獸繁殖五穀不
登禽獸偪人獸蹄鳥跡之
道交於中國堯獨憂之舉
舜而敷治焉舜使益掌火
益烈山澤而焚之禽獸逃
匿禹疏九河淪濟潔而注

are governed by others. Those who are governed by others support
them; those who govern others are supported by them." This is
a principle universally recognised.

7. 'In the time of Yâo, when the world had not yet been perfectly
reduced to order, the vast waters, flowing out of their channels, made
a universal inundation. Vegetation was luxuriant, and birds and
beasts swarmed. The various kinds of grain could not be grown.
The birds and beasts pressed upon men. The paths marked by the
feet of beasts and prints of birds crossed one another throughout
the Middle Kingdom. To Yâo alone this caused anxious sorrow. He
raised Shun to office, and measures to regulate the disorder were set
forth. Shun committed to Yî the direction of the fire to be employed,
and Yî set fire to, and consumed, *the forests and vegetation on* the
mountains and *in* the marshes, so that the birds and beasts fled away
to hide themselves. Yü separated the nine streams, cleared the
courses of the Tsî and T'â, and led them all to the sea. He opened

ficiency, and then he has abundantly everything
for profitable employment, and can without
anxiety support his children and parents.' This
gives a good enough meaning in the connexion,
but the signification attached to 備 is hardly
otherwise authorised. 而 路, 'and road
them,'—舜 走 道 路, 食, 4th tone, *tsze*.
7. 天下猶未平 carries us back to the
time antecedent to Yâo, and 天下 is to be
taken in the sense of 'world,' or 'earth.' There

is the idea of a wild, confused, chaotic state, on
which the successive sages had been at work,
without any great amount of success. Then in
the next paragraph we have Hâu-chî doing
over again the work of Shân-nâng and teaching
men husbandry. It is difficult to go beyond
Yâo for the founding of the Chinese kingdom.
The various questions which would arise here,
however, will be found discussed in the first
part of the Shû-ching. It is only necessary
to observe in reference to the calamity here
spoken of, that it is not presented as the
consequence of a deluge, or sudden accumulation of water, but from the natural river-

諸海決汝漢排淮泗而
注之江然後中國可得
而食也當是時也禹八
年於外三過其門而不
入雖欲耕得乎后稷教
民稼穡樹藝五穀五穀
熟而民人育人之有道
也飽食煖衣逸居而無
教則近於禽獸聖人有
憂之使契爲司徒教以

a vent also for the Zŭ and Han, and regulated the course of the Hwâi and Sze, so that they all flowed into the Chiang. When this was done, it became possible for the people of the Middle Kingdom to *cultivate the ground and* get food for themselves. During that time, Yŭ was eight years away from his home, and though he thrice passed the door of it, he did not enter. Although he had wished to cultivate the ground, could he have done so?

8. 'The Minister of Agriculture taught the people to sow and reap, cultivating the five kinds of grain. When the five kinds of grain were brought to maturity, the people all obtained a subsistence. But men possess a moral nature; and if they are well fed, warmly clad, and comfortably lodged, without being taught at the same time, they become almost like the beasts. This was a subject of anxious solicitude to the sage *Shun*, and he appointed Hsieh to be the Minister of Instruction, to teach the relations of humanity :— how, between father and son, there should be affection; between

channels being all broken up and disordered. 橫, in 4th tone, 'disobedient,' 'unreasonable.' 五穀, 'the five kinds of grains,' are 稻、黍、稷、麥, and 菽, 'paddy, millet, pannicled millet, wheat, and pulse,' but each of these terms must be taken as comprehending several varieties under it. 中國, in opposition to 天下, is the portion of country which was first settled, and regarded as a centre to all surrounding territories. 堯獨憂之,— the 獨 seems to refer to Yâo's position as sovereign, in which it belonged to him to feel this anxiety. For the labours of Shun, Yî, and Yŭ, see the Shû-ching, Parts I, II, III. 濟, in 3rd tone. 漯,—read Tâ. The nine streams all belonged to the Ho, or Yellow river. By them Yî led off a portion of its vast surging waters. The Chiang is the Yang-tsze. Chû Hsî observes that of the rivers mentioned as being led into the Chiang only the Han flows into that stream, while the Hwâi receives the Zŭ and the Sze, and makes a direct course to the sea. He supposes an error on the part of the recorder of Mencius's words. 8. Hâu-chî, now received as a proper name, is properly the official title of Shun's Minister of Agriculture, Ch'î (棄) 契 (read Hsieh) was the name

人倫父子有親君臣
有義夫婦有別長幼
有序朋友有信放勳
曰勞之來之匡之直
之輔之翼之使自得
之又從而振德之聖
人之憂民如此而暇
耕平堯以不得舜爲
己憂舜以不得禹皋
陶爲己憂夫以百畝

sovereign and minister, righteousness; between husband and wife, attention to their separate functions; between old and young, a proper order; and between friends, fidelity. The highly meritorious *sovereign* said to him, "Encourage them; lead them on; rectify them; straighten them; help them; give them wings :—thus causing them to become possessors of themselves. Then follow this up by stimulating them, and conferring benefits on them." When the sages were exercising their solicitude for the people in this way, had they leisure to cultivate the ground?

9. 'What Yâo felt giving him anxiety was the not getting Shun. What Shun felt giving him anxiety was the not getting Yü and Kâo Yâo. But he whose anxiety is about his hundred *mâu* not being properly cultivated, is a *mere* husbandman.

of his Minister of Instruction. For these men and their works, see the Shû-ching, Part II. 藝,—used synonymously with 蓺,—種 'to plant,' or 'sow.' foreigners generally try to construe this expression as they do the 民之爲道也 in the preceding chapter, par. 2, not having regard to the difference of 民 and 人, of 爲 and 有, and the five repetitions of 有 farther on in the paragraph. The interpretation which I have adopted is that of Chû Hsî, and every critic of note whom I have consulted. 聖人 is supposed to be plural,—'the sages.' This, however, cannot be, as the 使 immediately following must be understood with reference to Shun only. What has made 聖人 be taken as plural, is that the instructions addressed to Hsieh are said to be from 放 (3rd tone) 勳, which are two of the epithets applied to Yâo in the opening sentence of the Shû-ching, who is therefore supposed to be the speaker. Yet it was Shun who appointed Hsieh, and gave him his instructions, and may not Mencius intend *him* by 'The highly meritorious'? The address itself is not found in the Shû-ching. 勞 and 來 are both in 4th tone. In 夫婦有別, 別= 'separate functions,' according to which the husband is said to preside over all that is external, and the wife over all that is internal, while to the former it belongs to lead, and to the latter to follow. 9. An illustration of the 有大人之事, 有小人之事, in par. 6. 易,—read î, in 4th tone, in the sense of 治 (in 2nd tone). The Kâo of Kâo Yâo is generally written as in the text, but the proper form of it is 皋 It is difficult to determine whether to unite the two characters as a double surname, or to keep them apart as surname

夏變夷者未聞變於夷者也陳
其心哉亦不用於耕耳吾聞用
與焉堯舜之治天下豈無所用
君哉也舜巍巍乎有天下而不
惟堯則之蕩蕩乎民無能名焉
子曰大哉堯之為君惟天為大
為天下得人者謂之仁是故以
以財謂之惠敎人以善謂之忠
之不易為已憂者農夫也分人

10. 'The imparting by a man to others of his wealth, is called "kindness." The teaching others what is good, is called "the exercise of fidelity." The finding a man who shall benefit the kingdom, is called "benevolence." Hence to give the throne to another man would be easy; to find a man who shall benefit the kingdom is difficult.

11. 'Confucius said, "Great indeed was Yâo as a sovereign. It is only Heaven that is great, and only Yâo corresponded to it. How vast was his virtue! The people could find no name for it. Princely indeed was Shun! How majestic was he, having possession of the kingdom, and yet seeming as if it were nothing to him!" In their governing the kingdom, were there no subjects on which Yâo and Shun employed their minds? There were subjects, only they did not employ their minds on the cultivation of the ground.

12. 'I have heard of men using *the doctrines of* our great land to change barbarians, but I have never yet heard of any being changed

and name. 10. 為, in the 4th tone, 'on behalf of,'—who shall benefit. 易,—read as in the text, and meaning 'easy.' The difficulty spoken of arises from this, that to find the man in question requires the finder to go out of himself, and is beyond what is in his own power. The reader must bear in mind that 仁 is the name for the highest virtue, the combination of all possible virtues. Compare Analects, VI. xxviii. 11. See Analects, VIII. xviii and xix, which two chapters Mencius blends together with omissions and alterations. Observe the force of 亦 in the last clause. It = 'there were subjects on which they employed their minds, but still, &c.' 12. 夏 and 夷,—used as in Analects, III. v. 先,—the verb,

良楚產也悅周公仲尼之道、
比學於中國北方之學者、未
能或之先也、彼所謂豪傑之
士也子之兄弟事之數十年、
師死而遂倍之昔者孔子沒、○十三節
三年之外門人治任將歸入
揖於子貢相嚮而哭皆失聲
然後歸子貢反築室於場獨
居三年然後歸他日子夏子
張子游以有若似聖人欲以

by barbarians. Ch'an Liang was a native of Ch'û. Pleased with the doctrines of Châu-kung and Chung-nî, he came northwards to the Middle Kingdom and studied them. Among the scholars of the northern regions, there was perhaps no one who excelled him. He was what you call a scholar of high and distinguished qualities. You and your brother followed him some tens of years, and when your master died, you forthwith turned away from him.

13. 'Formerly, when Confucius died, after three years had elapsed, his disciples collected their baggage, and prepared to return to their several homes. But on entering to take their leave of Tsze-kung, as they looked towards one another, they wailed, till they all lost their voices. After this they returned to their homes, but Tsze-kung went back, and built a house for himself on the altar-ground, where he lived alone *other* three years, before he returned home. On another occasion, Tsze-hsiâ, Tsze-chang, and Tsze-yû, thinking that Yû Zo resembled the sage, wished to render to him the same

in 4th tone. 子之兄弟,—not 'your brothers,' but as in the translation; compare par. 2. 倍=背:—observe how Ch'û is here excluded from 'the Middle Kingdom' of Mencius's time. 13. On the death of Confucius, his disciples remained by his grave for three years, mourning for him as for a father, but without wearing the mourning dress. 治任,—both 2nd tone, 'looked after their burdens.' Tsze-

kung had acted to all his co-disciples as master of the ceremonies. Hence they took a formal leave of him. 場 is a flat place, an area scooped out upon the surface, and used primarily to sacrifice upon. Here it denotes such an area formed upon the sage's grave. There is a small wooden hut still shown in the Confucian cemetery, and said to be the apartment built by Tsze-kung for himself! I saw it in 1873. On Yû Zo's resemblance to Confucius, see the

之子是之學亦爲不善變矣。十七節
狄是膺荆舒是懲周公方且膺
喬木而入於幽谷者魯頌曰戎
出於幽谷遷于喬木者未聞下
師而學之亦異於曾子矣吾聞十五節
舌之人非先王之道子倍子之
鴃鴃乎不可尙已今也南蠻鴃
不可江漢以濯之秋陽以暴之、
所事孔子事之彊曾子曾子曰、

observances which they had rendered to Confucius. They tried to force the disciple Tsăng to join with them, but he said, "This may not be done. What has been washed in the waters of the Chiang and Han, and bleached in the autumn sun :—how glistening is it! Nothing can be added to it."

14. 'Now here is this shrike-tongued barbarian of the south, whose doctrines are not those of the ancient kings. You turn away from your master and become his disciple. Your conduct is different indeed from that of the philosopher Tsăng.

15. 'I have heard of *birds* leaving dark valleys to remove to lofty trees, but I have not heard of their descending from lofty trees to enter into dark valleys.

16. 'In the Praise-songs of Lû it is said,

"He smote the barbarians of the west and the north,
　He punished Ching and Shû."

Thus Châu-kung would be sure to smite them, and you become their disciple again ; it appears that your change is not good.'

17. *Ch'an Hsiang said,* 'If Hsü's doctrines were followed, then

Book of Rites, Bk. II. Sect. I. iii. 4. 彊,—in 3rd tone. 暴 is in the 4th tone. 鴃,—read *kwă*, in 2nd tone, or *kăo.* 尙=加. Compare 無以尙之, Analects, IV. vi. 1. 14. 鴃 —'the shrike, or butcher bird,' a strong epithet of contempt or dislike, as applied to Hsü Hsing. 倍,—as above. 15. 下,—used as a verb, in 4th tone. 16. See the Book of Poetry, IV. ii. Ode IV. st. 6. The two clauses quoted refer to

之道相率而爲僞者也惡能治
小屨同賈人豈爲之哉從許子
子比而同之是亂天下也巨屨
或相倍蓰或相什伯或相千萬
相若曰夫物之不齊物之情也
寡同則賈相若屨大小同則賈
絲絮輕重同則賈相若五穀多
欺布帛長短同則賈相若麻縷
僞雖使五尺之童適市莫之或
許子之道則市賈不貳國中無

there would not be two prices in the market, nor any deceit in the kingdom. If a boy of five cubits were sent to the market, no one would impose on him; linen and silk of the same length would be of the same price. So it would be with *bundles of* hemp and silk, being of the same weight; with the different kinds of grain, being the same in quantity; and with shoes which were of the same size.'

18. *Mencius* replied, 'It is the nature of things to be of unequal quality. Some are twice, some five times, some ten times, some a hundred times, some a thousand times, some ten thousand times as valuable as others. If you reduce them all to the same standard, that must throw the kingdom into confusion. If large shoes and small shoes were of the same price, who would make them? For people to follow the doctrines of Hsü, would be for them to lead one another on to practise deceit. How can they avail for the government of a State ?'

the achievements of the duke Hsi. Mencius uses them as if they expressed the approbation of his ancestor Châu-kung. 17. 賈,—read *chiâ*, 4th tone, —see Analects, VIII. vi. 麻縷絲絮 must be joined together, I think, in pairs, in opposition to the 布帛 above, the manufactured articles. 縷 is explained, in the 說文, by 綫,

'threads,' and may be used of silk or flax. 絮 is explained, also in the 說文, by 敝緜, 'spoiled, or bad, floss.' Its general application is to floss of an inferior quality. :8. 倍,— different from that in pars. 12, 15, meaning 'as much again.' 相=相去, 'are separated from each other,' or 'are to each other as.' The size of the shoes is mentioned as a thing more

國家。

墨者夷之因徐辟而求
見孟子。孟子曰、吾固願見、
今吾尚病、病愈我且往見、
夷子不來。又求見孟
子。孟子曰、吾今則可以見
矣、不直則道不見、我且直
之、吾聞夷子墨者、墨之治
喪也、以薄爲其道也、夷子
思以易天下、豈以爲非是

CHAP. V.　1. The Mohist, Î Chih, sought, through Hsü Pï, to see Mencius. Mencius said, 'I indeed wish to see him, but at present I am still unwell. When I am better, I will myself go and see him. He need not come here *again*.'

2. Next day, *Î Chih* again sought to see Mencius. Mencius said, 'To-day I am able to see him. But if I do not correct his errors, the *true* principles will not be fully evident. Let me first correct him. I have heard that this Î is a Mohist. Now Mo considers that in the regulation of funeral matters a spare simplicity should be the rule. Î thinks with *Mo's doctrines* to change *the customs of* the kingdom;—how does he regard them as if they were wrong, and not

palpable than their quality, and exposing more easily the absurdity of Hsü's proposition.

5. HOW MENCIUS CONVINCED A MOHIST OF HIS ERROR, THAT ALL MEN WERE TO BE LOVED EQUALLY, WITHOUT DIFFERENCE OF DEGREE. 1. Mo, by name 翟 (read Tï), was a heresiarch between the times of Confucius and Mencius. His most distinguishing principle was that of universal and equal love, which he contended would remedy all the evils of society ;—see next Part, chap. ix, *et al*. It has been contended, however, by the Rev. Dr. Edkins, that Mencius's account of Mo's views is unfair. See Journal of the North-China Branch of the Royal Asiatic Society, No. II. Some of Mo's writings remain, and some notice of them will be found in the prolegomena. 徐辟 (read Pï or Pï) was a disciple of Mencius. The philosopher, according to the opinion of Chû Hsî, was well enough, but feigned sick-

ness and told Î Chih that he need not come again to see him,—to try his sincerity. It is to be understood that Chih had intimated that he was dissatisfied with his Mohism, and Mencius would be guided in his judgment of his really being so, by testing his desire to obtain an interview with him. It is difficult to express the force of the particle 且;—'myself' comes near it. 夷子不來 is Mencius's remark, and Châo Ch'î is wrong, when he carries it on to the next paragraph, and construes—'Î in consequence did not then come, but another day, &c.' a. 他日, 'another day;' probably, 'next day.' The repetition of the application satisfied Mencius that Chih was really anxious to be instructed. 直, Chû Hsî says, = 盡言以相正, 'to expound the truth fully to correct him.' 不見 = 見, 4th tone. 我且直之, =

而不貫也然而夷子葬其
親厚則是以所賤事親也
徐子以告夷子夷子曰儒
者之道古之人若保赤子
此言何謂也之則以為愛
無差等施由親始徐子以
告孟子孟子曰夫夷子信
以為人之親其兄之子為
若親其鄰之赤子乎彼有
取爾也赤子匍匐將入井

honour them? Notwithstanding his views, Î buried his parents in a sumptuous manner, and so he served them in the way which *his doctrines* discountenance.'

3. The disciple Hsü informed Î of these remarks. Î said, '*Even according to* the principles of the learned, we find that the ancients *acted towards the people* "as if they were watching over an infant." What does this expression mean? To me it sounds that we are to love *all* without difference of degree; but the manifestation *of love* must begin with our parents.' Hsü reported this reply to Mencius, who said, 'Now, does Î really think that a man's affection for the child of his brother is *merely* like his affection for the infant of a neighbour? What is to be approved in that *expression* is simply this:—that if an infant crawling about is likely to fall into a well,

且 is here = 將, 'will.' The 備旨 says that 對未遽見言, 'it is used with reference to the not readily granting Î an interview.' Mencius wanted to put the applicant right, before conversing with him. We are to suppose that, after the acknowledgment in the concluding paragraph, he admitted Î to his presence. This principle about conducting funerals, or mourning generally, in a spare and inexpensive manner, was a subordinate point of Mo's teaching, and Mencius knowing that Î Chih had not observed it, saw how he could lead him on from it to see the error of the chief principle of the sect. 貫 and 賤 are both verbs. 3. Chih attempts to show that the classical doctrine likewise had the principle of equal and universal love. See the 若保赤子

quoted in the 'Great Learning,' Commentary, ix. 2. 之則.—之 is the name of the speaker. 差, read ts'ze, 'uneven.' 差等,—'uneven degrees.' Î Chih does not attempt to vindicate the sumptuous interment of his parents ;—he says 施由始親, not knowing what to say. 夫,—2nd tone. 彼有取爾 (=耳) 也, with what follows, requires to be supplemented by the reader :—'The child's falling into the well being thus from no perverse intent, but the consequence of its helplessness, people, liable to offend in ignorance, are to be dealt with in the same way ;—to be instructed and watched over. This is all that we can find

心達於面目蓋歸反
夫泚也非爲人泚中
其顙有泚睨而不視
狸食之蠅蚋姑嘬之
之於壑他日過之狐
者其親死則舉而委
上世嘗有不葬其親
而夷子二本故也。蓋
之生物也使之一本
非赤子之罪也且天

it is no crime in the infant. Moreover, Heaven gives birth to creatures in such a way that they have one root, and I makes them to have two roots. This is the cause *of his error.*

4. 'And, in the most ancient times, there were some who did not inter their parents. When their parents died, they took them up and threw them into some water-channel. Afterwards, when passing by them, *they saw* foxes and wild-cats devouring them, and flies and gnats biting at them. The perspiration started out upon their foreheads, and they looked away, unable to bear the sight. It was not on account of other people that this perspiration flowed. The emotions

in the words which he quotes.' Chão Ch'î makes 彼 refer to Î Chih :—' he only takes a part of the meaning. He loses the scope of the whole, and clings to the word infant.' This is ingenious, but does not seem sound. The 'one root' is the parents (and the seed in reference to inanimate things, but the subject is all about men, and hence the 備旨 says that 物 is to be taken as 一人), to whom therefore should be given a peculiar affection. Mo saying that other men should be loved as much, and in the same way, as parents, made two roots. The 故 is quite enigmatic, but it is explained as I have done. 4. 蓋, not exactly 'for,' but as a more general continuative. Julien translates the first clause :—' Porro in superioribus seculis nondum erant qui sepelirent suos parentes,' and he blames Noel for rendering —' quidam filii parentes suos tumulo non mandebant.' Mencius, he says, 'is treating of all men, and not of some only.' I cannot, however, get over the 者, which would seem to require the rendering given by Noel. Reference is made indeed to the highest antiquity (上世), when

the sages had not yet delivered their rules for ceremonies, but from the clause 非爲人泚 we may infer that even then all were not equally unobservant of what was proper. 過.—the 1st tone. The passing by is not to be taken as fortuitous. Their natural solicitude brought them to see how it was with the bodies. The 狐 is 'the fox.' 狸 or 貍 is a name given to different animals. We have the 貓貍, or 'wild cat ;' the 風貍, which appears to be the 'raccoon ;' and others. 姑, says Chû Hsî, has no meaning, but is a drawl between the words before and after it. Some would take it for 姑, a kind of cricket. 非爲人泚, —compare 非所以要譽云云, Bk. II. Pt. I. vi. 3. 中心 'their middle heart,' the very centre of their being. 蓋歸—蓋 = 'and forthwith,' but what follows contains a proof of what is said before—中心云云. 反虆梩, 'overturned baskets and shovels,'

曰　憮　夷　徐　必　掩　子　是　之　虆
命　然　子　子　有　其　仁　也　掩　梩
之　爲　夷　以　道　親　人　則　之　而
矣。閒　子　告　矣。亦　之　孝　誠　掩

of their hearts affected their faces and eyes, and instantly they went home, and came back with baskets and spades and covered the bodies. If *the covering them thus* was indeed right, you may see that the filial son and virtuous man, in interring *in a handsome manner* their parents, act according to a proper rule.'

5. The disciple Hsü informed Î of what Mencius had said. Î was thoughtful for a short time, and then said, 'He has instructed me.'

i. e. of earth. 虆,—read *lo* (not *lü*, as enjoined in the tonal notes in most editions of Mencius), in 2nd tone. The meaning of 梩 is obscure; that of a spade or shovel (wooden, of course) is given, however, to it. The conclusion of the argument is this, that what affection prompted in the first case, was prompted similarly in its more sumptuous exhibition in the progress of civilisation. If any interment was right, a handsome one must be right also. 5. 憮然, in the dictionary, is explained, as 'the appearance of being surprised.' In Analects, XVIII. vi. 4, Chû Hsî explains the phrase by 悵然, 'vexed-like.' I have there translated—'with a sigh.' 命之,—之 is again the speaker's name. 命 is in the sense of 教, 'to instruct.'

TĂNG WĂN KUNG. PART II.

尺見則侯二膝
士旌景爲而之宜陳文
不不公也直大若代公
忘至田三尋則小曰章
在將招孟宜以然不句
溝殺虞子若霸今見下
壑之人曰可且一諸
勇志以昔齊志王王小
       齊曰杜小以

CHAPTER I. 1. Ch'ăn Tâi said *to Mencius*, 'In not *going to* wait upon any of the princes, you seem to me to be standing on a small point. If now you were once to wait upon them, the result might be so great that you would make one of them sovereign, or, if smaller, that you would make one of them chief of all the other princes. Moreover, the History says, "By bending *only* one cubit, you make eight cubits straight." It appears to me like a thing which might be done.'

2. Mencius said, 'Formerly, the duke Ching of Ch'î, once when he was hunting, called his forester to him by a flag. *The forester* would not come, *and the duke* was going to kill him. *With reference to this incident,* Confucius said, "The determined officer never forgets

1. How MENCIUS DEFENDED THE DIGNITY OF RESERVE BY WHICH HE REGULATED HIS INTERCOURSE WITH THE PRINCES OF HIS TIME. To understand the chapter, it must be borne in mind, that there were many wandering scholars in the days of Mencius, men who went from court to court, recommending themselves to the various princes, and trying to influence the course of events by their counsels. They would stoop for place and employment. Not so with our philosopher. He required that there should be shown to himself a portion of the respect which was due to the principles of which he was the expounder. 1. Ch'ăn Tâi was one of Mencius's disciples. 不見=不往見 宜若小然,—'in reason is as if it were small like.' 大 is said to be 大用, 'if you were greatly employed,' and 小=小用. It is better to take these terms as in the translation. The clauses must be expanded—大則以其君王, 小則以其君霸. 王,—4th tone. 志,—see Pt. I. ii. 3. The 'thing that might be done' is Mencius's going to wait on the princes. 2. The 虞人 was an officer as old as the time of Shun, who appoints Yî (益), Shû-ching, II. i. 22, saying that 'he could rightly superintend the birds and beasts of the fields and trees on his hills, and in his forests.' In the Châu Lî, Pt. II. Bk. xvi, we have an account of the office, where it appears, that, on occasion of a great hunting, the forester had to clear the paths, and set up flags for the

士不忘喪其元孔
子奚取焉取非其
招不往也如不待
其招而往何哉且
夫枉尺而直尋者
以利言也如以利
則枉尋直尺而利
亦可爲與昔者趙
簡子使王良與嬖
奚乘終日而不獲

that his end may be in a ditch or a stream; the brave officer never forgets that he may lose his head." What was it *in the forester* that Confucius thus approved? He approved his not going *to the duke*, when summoned by the article which was not appropriate to him. If one go *to see the princes* without waiting to be invited, what can be thought of him?

3. 'Moreover, *that sentence*, "By bending *only* one cubit, you make eight cubits straight," is spoken with reference to the gain *that may be got*. If gain be the object, then, if it can be got by bending eight cubits to make one cubit straight, may we likewise do that?

4. 'Formerly, the officer Châo Chien made Wang Liang act as charioteer for his favourite Hsî, when, in the course of a whole day,

hunters to collect around. There the charges are the 'hills' and 'marshes,' and here, according to Châo Ch'î and Chû Hsî, they were the 'preserves and parks.' In those times, the various officers had their several tokens, which the prince's messenger bore when he was sent to call any of them. A forester's token was a fur cap, and the one in the text would not answer to a summons with a flag. See the incident in the 左傳，昭公，二十年, where the details, however, and Confucius's judgment on it, are different. It is there said:—'The prince of Ch'î was hunting in P'î and summoned the forester with a *bow*. As the forester did not come, the prince had him seized, when he excused himself, saying, *In the huntings of former princes*, 大夫 *have been summoned with a banner*; 士, *with a bow; and the forester with a fur cap. As I did not see the fur cap, I did not venture to approach.* The duke on this dismissed the man. Chung-ni said, *He observed the law of his office, rather than the ordinary rule of answering the summons. Superior men will approve of his act.'* 田,—used for 畋 or 佃. The observations which must be taken as made by Confucius are found nowhere else.

元,—here = 首, 'the head.' 不忘 is a difficult phrase in the connexion. I have made the best of it I could. The first 其招 is plain enough—the summons appropriate to him, i. e. to a forester. We cannot lay so much stress, however, on the 其 in the same phrase in the last sentence, the subject of the chapter being the question of Mencius's waiting on the princes without being called by them at all. 3. 且夫 (2nd tone) is more forcible and argumentative than 且 alone. 如以利 = 如以計利爲心. The question in 亦可爲與 is an appeal to Tâi's own sense of what was right. Admitting what I e asked in par. 1, any amount of evil might be done that good might come. Was he prepared to allow that? 4. The Chien (簡) in Châo Chien is the posthumous epithet. His name was 鞅 (*Yang*), a noble of Tsin, in the time of Confucius, and Wang Liang was his charioteer, famous for his skill. Liang appears in the histories of the time—the 左傳 and 國語—by different

破我不貫與小人乘請辭。
十詩云不失其馳舍矢如
獲一為之詭遇一朝而獲
吾為之範我馳驅終日不
與女乘謂王良良不可曰
之良工也簡子曰我使掌
獲十禽嬖奚反命曰天下
請復之彊而後可一朝而
賤工也或以告王良良曰
一禽嬖奚反命曰天下之

they did not get a single bird. The favourite Hsî reported this result, saying, "He is the poorest charioteer in the world." Some one told this to Wang Liang, who said, "I beg leave to *try again*." By dint of pressing, this was accorded to him, when in one morning they got ten birds. The favourite, reporting this result, said, "He is the best charioteer in the world." Chien said, "I will make him always drive your chariot for you." When he told Wang Liang so, *however*, Liang refused, saying, "I *drove* for him, strictly observing the proper rules for driving, and in the whole day he did not get one *bird*. I *drove* for him so as deceitfully to intercept *the birds*, and in one morning he got ten. It is said in the Book of Poetry,

'There is no failure in the management of their horses;
The arrows are discharged surely, like the blows of an axe.'

I am not accustomed to drive for a mean man. I beg leave to decline the office."

names. He is called 郵無恤 郵無 正, 郵展, as well as 王展;—see the 四書拓餘說, *in loc.* 與=為, 'for,' and 乘 (4th tone), 'a chariot,' is used as a verb, 'to drive a chariot.' 反命—see Pt. I. ii. 3. It is a phrase of form. 工,—'a mechanic,' 'an artist;' here = 'a charioteer.' 請復 (4th tone) 之,—'I beg to *again* it.' 彊 —2nd tone. 掌 與女 (=汝) 乘,—'to manage the chariot-driving for you.' It is not common in Chinese to separate, as here, the verb and its object. 展不可, 'Liang might not,' i.e. would not be induced to take the office. 吾為 (4th tone) 之範我馳驅, 'I for him *law-ed* my racing my horses and whipping them. 詩云,—see the Shih-ching, II. iii. Ode V. st. 6. Literally the two lines are, 'They err not in the galloping; they let go the arrows, as if rending.' 舍,—the 3rd tone. 貫,— used for 慣. 5 比,—4th tone, in the sense

未學禮乎丈夫之冠也父
曰、是焉得爲大丈夫乎子
侯懼安居而天下熄孟子
不誠大丈夫哉一怒而諸
二　景春曰、公孫衍張儀豈
者也。
過矣枉己者、未有能直人
如枉道而從彼何也且子
得禽獸雖若丘陵弗爲也。
御者、且羞與射者比、比而

5. ' *Thus* this charioteer even was ashamed, to bend improperly to the will of *such an* archer. Though, by bending to it, they would have caught birds and animals sufficient to form a hill, he would not do so. If I were to bend my principles and follow those *princes*, of what kind would my conduct be? And you are wrong. Never has a man who has bent himself been able to make others straight.'

CHAP. II. 1. Ching Ch'un said *to Mencius*, 'Are not Kung-sun Yen and Chang Î really great men? Let them once be angry, and all the princes are afraid. Let them live quietly, and the flames of trouble are extinguished throughout the kingdom.'

2. Mencius said, 'How can such men be great men? Have you not read the Ritual *Usages?*—"At the capping of a young man, his

of 'to flatter. 丘陵,—to be taken together, 'a mound,' 'a hill.' The 彼,—'that, or those,' referring to 諸侯 in par. 1. We must supply I, as the subject of 枉. The concluding remark is just, but hardly consistent with the allowances for their personal misconduct which Mencius was prepared to make to the princes.

2. MENCIUS'S CONCEPTION OF THE GREAT MAN. 1. Ching Ch'un was a man of Mencius's day, 'a practiser of the art of up-and-across' (爲 縱橫之術者), i.e. one who plumed himself on his versatility. Kung-sun Yen and Chang Î were also men of that age, natives of Wei (魏), and among the most celebrated of the ambitious scholars, who went from State to State, seeking employment, and embroiling the

princes;—see the 'Historical Records,' Book C, chap. x. 丈夫,—see Pt. I. i. 4. The phrase is used, however, in the next paragraph for ' a grown-up youth.' 熄 has, in the Shwo Wăn, the opposite meanings of ' feeding a fire' and ' extinguishing a fire.' The latter is its meaning here. 2. 是,—referring to Yen and Î with what is said about them above. 焉,—the interrogative, in 1st tone. The ' Rites ' or ' Book of Rites,' to which Mencius here chiefly refers, is not the compilation now received among the higher classics, under the name of the Lî Chî, but the Î Lî (儀禮). He throws various passages together, and, according to his wont, is not careful to quote correctly. In the Î Lî, not only does her mother admonish the bride, but her father also, and his concubines, and all to the effect

夫。威武不能屈此之謂大丈
富貴不能淫貧賤不能移。
民由之不得志獨行其道
位行天下之大道得志與
天下之廣居立天下之正
順爲正者妾婦之道也居
家必敬必戒無違夫子以
往送之門戒之曰往之女
命之女子之嫁也母命之

father admonishes him. At the marrying away of a young woman, her mother admonishes her, accompanying her to the door on her leaving, and cautioning her with these words, 'You are going to your home. You must be respectful; you must be careful. Do not disobey your husband.'" *Thus*, to look upon compliance as their correct course is the rule for women.

3. 'To dwell in the wide house of the world, to stand in the correct seat of the world, and to walk in the great path of the world ; when he obtains his desire *for office*, to practise his principles for the good of the people ; and when that desire is disappointed, to practise them alone ; to be above the power of riches and honours to make dissipated, of poverty and mean condition to make swerve from principle, and of power and force to make bend :—these characteristics constitute the great man.'

that she is to be obedient, though the husband (here called 夫子) is not expressly mentioned. See the 儀禮註疏, Bk. II. pp. 49, 50. For the ceremonies of Capping, see the same, Bk. I. In 送之門 and, more especially, in 往之女(汝)家 the 之 joins the verbs and nouns, and is construed as the verb,= 往. 妾婦 are to be taken together,—'a concubine-woman.' Mencius uses the term 妾 in his contempt for Yen and I, who, with all their bluster, only pandered to the passions of the princes. Obedience is the rule for all women, and specially so for secondary

wives. 3. 'The wide house of the world' is *benevolence* or *love*, the chief and home of all the virtues ; 'the correct seat' is *propriety ;* and 'the great path' is *righteousness.* 與民由之 (the 之 refers to the virtues so metaphorically indicated),—'walks according to them along with the people.' The paraphrase in the 日講 says :—'Getting his desire, and being employed in the world, he comes forth, and carries out these principles of benevolence, propriety, and righteousness towards the people, and pursues them along with them ' 此之謂—'this is what is called,'—such is the description of, a really 'great man.'

諸侯耕助以供粢盛

侯之失國家也禮曰

曰士之失位也猶諸

無君則弔不以急乎

三月無君則弔三月

質公明儀曰古之人

皇皇如也出疆必載

曰孔子三月無君則

子仕乎孟子曰仕傳

周霄問曰古之君

CHAP. III. 1. Châu Hsiâo asked *Mencius*, saying, 'Did superior men of old time take office?' Mencius replied, 'They did. The Record says, "If Confucius was three months without *being employed by some* ruler, he looked anxious and unhappy. When he passed from the boundary of a State, he was sure to carry with him his proper gift of introduction." Kung-ming Î said, "Among the ancients, if an officer was three months unemployed by a ruler, he was condoled with." '

2. *Hsiâo said*, 'Did not this condoling, on being three months unemployed by a ruler, show a too great urgency?'

3. *Mencius* answered, 'The loss of his place to an officer is like the loss of his State to a prince. It is said in the Book of Rites, "A prince ploughs himself, and is assisted *by the people*, to supply

3. OFFICE IS TO BE EAGERLY DESIRED, AND YET IT MAY NOT BE SOUGHT BUT BY ITS PROPER PATH. It will be seen that the questioner of Mencius in this chapter—a man of Wei, and one of the wandering scholars of the time—wished to condemn the philosopher for the dignity of reserve which he maintained in his intercourse with the various princes. Mencius does not evade any of his questions, and very satisfactorily vindicates himself. 1. 傳,—the 4th tone, the 'Record;' whatever it was, it is now lost. 無君,—'without a ruler,' i.e. without office. 皇皇如 is 'the appearance of one who is seeking for something and cannot find it.' It is appropriate to a mourner in the first stages of grief after bereavement. 質,—read chi, in 3rd tone, synonymous with 贄. Every person waiting on another,—a superior,—was supposed to pave his way by some introductory gift, and each official rank had its proper article

to be used for that purpose by all belonging to it. See the Lî Chî, Bk. I. Pt. II. iii. 19. Confucius carried this with him, that he might not lose any opportunity of getting to be in office again. Kung-ming Î, we are told by Châo Ch'î, was 'a worthy,' but of what time and what state, we do not know. An individual of the same surname is mentioned, Analects, XIV. xiv. Julien translates 則弔 incorrectly by—'tunc in luctu erant.' The paraphrase of the 日講 says:—'Then people all came to condole with and to comfort them.' 2. 以 is to be taken as synonymous with 已; 時不已急乎. 3. 國家,—the State, embracing the families of the nobles. In his quotations from the Lî Chî, Mencius combines and adapts to his purpose, with more, however, than his usual freedom, different passages. See Bk. XXI. Sect. ii. para. 5–7, and Bk. IV. Sect. I. iii. 12, Sect. II. i. 19. Chû Hsî, to illustrate the text, gives

農夫豈爲出疆舍其耒

之仕也猶農夫之耕也、

出疆必載質何也。曰士

不敢以宴亦不足弔乎。

衣服不備不敢以祭則

田、則亦不祭牲殺器皿、

不備不敢以祭惟士無

牲不成粢盛不潔衣服

夫人蠶繅以爲衣服、犧

the millet *for sacrifice*. His wife keeps silkworms, and unwinds their cocoons, to make the garments *for sacrifice*." If the victims be not perfect, the millet not pure, and the dress not complete, he does not presume to sacrifice. "And the scholar who, *out of office*, has no *holy* field, in the same way, does not sacrifice. The victims for slaughter, the vessels, and the garments, not being all complete, he does not presume to sacrifice, and then neither may he dare to feel happy." Is there not here sufficient ground also for condolence?'

4. *Hsido again asked*, 'What was the meaning of *Confucius's* always carrying his proper gift of introduction with him, when he passed over the boundaries *of the State where he had been*?'

5. 'An officer's being in office,' was the reply, 'is like the ploughing of a husbandman. Does a husbandman part with his plough, because he goes from one State to another?'

another summary of the passages in the Lî Chî, thus :—'It is said in the Book of Rites, The princes had their special field of 100 mâu, in which, wearing their crown, with its blue flaps turned up, they held the plough to commence the ploughing, which was afterwards completed with the help of the common people. The produce of this field was reaped and stored in the ducal granary, to supply the vessels of millet in the ancestral temple. They also caused the family women (世 婦) of their harem to attend to the silkworms, in the silk-worm house attached to the State mulberry trees, and to bring the cocoons to them. These were then presented to their wives, who received them in their sacrificial headdress and robe, soaked them, and thrice drew out a thread. They then distributed the cocoons among the ladies of the three palaces, to prepare the threads for the ornaments on the robes to be worn in sacrificing to the former kings and dukes.' 盛, the 2nd tone, 'the millet placed in the sacrificial vessel.' 犧牲,—牲, the victim, whatever it might be ; 犧, the victim, as pure and perfect. The officer's field is the 圭 field, Pt. I. iii. 16. 器皿 together = vessels. Chû Hsî says the 皿 were the covers of the 器. 以宴,—' to feast,' = to feel happy. The argument is that it was not the mere loss of office which was a proper subject for grief and condolence, but the consequences of it, especially in not being able to continue his proper sacrifices, as here set forth. 5. 舍,—the 3rd tone. 耒耜,—see Pt. I. iv. par. 2.

耕哉曰晉國亦仕國也未嘗聞
仕如此其急仕如此其急也君
子之難仕何也曰丈夫生而願
爲之有室女子生而願爲之有
家父母之心人皆有之不待父
母之命媒妁之言鑽穴隙相窺
踰牆相從則父母國人皆賤之
古之人未嘗不欲仕也又惡不
由其道不由其道而往者與鑽
穴隙之類也。

6. *Hsiáo* pursued, 'The kingdom of Tsin is one, as well as others,
of official employments, but I have not heard of anyone being
thus earnest about being in office. If there should be this urgency,
why does a superior man make any difficulty about taking it?'
Mencius answered, 'When a son is born, what is desired for
him is that he may have a wife; when a daughter is born, what is
desired for her is that she may have a husband. This feeling of
the parents is possessed by all men. If *the young people*, without
waiting for the orders of their parents, and the arrangements of the
go-betweens, shall bore holes to steal a sight of each other, or get
over the wall to be with each other, then their parents and all
other people will despise them. The ancients did indeed always
desire to be in office, but they also hated being so by any improper
way. *To seek office* by an improper way is of a class with *young
people's* boring holes.'

6. 'The kingdom of Tsin,'—see Bk. I. Pt. I. v. 1.
君子之難仕,—by the 君子, Hsiáo
evidently intends Mencius himself, who, however, does not notice the insinuation. 丈夫
and 女子,—here simply 'a son,' 'a daughter.'
A man marrying is said 有室, 'to have an
apartment,' and a woman marrying, 有家, 'to
have a family,' or 'home.' On the go-between, see
the Chāu Lī, Pt. II. Bk. vi. parr. 54–60; the Shih-
ching, I. viii. Ode VI. st. 4. The law of marriage
here referred to by Mencius still obtains, and
seems to have been the rule of the Chinese race
from time immemorial. 相從,—從=就,
而往,—往=往見諸侯.

子如通之則梓匠輪輿皆
足則農有餘粟女有餘布
子不通功易事以羨補不
否士無事而食不可也曰
不以爲泰子以爲泰乎曰
如其道則舜受堯之天下
道則一簞食不可受於人
侯不以泰乎孟子曰非其
從者數百人以傳食於諸
彭更問曰後車數十乘
四
一

CHAP. IV. 1. P'ǎng Kǎng asked *Mencius*, saying, 'Is it not an extravagant procedure to go from one prince to another and live upon them, followed by several tens of carriages, and attended by several hundred men?' Mencius replied, 'If there be not a proper ground *for taking it*, a single bamboo-cup of rice may not be received from a man. If there be such a proper ground, then Shun's receiving the kingdom from Yâo is not to be considered excessive. Do you think it was excessive?'

2. *Kǎng* said, 'No. But for a scholar *performing* no service to receive his support notwithstanding is improper.'

3. *Mencius* answered, 'If you do not have an intercommunication of the productions of labour, and an interchange of *men's* services, so that *one from his* overplus may supply the deficiency *of another*, then husbandmen will have a superfluity of grain, and women will have a superfluity of cloth. If you have such an interchange,

4. THE LABOURER IS WORTHY OF HIS HIRE, AND THERE IS NO LABOURER SO WORTHY AS THE SCHOLAR WHO INSTRUCTS MEN IN VIRTUE. 1. P'ǎng Kǎng was a disciple of Mencius. His object in addressing him, as in this chapter, seems to have been to stir him up to visit the princes and go into office. 乘,—4th tone, following 車, as a numeral or classifier. 從者-從, 4th tone, 'an attendant,' 'a follower,' not in a moral sense. 傳,—the 3rd tone, explained in the dictionary by 續, 'to connect,' 'succeed to.' 以傳, 'by succession.'—The phrase is felt to be a difficult one. Sun Shih explains it thus:— 'Mencius got his support from the princes, and the chariots and disciples got their support from Mencius. It came to this that the support of all was from the contributions of the princes, and hence it is said that by their mutual connexion they all lived on the princes.' 簞食-食 (tsze), 4th tone, 'ricecooked.' Compare Analects, VI. ix. 堯之天下, 'Yâo's world,' i.e. the kingdom from Yâo. 舜 may be construed very well as the nominative to the first 以爲. 3. 守先王之道以待後之學

得食於子、於此有人焉、入
則孝出則弟守先王之道、
以待後之學者而不得食
於子子何尊梓匠輪輿而
輕爲仁義者哉。四章、曰梓匠輪
輿其志將以求食也君子
之爲道也其志亦將以求
食與曰子何以其志爲哉
其有功於子可食而食之
矣且子食志乎、食功乎、曰。

carpenters and carriage-wrights may all get their food from you. Here now is a man, who, at home, is filial, and abroad, respectful to his elders; who watches over the principles of the ancient kings, awaiting *the rise of* future learners:—and yet you will refuse to support him. How is it that you give honour to the carpenter and carriage-wright, and slight him who practises benevolence and righteousness?'

4. *P'ång Kång* said, 'The aim of the carpenter and carriage-wright is *by their trades* to seek for a living. Is it also the aim of the superior man in his practice of principles thereby to seek for a living?' 'What have you to do,' returned *Mencius,* 'with his purpose? He is of service to you. He deserves to be supported, and should be supported. And *let me ask,*—Do you remunerate a man's intention, or do you remunerate his service.' *To this Kång* replied, 'I remunerate his intention.'

者,—the paraphrase in the 合講 is:—'He firmly guards the principles of benevolence and righteousness transmitted by the ancient kings, so that they do not get obscured or obstructed by perverse discourses, but hereby await future learners, and secure their having matter of instruction and models of imitation, whereby they may enter into truth and right. Thus he continues the past and opens the way for the future, and does service to the world.' 以 待 thus, = 'for the benefit of.' The 梓 and 匠 are both workers in wood, the 梓人's work being in smaller things, such as vessels and articles of furniture, and the 匠人's in large, such as building houses, &c. The 輪人 made the wheels and also the cover of a carriage; the 輿人 the other parts. 4. Observe how appropriately 將, expressive of futurity or object, follows 志. 可食而食之—here 食 and the three that follow, are read as in 一簞食, but with a different meaning, being = 'to feed' (active or passive), 'to give

牲也湯使遺之牛羊葛伯食
之曰何爲不祀曰無以供犧
鄰葛伯放而不祀湯使人問
之何孟子曰湯居亳與葛爲
行王政齊楚惡而伐之則如
萬章問曰宋小國也今將
食功也。
乎曰否曰然則子非食志也、
其志將以求食也則子食之
食志曰有人於此毀瓦畫墁、

5. *Mencius* said, 'There is a man here, who breaks your tiles, and draws *unsightly* figures on your walls;—his purpose may be thereby to seek for his living, but will you indeed remunerate him?' 'No,' said Kǎng; *and Mencius then* concluded, 'That being the case, it is not the purpose which you remunerate, but the work done.'

CHAP. V. 1. Wan Chang asked *Mencius*, saying, 'Sung is a small State. *Its ruler* is now setting about to practise the *true* royal government, and Ch'î and Ch'û hate and attack him. What in this case is to be done?'

2. *Mencius* replied, 'When Tang dwelt in Po, he adjoined to *the State of* Ko, the chief of which was living in a dissolute state and neglecting *his proper* sacrifices. Tang sent messengers to inquire why he did not sacrifice. He replied, "I have no means of supplying *the necessary* victims." *On this*, Tang caused oxen and sheep to be sent to him, but he ate them, and still continued not to sacrifice.

rice to.' 5. 畫 (4th tone) 墁,—墁 means 'ornaments on walls;'—we must therefore take 畫 in a bad sense, to correspond to the 毀. A man wishes to mend the roof, but he only breaks it; to ornament the wall, but he only disfigures it.

5. THE PRINCE WHO WILL SET HIMSELF TO PRACTISE A BENEVOLENT GOVERNMENT ON THE PRINCIPLES OF THE ANCIENT KINGS HAS NONE TO FEAR. 1. Wan Chang was a disciple of Mencius, the fifth book of whose Works is named from him. What he says here may surprise us,

because we know that the duke of Sung (its capital was in the present district of Shang-ch'iû [商邱], in the Kwei-teh department of Ho-nan), or king, as he styled himself, was entirely worthless and oppressive; see the 'Historical Records,' Book XXXVIII, 宋微子世家, towards the end. 2. Compare Bk. I. Pt. II. iii. 1, and xi. 2. Po, the capital of Tang (though there were three places of the same name), is referred to the same department of Ho-nan as the country of Ko, viz. that of

曰非富天下也爲匹夫匹　童子而征之四海之內皆　仇餉此之謂也爲其殺是　肉飼殺而奪之書曰葛伯　不授者殺之有童子以黍　要其有酒食黍稻者奪之　耕老弱饋食葛伯率其民　粢盛也湯使亳衆往爲之　之曰何爲不祀曰無以供　之又不以祀湯又使人問

Tang again sent messengers to ask him the same question as before, when he replied, "I have no means of obtaining the *necessary* millet." *On this*, Tang sent the mass of the people of Po to go and till the ground for him, while the old and feeble carried their food to them. The chief of Ko led his people to intercept those who were thus charged with wine, cooked rice, millet, and paddy, and took their stores from them, while they killed those who refused to give them up. There was a boy who had some millet and flesh for the labourers, who was thus slain and robbed. What is said in the Book of History, "The chief of Ko behaved as an enemy to the provision-carriers," has reference to this.

3. 'Because of his murder of this boy, *Tang* proceeded to punish him. All within the four seas said, "It is not because he desires the riches of the kingdom, but to avenge a common man and woman."

Kwei-teh. Its site is said to have been distant from the site of the supposed capital of Ko only about 100 li, so that Tang might easily render the services here mentioned to the 伯, chief or baron, of Ko. 無以供,—'no means of supplying,' i. e. of obtaining. 還, 4th tone, — 饋. 粢盛 (2nd tone),—see last chapter. 爲之,—爲, 4th tone. 饋食,—食 (tsze), 4th tone. 要, 1st tone;—we find it defined in the dictionary, by 'to meet with,' 'to extort,' which approximate to the meaning here. 酒 食, 一食, as above, 4th tone. 書曰,—see the Shû-ching, IV. ii. 6.—In the 四書拓餘 說, *in loc.*, 王厚齋 is quoted, to the effect that if Mencius had not been thus particular in explaining what is alluded to in the words of the Shû-ching, the interpretations of them would have been endless. But that in his time there were ancient books which could be appealed to. 3. 爲, 4th tone. 匹夫匹 婦,—'common men and women;'—see Analects, XIV. xviii. 3. The phrases are understood here, however, with a special application to the father and mother of the murdered boy.

婦復讐也湯始征自葛載十
一征而無敵於天下東面而
征西夷怨南面而征北狄怨
曰奚爲後我民之望之若大
旱之望雨也歸市者弗止芸
者不變誅其君弔其民如時
雨降民大悅書曰徯我后后
來其無罰有攸不爲臣東征
綏厥士女匪厥玄黃紹我周
王見休惟臣附于大邑周其

4. 'When T'ang began his work of executing justice, he commenced with Ko, and *though* he made eleven punitive expeditions, he had not an enemy in the kingdom. When he pursued his work in the east, the rude tribes in the west murmured. So did those on the north, when he was engaged in the south. Their cry was—"Why does he make us last." *Thus*, the people's longing for him was like their longing for rain in a time of great drought. The frequenters of the markets stopped not. Those engaged in weeding *in the fields* made no change *in their operations*. While he punished their rulers, he consoled the people. *His progress* was like the falling of opportune rain, and the people were delighted. It is said in the Book of History, "We have waited for our prince. When our prince comes, we may escape from the punishments *under which we suffer*."

5. 'There being some who would not become the subjects *of Châu*, *king Wû* proceeded to punish them on the east. He gave tranquillity to their people, who *welcomed him* with baskets full of their black and yellow silks, *saying*—"From henceforth we shall serve

4. Compare Bk. I. Pt. II. xi. a. There are, however, some variations in the phrases. 載=始. The quotation in the end is from a different part of the Shû-ching;—see Pt. IV. v. Section II. 5. The eleven punitive expeditions of T'ang cannot all be determined. From the Shih-ching and Shû-ching six only are made out, while by some their number is given as twenty-two, and twenty-seven;—see the 集證 *in loc.* 5. Down to 大邑周,—the substance of this paragraph is found in the Shû-ching;—see Pt. V. iii. 7; but this Book is confessed to require much emendation in its arrangement. 士女=男女. 匪,—used for 篚. 匪厥玄黃,—'basketed their azure and yellow silks.' It is said:—'Heaven is azure, and Earth is yellow. King Wû was

焉。欲以爲君齊楚雖大何畏
四海之內皆舉首而望之
不行王政云爾苟行王政
于殘殺伐用張于湯有光。
我武惟揚侵于之疆則取
中取其殘而已矣。太誓曰
迎其小人救民於水火之
君子其小人簞食壺漿以
君子實玄黃于匪以迎其

the sovereign of *our dynasty of* Châu, that we may be made happy by him." So they joined themselves, as subjects, to the great city of Châu. Thus, the men of station *of Shang* took baskets full of black and yellow *silks* to meet the men of station of *Châu*, and the lower classes of the one met those of the other with baskets of rice and vessels of congee. *Wû* saved the people from the midst of fire and water, seizing only their oppressors, *and destroying them.*'

6. 'In the Great Declaration it is said, "My power shall be put forth, and, invading the territories *of Shang*, I will seize the oppressor. I will put him to death to punish him:—so shall the greatness of my work appear, more glorious than that of Tang."

7. '*Sung* is not, as you say, practising *true* royal government, and so forth. If it were practising royal government, all within the four seas would be lifting up their heads, and looking for *its prince,* wishing to have him for their sovereign. Great as Ch'î and Ch'û are, what would there be to fear from them?'

able to put away the evils of the Yin rule, and gave the people rest. He might be compared to Heaven and Earth, overshadowing and sustaining all things in order to nourish men.' 紹 (we have 昭 in the Shû-ching),—'to continue.' We must understand a 'saying,' and bring out the meaning of 紹 thus:—'Formerly we served Shang, and now we continue to serve, but our service is to Châu.' 大邑周 literally, 'great city (or cities) Châu,' which is an irregular phrase, perhaps equal to Châu of the Great Capital. The 日讎 has 皆心悅誠服, 而盡歸附 於大邑周焉. From 其君子 onwards, Mencius explains the meaning of the Shû-ching. 6. This quotation from Pt. V. i. Sect. II. 8, is to illustrate the last clause of the preceding paragraph. 7. 云爾,—see Analects, VII. xviii. 云, however, does not here simply act as a particle closing the sentence, but also refers to the whole of Wan Chang's statement at the commencement of the conversation.

州善士也使之居於王所在
其楚亦不可得矣。子謂薛居
莊嶽之間數年雖日撻而求
其齊也不可得矣引而置之
之眾楚人咻之雖日撻而求
曰使齊人傅之曰一齊人傅
則使齊人傅諸使楚人傅諸
大夫於此欲其子之齊語也
之王之善與我明告子有楚
𡙇孟子謂戴不勝曰子欲子

CHAP. VI. 1. Mencius said to Tâi Pû-shăng, 'I see that you are desiring your king to be virtuous, and I will plainly tell you *how he may be made so.* Suppose that there is a great officer of Ch'û here, who wishes his son to learn the speech of Ch'î. Will he in that case employ a man of Ch'î as his tutor, or a man of Ch'û?' 'He will employ a man of Ch'î to teach him,' said *Pû-shăng*. *Mencius* went on, 'If *but* one man of Ch'î be teaching him, and there be a multitude of men of Ch'û continually shouting out about him, although *his father* beat him every day, wishing him to learn the speech of Ch'î, it will be impossible for him to do so. But in the same way, if he were to be taken and placed for several years in Chwang or Yo, though *his father* should beat him, wishing him to speak the language of Ch'û, it would be impossible for him to do so.

2. 'You supposed that Hsieh Chü-châu was a scholar of virtue, and you have got him placed in attendance on the king. Suppose

6. THE INFLUENCE OF EXAMPLE AND ASSOCIATION. THE IMPORTANCE OF HAVING VIRTUOUS MEN ABOUT A SOVEREIGN'S PERSON. 1. Tâi Pû-shăng was a minister of Sung, the descendant of one of its dukes who had received the posthumous epithet of Tâi, which had been adopted as their surname by a branch of his posterity. 子欲 … 與,—與, 2nd tone, the interrogative implying an affirmative reply. 欲其子之齊語, 'wishes the Ch'î speech of his son,'

i.e. wishes his son to learn Ch'î. 諸,—interrogative, and equal to 之乎. 咻, read *hsü*, = 讙, 'shouting,' 'clamorous.' Chwang and Yo were two well-known quarters in the capital of Ch'î, the former being the name of a street, and the latter the name of a neighbourhood; see the 四書拓餘說 in loc. 2. Hsieh Chü-châu was also a minister of Sung, a descendant of one of the princes of Hsieh, whose family had adopted the name

T 2

而辟之泄柳閉門而不
為臣不見段干木踰垣
侯何義孟子曰、古者、不
公孫丑問曰、不見諸
王何。
為善一薛居州、獨如宋
皆非薛居州也、王誰與
善在王所者、長幼卑尊、不
薛居州也、王誰與為不
於王所者、長幼卑尊、皆

that all in attendance on the king, old and young, high and low, were Hsieh Chü-châus, whom would the king have to do evil with? And suppose that all in attendance on the king, old and young, high and low, are not Hsieh Chü-châus, whom will the king have to do good with? What can one Hsieh Chü-châu do alone for the king of Sung?'

CHAP. VII. 1. Kung-sun Châu asked *Mencius*, saying, 'What is the point of righteousness involved in your not going to see the princes?' *Mencius* replied, 'Among the ancients, if one had not been a minister *in a State*, he did not go to see *the sovereign*.

2. 'Twan Kan-mû leaped over his wall to avoid the prince. Hsieh Liû shut his door, and would not admit the prince. These

of their original State as their surname. In the 萬姓通譜 we read :—'Tâi Pû-shâng said to Hsieh Chü-châu, "It is only the virtuous scholar (善士) who can set forth what is virtuous, and shut up the way of what is corrupt. You are a scholar of virtue; cannot you make the king virtuous?"' But this and what follows was probably constructed from Mencius's remark, and so I prefer to take 謂 as = 'supposed,' 'believed,' not 'said.' 長,—the 3rd tone. 居於王所,—'to dwell in the king's place,' i.e. to be about him.

7. MENCIUS DEFENDS HIS NOT GOING TO SEE THE PRINCES BY THE EXAMPLE AND MAXIMS OF THE ANCIENTS. 1. 何義 is not simply—'what is the meaning?' but 'what is the righteous?' Mencius, however, does not state distinctly the principle of the thing, but appeals to prescription and precedent. 不為臣=未為

臣, or 未仕於其國. In the Analects, XIV. xxii, we have an example of how Confucius, not then actually in office, but having been so, went to see the duke of Lû. 2. Twan Kan-mû was a scholar of Wei (魏), who refused to see the prince Wän (文). Wän was the posthumous title of 斯, B.C. 426–386. In the 'Historical Records,' it is mentioned that he received the writings of Tsze-hsiâ, and never drove past Kan-mû's house without bowing forward to the front bar of his carriage. 辟=避, 4th tone. 之 refers to the prince Wän. Hsieh Liû was a scholar of Lû, who refused to admit (內=納) the duke Mû (繆); see Bk. II. Pt. II. xi. 3. The incident referred to here must have been previous to the time spoken of there. 迫斯可以見矣,—literally, 'being urgent, this (or,

之所知也。由是觀之、則君子
同而言、觀其色赧赧然、非由
肩諂笑病于夏畦、子路曰、未
陽貨先豈得不見曾子曰、脅
矙其亡也、而往拜之、當是時、
亡也、而饋孔子蒸豚、孔子亦
則往拜其門、陽貨矙孔子之
夫有賜於士、不得受於其家、
陽貨欲見孔子、而惡無禮大
內、是皆已甚迫、斯可以見矣。

two, however, *carried their scrupulosity* to excess. When *a prince* is urgent, it is not improper to see him.

3. 'Yang Ho wished to get Confucius to go to see him, but disliked doing so by any want of propriety. *As it is the rule, therefore, that* when a great officer sends a gift to a scholar, if the latter be not at home to receive it, he must go to the *officer's* to pay his respects, Yang Ho watched when Confucius was out, and sent him a roasted pig. Confucius, in his turn, watched when Ho was out, and went to pay his respects to him. At that time, Yang Ho had taken the initiative;—how could *Confucius* decline *going* to see him?

4. 'Tsăng-tsze said, "They who shrug up their shoulders, and laugh in a flattering way, toil harder than the summer *labourer in the* fields." Tsze-lû said, "There are those who talk with people with whom they have no *great* community *of feeling*. If you look at their countenances, they are full of blushes. I do not *desire to* know such persons." By considering these *remarks*, the *spirit* which the superior man nourishes may be known.'

then) may be seen.' 3. 欲 見, 一 見, it is noted here, should be read in the 4th tone, with a *hiphil* sense. Compare Analects, XVII. i. 惡,—the verb, in 4th tone. 大夫有賜 云 云,—see the Lî Chî, XI. Sect. iii. 20. Mencius, however, does not quote the exact words. 亡 = 無, and so read. 4. 脅 肩, 'to rib,' i.e. to shrug, 'the shoulders.' 病, as in Bk. II. Pt. I. ii. 16. 夏畦 = 夏月治 畦之人. Chû Hsî makes 君子 to mean 'those two superior men,' referring to Tsăng and Tsze-lû. but this seems to be unnecessary.

義斯速已矣何待來年。待來年然後已如知其非道曰請損之月攘一雞以者或告之曰是非君子之曰今有人日攘其鄰之雞待來年然後已何如孟子之征今兹未能請輕之以

第九章 公都子曰外人皆稱夫

第八章 戴盈之曰什一去關市

之所養、可知已矣。

CHAP. VIII. 1. Tâi Ying-chih said to *Mencius*, 'I am not able at present and immediately to do with the levying of a tithe *only*, and abolishing the duties charged at the passes and in the markets. With your leave I will lighten, however, both the tax and the duties, until next year, and will then make an end of them. What do you think of such a course?'

2. Mencius said, 'Here is a man, who every day appropriates some of his neighbour's strayed fowls. Some one says to him, "Such is not the way of a good man;" and he replies, "With your leave I will diminish my appropriations, and will take only one fowl a month, until next year, when I will make an end of the practice."

3. 'If you know that the thing is unrighteous, then use all despatch in putting an end to it:—why wait till next year?'

CHAP. IX. 1. The disciple Kung-tû said to *Mencius*, 'Master, the people beyond *our school* all speak of you as being fond of

8. WHAT IS WRONG SHOULD BE PUT AN END TO AT ONCE, WITHOUT RESERVE AND WITHOUT DELAY. 1. Tâi Ying-chih was a great officer of Sung, supposed by some to be the same with Tâi Pûshâng, chap. vi. Mencius had, no doubt, been talking with him on the points indicated; see Bk. I. Pt. II. v. 3; Bk. II. Pt. I. v. 3; Bk. III. Pt. I. iii. 請, here and below, is simply the speaker's polite way of indicating his resolution. 2. 攘,—here as in Analects, XIII. xviii. 君子,—here, = 'a good man.' 損之 'diminish it,' i.e. the amount of his captures. 3. 斯 is used adverbially, = 'at once.' 已 in

all the paragraphs is the verb = 'have done with it,' 'put an end to it.'

9. MENCIUS DEFENDS HIMSELF AGAINST THE CHARGE OF BEING FOND OF DISPUTING. WHAT LED TO HIS APPEARING TO BE SO WAS THE NECESSITY OF THE TIME. Compare Bk. II. Pt. I. ii. 17. Mencius would appear from this chapter to have believed that the mantle of Confucius had fallen upon him, and that his position was that of a sage, on whom it devolved to live and labour for the world. 1. 外人,—'outside men,' i.e. people in general, all beyond his school, as the representative of orthodoxy in the kingdom. 敢問何, according to the gloss in the 備旨,

子好辯敢問何也。孟子
曰子豈好辯哉子不得
已也天下之生久矣、一
治一亂當堯之時、水逆
行氾濫於中國、蛇龍居
之民無所定下者爲巢、
上者爲營窟書曰、洚水
警余洚水者、洪水也。使
禹治之禹掘地而注之
海驅蛇龍而放之菹、水

disputing. I venture to ask whether it be so.' *Mencius* replied, Indeed, I am not fond of disputing, but I am compelled to do it.

2. 'A long time has elapsed since this world *of men* received its being, and there has been *along its history* now a period of good order, and now a period of confusion.

3. 'In the time of Yâo, the waters, flowing out of their channels, inundated the Middle Kingdom. Snakes and dragons occupied it, and the people had no place where they could settle themselves. In the low grounds they made nests for themselves *on the trees or raised platforms*, and in the high grounds they made caves. It is said in the Book of History, "The waters in their wild course warned me." Those "waters in their wild course" were the waters of the great inundation.

4. '*Shun* employed Yü to reduce the waters to order. Yü dug open *their obstructed channels*, and conducted them to the sea. He drove away the snakes and dragons, and forced them into the grassy

= 'I venture to ask why you are so fond of disputing,' as if Kung-tû admitted the charge of the outside people. But it is better to interpret as in the translation. The spirit of 子豈好辯哉 seems to be better given in English by dropping the interrogation. 2. Commentators are unanimous in understanding 天下之生 not of the material world, and taking 生＝生民. It is remarkable, then, that Mencius, in his review of the history of mankind, does not go beyond the time of Yâo (compare Pt. I. iv), and that at its commencement he places a period not of good order (治, 4th tone), but of confusion. 3. Mark the variations of phraseology here from Pt. I. iv. 7. 書曰,—see the Shû-ching, II. ii. 14, where for 警 we have 做. The 'nests' were huts on high-raised platforms. In the Lî Chî, VII. Sect. I. par. 8, these are said to have been the summer habitations of the earliest men, and 營窟, the winter. 營窟＝'artificial caves,' i.e. caves hollowed out from heaps of earth raised upon the ground. 洚水 is the same as the 水逆行 above. Chû Hsî explains it by 'deep and shoreless.' 4. 掘地, —'dug the earth,' but with the meaning in the translation. 菹 is read by Chû Hsî tsû,

又大亂周公相武王誅紂

而禽獸至及紂之身天下

行又作園囿汙池沛澤多

囿使民不得衣食邪說暴

民無所安息棄田以爲囿

君代作壞宮室以爲汙池

堯舜既沒聖人之道衰暴

消然後人得平土而居之。

險阻旣遠鳥獸之害人者

由地中行江淮河漢是也、

marshes. *On this,* the waters pursued their course through the country, even the waters of the Chiang, the Hwâi, the Ho, and the Han, and the dangers and obstructions which they had occasioned were removed. The birds and beasts which had injured the people *also* disappeared, and after this men found the plains *available for them,* and occupied them.

5. 'After the death of Yâo and Shun, the principles that mark sages fell into decay. Oppressive sovereigns arose one after another, who pulled down houses to make ponds and lakes, so that the people *knew* not where they could rest in quiet; they threw fields out of cultivation to form gardens and parks, so that the people could not get clothes and food. *Afterwards,* corrupt speakings and oppressive deeds became more rife; gardens and parks, ponds and lakes, thickets and marshes became more numerous, and birds and beasts swarmed. By the time of *the tyrant* Châu, the kingdom was again in a state of great confusion.

6. 'Châu-kung assisted king Wû, and destroyed Châu. He

but wrongly. With the meaning in the text, it is read *trieh.* 水由地中行—'the waters travelled in the middle or bosom of the earth,' i.e. ware no longer spread abroad over its surface. Chû Hsî makes 地中=兩涯 之閒, 'between their banks,' but that is not so much the idea, as that the waters pursued a course to the sea, through the land, instead of being spread over its surface. 5. In describing this period of confusion, Mencius seems to ignore the sageship of T'ang, and of the kings Wân and Wû;—especially that of T'ang.—in 4th tone. 浦, as associated with 澤 means thick marshy jungles, where beasts could find shelter. The 木 in its composition requires that we recognise the marshiness of the thickets or cover. But this account of the country down to the rise of the Châu dynasty implies that it was thinly peopled. 6. The kingdom of Yen is referred to a portion of the present district of Ch'û-fâu (曲阜) in Yen-

伐奄三年討其君驅飛廉
於海隅而戮之滅國者五
十驅虎豹犀象而遠之天
下大悅書曰丕顯哉文王
謨丕承哉武王烈佑啟我
後人咸以正無缺世衰道
微邪說暴行有作臣弑其
君者有之子弑其父者有
之孔子懼作春秋春秋天
子之事也是故孔子曰知

smote Yen, and after three years put its sovereign to death. He drove Fei-lien to a corner by the sea, and slew him. The States which he extinguished amounted to fifty. He drove far away also the tigers, leopards, rhinoceroses, and elephants;—and all the people was greatly delighted. It is said in the Book of History, "Great and splendid were the plans of king Wăn! Greatly were they carried out by the energy of king Wŭ! They are for the assistance and instruction of us who are of an after day. They are all in principle correct, and deficient in nothing."

7. 'Again the world fell into decay, and principles faded away. Perverse speakings and oppressive deeds waxed rife again. There were instances of ministers who murdered their sovereigns, and of sons who murdered their fathers.

8. 'Confucius was afraid, and made the "Spring and Autumn." What the "Spring and Autumn" contains are matters proper to the sovereign. On this account Confucius said, "Yes! It is the Spring

châu, Shan-tung. Châo Ch'î connects 三年 討其君 with 誅紂, but it seems to belong more naturally to 伐奄. Fei-lien was a favourite minister of Châu, who aided him in his enormities. In the 'Historical Records,' Bk. IV, 秦本記, at the beginning, he appears as 蜚廉, but without mention of his banishment and death. The place called 'a corner by the sea' cannot be determined. And it would be vain to try to enumerate the 'fifty kingdoms,' which Châu-kung ex-

tinguished. The 夷狄, in par. 11, must be supposed to have been among them. The 'tigers, leopards, &c.,' are the animals kept by Châu, not those infesting the country, as in the more ancient periods. 書曰,—see the Shû-ching, V. xxv. 6. 7. 行, 4th tone. 有 作,—有 read as, and = 又. 8. 'Spring and Autumn,'—annals of Lû for 242 years (B.C. 721-479), with Confucius's annotations, or rather, as is absurdly contended, adapted by him to express a correct judgment on every event and actor. They are composed as a sovereign

我者其惟春秋乎罪我者、
其惟春秋乎聖王不作諸
侯放恣處士橫議楊朱墨
翟之言盈天下天下之言
不歸楊則歸墨楊氏爲我
是無君也墨氏兼愛是無
父也無父無君是禽獸也
公明儀曰庖有肥肉廏有
肥馬民有饑色野有餓莩
此率獸而食人也楊墨之

and Autumn which will make men know me, and it is the Spring and Autumn which will make men condemn me."

9. '*Once more*, sage sovereigns cease to arise, and the princes of the States give the reins to their lusts. Unemployed scholars indulge in unreasonable discussions. The words of Yang Chû and Mo Tî fill the country. *If you listen to* people's discourses throughout it, *you will find that* they have adopted the views either of Yang or of Mo. Now, Yang's principle is—" each one for himself," which does not acknowledge *the claims of* the sovereign. Mo's principle is—" to love all equally," which does not acknowledge *the peculiar affection due to* a father. But to acknowledge neither king nor father is to be in the state of a beast. Kung-ming Î said, "In their kitchens, there is fat meat. In their stables, there are fat horses. But their people have the look of hunger, and on the wilds there are those who have died of famine. This is leading on beasts to devour men."

would have composed them. As Confucius was a sage without the throne, if one of the sovereign sages had written annals, he would have done so, as Confucius has done. Chû Hsî quotes from the commentator Hû (胡安國):—'Chung-nî made the *Spring and Autumn*, to lodge in it the true royal laws. There are the firm exhibition of the constant duties; the proper use of ceremonial distinctions; the assertion of Heaven's decree of favour to the virtuous; and the punishment of the guilty:—all these things, of which it may be said in brief that they are the business of the sovereign.' (Compare on Hû's language, the Shû-

ching, II. iii. 7.) It was by the study of this book, therefore, that Confucius wished himself to be known, though he knew that he exposed himself to presumption on account of the sovereign's point of view from which he looked at everything in it. This is the meaning of 罪我者其惟春秋乎, and not—'Those who condemn me (i. e. bad ministers and princes) will do so on account of my condemnations of them in it,' which is the view of Châo Ch'î. I have dropped the interrogations in the translation. 9. 處.—the 3rd tone, applied to a virgin dwelling in the seclusion of her apartments, and here to a scholar with-

兼夷狄驅猛獸而百姓寧、
禹抑洪水而天下平、周公
人復起不易吾言矣、昔者、
事作於其事害於其政、聖
不得作、作於其心、害於其
道距楊墨、放淫辭、邪說者
相食、吾爲此懼、閑先聖之
義充塞、則率獸食人、人將
邪說誣民、充塞仁義也、仁
道不息、孔子之道不著、是

If the principles of Yang and Mo be not stopped, and the principles of Confucius not set forth, then those perverse speakings will delude the people, and stop up *the path* of benevolence and righteousness. When benevolence and righteousness are stopped up, beasts will be led on to devour men, and men will devour one another.

10. 'I am alarmed by these things, and address myself to the defence of the doctrines of the former sages, and to oppose Yang and Mo. I drive away their licentious expressions, so that such perverse speakers may not be able to show themselves. *Their delusions* spring up in men's minds, and do injury to their practice of affairs. Shown in their practice of affairs, they are pernicious to their government. When sages shall rise up again, they will not change my words.

11. 'In former times, Yü repressed the vast waters *of the inundation*, and the country was reduced to order. Châu-kung's achievements extended even to the barbarous tribes of the east and north, and he drove away all ferocious animals, and the people enjoyed repose. Confucius completed the "Spring and Autumn," and rebellious ministers and villainous sons were struck with terror.

out public employment. Yang Chû, called also Yang Shû (成) and Yang Tsze-chû (子居), was a heresiarch of the times of Confucius and Lâo-tsze, of which last he is said to have been a disciple. In the days of Mencius, his principles appear to have been very rife. We may call his school the *selfish* school of China

(爲我,—爲, the 4th tone), as Mo's was the *transcendental*. 庖有肥肉云云,—see Bk. I. Pt. I. iv. 4. 10. 爲,—4th tone. 作於 其心云云,—see Bk. II. Pt. I. ii. 17. 11. 兼,—'embraced,' 'comprehended,' i. e. among the fifty States referred to above. 賊子,—

孔子成春秋、而亂臣賊子

懼詩云、戎狄是膺、荆舒是

懲則莫我敢承、無父無君

是周公所膺也、我亦欲正

人心息邪說距詖行放淫

辭以承三聖者、豈好辯哉、

予不得已也、能言距楊墨

者、聖人之徒也。

匡章曰陳仲子豈不誠

廉士哉、居於陵三日不食、

12. 'It is said in the Book of Poetry,

"He smote the barbarians of the west and the north;
He punished Ching and Shû;
And no one dared to resist. us."

These father-deniers and king-deniers would have been smitten by Châu-kung.

13. 'I also wish to rectify men's hearts, and to put an end to those perverse doctrines, to oppose their one-sided actions and banish away their licentious expressions;—and thus to carry on the work of the three sages. Do I do so because I am fond of disputing? I am compelled to do it.

14. 'Whoever is able to oppose Yang and Mo is a disciple of the sages.'

CHAP. X. 1. K'wang Chang said *to Mencius*, 'Is not Ch'ǎn Chung a man of true self-denying purity? He was living in Wû-ling, and for three days was without food, till he could neither hear

the parricides, mentioned in par. 7. 12. See Pt. I. iv. 16. The remark in the note there is equally applicable to the quotation here. 13. 詖行,—行, in and tone. Compare Bk. II. Pt. I. ii. 17. 14. This concluding remark is of a piece with the hesitancy shown by Mencius in Bk. II. Pt. I. ii, to claim boldly his place in the line of sages along with Confucius.

10. THE MAN WHO WILL AVOID ALL ASSOCIATION WITH, AND OBLIGATION TO, THOSE OF WHOM HE DOES NOT APPROVE, MUST NEEDS GO OUT OF THE WORLD. 1. Kw'ang Chang and Ch'ǎn Chung, called also

Ch'ǎn Tszĕ-chung (子終), were both men of Ch'î, the former high in the employment and confidence of the prince, the latter, as we learn from this chapter, belonging to an old and noble family of the State. His principles appear to have been those of Hsŭ Hsing (Pt. I. iv), or even more severe. We may compare him with the recluses of Confucius's time. Wû-ling (於 read wû) appears to have been a poor wild place, to which Chung and his wife, like-minded with himself, had retired. It is referred either to the district of Ch'ang-shan or that of Tszĕ-

耳無聞目無見也井上有李螬
食實者過半矣匍匐往將食之
三咽然後耳有聞目有見孟子
曰於齊國之士吾必以仲子爲
巨擘焉雖然仲子惡能廉充仲
子之操則蚓而後可者也夫蚓
上食槁壤下飲黃泉仲子所居
之室伯夷之所築與抑亦盜跖
之所築與所食之粟伯夷之所
樹與抑亦盜跖之所樹與是未

nor see. Over a well there grew a plum-tree, the fruit of which had been more than half eaten by worms. He crawled to it, and tried to eat *some of the fruit*, when, after swallowing three mouthfuls, he recovered his sight and hearing.'

2. Mencius replied, 'Among the scholars of Ch'î, I must regard Chung as the thumb *among the fingers*. But still, where is the self-denying purity *he pretends to*? To carry out the principles which he holds, one must become an earthworm, for so only can it be done.

3. 'Now, an earthworm eats the dry mould above, and drinks the yellow spring below. Was the house in which Chung dwells built by a Po-î? or was it built by a robber like Chih? Was the millet which he eats planted by a Po-î? or was it planted by a robber like Chih? These are things which cannot be known.'

ch'wan in the department of Tsî-nan. The 螬 is a worm proper to excrementitious matter. The term here is used, I suppose, to heighten our sense of the strait to which Chung was reduced by his self-denial. 咽, read yen, 4th tone, = 吞, 'to swallow.' 2. 充 = 推而滿之, 'to carry out fully.' 3. Po-î,—see Analects, V. xxii, et al. Chih was a famous robber chief of Confucius's time, a younger brother of Hûi of Liû-hsiâ. There was, however, it is said, in high antiquity in the times of Hwang-tî, a noted robber of the same name, which was given to Hûi's brother, because of the similarity of his course. Tâo Chih (the robber Chih) has come to be like a proper name. —As Chung withdrew from human society, lest he should be defiled by it, Mencius shows that unless he were a worm, he could not be independent of other men. Even the house he lived in, and the millet he ate, might be the result of the labour of a villain like Tâo-chih, or of a worthy like Po-î, for anything he could tell.

可知也。曰、是何傷哉、彼身織屨、
妻辟纑以易之也。曰、仲子齊之
世家也。兄戴蓋祿萬鍾、以兄之
祿爲不義之祿、而不食也。以兄
之室爲不義之室、而不居也。辟
兄離母、處於於陵。他日歸、則有
饋其兄生鵝者、己頻顣曰、惡用
是鶂鶂者爲哉。他日、其母殺是
鵝也、與之食之。其兄自外至、曰、
是鶂鶂之肉也、出而哇之。以母

4. 'But,' said *Chang*, 'what does that matter? He himself weaves sandals of hemp, and his wife twists and dresses threads of hemp to sell or exchange them.'

5. Mencius rejoined, 'Chung belongs to an ancient and noble family of Ch'î. His elder brother Tâi received from Kâ a revenue of 10,000 *chung*, but he considered his brother's emolument to be unrighteous, and would not eat of it, and in the same way he considered his brother's house to be unrighteous, and would not dwell in it. Avoiding his brother and leaving his mother, he went and dwelt in Wû-ling. One day afterwards, he returned *to their house*, when it happened that some one sent his brother a present of a live goose. He, knitting his eyebrows, said, "What are you going to use that cackling thing for?" By-and-by his mother killed the goose, and gave him some of it to eat. Just then his brother came into the house, and said, "It is the flesh of that cackling thing," upon which he went out and vomited it.

6. 'Thus, what his mother gave him he would not eat, but what

4. 何傷——compare 無傷 in Bk. I. Pt. I.
vii. 8. 織屨.—see Pt. I. iv. 辟 read pi,
=纑, 'to twist,' as threads of hemp on the
knee. This meaning is not found in the dic- | tionary, but Châo Ch'î explains it by 緝績,
and 績 by 績, 'to prepare for weaving.'
5. 蓋,—in 4th tone, as in Bk. II. Pt. II. vi. 1.
祿萬鍾.—see Bk. II. Pt. II. x. 3. 辟—

者 而 若 充 之 以 之 則 則
也。後 仲 其 是 於 室 食 不
　 充 子 類 尚 陵 則 之 食
　 其 者、也 爲 則 弗 以 以
　 操 蚓 乎、能 居 居 兄 妻

his wife gives him he eats. He will not dwell in his brother's house, but he dwells in Wû-ling. How can he in such circumstances complete the style of life which he professes? With such principles as Chung holds, a man must be an earthworm, and then he can carry them out.'

the name as 避. 頻顣 used for 顰蹙. 鶃 —read *ni*, the sound made by a goose. 是 鶃鶃者,—'this cackler.' 6. 以母則 不食 is expanded by Chû Hsî,—以 母 之食 爲不義 而不食, 'he considered what his mother gave him to eat not to be righteous, and would not eat it.' Similarly he brings out the force of the 以 in the other clauses. The glossarist of Châo Ch'î treats it more loosely, as in the translation.

BOOK IV.

LÎ LÂU. PART I.

之明公輸子之｜孟子曰離婁
能成方員師曠不｜之聰不以六律
巧不以規矩不
之聰不以六律
不能正五音堯
舜之道不以仁
政不能平治天
下今有仁心仁

CHAPTER I. 1. Mencius said, 'The power of vision of Lî Lâu, and skill of hand of Kung-shû, without the compass and square, could not form squares and circles. The acute ear of the music-master K'wang, without the pitch-tubes, could not determine correctly the five notes. The principles of Yâo and Shun, without a benevolent government, could not secure the tranquil order of the kingdom.

2. 'There are now *princes* who have benevolent hearts and a

With this Book commences what is commonly called the second or lower part of the works of Mencius, but that division is not recognised in the critical editions. It is named Lî Lâu, from its commencing with those two characters, and contains twenty-eight chapters, which are most of them shorter than those of the preceding Books.

1. THERE IS AN ART OF GOVERNMENT, AS WELL AS A WISH TO GOVERN WELL, TO BE LEARNED FROM THE EXAMPLE AND PRINCIPLES OF THE ANCIENT KINGS, AND WHICH REQUIRES TO BE STUDIED AND PRACTISED BY RULERS AND THEIR MINISTERS. 1. Lî Lâu, called also Lî Chû (朱), carries us back to a very high Chinese antiquity. He was, it is said, of the time of Hwang-tî, and so acute of vision, that, at the distance of too paces, he could discern the smallest hair. He is often referred to by the Taoist writer Chwang (莊) Some say that Lî Lâu was a disciple of Mencius, but this is altogether unlikely. Kung-shû, named Pan (written 班 and 般), was a celebrated mechanist of Lû, of the times of Confucius. He is fabled to have made birds of bamboo, that could continue flying for three days, and horses of wood, moved by springs, which could draw carriages. He is now the god of carpenters, and is worshipped by them; see the Lî Chî, Bk. II. Sect. II. ii. 21. There are some, however, who make two men of the name, an earlier and a later. K'wang, styled Tsze-yê (子野), was music-master and a wise counsellor of Tsin, a little prior to the time of Confucius;—see the 左傳襄公十四年. 六律, 'six pitch-tubes,' put by synecdoche for 十二律, or 'twelve tubes,' invented, it is said, in the earliest times, to determine by their various adjusted lengths the notes of the musical scale. Six of them go by the name of lü (呂), which are to be understood as comprehended under the phrase in the text. The five notes are the five full notes of the octave, neglecting the semitones. They are called 宮, 商, 角, 徵 (chî), 羽,—see on the Shû-ching, II. i. 24. 堯舜之道, —道 is to be taken 'emptily,' meaning the benevolent wish to govern well, such as animated Yâo and Shun. 仁政 in the same

勝用也既竭耳力焉繼
繩以爲方員平直不可
目力焉繼之以規矩準
者未之有也聖人既竭
舊章遵先王之法而過
行詩云不愆不忘率由
以爲政徒法不能以自
之道也故曰徒善不足
法於後世者不行先王
聞而民不被其澤不可

reputation for benevolence, while yet the people do not receive any benefits from them, nor will they leave any example to future ages;—all because they do not put into practice the ways of the ancient kings.

3. 'Hence we have the saying:—"Virtue alone is not sufficient for the exercise of government; laws alone cannot carry themselves into practice."

4. 'It is said in the Book of Poetry,

> "Without transgression, without forgetfulness,
> Following the ancient statutes."

Never has any one fallen into error, who followed the laws of the ancient kings.

5. 'When the sages had used the vigour of their eyes, they called in to their aid the compass, the square, the level, and the line, to make things square, round, level, and straight:—the use of the *instruments* is inexhaustible. When they had used their power

finding its embodiment,—the right art of government, having the same relation to it as the compass to circles, &c.   2. 聞,—4th tone. Observe the correlation of 者 and 也, the last clause assigning the reason of what is said in the preceding ones. 先王之道, —here, and below, the 道 must be taken differently from its application in the last paragraph, and = the 仁政 of that. The commentator 范 refers to king Hsüan of Ch'î (Bk. I. Pt. I. vii) as an instance of the princes who have a benevolent heart, and to the first emperor of the Liang dynasty (A. D. 502-556),

whose Buddhistic scrupulosity about taking life made him have a benevolent reputation. Yet the heart of the one did not advantage the State, nor the reputation of the other his empire.   3. 徒善,—here 'simply being good,' i.e. virtue without laws, and 徒法 = laws without virtue, the virtue, however, being understood of the 'benevolent heart.'   4. See the Shih-ching, Pt. III. ii. Ode V. st. 2.   5. 繼 之以,—literally, 'continued it with.' The line must be understood of the plumb-line, as well as of the marking-line. 準 is rightly translated,—'the level,' but I have not been able to ascertain its original form in China.

道揆也下無法守也朝

是播其惡於眾也上無

在高位不仁而在高位

謂智乎是以惟仁者宜

爲政不因先王之道可

因丘陵爲下必因川澤

覆天下矣故曰爲高必

之以不忍人之政而仁

勝用也既竭心思焉繼

之以六律正五音不可

of hearing to the utmost, they called in the pitch-tubes to their aid to determine the five notes:—the use of those *tubes* is inexhaustible. When they had exerted to the utmost the thoughts of their hearts, they called in to their aid a government that could not endure to witness the sufferings of men:—and their benevolence overspread the kingdom.

6. 'Hence we have the saying:—"To raise a thing high, we must begin from *the top of* a mound or a hill; to dig to a *great* depth, we must commence in *the low ground of* a stream or a marsh." Can he be pronounced wise, who, in the exercise of government, does not proceed according to the ways of the former kings?

7. 'Therefore only the benevolent ought to be in high stations. When a man destitute of benevolence is in a high station, he thereby disseminates his wickedness among all *below him*.

8. 'When the prince has no principles by which he examines *his administration*, and his ministers have no laws by which they

In the 前漢書, 本志, Bk. I, we read:— 'From the adjustment of weights and things sprang the *lever* (衡). The lever revolving produced the *circle*. The circle produced the *square*. The square produced the *line*. The line produced the *level*.' On the last sentence 韋昭 says:—'They set up the level to look at the line, using water as the equaliser.' 不可勝 (the 1st tone) 用,—see Bk. I. Pt. I. iii. 3. The subject of 可 is the whole of what

precedes from 繼. 不忍人, see Bk. II. Pt. I. vi. 1. 6. 因=依, 'to conform to,' i.e., here, to take advantage of. The saying is found in the Lî Chî. VIII. ii. 10. 8. This paragraph is an expansion of the last clause of the preceding, illustrating how the wickedness flows downwards, with its consequences. 上,—'the highest,' i.e. the prince. 下, the next 'below his ministers. 朝,—*ch'âo*, the 2nd tone, 'the court,' and 工, as opposed to it, the various officers, as having their 'work' to do. 君子

無義進退無禮言則非
泄泄泄猶沓沓也事君
詩曰天之方蹶無然泄
無學賊民興、喪無日矣。
非國之害也上無禮、下
也田野不辟貨財不聚、
完兵甲不多非國之災
存者幸也。故曰城郭不
犯義小人犯刑國之所
不信道工不信度君子

keep themselves *in the discharge of their duties*, then in the court obedience is not paid to principle, and in the office obedience is not paid to rule. Superiors violate the laws of righteousness, and inferiors violate the penal laws. It is only by a fortunate chance that a State in such a case is preserved.

9. 'Therefore it is said, "It is not the exterior and interior walls being incomplete, and the supply of weapons offensive and defensive not being large, which constitutes the calamity of a kingdom. It is not the cultivable area not being extended, and stores and wealth not being accumulated, which occasions the ruin of a State." When superiors do not observe the rules of propriety, and inferiors do not learn, then seditious people spring up, and *that State* will perish in no time.

10. 'It is said in the Book of Poetry,

"When such an overthrow *of Châu* is being produced by Heaven,
Be not ye so much at your ease!"

11. '"At your ease;"—that is, dilatory.

12. 'And so dilatory may *those officers* be deemed, who serve their prince without righteousness, who take office and retire from

and 小人,—with reference to station. The 也 at the end of the two clauses shows that they are both equally assertive, though the prince, governed and governing by principles of righteousness, will be a law to his ministers. 9. 城郭,—see Bk. II. Pt. II. i. 2. 辟=闢 as in Bk. I. Pt. I. vii. 16. 田野,—'fields and wilds.' 喪,—4th tone. 10. See the Shih-ching, III. ii. Ode X. 2. 蹶,—read kwei, the 4th tone. 泄,—i, 4th tone.—From this paragraph it is the ministers of a prince who are contemplated by Mencius. They have their duty to perform, in order that the benevolent government may be realised. 11. 猶沓沓,—we are to understand that this phrase was commonly used in Mencius's time with this acceptation. 12. 非,—used as a verb, 'to

U 2

先王之道者、猶沓沓也。故

<small>十三章</small>

曰、責難於君謂之恭、陳善

閉邪謂之敬、吾君不能謂

之賊。

<small>第二章</small>

孟子曰、規矩方員之至

也、聖人人倫之至也。欲爲

君、盡君道、欲爲臣、盡臣道、

二者皆法堯舜而已矣、不

以舜之所以事堯事君、不

敬其君者也。不以堯之所

it without regard to propriety, and who in their words disown the ways of the ancient kings.

13. 'Therefore it is said, "To urge one's sovereign to difficult achievements may be called showing respect for him. To set before him what is good and repress his perversities may be called showing reverence for him. *He who does not do these things, saying to himself,* —My sovereign is incompetent to this, may be said to play the thief with him."'

CHAP. II. 1. Mencius said, 'The compass and square produce perfect circles and squares. By the sages, the human relations are perfectly exhibited.

2. 'He who as a sovereign would perfectly discharge the duties of a sovereign, and he who as a minister would perfectly discharge the duties of a minister, have only to imitate—the one Yâo, and the other Shun. He who does not serve his sovereign as Shun served Yâo, does not respect his sovereign; and he who does not rule his people as Yâo ruled his, injures his people.

slander,' or 'disown.' 13. Compare Bk. II. Pt. II. ii. 4. We are obliged to supply considerably in the translation, to bring out the meaning of the last sentence. 賊 may be taken as a verb —'to injure, or as I have taken it.

2. A CONTINUATION OF THIS LAST CHAPTER;— THAT YÂO AND SHUN ARE THE PERFECT MODELS OF SOVEREIGNS AND MINISTERS, AND THE CONSEQUENCES OF NOT IMITATING THEM. 1. 'The compass and square are the perfection of squares and circles;'—but we must understand the mean-

ing as in the translation. So with the 2nd clause. 人倫,—see Bk. III. Pt. I. iv. 8. 2. 二者='these two' things, putting the above clauses abstractly, but we cannot do that so well in English. The force of 而已, according to the 備旨, is 'to show that there is no other way for the sovereign and minister to pursue.'—Of 'the human relations' only that of sovereign and minister is here adduced, because Mencius was speaking with reference

以治民治民賊其民者也。

孔子曰道二仁與不仁而

已矣暴其民甚則身弑國

亡不甚則身危國削名之

曰幽厲雖孝子慈孫百世

不能改也詩云殷鑒不遠

在夏后之世此之謂也。

孟子曰三代之得天下

也以仁其失天下也以不

3. 'Confucius said, "There are but two courses, *which can be pursued*, that of virtue and its opposite."

4. '*A ruler who* carries the oppression of his people to the highest pitch, will himself be slain, and his kingdom will perish. If one stop short of the highest pitch, his life will *notwithstanding* be in danger, and his kingdom will be weakened. He will be styled "The Dark," or "The Cruel," and though he may have filial sons and affectionate grandsons, they will not be able in a hundred generations to change *the designation*.

5. 'This is what is intended in the words of the Book of Poetry,
   "The beacon of Yin is not remote,
    It is in the time of the (last) sovereign of Hsiâ."'

CHAP. III. 1. Mencius said, 'It was by benevolence that the three dynasties gained the throne, and by not being benevolent that they lost it.

to the rulers of his time. 3. If the remark were Mencius's own, we should translate 仁 by 'benevolence.' The term in Confucius rather denotes 'perfect virtue.' By the course of virtue is intended the imitation of Yâo and Shun ; by its opposite, the neglect of them as models. 4. By sovereigns, who carry their oppression to the highest pitch. Mencius intends, as his examples, Chieh and Châu, the last kings of the Hsiâ and Yin dynasties. By 'The Dark' and 'The Cruel,' he intends the twelfth (B.C. 781) and tenth (B.C. 878) kings of the Châu dynasty, who received those posthumous indelible designations. I take 創 in the sense of 'weakened' (dictionary 弱), which it else-

where has in Mencius. 5. See the Shih-ching, III. iii. Ode I. st. 8, an ode of the time of the monarch Lî (厲), intended for his warning. The sovereign of Hsiâ is the tyrant Chieh, and by Yin is intended the tyrant Châu, by whose fate, though he neglected the lesson furnished him by that of Chieh, it is suggested that Lî should be admonished.

3. THE IMPORTANCE TO ALL, AND SPECIALLY TO RULERS, OF EXERCISING BENEVOLENCE. 1. 'The three dynasties' are the Hsiâ, the Shang, and the Châu. It is a bold utterance, seeing the Châu dynasty was still existing in the time of Mencius, though he regarded it as old and ready to vanish away. He has a reference, according to Chû Hsî, to the sovereigns Lî and Yû, men-

反其仁治人不治反　孟子曰愛人不親　惡醉而強酒。　死亡而樂不仁是猶　不仁不保四體今惡　仁不保宗廟士庶人　不保社稷卿大夫不　不保四海諸侯不仁　亡者亦然天子不仁　仁國之所以廢興存

2. 'It is by the same means that the decaying and flourishing, the preservation and perishing, of States are determined.

3. 'If the sovereign be not benevolent, he cannot preserve the throne *from passing from him.* If the Head of a State be not benevolent, he cannot preserve his rule. If a high noble or great officer be not benevolent, he cannot preserve his ancestral temple. If a scholar or common man be not benevolent, he cannot preserve his four limbs.

4. 'Now they hate death and ruin, and yet delight in being not benevolent ;—this is like hating to be drunk, and yet being strong *to drink* wine.'

CHAP. IV. 1. Mencius said, 'If a man love others, and no *responsive* attachment is shown to him, let him turn inwards and examine his own benevolence. If he *is trying to* rule others, and his government is unsuccessful, let him turn inwards and examine his wisdom. If he treats others politely, and they do not return his

tioned in the last chapter. 3. 四海,—'the four seas,' i.e. all with them, as subject to the sovereign's jurisdiction. There is a special reference, however, to the sovereign's right to offer all sacrifices :—those peculiar to himself, and those open to others. 社稷,—'the spirits of the land and the grain,' i.e. the spirits securing the stability and prosperity of a particular State, which it was the prerogative of the ruler to sacrifice to. Hence the expression is here used figuratively. See the Lî Chî, Bk. III. iii. 6. 4. 惡,—the verb, in 4th tone, 'to hate, dislike.' 強 (in 2nd tone) 酒,—like the Hebrew idiom, Isa. v. 22. This is spoken with reference to the princes of Mencius's time.

4. WITH WHAT MEASURE A MAN METES IT WILL BE MEASURED TO HIM AGAIN, AND CONSEQUENTLY BEFORE A MAN DEALS WITH OTHERS, EXPECTING THEM TO BE AFFECTED BY HIM, HE SHOULD FIRST DEAL WITH HIMSELF. The sentiment is expressed quite generally, but a particular reference is to be understood to the princes of Mencius's time. 1. 反 is used in a manner common in Mencius, = 'to turn back from the course being pursued, and then to turn inwards to the work of examination and correction.' In the next paragraph, we have it followed by another verb, 求. In 治人, 治 is in 2nd tone, 'to regulate,' 'to try to rule ;' in 不治, 治 is in 4th tone, 'to be regulated,' the government being effective. The clauses—愛人不親, &c., are very concise. The paraphrase in the 備旨 thus expands :—為治者體仁

其智禮人不答反其敬。
行有不得者皆反求諸
己其身正而天下歸之。
詩云永言配命自求多
福。

孟子曰人有恆言皆
曰天下國家天下之本
在國國之本在家家之
本在身。

孟子曰爲政不難不

politeness, let him turn inwards and examine his own *feeling of respect*.

2. 'When we do not, by what we do, realise *what we desire*, we must turn inwards, and examine ourselves in every point. When a man's person is correct, the whole kingdom will turn to him *with recognition and submission*.

3. 'It is said in the Book of Poetry,
"Be always studious to be in harmony with the ordinances *of God*,
And you will obtain much happiness."'

CHAP. V. Mencius said, 'People have this common saying,—"The kingdom, the State, the family." The root of the kingdom is in the State. The root of the State is in the family. The root of the family is in the person *of its Head*.'

CHAP. VI. Mencius said, 'The administration of government is not difficult ;—it lies in not offending the great families. He whom

以愛人, 宜乎人之我親矣, 而顧有不親焉, 則必反其 仁, 恐我之愛人有未至也, 云云, 'He who administers government embodies benevolence to love men, and it is to be expected men will love him. Should he find however that they do not, he must turn in and examine his benevolence, lest it should be imperfect,' &c. 2. 不得=不得其 所欲, 'does not get what he wishes.' 皆 —'all,' with reference to the general form of the preceding clause. 3. See Bk. II. Pt. I. iv. 6.

5. PERSONAL CHARACTER IS NECESSARY TO ALL GOOD INFLUENCE. Compare 'The Superior Learning,' text of Confucius, par. 4. The common saying repeated by all probably means :—the kingdom is made up of its component States, and of their component families ;—i.e. the families of the great officers. But Mencius takes its meaning more generally, and carries it out a step farther.

6. THE IMPORTANCE TO A RULER OF SECURING THE ESTEEM AND SUBMISSION OF THE GREAT HOUSES. The 'not offending' is to be taken in a moral sense ;—the ruler's doing nothing but what will command the admiring approbation of the old and great families in the State. In illustration of the sentiment, a story is related from Liû Hsiang of the duke Hwan of Ch'î. Lighting, one day in hunting, on an old man

既不能令又不受命是
存逆天者亡齊景公曰
強斯二者天也順天者
天下無道小役大弱役
德役大德小賢役大賢
☐孟子曰天下有道小
教溢乎四海。
慕天下慕之故沛然德
慕一國慕之一國之所
得罪於巨室巨室之所

the great families affect, will be affected by the whole State; and he whom *any* one State affects, will be affected by the whole kingdom. When this is the case, such an one's virtue and teachings will spread over all within the four seas like the rush of water.'

CHAP. VII. 1. Mencius said, 'When right government prevails in the kingdom, *princes of* little virtue are submissive to *those of* great, and *those of* little worth to those of great. When bad government prevails in the kingdom, *princes of* small power are submissive to those of great, and the weak to the strong. Both these cases are *the rule of* Heaven. They who accord with Heaven are preserved, and they who rebel against Heaven perish.

2. 'The duke Ching of Ch'î said, "Not to be able to command others, and at the same time to refuse to receive their commands, is to cut one's self off from all intercourse with others." His tears

of eighty-three, the duke sought his blessing, that he might attain a like longevity. The old man then prayed, 'May my ruler enjoy great longevity, despising gems and gold, and making men his jewels!' At the duke's request he prayed a second time, that he might not be ashamed to learn even from his inferiors, and a third time, 'May my ruler not offend against his ministers and the people!' This answer offended the duke. 'A son,' he said, 'may offend against his father, and a minister against his ruler. But how can a ruler offend against his ministers?' The old man replied, 'An offending son may get forgiveness through the intercessions of aunts and uncles. An offending minister may be forgiven by the intercession of the ruler's favourites and attendants. But when Chieh offended against Tang, and Châu offended against Wû;—those were cases in point. There was no forgiveness

for them.' 所慕,—'whom they affect,' not what. Observe the force of 故.

7. HOW THE SUBJECTION OF ONE STATE TO ANOTHER IS DETERMINED AT DIFFERENT TIMES. A PRINCE'S ONLY SECURITY FOR SAFETY AND PROSPERITY IS IN BEING BENEVOLENT. 1. Many commentators say that by 大德 and 大賢 reference is made to the sovereign, but the declarations may as well be taken generally. 斯二者天也,—'Heaven,' it is said, 'embraces here the ideas of what must be in reason, and the different powers of the contrasted States (兼理勢言).' This is true, but why sink the idea of a Providential government which is implied in 'Heaven?' 2. 景公,—see Analects, XII. xi. 絕物,—物.

命侯于周服侯服于
子其麗不億上帝旣
天下矣詩云商之孫
小國七年必爲政於
王師文王大國五年、
也如恥之莫若師文
子而恥受命於先師
而恥受命焉是猶弟
吳今也小國師大國
絶物也涕出而女於

flowed forth while he gave his daughter to be married to *the prince of* Wû.

3. 'Now the small States imitate the large, and yet are ashamed to receive their commands. This is like a scholar's being ashamed to receive the commands of his master.

4. 'For a prince who is ashamed of this, the best plan is to imitate king Wăn. Let one imitate king Wăn, and in five years, if his State be large, or in seven years, if it be small, he will be sure to give laws to the kingdom.

5. 'It is said in the Book of Poetry,

"The descendants of *the sovereigns of* the Shang dynasty,
　　Are in number more than hundreds of thousands,
But, God having passed His decree,
　　They are all submissive to Châu.
They are submissive to Châu,
　　Because the decree of Heaven is not unchanging.
The officers of Yin, admirable and alert,
　　Pour out the libations, and assist in the capital *of Châu*."

is taken as used for 人, 'men,' but the phrase is a contracted one, and = 與人睽絶, 'separated from other men,' or 絶 may be taken actively, which I prefer, and similarly supplemented. 女,—in 4th tone, 'to give a daughter in marriage.' Wû, corresponding to the northern part of the present Cheh-chiang, and the south of Chiang-sû, was in Confucius's time still reckoned a barbarous territory, and the princes of the Middle Kingdom were ashamed to enter into relations with it. The duke Ching, however, yielded to the force of circumstances and so saved himself. The daughter so married soon died. She pined away for her father and her native Ch'î, and was followed to the grave by her husband. The old king of Wû, barbarian as he was, showed much sympathy for his young daughter-in-law. 3. 師,—'to imitate,' 'to make a master of.' Mencius's meaning is that the smaller States followed the example of the larger ones in what was evil, and yet did not like to submit to them. 弟子,—'a youth,' here, = a pupil. 4. 爲政,—'be exercising government,'=giving law to. 5. See the Shih-ching, III. i. Ode I. st. 4, 5. 不億 = 不止於億, 'not hundreds of thousands only.' 侯于周服 is an inversion for 侯服于周. 侯 is here an introductory particle,

周天命靡常殷士膚敏裸將

于京孔子曰仁不可爲衆也

夫國君好仁天下無敵今也

欲無敵於天下而不以仁是

猶執熱而不以濯也詩云誰

能執熱逝不以濯。

⊠子孟子曰不仁者可與言哉

安其危而利其菑樂其所以

亡者不仁而可與言則何亡

Confucius said, "*As against so benevolent a sovereign, they could not be deemed a multitude.*" Thus, if the prince of a State love benevolence, he will have no opponent in all the kingdom.

6. 'Now they wish to have no opponent in all the kingdom, but they *do not seek to attain this* by being benevolent. This is like a man laying hold of a heated substance, and not having *first* dipped it in water. It is said in the Book of Poetry,

"Who can take up a heated substance,
Without first dipping it (in water)?"'

CHAP. VIII. 1. Mencius said, 'How is it possible to speak with those *princes* who are not benevolent? Their perils they count safety, their calamities they count profitable, and they have pleasure in the things by which they perish. If it were possible to talk with them who so violate benevolence, how could we have such destruction of States and ruin of Families?

-惟. 仁不可爲衆 is to be understood as a remark of Confucius on reading the portion of the Shih-ching just quoted;—'against a benevolent prince, like king Wǎn, the myriads of the adherents of Shang ceased to be myriads. They would not act against him.' The expansion in the 日講—'numerous as the adherents of Shang were, 以我周之人, 是衆 不可爲(=以爲)衆.' 6. See the Shih-ching, III. iii. Ode III. st. 5. The ode is referred to the time of the sovereign Lî, when the kingdom was hastening to ruin, and in the lines quoted, the author deplores that there was no resort to proper measures. 逝 is taken as a mere particle of transition.

8. THAT A PRINCE IS THE AGENT OF HIS OWN RUIN BY HIS VICIOUS WAYS AND REFUSING TO BE COUNSELLED. 1. Stress must be laid always on the 不 in 不仁. The expression does not

國敗家之有。有孺子歌曰、滄
浪之水清兮、可以濯我纓、滄
浪之水濁兮、可以濯我足。孔
子曰、小子聽之。清斯濯纓、濁
斯濯足矣。自取之也。夫人必
自侮、然後人侮之、家必自毀、
而後人毀之、國必自伐、而後
人伐之。太甲曰、天作孽、猶可
違、自作孽、不可活。此之謂也。
孟子曰、桀紂之失天下也、

2. 'There was a boy singing,

> "When the water of the Ts'ang-lang is clear,
> It does to wash the strings of my cap;
> When the water of the Ts'ang-lang is muddy,
> It does to wash my feet."

3. 'Confucius said, "Hear what he sings, my children. When clear, then he will wash his cap-strings; and when muddy, he will wash his feet with it. This *different application* is brought *by the water* on itself."

4. 'A man must first despise himself, and then others will despise him. A family must first destroy itself, and then others will destroy it. A State must first smite itself, and then others will smite it.

5. 'This is illustrated in the passage of the T'ai Chiă, "When Heaven sends down calamities, it is still possible to escape them. When we occasion the calamities ourselves, it is not possible any longer to live."'

CHAP. IX. 1. Mencius said, 'Chieh and Châu's losing the

denote merely the want of benevolence, but the opposite of it. 言-忠言 'to give faithful advice to.' 2. The name Ts'ang-lang (in 2nd tone) is found applied to different streams in different places. That in the text was probably in Shan-tung. 3. 聽之,-之 referring to the words of the song. 斯,-'this,' intensive, or we may take it adverbially:—'when clear, then it serves to wash the cap-strings, &c.' 4, 5. See Bk. II. Pt. I. iv. 4-6.

9. ONLY BY BEING BENEVOLENT CAN A PRINCE RAISE HIMSELF TO BE SOVEREIGN, OR EVEN AVOID RUIN. 1. 與之聚之-與之、富

失其民也失其民者失其心
也得天下有道得其民斯得
天下矣得其民有道得其心
斯得民矣得其民有道所欲
與之聚之所惡勿施爾也民
之歸仁也猶水之就下獸之
走壙也故爲淵敺魚者獺也
爲叢敺爵者鸇也爲湯武敺
民者桀與紂也今天下之君
有好仁者則諸侯皆爲之敺

throne, arose from their losing the people, and to lose the people means to lose their hearts. There is a way to get the kingdom :—get the people, and the kingdom is got. There is a way to get the people :—get their hearts, and the people are got. There is a way to get their hearts :—it is simply to collect for them what they like, and not to lay on them what they dislike.

2. 'The people turn to a benevolent rule as water flows downwards, and as wild beasts fly to the wilderness.

3. 'Accordingly, *as* the otter aids the deep waters, driving the fish into them, and the hawk aids the thickets, driving the little birds to them, *so* Chieh and Châu aided T'ang and Wû, driving the people to them.

4. 'If among the present rulers of the kingdom, there were one who loved benevolence, all the *other* princes would aid him, by

民. Châo Ch'î interprets it,—聚其所欲而與之, taking 與 in the sense of 'to give,' but this does not appear to be admissible here. To collect for the people what they like, is to govern in such a way that they shall enjoy their lives. One has illustrated the meaning from 晁 (Châo) 錯, of the Han dynasty, who did service in the recovery of the ancient books, thus :—'Men like long life, and the founders of the three dynasties cherished men's lives and kept them from harm : men love wealth, and those kings enriched them, and kept them from straits, &c. &c.' 2. It is best to take 仁 here in the concrete. 走, as it is marked, is in the 4th tone. The dictionary gives it in the same in Bk. I. Pt. I. iii. 2. 3. 爲—in 4th tone. 敺=驅. 爲淵敺魚者,—'he or that which drives the fish for the deep waters.' The 獺 is the otter. For a curious particular about it, see the Lî Chî, IV. (月令) Sect. i. I. 8. 爵 is given in the dictionary as 鳥名, 'the name of a bird.' Chû Hsî takes it, how-

矣雖欲無王不可得已今
之欲王者猶七年之病求
三年之艾也苟爲不畜終
身不得苟不志於仁終身
憂辱以陷於死亡詩云其
何能淑載胥及溺此之謂
也。

孟子曰自暴者不可與
有言也自棄者不可與有
爲也言非禮義謂之自暴

driving *the people to him*. Although he wished not to become sovereign, he could not avoid becoming so.

5. 'The case of *one of* the present princes wishing to become sovereign is like the having to seek for mugwort three years old, to cure a seven years' sickness. If it have not been kept in store, the patient may all his life not get it. If the princes do not set their wills on benevolence, all their days will be in sorrow and disgrace, and they will be involved in death and ruin.

6. 'This is illustrated by what is said in the Book of Poetry,
"How *otherwise* can you improve *the kingdom*?
You will only with it go to ruin."'

CHAP. X. 1. Mencius said, 'With those who do violence to themselves, it is impossible to speak. With those who throw themselves away, it is impossible to do anything. To disown in his conversation propriety and righteousness, is what we mean by doing violence to one's self. *To say*—"*I* am not able to dwell in bene-

ever, as = 雀, a general name for small birds. 4. 王,—in 4th tone, and in next paragraph also. 5. 苟爲不畜, 終身不得 is by most commentators interpreted:—'If you now, feeling its want, begin to collect it, it may be available for the cure. You can hold on till it is so. If you do not at once set about it, your case is hopeless.' Perhaps the 爲 and 不 should determine in favour of this view. Chāo Ch'î interprets as in the translation. The down of the mugwort, burnt on the skin, is used for

purposes of cautery. The older the plant, the better. 6. The quotation from the Shih-ching is of the two lines immediately following the last quotation in chap. vii. 載,—a particle, = 則.

10. A WARNING TO THE VIOLENTLY EVIL, AND THE WEAKLY EVIL. 1. 自暴者, 'those who are cruel to themselves,' i.e. those who deny, and act contrary to their own nature. 非, a verb, 'to disown,' 'to condemn.' 與有言, 有

也吾身不能居仁由義謂
之自棄也。仁人之安宅也、
義、人之正路也。曠安宅而
不居舍正路而弗由、哀哉。
孟子曰、道在爾而求諸
遠、事在易而求諸難。人人
親其親長其長、而天下平。
孟子曰、居下位而不獲
於上民不可得而治也。獲
於上有道、不信於友、弗獲

volence or pursue the path of righteousness," is what we mean by throwing one's self away.

2. 'Benevolence is the tranquil habitation of man, and righteousness is his straight path.

3. 'Alas for them, who leave the tranquil dwelling empty and do not reside in it, and who abandon the right path and do not pursue it?'

CHAP. XI. Mencius said, 'The path *of duty* lies in what is near, and men seek for it in what is remote. The work *of duty* lies in what is easy, and men seek for it in what is difficult. If each man would love his parents and show the due respect to his elders, the whole land would enjoy tranquillity.'

CHAP. XII. 1. Mencius said, 'When those occupying inferior situations do not obtain the confidence of the sovereign, they cannot succeed in governing the people. There is a way to obtain the confidence of the sovereign:—if one is not trusted by his friends, he will not obtain the confidence of his sovereign. There is a way

爲—'to have conversation (words), to have action (doing) with them.' 3. 舍—for 捨, in 3rd tone. The lamentation is to be understood as for the 自暴者 and the 自棄者—It is observed that 'this chapter shows that what is right and true (道) do really belong to man, but he extirpates them himself. Profound is the admonition, and learners should give most earnest heed to it.'

11. THE TRANQUIL PROSPERITY OF THE KINGDOM DEPENDS ON THE DISCHARGE OF THE COMMON RELATIONS OF LIFE. 爾-邇, with which it was anciently interchanged. 長, in 3rd tone, comprehends elders and superiors, as in the Chung Yung, i. 1.

12. THE GREAT WORK OF MEN SHOULD BE TO STRIVE TO ATTAIN PERFECT SINCERITY. See the Chung Yung, xx. para. 17, 18, which are here substantially quoted. As the twentieth chapter of

來吾聞西伯善養老者太公
之濱聞文王作興曰盍歸乎
孟子曰伯夷辟紂居北海
有也不誠未有能動者也
之道也至誠而不動者未之
故誠者天之道也思誠者人
道不明乎善不誠其身矣是
身不誠不悅於親矣誠身有
悅弗信於友矣悅親有道反
於上矣信於友有道事親弗

of being trusted by one's friends:—if one do not serve his parents
so as to make them pleased, he will not be trusted by his friends.
There is a way to make one's parents pleased:—if one, on turning
his thoughts inwards, finds a want of sincerity, he will not give
pleasure to his parents. There is a way to the attainment of sincerity in one's self:—if a man do not understand what is good, he
will not attain sincerity in himself.

2. 'Therefore, sincerity is the way of Heaven. To think *how*
to be sincere is the way of man.

3. 'Never has there been one possessed of complete sincerity,
who did not move others. Never has there been one who had not
sincerity who was able to move others.'

CHAP. XIII. 1. Mencius said, 'Po-î, that he might avoid Châu,
was dwelling on the coast of the northern sea. When he heard
of the rise of king Wăn, he roused himself, and said, " Why should
I not go and follow him? I have heard that the chief of the West
knows well how to nourish the old." Tâi-kung, that he might

the Chung Yung, however, is found also in the
'Family Sayings.' Mencius may have had that,
or the fragmentary memorabilia of Confucius,
from which it is compiled, before him, and not
the Chung Yung.

15. THE INFLUENCE OF GOVERNMENT LIKE THAT
OF KING WĂN. 1. Po-î,—see Analects, V. xxii,
et al. Tâi-kung was Lî Shang (呂尚), a
great counsellor of the kings, Wăn and Wû.

He was descended from one of Yü's assistants
in the regulation of the waters, and on his first
rencontre with king Wăn, when he appeared
to be only a fisherman, Wăn said 吾太公
望子久矣, 'My grandfather looked for
you long ago.' This led to his being styled
太公望, or 'Grandfather's Hope.' See the

辟紂、居東海之濱、聞文王
作興曰、盍歸乎來、吾聞西
伯善養老者。二老者天下
之大老也、而歸之、是天下
之父歸之也、天下之父歸
之、其子焉往、諸侯有行文
王之政者、七年之內、必爲
政於天下矣。

孟子曰、求也爲季氏宰、
無能改於其德、而賦粟倍

avoid Châu, was dwelling on the coast of the eastern sea. When he heard of the rise of king Wăn, he roused himself, and said, "Why should I not go and follow him? I have heard that the chief of the West knows well how to nourish the old."

2. 'Those two old men were the greatest old men of the kingdom. When they came to follow king Wăn, it was the fathers of the kingdom coming to follow him. When the fathers of the kingdom joined him, how could the sons go *to any other*?

3. 'Were any of the princes to practise the government of king Wăn, within seven years he would be sure to be giving laws to the kingdom.'

CHAP. XIV. 1. Mencius said, 'Ch'iû acted as chief officer to the head of the Chî family, whose *evil* ways he was unable to change,

---

'Historical Records,' Bk. XXXII, 齊太公世家, at the beginning. Though Po-î and T'ai-kung were led in the same way to follow king Wăn, their subsequent courses were very different. 辟=避. Wăn was appointed by Châu chief or baron (伯), his viceroy in the West, to be leader of all the princes in that part of the kingdom. The commentators say this is referred to in 文王作. I should rather interpret 作 of Wăn's 'movements,' style of administration. With 善養老者, compare the account of king Wăn's government in Bk. I. Pt. II. v. 3. 盍歸乎來=盍歸來乎

Still the 來 is somewhat embarrassing. a. I like the expansion of this paragraph in the 日講:—'Moreover, these two old men were not ordinary men. Distinguished alike by age and virtue, they were the greatest old men of the kingdom. Fit to be so named, the hopes of all looked to them, and the hearts of all were bound to them. All looked up to them as fathers, and felt as their children, so that when they were moved by the government of king Wăn, and came from the coasts of the sea to him, how could the children leave their fathers and go to any others?' 3. 爲政,—as in chap. vii. 4. Compare Analects, XIII. x-xii, where Confucius thinks he could have accomplished a similar result in shorter time.

14. AGAINST THE MINISTERS OF HIS TIME WHO

刑連諸侯者次之辟草
容於死故善戰者服上
率土地而食人肉罪不
以戰殺人盈城此所謂
地以戰殺人盈野爭城
者也況於爲之强戰爭
政而富之皆棄於孔子
也由此觀之君不行仁
也小子鳴鼓而攻之可
他日孔子曰求非我徒

while he exacted from the people double the grain formerly paid. Confucius said, "He is no disciple of mine. Little children, beat the drum and assail him."

2. 'Looking at the subject from this case, *we perceive that* when a prince was not practising benevolent government, all *his ministers* who enriched him were rejected by Confucius:—how much more *would he have rejected* those who are vehement to fight for their *prince!* When contentions about territory are the ground on which they fight, they slaughter men till the fields are filled with them. When some struggle for a city is the ground on which they fight, they slaughter men till the city is filled with them. This is what is called "leading on the land to devour human flesh." Death is not enough for such a crime.

3. 'Therefore, those who are skilful to fight should suffer the highest punishment. Next to them *should be punished* those who unite *some* princes in leagues *against others;* and next to them,

PURSUED THEIR WARLIKE AND OTHER SCHEMES, REGARDLESS OF THE HAPPINESS OF THE PEOPLE. 1. See Analects, XI. xvi. Here is a plain instance of 德 used in a bad sense. 2. 爲之强戰,—爲, in 4th tone. 强 I take as in the 3rd tone, and the phrase 强戰 after the analogy of 强酒, chap. iii. 4. Chû Hsî and others take 强 in the 2nd tone, and make the phrase = 'who fight trusting in the powerfulness of weapons and strength (恃兵力之强而戰).' The proposed interpretation seems much preferable. With the whole phrase compare 爲之聚歛, Analects, XI. xvi. The force of the 爲之, it seems to me, must be to make the whole equal to the rendering of Noel, which Julien condemns—'qui suum principem ad arma adstimulant.' To be strong to fight for his prince, is a minister's duty. But to encourage a warlike spirit in him, is injurious to the country. 罪不容於死=其罪大死刑不足以容之 'his crime is so great that even capital punishment is not sufficient to contain it.' 3. Here we have three classes of adventurers who were rife in Mencius's time, and who recommended themselves to the

萊、任土地者次之。

辟草孟子曰存乎人者、莫

良於眸子眸子不能掩

其惡胸中正則眸子瞭

焉胸中不正則眸子眊

焉。聽其言也觀其眸子、

人焉廋哉。

丈孟子曰恭者不侮人、

儉者不奪人侮奪人之

君惟恐不順焉惡得爲

those who take in grassy commons, imposing the cultivation of the ground *on the people.*'

CHAP. XV. 1. Mencius said, 'Of all the parts of a man's body there is none more excellent than the pupil of the eye. The pupil cannot *be used to* hide a man's wickedness. If within the breast all be correct, the pupil is bright. If within the breast all be not correct, the pupil is dull.

2. 'Listen to a man's words and look at the pupil of his eye. How can a man conceal his character?'

CHAP. XVI. Mencius said, 'The respectful do not despise others. The economical do not plunder others. The prince who treats men with despite and plunders them, is only afraid that they may not prove obedient to him:—how can he be regarded as

prince in the ways described, pursuing their own ends, regardless of the people. Some advanced themselves by their skill in war; some by their talents for intrigue; and some by plans to make the most of the ground, turning every bit of it to account, but for the good of the ruler, not of the people. 辟-闢. 萊,—'a kind of creeper,' 'weeds,' = fields lying fallow or uncultivated. 任土地,—the 土地 is what had been occupied by the 草萊. Chû Hsî expands the phrase thus :—'任土地 means, —to divide this land and give it to the people, making them undertake the charge of cultivating it.'

15. THE PUPIL OF THE EYE THE INDEX OF THE HEART. 1. 存乎人者,—存-在, 'the things that are in man,' i.e. in his body. The

excellence of the pupil is from its truthfulness as an index of the heart. The whole is to be understood as spoken by Mencius for the use of those who thought they had only to hear man's words to judge of them. 2. Compare Analects, II. x.

16. DEEDS, NOT WORDS OR MANNERS, NECESSARY TO PROVE MENTAL QUALITIES. 恭者, 儉者, though I have translated them generally, are yet spoken with a reference to the 君 that follows. The princes of Mencius's time made great pretensions, of which their actions proved the insincerity. 侮 and 不奪 are to be understood of the disposition :—'not wish to contemn, &c.' 奪 directly governing 人, is remarkable. 爲恭儉-爲-以爲 or 名爲, 'to be regarded,' 'to be styled.' The

CH. XVII.] THE WORKS OF MENCIUS. 307

恭儉恭儉豈可以聲音笑
貌爲哉。
曰淳于髠曰男女授受不
親禮與孟子曰禮也。曰嫂
溺則援之以手乎。曰嫂溺
不援是豺狼也。男女授受
不親禮也。嫂溺援之以手
者權也。曰今天下溺矣。夫
子之不援何也。曰天下溺
援之以道嫂溺援之以手。

respectful or economical? How can respectfulness and economy be made out of tones of the voice, and a smiling manner?'

CHAP. XVII. 1. Shun-yü K'wăn said, 'Is it the rule that males and females shall not allow their hands to touch in giving or receiving anything?' Mencius replied, 'It is the rule.' *K'wăn* asked, 'If a man's sister-in-law be drowning, shall he rescue her with his hand?' Mencius said, 'He who would not so rescue the drowning woman is a wolf. For males and females not to allow their hands to touch in giving and receiving is the *general* rule; when a sister-in-law is drowning, to rescue her with the hand is a peculiar exigency.'

2. *K'wăn* said, 'The whole kingdom is drowning. How strange it is that you will not rescue it!'

3. *Mencius* answered, 'A drowning kingdom must be rescued with right principles, as a drowning sister-in-law has to be rescued with the hand. Do you wish me to rescue the kingdom with my hand?'

final 爲＝作爲, and in the passive, 'to be made.' 聲音, 'tones'＝words.

17. HELP—EFFECTUAL HELP—CAN BE GIVEN TO THE WORLD ONLY IN HARMONY WITH RIGHT AND PROPRIETY. 1. Shun-yü K'wăn was a native of Ch'í, a famous sophist, and otherwise a man of note in his day; see the 'Historical Records,' Bk. CXXVI, 列傳, lxvi. He here tries to entrap Mencius into a confession that he did not well in maintaining his dignity of reserve. For the rule of propriety referred to, see the Lî Chî, I. Sect. I. iii. 31. 不親＝不以手

相親接. 權—see Analects, IX. xxix; XVIII. viii.—豺狼 may be taken together as—'a wolf.' The names belong to different animals of the same species. See on Bk. VI. Pt. I. xiv. 4. 2. 夫子 is complimentary, as K'wăn was not a disciple of Mencius. 3. Chû Hsî expands here:—'The drowning kingdom can be rescued only by right principles;—the case is different from that of a drowning sister-in-law who can be rescued by the hand. Now you, wishing to rescue the kingdom, would have me, in violation of right principles, seek alliance with the princes, and so begin by losing the

X 2

而教之父子之間不責
相夷則惡矣古者易子
則是父子相夷也父子
以正夫子未出於正也
怒則反夷矣夫子教我
不行繼之以怒繼之以
行也教者必以正以正
教子何也孟子曰勢不
公孫丑曰君子之不
子欲手援天下乎。

CHAP. XVIII. 1. Kung-sun Ch'âu said, 'Why is it that the superior man does not *himself* teach his son?'

2. Mencius replied, 'The circumstances of the case forbid its being done. The teacher must inculcate what is correct. When he inculcates what is correct, and his lessons are not practised, he follows them up with being angry. When he follows them up with being angry, then, contrary to what should be, he is offended with his son. *At the same time, the pupil says,* "My master inculcates on me what is correct, and he himself does not proceed in a correct path." The result of this is, that father and son are offended with each other. When father and son come to be offended with each other, the case is evil.

3. 'The ancients exchanged sons, and one taught the son of another.

4. 'Between father and son, there should be no reproving ad-

means wherewith to rescue it. Do you wish to make me save the kingdom with my hand?' I hardly see the point of the last question.

18. How A FATHER MAY NOT HIMSELF TEACH HIS SON. 1. This proposition is not to be taken in all its generality. Confucius taught his son, and so did other famous men their sons. We are to understand the first clause of the second paragraph,—勢不行也, as referring to the case of a stupid or perverse child. As to what is said in the third paragraph of the custom of the ancients, I have seen no other proof adduced of it. 2. 反,—'contrary,' i.e. to the affection which should rule between father and son. 夷,—in the sense of 傷, which, however, we must take passively; not 'to wound,'

but 'to be wounded,' that is, to be offended. We might take it actively in the first instance; —'contrary to what should be, he wounds—i.e. beats—his son.' But below, in 父子相夷, we cannot give it such an active signification as to suppose that the son will proceed to beat his father. 傷 may well be taken passively, as in the common saying, 眼見心傷. 夫子教我, 云云,—this is to be understood as the resentful murmuring of the son, whose feeling is strongly indicated by the use of 夫子, 'my master,' as applied to his father. 3. The commentators all say, that this only means that the ancients sent out their sons to be taught away from home by masters.

善、貴善則離、離則不祥莫大
焉。
孟子曰事孰爲大事親爲
大守孰爲大守身爲大不失
其身而能事其親者吾聞之
矣失其身而能事其親者吾
未之聞也孰不爲守守身守
之本也孰不爲事事親事
之本也曾子養曾晳必有酒肉
將徹必請所與問有餘必曰.

monitions to what is good. Such reproofs lead to alienation, and than alienation there is nothing more inauspicious.'

CHAP. XIX. 1. Mencius said, ' Of services, which is the greatest ? The service of parents is the greatest. Of charges, which is the greatest ? The charge of one's self is the greatest. That those who do not fail to keep themselves are able to serve their parents is what I have heard. But I have never heard of any, who, having failed to keep themselves, were able *notwithstanding* to serve their parents.

2. ' There are many services, but the service of parents is the root of all others. There are many charges, but the charge of one's self is the root of all others.

3. ' The philosopher Tsăng, in nourishing Tsăng Hsî, was always sure to have wine and flesh provided. And when they were being

But this is explaining away the 易. 4. 責 善-以善責之使行, ' laying what is good on them, and causing them to do it.'

19. THE RIGHT MANNER OF SERVING PARENTS, AND THE IMPORTANCE OF WATCHING OVER ONE'S SELF, IN ORDER TO DO SO. 1. 事孰爲大. —literally, ' of services—i.e. duties of service which a man has to pay to others—which is great ?' 守,—charges, what a man has to guard and keep. The keeping one's self from

all that is contrary to righteousness. 2. 孰 不爲事,—' what is not a service ?' i.e. the services a man has to perform are many. 本, —in the sense of ' root,' according to the Chinese way of developing all other services from filial piety; see the HaiĂo-ching (孝經), passim. There is more truth in the second part of the paragraph. 3. Hsî was Tsăng Shăn's father; see Analects, XI. xxv. 養,—in 4th tone. ' Nourishing the will,' i.e. gratifying and carrying

有曾晳死曾元養曾子
必有酒肉將徹不請所
與問有餘曰亡矣將以
復進也此所謂養口體
者也若曾子則可謂養
志也事親若曾子者可
也。

二十孟子曰人不足與適
也政不足閒也惟大人
爲能格君心之非君仁

removed, he would ask respectfully to whom he should give *what was left*. If *his father* asked whether there was anything left, he was sure to say, "There is." After the death of Tsǎng Hsî, when Tsǎng Yüan came to nourish Tsǎng-tsze, he was always sure to have wine and flesh provided. But when the things were being removed, he did not ask to whom he should give *what was left*, and if *his father* asked whether there was anything left, he would answer "No;"—intending to bring them in again. This was what is called—"nourishing the mouth and body." We may call Tsǎng-tsze's practice—"nourishing the will."

4. 'To serve one's parents as Tsǎng-tsze served his, may be accepted *as filial piety*.'

CHAP. XX. Mencius said, 'It is not enough to remonstrate with a *sovereign* on account of *the mal-employment of* ministers, nor to blame *errors of* government. It is only the great man who can rectify what is wrong in the sovereign's mind. Let the prince be

out the father's wishes. 4. The 可也 at the end occasions some difficulty. Chû Hsî quotes from one of the brothers Ch'âng these words :— 'To serve one's parents as Tsǎng Shǎn did his, may be called the height of filial piety, and yet Mencius only says that it might be accepted as such—可也 : did he really think that there was something supererogatory in Tsǎng's service?' Possibly, Mencius may have been referring to Tsǎng's disclaimer of being deemed a model of filial piety. See the Lî Chî, XXI (祭義) ii. 10, where he says :—'What the superior man calls filial piety, is to anticipate the wishes, and carry out the mind of his

parents, always leading them on in what is right and true. I am only one who nourishes his parents. How can I be deemed filial?'

20. A TRULY GREAT MINISTER WILL BE SEEN IN HIS DIRECTING HIS EFFORTS, NOT TO THE CORRECTION OF MATTERS IN DETAIL, BUT OF THE SOVEREIGN'S CHARACTER. 適,—read chih, = 謫, 'to reprehend.' 閒,—*chien*, in 4th ton 人 and 政 are to be taken as in the objective governed by 適 and 閒, and 不足 as used impersonally. 與=與君, 'with the sovereign.' Châo Ch'î introduces 與 before 閒 as well. He seems

莫不仁君義莫不義君

正莫不正一正君而國

定矣。

〇孟子曰、有不虞之譽、

有求全之毀。

〇孟子曰、人之易其言

也無責耳矣。

〇孟子曰、人之患在好

為人師。

〇樂正子從於子敖之

benevolent, and all *his acts* will be benevolent. Let the prince be righteous, and all *his acts* will be righteous. Let the prince be correct, and everything will be correct. Once rectify the ruler, and the kingdom will be firmly settled.'

CHAP. XXI. Mencius said, 'There are cases of praise which could not be expected, and of reproach when the parties have been seeking to be perfect.'

CHAP. XXII. Mencius said, 'Men's being ready with their tongues arises simply from their not having been reproved.'

CHAP. XXIII. Mencius said, 'The evil of men is that they like to be teachers of others.'

CHAP. XXIV. 1. The disciple Yo-chǎng went in the train of Tsze-âo to Ch'î.

to interpret differently, from the translation, making 人 (= 小人, 'little men') the subject of 不足 :—'little men are not fit to remonstrate with their sovereign.' This is plainly wrong, because we cannot carry it on to the next clause, 格=正, 'to correct.'—The sentiment of the chapter is illustrated by an incident related of Mencius by the philosopher 荀 (about B.C. 250):—'As Mencius thrice visited Ch'î, without speaking to the king about the errors of his government, his disciples were surprised, but he simply said, I *must first correct his evil heart.*'

21. PRAISE AND BLAME ARE NOT ALWAYS ACCORDING TO DESERT. 虞,—in the sense of 度, 'to calculate,' 'to measure.' For 毀 in

the sense here, 譽 is often used in modern language.

22. THE BENEFIT OF REPROOF. 易,—read 4, in 4th tone, 'easy.' Chû Hsî supposes that this remark was spoken with some particular reference. This would account for the 耳矣, 'simply.'

23. BE NOT MANY MASTERS. Commentators suppose that Mencius's lesson was that such a liking indicated a self-sufficiency which put an end to self-improvement.

24. HOW MENCIUS REPROVED YO-CHĂNG FOR ASSOCIATING WITH AN UNWORTHY PERSON, AND BEING REMISS IN WAITING ON HIMSELF. 1. Yo-chǎng,—see Bk. I. Pt. II. xvi. 2. Tsze-âo was the designation of Wang Hwan, mentioned in Bk. II. Pt. II. vi. From that chapter we may understand that Mencius would not be pleased with one of his disciples associating with such

子學古之道而以餔啜也。
於子敖來徒餔啜也我不意
孟子謂樂正子曰子之從
乎曰克有罪。
之也舍館定然後求見長者
亦宜乎曰舍館未定曰子聞
者曰昔者則我出此言也不
此言也曰子來幾日矣曰昔
亦來見我乎曰先生何爲出
齊樂正子見孟子孟子曰子

2. He came to see Mencius, who said to him, 'Are you also come to see me?' Yo-chăng replied, 'Master, why do you speak such words?' 'How many days have you been here?' asked Mencius. 'I came yesterday.' 'Yesterday! Is it not with reason then that I thus speak?' 'My lodging-house was not arranged.' 'Have you heard that *a scholar's* lodging-house must be arranged before he visit his elder?'

3. *Yo-chăng* said, 'I have done wrong.'

CHAP. XXV. Mencius, addressing the disciple Yo-chăng, said to him, 'Your coming here in the train of Tsze-âo was only because of the food and the drink. I could not have thought that you, having learned the doctrine of the ancients, would have acted with a view to eating and drinking.'

a person. 之,—the verb, = 往. 2. The name is repeated at the beginning of this paragraph, the former being narrative, and introductory merely. 亦來,—the 亦, 'also,' is directed against Tsze-âo. Chû Hsî explains 昔者 by 前日, which, in common parlance, means 'the day before yesterday.' But I do not see that it should have that meaning here. 昔 properly means 'formerly,' and may extend to the remotest antiquity. It is used also for yesterday, the time separated from the present by one rest — 息, as if the same sound of the two characters (昔息) determined the meaning. 長 (in 3rd tone) 者 is used before by Mencius of himself—Bk. II. Pt. II. xi. 4.

25. A FURTHER AND MORE DIRECT REPROOF OF YO-CHĂNG. 餔啜 are both contemptuous terms, — our application of 'the loaves and fishes.' 而以餔啜 = 而以餔啜 爲也.

孟子曰、不
孝有三、無後
爲大。舜不告
而娶、爲無後
也。君子以爲
猶告也。
孟子曰、仁
之實、事親是
也。義之實、從
兄是也。智之

CHAP. XXVI. 1. Mencius said, 'There are three things which are unfilial, and to have no posterity is the greatest of them.

2. 'Shun married without informing his parents because of this,—*lest he should have* no posterity. Superior men consider that his doing so was the same as if he had informed them.'

CHAP. XXVII. 1. Mencius said, 'The richest fruit of benevolence is this,—the service of one's parents. The richest fruit of righteousness is this,—the obeying one's elder brothers.

2. 'The richest fruit of wisdom is this,—the knowing those two

26. SHUN'S EXTRAORDINARY WAY OF CONTRACTING MARRIAGE JUSTIFIED BY THE MOTIVE. 1. The other two things which are unfilial are, according to Châo Ch'î, first, by a flattering assent to encourage parents in unrighteousness; and secondly, not to succour their poverty and old age by engaging in official service. To be without posterity is greater than those faults, because it is an offence against the whole line of ancestors, and terminates the sacrifices to them.—In Pt. II. xxx, Mencius specifies five things which were commonly deemed unfilial, and not one of these three is among them. It is to be understood that here 不孝有三 is spoken of from the point of view of the superior man, and, moreover, that the first paragraph simply lays down the ground for the vindication of Shun. 2. 爲無後一爲, in 4th tone. 告 implies getting the parents' permission, as well as informing them. But Shun's parents were so evil, and hated him so much, that they would have prevented his marriage had they been told of it.

27. FILIAL PIETY AND FRATERNAL OBEDIENCE IN THEIR RELATION TO BENEVOLENCE, RIGHTEOUSNESS, WISDOM, PROPRIETY, AND MUSIC. 1. 實 is sometimes opposed to 虛, 'what is solid to what is empty, shadowy;' sometimes to 名, 'what is real to what is nominal;' and sometimes to 華, 'what is substantial to what is ornamental,' 'fruit to flower.' In the text it is used in the last way, and I cannot express it better than by the 'richest fruit.' 是也 is emphatic;—'the fruit of benevolence is the

service of parents;—*it is*.' So in the other instances. Benevolence, righteousness, &c., are the principles of those, the capabilities of them in human nature, which may have endless manifestations, but are chiefly and primarily to be seen in the two virtues spoken of.—What strikes us as strange is the subject of music. The difficulty has not escaped native commentators. The author of the 集註本義匯參 says, *in loc.*:—'Benevolence, righteousness, propriety, and knowledge are the four virtues, but this chapter proceeds to speak of music. For the principles of music are really a branch of propriety, and when the ordering and adorning which belong to that are perfect, then harmony and pleasure spring up as a matter of course. In this way we have propriety mentioned first, and then music. Moreover, the fervancy of benevolence, the exactness of righteousness, the clearness of knowledge, and the firmness of maintenance, must all have their depth manifested in music. If the chapter had not spoken of music, we should not have seen the whole amount of achievement.' The reader may try to conceive the exact meaning of this writer, who also points out another peculiarity in the chapter, which many have overlooked. Instead of 是也 after 樂斯二者, as at the end of the other clauses, we have 樂則生矣, 云云, 'showing,' says he, 'most vividly how his admiration was stirred. It is as if from every sentence there floated up a 是也 upon the paper, so true is it that perfect filial piety and fraternal duty reach to spiritual beings, and shed a light over

實知斯二者、弗去是也、禮
之實節文斯二者是也、樂
之實樂斯二者、樂則生矣、
生則惡可已也、惡可已、則
不知足之蹈之、手之舞之。
孟子曰、天下大悦而將
歸己視天下悦而歸己、猶
草芥也、惟舜為然、不得乎
親不可以為人、不順乎親、

things, and not departing from them. The richest fruit of propriety is this,—the ordering and adorning those two things. The richest fruit of music is this,—the rejoicing in those two things. When they are rejoiced in, they grow. Growing, how can they be repressed? When they come to this state that they cannot be repressed, then unconsciously the feet begin to dance and the hands to move.'

CHAP. XXVIII. 1. Mencius said, 'Suppose the case of the whole kingdom turning in great delight to an individual to submit to him.—To regard the whole kingdom *thus* turning to him in great delight but as a bundle of grass;—only Shun was capable of this. *He considered* that if one could not get *the hearts of* his parents he could not be considered *a man*, and that if he could not get to an entire accord with his parents, he could not be considered a son.

the world, and then do we know that in the greatest music there is a harmony with heaven and earth.' 2. Julien translates 去 by *objicere*. To have that meaning, it must have been in the 3rd tone, which it is not. The first 樂 is yŏ, 'music;' the other two are lŏ, 'to enjoy.' 不知 is used absolutely, = 'unconsciously,' though we might make 知 personal also,— 'we do not know.' 足之蹈之,—'the feet's stamping it.' So the next clause.

28. How SHUN VALUED AND EXEMPLIFIED FILIAL PIETY. 1. The first sentence is to be taken generally, and not with reference to Shun simply. It is incomplete. The conclusion would be something like—'this would be accounted the greatest happiness and glory.' 芥 is properly 'the mustard plant,' but it is sometimes, as here, only synonymous with 草. 不得, 云 云,—all this is the reasoning of Shun's mind. 不得乎,—like 不獲於, in chap. 12. 不順, 'not to obey,' 'not to accord with,' but Chû Hsî and others labour hard to make it out to mean,—' to bring the parents to accord with what is right, so as to be able then

大孝。者定此之謂下之爲父子瞍底豫而天而天下化瞽豫瞽瞍底道而瞽瞍底舜盡事親之不可以爲子。

2. 'By Shun's completely fulfilling everything by which a parent could be served, Kû-sâu was brought to find delight *in what was good*. When Kû-sâu was brought to find that delight, the whole kingdom was transformed. When Kû-sâu was brought to find that delight, all fathers and sons in the kingdom were established *in their respective duties*. This is called great filial piety.'

fully to accord with them.' 2. Shun's father is known by the name of Kû-sâu, but both the characters denote 'blind,' and he was so styled, it is said, because of his mental blindness and opposition to all that was good. 豫, in the sense of 'to be pleased,' 'joyful,' understood here with a moral application. 'All fathers and sons, &c.,'—i. e. all sons were made to see, that, whatever might be the characters of their parents, they had only to imitate Shun, and fathers, even though they might be like Kû-sâu, were ashamed to reformation.

LÌ LÂU. PART II.

相後也千有餘
千有餘也千有餘
也地之相去也
畢郢西夷之人
生於岐周卒於
夷之人也文王
夏卒於鳴條東
於諸馮遷於負
孟子曰舜生
離婁章句下

CHAPTER I. 1. Mencius said, 'Shun was born in Chû-făng, removed to Fû-hsiâ, and died in Ming-t'iâo;—a man near the wild tribes on the east.

2. 'King Wăn was born in Châu by *mount* Ch'î, and died in Pî-ying;—a man near the wild tribes on the west.

3. 'Those regions were distant from one another more than a thousand *lì*, and the age of the one *sage* was posterior to that of the other more than a thousand years. But when they got their wish,

1. THE AGREEMENT OF SAGES NOT AFFECTED BY PLACE OR TIME. 1. The common view derived from the 'Historical Records,' Book I, is, that Shun was a native of Chî-châu, corresponding to the modern Shan-hsî, to which all the places in the text are accordingly referred. Some, however, and especially Tsăng Tsze-kû (曾子固), of the Sung dynasty, find his birthplace in Chî-nan in Shan-tung, and this would seem to be supported by Mencius in this passage. There is considerable difficulty with Ming-t'iâo, as we read in the 'Historical Records,' that in the thirty-ninth year of his reign, Shun died, while on a tour of inspection to the south, in the wilderness of Ts'ang-wû (蒼梧), and was buried on the Chiû-î (九疑) hills in Chiang-nan, which are in Ling-ling (零陵). The discussions on the point are very numerous. See the 集證 and 四書拓餘說, *in loc.*; see also on the Shû-ching, Pt. II. No doubt, Mencius was not speaking without book. 東夷之人, literally, 'a man of the eastern Î, or barbarians,' but the meaning can only be what I have given in the translation. So 西夷之人. 2. Châu, the original seat of the House of Châu, was in the present department of Fung-ts'iang, in Shen-hsî. Pî-ying is to be distinguished from Ying which was the capital of Ch'û, and with which the paraphrast of Chao Ch'î strangely confounds it. Chû Hsî says it was near to Făng (豐) and Hâo (鎬), the successive capitals of king Wû. The former was in Hû-hsien (鄠縣), and the latter in Hsien-yang (咸陽), both in the department of Hsî-an. Pî-ying was in the district of Hsien-ning (咸寧) of the same department, and there the grave of king Wû, or the place of it, is still pointed out. 3 得志行乎中國,—'when they got their wishes carried out in the Middle Kingdom.' We are to understand that their aim was to carry out their principles, not to get the throne. 符 should be called a tally or token perhaps, rather than 'a seal.' Anciently, the sovereign delivered, as the token of investiture, one half of a tally of wood or some precious stone, reserving the other half in his own keeping. It was cut right

歲得志行乎中國若
合符節先聖後聖其
揆一也。
子産聽鄭國之政
以其乘輿濟人於溱
洧孟子曰惠而不知
爲政歲十一月徒杠
成十二月輿梁成民
未病涉也君子平其

and carried their principles into practice throughout the Middle
Kingdom, it was like uniting the two halves of a seal.

4. '*When we examine* those sages, both the earlier and the later,
their principles are found to be the same.'

CHAP. II.   1. When Tsze-ch'an was chief minister of the State
of Chăng, he would convey people across the Chăn and Wei in his
own carriage.

2. Mencius said, 'It was kind, but showed that he did not
understand the practice of government.

3. 'When in the eleventh month of the year the foot-bridges
are completed, and the carriage-bridges in the twelfth month, the
people have not the trouble of wading.

4. 'Let a governor conduct his rule on principles of equal justice,

through a line of characters, indicating the
commission, and their halves fitting each other
when occasion required, was the test of truth
and identity. Originally as we see from the
formation of the character (符), the tally must
have been of bamboo. 4 先聖後聖 is
to be understood generally, and not of Shun
and Wăn merely. 其揆一揆 is taken
as a verb = 度 'to reckon,' 'to estimate,' and
is understood of the mental exercises of the
sages. 其揆,—'their mindings,' the principles which they cherished.

2. GOOD GOVERNMENT LIES IN EQUAL MEASURES
FOR THE GENERAL GOOD, NOT IN ACTS OF FAVOUR
TO INDIVIDUALS. 1. Tsze-ch'an,—see Analects,
V. xv. The Chăn and Wei were two rivers of
Chăng, said to have their rise in the Mă-ling
(馬嶺) hills, and to meet at a certain point,
after which the common stream seems to have
borne the name of both the feeders. They are
referred to the department of Ho-nan in Ho-

nan province. 聽政,—'was hearing the
government,' i.e. was chief minister. 乘,
4th tone. Chû Hsi explains 以其乘輿
by 以其所乘之輿, but 乘 so used is
in and tone. He so expands, however, probably
from remembering a conversation on Tsze-
ch'an between Confucius and Tsze-yû, related
in the *Chiâ-yû*, Bk. IV. iv, near the end, and to
which Mencius has reference. The sage held
that Tsze-ch'an was kind, but only as a mother,
loving but not teaching the people, and, in
illustration of his view, says that Tsze-ch'an,
以所乘之車濟冬涉, 'used the
carriage in which he rode to convey over those
who were wading through the water in the
winter.' 2. The subject here is the action, not
the man. The practice of government is to be
seen not in acts of individual kindness and
small favours, but in the administration of just
and beneficent laws. 3. The eleventh and
twelfth months here correspond to the ninth
and tenth of the present calendar, which follows

政行辟人可也焉得人人而
濟之故爲政者每人而
悅之日亦不足矣。
曰孟子告齊宣王曰君之
視臣如手足則臣視君如
腹心君之視臣如犬馬則
臣視君如國人君之視臣
如土芥則臣視君如寇讐。
王曰禮爲舊君有服何如
斯可爲服矣曰諫行言聽

and, when he goes abroad, he may cause people to be removed out of his path. But how can he convey everybody across the rivers?

5. 'It follows that if a governor will *try to* please everybody, he will find the days not sufficient *for his work.*'

CHAP. III. 1. Mencius said to the king Hsüan of Ch'î, 'When the prince regards his ministers as his hands and feet, his ministers regard their prince as their belly and heart; when he regards them as his dogs and horses, they regard him as any other man; when he regards them as the ground or as grass, they regard him as a robber and an enemy.'

2. The king said, 'According to the rules of propriety, a minister wears mourning when he has left the service of a prince. How must *a prince* behave that his *old ministers* may thus go into mourning?'

3. Mencius replied, 'The admonitions *of a minister* having been

the Hsiâ division of the year;—see Analects, XV. x. Mencius refers to a rule for the repair of the bridges, on the termination of agricultural labours. 4. 君子·爲政者, 'a chief minister.' 辟, read as 闢. Removing people from the way, when the prince went forth, was likewise a rule of the Châu dynasty; and not only did it extend to the prince, but to many officers and women. See the Châu-lî, Pt. I. vii. 32. 5. 'The days not sufficient,'—i.e. he will not have time for all he has to do.

3. WHAT TREATMENT SOVEREIGNS GIVE TO THEIR MINISTERS WILL BE RETURNED TO THEM BY A CORRESPONDING BEHAVIOUR. 1. 'As his hands and feet,'—i.e. with kindness and attention. 'As

their belly and heart,'—i.e. with watchfulness and honour. 'As his dogs and horses,'—i.e. without respect, but feeding them. 'As any other man,'—literally, 'as a man of the kingdom,' i.e. without any distinction or reverence. 'As ground or as grass,'—i.e. trampling on them, cutting them off. 2. The Lî here referred to is mentioned in the 'Ritual Usages;'—see Bk. XI (卷二十三), 66; et al. The passage, however, is obscure. 爲舊君,—'for an old prince,' i.e. a prince whose service he has left. The king falls back on this rule, thinking that Mencius had expressed himself too strongly. 3. 膏澤,—'fat and moistening influences,'

膏澤下於民、有故而去、則君
使人導之出疆、又先於其所
往去三年不反、然後收其田
里、此之謂三有禮焉、如此則
爲之服矣。今也爲臣諫則不
行言則不聽膏澤不下於民、
有故而去、則君博執之、又極
之於其所往去之日、遂收其
田里、此之謂寇讎寇讎何服
之有。

followed, and his advice listened to, so that blessings have descended on the people, if for some cause he leaves *the country*, the prince sends an escort to conduct him beyond the boundaries. He also anticipates *with recommendatory intimations* his arrival in the country to which he is proceeding. When he has been gone three years and does not return, *only* then at length does he take back his fields and residence. This treatment is what is called a "thrice-repeated display of consideration." When a prince acts thus, mourning will be worn on leaving his service.

4. 'Now-a-days, the remonstrances of a minister are not followed, and his advice is not listened to, so that no blessings descend on the people. When for any cause he leaves the country, the prince tries to seize him and hold him a prisoner. He also pushes him to extremity in the country to which he has gone, and on the very day of his departure, takes back his fields and residence. This treatment shows him to be what we call "a robber and an enemy." What mourning can be worn for a robber and an enemy?'

=blessings. 先於其所往 must be sup-plemented by 稱揚其賢、欲其收用之, 'mentions and commends his worth, wishing him to be received and used.' 田,—'fields,'=emoluments. 里,—used for an individual residence. We have not had the character in this sense before. The 'thrice-repeated display of consideration' refers, first, to the escort as a protection from danger; secondly, to the anticipatory recommendations; and thirdly, to the long-continued emoluments, in expectation of the minister's return. 4. Here and above, 有故 is not to be taken as 大故; in Bk. III. Pt. I. ii. 1. We must under-

孟子曰、無罪而殺士
則大夫可以去、無罪而
戮民則士可以徙。
孟子曰、君仁莫不仁、
君義莫不義。
孟子曰、非禮之禮、非
義之義、大人弗爲。
孟子曰、中也養不中、
才也養不才、故人樂有
賢父兄也、如中也棄不

CHAP. IV. Mencius said, 'When scholars are put to death without any crime, the great officers may leave *the country*. When the people are slaughtered without any crime, the scholars may remove.'

CHAP. V. Mencius said, 'If the sovereign be benevolent, all will be benevolent. If the sovereign be righteous, all will be righteous.'

CHAP. VI. Mencius said, 'Acts of propriety which are not *really* proper, and acts of righteousness which are not *really* righteous, the great man does not do.'

CHAP. VII. Mencius said, 'Those who keep the Mean, train up those who do not, and those who have abilities, train up those who have not, and hence men rejoice in having fathers and elder brothers who are possessed of virtue and talent. If they who keep

stand 'wishes to,' or 'tries to,' before 搏執 之, for if the minister were really imprisoned, he could not go to another kingdom.

4. PROMPT ACTION IS NECESSARY AT THE RIGHT TIME. 可以, 'may,'=it is time to. If the opportunity be not taken, while the injustice of the ruler is exercised on those below them, it will soon come to themselves, and it will be too late to escape. The 日講 concludes its paraphrase thus :—'We may see how the ruler should prize virtue, and be slow to punish ; and how he should be cautious in execution of the laws, ever trying to practise benevolence. If he can indeed embody the mind of God, who loves all living things, and make the compassion of the ancient sages his rule, then both officers and people will be grateful to him as to

Heaven, and long repose and protracted good order will be the result.'

5. THE INFLUENCE OF THE RULER'S EXAMPLE. See Pt. I. xx, where the same words are found, but their application is to stimulate ministers to do their duty in advising, or remonstrating with, their sovereign.

6. THE GREAT MAN MAKES NO MISTAKES IN MATTERS OF PROPRIETY AND RIGHTEOUSNESS. 非 禮之禮 非義之義, expressions in themselves contradictory, must be taken with some latitude. 'Respect,' it is said, 'belongs to propriety, but it may be carried so far as to degenerate into flattery,' &c. &c.

7. WHAT DUTIES ARE DUE FROM, AND MUST BE RENDERED BY, THE VIRTUOUS AND TALENTED TO THE YOUNG AND IGNORANT. 中也、才也

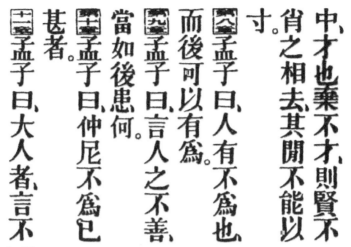

中、才也棄不才、則賢不
肖之相去其閒不能以
寸。

〔八〕孟子曰人有不爲也、
而後可以有爲。

〔九〕孟子曰言人之不善、
當如後患何。

〔十〕孟子曰仲尼不爲已
甚者。

〔十一〕孟子曰大人者言不

the Mean spurn those who do not, and they who have abilities spurn those who have not, then the space between them—those so gifted and the ungifted—will not admit an inch.'

CHAP. VIII. Mencius said, 'Men must be decided on what they will NOT do, and then they are able to act with vigour *in what they ought to do.*'

CHAP. IX. Mencius said, 'What future misery have they and ought they to endure, who talk of what is not good in others!'

CHAP. X. Mencius said, 'Chung-nî did not do extraordinary things.'

CHAP. XI. Mencius said, 'The great man does not think before-

—'given the Mean,' 'given abilities.' 中,—the Mean, the rightly ordered course of conduct. Both it and 才 must be taken here in the concrete. 父兄,—as in Bk. III. Pt. I. ii. 3. 如中也,云云,—by neglecting their duty, the one class bring themselves to the level of the other. 賢 embraces both the 中 and the 才 above. 不肖,—see the Doctrine of the Mean, iv. 以寸,—'with an inch,' i. e. be measured with an inch.

8. CLEAR DISCRIMINATION OF WHAT IS WRONG AND RIGHT MUST PRECEDE VIGOROUS RIGHT-DOING. Literally, 'men have the not-do, and afterwards they can have the do.' 有爲 implies vigour in the action. Châo Ch'î's commentary is :—'If a man will not condescend to take in any irregular way, he will be found able to yield a thousand chariots.'

9. EVIL SPEAKING IS SURE TO BRING WITH IT EVIL CONSEQUENCES. The 富 here, followed by 如何, creates a difficulty. Chû Hsî supposes the remark was made with some peculiar reference. If we know that, the difficulty would vanish. The original implies, I think, all that I have expressed in the translation.

10. THAT CONFUCIUS KEPT THE MEAN. 已甚者,—i. e. 'excessive things,' but 'extraordinary' rather approaches the meaning. It may strike the student that the meaning is—'Confucius's inaction (=slowness to act) was excessive,' but in that case we should have had 矣, and not 者, at the end. We may compare with the sentiment the Doctrine of the Mean, xi, xiii ; Analects, VII. xx, et al.

11. WHAT IS RIGHT IS THE SUPREME PURSUIT OF THE GREAT MAN. Compare Analects, IV. x. 不必,—'does not *must*,' he is beyond the habit of caring for that. 惟義所在,—

必信行不必果惟義所在。孟子曰大人者不失其赤子之心者也。孟子曰養生者不足以當大事惟送死可以當大事。孟子曰君子深造之以道欲其自得之也自得之則居之安

hand of his words that they may be sincere, nor of his actions that they may be resolute;—he simply *speaks and does* what is right.'

CHAP. XII. Mencius said, 'The great man is he who does not lose his child's-heart.'

CHAP. XIII. Mencius said, 'The nourishment of *parents when* living is not sufficient to be accounted the great thing. It is only in the performing their obsequies when dead that we have what can be considered the great thing.'

CHAP. XIV. Mencius said, 'The superior man makes his advances *in what he is learning* with deep earnestness and by the proper course, wishing to get hold of it as in himself. Having got

'only that in which righteousness is;' that only is his concern. In fact he can hardly be said to be concerned about this. It is natural to him to pursue the right.

12. A MAN IS GREAT BECAUSE HE IS CHILDLIKE. Châo Ch'î makes 'the great man' to be 'a sovereign,' and 其赤子, 'his children,' i.e. his people, and the sentiment is that the true sovereign is he who does not lose his people's hearts. I mention this interpretation, as showing how learned men have varied and may vary in fixing the meaning of these books. It is sufficiently absurd, and has been entirely displaced by the interpretation which is given in the version. The sentiment may suggest the Saviour's words,—'Except ye be converted, and become as little children, ye shall not enter into the kingdom of heaven.' But Christ speaks of the child's-heart as a thing to be regained; Mencius speaks of it as a thing not to be lost. With Christ, to become as children is to display certain characteristics of children. With Mencius, 'the child's-heart' is the ideal moral condition of humanity. Chû Hsî says:—'The mind of the great man comprehends all changes of phenomena, and the mind of the child is nothing but a pure simplicity, free from all hypocrisy. Yet the great man is the great man, just as he is not led astray by external things,

but keeps his original simplicity and freedom from hypocrisy. Carrying this out, he becomes omniscient and omnipotent, great in the highest degree.' We need not suppose that Mencius would himself have expanded his thought in this way.

13. FILIAL PIETY SEEN IN THE OBSEQUIES OF PARENTS. 養生者—者字指養生之事,—'the character 者 refers to the ways by which the living may be nourished.' It belongs to the phrase 養生生 alone. 當=爲,—'to be considered,' 'to constitute.' 送死,—literally, 'to accompany the dead,' but denoting all the last duties to them. It = 慎終, Analects, I. ix. The sentiment needs a good deal of explaining and guarding. The obsequies are done, it is said, once for all. If done wrong, the fault cannot be remedied. Probably the remark had a peculiar reference. The 日講 supposes it was spoken against the Mohist practice of burying parents with a spare simplicity;—see III. Pt. I. v.

14. THE VALUE OF LEARNING THOROUGHLY IN-

居之安、則資之深、資
之深、則取之左右逢
其原、故君子欲其自
得之也。

臺孟子曰、博學而詳
說之、將以反說約也。

因孟子曰、以善服人
者、未有能服人者也、
以善養人然後能服
天下天下不心服而

hold of it in himself, he abides in it calmly and firmly. Abiding in it calmly and firmly, he reposes a deep reliance on it. Reposing a deep reliance on it, he seizes it on the left and right, meeting everywhere with it as a fountain *from which things flow.* It is on this account that the superior man wishes to get hold of what he is learning as in himself.'

CHAP. XV. Mencius said, 'In learning extensively and discussing minutely what is learned, the object *of the superior man* is that he may be able to go back and set forth in brief what is essential.'

CHAP. XVI. Mencius said, 'Never has he who would by his excellence subdue men been able to subdue them. Let *a prince* seek by his excellence to nourish men, and he will be able to subdue the whole kingdom. It is impossible that any one should become ruler of the people to whom they have not yielded the subjection of the heart.'

WROUGHT INTO THE MIND. 深造之—造 read *ts'âo*, 4th tone, 'to arrive at;' 之 must refer to the 理, or principles of the subject which is being learnt. 以道 is understood of the proper course or order, the successive steps of study,—依着次序. 其自得 gives the key to the chapter;—'his self-getting,' i.e. his getting hold of the subject so that his knowledge of it becomes a kind of intuition. 資—藉, 'to rely on.' The subject so apprehended in its principles is capable of indefinite application. 'He seizes it on the right and left,'—i.e. he no longer needs his early efforts to apprehend it. It underlies numberless phenomena, in all which he at once detects it, just as water below the earth is found easily and anywhere, on digging the surface.—One may read scores of pages in the Chinese commentators, and yet not get a clear idea in his own

mind of the teaching of Mencius in this chapter. Châo Ch'î gives 道 a more substantive meaning than in the translation; thus:—'The reason why the superior man pursues with earnestness to arrive at the depth and mystery of 道, is from a wish to get hold for himself of its source and root, as something belonging to his own nature.' Most critics understand the subject studied to be man's own self, not things external to him. We must leave the subject in its own mist.

15. Chû Hsî says, apparently with reason, that this is a continuation of the last chapter, showing that the object of the superior man in the extensive studies which he pursues, is not vain-glory, but to get to the substance and essence of things. 的 conveys the two ideas of condensation and importance.

16. The object of this chapter, say commentators, is to stimulate rulers to do good in sincerity, with a view, that is, to the good of

有本者如是是之取
科而後進放乎四海
泉混混不舍晝夜盈
取於水也孟子曰原
於水曰水哉水哉何
徐子曰仲尼亟稱
當之。
祥不祥之實蔽賢者
孟子曰言無實不
王者未之有也。

CHAP. XVII. Mencius said, 'Words which are not true are inauspicious, and the words which are most truly obnoxious to the name of inauspicious, are those which throw into the shade men of talents and virtue.'

CHAP. XVIII. 1. The disciple Hsü said, 'Chung-ni often praised water, saying, "O water! O water!" What did he find in water *to praise?*'

2. Mencius replied, 'There is a spring of water; how it gushes out! It rests not day nor night. It fills up every hole, and then advances, flowing on to the four seas. Such is water having a spring! It was this which he found in it to praise.

others. I confess it is to me very enigmatical. Paul's sentiment,—'Scarcely for a righteous man will one die, yet peradventure for a good man some would even dare to die,'—occurs to the mind on reading it, but this is clashed with by its being insisted on that 養人以善 has no reference to the nourishing men's bodies, but is the bringing them to the nourisher's own moral excellence. Châo Ch'î takes the first 善 as meaning 威力, 'majesty and strength.' But this is inadmissible. The point of the chapter is evidently to be found in the contrast of 服 and 養.

17. The translation takes 無實 as an adjective qualifying 言, and there is a play on the term in the use of 實 in the two parts. Chû Hsî mentions another view making 無實 an adverb joined to 不祥, 'there are no words really inauspicious;' i.e. generally speaking, 'only those are obnoxious to be

regarded as really inauspicious which throw into,' &c. He says he is unable to decide between the two interpretations, and thinks the text may be mutilated. 者 has reference to 言, and not to 人, to 'words,' not to 'men.'

18. How MENCIUS EXPLAINED CONFUCIUS'S PRAISE OF WATER. 1. 亟,—read *chi*, the 2nd tone, 'often.' 稱 (in the sense of 'to praise') 於 水=於 marking the objective case, or = found something to praise in water. See Analects, IX. xvi, though we have not there the exact words of this passage. 2. 科=坎, 'a pit,' i.e. every hollow in its course. 是 之 取 爾, '*it was* just the seizing of this.' One commentator brings out the 是 之 in this way—以 是 之 故 而 取 之 爾. 3. Here, again, the months are those of Châu, corresponding to the present

察存希以囚而皆月爾
於之庶異孟待盈之苟
人舜民於子也其閒為
倫明去禽曰故涸雨無
由於之獸人聲也集本
仁庶君者之聞可溝七
義物子幾所過立澮八

情
君
子
恥
之

3. 'But suppose that the water has no spring.—In the seventh
and eighth months when the rain falls abundantly, the channels in
the fields are all filled, but their being dried up again may be
expected in a short time. So a superior man is ashamed of a
reputation beyond his merits.'

CHAP. XIX. 1. Mencius said, 'That whereby man differs from
the lower animals is but small. The mass of people cast it away,
while superior men preserve it.

2. 'Shun clearly understood the multitude of things, and closely
observed the relations of humanity. He walked along the path of
benevolence and righteousness; he did not *need to* pursue benevolence and righteousness.'

third and sixth. 雨集 'the rains are collected.' 溝澮 were channels belonging to
the irrigation of the lands divided on the nine-
squares system. 可立而待—we might
translate as='one may stand and wait till
they are dry,' but 立 is often used='quickly.'
情=實, as in the Great Learning, Commentary, chap. iv.

19. WHEREBY SAGES ARE DISTINGUISHED FROM
OTHER MEN;—ILLUSTRATED IN SHUN. 1. It is to be
wished that Mencius had said distinctly what
the small (幾, the 1st tone, 希) point distinguishing men from birds and beasts was.
According to Chû Hsî, men and creatures have
the 理 (intellectual and moral principle) of
Heaven and Earth to form their *nature*, and
the 氣 (matter) of Heaven and Earth to form
their *bodies*, only men's 氣 is more correct than
that of beasts, so that they are able to fill up
the capacity of their nature. This denies any
essential difference between men and animals,
and what difference it allows is corporeal or
material. Châo Ch'î says:—幾希,無幾

也知義與不知義之閒耳.
幾希 means not much. It is simply the
interval between the knowledge of righteousness, and the want of that knowledge.' This
is so far correct, but the difference which it
indicates cannot be said to be 'not great.'—
But it is not the object of Mencius to indicate
the character of that which differences men
and animals, and not its amount? 幾希=
is something minute. One commentator refers
us to the expression in the Shû-ching,—人
心惟危道心惟微 (II. ii. 15), as
forming a key to the passage. In that, 人心
is the mind prone to err, in distinction from the
道心, 'the mind of reason,' which it is said
is minute. 2. Shun preserving and cultivating
this distinctive endowment was led to the
character and achievements which are here
briefly described. The phrase 庶物, it is
said, 該得廣,凡天地閒事物
皆是, 'covers a wide extent of meaning,
embracing all matters and things in heaven
and earth.' The 日講 refers to it all the

行非行仁義也。

孟子曰禹惡旨酒

而好善言湯執中立

賢無方文王視民如

傷望道而未之見武

王不泄邇不忘遠周

公思兼三王以施四

事其有不合者仰而

思之夜以繼日幸而

CHAP. XX. 1. Mencius said, 'Yü hated the pleasant wine, and loved good words.

2. 'T'ang held fast the Mean, and employed men of talents and virtue without regard to where they came from.

3. 'King Wăn looked on the people as *he would on a man who was* wounded, and he looked towards the right path as if he could not see it.

4. 'King Wŭ did not slight the near, and did not forget the distant.

5. 'The duke of Châu desired to unite in himself *the virtues* of those kings, *those founders of the* three *dynasties*, that he might display in his practice the four things *which they did*. If he saw anything in them not suited *to his time*, he looked up and thought about it, from daytime into the night, and when he was fortunate enough to master the difficulty, he sat waiting for the morning.'

governmental achievements of Shun related in the Shû-ching.

20. THE SAME SUBJECT;—ILLUSTRATED IN Yü, T'ĂNG, WĂN, WÛ, AND CHÂU-KUNG. 1. In the Chan Kwo Ts'ê (戰國策), which fills up in a measure the space between the period of the Ch'un Ch'iû and the Han dynasty, Part VI, Article 11, we read that anciently a daughter of the Tî (probably Yâo or Shun) caused Î-tî to make wine (? spirits), and presented it to Yü, who drank some of it, and pronounced it to be pleasant. Then, however, he frowned on Î-tî, and forbade the use of the pleasant liquor, saying, 'In future ages, rulers will through this liquor ruin their States.' Yü's love of good words is commemorated in the Shû-ching, II. ii. 21.

2. 無方 may be understood with reference to class or place;—compare the Shû-ching, IV. ii. 5, 8. 3. 'As he would on one who was wounded,' i.e. he regarded the people with compassionate tenderness. 而 is to be read as 如, with which, according to Chû Hsî, it was anciently interchanged. See the Shû-ching, V. xvi. 11, 12, for illustrations of Wăn's care of the people, and the Shû-ching, III. i. Ode VI, for illustration of the other characteristic. 4. 泄, read Asieh (as 渫), and defined by Châo Ch'î as meaning 狎, 'to slight.' The adjectives are to be understood both of persons and things. 5. 三王,—i.e. Yü, T'ăng, and the kings Wăn and Wû, who are often classed together as the one founder of the Châu dynasty. 'The four things' are what have been stated in the preceding paragraphs. 其事 for its antecedent. 得之,— 'apprehended it,' understood the matter in its principles, so as to be able to bring into his own practice the spirit of those ancient sages.

世而斬小人之澤五世　孟子曰君子之澤五　曰其義則丘竊取之矣。　桓晉文其文則史孔子　之春秋一也其事則齊　作。晉之乘楚之檮杌魯　而詩亡詩亡然後春秋　孟子曰王者之迹熄　得之坐以待旦。

CHAP. XXI. 1. Mencius said, 'The traces of sovereign rule were extinguished, and the *royal* odes ceased to be made. When those odes ceased to be made, then the Ch'un Ch'iû was produced.

2. 'The Shǎng of Tsin, the Tâo-wû of Ch'û, and the Ch'un Ch'iû of Lû were books of the same character.

3. 'The subject of *the* Ch'un Ch'iû was the affairs of Hwan of Ch'î and Wǎn of Tsin, and its style was the historical. Confucius said, "Its *righteous* decisions I ventured to make."'

CHAP. XXII. 1. Mencius said, 'The influence of a sovereign sage terminates in the fifth generation. The influence of a mere sage does the same.

21. THE SAME SUBJECT ;—ILLUSTRATED IN CONFUCIUS. 1. The extinction of the true royal rule of Châu dates from the transference of the capital from Fǎng and Hâo to Lo by the sovereign Ping, B.C. 769. From that time, the sovereigns of Châu had the name without the rule. By the 詩 is intended, not the Book of Poems, but the YA (雅) portion of them, descriptive of the royal rule of Châu, and to be used on great occasions. 亡 does not mean that the YA were lost, but that no additions were made to them, and they degenerated into mere records of the past, and were no longer descriptions of the present. Confucius edited the annals of Lû to supply the place of the YA. See Bk. III. Pt. II. ix. 8. 2. Each State had its annals. Those of Tsin were compiled under the name of Shǎng (4th tone), 'The Carriage;' those of Ch'û under that of Tâo-wû, which is explained as the name of a ferocious animal, and more anciently as the denomination of a vile and lawless man. The annals of Lû had the name of 'Spring and Autumn,' two seasons for the whole. 其 refers only to the annals of Lû. They did not contain only the affairs of Hwan and Wǎn, but these occupied an early and prominent place in them. 竊,—see Bk. II. Pt. I. ii. so. 取 makes the expression still more humble, as if Confucius had 'taken' the judgments from the historians, and not made them himself.

22. THE SAME SUBJECT ;—ILLUSTRATED IN MENCIUS HIMSELF. 1. Here 君子=聖賢有位者, 'the sage and worthy, who has position,' i. e. who occupies the throne, and 小人 =聖賢無位者, 'the sage and worthy, who has no position.' We might suppose that the influence of the former would be more permanent, but Mencius is pleased to say their influence lasts the same time. 澤 is to be taken as='influence,' it being understood to

亦羿有罪焉公明儀曰
己於是殺羿孟子曰是
之道思天下惟羿爲愈
逄蒙學射於羿盡羿
可以無死死傷勇。
以無取與傷惠可以死
無取取傷廉可以與可以
孟子曰可以取可以
也、子私淑諸人也。
而斷。子未得爲孔子徒

2. 'Although I could not be a disciple of Confucius himself, I have endeavoured to cultivate my virtue by means of others *who were.*'

CHAP. XXIII. Mencius said, 'When it appears proper to take a thing, and *afterwards* not proper, to take it is contrary to moderation. When it appears proper to give a thing and *afterwards* not proper, to give it is contrary to kindness. When it appears proper to sacrifice one's life, and *afterwards* not proper, to sacrifice it is contrary to bravery.'

CHAP. XXIV. 1. P'ang Măng learned archery of Î. When he had acquired completely all the science of Î, he thought that in all the kingdom only Î was superior to himself, and so he slew him. Mencius said, 'In this case Î also was to blame. Kung-ming Î *indeed* said, "It would appear as if he were not to be blamed," but

be of a beneficial character. 2. From the death of Confucius to the birth of Mencius there would be nearly a hundred years, so that, though Mencius could not learn his doctrines from the sage himself, he did so from his grandson Tsze-sze, or some of his disciples. 私=竊 in last chapter. 淑=菽 taken actively. 諸人= 於人, the 人 referring to Tsze-sze and his school. This and the three preceding chapters should be considered as one, whose purpose is much the same as Bk. III. Pt. II. ix, showing us that Mencius considered himself the successor of Confucius in the line of sages.

23. FIRST JUDGMENTS ARE NOT ALWAYS CORRECT. IMPULSES MUST BE WEIGHED IN THE BALANCE OF REASON, AND WHAT REASON DICTATES MUST BE FOLLOWED. Such is the meaning of this chapter, in translating the separate clauses of which, we must supplement them by introducing 'afterwards.'

24. THE IMPORTANCE OF BEING CAREFUL OF WHOM WE MAKE FRIENDS. The sentiment is good, but Mencius could surely have found better illustrations of it than the second one which he selected. 1. Of Î, see Analects, XIV. xlviii. 逄 (P'ang, as formed with 夆, not 夅) 蒙 is said both by Chào Ch'î and Chû Hsî to refer to Î's servants (家衆), but one man is evidently denoted by the name. Î's servants did indeed make themselves parties to his murder, but P'ang Măng is the same, I suppose, with Han Tsû, the principal in it. 云爾,— see Bk. II. Pt. II. ii. 4, and Analects, VII. xviii. 曰薄乎云爾 'saying, (meaning to say),'

庾公之斯至、曰、夫子何爲不執弓、曰、
夫尹公之他、端人也、其取友必端矣。
射於尹公之他、尹公之他學射於我、
夫子曰、吾生、何謂也、曰、庾公之斯學
矣。其僕曰、庾公之斯、衞之善射者也、
者誰也。其僕曰、庾公之斯也。曰、吾生
可以執弓、吾死矣夫、問其僕曰、追我
斯追之、子濯孺子曰、今日我疾作、不
鄭人使子濯孺子侵衞、衞使庾公之
宜若無罪焉、曰、薄乎云爾、惡得無罪。

he thereby only meant that his blame was slight. How can he be held without *any* blame?'

2. 'The people of Chăng sent Tsze-cho Yü to make a stealthy attack on Wei, which sent Yü-kung Sze to pursue him. Tsze-cho Yü said, "To-day I feel unwell, so that I cannot hold my bow. I am a dead man!" *At the same time* he asked his driver, "Who is it that is pursuing me?" The driver said, "It is Yü-kung Sze," *on which* he exclaimed, "I shall live." The driver said, "Yü-kung Sze is the best archer of Wei, what do you mean by saying 'I shall live?'" Yü replied, "Yü-kung Sze learned archery from Yin-kung T'o, who again learned it from me. Now, Yin-kung T'o is an upright man, and the friends of his selection must be upright *also*." When Yü-kung Sze came up, he said, "Master, why are you not holding your bow?"

It was slighter than ... simply.' 2. 侵, 'to attack stealthily.' An incursion made with music, and the pomp of war, is called 伐, and the one without these, 侵. The 之 in the names—庾公之斯 and 尹公之佗, are mere vocal particles. 他,—read t'o. The name is elsewhere found 尹公佗. In the 左傳, under the fourteenth year of duke

今日我疾作不可以執弓。
曰小人學射於尹公之他
尹公之他學射於夫子我
不忍以夫子之道反害夫
子雖然今日之事君事也
我不敢廢抽矢扣輪去其
金發乘矢而後反。
蓋孟子曰西子蒙不潔則
人皆掩鼻而過之雖有惡
人齊戒沐浴則可以祀上

Yü answered him, "To-day I am feeling unwell, and cannot hold my bow." *On this* Sze said, "I learned archery from Yin-kung T'o, who again learned it from you. I cannot bear to injure you with your own science. The business of to-day, however, is the prince's business, which I dare not neglect." He then took his arrows, knocked off their steel points against the carriage-wheel, discharged four of them, and returned.'

CHAP. XXV. 1. Mencius said, 'If the lady Hsï had been covered with a filthy *head-dress*, all people would have stopped their noses in passing her.

2. 'Though a man may be wicked, yet if he adjust his thoughts, fast, and bathe, he may sacrifice to God.'

襄, we have a narrative bearing some likeness to this account of Mencius, and in which 尹公佗 and 庾公差 figure as famous archers of Wei. It is hardly possible, however, to suppose that the two accounts are of the same thing. 乘, 4th tone, 'a team of four horses,' here used for a set of four arrows.

25. IT IS ONLY MORAL BEAUTY THAT IS TRULY EXCELLENT AND ACCEPTABLE. 1. Hsï-tsze, or 'Western lady,' was a poor girl of Yüeh, named Shih î (施夷), of surpassing beauty, presented by the king of Yüeh to his enemy the king of Wû, who became devotedly attached to her, and neglected all the duties of his government. She was contemporary with Confucius. The common account is that she was called 'The western lady,' because she lived on the western bank of a certain stream. If we may receive the works of 管子, however, as having really proceeded from that scholar and statesman, there had been a celebrated beauty named Hsï-tsze, two hundred years before the one of Yüeh. In translating 蒙 不潔, I have followed Chào Ch'î. 2. 惡 both by Chào Ch'î and Chû Hsï, is taken in the sense of 'ugly,' in opposition to the beauty of the lady Hsï. I cannot but think Mencius intended it in the sense of 'wicked,' and that his object was to encourage men to repentance and well-doing. 齊—read châi. See Analects, VII. xii, *et al.* By the laws of China, it was competent for the sovereign only to sacrifice to God. The language of Mencius, in connexion with this fact, very strikingly shows the virtue he attached to penitent purification.

高也星辰之遠也苟求
無事則智亦大矣天之
事也如智者亦行其所
禹之行水也行其所
行水也則無惡於智矣
其鑿也如智者若禹之
利爲本所惡於智者爲
也則故而已矣故者以
孟子曰天下之言性
帝。

CHAP. XXVI. 1. Mencius said, 'All who speak about the natures *of things*, have in fact only their phenomena *to reason from*, and the value of a phenomenon is in its being natural.

2. 'What I dislike in your wise men is their boring out *their conclusions*. If those wise men would only act as Yü did when he conveyed away the waters, there would be nothing to dislike in their wisdom. The manner in which Yü conveyed away the waters was by doing what gave him no trouble. If your wise men would also do that which gave them no trouble, their knowledge would also be great.

3. 'There is heaven so high; there are the stars so distant. If

26. How knowledge ought to be pursued by the careful study of phenomena. Mencius here points out correctly the path to knowledge. The rule which he lays down is quite in harmony with that of Bacon. It is to be regretted that in China, more perhaps than in any other part of the world, it has been disregarded. 1. 性 is here to be taken quite generally. Julien finds fault with Noel for translating it by *rerum natura*, which appears to be quite correct. Chû Hsî makes it = 人物所得以生之理, than which nothing could be more general. Possibly Mencius may have had in view the disputes about the nature of man which were rife in his time, but the references to Yü's labours with the waters, and to the studies of astronomers, show that the term is used in its most general signification. 故 = our 'phenomenon,' the nature in its development. The character is often used as synonymous with 事, 'facts.' 則 is more than a simple con-junction, and is to be taken in close connexion with the 而已; Châo Ch'î explains—則以故而已, 'can only do so by the 故.' And phenomena, to be valuable, must be natural. 利=順, 'following easily,' 'unconstrained. 2. 智者 is the would-be wise='your wise men.' 其鑿, 'their chiselling,' or 'boring,' i.e. their forcing things, instead of 'waiting' for them, which is a 行其所事, 'doing that in which they have every affairs, or much to do.' Yü is said 行水, rather than, according to the common phraseology about his labours, 治水, because 行 more appropriately represents the mode of his dealing with the waters, according to their nature, and not by a system of force. 3. 千歲之日至, according to modern scholars, refers to the winter solstice, from the midnight of which, it

朝　是　與　言　右　言　往　　致
廷　簡　驩　右　師　者　弔　公　也
不　驩　言　師　言　有　入　行
歷　也　孟　不　者　就　門　子　其
位　孟　子　悅　孟　右　有　有　故
而　子　獨　曰　子　師　進　子　千
相　聞　不　諸　不　之　而　之　歲
與　之　與　君　與　位　與　喪　之
言　曰　驩　子　右　而　右　右　日
不　禮　言　皆　師　與　師　師　至
　　　　　　　　　　　　　　　　可
　　　　　　　　　　　　　　　　坐
　　　　　　　　　　　　　　　　而

we have investigated their phenomena, we may, while sitting *in our places*, go back to the solstice of a thousand years *ago*.'

CHAP. XXVII. 1. The officer Kung-hang having on hand the funeral of one of his sons, the Master of the Right went to condole with him. When *this noble* entered the door, some called him to them and spoke with him, and some went to his place and spoke with him.

2. Mencius did not speak with him, so that he was displeased, and said, 'All the gentlemen have spoken with me. There is only Mencius who does not speak to me, thereby slighting me.'

3. Mencius having heard of this remark, said, 'According to the prescribed rules, in the court, individuals may not change their places to speak with one another, nor may they pass from their ranks to

is supposed, the first calculation of time began; 一致是推致而得之, 'we may calculate up to and get it.' Châo Ch'î, however, makes the meaning to be simply :—'We may sit and determine on what day the solstice occurred a thousand years ago.' See the 四書拓餘說, where this view is approved.

27. HOW MENCIUS WOULD NOT IMITATE OTHERS IN PAYING COURT TO A FAVOURITE. 1. Kung-hang (and tone, 'a rank,' 'a row;' various accounts are given of the way in which the term passed along with 公 into a double surname) was an officer of Ch'î, who 'had the funeral of a son.' Neither Châo Ch'î nor Chû Hsî offers any remark on the phrase, but some scholars of the Sung dynasty, subsequent to Chû Hsî, explained it as meaning, 有人子之喪, 'had the funeral duty that devolves on a son,' i. e. was occupied with the funeral of one of his parents, and nearly all commentators have since followed that view. The author of the 四書拓餘說, *in loc.*, shows clearly however, that it is incorrect, and that the true interpretation is the more natural one given in the translation. The Master of the Right here was Wang Hwan (see Bk. II. Pt. II. vi), styled Tsze-áo. At the royal court there were the high nobles, called 太師 and 少師, 'Grand Master' and 'Junior Master.' In the courts of the princes, the corresponding nobles were called 左師 and 右師, 'Master of the Left' and 'Master of

物奚宜至哉其自反而仁矣、

也我必不仁也必無禮也此

待我以橫逆則君子必自反

人者人恆敬之有人於此其

者敬人愛人者人恆愛之敬

心以禮存心仁者愛人有禮

者以其存心也君子以仁存

二 孟子曰君子所以異於人

敖以我爲簡不亦異乎。

踰階而相揖也我欲行禮子

bow to one another. I was wishing to observe this rule, and Tsze-ao understands it that I was slighting him :—is not this strange!'

Chap. XXVIII. 1. Mencius said, 'That whereby the superior man is distinguished from other men is what he preserves in his heart;—namely, benevolence and propriety.

2. 'The benevolent man loves others. The man of propriety shows respect to others.

3. 'He who loves others is constantly loved by them. He who respects others is constantly respected by them.

4. 'Here is a man, who treats me in a perverse and unreasonable manner. The superior man in such a case will turn round upon himself—"I must have been wanting in benevolence; I must have been wanting in propriety;—how should this have happened to me?"

5. 'He examines himself, and is *specially* benevolent. He turns

the Right.' 進,—as in Analects, VII. xxx. 2. It is to be understood that all the condolers made their visit by the prince's order, and were consequently to observe the court rules. This is the explanation of Mencius's conduct. 3. 禮 refers to the established usages of the court; see the Châu Lî, Bk. III. v. 65-67; Bk. IV. iv. 3-14; et al. 階, 'steps,' or 'stairs,' but here for the ranks of the officers arranged with reference to the steps leading up to the hall.

28. How the superior man is distinguished by the cultivation of moral excellence, and is placed thereby beyond the reach of calamity. 1. 存心 must not be understood— 'he preserves his heart.' The first definition of 存 in K'ang-hsî's dictionary is 在, 'to be in.' It is not so much an active verb, 'to preserve,' as = 'to preserve in.' 4. 橫 (4th tone) 逆 presuppose the exercise of love and respect, which are done despite to. 此物=此事 5. 由 is used for 猶, as often elsewhere. 忠, in

則可憂也憂之如何如舜而已
於後世我由未免爲鄉人也是
我亦人也舜爲法於天下可傳
患也。乃若所憂則有之舜人也
故君子有終身之憂無一朝之
獸奚擇哉於禽獸又何難焉
此亦妄人也已矣如此則與禽
而忠矣其橫逆由是也君子曰
君子必自反也我必不忠自反
自反而有禮矣其橫逆由是也

round upon himself, and is *specially* observant of propriety. The perversity and unreasonableness of the other, *however*, are still the same. The superior man will *again* turn round on himself— "I must have been failing to do my utmost."

6. 'He turns round upon himself, and proceeds to do his utmost, but still the perversity and unreasonableness of the other are repeated. *On this* the superior man says, "This is a man utterly lost indeed! Since he conducts himself so, what is there to choose between him and a brute? Why should I go to contend with a brute?"

7. 'Thus it is that the superior man has a life-long anxiety and not one morning's calamity. As to what is matter of anxiety to him, that *indeed* he has.—He *says*, "Shun was a man, and I also am a man. *But* Shun became an example to all the kingdom, and *his conduct* was worthy to be handed down to after ages, while I am nothing better than a villager." This indeed is the proper matter of anxiety to him. And in what way is he anxious about it? Just that he may be like

the sense of 盡已, 'doing one's utmost.' 6. 難, 4th tone,—校, 'to compare with.' It is explained in the dictionary, with reference to this passage, by 責, 'to charge,' 'to reprove.' 7. 豎,—proceeding from within; 患,— coming from without. 一朝之患 must be understood from the expressions below:— There may be calamity, but the superior man is superior to it. 乃, 'but.' We must supply, —'He should be without anxiety, *but* he has anxiety.' 若夫,—夫, and tone. 亡—無

之也稷思天下有飢者由已
道禹思天下有溺者由己溺
子賢之孟子曰禹稷顏回同
不堪其憂顏子不改其樂孔
居於陋巷一簞食一瓢飲人
不入孔子賢之顏子當亂世
禹稷當平世三過其門而
一朝之患則君子不患矣。
仁無爲也非禮無行也如有
矣若夫君子所患則亡矣非

Shun :—then only will he stop. As to what the superior man would feel to be a calamity, there is no such thing. He does nothing which is not according to propriety. If there should befall him one morning's calamity, the superior man does not account it a calamity.'

CHAP. XXIX. 1. Yü and Chî, in an age when the world was being brought back to order, thrice passed their doors without entering them. Confucius praised them.

2. The disciple Yen, in an age of disorder, dwelt in a mean narrow lane, having his single bamboo-cup of rice, and his single gourd-dish of water; other men could not have endured the distress, but he did not allow his joy to be affected by it. Confucius praised him.

3. Mencius said, 'Yü, Chî, and Yen Hûi agreed in the principle of their conduct.

4. 'Yü thought that if any one in the kingdom were drowned, it was as if he drowned him. Chî thought that if any one in the kingdom suffered hunger, it was as if he famished him. It was on this account that they were so earnest.

29. A RECONCILING PRINCIPLE WILL BE FOUND TO UNDERLIE THE OUTWARDLY DIFFERENT CONDUCT OF GREAT AND GOOD MEN;—IN HONOUR OF YEN HÛI, WITH A REFERENCE TO MENCIUS HIMSELF. 1. See Bk. III. Pt. I. iv. 6, 7, 8. The thrice passing his door without entering it was proper to Yü, though it is here attributed also to Chî. 賢,—used as a verb, 'to pronounce a worthy,' = 'to praise.' 2. See Analects, VI. ix. 平世 and 亂世 are contrasted, but a tranquil age was not a characteristic of Yü and Chî's time. It was an age of tranquillization. 3. 同道,—道-理 之當然, 'what was proper in principle.' 4. 由,—used for 猶.

飢之也、是以如是其急
也、禹稷顏子、易地則皆
然、今有同室之人鬬者、
救之、雖被髮纓冠而救
之、可也、鄉鄰有鬬者、被
髮纓冠而往救之、則惑
也、雖閉戶可也。
公都子曰、匡章通國
皆稱不孝焉、夫子與之
遊、又從而禮貌之、敢問

5. 'If Yü and Chî, and Yen-tsze, had exchanged places, each would have done what the other did.

6. 'Here now in the same apartment with you are people fighting:—*you ought to* part them. Though you part them with your cap simply tied over your unbound hair, your conduct will be allowable.

7. 'If the fighting be *only* in the village or neighbourhood, if you go to put an end to it with your cap tied over your hair unbound, you will be in error. Although you should shut your door *in such a case*, your conduct would be allowable.'

CHAP. XXX. 1. The disciple Kung-tû said, 'Throughout the whole kingdom everybody pronounces K'wang Chang unfilial. But you, Master, keep company with him, and moreover treat him with politeness. I venture to ask why you do so.'

5. 則皆然, literally, 'then all so,' the meaning being as in the translation. Yen Hûi, in the circumstances of Yü and Chî, would have been found labouring with as much energy and self-denial for the public good as they showed; and Yü and Chî, in the circumstances of Hûi, would have lived in obscurity, contented as he was, and happy in the pursuit of the truth and in cultivation of themselves. 6. 被,—read p'ï, and tone. The rules anciently prescribed for dressing were very minute. Much had to be done with the hair before the final act of putting on the cap, and tying its strings (纓) under the chin, could be performed. In the case in the text, all this is neglected. The urgency of the case, and the intimacy of the individual with the parties quarrelling, justify such neglect. 救之,—literally, 'to save

them,' i.e. to part them. This was the case of Yü and Chî, in their relation to their times, while that in the next paragraph is supposed to illustrate the case of Yen Hûi in relation to his. But Mencius's illustrations are generally happier than these.

30. HOW MENCIUS EXPLAINED HIS FRIENDLY INTERCOURSE WITH A MAN CHARGED WITH BEING UNFILIAL. 1. K'wang Chang was an officer of Chî. His name, according to 顧麟士, was Chang, and designation Chang-tsze, so that Kung-tû calls him by his name, and Mencius by his designation. In opposition to this, 蔡虛齋 says that Kung-tû merely drops a part of the designation, just as when Yen Hûi is called Yen Yüan, instead of Yen Tsze-yüan. But both these explanations are to be rejected. Chang was the name, and the

何也。孟子曰、世俗所謂不孝
者五、惰其四支、不顧父母之
養、一不孝也、博奕好飲酒不
顧父母之養、二不孝也、好貨
財私妻子不顧父母之養三
不孝也、從耳目之欲、以爲父
母戮、四不孝也、好勇鬭狠、以
危父母、五不孝也、章子有一
於是乎、夫章子、子父責善、而
不相遇也。責善朋友之道也。

2. Mencius replied, ' There are five things which are pronounced in the common usage of the age to be unfilial. The first is laziness in the use of one's four limbs, without attending to the nourishment of his parents. The second is gambling and chess-playing and being fond of wine, without attending to the nourishment of his parents. The third is being fond of goods and money, and selfishly attached to his wife and children, without attending to the nourishment of his parents. The fourth is following the desires of one's ears and eyes, so as to bring his parents to disgrace. The fifth is being fond of bravery, fighting and quarrelling so as to endanger his parents. Is Chang guilty of any one of these things?

3. ' Now between Chang and his father there arose disagreement, he, the son, reproving his father, to urge him to what was good.

4. ' To urge one another to what is good by reproofs is the way of friends. But such urging between father and son is the greatest injury to the kindness, *which should prevail between them*.

子 in 章子 is simply equivalent to our Mr. 與之遊, 'ramble with him,' i.e. as commonly understood, 'allow him to come about your gate, your school.' 又從, 'and moreover from that,' i.e. in addition to that. 博奕, may be taken together, simply = 'chess-playing,' or separately, as in the translation; see Analects, XVII. xxii 私妻子 'selfishly—i.e. partially putting them out of their due place, above his parents, - loving wife and children.' I cannot see why some should give a sensual meaning to 私 here. The advance of meaning from 戮 to 危 shows that the former is to be taken in the lighter sense of 'disgrace.' 3, 4. Compare Pt. I. xviii. 子父責善.—子 precedes 父 here to show that K'wang Chang had been the aggressor.

父子責善賊恩之大者夫章
子豈不欲有夫妻子母之屬
哉爲得罪於父不得近出妻
屏子終身不養焉其設心以
爲不若是是則罪之大者是
則章子已矣。
曾子居武城有越寇或曰、
寇至盍去諸曰無寓人於我
室毀傷其薪木寇退則曰脩
我牆屋我將反寇退曾子反

5. 'Moreover, did not Chang wish to have *in his family* the relationships of husband and wife, child and mother ? But because he had offended his father, and was not permitted to approach him, he sent away his wife, and drove forth his son, and all his life receives no cherishing attention from them. He settled it in his mind that if he did not act in this way, his would be one of the greatest of crimes.—Such and nothing more is the case of Chang.'

CHAP. XXXI. 1. When the philosopher Tsăng dwelt in Wŭ-ch'ăng, there came a band from Yüeh to plunder it. Some one said *to him*, 'The plunderers are coming :—why not leave this ?' Tsăng *on this left the city*, saying to *the man in charge of the house*, 'Do not lodge any persons in my house, lest they break and injure the plants and trees.' When the plunderers withdrew, he sent word to him, saying, 'Repair the walls of my house. I am about to return.'

5. 屏, 3rd tone. Readers not Chinese will think that Chang's treatment of his wife and son was more criminal than his conduct to his father. 是則罪之大者,—是 'this,' embracing the two things, his giving offence to his father, and still continuing to enjoy the comforts of wife and son.

31. How MENCIUS EXPLAINED THE DIFFERENT CONDUCT OF TSĂNG-TSZE AND OF TSZE-SZE IN SIMILAR CIRCUMSTANCES. 1. Wŭ-ch'ăng, as in Analects, VI. xii. It appears below that Tsăng had opened a school or lecture-room in the place. Many understand that he had been invited to

do so,—to be a 賓師, 'guest and teacher,'— by the commandant. Wŭ-ch'ăng is probably to be referred to a place in the district of 嘉 祥 in the department of Yen-châu. It was thus in the south of Shan-tung. South from it, and covering the present Chiang-sŭ and part of Cheh-chiang, were the possessions of Wŭ (吳) and Yüeh, all in Tsăng-tsze's time subject to Yüeh. See in the 集證, *in loc.*, a somewhat similar incident in Tsăng's life (probably a different version of the same), in

左右曰、待先生如此其忠
且敬也、寇至、則先去以爲
民望寇退、則反殆於不可。
沈猶行曰、是非汝所知也。
昔沈猶有負芻之禍、從先
生者七十人、未有與焉。子
思居於衞、有齊寇。或曰、寇
至、盍去諸。子思曰、如伋去、
君誰與守。孟子曰、曾子子
思同道、曾子師也父兄也

When the plunderers retired, the philosopher Tsăng returned *accordingly*. His disciples said, 'Since our master was treated with so much sincerity and respect, for him to be the first to go away on the arrival of the plunderers, so as to be observed by the people, and then to return on their retiring, appears to us to be improper.' Ch'ăn-yü Hsing said, 'You do not understand this matter. Formerly, when Ch'ăn-yü was exposed to the outbreak of the grass-carriers, there were seventy disciples in our master's following, and none of them took part in the matter.'

2. When Tsze-sze was living in Wei, there came a band from Ch'î to plunder. Some one said to him, 'The plunderers are coming;—why not leave this?' Tsze-sze said, 'If I go away, whom will the prince have to guard *the State* with?'

3. Mencius said, 'The philosophers Tsăng and Tsze-sze agreed in

which the plunderers are from Lû. 曰、無 寓、云 云,—the translation needs to be supplemented here considerably to bring out the meaning. 薪 is explained in the K'ang-hsî Dictionary, with reference to this passage, by 草, 'grass,' or small plants generally. 寇 退 則 曰,—this 曰 must = 'sent word to.' 牆 屋,—we should rather expect 屋 牆; but 屋 perhaps has to be taken in the sense of 'roof.' The two characters, however, = 'house.' If 待 be translated actively, we must supply as a nominative—'the governor of the city.'

Ch'ăn- (沈 is pronounced as 審; so commonly; but the point is doubtful; see the 集 證, *in loc*.) yü Hsing is supposed to have been a disciple of Tsăng, and a native of Wû-ch'ăng. The Ch'ăn-yü whom he mentions below was another person of the same surname with whom Tsăng and his disciples (從 者 = 左 右 above) were living. Perhaps he was the Head of the Ch'ăn-yü Family or Clan. 與, 4th tone. Ch'ăn-yü Hsing adduces this other case, as analogous to Tsăng's leaving Wû-ch'ăng, intimating that he acted on a certain principle which justified his conduct. 2. 伋 was Tsze-sze's name. 'Was living in Wei,'—i.e. was

人盡富貴也其妻告其妾曰良
出則必饜酒肉而後反問

後反其妻問所與飲食者則
者其良人出則必饜酒肉而
齊人有一妻一妾而處室
異於人哉堯舜與人同耳。
有以異於人乎孟子曰何以
儲子曰王使人瞯夫子果
地則皆然。
子思臣也微也曾子子思易

the principle of their conduct. Tsăng was a teacher;—in the place of a father or elder brother. Tsze-sze was a minister;—in a meaner place. If the philosophers Tsăng and Tsze-sze had exchanged places, the one would have done what the other did.'

CHAP. XXXII. The officer Ch'û said *to Mencius,* 'Master, the king sent persons to spy out whether you were really different from other men.' Mencius said, 'How should I be different from other men? Yâo and Shun were just the same as other men.'

CHAP. XXXIII. 1. A man of Ch'î had a wife and a concubine, and lived together with them in his house. When their husband went out, he would get himself well filled with wine and flesh, and then return, and, on his wife's asking him with whom he ate and drank, they were sure to be all wealthy and honourable people. The wife informed the concubine, saying, 'When our good man goes out, he is sure to come back having partaken plentifully of wine and flesh. I asked with whom he ate and drank, and they are all, *it seems,* wealthy and honourable people. And yet no people

living and sustaining office. But the attack of Wei by Ch'î is not easily verified. 3. The reader can judge how far the defence of Tsăng's conduct is satisfactory.

32. SAGES ARE JUST LIKE OTHER MEN. This Ch'û was a minister of Ch'î. We must suppose that it was the private manners and way of living of Mencius, which the king wanted to spy out, unless the thing occurred on Mencius's first arrival in Ch'î, and before he had any interview with the king.

33. THE DISGRACEFUL MEANS WHICH SOME MEN TAKE TO SEEK FOR THEIR LIVING, AND FOR WEALTH. 1. As Chû Hsî observes, there ought to be, at the beginning of the chapter, 孟子曰, 'Mencius said.' The phrase 而處 (3rd tone) 室者 is not easily managed in translating.

其與飲食者、盡富貴也。而未嘗有
顯者來、吾將瞯良人之所之也。蚤
起、施從良人之所之、徧國中、無與
立談者。卒之東郭墦間之祭者、乞
其餘不足、又顧而之他、此其為饜
足之道也。其妻歸告其妾曰、良人
者、所仰望而終身也、今若此、與其
妾訕其良人、而相泣於中庭、而良
人未之知也、施施從外來、驕其妻
妾。由君子觀之、則人之所以求富

of distinction ever come here. I will spy out where our good man goes.' *Accordingly*, she got up early in the morning, and privately followed wherever her husband went. Throughout the whole city, there was no one who stood or talked with him. At last, he came to those who were sacrificing among the tombs beyond the outer wall on the east, and begged what they had over. Not being satisfied, he looked about, and went to another party;—and this was the way in which he got himself satiated. His wife returned, and informed the concubine, saying, 'It was to our husband that we looked up in hopeful contemplation, with whom our lot is cast for life;—and now these are his ways!' On this, along with the concubine she reviled their husband, and they wept together in the middle hall. In the meantime the husband, knowing nothing of all this, came in with a jaunty air, carrying himself proudly to his wife and concubine.

2. In the view of a superior man, as to the ways by which men

The subject of it is the 'man of Ch'î,' and not 'the wife and concubine.' It is descriptive of him as living with them, and being the head of a family,—有刑家之責, as is said in the 備旨, 'having the duty of setting an example to its members.' 良人,—corresponding to the Scottish term of 'goodman' for husband. 所與飲食者,—not 'who

希 者 相 而 羞 妾 其 達
矣。幾 泣 不 也。不 妻 者、利
貴

seek for riches, honours, gain, and advancement, there are few of
their wives and concubines who would not be ashamed and weep
together *on account of them*.

gave him to drink and eat,' as Julien makes
it. 所之,-之, the verb, as also below,
and in 之東,之他 施從,-施 read
ì, either 2nd or 4th tone. 國,—plainly used

for 'city.' 郭,—see Bk. II. Pt. II. i. 2 之
他, 'went to another place,' = 'another party.'
2. 幾希, as in chap. xix. 1, but it is here
an adjective, 'few.'

BOOK V.

WAN CHANG. PART I.

怨 而 忘 母 慕 泣 旻 往 二
乎。不 父 愛 也。也。天 于 萬
曰 怨 母 之 萬 孟 何 田、章
長 然 惡 喜 章 子 爲 號 問
息 則 之 而 曰、曰、其 泣 曰、
問 舜 勞 不 父 怨 號 于 舜

萬
章
句
上

CHAPTER I. 1. Wan Chang asked *Mencius*, saying, '*When* Shun
went into the fields, he cried out and wept towards the pitying
heavens. Why did he cry out and weep?' Mencius replied, 'He
was dissatisfied, and full of earnest desire.'

2. Wan Chang said, 'When his parents love him, a son rejoices
and forgets them not. When his parents hate him, though they
punish him, he does not murmur. Was Shun then murmuring

This Book is named from the chief interlocutor in it, Wan Chang (see Bk. III. Pt. II.
v). The tradition is that it was in company
with Wan Chang's disciples, that Mencius,
baffled in his hopes of doing public service, and
having retired into privacy, composed the seven
Books, which constitute his Works. The first
part of this Book is occupied with discussions
about Shun, and other ancient worthies.

1. SHUN'S GREAT FILIAL PIETY:—HOW IT CAR-
RIED HIM INTO THE FIELDS TO WEEP AND DEPLORE
HIS INABILITY TO SECURE THE AFFECTION AND
SYMPATHY OF HIS PARENTS. 1. 號, 2nd tone,
'to cry out.' It has another signification in
the same tone,—'to wail,' which would answer
equally well. See the incident related in the
Shû-ching, II. ii. 21, from which we learn that

於公明高曰、舜往于田、
則吾既得聞命矣號泣
于旻天、于父母、則吾不
知也。公明高曰、是非爾
所知也。夫公明高以孝
子之心爲不若是恝我
竭力耕田共爲子職而
已矣父母之不我愛於
我何哉帝使其子九男
二女百官牛羊倉廩備

against his parents?' Mencius answered, 'Ch'ang Hsî asked Kung-ming Kâo, saying, "As to Shun's going into the fields, I have received your instructions, but I do not know about his weeping and crying out to the pitying heavens and to his parents." Kung-ming Kâo answered him, "You do not understand that matter." Now, Kung-ming Kâo supposed that the heart of the filial son could not be so free of sorrow. *Shun would say,* "I exert my strength to cultivate the fields, but I am thereby only discharging my office as a son. What can there be in me that my parents do not love me?"

3. 'The Tî caused his own children, nine sons and two daughters, the various officers, oxen and sheep, storehouses and granaries, *all*

such behaviour was a characteristic of his earlier life, when he was 'ploughing' at the foot of the Lî hill. 旻天,—the name given to the autumnal sky or heavens. Two meanings have been assigned to 旻: 'the variegated,' with reference to the beautiful tints (文章) of matured nature; and 'the compassionate,' as if it were 慜, with reference to the decay of nature. This latter is generally acquiesced in. I have translated 于 by 'towards,' but the paraphrase in the 日講 is :—'He cried out and called upon pitying Heaven, that lovingly overshadows and compassionates this lower world, weeping at the same time.' 怨慕—simply, 'he was murmuring and desiring.' The murmuring was at himself, but this is purposely kept in the background, and Chang supposed that he was murmuring at his parents. a 父母…不怨,—see

Analects, IV. xviii. Kung-ming Kâo is generally understood to have been a disciple of Tsäng Shän, and Ch'ang Hsî again to have been a disciple of Kâo. 吾既得聞命, 'I have received your *commands;*'—'commands,' said deferentially for 'instructions,' as in Bk. III. Pt. I. v. 5. 于父母 is also from the Shû-ching, though omitted above in par. 1. In translating we must reverse the order of 號泣, 'he wept and cried out,—to heaven, to his parents.' 是非爾所知也,—see Bk. IV. Pt. II. xxxi. 1. 不若是恝 'not so without sorrow,' i.e. not so, as common people would have it, and as Ch'ang Hsî thought would have been right, that he could refrain from weeping and crying out. 我竭云云 are the thoughts supposed to pass through Shun's mind. 共=耕, the 1st tone. 3. See the Shû-ching, I. par. 12, but the various incidents of the particular honours conferred

解憂人悅之好色富貴無足
之所欲貴爲天子而不足以
有天下而不足以解憂貴人之所欲富
不足以解憂富人之所欲富
色人之所欲妻帝之二女而
之所欲也而不足以解憂好
人無所歸天下之士悅之人
遷之焉爲不順於父母如窮
士多就之者帝將胥天下而
以事舜於畎畝之中天下之

to be prepared, to serve Shun amid the channelled fields. Of the
scholars of the kingdom there were multitudes who flocked to him.
The sovereign designed that *Shun* should superintend the kingdom
along with him, and then to transfer it to him entirely. But
because his parents were not in accord with him, he felt like a poor
man who has nowhere to turn to.

4. 'To be delighted in by all the scholars of the kingdom, is
what men desire, but it was not sufficient to remove the sorrow *of
Shun*. The possession of beauty is what men desire, and *Shun* had
for his wives the two daughters of the Tî, but this was not sufficient
to remove his sorrow. Riches are what men desire, and the kingdom
was the rich property *of Shun*, but this was not sufficient to remove
his sorrow Honours are what men desire, and *Shun* had the dignity
of being sovereign, but this was not sufficient to remove his sorrow.
The reason why the being the object of men's delight, with the

on Shun, and his influence, are to be collected
from the general history of him and Yâo.
There is, however, an important discrepancy
between Mencius's account of Shun, and that
in the Shû-ching. There, when he is first
recommended to Yâo by the high officers, they
base their recommendation on the fact of his
having overcome the evil that was in his
parents and brother, and brought them to self-
government. The Shû-ching, moreover, mentions only one son of Yâo, Tan Chû (丹朱),
and says nothing of the nine who are here
said to have been put under the command of

Yâo. They are mentioned, however, in the
'Historical Records,' 虞史記. 帝將
胥天下-將與之胥(-相)視
天下. 而遷之-自移以與之.
不順於父母,—see Bk. IV. Pt. II.
xviii 1. 4. 色,—色 is here = our 'a beauty,
'beauties.' 妻, in 2nd tone, here as a verb,
'to wive,' 'to have for wife.' Observe the force

以解憂者、惟順於父母可
以解憂人少、則慕父母、知
好色則慕少艾、有妻子、則
慕妻子、仕則慕君、不得於
君、則熱中大孝終身慕父
母、五十而慕者予於大舜
見之矣。
[二]萬章問曰詩云、娶妻如
之何必告父母、信斯言也、
宜莫如舜舜之不告而娶

possession of beauty, riches, and honours were not sufficient to remove his sorrow, was that it could be removed only by his getting his parents to be in accord with him.

5. 'The desire of the child is towards his father and mother. When he becomes conscious of the attractions of beauty, his desire is towards young and beautiful women. When he comes to have a wife and children, his desire is towards them. When he obtains office, his desire is towards his sovereign :—if he cannot get the regard of his sovereign, he burns within. *But* the man of great filial piety, to the end of his life, has his desire towards his parents. In the great Shun I see the case of one whose desire at fifty years was towards them.'

CHAP. II. 1. Wan Chang asked *Mencius*, saying, 'It is said in the Book of Poetry,

"In marrying a wife, how ought a man to proceed? He must inform his parents."

If the rule be indeed as here expressed, no man ought to have illustrated it so well as Shun. How was it that Shun's marriage took place without his informing *his parents?*' Mencius replied, 'If he had informed them, he would not have been able to marry. That

of 者, leading on to what follows as the explanation of the preceding circumstances. 5. 少, 4th tone, 'young,' 'little.' 好色,— the term has a different acceptation from that in the preceding paragraph, though I have translated it in the same way. 艾,—in the sense of 美, 'beautiful.'

2. DEFENCE OF SHUN AGAINST THE CHARGES OF VIOLATING THE PROPER RULE IN THE WAY OF HIS MARRYING, AND OF HYPOCRISY IN HIS CONDUCT TO HIS BROTHER. 1, 2. Compare IV. Part I. xxvi. 詩云,—see the Shih-ching, I. viii. Ode VI. st. 3 告, 4th tone, as in Analects, III. xvii. 信=誠, 'if indeed.' 以懟父母,—if

都君咸我績、牛羊父母、倉廩
浚井出從而揜之象曰、謨蓋
使舜完廩、捐階瞽瞍焚廩、使
焉則不得妻也萬章曰、父母
舜而不告何也。曰、帝亦知告
娶則吾既得聞命矣、帝之妻
不告也萬章曰、舜之不告而
廢人之大倫以懟父母、是以
女居室人之大倫也、如告則
何也。孟子曰、告則不得娶、男

male and female should dwell together, is the greatest of human relations. If *Shun* had informed his parents, he must have made void this greatest of human relations, thereby incurring their resentment. On this account, he did not inform them.'

2. Wan Chang said, 'As to Shun's marrying without informing his parents, I have heard your instructions; but how was it that the Tî Yâo gave him his daughters as wives without informing *Shun's parents?*' *Mencius* said, 'The Tî also knew that if he informed them, he could not marry his daughters to him.'

3. Wan Chang said, 'His parents set Shun to repair a granary, to which, the ladder having been removed, Kû-sâu set fire. They *also* made him dig a well. He got out, but they, *not knowing that*, proceeded to cover him up. Hsiang said, "Of the scheme to cover up the city-forming prince, the merit is all mine. Let my parents have his oxen and sheep. Let them have his storehouses and granaries.

he had not married, then his parents would have had cause to be angry with him, for allowing the line of the family to terminate. This seems to be the meaning of the phrase. 聞命,—as in the last chapter. 帝...而 不告,—告 here is understood as='requiring Shun to inform his parents.' 3. Shun's half-brother is understood to have been the instigator in the attempts on his life here mentioned. The incidents, however, are taken from tradition, and not from the Shû-ching. Shun covered himself with two bamboo screens, and made his way through the fire. In the second case, he found a hole or passage in the side of the wall, and got away by means of it. 都君, —it is mentioned in the last chapter, how the scholars of the kingdom flocked to Shun. They say that if he lived in one place for a year, he formed a 聚, or 'assemblage;' in two years, he formed a 邑, or 'town,' and in three, a 都, or 'capital.' With reference to this, Hsiang

父母干弋朕琴朕弤朕二嫂使
治朕棲象往入舜宮舜在牀琴
象曰鬱陶思君爾忸怩舜曰惟
諸臣庶汝其于予治不識舜不
知象之將殺己與曰奚而不知
也象憂亦憂象喜亦喜曰然則
舜僞喜者與曰否昔者有饋生
魚於鄭子產子產使校人畜之
池校人烹之反命曰始舍之圉
圉焉少則洋洋焉攸然而逝予

His shield and spear shall be mine. His lute shall be mine. His bow shall be mine. His two wives I shall make attend for me to my bed." Hsiang then went away into Shun's palace, and there was Shun on his couch playing on his lute. Hsiang said, "I am come simply because I was thinking anxiously about you." *At the same time*, he blushed deeply. Shun said to him, "There are all my officers:—do you undertake the government of them for me." I do not know whether Shun was ignorant of Hsiang's wishing to kill him.' *Mencius* answered, 'How could he be ignorant of that? But when Hsiang was sorrowful, he was also sorrowful; when Hsiang was joyful, he was also joyful.'

4. *Chang* said, 'In that case, then, did not Shun rejoice hypocritically?' Mencius replied, 'No. Formerly, some one sent a present of a live fish to Tsze-ch'an of Chǎng. Tsze-ch'an ordered his pond-keeper to keep it in the pond, but that officer cooked it, and reported the execution of his commission, saying, "When

calls him 都君. 朕, now confined to the imperial wě, was anciently used by high and low. 弤, 'a carved bow,' said to have been given to Shun by Yâo, as a token of his associating him with him on the throne. 二嫂 —literally, 'the two sisters-in-law.' 棲＝牀 'a bed,' or 'couch.' 鬱陶思君爾 一爾＝耳, as a final particle, 'only.' The expression literally is,—'with suppressed anxiety thinking of you only.' 4. 校 (read Asiâo, 4th tone) 人 is taken by all the commentators as

產曰、得其所哉、得其所哉、
校人出曰、孰謂子產智子
既烹而食之曰、得其所哉、
得其所哉、故君子可欺以
其方難罔以非其道彼以
愛兄之道來故誠信而喜
之奚偽焉。

三、萬章問曰、象日以殺舜
為事立為天子、則放之何
也。孟子曰封之也或曰放

I first let it go, it appeared embarrassed. In a little while, it seemed to be somewhat at ease, and then it swam away joyfully." Tsze-ch'an observed, "It had got into its element! It had got into its element!" The pond-keeper then went out and said, "Who calls Tsze-ch'an a wise man? After I had cooked and eaten the fish, he says, "It had got into its element! It had got into its element!" Thus a superior man may be imposed on by what seems to be as it ought to be, but he cannot be entrapped by what is contrary to right principle. Hsiang came in the way in which the love of his elder brother would have made him come; therefore *Shun* sincerely believed him, and rejoiced. What hypocrisy was there?'

CHAP. III. 1. Wan Chang said, 'Hsiang made it his daily business to slay Shun. When *Shun* was made sovereign, how was it that he *only* banished him?' Mencius said, 'He raised him to be a prince. Some supposed that it was banishing him?'

主池沼小吏, 'a small officer over the ponds,' but I do not know that this meaning of the phrase is found elsewhere. 反命,—as in Bk. III. Pt. I. ii. 3. 故君子可欺以其方,—compare Analects, VI. xxiv. 以其方, 'by its class,' the meaning being as in the translation.—Chû Hsî says :—'Mencius says that Shun knew well that Hsiang wished to kill him, but when he saw him sorrowful, he was sorrowful, and when he saw him joyful, he was joyful. The case was that his brotherly feeling could not be repressed. Whether the things mentioned by Wan Chang really occurred or not, we do not know. But Mencius was able to know and describe the mind of Shun, and that is the only thing here worth discussing about.'

3. EXPLANATION AND DEFENCE OF SHUN'S CONDUCT IN THE CASE OF HIS WICKED BROTHER HSIANG; —HOW HE BOTH DISTINGUISHED HIM, AND KEPT HIM UNDER RESTRAINT. 1. 放 = 置, 'to place,' with the idea of keeping in the place, = 'to banish.' Chang's thought was that Hsiang should have been put to death, and not merely banished. 或曰,—it seems best to understand 曰 as meaning 'supposed,' and not 'said.'

之欲其富也封之有庳富貴
之而已矣親之欲其貴也愛
也不藏怒焉不宿怨焉親愛
在弟則封之曰仁人之於弟
人固如是乎在他人則誅之
之有庳有庳之人奚罪焉仁
咸服誅不仁也象至不仁封
危殛鯀于羽山四罪而天下
放驩兜于崇山殺三苗于三
焉萬章曰舜流共工于幽州

2. Wan Chang said, 'Shun banished the superintendent of works
to Yû-châu; he sent away Hwan-tâu to tle mountain Ch'ung; he
slew *the prince of* San-miâo in San-wei; ai d he imprisoned K'wăn
on the mountain Yü. When the crimes of those four were thus
punished, the whole kingdom acquiesced:—it was a cutting off of men
who were destitute of benevolence. But Hsiang was *of all men* the
most destitute of benevolence, and *Shun* raised him to be the prince
of Yû-pî;—of what crimes had the people of Yû-pî been guilty?
Does a benevolent man really act thus? In the case of other men,
he cut them off; in the case of his brother, he raised him to be
a prince.' *Mencius* replied, 'A benevolent man does not lay up anger,
nor cherish resentment against his brother, but only regards him
with affection and love. Regarding him with affection, he wishes
him to be honourable: regarding him with love, he wishes him to
be rich. The appointment *of Hsiang* to be the prince of Yû-pî was
to enrich and ennoble him. If while *Shun* himself was sovereign, his-

2. The different individuals mentioned here
are all spoken of in the Shû-ching, Pt. II. i. 12,
which see. 共工 is a name of office. The
surname or name of the holder of it is not found
in the Shû-ching. Hwan-tâu was the name of
the 司徒, 'Minister of Instruction.' He
appears in the Shû-ching, as the friend of the
共工, recommending him to Yâo; hence
Chû Hsî says that these two were confederate

in evil. 三苗 is to be understood, in the
text, as 'the prince of San-miâo,' which was the
name of a State, near the Tung-t'ing lake, embracing the present department of 岳州, and
extending towards Wû-ch'ang. K'wăn was the
name of the father of Yü. The places mentioned are difficult of identification. Yû-pî is
referred to the present 道州, and the district of Ling-ling, in the department of 永州,

之也身爲天子弟爲匹夫
可謂親愛之乎敢問或曰
放者何謂也曰象不得有
爲於其國天子使吏治其
國而納其貢稅焉故謂之
放豈得暴彼民哉雖然欲
常常而見之故源源而來
不及貢以政接於有庫此
之謂也。
咸丘蒙問曰語云盛德

brother had been a common man, could he have been said to regard
him with affection and love?'

3. *Wan Chang* said, 'I venture to ask what you mean by saying
that some supposed that it was a banishing of Hsiang?' *Mencius*
replied, 'Hsiang could do nothing in his State. The Son of Heaven
appointed an officer to administer its government, and to pay over its
revenues to him. This treatment of him led to its being said that
he was banished. How *indeed* could he be allowed the means of
oppressing the people? Nevertheless, *Shun* wished to be continually
seeing him, and by this arrangement, he came incessantly *to court*, as
is signified in that expression—"He did not wait for the rendering of
tribute, or affairs of government, to receive the prince of Yû-pî."'

CHAP. IV. 1. Hsien-ch'iû Măng asked *Mencius*, saying, 'There

in Hû-nan. 殛 is said by Chû Hsî to = 誅
'to cut off,' but that is too strong. 四罪 =
治此四凶之罪, taking 罪 as mean-
ing 'crimes.' 服, 'submitted,' i.e. acknowledged the justice of the punishments inflicted.
在他人 … 誅之 appears to be incom-
plete, as if Mencius had not permitted his
disciple to finish what he had to say. 宿怨
'to lodge, as if for a night, resentment;'
compare 宿諾, Analects, XII. xii. 2. 3 不
得有爲 'did not get to have doing,' i. e.
was not allowed to act independently 其貢

稅=其國所賦 (taking 貢 as a verb)
之稅. 源源, 'the uninterrupted flowing
of a stream.' 不及貢 … 有庫 is a
quotation by Mencius from some book that is
now lost. There were regular seasons for the
princes in general to repair to court, and emer-
gencies of government which required their
presence, but Shun did not wish his brother to
wait for such occasions, but to be often with
him. The 不 extends over the two clauses,
which = 不及貢期而見 不以
政事而見.
4. EXPLANATION OF SHUN'S CONDUCT WITH
REFERENCE TO THE SOVEREIGN YÂO, AND HIS FATHER

堯老而舜攝也堯典曰
之言齊東野人之語也
哉。孟子曰否此非君子
岌乎不識此語誠然乎
於斯時也天下殆哉岌
瞽瞍其容有蹙孔子曰
瞍亦北面而朝之舜見
帥諸侯北面而朝之瞽
得而子舜南面而立堯
之士君不得而臣父不

is the saying, "A scholar of complete virtue may not be employed as a minister by his sovereign, nor treated as a son by his father. Shun stood with his face to the south, and Yâo, at the head of all the princes, appeared before him at court with his face to the north. Kû-sâu also did the same. When Shun saw Kû-sâu, his countenance became discomposed. Confucius said, At this time, in what a perilous condition was the kingdom! Its state was indeed unsettled."—I do not know whether what is here said really took place.' Mencius replied, 'No. These are not the words of a superior man. They are the sayings of an uncultivated person of the east of Ch'î. When Yâo was old, Shun was associated with him in the government. It is said in the Canon of Yâo, "After twenty and eight years, the Highly Meritorious one deceased. The people acted as if

Kû-sâu. 1. Hsien-ch'iû Mång was a disciple of Mencius. The surname Hsien-ch'iû was derived from a place of that name where his progenitors had resided. The saying which Mång adduces extends to 岌岌乎. Two entirely contrary interpretations of it have been given. One is that given in the translation. It is the view of Châo Ch'î, and is found in the modern Pî-chih (備旨), or 'Complete Digest of Annotations on the Four Books.' Most modern commentaries, however, take an opposite view:—'The scholar of complete virtue cannot employ his sovereign as a minister, or treat his father as a son.' This view is preferred by Julien, who styles the other very bad. I am satisfied, however, that the other is the correct one If it were not, why should Mencius condemn the sentiment as that of an uninstructed man. 舜南面, 云云, follows as a direct example of the principle announced. Shun was the scholar of complete virtue, and therefore the sovereign Yâo, and his father, Kû-sâu, both appeared before him as subjects. 舜見, 云云, and the remarks of Confucius are to be taken as a protest against the arrangements described in the preceding paragraphs. 南面, 北面,—see Analects, VI. i. 野 is to be joined as an adjective with 人, and not as a noun with 東. The passage quoted from the Shû-ching is now found in the canon of Shun, and not that of Yâo;—see II. i. 13. 有, 4th tone. 載, 3rd tone, 'a year.' 放 (3rd tone - see Bk. III. Pt. I. iv. 8) 勤 is not in the classic. 徂 (= 殂) 落.—Chû Hsî makes

王臣而舜既爲天子矣敢
莫非王土率土之濱莫非
得聞命矣詩云普天之下
蒙曰舜之不臣堯則吾既
三年喪是二天子矣咸丘
矣又帥天下諸侯以爲堯
曰民無二王舜既爲天子
過密八音孔子曰天無二
百姓如喪考妣三年四海
二十有八載放勳乃徂落

they were mourning for a father or mother for three years, and up
to *the borders of* the four seas every sound of music was hushed."
Confucius said, "There are not two suns in the sky, nor two sovereigns over the people." Shun having been sovereign, and, moreover,
leading on all the princes to observe the three years' mourning for
Yâo, there would have been in this case two sovereigns.'

2. Hsien-ch'iû Măng said, 'On the point of Shun's not treating
Yâo as a minister, I have received your instructions. *But* it is
said in the Book of Poetry,

"Under the whole heaven,
Every spot is the sovereign's ground;
To the borders of the land,
Every individual is the sovereign's minister;"

—and Shun had become sovereign. I venture to ask how it was
that Kû-sâu was not one of his ministers.' *Mencius* answered,

殂=升, 'to ascend.' The *animus* ascends at death, and the anima 落, 'descends;'—hence the combination = 'dissolution,' 'decease.' The dictionary, however, makes 殂 simply = 往, and the phrase = 'vanish away.' 百姓 is the people within the royal domain; the 四海 denotes the rest of the kingdom, beyond that. Some, however, approved by the 日講, make 百姓=百官, 'the officers,' and 四海 = 'all the people.' 考妣,—the terms for a deceased father and mother. 三年,—for the classic has 載. The 八音, 'eight sounds,' are all instruments of music, formed of metal, stone, cord, bamboo, calabash, earthen-ware, leather, or wood.—The meaning is that up to the time of Yâo's decease, Shun was only vice-king, and, therefore, Yâo never could have appeared before him in the position of a subject. 2 舜之不臣堯 is not to be taken with reference to the phrase 君不得而臣, but to the general scope of the preceding para-

問瞽瞍之非臣如何。曰、是詩
也、非是之謂也、勞於王事而
不得養父母也、曰、此莫非王
事、我獨賢勞也、故說詩者、不
以文害辭、不以辭害志以意
逆志是爲得之、如以辭而已
矣、雲漢之詩曰、周餘黎民靡
有孑遺信斯言也、是周無遺
民也孝子之至莫大乎尊親、
尊親之至莫大乎以天下養。

'That ode is not to be understood in that way:—it speaks of being
laboriously engaged in the sovereign's business, so as not to be able
to nourish one's parents, *as if the author* said, "This is all the sovereign's business, and *how is it that* I alone am supposed to have ability,
and am made to toil in it?" Therefore, those who explain the odes,
may not insist on one term so as to do violence to a sentence, nor on
a sentence so as to do violence to the general scope. They must try
with their thoughts to meet that scope, and then we shall apprehend it. If we simply take single sentences, there is that in the ode
called "The Milky Way,"—

"Of the black-haired people of the remnant of Châu,
There is not half a one left."

If it had been really as thus expressed, then not an individual of
the people of Châu was left.

3. 'Of all which a filial son can attain to, there is nothing greater
than his honouring his parents. And of what can be attained to

graph, and especially to Mencius's explanation.
The restricting it to the former, in opposition
to the maxim—不以辭害志, has led
to the erroneous view of the whole passage
animadverted on above. Măng is now convinced that it was only on Yâo's death that
Shun became full sovereign, but after that
event there still remained the relation between
him and Kû-sâu, and how could he be at once
sovereign and son to him? How was it that Kû-

sâu would be at once father and subject to him?
詩云,—see the Shih-ching, II. vi. Ode I. st. a.
雲漢之詩, —see the Shih-ching, III. iii.
Ode IV. st. 3. 志, 'the scope,' i. e. the mind
or aim of the writer. 3. 詩曰,—see the
Shih-ching, III. i. Ode IX. st. 3, celebrating the
praises of king Wû.—This paragraph shows that
Shun, by his exaltation. honoured his father
only the more exceedingly. He was the more

為天子父尊之至也以天
下養養之至也詩曰永言
孝思孝思維則此之謂也。
書曰祇載見瞽瞍夔夔齊
栗瞽瞍亦允若是為父不
得而子也。

萬章曰堯以天下與舜
有諸孟子曰否天子不能
以天下與人然則舜有天
下也孰與之曰天與之

in the honouring one's parents, there is nothing greater than the
nourishing them with the whole kingdom. Kû-sâu was the father of
the sovereign;—this was the height of honour. *Shun* nourished
him with the whole kingdom;—this was the height of nourishing.
In this was verified the sentiment in the Book of Poetry,

"Ever cherishing filial thoughts,
　Those filial thoughts became an example *to after ages*."

4. 'It is said in the Book of History, "Reverently performing
his duties, he waited on Kû-sâu, and was full of veneration and
awe. Kû-sâu also believed him and conformed to virtue."—This
is the *true* case of *the scholar of complete virtue* not being treated as
a son by his father.'

CHAP. V. 1. Wan Chang said, 'Was it the case that Yâo
gave the throne to Shun?' Mencius said, 'No. The sovereign
cannot give the throne to another.'

2. 'Yes;—but Shun had the throne. Who gave it to him?'
'Heaven gave it to him,' was the answer.

'a son' to Kû-sâu. 4. 書曰,—see the Shû-
ching, II. ii. 15. 齊 (read châi) 栗 (the classic
has 栗),—this seems to be a supplement by
Mencius, as if he said, 'There is indeed a meaning in that saying that a scholar of complete
virtue cannot be treated as a son by his father,
for in the case of Shun and Kû-sâu we see that
the father was affected by the son, and not the
son by the father.'

5. How SHUN GOT THE THRONE BY THE GIFT OF
HEAVEN. VOX POPULI VOX DEI. 1. 有諸,—

see Bk. I. Pt. II. ii, 有之乎. 2. 天與
之,—is it not plain that by 'Heaven' in this
chapter we are to understand GOD? Many commentators understand by it 理, 'reason,' or
'the truth and fitness of things,' saving in the
expression 故曰天, in par. 7, where they
take it as 數, 'fate.' On this the author of
the 四書諸儒輯要, 'A collection of
the most important comments of the Learned

與之者、諄諄然命之乎。曰
否。天不言、以行與事示之
而已矣。曰以行與事示之
者、如之何。曰天子能薦人
於天、不能使天與之天下、
諸侯能薦人於天子、不能
使天子與之諸侯、大夫能
薦人於諸侯、不能使諸侯
與之大夫。昔者堯薦舜於
天、而天受之、暴之於民、而

3. '"Heaven gave it to him:"—did *Heaven* confer its appointment on him with specific injunctions?'

4. *Mencius* replied, 'No. Heaven does not speak. It simply showed its will by his personal conduct and his conduct of affairs.'

5. '"It showed its will by his personal conduct and his conduct of affairs:"—how was this?' Mencius's answer was, 'The sovereign can present a man to Heaven, but he cannot make Heaven give that man the throne. A prince can present a man to the sovereign, but he cannot cause the sovereign to make that man a prince. A great officer can present a man to his prince, but he cannot cause the prince to make that man a great officer. Yâo presented Shun to Heaven, and Heaven accepted him. He presented him to the people, and the people accepted him. Therefore I say, "Heaven does not

on the Four Books,' says—盧齊獨以此一天字指數言, 其餘天字指理言, 大謬. 此章天字以上帝之主宰言, 理與數皆在其中 (故曰天) the word Heaven means fate. But this is a great error. In this chapter "Heaven" signifies the government of God, within which are included both reason and fate.' 3. 天與之者,—者, = 'as to what you say.' 諄 (the 1st tone) 諄然, 'with repetitions.'—The paraphrase in the 日講 is:—'As to what you say, *Heaven gave it to him*, did Heaven indeed express its instructions and commands to him again and again? If it did not do so, where is the ground for what you say?' 4. 行, 4th tone, 'conduct,' as opposed to 事, 'the conduct of affairs.' 示之, 'showed it,' i.e. its will to give him the throne. The character 示 takes here the place of 命, because 命 would require the use of language, whereas 示 is the simple indication of the will. 5. 百神, 'the hundred' (= all the) 'spirits,' is explained as 天地山川之神 'the spirits of heaven, earth, the mountains, and the rivers,' i.e. all

A a 2

民受之故曰天不言以行
與事示之而已矣曰敢問
薦之於天而天受之暴之
於民而民受之如何曰使
之主祭而百神享之是天
受之使之主事而事治百
姓安之是民受之也天與
之人與之故曰天子不能
以天下與人舜相堯二十
有八載非人之所能爲也

speak. It simply indicated its will by his personal conduct and his conduct of affairs."'

6. *Chang* said, 'I presume to ask how it was that *Yâo* presented *Shun* to Heaven, and Heaven accepted him; and that he exhibited him to the people, and the people accepted him.' *Mencius* replied, 'He caused him to preside over the sacrifices, and all the spirits were well pleased with them;—thus Heaven accepted him. He caused him to preside over the conduct of affairs, and affairs were well administered, so that the people reposed under him;—thus the people accepted him. Heaven gave *the throne* to him. The people gave it to him. Therefore I said, "The sovereign cannot give the throne to another."

7. 'Shun assisted Yâo *in the government* for twenty and eight years;—this was more than man could have done, and was from

spiritual beings, real or supposed. In the Shû-ching, II. i. 6, a distinction is made between the 羣神, 'host of spirits,' and 上帝, 六宗, and 山川, but the phrase here is to be taken as inclusive of all. The sovereign is 百神之主, and Shun entered into all the duties of Yâo, even while Yâo was alive. How the spirits signified their approbation of the sacrifices, we are not told.—Modern critics take the 百神 here as exclusive of Heaven and subordinate to it, being equivalent to the 鬼神, 'the energetic operations of Heaven.' But such views were long subsequent to Mencius's

time. 6. 諸侯 is very plainly in the singular notwithstanding the 諸;—'one of the princes.' I leave the 昔者, 'formerly,' out of the translation. 暴—read pû, 'to manifest,' 'to exhibit.' 7. 相, 4th tone. 載, 2nd tone. 有, 4th tone. In 天地天, it is said, 以氣數言, 'Heaven means destiny.' But why suppose a different meaning of the term? Twenty-eight years were, indeed, a long time for Shun to occupy the place of vice-sovereign as he did, and showed wonderful gifts. I consider that this is an additional illus-

天也堯崩三年之喪畢舜避
堯之子於南河之南天下諸
侯朝覲者不之堯之子而之
舜訟獄者不之堯之子而之
舜謳歌者不謳歌堯之子而
謳歌舜故曰天也夫然後之
中國踐天子位焉而居堯之
宮逼堯之子是篡也非天與
也泰誓曰天視自我民視天
聽自我民聽此之謂也。

Heaven. After the death of Yâo, when the three years' mourning
was completed, Shun withdrew from the son of Yâo to the south
of South river. The princes of the kingdom, however, repairing to
court, went not to the son of Yâo, but they went to Shun. Litigants went not to the son of Yâo, but they went to Shun. Singers
sang not the son of Yâo, but they sang Shun. Therefore I said,
"Heaven *gave him the throne.*" It was after these things that he
went to the Middle Kingdom, and occupied the seat of the Son of
Heaven. If he had, *before these things*, taken up his residence in
the palace of Yâo, and had applied pressure to the son of Yâo, it
would have been an act of usurpation, and not the gift of Heaven.

8. This sentiment is expressed in the words of The Great Declaration,—"Heaven sees according as my people see ; Heaven
hears according as my people hear."'

tration of the 行 above, by which Heaven
intimated its will about Shun. The south of
the South river (probably the most southern of
the nine streams which Yü opened) would be
in the present Ho-nan. Thither Shun retired
from Chî-châu, the present Shan-hsî, where
Yâo's capital was. For the difference between
朝 (ch'do, and tone) and 覲, see the Lî-chî,
I. Sect. II. ii. 11, and notes thereon. 之堯
之舜之中國,—之 = 往, the verb.
訟獄,—see Analects, XII. xiii, but Chû Hsî

makes no distinction between the terms here,
and explains 訟獄謂獄不決而訟
之. 謳歌,—these two terms must be taken
together. 歌 is the more general name of the
two. The 說文 says that 謳 is 齊歌
'the singing of many together.' The 正字
通 makes 謳 to be the several tunes of the
singers. 而若, or 使. 8. 泰誓曰,
—see the Shû-ching, V. i. Sect. II. 7.

於箕山之陰朝覲訟獄者不之
禹崩三年之喪畢益避禹之子
子而從舜也禹薦益於天七年
民從之若堯崩之後不從堯之
畢禹避舜之子於陽城天下之
於天十有七年舜崩三年之喪
賢天與子則與子昔者舜薦禹
孟子曰否不然也天與賢則與
德衰不傳於賢而傳於子有諸。
萬章問曰人有言至於禹而

CHAP. VI. 1. Wan Chang asked *Mencius*, saying, 'People say, "When *the disposal of the kingdom* came to Yü, his virtue was inferior to that of *Yâo and Shun*, and he transmitted it not to the worthiest but to his son." Was it so?' Mencius replied, 'No; it was not so. When Heaven gave the kingdom to the worthiest, it was given to the worthiest. When Heaven gave it to the son *of the preceding sovereign*, it was given to him. Shun presented Yü to Heaven. Seventeen years elapsed, and Shun died. When the three years' mourning was expired, Yu withdrew from the son of Shun to Yang-ch'âng. The people of the kingdom followed him just as after the death of Yâo, instead of following his son, they had followed Shun. Yü presented Yî to Heaven. Seven years elapsed, and Yü died. When the three years' mourning was expired, Yî withdrew from the son of Yü to the north of mount Ch'î. The *princes*, repairing to court, went not to Yî, but they went to Ch'î. Litigants did not go

6. HOW THE THRONE DESCENDED FROM YÜ TO HIS SON, AND NOT TO HIS MINISTER YÎ; THAT YÜ WAS NOT TO BE CONSIDERED ON THAT ACCOUNT AS INFERIOR IN VIRTUE TO YÂO AND SHUN. 1. 至 於,—'coming to;' we must understand, 'From Yâo and Shun,' or translate somehow as I have done. Some say that 與賢, 與子 are not to be taken with special reference to Shun and Yü, and to Ch'î, but it seems best to do so.

A general inference may be drawn as well from the special cases. 有諸, 'was it so?' I.e. was his virtue inferior, and his transmitting the throne to his son a proof that it was so? 昔者,—omitted in translating, as before. Chû Hsî says, 'Yang-ch'âng and the north of mount Ch'î were both at the foot of the Sung mountains, places fit for retirement, within deep valleys.' By many they are held to have

益而之啟曰吾君之子也謳歌
者不謳歌益而謳歌啟曰吾君
之子也丹朱之不肖舜之子亦
不肖舜之相堯禹之相舜也歷
年多施澤於民久啟賢能敬承
繼禹之道益之相禹也歷年少
施澤於民未久舜禹益相去久
遠其子之賢不肖皆天也非人
之所能爲也莫之爲而爲者天
也莫之致而至者命也匹夫而

to Yî, but they went to Ch'î, saying, "He is the son of our sove-reign;" the singers did not sing Yî, but they sang Ch'î, saying. "He is the son of our sovereign."

2. 'That Tan-chû was not equal *to his father*, and Shun's son not equal *to his*; that Shun assisted Yâo, and Yü assisted Shun, for many years, conferring benefits on the people for a long time; that *thus* the length of time during which Shun, Yü, and Yî *assisted in the government* was so different; that Ch'î was able, as a man of talents and virtue, reverently to pursue the same course as Yü; that Yî assisted Yü only for a few years, and had not long conferred benefits on the people; that the periods of service of the three were so different; and that the sons were one superior, and the other superior:—all this was from Heaven, and what could not be brought about by man. That which is done without man's doing is from Heaven. That which happens without man's causing is from the ordinance *of Heaven*.

3. 'In the case of a private individual obtaining the throne, there

been the same place, and that 陰 is a mistake for 鄐. They were certainly near each other, and are referred to the district of Tăng-fang (登封), in the department of Ho-nan, in Ho-nan. Yî was Yü's great minister, raised to that dignity after the death of Kâo-yâo;—see the Shû-ching, II. iv. Ch'î was Yü's son, who succeeded him on the throne. 2. Tan-chû was the son of Yâo; see the Shû-ching, I. 9. The son of Shun is not mentioned in the classic. His name was I-chün (義均), and often appears as Shang Chün, he having been appointed to the principality of Shang (商). In 之相.

甲悔過自怨自艾於桐處

刑伊尹放之於桐三年太

壬四年太甲顚覆湯之典

崩太丁未立外丙二年仲

伊尹相湯以王於天下湯

故益伊尹周公不有天下。

天之所廢必若桀紂者也

不有天下繼世以有天下

又有天子薦之者故仲尼

有天下者德必若舜禹而

must be in him virtue equal to that of Shun or Yü; and moreover there must be the presenting of him *to Heaven* by the *preceding* sovereign. It was on this account that Confucius did not obtain the throne.

4. 'When the kingdom is possessed by *natural* succession, the sovereign who is displaced by Heaven must be like Chieh or Châu. It was on this account that Yî, Î Yin, and Châu-kung did not obtain the throne.

5. 'Î Yin assisted T'ang so that he became sovereign over the kingdom. After the demise of T'ang, T'âi-ting having died before he could be appointed sovereign, Wâi-ping reigned two years, and Chung-zän four. T'âi-chiâ was then turning upside down the statutes of T'ang, when Î Yin placed him in T'ung for three years. *There* T'âi-chiâ repented of his errors, was contrite, and reformed himself. In T'ung he came to dwell in benevolence and walk in

the 相 is in 4th tone. In this paragraph we have a longer sentence than is commonly found in Chinese composition, the 皆 in 皆天也 resuming all the previous clauses, which are in apposition with one another :—'Tan Chû's not being like his father, Shun's son's not being like him,' &c. 相去久遠=歷年久遠 之相去 莫之爲而爲=人莫 (=不)爲之而爲, the first 爲 is active; implying the purpose of man, the second is passive ; so, as is indicated by the terms, with 致 and 至 in the next sentence. 4. Î Yin was the chief minister of T'ang (see Analects,

XII. xxii. 6), and Châu-kung or the duke of Châu, the well-known assistant of his brother, king Wû. 5. 相, in 4th tone. 王, in 3rd tone. 太丁 ... 四年,—I have translated here according to Châo Ch'î. One of the Ch'ings gives a different view:—'On the death of T'ang, Wâi-ping was only two years old, and Chung-zän was but four. T'âi was somewhat older, and therefore was put on the throne ;' and between this view and the other, Chû Hsî professes himself unable to decide. The first view appears to me much the more natural, and is founded moreover on the account in the 'Historical Records,' though the histories have been arranged according to the other, and T'âi-chiâ appears as the successor of T'ang. This arrange-

仁遷義二年以聽
伊尹之訓己也復
歸于亳周公之不
有天下猶益之於
夏伊尹之於殷也。
孔子曰唐虞禪夏
后殷周繼其義一
也。　萬章問曰人有
言伊尹以割烹要

righteousness, during those three years, listening to the lessons given to him by Î Yin. Then *Î Yin* again returned *with him* to Po.

6. 'Châu-kung's not getting the throne was like the case of Yî and *the throne of* Hsiâ, or like that of Î Yin and *the throne of* Yin.

7. 'Confucius said, "T'ang and Yü resigned the throne *to their worthy ministers*. The sovereign of Hsiâ and *those of* Yin and Châu transmitted it to their sons. The principle of righteousness was the same *in all the cases*."'

CHAP. VII. 1. Wan Chang asked *Mencius*, saying, 'People say that Î Yin sought an introduction to T'ang by his knowledge of cookery. Was it so?'

ment of the chronology seems indeed required by the statements in the Shû-ching, IV. iv, which do not admit of any reign or reigns being interposed between T'ang and T'âi-chiâ. The author of the 四書拓餘說 proposes the following solution:—'Châo Ch'i's view is inadmissible, being inconsistent with the Shû-ching. The scholar Ch'ing's view is also to be rejected. For how can we suppose that T'ang, dying over a hundred years old, would leave children of two and four years? And, moreover, on this view Chung-sin was the elder brother, and Mencius would have mentioned him first. But there is a solution which meets all the difficulties of the case. First, we assume, with the old explanation, that Wâi-ping and Chung-sin were both dead when T'âi-chiâ succeeded to the throne. Then, with Ch'ing, we take 年 in the sense of 歲, years of life, and not of reign;—and the meaning thus comes out, that T'âi-ting died before his father, and his brothers Wâi-ping and Chung-sin died also, the one at the age of two, and the other of four years.' 刑,—in the sense of laws. Tung was the place where T'ang had been buried, and Po the name of his capital. There is some controversy about the time of T'âi-chiâ's detention in Tung, whether the three years are to be reckoned from his accession, or from the con-

clusion of the three years of mourning. The 'Historical Records' sanction the latter view, but the former is generally received, as more in accordance with the Shû-ching. 7. We must understand Confucius's saying,—the second clause of it,—as referring to the first sovereigns of the dynasties mentioned, and 繼, opposed to 禪,=傳, 'to transmit to,' i.e. their sons. 唐 and 虞 are Yâo and Shun; see the Shû-ching, I. II. 夏后,—see Analects, III. xxxi. 1. Yü originally was the 伯, or Baron, of Hsiâ, a district in the present department of K'âi-fâng. The one principle of righteousness was accordance with the will of Heaven, as expressed in par. 1, 天與賢, 則與賢, 天與子, 則與子.

7. VINDICATION OF Î YIN FROM THE CHARGE OF INTRODUCING HIMSELF TO THE SERVICE OF T'ANG BY AN UNWORTHY ARTIFICE. 1. 要, the 1st tone, =求, or 干, 'to seek,' i.e. an introduction to, or the favour of. 伊 (伊 is the surname) Yin (尹, the 'regulator,' is the designation) was the chief minister of T'ang. The popular account (found also in the 'Historical Records')

湯有諸孟子曰否不然伊尹
耕於有莘之野而樂堯舜之
道焉非其義也非其道也祿
之以天下弗顧也繫馬千駟
弗視也非其義也非其道也
一介不以與人一介不以取
諸人湯使人以幣聘之囂囂
然曰我何以湯之聘幣爲哉
我豈若處畎畝之中由是以
樂堯舜之道哉湯三使往聘

2. Mencius replied, 'No, it was not so. Î Yin was a farmer in the lands of the prince of Hsin, delighting in the principles of Yâo and Shun. In any matter contrary to the righteousness which they prescribed, or contrary to their principles, though he had been offered the throne, he would not have regarded it; though there had been yoked for him a thousand teams of horses, he would not have looked at them. In any matter contrary to the righteousness which they prescribed, or contrary to their principles, he would neither have given nor taken a single straw.

3. 'T'ang sent persons with presents of silk to entreat him to enter his service. With an air of indifference and self-satisfaction he said, "What can I do with those silks with which T'ang invites me? Is it not best for me to abide in the channelled fields, and so delight myself with the principles of Yâo and Shun?"

4. 'T'ang thrice sent messengers to invite him. After this, with

in the times of Mencius was, that Î Yin came to Po in the train of a daughter of the prince of Hsin, whom T'ang was marrying, carrying his cooking-instruments with him, that by 'cutting and boiling,' he might recommend himself to favour. 2. 有莘之野 —Î Yin was a native of Hsin, the same territory which under the Châu dynasty was called Kwo, the present Shen-châu (陝州) of Ho-nan. It was not far distant from T'ang's original seat of Po, also in the present Ho-nan. 有莘=有莘氏, 'the surname, i.e. the prince, holding Hsin.' 非其義也, 非其道也 are in apposition, the one explanatory of the other. 祿之一 literally, 'emolument him.' 駟, 'a team of four horses.' 介=芥. 3. 聘, 'to ask,' often used for 'to ask in marriage;' here, 'to ask to be minister.' 4. 囂曰 may be 囂

之既而幡然改曰與我處畎畝
之中由是以樂堯舜之道吾豈
若使是君為堯舜之君哉吾豈
若使是民為堯舜之民哉吾豈
若於吾身親見之哉天之生此〇五節
民也使先知覺後知使先覺覺
後覺也予天民之先覺者也予
將以斯道覺斯民也非予覺之
而誰也。思天下之民匹夫匹婦〇六節
有不被堯舜之澤者若己推而

the change of resolution displayed in his countenance, he spoke in a different style,—" Instead of abiding in the channelled fields and thereby delighting myself with the principles of Yáo and Shun, had I not better make this prince a prince like Yáo or Shun, and this people like the people of Yáo or Shun? Had I not better in my own person see these things for myself?

5. '"Heaven's plan in the production of mankind is this :—that they who are first informed should instruct those who are later in being informed, and they who first apprehend principles should instruct those who are slower to do so. I am one of Heaven's people who have first apprehended ;—I will take these principles and instruct this people in them. If I do not instruct them, who will do so?"

6. 'He thought that among all the people of the kingdom, even the private men and women, if there were any who did not enjoy

其計曰, 'changed his plan, and said,' or 改其言曰, 'changed his words, and said.' 堯舜之君, 'a prince of, = like to, Yáo and Shun.' I do not see exactly the force of 於吾身 in the last sentence, and have therefore simply translated the phrase literally. 5. This paragraph is to be understood as spoken by Î Yin. The meaning of 覺, 'to apprehend,' 'to understand,' is an advance on that of 知, simply 'to know.' The student will observe also that it is used actively three times, — 'to instruct.' In 生此民, the 此民, 'this people,' = 'mankind.' 6. 內,—read as, and = 納. 說,—read shwuy, in 4th tone, 'to advise,'

造攻自牧宮朕載自亳。
未聞以割烹也、伊訓曰、天誅
矣、吾聞其以堯舜之道要湯、
或去或不去、歸潔其身而已
聖人之行不同也、或遠或近、
者也、況辱己以正天下者乎、
夏救民吾未聞枉己而正人
重如此、故就湯而說之以伐
内之溝中、其自任以天下之

such benefits as Yâo and Shun conferred, it was as if he himself pushed them into a ditch. He took upon himself the heavy charge of the kingdom in this way, and therefore he went to T'ang, and pressed upon him the subject of attacking Hsiâ and saving the people.

7. 'I have not heard of one who bent himself, and at the same time made others straight;—how much less could one disgrace himself, and thereby rectify the whole kingdom? The actions of the sages have been different. Some have kept remote *from court*, and some have drawn near *to it;* some have left their offices, and some have not done so:—that to which those different courses all agree is simply the keeping of their persons pure.

8. 'I have heard that Î Yin sought an introduction to T'ang by the doctrines of Yâo and Shun. I have not heard that he did so by his knowledge of cookery.

9. 'In the "Instructions of Î," it is said, "Heaven destroying Chieh commenced attacking him in the palace of Mû. I commenced in Po."'

'to persuade.' 說之以, 'advised him about.' 7. Compare Bk. III. Pt. II. i. 1, 5. 歸 =要歸, 'if we seek where they came to, where they centered.' 8. 要,—as in paragraph 1. 9. See the Shû-ching, IV. iv. 2, but the classic and this text are so different that many suppose Mencius to quote from some form of the book referred to which Confucius disallowed. The meaning is that Chieh's atrocities in his palace in Mû led Heaven to destroy him, while Î Yin, in accordance with the will of Heaven, advised T'ang in Po to take action against him. 造 and 載, both = 始, 'to begin.'

萬章問曰、或謂孔子於
衞主癰疽、於齊主侍人瘠
環、有諸乎孟子曰、否不然
也好事者爲之也。於衞主
顏讐由彌子之妻與子路
之妻兄弟也、彌子謂子路
曰孔子主我彌卿可得也。
子路以告孔子孔子曰有命、
子進以禮退以義得之不
得曰有命而主癰疽與侍

CHAP. VIII. 1. Wan Chang asked *Mencius*, saying, 'Some say that Confucius, when he was in Wei, lived with the ulcer-doctor, and when he was in Ch'î, with the attendant, Ch'î Hwan ;—was it so ?' Mencius replied, 'No ; it was not so. Those are the inventions of men fond of strange things.

2. 'When he was in Wei, he lived with Yen Ch'âu-yû. The wives of the officer Mî and Tsze-lû were sisters, and Mî told Tsze-lû, "If Confucius will lodge with me, he may attain to the dignity of a high noble of Wei." Tsze-lû informed Confucius of this, and he said, "That is as ordered *by Heaven*." Confucius went into office according to propriety, and retired from it according to righteousness. In regard to his obtaining office or not obtaining it, he said, "That is as ordered." But if he had lodged with the attendant

8. VINDICATION OF CONFUCIUS FROM THE CHARGE OF LODGING WITH UNWORTHY CHARACTERS. 1. 癰, 'a swelling,' 'an ulcer,' and 疽 (read *tsü*, in 1st tone), 'a deep-seated ulcer.' Chû Hsî, after Châo Ch'î, takes the two terms as in the translation. Some, however, take the characters as a man's name, called also 雍渠, 雍雎, and 雍鉏 They are probably right. The 'Historical Records' make 雍渠 to have been the eunuch in attendance on the duke of Wei, when he rode through the market-place with the duchess, followed by the sage,— to his great disgust. 侍人＝奄人, 'the eunuch.' Eunuchs were employed during the Châu dynasty. Both the men referred to were unworthy favourites of their respective princes. 好 (in 3rd tone) 事者, 'one who is fond of raising trouble,' and in a lighter sense, as here, 'one who is fond of saying, and doing, strange things.' 主＝舍於其家, 'lodged in his house,' literally, 'hosted him.' In par. 4, 以其所爲主, 'by those of whom they are hosts ;' 以其所主, 'by those whom they host,' i. e. make their hosts. 2. Yen Ch'âu-yû, called also 顏濁鄒, was a worthy officer of Wei. One account has it, that he was brother to Tsze-lû's wife, but this is probably incorrect. Mî, with the name Hsiá (瑕), was an unworthy

自鬻於秦養牲者五羊之　萬章問曰或曰百里奚　與侍人瘠環何以爲孔子　以其所主若孔子主癰疽　近臣以其所爲主觀遠臣　貞子爲陳侯周臣吾聞觀　宋是時孔子當阨主司城　馬將要而殺之微服而過　子不悅於魯衞遭宋桓司　人瘠環是無義無命也孔

Chî Hwan, that would neither have been according to righteousness, nor any ordering *of Heaven*.

3. 'When Confucius, being dissatisfied in Lû and Wei, *had left those States*, he met with the attempt of Hwan, the Master of the Horse, of Sung, to intercept and kill him. He assumed, however, the dress of a common man, and passed by Sung. At that time, though he was in circumstances of distress, he lodged with the city-master Ch'ăng, who was *then* a minister of Châu, the marquis of Ch'ăn.

4. 'I have heard that *the characters of* ministers about court may be discerned from those whom they entertain, and those of stranger officers, from those with whom they lodge. If Confucius had lodged with the ulcer-doctor, and with the attendant Chî Hwan, how could he have been Confucius?'

CHAP. IX. 1. Wan Chang asked *Mencius*, 'Some say that Pâi-lî Hsî sold himself to a cattle-keeper of Ch'in for the skins of

favourite of the duke Ling. 3. Compare Analects, VII. xxii; Hwan is the Hwan T'âi there. 要, in 1st tone, = 攔截, 'to intercept.' 微服, 'small clothes,' i.e. the dress of a common man. 貞, 'the Pure,' is the honorary epithet of the officer who was Confucius's host, and 周 was the proper name of the prince of Ch'ăn, with whom indeed the independence of the State terminated. Ch'ăng, it is said, afterwards became 'city-master' in Sung, and was known as such;—hence he is so styled here at an earlier period of his life. 4. 近遠 here

have a different application from what belongs to them in the last chapter, par. 7.

9. VINDICATION OF PÂI-LÎ HSÎ FROM THE CHARGE OF SELLING HIMSELF AS A STEP TO HIS ADVANCEMENT. 1. Pâi-lî Hsî was chief minister to the duke Mû (穆 = 'the diffuser of virtue, and maintainer of integrity'), B.C. 659–620. His history will be found interestingly detailed in the twenty-fifth and some subsequent Books of the 'History of the Several States' (列國志), though the incidents there are, some of them, different from Mencius's statements about him. With regard to that in this paragraph, it is not easy to understand the popular

皮食牛以要秦穆公信乎。

孟子曰否不然好事者爲

之也百里奚虞人也晉人

以垂棘之璧與屈產之乘。

假道於虞以伐虢宮之奇

諫百里奚不諫知虞公之

不可諫而去之秦年已七

十矣曾不知以食牛干秦

穆公之爲汙也可謂智乎、

不可諫而不諫可謂不智

five rams, and fed his oxen, in order to find an introduction to the duke Mû of Ch'in ;—was this the case ?' Mencius said, ' No; it was not so. This story was invented by men fond of strange things.

2. 'Pâi-lî Hsî was a man of Yü. The people of Tsin, by the inducement of a round piece of jade from Ch'ûi-chî, and four horses of the Ch'ü breed, borrowed a passage through Yü to attack Kwo. *On that occasion*, Kung Chih-ch'î remonstrated *against granting their request*, and Pâi-lî Hsî did not remonstrate.

3. ' When he knew that the duke of Yü was not to be remonstrated with, and, leaving that State, went to Ch'in, he had reached the age of seventy. If by that time he did not know that it would be a mean thing to seek an introduction to the duke Mû of Ch'in by feeding oxen, could he be called wise ? But not remonstrating where it was of no use to remonstrate, could he be said not to be

account referred to. The account in the 'Historical Records,' 秦本記, is, that, after the subversion of Yü, Hsî followed its captive duke to Tsin, refusing to take service in that State, and was afterwards sent to Ch'in in a menial capacity, in the train of the eldest daughter of the house of Tsin, who was to become the wife of the duke Mû. Disgusted at being in such a position, Hsî absconded on the road, and fleeing to Ch'û, he became noted for his skill in rearing cattle. The duke Mû somehow heard of his great capacity, and sent to Ch'û, to reclaim him as a runaway servant, offering also to pay for his ransom five rams' skins. He was afraid to offer a more valuable ransom, lest he should awaken suspicions in Ch'û that he wanted to get Hsî

on account of his ability ; and on obtaining him, he at once made him his chief minister. 食,—read tsze, 4th tone, = 飼, 'to feed.' 要, —as in chap. 7, the 1st tone. 好事者,— as in last chapter. 2. Ch'ûi-chî and Ch'ü were the names of places in Tsin, the one famous for its jade, the other for its horses. 乘, 4th tone, 'a team of four horses.' Kwo and Yü were small States, adjoining each other, and only safe against the attacks of their more powerful neighbour, Tsin, by their mutual union. Both the officers of Yü, Kung Chih-ch'î and Pâi-lî Hsî, saw this, but Hsî saw also that no remonstrances would prevail with the duke of Yü against the bribes of Tsin. 3. 去

謂賢者爲之乎。
鄉黨自好者不爲而
之乎自鬻以成其君、
傳於後世、不賢而能
而顯其君於天下、可
之可謂不智乎、相秦、
之可與有行也、而相
也時舉於秦知穆公
先去之不可謂不智
乎、知虞公之將亡、而

wise? Knowing that the duke of Yü would be ruined, and leaving him before that event, he cannot be said not to have been wise. Being then advanced in Ch'in, he knew that the duke Mû was one with whom he would enjoy a field for action, and became minister to him;—could he, *acting thus*, be said not to be wise? Having become chief minister of Ch'in, he made his prince distinguished throughout the kingdom, and worthy of being handed down to future ages;—could he have done this, if he had not been a man of talents and virtue? As to selling himself in order to accomplish all the aims of his prince, even a villager who had a regard for himself would not do such a thing; and shall we say that a man of talents and virtue did it?'

之秦,—之-往, the verb. 而先去 之,—this may have been prudent, but was not honourable. It is contrary to other accounts of Hsî's conduct. He *is* said to have urged Chih-ch'î to leave Yü after his remonstrance, while he remained himself to be with the duke in the evil day which he saw approaching. 鄉黨 are to be taken together.

WAN CHANG. PART II.

伯夷之風者頑夫廉懦夫
濱以待天下之清也故聞
炭也當紂之時居北海之
處如以朝衣朝冠坐於塗
所止不忍居也思與鄉人
則退橫政之所出橫民之
事非其民不使治則進亂
色耳不聽惡聲惡君不
孟子曰伯夷目不視惡
萬章章句下

CHAPTER I. 1. Mencius said, ‘Po-î would not allow his eyes to look on a bad sight, nor his ears to listen to a bad sound. He would not serve a prince whom he did not approve, nor command a people whom he did not esteem. In a time of good government he took office, and on the occurrence of confusion he retired. He could not bear to dwell either in *a court* from which a lawless government emanated, or among lawless people. He considered his being in the same place with a villager, as if he were to sit amid mud and coals with his court robes and court cap. In the time of Châu he dwelt on the shores of the North sea, waiting the purification of the kingdom. Therefore when men *now* hear the character of Po-î, the corrupt become pure, and the weak acquire determination.

1. How Confucius differed from and was superior to all other sages. 1. Compare Bk. II. Pt. I. ii. 22, and ix ; Bk. IV. Pt. I. xiii. 1. 橫政之所出, ‘the place whence perverse government issues,’ i.e. a court. 橫民之所止, ‘the place where perverse people stop.’ 頑 is properly ‘stupid,’ ‘obstinate,’ but here as opposed to 廉, we must take it in the sense of ‘corrupt.’ Julien, indeed, takes 廉 in the sense of ‘*habere vim discernendi.*’ But it is better to retain its proper signification, and to alter that of 頑, with the gloss in the

其道遺佚而不怨阨窮而不憫
汙君不辭小官進不隱賢必以
任以天下之重也柳下惠不羞
澤者若己推而內之溝中其自
民匹夫匹婦有不與被堯舜之
將以此道覺此民也思天下之
覺後覺予天民之先覺者也予
斯民也使先知覺後知使先覺
非民治亦進亂亦進曰天之生
有立志伊尹曰、何事非君、何使

2. 'Î Yin said, "Whom may I not serve? My serving him makes him my sovereign. What people may I not command? My commanding them makes them my people." In a time of good government he took office, and when confusion prevailed, he also took office. He said, "Heaven's plan in the production of mankind is this:—that they who are first informed should instruct those who are later in being informed, and they who first apprehend principles should instruct those who are slower in doing so. I am the one of Heaven's people who has first apprehended;—I will take these principles and instruct the people in them." He thought that among all the people of the kingdom, even the common men and women, if there were any who did not share in the enjoyment of such benefits as Yâo and Shun conferred, it was as if he himself pushed them into a ditch;—for he took upon himself the heavy charge of the kingdom.

3. 'Hûi of Liû-hsiâ was not ashamed to serve an impure prince, nor did he think it low to be an inferior officer. When advanced to employment, he did not conceal his virtue, *but* made it a point to

備旨、頑夫無知覺、必貪昧 | 澤者, we have 有不與被…澤者,
晤利、故與廉反. a. Compare Bk. | = 'if there were any who did not have part in
II. Pt. I. ii. 23; and Bk. V. Pt. I. vii. 2-6. | the enjoyment,' &c. 3. Compare Bk. II. Pt. I.
Observe, that here instead of 有不被… | ix. a. The clause 與鄉人, 云云, which

清者也伊尹聖之任者也柳
仕孔子也孟子曰伯夷聖之
而久可以處而處可以仕而
之道也可以速而速可以久
魯曰遲遲吾行也去父母國
敦孔子之去齊接淅而行去
柳下惠之風者、鄙夫寬薄夫
於我側爾焉能浼我哉故聞
爾爲爾我爲我雖袒裼裸裎
與鄉人處、由由然不忍去也、

carry out his principles. When dismissed and left without office, he did not murmur. When straitened by poverty, he did not grieve. When thrown into the company of village people, he was quite at ease and could not bear to leave them. *He had a saying,* "You are you, and I am I. Although you stand by my side with breast and arms bare, or with your body naked, how can you defile me?" Therefore when men now hear the character of Hûi of Liû-hsiâ, the mean become generous, and the niggardly become liberal.

4. 'When Confucius was leaving Ch'î, he strained off with his hand the water in which his rice was being rinsed, *took the rice,* and went away. When he left Lû, he said, "I will set out by-and-by:" —it was right he should leave the country of his parents in this way. When it was proper to go away quickly, he did so; when it was proper to delay, he did so; when it was proper to keep in retirement, he did so; when it was proper to go into office, he did so:— this was Confucius.'

5. Mencius said, 'Po-î among the sages was the pure one; Î Yin

is wanting there, makes the 故曰 of that place more plain. 袒 is 'to have the arms bare,' and 裼, 'to put off all the upper garment.' 裸裎 together, is 'to have the body naked.' Here and in par. 1, 風 is expressed more nearly

by 'character,' than by any other English term. 4. 淅, 'to rinse or wash rice,' 'the water in which rice is washed.' The latter is the sense here. 遲遲吾行 was the answer given by Confucius to Tsze-lû, who wished to hurry him away. 5. I have invented the adjective

下惠聖之和者也、孔子、聖之
時者也、孔子之謂集大成、集
大成也者、金聲而玉振之也。
金聲也者、始條理也、玉振之
也者、終條理也、始條理者、智
之事也、終條理者、聖之事也。
智譬則巧也、聖譬則力也、由
射於百步之外也、其至、爾力
也、其中、非爾力也。

was the one most inclined to take office; Hûi of Liû-hsiâ was the
accommodating one; and Confucius was the timeous one.

6. 'In Confucius we have what is called a complete concert.
A complete concert is when the *large* bell proclaims the *commencement of the music*, and the ringing stone proclaims its close. The
metal sound commences the blended harmony of all the instruments,
and the winding up with the stone terminates that blended harmony. The commencing that harmony is the work of wisdom.
The terminating it is the work of sageness.

7. 'As a comparison for wisdom, we may liken it to skill, and as
a comparison for sageness, we may liken it to strength;—as in the
case of shooting at a mark a hundred paces distant. That you reach
it is owing to your strength, but that you hit the mark is not owing
to your strength.'

'timeous' to translate the 時 here, meaning
that Confucius did at *every time* what the circumstances of it required, possessing the qualities
of all other sages, and displaying them, at the
proper time and place. 6. The illustration of
Confucius here is from a grand performance of
music, in which all the eight kinds of musical
instruments are united. One instrument would
make a 小成, 'small performance.' Joined,
they make a 集大成, 'a collected great
performance,'—'a concert.' 聲始, and 終
are all used as verbs. 條理, 'discriminated
rules,' indicates the separate music of the
various instruments blended together. 金
聲 and 振之 are not parts of the concert,
but the signals of its commencement and close,
the 之 referring to 集大聲. 7. Observe
the comma after 智 and 聖. 由-猶
'The other three worthies,' it is observed, 'carried one point to an extreme, but Confucius was
complete in everything. We may compare
each of them to one of the seasons, but Con-

位中士一位下士一位
一位大夫一位上士一
位凡五等也君一位卿
一位伯一位子男同一
也天子一位公一位侯
籍然而軻也嘗聞其畧
惡其害己也而皆去其
其詳不可得聞也諸侯
爵祿也如之何孟子曰
比宮錡問曰周室班

CHAP. II. 1. Pêi-kung Î asked *Mencius*, saying, 'What was the arrangement of dignities and emoluments determined by the House of Châu?'

2. Mencius replied, 'The particulars of that arrangement cannot be learned, for the princes, disliking them as injurious to themselves, have all made away with the records of them. Still I have learned the general outline of them.

3. 'The SON OF HEAVEN constituted one dignity; the KUNG one; the HÂU one; the PÂI one; and the TSZE and the NAN each one of equal rank:—altogether making five degrees of rank. The RULER *again* constituted one dignity; the CHIEF MINISTER one; the GREAT OFFICERS one; the SCHOLARS OF THE FIRST CLASS one; THOSE OF THE MIDDLE CLASS one; and THOSE OF THE LOWEST CLASS one:—altogether making six degrees of dignity.

fucius was the grand, harmonious air of heaven, flowing through all the seasons.'

2. THE ARRANGEMENT OF DIGNITIES AND EMOLU-MENTS ACCORDING TO THE DYNASTY OF CHÂU. 1. Pêi-kung Î was an officer of the State of Wei. The double surname, 'Northern-palace,' had probably been given to the founder of the family from his residence. 2. Many passages might be quoted from the Lî Chî, the Châu Lî, and the Shû-ching, illustrating, more or less, the dignities of the kingdom and their emoluments, but it would be of little use to adduce them after Mencius's declaration that only the general outline of them could be ascertained. It is an important fact which he mentions, that the princes had destroyed (去, 3rd tone) many of the records before his time. The founder of the Ch'in dynasty had had predecessors and patterns. 惡, 4th tone, 'to hate.'

3. 公, 侯, 伯, 子, 男 have been rendered 'duke, marquis, earl, viscount, and baron,' and also 'duke, prince, count, marquis, and baron,' but they by no means severally correspond to those dignities. It is better to retain the Chinese designations, which, no doubt, were originally meant to indicate certain qualities of those bearing them. 公 = 'just, correct, without selfishness.' 侯, 'taking care of,'— 侯, in the sense of 'guarding the borders and important places against banditti; possessed of the power to govern.' 伯 conveys the idea of 'elder and intelligent,' 'one capable of presiding over others.' 子 = 孳, 'to nourish,' 'one who genially cherishes the people.' 男 (from 田, 'field,' and 力, 'strength'), 'one adequate to

凡六等天子之制地
方千里公侯皆方百
里伯七十里子男五
十里凡四等不能五
十里不達於天子附
於諸侯曰附庸天子
之卿受地視侯大夫
受地視伯元士受地
視子男大國地方百
里君十卿祿卿祿四

4. 'To the Son of Heaven there was allotted a territory of a thousand *li* square. A Kung and a Hâu had each a hundred *li* square. A Pâi had seventy *li*, and a Tsze and a Nan had each fifty *li*. The assignments altogether were of four amounts. Where the territory did not amount to fifty *li*, the chief could not have access himself to the Son of Heaven. His land was attached to some Hâu-ship, and was called a Fû-YUNG.

5. 'The Chief ministers of the Son of Heaven received an amount of territory equal to that of a Hâu; a Great officer received as much as a Pâi; and a scholar of the first class as much as a Tsze or a Nan.

6. 'In a great State, where the territory was a hundred *li* square, the ruler had ten times as much income as his Chief ministers;

office and labour.' The name of 君, 'ruler,' 'sovereign,' is applicable to all the dignities enumerated, and under each of them are the secondary or ministerial dignities. 卿=彰夫=扶, 'to support,' 'to sustain;'—大夫, 'a great sustainer.' 士, 'a scholar,' 'an officer;'—任事之稱, 'the designation of one entrusted with business.' 4. 地方千里,—this means, according to the commentator 彭絲, 橫千里, 直千里, 共一百萬里也, '1,000 lî in breadth, and 1,000 lî in length, making an area of 1,000,000 lî.' On this, however, the following judgment is given by the editors of the imperial edition of the five *Ching* of the present dynasty:—'Where we find the word *square* (方) we are not to think of an exact square, but simply that, on a calculation, the amount of territory is equal to so many square *lî*. For instance, we are told by the minister Tsan that, at the western capital of Châu, the territory was 800 lî square. The meaning is that there were 8×8 squares of 100 lî. At the eastern capital again, the territory was 600 lî square, or 6×6 squares of 100 lî. Putting these two together, we get the total of 1,000 lî square. So in regard to the various States of the princes, we are to understand that, however their form might be varied by the hills and rivers, their area, in round numbers, amounted to so much;'—see in the Lî Chî, III. i, 2, where the text, however, is not at all perspicuous. 附, attached;' 庸, 'meritoriousness.' These States were too small to bear the expenses of appearing before the sovereign, and therefore, the names and surnames of their chiefs were sent into court by the great princes to whom they were *attached*, or perhaps they appeared in their train;—see on Analects, XVI. i. 1. 5. 元士, 'Head scholar,' could only be applied to the scholars of the first class in the sovereign's immediate government. 6. 庶人在官 would be runners, clerks, and other subor-

大夫、大夫倍上士、上士倍

中士、中士倍下士、下士與

庶人在官者同祿、祿足以

代其耕也。次國地方七十

里君十卿祿、卿祿三大夫、

大夫倍上士、上士倍中士、

中士倍下士、下士與庶人

在官者同祿、祿足以代其

耕也。小國地方五十里君

十卿祿、卿祿二大夫、大夫

a Chief minister four times as much as a Great officer; a Great officer twice as much as a scholar of the first class; a scholar of the first class twice as much as one of the middle; a scholar of the middle class twice as much as one of the lowest; the scholars of the lowest class, and such of the common people as were employed about the government offices, had for their emolument as much as was equal to what they would have made by tilling the fields.

7. 'In a State of the next order, where the territory was seventy *li* square, the ruler had ten times as much revenue as his Chief minister; a Chief minister three times as much as a Great officer; a Great officer twice as much as a scholar of the first class; a scholar of the first class twice as much as one of the middle; a scholar of the middle class twice as much as one of the lowest; the scholars of the lowest class, and such of the common people as were employed about the government offices, had for their emolument as much as was equal to what they would have made by tilling the fields.

8. 'In a small State, where the territory was fifty *li* square, the ruler had ten times as much revenue as his Chief minister; a Chief minister had twice as much as a Great officer; a Great officer twice as much as a scholar of the highest class; a scholar of the highest class twice as much as one of the middle; a scholar of

dinates, which appear in the Châu Lî, as 府, 史, 胥, and 徒. Chû Hsî gives his opinion, that, from the sovereign downwards, all who had lands received their incomes from them, as cultivated on the system of mutual aid, while the landless scholars and other subordinates received according to the income

倍上士、上士倍中士、中士倍下
士、下士與庶人在官者同祿、祿
足以代其耕也、耕者之所獲、一
夫百畝、百畝之糞、上農夫食九
人、上次食八人、中食七人、中次
食六人、下食五人、庶人在官
者、其祿以是爲差。

萬章問曰、敢問友、孟子曰、不
挾長、不挾貴、不挾兄弟而友、友
也者、友其德也、不可以有挾也。

the middle class twice as much as one of the lowest; scholars of the lowest class, and such of the common people as were employed about the government offices, had the same emolument;—as much, namely, as was equal to what they would have made by tilling the fields.

9. 'As to those who tilled the fields, each husbandman received a hundred mâu. When those mâu were manured, the best husbandmen of the highest class supported nine individuals, and those ranking next to them supported eight. The best husbandmen of the second class supported seven individuals, and those ranking next to them supported six; while husbandmen of the lowest class only supported five. The salaries of the common people who were employed about the government offices were regulated according to these differences.'

CHAP. III. 1. Wan Chang asked *Mencius*, saying, 'I venture to ask *the principles of* friendship.' Mencius replied, 'Friendship should be maintained without any presumption on the ground of one's superior age, or station, or *the circumstances of his* relatives. Friendship *with a man* is friendship with his virtue, and does not admit of assumptions of superiority.

from the land. 9. 食,—read *tsze.* 差,—read *ts'ze*, 'uneven,' 'different.'

3. FRIENDSHIP MUST HAVE REFERENCE TO THE VIRTUE OF THE FRIEND. THERE MAY BE NO ASSUMPTION ON THE GROUND OF ONE'S OWN ADVAN-

TAGES. 1. 問友=問交友之道. 長, 3rd tone, having reference to age. 兄弟, 'one's brethren,' in the widest acceptation of that term. Observe how 也者 takes up

國之君爲然也雖大國之君亦
王順長息則事我者也非惟小
則師之矣吾於顏般則友之矣
君亦有之費惠公曰吾於子思
惟百乘之家爲然也雖小國之
有獻子之家則不與之友矣非
無獻子之家者也此五人者亦
之矣獻子之與此五人者友也
焉樂正裘牧仲其三人則予忘
孟獻子百乘之家也有友五人

2. 'There was Măng Hsien, *chief of* a family of a hundred chariots. He had five friends, namely, Yŏ-chăng Chiŭ, Mŭ Chung, and three others *whose names* I have forgotten. With those five men Hsien maintained a friendship, because they thought nothing about his family. If they had thought about his family, he would not have maintained his friendship with them.

3. 'Not only has the *chief of* a family of a hundred chariots acted thus. The same thing was exemplified by the sovereign of a small State. The duke Hŭi of Pĭ said, "I treat Tsze-sze as my Teacher, and Yen Pan as my Friend. As to Wang Shun and Ch'ang Hsĭ, they serve me."

4. 'Not only has the sovereign of a small State acted thus. The same thing has been exemplified by the sovereign of a large State.

the preceding 友, and goes on to its explanation. 其 refers to the individual who is the object of the 友 ; friendship with him as virtuous will tend to help our virtue. 有挾, 'to have presumptions,' with reference of course to the three points mentioned, but as of those the second most readily comes into collision with friendship, it alone is dwelt upon in the sequel. 2. Măng Hsien,—see 'Great Learning,' Comm. x. 22. 3. 費, read Pĭ,—see Analects,

VI. vii. We must suppose that, after the time of Confucius, some chief had held this place and district with the title of Kung. 'The Kind (惠),' is the honorary epithet. Tsze-sze is Confucius's grandson. 般,—read pan. Yen Pan appears to have been the son of the sage's favourite disciple. 4. P'ing ('The Pacificator') was the honorary epithet of the duke 彪, B.C. 556-531. Hsĭ Tang was a famous worthy of his State. 入云, 'enter being said.' 琥

有之晉平公之於亥唐也入
云則入坐云則坐食云則食
雖疏食菜羹未嘗不飽蓋不
敢不飽也然終於此而已矣
弗與共天位也弗與治天職
也弗與食天祿也士之尊賢
者也非王公之尊賢也舜尚
見帝帝館甥于貳室亦饗舜
迭為賓主是天子而友匹夫

There was the duke P'ing of Tsin with Hâi T'ang:—when *T ang* told him to come into his house, he came; when he told him to be seated, he sat; when he told him to eat, he ate. There might only be coarse rice and soup of vegetables, but he always atè his fill, not daring to do otherwise. Here, however, he stopped, and went no farther. He did not call him to share any of Heaven's places, or to govern any of Heaven's offices, or to partake of any of Heaven's emoluments. His conduct was but a scholar's honouring virtue and talents, not the honouring them proper to a king or a duke.

5. 'Shun went up to *court* and saw the sovereign, who lodged him as his son-in-law in the second palace. The sovereign also enjoyed there Shun's hospitality. Alternately he was host and guest. Here was the sovereign maintaining friendship with a private man.

食, 一食, read *tsze*, 4th tone. The 之 after 平公 and 王公 is wanting in many copies. 與其天位云云 would seem to be a complaint that the duke did not share with the scholar his own rank, &c., but the meaning in the translation, which is that given by the commentator, is perhaps the correct one. Rank, station, and revenue are said to be Heaven's, as entrusted to the ruler to be conferred on individuals able to occupy in them for the public good. 5. In this paragraph, Mencius advances another step, and exemplifies the highest style of friendship. Chû Hsî, after

Châo Ch'î, explains 尚 by 上, as if it were 'to go up to,' i. e. to court. 貳室＝副宮, 'attached or supplemental palace.' 饗是就舜宮而饗其食, '饗 means that he went to Shun's palace, and partook of his food.' The more common meaning of 饗 however, is 'to entertain.' 迭為—the subject is only Yâo. 賓, 'made a guest' of Shun, was the host. 主, 'made a host' of Shun,

也用下敬上謂之貴貴用
上敬下謂之尊賢貴貴尊
賢其義一也。
萬章問曰敢問交際何
心也孟子曰恭也曰郤之
郤之爲不恭何哉曰尊者
賜之曰其所取之者義乎
不義乎而後受之以是爲
不恭故弗郤也曰請無以
辭郤之以心郤之曰其取

6. 'Respect shown by inferiors to superiors is called giving to the noble the observance due to rank. Respect shown by superiors to inferiors is called giving honour to talents and virtue. The rightness in each case is the same.'

CHAP. IV. 1. Wan Chang asked *Mencius*, saying, 'I venture to ask what *feeling of the* mind is expressed in the presents of friendship?' Mencius replied, '*The feeling of* respect.'

2. 'How is it,' pursued *Chang*, 'that the declining a present is accounted disrespectful?' The answer was, 'When one of honourable rank presents a gift, to say *in the mind*, "Was the way in which he got this righteous or not? I must know this before I can receive it;"—this is deemed disrespectful, and therefore presents are not declined.'

3. *Wan Chang* asked *again*, 'When one does not take on him in so many express words to refuse the gift, but having declined it

was the guest. 6. 用＝以, 'for.' 義＝事 之宜, 'the rightness or propriety of things.'

4. How MENCIUS DEFENDED THE ACCEPTING PRESENTS FROM THE PRINCES, OPPRESSORS OF THE PEOPLE. 1. 際 is explained by 接, but that term is not to be taken in the sense of 'to receive,' but as a synonym of 交. If we distinguish the two words, we may take 交 as = the 友 of the last chapter, and 際 the gift, expressive of the friendship. 2. Chû Hsî says he does not understand the repetition of 郤之. It has probably crept into the text

through the oversight of a transcriber, unless we suppose, with the 合講, that the repetition indicates the firmness and decision with which the gift is refused, but the introduction of that element seems out of place. 曰,其 (referring to 尊者) 所 (所以) 取之 —曰 is the reflection passing in the mind, as in the next paragraph also. We must suppose 人 as the nominative in 以是爲不 恭. 3. 請 is not to be understood of Wan Chang, but as indicating the hesitancy and delicacy of the scholar to whom a gift is offered.

諸民之不義也而以他辭
無受不可乎曰其交也以
道其接也以禮斯孔子受
之矣萬章曰今有禦人於
國門之外者其交也以道
其餽也以禮斯可受禦與
曰不可康誥曰殺越人於
貨閔不畏死凡民罔不譈
是不待教而誅者也殷受
夏周受殷所不辭也於今

in his heart, saying, "It was taken by him unrighteously from the people," and then assigns some other reason for not receiving it;—is not this a proper course?' *Mencius* said, 'When the donor offers it on a ground of reason, and his manner of doing so is according to propriety;—in such a case Confucius would have received it.'

4. Wan Chang said, 'Here now is one who stops and robs people outside the gates of the city. He offers his gift on a ground of reason, and does so in a manner according to propriety;—would the reception of it so acquired by robbery be proper?' Mencius replied, 'It would not be proper. In "The Announcement to K'ang" it is said, "When men kill others, and roll over their bodies to take their property, being reckless and fearless of death, among all the people there are none but detest them:"—thus, such characters are to be put to death, without waiting to give them warning. Yin received *this rule* from Hsiâ, and Châu received it from Yin. It cannot

其交也，以道，–其 still referring to 尊者, and 道 to the deservingness of the scholar, or something in his circumstances which renders the gift proper and seasonable. Compare Bk. II. Pt. II. iii. 3, 4. The meaning of 接 is determined (contrary to Châo Ch'î) by the 餽, which takes its place in the next paragraph. 4. 國門之外–國 as in Bk. IV. Pt. II. xxxiii. 1. 斯可受之與,–斯, as in the last paragraph, adverbially, =

'in this case.' 康誥曰, see the Shû-ching, Bk. V. x. 15, though the text is somewhat altered in the quotation, and 閔 and 譈 take the place of 暋 and 懟. 于 = 'for the sake of,' i.e. to take. 殷...烈 is a passage of which the meaning is much disputed. Chû Hsî supposes it a gloss that has crept into the text. I have given it what seemed the most likely translation. 其受之,–其 is the party to whom the gift is offered, and 之, the fruit

爲烈如之何其受之曰今之
諸侯取之於民也猶禦也苟
善其禮際矣斯君子受之敢
問何說也曰子以爲有王者
作將比今之諸侯而誅之乎
其教之不改而後誅之乎夫
謂非其有而取之者盜也充
類至義之盡也孔子之仕於
魯也魯人獵較孔子亦獵較
獵較猶可而況受其賜乎曰

be questioned, and to the present day is clearly acknowledged. How can the gift *of a robber* be received?'

5. *Chang* said, 'The princes of the present day take from their people just as a robber despoils his victim. Yet if they put a good face of propriety on their gifts, then the superior man receives them. I venture to ask how you explain this.' *Mencius* answered, 'Do you think that, if there should arise a truly royal sovereign, he would collect the princes of the present day, and put them all to death? Or would he admonish them, and then, on their not changing their ways, put them to death? Indeed, to call every one who takes what does not properly belong to him a robber, is pushing a point of resemblance to the utmost, and insisting on the most refined idea of righteousness. When Confucius was in office in Lù, the people struggled together for the game taken in hunting, and he also did the same. If that struggling for the captured game was proper, how much more may the gifts of the princes be received!'

6. *Chang* urged, 'Then are we to suppose that when Confucius

of robbery. 5. 斯—as above. By 君子 Chang alludes to Mencius himself. 比,—4th tone, 'to take together.' 充類至義之盡,—literally, 'filling up a resemblance to the extremity of righteousness;' the meaning is as in the translation. 獵較 (chio) is unin-

telligible to Chû Hsî. I have given the not unlikely explanation of Châo Ch'î. But to get rid of the declaration that Confucius himself joined in the struggling, the critics all say it only means that he allowed the custom.—The introduction of this yielding on the part of Confucius to a vulgar practice is an adroit manœuvre by Mencius. The offence of the people against propriety in struggling for the game,

桓　可　孔　以　不　以　也　與　然
子　之　子　未　去　四　曰　曰　則
見　仕　有　嘗　也　方　孔　事　孔
行　有　見　有　曰　之　子　道　子
可　公　行　所　爲　食　先　也　之
之　養　可　終　之　供　簿　事　仕
仕　之　之　三　兆　簿　正　道　也
也　仕　仕　年　也　正　祭　奚　非
於　於　有　淹　兆　曰　器　獵　事
衞　季　際　也　足　奚　不　較　道

held office, it was not with the view to carry his doctrines into practice?' 'It was with that view,' *Mencius* replied, and *Chang* rejoined, 'If the practice of his doctrines was his business, what had he to do with that struggling for the captured game?' *Mencius* said, 'Confucius first rectified his vessels of sacrifice according to the registers, and did not fill them so rectified with food gathered from every quarter.' 'But why did he not go away?' 'He wished to make a trial *of carrying his doctrines into practice*. When that trial was sufficient to show that they could be practised and they were still not practised, then he went away, and thus it was that he never completed in any State a residence of three years.

7. 'Confucius took office when he saw that the practice *of his doctrines* was likely; he took office when his reception was proper; he took office when he was supported by the State. In the case of his relation to Chî Hwan, he took office, seeing that the practice of

and the offence of the princes in robbing their people, were things of a different class. Yet Mencius's defence of himself in the preceding part of the paragraph is ingenious. It shows that he was eminently a practical man, acting in the way of expediency. How far that way may be pursued will always depend on circumstances. 6. 非事道與 (and tone, interrogative) = 非以行道爲事與 事道奚獵較 is evidently a question of Chang. 先簿正祭器 is unintelligible to Chû Hsî. The translation is after the commentator Hsü (徐氏). 'Food gathered from every quarter,'—i.e. gathered without discrimination. It would appear that the practice of 獵較 had some connexion with the offering of sacrifices, and that Confucius thought that if he only rectified the rules for sacrifice, the practice would fall into disuse. But the whole passage and its bearing on the struggling for game is obscure. 兆,—'a prognostic,' 'an omen,' used figuratively. 7. See the 'Life of Confucius,' though it is only here that we have mention of the sage's connexion with the duke Hsiâo. Indeed no duke appears in the annals of Wei with such a posthumous title. Chû Hsî supposes that the duke Ch'ô (see Analects, VII. xiv, note) is intended, in which the author of

嘗為委吏矣曰會計　宜乎抱關擊柝孔子　居卑辭富居貧惡乎　居卑辭富居貧辭尊　乎為養為貧者辭尊　妻非為養也而有時　也而有時乎為貧娶　孟子曰仕非為貧　衞孝公公養之仕也　靈公際可之仕也於

his doctrines was likely. With the duke Ling of Wei he took office, because his reception was proper. With the duke Hsiâo of Wei he took office, because he was maintained by the State.'

CHAP. V. 1. Mencius said, 'Office is not *sought* on account of poverty, yet there are times when one seeks office on that account. Marriage is not entered into for the sake of being attended to by the wife, yet there are times when one marries on that account.

2. 'He who *takes office* on account of his poverty must decline an honourable situation and occupy a low one; he must decline riches and prefer to be poor.

3. 'What office will be in harmony with this declining an honourable situation and occupying a low one, this declining riches and preferring to be poor? *Such an one as* that of guarding the gates, or beating the watchman's stick.

4. 'Confucius was once keeper of stores, and he then said, "My calculations must be all right. That is all I have to care about."

the 四書拓餘說 acquiesces. The text mentions Chî Hwan, and not duke Ting, because the duke and his government were under the control of that nobleman.

5. HOW OFFICE MAY BE TAKEN ON ACCOUNT OF POVERTY, BUT ONLY ON CERTAIN CONDITIONS. 1. 仕 and 娶妻,—it is as well to translate here abstractly, 'office,' and 'marriage.' 為 4th tone, 'for,' 'on account of.' The proper motive for taking office is supposed to be the carrying principles—the truth, and the right—into practice, and the proper motive for marriage is the begetting of children, or rather of a son, to continue one's line. 乎,—not interrogative, but serving as a pause for the voice. 養 4th tone, 'the being supported,' but we may take it

generally, as in the translation. 2. 尊,—i. e. 尊位, 'an honourable situation,' and 富 富祿, 'rich emolument.' 3. 惡, the 1st tone, 'how.' The first 乎 as above, and helping the rhythm of the sentence. 抱關 (going round the barrier-gates, 'embracing' them, as it were) and 擊柝 are to be taken together, and not as two things, or offices; see the Yî-ching, App. III. Sect. II. 18. 4. In Sze-mâ Ch'ien's History of Confucius, for 委 (4th tone) 吏 we have 季氏史, but in a case of this kind the authority of Mencius is to be followed. 會, —read *kwei*, 3rd tone, 'entries in a book.' Annual calculations of accounts are denomin-

當而已矣嘗爲乘田
矣曰牛羊茁壯長而
已矣位卑而言高罪
也立乎人之本朝而
道不行恥也。
圀萬章曰士之不託
諸侯何也孟子曰不
敢也諸侯失國而後
託於諸侯禮也士之
託於諸侯非禮也萬

He was once in charge of the public fields, and he then said, "The oxen and sheep must be fat and strong, and superior. That is all I have to care about."

5. 'When one is in a low situation, to speak of high matters is a crime. When a scholar stands in a prince's court, and his principles are not carried into practice, it is a shame to him.'

CHAP. VI. 1. Wan Chang said, 'What is the reason that a scholar does not accept a stated support from a prince?' Mencius replied, 'He does not presume to do so. When a prince loses his State, and then accepts a stated support from another prince, this is in accordance with propriety. But for a scholar to accept such support from any of the princes is not in accordance with propriety.'

2. Wan Chang said, 'If the prince send him a present of grain,

ated 會, and monthly, 計, when a distinction is made between the terms. 富, 4th tone. 乘 (4th tone) 田＝主 苑 囿 芻 牧 之 吏, but I do not understand the use of 乘 in this sense. Here again the history has 爲 司 職 (是＝檄) 吏. These were the first offices Confucius took, before the death of his mother, and while they were yet struggling with poverty.

5. 立 乎 (＝于) 人 之 本 朝 (ch'āou, 2nd tone),—it is difficult to express the force of the 本; 'to stand in a man's proper court,' i.e. the court of the prince who has called him to office, and where he ought to develop and carry out his principles. It is said that this paragraph gives the reasons why he who takes office for poverty must be content with a low situation and small emolument, but the connexion is somewhat difficult to trace. The 四

書 味 根 錄 says:—'Why did Confucius confine himself to having his calculations exact, and his cattle sleek and fat? Because in his humble position he had nothing to do with business of the State, and he would not incur the crime of usurping a higher office. If, making a pretence of poverty, a man keep long clinging to high office, he stands in his prince's court, but carries not principles into practice:—can he lay his hand on his heart, and not feel the shame of making his office of none effect?' This is true, but it is not necessary that he who takes office because he is poor should continue to occupy it simply with the desire to get rich.

6. HOW A SCHOLAR MAY NOT BECOME A DEPENDENT BY ACCEPTING PAY WITHOUT OFFICE, AND HOW THE REPEATED PRESENTS OF A PRINCE TO A SCHOLAR MUST BE MADE. 1. 士 is here the scholar, the candidate for public office and use, still unemployed. 不 託, 'does not depend on,' i.e. assure himself of a regular support by receiving regular pay though not in office. On one prince,

乎。曰、繆公之於子思也亟
餽之則受之不識可常繼
於上者、以爲不恭也。曰君
職以食於上無常職而賜
也。曰抱關擊柝者、皆有常
不敢也。曰、敢問其不敢、何
則受賜之則不受、何也。
之於氓也固周之曰、周之
曰受之。受之何義也曰、君
章曰君餽之粟、則受之乎。

for instance, does he accept it?' 'He accepts it,' answered *Mencius*. 'On what principle of righteousness does he accept it?' 'Why—the prince ought to assist the people in their necessities.'

3. *Chang* pursued, 'Why is it that the scholar will *thus* accept the prince's help, but will not accept his pay?' The answer was, 'He does not presume to do so.' 'I venture to ask why he does not presume to do so.' 'Even the keepers of the gates, with their watchmen's sticks, have their regular offices for which they can take their support from the prince. He who without a regular office should receive the pay of the prince must be deemed disrespectful.'

4. Chang asked, 'If the prince sends a scholar a present, he accepts it;—I do not know whether this present may be constantly repeated.' *Mencius* answered, 'There was the conduct of the duke

driven from his State, finding an assured and regular support with another, see the Lî-chî, IX. Sect. I. i. 13. It is only stated there, however, that a prince did not employ another refugee prince as a minister. We know only from Mencius, so far as I am aware, that a prince driven from his own dominions would find maintenance in another State, according to a sort of law. 2. 何義 'what is the principle of righteousness?' or simply—'what is the explanation of?' 周=賙 'to give alms,' and generally to help the needy. 氓,—see Bk. II. Pt. I. v. 5. A scholar not in office is only one of the people. 3. 賜之 'if he give him,' i.e. 賜之祿 'give him pay.' This brings out all the meaning that is in 託. 賜於上,—賜 is passive, or = 'to receive pay.' 不恭, 'disrespectful,' is to be taken in its implication of a want of humility in the scholar, who is only one of the people having no office, and yet is content to take pay, as if he had. 4. 亟, read *ch'î*, 4th tone (below, the same), 'frequently.' 鼎肉 'caldron flesh,' i.e. flesh cooked. 摽—*piâo*, the 1st tone, 'to motion with the hand.' 使者—使, 4th tone. 伋 was Tsze-sze's name. To bow, raising the

受其後廩人繼粟庖人繼
以君命將之再拜稽首而
君子如何斯可謂養矣。曰
悅賢乎曰敢問國君欲養
不能舉又不能養也可謂
伋蓋自是臺無餽也悅賢
曰今而後知君之犬馬畜
外比面稽首再拜而不受。
卒也摽使者出諸大門之
問亟餽鼎肉子思不悅於

Mû to Tsze-sze—He made frequent inquiries after Tsze-sze's health, and sent him frequent presents of cooked meat. Tsze-sze was displeased; and at length, having motioned to the messenger to go outside the great door, he bowed his head to the ground with his face to the north, did obeisance twice, and declined the gift, saying, "From this time forth I shall know that the prince supports me as a dog or a horse." And so from that time no servant was no more sent with the presents. When a prince professes to be pleased with a man of talents and virtue, and can neither promote him to office, nor support him *in the proper way*, can he be said to be pleased with him?'

5. Chang said, 'I venture to ask how the sovereign of a State, when he wishes to support a superior man, must proceed, that he may be said to do so in the proper way?' Mencius answered, '*At first*, the present must be offered with the prince's commission, and the scholar, making obeisance twice with his head bowed to the ground, will receive it. But after this the storekeeper will continue

hands to the bent forehead, was called 拜手; lowering the hands in the first place to the ground, and then raising them to the forehead, was called 拜; bowing the head to the earth was called 稽首. Tsze-sze appears on this occasion to have first performed the most profound expression of homage, as if in the prince's presence, and then to have bowed twice, with his hands to the ground, in addition. All this he did, outside the gate, which was the appropriate place in the case of declining the gifts.

If they were received, the party performed his obeisances inside. To bring out the meaning of 'for,' that properly belongs to 蓋, we must translate it here by 'and so.' 臺,—the designation of an officer or servant of a very low class. 5. 以君命將之,-將=奉. 君命 'a message from the prince,' reminding of course the scholar of his obligation. 僕僕爾 — an adverb, 'the appearance of being troubled.'

臣在野曰草莽之臣皆謂庶

義也孟子曰在國曰市井之

萬章曰敢問不見諸侯何

故曰王公之尊賢者也。

畎畝之中後舉而加諸上位、

百官牛羊倉廩備以養舜於

使其子九男事之二女女焉、

養君子之道也堯之於舜也、

鼎肉使已僕僕爾亟拜也非

肉不以君命將之子思以爲

to send grain, and the master of the kitchen to send meat, presenting it as if without the prince's express commission. Tsze-sze considered that the meat from the prince's caldron, giving him the annoyance of constantly doing obeisance, was not the way to support a superior man.

6. 'There was Yâo's conduct to Shun:—He caused his nine sons to serve him, and gave him his two daughters in marriage; he caused the various officers, oxen and sheep, storehouses and granaries, *all* to be prepared to support Shun amid the channelled fields, and then he raised him to the most exalted situation. From this we have the expression—"The honouring of virtue and talents proper to a king or a duke."'

CHAP. VII. 1. Wan Chang said, 'I venture to ask what principle of righteousness is involved in *a scholar's* not going to see the princes?' Mencius replied, 'A scholar residing in the city is called "a minister of the market-place and well," and one residing in the country is called "a minister of the grass and plants." In both cases he is a common man, and it is the rule of propriety that common

6. See Pt. I. i. 3. 二女女焉,—the second 女 is read *sü*, in 4th tone.

7. WHY A SCHOLAR SHOULD DECLINE GOING TO SEE THE PRINCES, WHEN CALLED BY THEM. Compare Bk. III. Pt. II. i, *et al.* 1. We supply 士 as the subject of 見; and other verbal

characters; Wan Chang evidently intends Mencius himself. 國, 'city,' as in chap. iv. par. 4. 莽,—here as a synonym, in apposition with 草. 臣 in 市井,草莽之臣 is different from the 爲臣 below. Every in-

而召之也。繆公亟見於子思
爲其賢也。則吾未聞欲見賢
則天子不召師而況諸侯乎。
也爲其賢也。曰爲其多聞也
之也何爲也哉曰爲其多聞
也往見不義也。且君之欲見
則不往見不義也。何也。且君之欲見義
之役則往役君欲見之召之
於諸侯禮也。萬章曰庶人召
人庶人不傳質爲臣不敢見

men, who have not presented the introductory present and become ministers, should not presume to have interviews with the prince.'

2. Wan Chang said, 'If a common man is called to perform any service, he goes and performs it;—how is it that a scholar, when the prince, wishing to see him, calls him to his presence, refuses to go?' Mencius replied, 'It is right to go and perform the service; it would not be right to go and see the prince.'

3. 'And,' *added Mencius,* 'on what account is it that the prince wishes to see *the scholar?*' 'Because of his extensive information, or because of his talents and virtue,' was the reply. 'If because of his extensive information,' said Mencius, 'such a person is a teacher, and the sovereign would not call him;—how much less may any of the princes do so? If because of his talents and virtue, then I have not heard of any one wishing to see a person with those qualities, and calling him to his presence.'

4. 'During the frequent interviews of the duke Mû with Tsze-sze,

dividual may be called a 臣, as being a subject, and bound to serve the sovereign, and this is the meaning of the term in those two phrases. In the other case it denotes one who is officially 'a minister.' 傳=通. 質,—*chi*, in 3rd tone; see Bk. III. Pt. II. iii. 1, and notes. There is a force in the 於, in 見於諸侯, which it is difficult to indicate in another language. 2. 'It is right to go and perform the service,'

i.e. it is right in the common man, to perform service being his 戩, or office. And so with the scholar. He will go when called as a scholar should be called, but only then. 3. The 爲 are all in the 4th tone. It must be borne in mind that the conversation is all about a scholar who is not in office; compare par. 9. 4. 千乘 (in 4th tone) 之國=千乘之君

曰、古千乘之國以友士、何如。子
思不悅曰、古之人有言曰、事之
云乎、豈曰友之云乎、子思之不
悅也、豈不曰以位則子君也、我
臣也、何敢與君友也、以德則子
事我者也、奚可以與我友千乘
之君求與之友、而不可得也、而
況可召與齊景公田、招虞人以
旌不至、將殺之、志士不忘在溝
壑勇士不忘喪其元孔子奚取

○五節

he *one day* said to him, " Anciently, princes of a thousand chariots have yet been on terms of friendship with scholars;—what do you think *of such an intercourse?*" Tsze-sze was displeased, and said, " The ancients have said, ' The scholar should be served:' how should they have merely said that *he should be made a friend of?*" When Tsze-sze was thus displeased, did he not say *within himself,*—" With regard to our stations. you are sovereign, and I am subject. How can I presume to be on terms of friendship with my sovereign? With regard to our virtue, you ought to make me your master. How can you be on terms of friendship with me?" *Thus,* when a ruler of a thousand chariots sought to be on terms of friendship with a scholar, he could not obtain his wish:—how much less could he call him to his presence!

5. 'The duke Ching of Ch'î, once, when he was hunting, called his forester to him by a flag. *The forester* would not come, *and the duke* was going to kill him. *With reference to this incident, Confucius said,* " The determined officer never forgets that *his end*

below; 以 =with all his dignity, 'yet.' 乎-云爾, Bk. IV. Pt. II. xxiv. 1, *et al.*, but the second 乎 also responds to 豈. The paraphrase in the 日講 is:—古之人 有言、人君於士、當師事之、豈但如君所言友之云乎

5. See Bk. III. Pt. II. i. 2. 6. The explanation of the various flags here is from Chù Hsî, after

路也禮門也惟君子能由
欲其入而閉之門也夫義
欲見賢人而不以其道猶
以不賢人之招招賢人乎。
庶人庶人豈敢往哉況乎
人死不敢往以士之招招
旌。以大夫之招招虞人虞
庶人以旃士以旂大夫以
問招虞人何以。曰以皮冠。
焉取非其招不往也。曰敢

may be in a ditch or a stream; the brave officer never forgets that he may lose his head." What was it *in the forester* that Confucius thus approved? He approved his not going *to the duke*, when summoned by the article which was not appropriate to him.'

6. Chang said, 'May I ask with what a forester should be summoned?' Mencius replied, 'With a skin cap. A common man *should be summoned* with a plain banner; a scholar *who has taken office*, with one having dragons embroidered on it; and a Great officer, with one having feathers suspended from the top of the staff.

7. 'When the forester was summoned with the article appropriate to the summoning of a Great officer, he would have died rather than presume to go. If a common man were summoned with the article appropriate to the summoning of a scholar, how could he presume to go? How much more may we expect this refusal to go, when a man of talents and virtue is summoned in a way which is inappropriate to his character!

8. 'When a prince wishes to see a man of talents and virtue, and does not take the proper course *to get his wish*, it is as if he wished him to enter *his palace*, and shut the door against him.

the Châu Lî. The dictionary may be consulted about them. 何以＝何用. 7. A man of talents and virtue ought not to be called at all; the prince ought to go to *him*. 8. 閉之門, —this is another case of a verb followed by the pronoun and another objective;—literally, 'shut him the door.' 詩云, —see the Shih-ching, II. v. Ode IX. st. 1. Julien condemns the translating 周道 by 'the way to Châu,' but that is the meaning of the terms in the ode; and, as the royal highway, it is used to indicate figuratively the great way of righteousness. 底, —in the ode 砥 (*chih*), the 3rd tone. The ode is attributed to an officer of one of the

是路出入是鬥也詩云周
道如底其直如矢君子所
履小人所視萬章曰孔子
君命召不俟駕而行然則
孔子非與曰孔子當仕有
官職而以其官召之也
孟子謂萬章曰一鄉之
善士斯友一鄉之善士一
國之善士斯友一國之善
士天下之善士斯友天下

Now, righteousness is the way, and propriety is the door, but it is only the superior man who can follow this way, and go out and in by this door. It is said in the Book of Poetry,

> "The way to Châu is level like a whetstone,
> And straight as an arrow.
> The officers tread it,
> And the lower people see it."'

9. Wan Chang said, 'When Confucius received the prince's message calling him, he went without waiting for his carriage. Doing so, did Confucius do wrong?' Mencius replied, 'Confucius was in office, and had to observe its appropriate duties. And moreover, he was summoned on the business of his office.'

CHAP. VIII. 1. Mencius said to Wan Chang, 'The scholar whose virtue is most distinguished in a village shall make friends of all the virtuous scholars in the village. The scholar whose virtue is most distinguished throughout a State shall make friends of all the virtuous scholars of that State. The scholar whose virtue is most distinguished throughout the kingdom shall make friends of all the virtuous scholars of the kingdom.

eastern States, mourning over the oppressive and exhausting labours which were required from the people. The 'royal highway' presents itself to him, formerly crowded by officers hastening to and from the capital, and the people hurrying to their labours, but now toiled slowly and painfully along. 9. See Analects, X. xiii. 4.

8. THE REALIZATION OF THE GREATER ADVAN-TAGES OF FRIENDSHIP, AND THAT IT IS DEPENDENT ON ONE'S SELF. 1. 'The virtuous scholar of one village,—he shall make friends of the virtuous scholars of (that) one village:'—the first 善 is in the superlative degree, and 友 is not only 'to be friends with,' but also 'to realize the uses of friendship.' The eminence attained by the individual attracts all the others to him,

則易位王勃然變乎色曰王

有大過則諫反覆之而不聽

卿王曰請問貴戚之卿曰君

不同有貴戚之卿有異姓之

卿之問也王曰卿不同乎曰

齊宣王問卿孟子曰王何

論其世也是尚友也。

讀其書不知其人可乎是以

未足又尚論古之人頌其詩。

之善士以友天下之善士為

2. 'When a scholar feels that his friendship with all the virtuous scholars of the kingdom is not sufficient *to satisfy him*, he proceeds to ascend to consider the men of antiquity. He repeats their poems, and reads their books, and as he does not know what they were as men, to ascertain this, he considers their history. This is to ascend and make friends *of the men of antiquity*.'

CHAP. IX. 1. The king Hsüan of Ch'î asked about *the office of* high ministers. Mencius said, 'Which high ministers is your Majesty asking about?' 'Are there differences among them?' inquired the king. 'There are,' was the reply. 'There are the high ministers who are noble and relatives *of the prince*, and there are those who are of a different surname.' The king said, 'I beg to ask about the high ministers who are noble and relatives of the prince.' Mencius answered, 'If the prince have great faults, they ought to remonstrate with him, and if he do not listen to them after they have done so again and again, they ought to dethrone him.'

2. The king on this looked moved, and changed countenance.

and he has thus the opportunity of learning from them, which no inflation because of his own general superiority prevents him from doing. a. 尚=上. 又尚, 'he proceeds and ascends.' 頌=誦, 'to repeat,' 'croon over.' 可乎=可否, 'proper or not?' 其世, 'their age,' i. e. what they were in

their age.—We are hardly to understand the poetry and books here generally. Mencius seems to have had in his eye the Book of Poetry, and the Book of History.

9. THE DUTIES OF THE DIFFERENT CLASSES OF HIGH MINISTERS. 1. 君有大過—such ministers will overlook small faults. To animadvert on them would be inconsistent with

則之則曰異然對敢問勿
去而諫君姓後王不臣異
。不反有之請色以臣也
聽覆過卿問定正不王

3. Mencius said, 'Let not your Majesty be offended. You asked me, and I dare not answer but according to truth.'

4. The king's countenance became composed, and he then begged to ask about high ministers who were of a different surname *from the prince.* Mencius said, 'When the prince has faults, they ought to remonstrate with him; and if he do not listen to them after they have done this again and again, they ought to leave *the State.*'

their consanguinity. No distinction is made of faults, as great or small, when the other class of ministers is spoken of. 'Great faults' are such as endanger the safety of the State.

3 勿異, 'don't think it strange,' but = 'don't be offended.'—We may not wonder that duke Hsüan should have been moved and surprised by the doctrines of Mencius as announced in this chapter. It is true that the members of the family of which the ruler is the Head have the nearest interest in his ruling well, but to teach them that it belongs to them, in case of his not taking their advice, to proceed to dethrone him, is likely to produce the most disastrous effects. Chû Hsi notices that the able and virtuous relatives of the tyrant Châu (紂) were not able to do their duty as here laid down, while Ho Kwang, a minister of another surname, was able to do it in the case of the king of Ch'ang-yî (昌邑王), whom he placed in B.C. 74, though not the proper heir, on the throne in succession to the emperor Châo. His nominee, however, proved unequal to his position. See the Memoir of Ho Kwang in the Thirty-eighth Book of the Biographies of the first Han dynasty.

BOOK VI.

KÁO TSZE. PART I.

而　乎　性　子　爲　仁　棬　杞　圖　告
後　將　而　能　桮　義　也　柳　一　子　告
以　戕　以　順　棬　猶　以　也　告　曰　子
爲　賊　爲　杞　孟　以　人　義　子　性　章
桮　杞　桮　柳　子　杞　性　猶　曰　猶　句
棬　柳　棬　之　曰　柳　爲　桮　　　　上

CHAPTER I. 1. The philosopher Káo said, '*Man's* nature is like the *ch'i*-willow, and righteousness is like a cup or a bowl. The fashioning benevolence and righteousness out of man's nature is like the making cups and bowls from the *ch'i*-willow.'

2. Mencius replied, 'Can you, leaving untouched the nature of the willow, make with it cups and bowls? You must do violence and injury to the willow, before you can make cups and bowls with

Káo, from whom this Book is named, is the same who is referred to in Bk. II. Pt. I. ii. His name was Pǔ-hai (不害), a speculatist of Mencius's day, who is said to have given himself equally to the study of the orthodox doctrines and those of the heresiarch Mo (Bk. III. Pt. I. v; Pt. II. ix). See the 四書拓餘說, on Mencius. Vol. I. Art. xxix. He appears from this Book to have been much perplexed respecting the real character of human nature in its relations to good and evil. This is the principal subject discussed in this Book. For his views of human nature as here developed, Mencius is mainly indebted for his place among the Sages of his country. 'In the first Part,' says the 四書味根錄, 'he treats first *of the nature*, then *of the heart*, and then of *instruction*, the whole being analogous to the lessons in the Doctrine of the Mean. The second Part continues to treat of the same subject, and a resemblance will generally be found between the views of the parties there combated, and those of the scholar Káo.'

1. THAT BENEVOLENCE AND RIGHTEOUSNESS ARE NO UNNATURAL PRODUCTS OF HUMAN NATURE. There underlie the words of Káo here, says Chû Hsî,

the view of the philosopher Hsün (荀) that human nature is evil (性惡). This is putting the case too strongly. It is an induction from his words, which Káo would probably have disallowed. Hsün (see the *prolegomena*, and Morrison under the character 子), accounted by many the most distinguished scholar of the Confucian school, appears to have maintained positively that all good was foreign to the nature of man;—人之性惡,其善者僞也, 'man's nature is bad; his good is artificial.' 1. The 杞 and the 柳 are taken by some as two trees, but it is better to take them together, the first character giving the species of the other. It is described as 'growing by the water-side, like a common willow, the leaf coarse and white, with the veins small and reddish.' 2. 順, 'according with,' 'following,' i.e. 'leaving untouched,' 'doing no violence to.' 戕賊人-人-人性, 'man's nature,' humanity. Káo had said that man's nature could be *made into* benevolence and righteousness, and Mencius exposes the error

東西無分於上下乎人性
西也孟子曰水信無分於
不善也猶水之無分於東
則西流人性之無分於善
諸東方則東流決諸西方
第二章 告子曰性猶湍水也決
仁義者必子之言夫。
仁義與率天下之人而禍
桮棬則亦將戕賊人以爲
也如將戕賊杞柳而以爲

it. If you must do violence and injury to the willow in order to
make cups and bowls with it, *on your principles* you must in the
same way do violence and injury to humanity in order to fashion
from it benevolence and righteousness! Your words, alas! would
certainly lead all men on to reckon benevolence and righteousness
to be calamities.'

CHAP. II. 1. The philosopher Kâo said, '*Man's* nature is like
water whirling round *in a corner*. Open a passage for it to the
east, and it will flow to the east; open a passage for it to the west,
and it will flow to the west. Man's nature is indifferent to good
and evil, just as the water is indifferent to the east and west.'

2. Mencius replied, 'Water indeed *will flow* indifferently to the
east or west, but will it flow indifferently up or down? The

by here substituting 戕賊 for 爲, in doing
which he is justified by the nature of the action
that has to be put forth on the wood of the
willow. 禍仁義, 'calamitize benevolence
and righteousness.' I take the meaning to be
as in the translation. If their nature must be
hacked and bent to bring those virtues from
it, men would certainly account them to be
calamities.

2. MAN'S NATURE IS NOT INDIFFERENT TO GOOD
AND EVIL. ITS PROPER TENDENCY IS TO GOOD. That
man is indifferent to good and evil, or that the
tendencies to these are both blended in his
nature, was the doctrine of Yang Hsiung (楊
雄), a philosopher about the beginning of our

era (B.C. 53–A.D. 18). We have the following
sentence from him:—'In the nature of man
good and evil are mixed. The cultivation of the
good in it makes a good man; the cultivation of
the evil makes a bad man. The passion-nature
in its movements may be called the horse of good
or evil.' (十子全書楊子修身
篇) 人無有不善 is the sum of the
chapter on Mencius's part. His opponent's views
were wrong, but did he himself have the whole
truth? 1. 湍水, as explained in the dictionary, 'water flowing rapidly,' and 'water
rippling over the sand.' Châo Ch'î, followed by
Chû Hsî, explains it as in the translation, which
is certainly better adapted to the passage. 2.
信,—as an adverb, 'truly.' 人性之善,

白與曰然白羽之白也猶
曰生之謂性也猶白之謂
告子曰生之謂性孟子
是也。
之可使爲不善其性亦猶
水之性哉其勢則然也人
激而行之可使在山是豈
夫水搏而躍之可使過顙
無有不善水無有不下今
之善也猶水之就下也人

tendency of man's nature to good is like the tendency of water to
flow downwards. There are none but have this tendency to good,
just as all water flows downwards.

3. 'Now by striking water and causing it to leap up, you may
make it go over your forehead, and, by damming and leading it,
you may force it up a hill;—but are such movements according to
the nature of water? It is the force applied which causes them.
When men are made to do what is not good, their nature is dealt
with in this way.'

CHAP. III. 1. The philosopher Kâo said, 'Life is what we call
nature.'

2. Mencius asked him, 'Do you say that by nature you mean
life, just as you say that white is white?' 'Yes, I do,' was the reply.
Mencius added, 'Is the whiteness of a white feather like that of

—literally, 'the goodness of man's nature,' but
we must take 善 as = 'tendency to good.' 3.
激, to provoke,' 'to fret,' the *consequence of a
dam.* 激而行之,—'dam and walk it,'
i.e. by gradually leading it from dam to dam.
Chû Hsî says:—'This chapter tells us that the
nature is properly good, and if we accord with
it, we shall do nothing which is not good ; that
it is properly without evil, and we must violate
it therefore, before we can do evil. It shows
that the nature is properly not without a decided
character, or that it may do good or evil indifferently.'

3. THE NATURE IS NOT TO BE CONFOUNDED WITH

THE PHENOMENA OF LIFE. 1. 'By 生,' says Chû
Hsî, 'is intended that whereby men and animals
perceive and move,' and the sentiment, he adds,
is analogous to that of the Buddhists, who make
作用, 'doing and using,' to be the nature.
We must understand by the term, I think, the
phenomena of life, and Kâo's idea led to the
ridiculous conclusion that wherever there were
the phenomena of life, the nature of the subjects
must be the same. At any rate, Mencius here
makes him allow this. 2, 3. The 與, 4th tone,
all interrogative, and = 'you allow this, I suppose.'—We find it difficult to place ourselves in
sympathy with Kâo in this conversation, or to

之從其白於外也故謂之
長於我也猶彼白而我白
也。曰彼長而我長之非有
孟子曰何以謂仁內義外
也非外也義外也非內也。
告子曰食色性也仁內
之性與。
性猶牛之性牛之性猶人
玉之白與。曰然。然則犬之
白雪之白白雪之白猶白

white snow, and the whiteness of white snow like that of white jade?' *Kâo again* said 'Yes.'

3. 'Very well,' *pursued Mencius.* 'Is the nature of a dog like the nature of an ox, and the nature of an ox like the nature of a man?'

CHAP. IV. 1. The philosopher Kâo said, '*To enjoy* food and *delight in* colours is nature. Benevolence is internal and not external; righteousness is external and not internal.'

2. Mencius asked him, 'What is the ground of your saying that benevolence is internal and righteousness external?' He replied, 'There is a man older than I, and I give honour to his age. It is not that there is *first* in me a principle of such reverence to age. It is just as when there is a white man, and I consider him white;— according as he is so externally to mê. On this account, I pronounce of righteousness that it is external.'

follow Mencius in passing from the second paragraph to the third. His questions in paragraph 2 all refer to qualities, and then he jumps to others about the nature.

4. THAT THE BENEVOLENT AFFECTIONS AND THE DISCRIMINATIONS OF WHAT IS RIGHT ARE EQUALLY INTERNAL. 1. 食色=甘食悅色. We might suppose that 色 here denoted 'the appetite of sex.' But another view is preferred. Thus the commentator 周熙 observes:— 'The infant knows to drink the breast, and to look at fire, which illustrates the text 食色

性.' It is important to observe that by 義 is denoted 事物之宜, 'the determining what conduct in reference to them is required by men and things external to us, and giving it to them.' Kâo contends that as we are moved by our own internal impulse to food and colours, so we are also in the exercise of benevolence, but not in that of righteousness. 2. 長 always 3rd tone. In 彼長 it is the adjective, but in the other cases it is the verb. 非有長於我-非先有長之之心在我. The second 白 is also a verb.

是以長爲悅者也故謂
楚人之長亦長吾之長
爲悅者也故謂之內長
之弟則不愛也是以我
乎曰吾弟則愛之秦人
謂長者義乎長之者義
以異於長人之長與且
也不識長馬之長也無
也無以異於白人之白
外也。曰異於白馬之白

3. *Mencius* said, 'There is no difference between our pronouncing a white horse to be white and our pronouncing a white man to be white. But is there no difference between the regard with which we acknowledge the age of an old horse and that with which we acknowledge the age of an old man? And what is it which is called righteousness?—the fact of a man's being old? or the fact of our giving honour to his age?'

4. *Kâo* said, 'There is my younger brother;—I love him. But the younger brother of a man of Ch'in I do not love: that is, the feeling is determined by myself, and therefore I say that benevolence is internal. *On the other hand*, I give honour to an old man of Ch'û, and I also give honour to an old man of my own *people*: that is, the feeling is determined by the age, and therefore I say that righteousness is external.'

3. 異於, at the commencement, have crept by some oversight into the text. They must be disregarded. 白馬,白人,長馬,長人,—白 and 長 are the verbs,—the 長之 below. 且謂 云云, 'and do you say? &c.,' but the meaning comes out better by expanding the words a little. The 日講 says :—'The recognition of the whiteness of a horse is not different from the recognition of the whiteness of a man. So indeed it is. But when we acknowledge the age of a horse, we simply acknowledge the age of a horse. In acknowledging, however, the age of a man, there is at the same time the feeling of respect in the mind. The case is different from our recognition of the age of a horse.' 4. 秦人.

楚人,— indifferent people, strangers. 以我爲悅以長爲悅,—the meaning is, no doubt, as in the translation, but the use of 悅 in both cases occasions some difficulty. Here again I may translate from the 日講 悅 which attempts to bring out the meaning of 悅 :—'I love my younger brother and do not love the younger brother of a man of Ch'in ; that is, the love depends on me. Him with whom my heart is pleased, I love (悅乎我之心,則愛之), and him with whom my heart is not pleased, I do not love. But the reverence is in both cases determined by the age. Wherever we meet with age, there we

此所長在彼果在外非由
誰先。曰先酌鄉人所敬在
一歲則誰敬曰敬兄。酌則
謂之內也。鄉人長於伯兄
以謂義內也。行吾敬故
孟季子問公都子曰何
外與。
有然者也然則者炙亦有
以異於者吾炙夫物則亦
之外也。者秦人之炙無

5. *Mencius* answered him, 'Our enjoyment of meat roasted by a man of Ch'in does not differ from our enjoyment of meat roasted by ourselves. Thus, *what you insist on* takes place also in the case of such things, and will you say likewise that our enjoyment of a roast is external?'

CHAP. V. 1. The disciple Măng Chî asked Kung-tû, saying, On what ground is it said that righteousness is internal?'

2. Kung-tû replied, 'We *therein* act out our feeling of respect, and therefore it is said to be internal.'

3. *The other objected,* 'Suppose the case of a villager older than your elder brother by one year, to which of them would you show the *greater* respect?' 'To my brother,' was the reply. 'But for which of them would you first pour out wine *at a feast*?' 'For the villager.' *Măng Chî argued,* '*Now* your feeling of reverence rests on the one, and *now* the honour due to age is rendered to the other; —this is certainly determined by what is without, and does not proceed from within.'

have the feeling of complacency (凡遇長皆在所悅), and it does not necessarily proceed from our own mind.' After reading all this, a perplexity is still felt to attach to the use of 悅. 5. 者=嗜.—Mencius silences his opponent by showing that the same difficulty would attach to the principle with which he himself started; namely, that the enjoyment of food was internal, and sprang from the inner springs of our being.

5. THE SAME SUBJECT;—THE DISCRIMINATIONS OF WHAT IS RIGHT ARE FROM WITHIN. 1. Măng Chî was a younger brother of Măng Chung, mentioned in Bk. II. Pt. II. ii. 3. Their relation to each other in point of age is determined by the characters 仲 and 季. Măng Chî had heard the previous conversation with Kâo, or heard of it, and feeling some doubts on the subject he applied to Kung-tû (Bk. II. Pt. II. v. 4) for their solution. 'On what ground is it said?'—i. e. by our master, by Mencius. 3. The questions here are evidently by Măng Chî

內也。公都子不能答以告孟
子。孟子曰敬叔父乎。敬弟乎。
彼將曰敬叔父曰弟爲尸、則
誰敬彼將曰敬弟子曰惡在
其敬叔父也彼將曰在位故
也子亦曰在位故也庸敬在
兄斯須之敬在鄉人季子聞
之曰敬叔父則敬敬弟則敬
果在外非由內也公都子曰
冬日則飲湯夏日則飲水然

4. Kung-tû was unable to reply, and told the conversation to Mencius. Mencius said, '*You should ask him*, "Which do you respect most,—your uncle, or your younger brother?" He will answer, "My uncle." Ask him *again*, "If your younger brother be personating a dead ancestor, to which do you show the greater respect,—*to him or to your uncle?*" He will say, "To my younger brother." You can go on, "But where is the respect due, as you said, to your uncle?" He will reply to this, "*I show the respect to my younger brother, because of the position which he occupies,*" and you can likewise say, "*So my respect to the villager is* because of the position which he occupies. Ordinarily, my respect is rendered to my elder brother; for a brief season, *on occasion*, it is rendered to the villager."'

5. *Măng* Chî heard this and observed, 'When respect is due to my uncle, I respect him, and when respect is due to my younger brother, I respect him;—the thing is certainly determined by what is without, and does not proceed from within.' Kung-tû replied, 'In winter we drink things hot, in summer we drink things cold; and

伯 is in the general sense of 長, 'elder.'
4. The translation needs to be supplemented, to show that Mencius gives his decision in the form of a dialogue between the two disciples. 叔父, 'a father's younger brother,' but used generally for 'an uncle.' 弟爲尸,—in sacrificing to the departed, some one—a certain one of the descendants, if possible—was made the 尸, or 'personator of the dead,' into whom the spirit of the other was supposed to descend to receive the worship. 惡在其敬—the 其 = 'as you said.' 斯須=暫時; compare the 'Doctrine of the Mean,' i. 2. 5. 湯, 水, 'hot

則飲食亦在外也。

公都子曰告子曰性無

善無不善也或曰性可以

爲善可以爲不善是故文

武興則民好善幽厲興則

民好暴或曰有性善有性

不善是故以堯爲君而有

象以瞽瞍爲父而有舜以

紂爲兄之子且以爲君而

有微子啟王子比干今曰

so, *on your principle*, eating and drinking also depend on what is external !'

CHAP. VI. 1. The disciple Kung-tû said, ' The philosopher Kâo says, "*Man's* nature is neither good nor bad."

2. 'Some say, "*Man's* nature may be made to practise good, and it may be made to practise evil, and accordingly, under Wăn and Wû, the people loved what was good, *while* under Yû and Lì, they loved what was cruel."

3. 'Some say, " The nature of some is good, and the nature of others is bad. Hence it was that under such a sovereign as Yâo there yet appeared Hsiang ; that with such a father as Kû-sâu there yet appeared Shun ; and that with Châu for their sovereign, and the son of their elder brother besides, there were found Ch'ì, the viscount of Wei, and the prince Pì-kan.

4. ' And now you say, "The nature is good." Then are all those wrong ?'

water,' or ' soup,' and ' water ;' 水 must be taken as ' cold ' water. Kung-tû answers after the example of his master in the last paragraph of the preceding chapter.

6. EXPLANATION OF MENCIUS'S OWN DOCTRINE THAT MAN'S NATURE IS GOOD. '1. Chû Hsî says that the view of Kâo, as here affirmed, had been advocated by Sû Tung-p'o (東坡) and Hû, styled Wăn-ting Kung (胡文定公), near to his own times. 2. This is the view propounded by Kâo in the second chapter.

is explained by 智, and 可以爲=可 以使爲. 3. 啟 was the name of the viscount of Wei ; see Analects, XVIII. i. Both he and Pì-kan are here made to be uncles of Châu, while Ch'ì, according to the Shû-ching, was his half-brother. Chû Hsî supposes some error to have crept into the text. For convenience in translating, I have changed the order of 爲兄之子, 且以爲君 王子, —as the sons of the princes of States were called 爲公子.—This view of human nature found

性善然則彼皆非與孟
子曰乃若其情則可以
爲善矣乃所謂善也若
夫爲不善非才之罪也
惻隱之心人皆有之羞
惡之心人皆有之恭敬
之心人皆有之是非之
心人皆有之惻隱之心
仁也羞惡之心義也恭
敬之心禮也是非之心

5. Mencius said, 'From the feelings proper to it, it is constituted for the practice of what is good. This is what I mean in saying that *the nature* is good.

6. 'If men do what is not good, the blame cannot be imputed to their natural powers.

7. 'The feeling of commiseration belongs to all men; so does that of shame and dislike; and that of reverence and respect; and that of approving and disapproving. The feeling of commiseration *implies the principle of* benevolence; that of shame and dislike, the principle of righteousness; that of reverence and respect, the principle of propriety; and that of approving and disapproving the principle of knowledge. Benevolence, righteousness, propriety, and knowledge are not infused into us from without. We are certainly

an advocate afterwards in the famous Han Wăn-kung (韓文公) of the T'ang dynasty.

4, 5. 乃若,—'as to,' 'looking at.' Chû Hsî calls them an initial particle. The 其, of course, refers to 性 or 'nature,' which is the subject of the next clause—可以爲善 This being the amount of Mencius's doctrine, that by the study of our nature we may see that it is formed for goodness, there seems nothing to object to in it. By 情 is denoted 性之動 'the movements of the nature,' i.e. the inward feelings and tendencies, 'stirred up.'—Chảo Ch'î takes 若 here in the sense of 順, 'to obey,' 'to accord with,' on which the translation would be—'If it act in accordance with its feelings, or emotional tendencies. The mean-

ing, however, is the same on the whole. 可以爲善 is not so definite as we could wish. Chû Hsî expands it:—人之情本但可以爲善, 而不可以爲惡 'the feelings of man may properly be used only to do good, and may not be used to do evil.' This seems to be the meaning. 6. 才=材 質, 人之能也, 'man's ability,' 'his natural powers.' 若夫 (in and tone),—'as to,' 'in the case of.' 7. Compare Bk. II. Pt. I. vi. 4, 5. 恭敬之心 however, takes the place of 辭讓之心 there. 弗思耳 is the *apodosis* of a sentence, and the *protasis* must be supplied as in the translation. 舍

智也、仁義禮智非由外鑠我
也我固有之也弗思耳矣故
曰求則得之舍則失之或相
倍蓰而無算者不能盡其才
者也詩曰天生蒸民有物有
則民之秉夷好是懿德孔子
曰爲此詩者其知道乎故有
物必有則民之秉夷也故好
是懿德。

furnished with them. *And a different view* is simply owing to want of reflection. Hence it is said, "Seek and you will find them. Neglect and you will lose them." Men differ from one another in regard to them;—some as much again as others, some five times as much, and some to an incalculable amount:—it is because they cannot carry out fully their *natural* powers.

8. 'It is said in the Book of Poetry,

"Heaven in producing mankind,
　Gave them their *various* faculties and relations with *their specific* laws.
These are the invariable rules of nature for all to hold,
And *all* love this admirable virtue."

Confucius said, "The maker of this ode knew indeed the principle *of our nature!*" We may thus see that every faculty and relation must have its law, and since there are invariable rules for all to hold, they consequently love this admirable virtue.'

一擒, 3rd tone. 或相倍云云一與 蓰相去, 或一倍云云 'they lose them so that they depart from what is good, some as far again as others, &c.' 8. 詩曰, see the Shih-ching, III. Pt. III. Ode VI. st. 1, where we have 烝 for 蒸, and 彝 for 夷. 有物有則,—'have things, have laws,' but the things specially intended are our constitution with reference to the world of sense, and the various circles of relationship. The quotation is designed specially to illustrate par. 5, but the conclusion drawn is stronger than the statement there. It is said the people actually love (好, 4th tone), and are not merely constituted to love, the admirable virtue.

不齊也故凡同類者舉相
有肥磽雨露之養人事之
時皆熟矣雖有不同則地
同浡然而生至於日至之
而耰之其地同樹之時又
心者然也今夫麰麥播種
才爾殊也其所以陷溺其
凶歲子弟多暴非天之降
孟子曰富歲子弟多賴

CHAP. VII. 1. Mencius said, 'In good years the children of the
people are most of them good, while in bad years the most of them
abandon themselves to evil. It is not owing to any difference of their
natural powers conferred by Heaven that they are thus different.
The abandonment is owing to the circumstances through which they
allow their minds to be ensnared and drowned *in evil.*

2. 'There now is barley.—Let it be sown and covered up; the
ground being the same, and the time of sowing likewise the same,
it grows rapidly up, and, when the full time is come, it is all found
to be ripe. Although there may be inequalities *of produce,* that is
owing to the *difference of the* soil, as rich or poor, to the *unequal*
nourishment afforded by the rains and dews, and to the different
ways in which man has performed his business *in reference to it.*

3. 'Thus all things which are the same in kind are like to one

7. ALL MEN ARE THE SAME IN MIND ;—SAGES
AND OTHERS. IT FOLLOWS THAT THE NATURE
OF ALL MEN, LIKE THAT OF THE SAGES, IS GOOD.
1. 富歲, 'rich years,'=豐年, 'plentiful
years.' 賴 is given by Châo Ch'î as=善,
'good,' and 暴=惡, 'evil.' But 暴=the
Mencian phrase—自暴, 'self-abandonment,'
and there is the proper meaning of 賴, 'to
depend on,' also in that term. 'In rich years,
子弟 (sons and brothers, i.e. the young
whose characters are plastic) *depend on* the
plenty and are good.' Temptations do not
lead them from their natural bent. 爾殊

也,—the use of 爾 here is peculiar. Most
take it as=如此, 'thus;'—see Wang Yän-
chih, *in voc.* Some take it in its proper pronominal meaning, as if Mencius in a lively
manner turned to the young :—'It is not from
the powers conferred by Heaven that you are
different.' 然, 'so,' referring specially to the
self-abandonment. 2. 麰麥 go together=
'barley.' 播種 (3rd tone, the noun), 'sow
the seeds.' 耰, properly, 'a kind of harrow.'
日至, not 'the solstice,' but 'the days (i.e.
the time, harvest-time) are come.' 3. 舉=

似也何獨至於人而疑之聖
人與我同類者故龍子曰不
知足而爲屨我知其不爲蕢
也屨之相似天下之足同也。
口之於味有同耆也易牙先
得我口之所耆者也如使口
之於味也其性與人殊若犬
馬之與我不同類也則天下
何耆皆從易牙之於味也至
於味天下期於易牙是天下

another;—why should we doubt in regard to man, as if he were a solitary exception to this? The sage and we are the same in kind.

4. 'In accordance with this the scholar Lung said, "If a man make hempen sandals without knowing *the size of people's* feet, *yet* I know that he will not make *them like* baskets." Sandals are all like one another, because all men's feet are like one another.

5. '*So* with the mouth and flavours;—all mouths have the same relishes. Yî-yâ *only* apprehended before me what my mouth relishes. Suppose that his mouth in its relish for flavours differed from that of other men, as is the case with dogs or horses which are not the same in kind with us, why should all men be found following Yî-yâ in their relishes? In the matter of tastes all the people model themselves after Yî-yâ; that is, the mouths of all men are like one another.

皆, 'all.' 何獨, 云云, 'why only come to man and doubt it?' 4. 故, illustrating, not inferring. So, below; except perhaps in the last instance of its use. Of the Lung who is quoted nothing seems to be known;—see Bk. III. Pt. I. iii 7. 屨, see Bk. III. Pt. I. iv. 1. 5 耆=嗜. 口之於味有同耆也, literally, 'The relation of mouths to tastes is that they have the same relishes.' Yî-yâ was the cook of the famous duke Hwan of Ch'î (B.C. 684-642), a worthless man, but great in his art. 先得 云云, is better translated 'apprehended before me,' than 'was the first to apprehend,' &c., and *only* is evidently to be supplied. 如使口之於味,—the 口 here is to be understood with reference to Yî-yâ. 其性, 'its nature,' i.e. its likings and dislikings in the matter of tastes. 天下期於易牙,—期, 'to fix a limit,' or 'to aim at.'

謂理也義也聖人先得我心
同然乎心之所同然者何也
也有同美焉至於心獨無所
於聲也有同聽焉目之於色
口之於味也有同耆焉耳之
子都之姣者無目者也故曰
都天下莫不知其姣也不知
耳相似也惟目亦然至於子
聲天下期於師曠是天下之
之口相似也惟耳亦然至於

6. 'And so also it is with the ear. In the matter of sounds, the whole people model themselves after the music-master K'wang; that is, the ears of all men are like one another.

7. 'And so also it is with the eye. In the case of Tsze-tû, there is no man but would recognise that he was beautiful. Any one who would not recognise the beauty of Tsze-tû must have no eyes.

8. 'Therefore I say,—*Men's* mouths agree in having the same relishes; their ears agree in enjoying the same sounds; their eyes agree in recognising the same beauty:—shall their minds alone be without that which they similarly approve? What is it then of which they similarly approve? It is, I say, the principles *of our nature*, and the determinations of righteousness. The sages only apprehended before me that of which my mind approves along with other men. Therefore the principles of our nature and the deter-

6. 惟耳亦然.—惟 is here in the sense of our *but*, from *botan*, the connective particle, though it often corresponds to our other *but*, a disjunctive, or exceptive, = 'only.' see Bk. IV. Pt. I.i 1. 7. Tsze-tû was the designation of Kung-sun O (公孫閼), an officer of Chăng about B.C. 700, distinguished for his beauty. See his villainy and death in the seventh chapter of the 'History of the Several States.' 8. 無所同然乎.—然 is to be taken as a verb, 'to approve.' 謂 merely indicates the answers to the preceding question. It is not so much as 'I say' in the translation. 理=心之體, 'the mental constitution,' the moral nature, and 義=心之用, that constitution or nature, acting outwardly. 芻 'hay,' 'fodder,' used for 'grass-fed animals,' such as sheep and oxen. 豢 = 'corn or rice-fed animals,' such as dogs and pigs.

之所同然耳故理義之悅我心
猶芻豢之悅我口。
八章 孟子曰牛山之木嘗美矣以
其郊於大國也斧斤伐之可以
爲美乎是其日夜之所息雨露
之所潤非無萌蘗之生焉牛羊
又從而牧之是以若彼濯濯也
人見其濯濯也以爲未嘗有材
焉此豈山之性也哉雖存乎人
者豈無仁義之心哉其所以放

minations of righteousness are agreeable to my mind, just as the flesh of grass and grain-fed animals is agreeable to my mouth.'

CHAP. VIII. 1. Mencius said, ' The trees of the Niû mountain were once beautiful. Being situated, however, in the borders of a large State, they were hewn down with axes and bills;—and could they retain their beauty? Still through the activity of the vegetative life day and night, and the nourishing influence of the rain and dew, they were not without buds and sprouts springing forth, but then came the cattle and goats and browsed upon them. To these things is owing the bare and stripped appearance *of the mountain*, and when people *now* see it, they think it was never finely wooded. But is this the nature of the mountain?

2. ' And so *also of* what properly belongs to man;—shall it be said that the mind *of any man* was without benevolence and righteous-

8. HOW IT IS THAT THE NATURE PROPERLY GOOD COMES TO APPEAR AS IF IT WERE NOT SO;—FROM NOT RECEIVING ITS PROPER NOURISHMENT. 1. The Niû mountain was in the south-east of Ch'l. It is referred to the present district of Lin-tsze (臨淄) in the department of Ch'ing-châu. 以其郊於大國=以其所生之郊在于大國. 可以爲美乎,—'could they be beautiful?' i. e. 'could they retain their beauty?' 是其日夜之所息,—the 是 is difficult;—'there is what they grow day and night,' the 息 referring to the 氣化生物, what we may call 'vegetative life.' The use of 濯濯 here is peculiar. 材=材木, 'trees of materials,' fine trees. 2. The connexion indicated by 雖,

以爲未嘗有才焉者是豈人
獸不遠矣人見其禽獸也而
存夜氣不足以存則其違禽
梏之反覆則其夜氣不足以
其旦晝之所爲有梏亡之矣
好惡與人相近也者幾希則
其日夜之所息平旦之氣其
也旦旦而伐之可以爲美乎
其良心者亦猶斧斤之於木

ness? The way in which a man loses his proper goodness of mind is like the way in which the trees are denuded by axes and bills. Hewn down day after day, can it—*the mind*—retain its beauty? But there is a development of its life day and night, and in the *calm* air of the morning, just between night and day, the mind feels in a degree those desires and aversions which are proper to humanity, but the feeling is not strong, and it is fettered and destroyed by what takes place during the day. This fettering taking place again and again, the restorative influence of the night is not sufficient to preserve *the proper goodness of the mind;* and when this proves insufficient for that purpose, the nature becomes not much different from that of the irrational animals, and when people *now* see it, they think that it never had those powers *which I assert.* But does this condition represent the feelings proper to humanity?

'although,' may be thus traced :—'Not only is such the case of the Niû mountain. Although we speak of what properly belongs to man (存=在), we shall find that the same thing obtains.' The next clause is to be translated in the past tense, the question having reference to a mind or nature, which has been allowed to run to waste. 其, 'he,'='a man.' 放失 戾心—'the good mental constitution or nature. 平, 'even,' indicates the time that lies *evenly* between the night and day. It is difficult to catch the exact idea conveyed by 氣, in this clause, and where it occurs below, the calm of the air, the corresponding calm of the spirit, and the moral invigoration from the repose of the night, being blended in it. The next clause is difficult. Châo Ch'î makes it :—'The mind is not far removed in its likings and dislikings (好, 惡, both in 4th tone) from those which are proper to humanity.' The more common interpretation is that which I have given. 幾 希,—see Bk. IV. Pt. II.

見亦罕矣吾退而寒之

寒之未有能生者也吾

之物也一日暴之十日

不智也雖有天下易生

孟子曰無或乎王之

其鄉惟心之謂與

舍則亡出入無時莫知

物不消孔子曰操則存

無物不長苟失其養無

之情也哉故苟得其養

3. 'Therefore, if it receive its proper nourishment, there is nothing which will not grow. If it lose its proper nourishment, there is nothing which will not decay away.

4. 'Confucius said, "Hold it fast, and it remains with you. Let it go, and you lose it. Its outgoing and incoming cannot be defined as to time or place." It is the mind of which this is said!'

CHAP. IX. 1. Mencius said, 'It is not to be wondered at that the king is not wise!

2. 'Suppose the case of the most easily growing thing in the world;—if you let it have one day's genial heat, and then expose it for ten days to cold, it will not be able to grow. It is but seldom that I have an audience of the king, and when I retire, there come

xix. 1. 旦晝＝一日間. 3. 無物＝物 embraces both things in nature, and the nature of man. 4. This is a remark of Confucius for which we are indebted to Mencius. 舍＝捨 出入云云,—'its outgoings and incomings have no *set* time; no one knows its direction.' 與, and tone, = 'is it not?' or an exclamation. This paragraph is thus expanded by Chû Hsî :—'Confucius said of the mind, "If you hold it fast, it is here; if you let it go, it is lost and gone: so without determinate time is its outgoing and incoming, and also without determinate place." Mencius quoted his words to illustrate the unfathomableness of the spiritual and intelligent mind, how easy it is to have it or to lose it, and how difficult to preserve and keep it, and how it may not be left unnourished for an instant. Learners ought constantly to be exerting their strength to insure the pureness of its spirit, and the settledness of its passion-nature, as in the calm of the morning, then will the mind always be preserved, and everywhere and in all circumstances its manifestations will be those of benevolence and righteousness.'

9. ILLUSTRATING THE LAST CHAPTER.—HOW THE KING OF CH'Î'S WANT OF WISDOM WAS OWING TO NEGLECT AND BAD ASSOCIATIONS. 1. 或 is used for 惑, 'to be perplexed.' 乎 is an exclamation. The king is understood to be the king Hsüan of Ch'î; see I. ii. 2. 暴＝曝, often written 曝, 'to dry in the sun,' here＝溫, 'to warm genially.' 未有 云云,—the 未, 'not yet,' 'never,' puts the general truth as an inference from the past. 見,—the 4th tone, hsien. Chû Hsî points the last clause— 吾, 如有萌焉, 何哉, 'though there

是其智弗若與曰非然也。

之雖與之俱學弗若之矣爲

有鴻鵠將至思援弓繳而射

爲聽一人雖聽之一心以爲

其一人專心致志惟弈秋之

善弈者也使弈秋誨二人弈

致志則不得也弈秋通國之

夫弈之爲數小數也不專心

者至矣吾如有萌焉何哉今

all those who act upon him like the cold. Though I succeed in
bringing out some buds *of goodness*, of what avail is it?

3. 'Now chess-playing is but a small art, but without his whole
mind being given, and his will bent, to it, a man cannot succeed at
it. Chess Ch'iû is the best chess-player in all the kingdom. Suppose
that he is teaching two men to play.—The one gives to the subject
his whole mind and bends to it all his will, doing nothing but
listening to Chess Ch'iû. The other, although *he seems to be* listening to him, has his whole mind running on a swan which he thinks
is approaching, and wishes to bend his bow, adjust the string to the
arrow, and shoot it. Although he is learning along with the other,
he does not come up to him. Why?—because his intelligence is
not equal? Not so.'

may be sprouts of goodness, what can I do?'
In this way, 吾 and 何哉 are connected,
and there is the intermediate clause between
them, which is an unusual thing in Chinese.
Feeling this difficulty, Chao Ch'î makes 吾
the nominative to 有萌 and interprets,—
'Although I wish to encourage the sprouting of
his goodness, how can I do so?' I have followed
this construction, taking the force of the terms,
however, differently. 3. 今夫 (2nd tone),
云云,—'now the character of chess-playing

as an art, is that it is a small art.' 奕秋,—
Ch'iû was the man's name, and he was called
Chess Ch'iû from his skill at the game. 鴻鵠
'a great *kû*,' which is also called 'the heavenly
goose'—the swan. 繳 (cho) 而射 (shih)
之;—see Analects, VII. xxvi. 爲 (4th tone)
是其智弗若與 (2nd tone),—'Is it
because of this, the inferiority of his (*natural*)
intelligence?' 是 and the following words
being in apposition.

王子曰、魚我所欲也、熊掌
亦我所欲也、二者不可得兼、
舍魚而取熊掌者也、生亦我
所欲也、義亦我所欲也、二者、
不可得兼、舍生而取義者也。
生亦我所欲所欲有甚於生
者、故不爲苟得也、死亦我所
惡、所惡有甚於死者、故患有
所不辟也、如使人之所欲莫
甚於生、則凡可以得生者、何

CHAP. X. 1. Mencius said, 'I like fish, and I also like bear's paws. If I cannot have the two together, I will let the fish go, and take the bear's paws. So, I like life, and I also like righteousness. If I cannot keep the two together, I will let life go, and choose righteousness.

2. 'I like life indeed, but there is that which I like more than life, and therefore, I will not seek to possess it by any improper ways. I dislike death indeed, but there is that which I dislike more than death, and therefore there are occasions when I will not avoid danger.

3. 'If among the things which man likes there were nothing which he liked more than life, why should he not use every means

10. THAT IT IS PROPER TO MAN'S NATURE TO LOVE RIGHTEOUSNESS MORE THAN LIFE, AND HOW IT IS THAT MANY ACT AS IF IT WERE NOT SO. 1. 'Bear's palms' have been a delicacy in China from the earliest times. They require a long time, it seems, to cook them thoroughly. The king Ch'ăng of Ch'û, B. C. 625, being besieged in his palace, requested that he might have a dish of bear's palms before he was put to death,— hoping that help would come while they were being cooked. 2. 生亦我所欲,—the 亦 is retained from the preceding paragraph. We may render it by 'indeed.' 所欲 云 云, is to be translated indicatively. It is explanatory of the conclusion of the last paragraph, 舍生而取義 不爲 (emphatic) 苟得, 'I won't do improper getting,' i. e. of life. The paraphrasts mostly say—不 爲苟且以得生, 'I will not act improperly to get life.' 患, 'sorrow,' 'calamity,' =danger of death. 辟=避. It seems better to construe as I have done, making 患 governed by 辟, than to make 患=a clause by itself, and suppose 死 as the object of 辟

不用也使人之所惡莫甚
於死者則凡可以辟患者
何不爲也由是則生而有
不用也由是則可以辟患
而有不爲也是故所欲有
甚於生者所惡有甚於死
者非獨賢者有是心也人
皆有之賢者能勿喪耳一
簞食一豆羹得之則生弗
得則死嘑爾而與之行道

by which he could preserve it? If among the things which man dislikes there were nothing which he disliked more than death, why should he not do everything by which he could avoid danger?

4. 'There are cases when men by a certain course might preserve life, and they do not employ it; when by certain things they might avoid danger, and they will not do them.

5. 'Therefore, men have that which they like more than life, and that which they dislike more than death. They are not men of distinguished talents and virtue only who have this mental nature. All men have it; what belongs to such men is simply that they do not lose it.

6. 'Here are a small basket of rice and a platter of soup, and the case is one in which the getting them will preserve life, and the want of them will be death;—if they are offered with an insulting

4. I translate here differently both from Châo Ch'î and Chû Hsî. They take 由是 to be = 'From this righteousness-loving nature so displayed,' as if the paragraph were merely an inference from the two preceding. I understand the paragraph to be a repetition of the two preceding, and introductory to the one which follows. 由是則生, 'by this course (any particular course) there is life,' 而有不用, 'and yet in cases it is not used.' This gives a much easier and more legitimate construction. 5. 能勿喪 (4th tone),—stress must not be laid on the 能. 勿 is simply negative, not prohibitive. 6. 嘑 4th tone. 嘑爾 is explained 幽 呼之貌, 'the appearance of reproachful clamour,' but the 蹴爾 shows that more than the idea of 'appearance,' or demonstration is intended. 行道之人=乞人, below, and not simply 'any ordinary man upon the way,' as Chû Hsî makes it. 不屑, see Bk. II. Pt. I. ix. 1.—This paragraph is intended to illustrate the 人皆有之 of the preceding. Even in the poorest and most distressed of men,

身死而不受今爲所識窮
今爲妻妾之奉爲之鄉爲
美爲之鄉爲身死而不受
身死而不受今爲宮室之
所識窮乏者得我與鄉爲
焉爲宮室之美妻妾之奉
義而受之萬鍾於我何加
人不屑也萬鍾則不辨禮
之人弗受蹴爾而與之乞

voice, even a tramper will not receive them, or if you first tread upon them, even a beggar will not stoop to take them.

7. '*And yet* a man will accept of ten thousand chung, without any consideration of propriety or righteousness. What can the ten thousand chung add to him? *When he takes them,* is it not that he may obtain beautiful mansions, that he may secure the services of wives and concubines, or that the poor and needy of his acquaintance may be helped by him?

8. 'In the former case *the offered bounty* was not received, though it would have saved from death, and now *the emolument* is taken for the sake of beautiful mansions. *The bounty* that would have preserved from death was not received, and *the emolument* is taken to get the service of wives and concubines. *The bounty* that would

the 羞惡之心 will show itself. 7. 萬
鍾,—see Bk. II. Pt. II. x. 3. 萬鍾於
我何加焉,—'what do they add to me?'
There is here a contrast with the case in the
former paragraph, which was one of life or
death. The large emolument was not an absolute necessity. But also there is the lofty, and
true, idea, that a man's personality is something
independent of, and higher than, all external
advantages. The meaning is better brought out
in English by changing the person from the first
to the third. 爲妻妾之奉, 'because
of the services of wives and concubines.' 妻
is plural as well as 妾, though according to

the law of China there could be only one wife,
however many concubines there might be. 所
識窮乏者得我=所知識窮
乏者感我之惠, 'that the poor of his
acquaintance may be grateful for his kindness.'
A gloss in the 四書味根錄 says:—
'The thinking of the poor would seem to be a
thought of kindly feeling, but the true nature
of it is shown in the 得我, may get me. The
idea is not of benevolence, but selfishness.'
8. 鄉, the 4th tone,=向. 爲 (4th tone)
身死, 'for the body dying,' i. e. to save from
dying. 是亦不可以已乎=是 is

乏者得我而爲之是亦不
可以已乎、此之謂失其本
心。

二　孟子曰、仁人心也義人
路也。舍其路而弗由、放其
心而不知求哀哉。人有雞
犬放、則知求之、有放心而
不知求。學問之道無他、求
其放心而已矣。

三　孟子曰、今有無名之指、

have saved from death was not received, and *the emolument* is taken that one's poor and needy acquaintance may be helped by him. Was it then not possible likewise to decline this? This is a case of what is called—"Losing the proper nature of one's mind."'

CHAP. XI. 1. Mencius said, 'Benevolence is man's mind, and righteousness is man's path.

2. 'How lamentable is it to neglect the path and not pursue it, to lose this mind and not know to seek it again!

3. 'When men's fowls and dogs are lost, they know to seek for them again, but they lose their mind, and do not know to seek for it.

4. 'The great end of learning is nothing else but to seek for the lost mind.'

CHAP. XII. 1. Mencius said, 'Here is a *man whose* fourth finger is bent and cannot be stretched out straight. It is not painful, nor

emphatic,—this large emolument, taken for such purposes.—For an example in point to illustrate par. 6, see the Lî-chî, II. Sect. II. iii. 17.

11. HOW MEN HAVING LOST THE PROPER QUALITIES OF THEIR NATURE SHOULD SEEK TO RECOVER THEM. 1. 'Benevolence is man's mind, or heart,' i.e. it is the proper and universal characteristic of man's nature, as the 正義 on Châo Ch'î says,—人人有之, 'all men have it.' 'Benevolence' would seem to include here all the other moral qualities of humanity. Chû Hsî says 仁者心之德; yet we have the usual Mencian specification of 'righteousness' along with it. 4. 學問之道,—道=切

要, 'that which is most important in.'—The Chinese sages always end with the recovery of 'the old heart;' the idea of 'a new heart' is unknown to them. One of the Ch'ăng says:— 'The thousand words and ten thousand sayings of the sages and worthies are simply designed to lead men to get hold of their lost minds, and make them again enter their bodies. This accomplished, they can push their inquiries upwards, and from the lowest studies acquire the highest knowledge.'

12. HOW MEN ARE SENSIBLE OF BODILY, AND NOT OF MENTAL OR MORAL, DEFECTS. 1. 無名之指, 'the nameless finger,' i.e. the fourth, reckoning from the thumb as the first. It is

屈而不信非疾痛害事也、
如有能信之者則不遠秦
楚之路爲指之不若人也。
指不若人則知惡之心不
若人則不知惡此之謂不
知類也。

孟子曰拱把之桐梓人
苟欲生之皆知所以養之
者至於身而不知所以養
之者豈愛身不若桐梓
哉。

does it incommode his business, and yet if there be any one who can make it straight, he will not think the way from Ch'in to Ch'û far *to go to him;* because his finger is not like the finger of other people.

2. 'When a man's finger is not like those of other people, he knows to feel dissatisfied, but if his mind be not like that of other people, he does not know to feel dissatisfaction. This is called—"Ignorance of the relative *importance of things.*"'

CHAP. XIII. Mencius said, 'Anybody who wishes to cultivate the *t'ung* or the *tsze,* which may be grasped with both hands, *perhaps* with one, knows by what means to nourish them. In the case of their own persons, men do not know by what means to nourish them. Is it to be supposed that their regard of their own persons is inferior to their regard for a *t'ung* or *tsze?* Their want of reflection is extreme.'

so styled, as of less use than the others, and less needing a name. 信,—read as, and with the meaning of, 伸 (*shin*). 不遠秦楚之路＝雖越秦楚相去之路不以爲遠, 'though he should pass over all the way between Ch'in and Ch'û, he will not think it far.' 2. 不知類,—'not knowing kinds,' or degrees. 類＝等.

13. MEN'S EXTREME WANT OF THOUGHT IN REGARD TO THE CULTIVATION OF THEMSELVES. The *t'ung* and *tsze* resemble each other. The latter is called by the Chinese 'the king of trees,' and its wood is well adapted for their block-engraving. Of the *t'ung* there are various arrangements, some making three kinds of it, some four, and some seven. The wood of the first kind, or white *t'ung* (白桐), is the best for making musical instruments like the lute. Bretschneider makes the *t'ung* to be the *paulownia;* and the *tsze,* the *rottlera Japonica,* or the *catalpa.* 至於身＝身, 'the body,' but here 'the person,' the whole human being. 豈...哉＝'is it to be supposed?' A supplementary note in the 備旨 says that 'by

有場師舍其梧檟養其樲棘
爲小人養其大者爲大人今
害大無以賤害貴養其小者
矣。體有貴賤有小大無以小
者豈有他哉於己取之而已
膚不養也所以考其善不善
寸之膚不愛焉則無尺寸之
愛兼所愛則兼所養也無尺
孟子曰人之於身也兼所
弗思甚也。

CHAP. XIV. 1. Mencius said, 'There is no part of himself which a man does not love, and as he loves all, so he must nourish all. There is not an inch of skin which he does not love, and so there is not an inch of skin which he will not nourish. For examining whether *his way of nourishing* be good or not, what other rule is there but this, that he determine by *reflecting on* himself where it should be applied?

2 'Some parts of the body are noble, and some ignoble; some great, and some small. The great must not be injured for the small, nor the noble for the ignoble. He who nourishes the little belonging to him is a little man, and he who nourishes the great is a great man.

3. 'Here is a plantation-keeper, who neglects his *wû* and *chiâ*, and cultivates his sour jujube-trees;—he is a poor plantation-keeper.

nourishing the 身 here is intended the ruling of the mind, to nourish our inner man, and paying careful attention to the body, to nourish our outer man.'

14. THE ATTENTION GIVEN BY MEN TO THE NOURISHMENT OF THE DIFFERENT PARTS OF THEIR NATURE MUST BE REGULATED BY THE RELATIVE IMPORTANCE OF THOSE PARTS. 1. 身,—as in the last chapter, but with more special reference to the body. 兼所愛, 'unites what he loves,' i.e. loves all. 尺寸, 'a cubit or an inch,' but the meaning is—the least bit of. = our 'an inch.' 所以考, 云云, requires to be

supplemented a good deal in translating. The meaning is plain:—A man is to determine for himself, by reflection on his constitution, what parts are more important and should have the greater attention paid to them. Compare the two last paragraphs of Analects, VI. xxviii. a 體, 'the members of the body,' but the character, like 身, is to be understood with a tacit reference to the mental part of our constitution as well. 3. The 場人 was an officer under the Châu dynasty, who had the superintendence of the ruler's plantations and orchards;—see the Châu Lî, II. Pt. XVI. xxiii. 1. The wû (the *sterculia platanifolia*, according to Bretschneider) and the

體爲小人。曰鈞是人也。或從
曰從其大體爲大人從其小
爲大人或爲小人何也。孟子
☐公都子問曰鈞是人也或
爲尺寸之膚哉。
之人、無有失也則口腹豈適
矣、爲其養小以失大也飲食
疾人也飲食之人、則人賤之
失其肩背而不知也則爲狼
則爲賤場師焉。養其一指而

4. 'He who nourishes one of his fingers, neglecting his shoulders or his back, without knowing *that he is doing so*, is a man *who resembles* a hurried wolf.

5. 'A man who *only* eats and drinks is counted mean by others;—because he nourishes what is little to the neglect of what is great.

6. 'If a man, *fond of his* eating and drinking, were not to neglect *what is of more importance*, how should his mouth and belly be considered as no more than an inch of skin?'

CHAP. XV. 1. The disciple Kung-tû said, 'All are equally men, but some are great men, and some are little men;—how is this?' Mencius replied, 'Those who follow that part of themselves which is great are great men; those who follow that part which is little are little men.'

2. Kung-tû pursued, 'All are equally men, but some follow

chiû are used like *t'ung* and *tsze* in the last chapter; or, as some make out, the *sterculia platanifolia* and the *catalpa Japonica*. Two valuable trees are evidently intended by them. 梧棘 go together, 梧 indicating the species. 棘 is generally used with the general meaning of thorns;—but it here indicates a kind of small wild date-tree. The date-tree proper is 棗; this wild tree, 棘; the different forms indicating the *high* tree and the *low bushy* shrub respectively. See the 集證, *in loc.* 4. 失 =

狼疾, 'a wolf hurried,' i. e. chased, and so unable to exercise the quick sight for which it is famous. 6. The meaning is that the parts considered small and ignoble may have their due share of attention, if the more important parts are first cared for, as they ought to be.

15. HOW SOME ARE GREAT MEN, LORDS OF REASON, AND SOME ARE LITTLE MEN, SLAVES OF SENSE. 1. 鈞=均, 'all equally.' 體, 'the members,' but here, more evidently than in the last chapter, it is spoken of our whole constitution, mental as well as physical. 2. 耳目之官 'the offices of the ears and eyes.' We might

其大體或從其小體何
也曰耳目之官不思而
蔽於物物交物則引之
而已矣心之官則思思
則得之不思則不得也
此天之所與我者先立
乎其大者則其小者不
能奪也此為大人而已
矣。
孟子曰有天爵者有

that part of themselves which is great, and some follow that part which is little;—how is this?' Mencius answered, 'The senses of hearing and seeing do not think, and are obscured by *external* things. When one thing comes into contact with another, as a matter of course it leads it away To the mind belongs the office of thinking. By thinking, it gets *the right view of things;* by neglecting to think, it fails to do this. These—*the senses and the mind*—are what Heaven has given to us. Let a man first stand fast in *the supremacy of* the nobler part of his constitution, and the inferior part will not be able to take it from him. It is simply this which makes the great man.'

CHAP. XVI.   1. Mencius said, 'There is a nobility of Heaven,

suppose that the senses are so styled, as being conceived to be subject to the control of the ruling mind. We have below, however, the expression 心之官, and 官 is to be taken in both cases as = 'prerogative,' 'business.' Châo Ch'î and his glossarist do not take 耳目之官 as the subject of 思 in 不思, but interpret thus:—'The senses, if there be not the exercise of thought by the mind, are obscured by external things.' But the view of Chû Hsî, as in the translation, is preferable. It is very evident that 心 indicates our whole mental constitution. 物交物,—the first 物 is the external objects, what is heard and seen; the second denotes the senses themselves, which are only things. 引之而已,—而已 = 'as a matter of course.' 得之,—之 = 事物之理, 'the mind apprehends the true nature of the

objects of sense,' and of course can guard against their deluding influence. 其大者, 'his what is great,' the nobler part of his constitution, i.e. the mind.—Kung-tû might have gone on to inquire,—'All are equally men. Some stand fast in the nobler part of their constitution, and some allow its supremacy to be snatched away by the inferior part. How is this?' and Mencius would have tried to carry the difficulty a step farther back, and after all have left it where it originally was. His saying that the nature of man is good may be reconciled with the doctrines of evangelical Christianity, but his views of human nature as a whole are open to the three objections stated in the note to the twenty-first chapter of the *Chung Yung.*

16. THERE IS A NOBILITY THAT IS OF HEAVEN, AND A NOBILITY THAT IS OF MAN. THE NEGLECT OF THE FORMER LEADS TO THE LOSS OF THE LATTER.

1. 忠 is the *heart* true in itself, loyal to benevolence and righteousness, and 信 is the conduct

同心也人人有貴於己
孟子曰欲貴者人之
必亡而已矣。
爵則惑之甚者也終亦
爵既得人爵而棄其天
之人修其天爵以要人
其天爵而人爵從之今
夫此人爵也古之人修
不倦此天爵也公卿大
人爵者仁義忠信樂善

and there is a nobility of man. Benevolence, righteousness, self-consecration, and fidelity, with unwearied joy in *these* virtues;—these constitute the nobility of Heaven. To be a kung, a ch'ing, or a tâ-fû ;—this constitutes the nobility of man.

2. 'The men of antiquity cultivated their nobility of Heaven, and the nobility of man came to them in its train.

3. 'The men of the present day cultivate their nobility of Heaven in order to seek for the nobility of man, and when they have obtained that, they throw away the other :—their delusion is extreme. The issue is simply this, that they must lose *that nobility of man* as well.'

CHAP. XVII. 1. Mencius said, 'To desire to be honoured is the common mind of men. And all men have in themselves that which is *truly* honourable. Only they do not think of it.

true to them. 公卿大夫,—see Bk. V. Pt. II. ii. 3-7. 3. 要, the 1st tone,—求; 'their delusion is extreme,'—this is well set forth in the 日講:—夫修天爵以 要人爵是脩之之日,原先有 棄之之心,已不免於惑矣,是 至得人爵而棄天爵是得 之之後,其不及要之之時, 則惑之甚者也, 'Now when the nobility of Heaven is cultivated in order to seek for the nobility of man, at the very time it is cultivated, there is a previous mind to throw it away;—showing the existence of delusion. Then when the nobility of man has been got, to throw away the nobility of Heaven, exhibits conduct after attainment not equal to that in the time of search, so that the delusion is extreme.' 終亦必亡而已矣—亡 has reference to the nobility of man, and is best translated as an active verb, to which the 亦 also points.—Many commentators observe that facts may be referred to, apparently inconsistent with the assertions in this chapter, and then go on to say that such inconsistency is but a lucky accident; the issue *should* always be as Mencius says. Yes; but all moral teachings must be imperfect where the thoughts are bounded by what is seen and temporal.

17. THE TRUE HONOUR WHICH MEN SHOULD DESIRE. 1. 爵 in the last chapter is the material dignity; 貴 in this is the honour,

以一杯水救一車薪之火
猶水勝火今之爲仁者猶
孟子曰仁之勝不仁也。
願人之文繡也。
令聞廣譽施於身所以不
以不願人之膏粱之味也
飽以德言飽乎仁義也所
能賤之詩云既醉以酒既
良貴也趙孟之所貴趙孟
者弗思耳人之所貴者非

2. 'The honour which men confer is not good honour. Those whom Châo the Great ennobles he can make mean *again*.

3. 'It is said in the Book of Poetry,

"He has filled us with his wine,
He has satiated us with his goodness."

"*Satiated us with his goodness*," that is, satiated us with benevolence and righteousness, and he who is so satiated, consequently, does not wish for the fat meat and fine millet of men. A good reputation and far-reaching praise fall to him, and he does not desire the elegant embroidered garments of men.'

CHAP. XVIII. 1. Mencius said, 'Benevolence subdues its opposite just as water subdues fire. Those, however, who now-a-days practise benevolence *do it* as if with one cup of water they could save a whole waggon-load of fuel which was on fire, and when

such as springs from such dignity. 2. 人之 所貴.—人 here and in the next paragraph refers to those who confer dignities. It is not to be understood—'what men consider honour.' 趙孟, 'Châo, the chief.' This title was borne by four ministers of the family of Châo, who at different times held the chief sway in Tsin. They were a sort of 'king-making War-wicks.' In the time of Mencius, the title had become associated with the name of the house. 3. 詩云—see the Shih-ching, III. ii. Ode III. st. 1. The ode is one responsive from 'his fathers and brethren' to the sovereign who has

entertained them. Mencius's application of it is a mere accommodation.

18. IT IS NECESSARY TO PRACTISE BENEVOLENCE WITH ALL ONE'S MIGHT. THIS ONLY WILL PRESERVE IT. 1. 不熄 則謂之.—謂之—'were to say of it.' 與 is said by Chû Hsî to—膊, 'to aid.' The 甚 is joined to 與, and not to 不仁. Bad men seeing the ineffectiveness of feeble endeavours to do good are only encouraged in their own course. This mean-ing of 與 is found elsewhere. Châo Ch'î interprets:—'This also is worse than the case of those who practise what is not benevolent.' But both the sentiment and construction of

亦必以規矩。
大匠誨人必以規矩學者
至於穀學者亦必志於穀。
孟子曰羿之教人射必
夫仁亦在乎熟之而已矣。
者也苟爲不熟不如荑稗
孟子曰五穀者種之美
亦終必亡而已矣。
此又與於不仁之甚者也。
也不熄則謂之水不勝火、

the flames were not extinguished, were to say that water cannot subdue fire. This conduct, moreover, greatly encourages those who are not benevolent.

2. 'The final issue will simply be this—the loss *of that small amount of benevolence.*'

CHAP. XIX. Mencius said, 'Of all seeds the best are the five kinds of grain, yet if they be not ripe, they are not equal to the *tî* or the *pâi.* So, the value of benevolence depends entirely on its being brought to maturity.'

CHAP. XX. 1. Mencius said, 'Î, in teaching men to shoot, made it a rule to draw the bow to the full, and his pupils also did the same.

2. 'A master-workman, in teaching others, uses the compass and square, and his pupils do the same.'

this are more difficult than the other. 2. Compare chapter xvi. 3.

19. BENEVOLENCE MUST BE MATURED. 1. 'The five kinds of grain;'—see Bk. III. Pt. I. iv. 7. The *tî* and *pâi* are two plants closely resembling one another. They are a kind of spurious grain, 'yielding a rice-like seed, but small. They are to be found at all times, in wet situations and dry, and when crushed and roasted, may satisfy the hunger in a time of famine.' Mencius's vivacity of mind and readiness at illustration lead him at times to broad unguarded statements, of which this seems to be one.

20. LEARNING MUST NOT BE BY HALVES. 1. 志,—see Bk. IV. Pt. II. xxiv. 1. 志—used as 期 in chap. vii. 5. 必志 'found it necessary to,' or simply the past tense emphatic. So, in the next paragraph. 2. 大匠＝工師, 'a master-workman.' Chû Hsî says:—'This chapter shows that affairs must be proceeded with according to their laws, and then they can be completed. But if a master neglect these, he cannot teach; and if a pupil neglect these, he cannot learn. In small arts it is so:—how much more with the principles of the sages!'

KÂO TSZE. PART II.

告子章句下

一

任人有問屋廬
子曰禮與食孰重。
曰禮重色與禮孰
重曰禮重曰以禮
食則飢而死不以
禮食則得食必以
禮乎親迎則不得
妻不親迎則得妻
必親迎乎屋廬子

CHAPTER I. 1. A man of Zăn asked the disciple Wû-lû, saying, 'Is *an observance of* the rules of propriety *in regard to eating,* or eating *merely,* the more important?' The answer was, '*The observance of* the rules of propriety is the more important'

2. 'Is *the gratifying* the appetite of sex, or *the doing so only* according to the rules of propriety, the more important?' The answer *again* was, '*The observance of* the rules of propriety *in the matter* is the more important.'

3. *The man* pursued, 'If the result of eating only according to the rules of propriety will be death by starvation, while by disregarding those rules we may get food, must they *still* be observed *in such a case?* If according to the rule that he shall go in person to meet his wife a man cannot get married, while by disregarding that rule he may get married, must he *still* observe the rule *in such a case?*'

4. Wû-lû was unable to reply to *these questions,* and the next

1. THE IMPORTANCE OF OBSERVING THE RULES OF PROPRIETY, AND, WHEN THEY MAY BE DISREGARDED, THE EXCEPTION WILL BE FOUND TO PROVE NOT BE THE RULE. EXTREME CASES MAY NOT BE PRESSED TO INVALIDATE THE PRINCIPLE. 1. 任 (in 2nd tone) was a small State, referred to the present Tsî-ning (濟寧) châu, of the department of Yen-châu, in Shan-tung. It was not far from Mencius's native State of Tsâu, the distance being only between twenty and thirty li. The disciple Wû-lû, who is said to have published books on the doctrines of Lâo-tsze, was a native of the State of Tsin. His name was Lien (連). His questions are not to be understood of propriety in the abstract, but of the rules of propriety understood to regulate the other things which he mentions. 2. 色 is to be understood as in the translation, and this is its common signification in Mencius. I include the 曰禮重, in this paragraph. 3. 以禮食,—see the Lî Chî, XXVII. 26, et al. 親迎 (4th tone),—see the Lî Chî XXVII. 38. 4. 之鄰=之=往 Châo Ch'î

不　子　不　之　於　與　與　食　輕　應
能　。　揣　木　羽　羽　禮　重　者　之
對　孟　其　可　者　之　之　取　而　曰
明　子　本　使　豈　謂　輕　色　比　紾
日　曰　而　高　謂　哉　者　之　之　兄
之　於　齊　於　一　。　而　重　奚　之
鄒　答　其　岑　鉤　取　比　者　翅　臂
以　是　末　樓　金　食　之　與　色　而
告　也　方　金　與　之　奚　禮　重　奪
孟　何　寸　重　一　重　翅　之　往　之
　　有　　　　　者　　　

day he went to Tsâu, and told them to Mencius. Mencius said, 'What difficulty is there in answering these inquiries?

5. 'If you do not adjust them at their lower extremities, but only put their tops on a level, a piece of wood an inch square may be made to be higher than the pointed peak of a high building.

6. 'Gold is heavier than feathers;—but does that saying have reference, on the one hand, to a single clasp of gold, and, on the other, to a waggon-load of feathers?

7. 'If you take a case where the eating is of the utmost importance and the observing the rules of propriety is of little importance, and compare the things together, why stop with saying merely that the eating is more important? *So*, taking the case where the gratifying the appetite of sex is of the utmost importance and the observing the rules of propriety is of little importance, why stop with merely saying that the gratifying the appetite is the more important?

8. 'Go and answer him thus, "If, by twisting your elder brother's

reads 於 as 烏 (wû, 1st tone), making it an exclamation—'oh!' 5. 揣, 'to measure, or feel with the hand.' 本 and 末 are used for 下 and 上. 岑 (ch'ân), 'a high and pointed small hill.' Châo Ch'î takes 岑樓 together as meaning 'a peaked ridge of a hill,' and the dictionary gives this signification to the phrase. The view of Chû Hsî, which I have followed,

is better. 6. 金 ... 者—者 indicates the clause to be a common saying, and carries us on to some explanation of it. 豈謂 ... 之謂, 'How does it say (mean) the saying (meaning) of the gold of one hook, and the feathers of one waggon?' Compare Bk. I. Pt. I. vii. 10. 7. 奚翅 (-啻)—何但. 8. 紾 (read ch'ân, 3rd tone), both by Châo Ch'î and Chû Hsî, is explained by 戾, 'to bend.' I prefer

食則得食不綯則不得
食則將綯之乎踰東家
牆而摟其處子則得妻
不摟則不得妻則將摟
之乎。
曹交問曰人皆可以
爲堯舜有諸孟子曰然。
交聞文王十尺湯九尺
今交九尺四寸以長
粟而已如何則可曰奚

arm, and snatching from him what he is eating, you can get food for yourself, while, if you do not do so, you will not get anything to eat, will you so twist his arm? If by getting over your neighbour's wall, and dragging away his virgin daughter, you can get a wife, while if you do not do so, you will not be able to get a wife, will you so drag her away?"'

CHAP. II.   1. Chiâo of Tsâo asked *Mencius*, saying, ' *It is said,* " All men may be Yâos and Shuns ;"—is it so ?' Mencius replied, ' It is.'

2. *Chiâo went on,* 'I have heard that king Wăn was ten cubits *high*, and T'ang nine. Now I am nine cubits four inches in height. *But* I can do nothing but eat *my* millet. What am I to do to realize that saying ?'

3. *Mencius* answered him,' What has this—*the question of size—*

the first meaning of the character given in the dictionary,—that of 轉, 'to turn,' here = 'to twist.' 而奪之食,—here 奪 is followed by two objectives, 之 being = 'from him.' Julien errs strangely in rendering ' *Si, rumpens fratris majoris brachium, rapuas illud comedendium.*' 東家牆, 'the wall of the house on the east,' i. e. a neighbour's wall. 東家 is a common designation for the master of a house, and I do not know of any instance of its use by a writer earlier than Mencius. 處 (3rd tone) 子, 'a virgin daughter,' one *dwelling* in the harem. 子, as sometimes elsewhere, is feminine.

2. ALL MAY BECOME Yâos AND SHUNS, AND TO

BECOME SO, THEY HAVE ONLY SINCERELY, AND IN THEMSELVES, TO CULTIVATE Yâo AND SHUN'S PRINCIPLES AND WAYS. 1. Châo Ch'î says that Chiâo was a brother of the prince of Ts'âo, but the principality of Ts'âo had been extinguished before the time of Mencius. The descendants of the ruling house had probably taken their surname from their ancient patrimony. Ts'âo is referred to the present district of T'ing-t'âo (定陶) in the department of Ts'âo-châu, in Shan-tung. 有諸,—compare Bk. I. Pt. II. ii. 1, *et al.* 2. On the heights mentioned here, see Analects, VIII. vi. 以長, 'for my height.' The 以, however, may be taken as simply euphonic. Chiâo's idea is, that physically he was between Wăn and T'ang, who might be considered as having become Yâos or Shuns, and therefore he also might become such, if he

有於是亦爲之而已矣有
人於此力不能勝一匹雛
則爲無力人矣今日舉百
鈞則爲有力人矣然則舉
烏獲之任是亦爲烏獲而
已矣夫人豈以不勝爲患
哉弗爲耳徐行後長者謂
之弟疾行先長者謂之不
弟夫徐行者豈人所不能
哉所不爲也堯舜之道孝

to do with the matter? It all lies simply in acting as such. Here is a man, whose strength was not equal to lift a duckling:—he was *then* a man of no strength. But to-day he says, "I can lift 3,000 catties' weight," and he is a man of strength. And so, he who can lift the weight which Wû Hwo lifted is just another Wû Hwo. Why should a man make a want of ability the subject of his grief? It is only that he will not do the thing.

4. 'To walk slowly, keeping behind his elders, is to perform the part of a younger. To walk quickly and precede his elders, is to violate the duty of a younger brother. Now, is it what a man cannot do—to walk slowly? It is what he does not do. The course of Yâo and Shun was simply that of filial piety and fraternal duty.

were shown the right way. 3. 於是,一是 referring to the height, or body generally. 爲之,一之 referring to Yâo and Shun. 匹, is said to be an abbreviation for 鴄=鶩, 'a wild duck.' I do not see why it should not be taken simply as a numeral or classifier, and 一匹雛='a chicken.' Wû Hwo was a man noted for his strength. He is mentioned in connexion with the king Wú of Ts'in (B.C. 309-306). Accounts go that he made light of 30,000 catties! 4. 後 and 先 (4th tone) are verbs; 弟=悌. Chû Hsî here quotes from the commentator Ch'ân (陳氏):—'Filial piety and fraternal duty are the natural out-goings of the nature, of which men have an intuitive knowledge, and for which they have an intuitive ability (良知良能). Yâo and Shun showed the perfection of the human relations, but yet they simply acted in accordance with this nature. How could they add a hair's point to it?' He also quotes another (陽氏), who says:—'The way of Yâo and Shun was great, but the pursuit of it lay simply in the rapidity or slowness of their walking and stopping, and not in things that were very high and difficult. It is present to the common people in their daily usages, but they do not

弟而已矣子服堯之服誦堯
之言行堯之行是堯而已矣
子服桀之服誦桀之言行桀
之行是桀而已矣曰交得見
於鄒君可以假館願留而受
業於門曰夫道若大路然豈
難知哉人病不求耳子歸而
求之有餘師。
公孫丑問曰高子曰小弁、
小人之詩也孟子曰何以言

5. 'Wear the clothes of Yâo, repeat the words of Yâo, and do the actions of Yâo, and you will just be a Yâo. And, if you wear the clothes of Chieh, repeat the words of Chieh, and do the actions of Chieh, you will just be a Chieh.'

6. Chiâo said, 'I shall be having an interview with the prince of Tsâu, and can ask him to let me have a house to lodge in. I wish to remain here, and receive instruction at your gate.'

7. Mencius replied, 'The way of truth is like a great road. It is not difficult to know it. The evil is only that men will not seek it. Do you go home and search for it, and you will have abundance of teachers.'

CHAP. III. 1. Kung-sun Ch'âu asked *about an opinion of the scholar Kâo*, saying, 'Kâo observed, "The Hsiâo P'an is the ode of a little man."' Mencius asked, 'Why did he say so?' 'Because of the murmuring *which it expresses*,' was the reply.

know it.' 5. The meaning is simply—Imitate the men, do what they did, and you will be such as they were. 6. 變得見 (4th tone), —it is better not to translate this conditionally, as it shows how Chiâo was presuming on his nobility. 7. 夫道, 'Now, the way'—i.e. the way of Yâo and Shun, or generally 'of truth.'

3. EXPLANATION OF THE ODES HSIÂO P'AN AND K'ÂI FÂNG. DISSATISFACTION WITH A PARENT IS NOT NECESSARILY UNFILIAL. 1. Kâo appears to have been a disciple of Tsze-hsiâ, and lived to Mencius's time. From the expression 高叟 in par. 2, it is plain, he is not to be confounded with Mencius's own disciple of the same surname, mentioned in Bk. II. Pt. II. xii. 2. 小弁,—see the Shih-ching, II. v. Ode III. 3. The ode is commonly understood to have been written by the master of I-ch'iû (宜白) the son and heir-apparent of the sovereign Yû (B.C. 780-770). Led away by the arts of a

怨曰凱風親之過小者
爲詩也、曰凱風何以不
親仁也、固矣夫高叟之
也小弁之怨親親也、親
涕泣而道之、無他戚之
兄關弓而射之、則己垂
而道之、無他疏之也、其
關弓而射之、則已談笑
爲詩也有人於此越人
之曰、怨曰固哉高叟之

2. *Mencius* answered, 'How stupid was that old Kâo in dealing with the ode! There is a man here, and a native of Yüeh bends his bow to shoot him. I will advise him *not to do so*, but speaking calmly and smilingly;—for no other reason but that he is not related to me. *But* if my own brother be bending his bow to shoot the man, then I will advise him not to do so, weeping and crying the while;—for no other reason than that he is related to me. The dissatisfaction expressed in the Hsiâo P'án is the working of relative affection, and that affection shows benevolence. Stupid indeed was old Kâo's criticism on the ode.'

3. *Ch'âu then said*, 'How is it that there is no dissatisfaction expressed in the K'âi Fäng?'

4. Mencius replied, 'The parent's fault referred to in the K'âi

mistress, the sovereign degraded Î-ch'iû and his mother, and the ode expresses the sorrow and dissatisfaction which the son could not but feel in such circumstances. Châo Ch'î, however, assigns it another authorship, but on this and other questions, connected with it, see the Shih-ching, *in loc.* 2. 固 is explained by Châo Ch'î by 陋, 'narrow,' and by Chû Hsî by 就 滯不通, 'bigoted and not penetrating.' 爲詩=治詩. 有人… 戚之— here 已 is to be understood of the speaker or beholder, and 其兄 of his—the speaker's—brother. In 道 (=言, the verb) 之, 疏 之, 戚之 之 refers to the shooter. 關, read *wan*, = 彎. The paraphrast of Châo Ch'î

points, however, and understands differently— 'Here is a man of Yüeh, who is about to be shot by another man. I see it and advise the man not to shoot, but coolly and smilingly, because I am not related to the man of Yüeh. But if my brother is about to be shot, &c.' This is ingenious, but not so apt to the subject of the Hsiâo Fân. When native scholars can construe a passage so differently, we may be sure it is not very definitely expressed. 3. 凱風 —see the Shih-ching, I. iii. Ode VII. The ode is supposed to be the production of seven sons, bewailing the conduct of their widowed mother, who could not live quietly and chastely at home, but they take all the blame to themselves, and express no dissatisfaction with her. 4. We must think there was room enough for dissatisfaction in both cases. And indeed, many commentators say that the received account of the subject of the K'âi Fäng must be wrong, or that Mencius's decision on it is

說而罷之楚王不悅我將
聞秦楚搆兵我將見楚王
石丘曰先生將何之曰吾
宋牼將之楚孟子遇於
【四】
矣五十而慕。
不孝也孔子曰舜其至孝
也愈疏不孝也不可磯亦
親之過小而怨是不可磯
之過大而不怨是愈疏也
也小弁親之過大者也親

Fang is small; that referred to in the Hsiâo P'ân is great. Where the parent's fault was great, not to have murmured on account of it would have increased the want of natural affection. Where the parent's fault was small, to have murmured on account of it would have been to act like water which frets and foams about a stone that interrupts its course. To increase the want of natural affection would have been unfilial, and to fret and foam in such a manner would also have been unfilial.

5. 'Confucius said, "Shun was indeed perfectly filial! *And yet*, when he was fifty, he was full of longing desire about his parents."'

CHAP. IV. 1. Sung K'ang being about to go to Ch'û, Mencius met him in Shih-ch'iû.

2. 'Master, where are you going?' asked *Mencius*.

3. *K'ang* replied, 'I have heard that Ch'in and Ch'û are fighting together, and I am going to see the king of Ch'û and persuade him to cease hostilities. If he shall not be pleased *with my advice*,

absurd. But here again, see the Shih-ching, *in loc.* 愈疏, 'mores' (if we had such a verb), 'the distance.' The father's act was unkind; if the son responded to it with indifference, that would increase the distance and alienation between them. 是不可磯也,—the three characters 不可磯 are to be taken together. The mother is compared to a rock or stone in a stream, and the sons to the water fretting about it. But the case in the text is one where the children's affections should flow on undisturbed. 5. Compare Bk. V. Pt. I. i.

4. MENCIUS'S WARNINGS TO SUNG K'ANG ON THE ERROR AND DANGER OF COUNSELLING THE PRINCES FROM THE GROUND OF PROFIT, THE PROPER GROUND BEING THAT OF BENEVOLENCE AND RIGHTEOUSNESS. Compare Bk. I. Pt. I. i, *et al.* 1. K'ang was one of the travelling scholars of the times, who went from State to State, making it their business to counsel (說, *shûi*, 4th tone) the princes, with a view for the most part, though not apparently with him, to exalt themselves. Shih-ch'iû was in the State of Sung. Here, and also in the next paragraph, 之 is the verb.

3. 搆 (=戰) 兵 ~ 'battling weapons.' 罷

見秦王、說而罷之、二王、我將有
所遇焉、曰、軻也、請無問其詳、願
聞其指、說之、將何如、曰、我將言
其不利也、曰、先生之志則大矣、
先生之號、則不可、先生以利、說
秦楚之王、秦楚之王、悅於利以
罷三軍之師、是三軍之士、樂罷
而悅於利也、爲人臣者、懷利以
事其君、爲人子者、懷利以事其
父爲人弟者、懷利以事其兄、是

I shall go to see the king of Ch'in, and persuade him in the same
way. Of the two kings I shall *surely* find that I can succeed with
one of them.'

4. *Mencius* said, 'I will not venture to ask about the particulars,
but I should like to hear the scope of your plan. What course will
you take to try to persuade them?' *K'ang* answered, 'I will tell
them how unprofitable their course is to them.' 'Master,' said
Mencius, 'your aim is great, but your argument is not good.

5. 'If you, starting from the point of profit, offer your persuasive
counsels to the kings of Ch'in and Ch'ŭ, and if those kings are
pleased with the consideration of profit so as to stop the movements
of their armies, then all belonging to those armies will rejoice in
the cessation *of war*, and find their pleasure in *the pursuit of* profit.
Ministers will serve their sovereign for the profit of which they
cherish the thought; sons will serve their fathers, and younger
brothers will serve their elder brothers, from the same consideration:—and the issue will be, that, abandoning benevolence and

之, 'make an end of it.' 所遇,—see Bk. I. | the two States. 號.—I take the word 'argu-
Pt. II. xv. 3. 4. 請 = our 'if you'll allow me.' | ment' from Julien. The gloss in the 備旨
Then follows—'not asking the particulars, I | is—號是不利之名號, 號 is the
should like,' &c. 其不利—其 refers to | name and title of *unprofitable*.' 5. 三軍之

君臣父子兄弟終去仁義懷利
以相接然而不亡者未之有也。
先生以仁義說秦楚之王秦楚
之王悅於仁義而罷三軍之師、
是三軍之士樂罷而悅於仁義
也爲人臣者懷仁義以事其君、
爲人子者懷仁義以事其父、
人弟者懷仁義以事其兄是君
臣父子兄弟去利懷仁義以相
接也然而不王者未之有也何

六章

righteousness, sovereign and minister, father and son, younger brother and elder, will carry on all their intercourse with this thought of profit cherished in their breasts. But never has there been such a state *of society*, without ruin being the result of it.

6. 'If you, starting from the ground of benevolence and righteousness, offer your counsels to the kings of Ch'in and Ch'û, and if those kings are pleased with the consideration of benevolence and righteousness so as to stop the operations of their armies, then all belonging to those armies will rejoice in the stopping *from war*, and find their pleasure in benevolence and righteousness. Ministers will serve their sovereign, cherishing the principles of benevolence and righteousness; sons will serve their fathers, and younger brothers will serve their elder brothers, in the same way:—and so, sovereign and minister, father and son, elder brother and younger, abandoning *the thought of* profit, will cherish the principles of benevolence and righteousness, and carry on all their intercourse upon them. But never has there been such a state *of society*, without the State where it prevailed rising to the royal sway. Why must you use that word "profit."'

師, 'the multitudes of the three armies;' see the Analects, VII. I. 士 embraces both 'officers and soldiers.' 6. 然而不王 (4th tone) 者未之有,—here the translation needs to be supplemented considerably. ·

相與曰非也書曰享多儀　子之齊不見儲子爲其爲　閒矣問曰夫子之任見季　見儲子屋廬子喜曰連得　見季子由平陸之齊不　受之而不報他日由鄒之齊不　於平陸儲子爲相以幣交　守以幣交受之而不報處　孟子居鄒季任爲任處　必曰利。

CHAP. V. 1. When Mencius was residing in Tsâu, the younger brother of the chief of Zǎn, who was guardian of Zǎn at the time, paid his respects to him by *a present of* silks, which Mencius received, not *going* to acknowledge it. When he was sojourning in P'ing-lû, Ch'û, who was prime minister of the State, sent him a similar present, which he received in the same way.

2. Subsequently, going from Tsâu to Zǎn, he visited the guardian; but when he went from P'ing-lû to *the capital of* Ch'î, he did not visit the minister Ch'û. The disciple Wû-lû was glad, and said, 'I have got an opportunity *to obtain some instruction.*'

3. He asked *accordingly*, 'Master, when you went to Zǎn, you visited the chief's brother; and when you went to Ch'î, you did not visit Ch'û. Was it not because he is *only* the minister?'

4. *Mencius* replied, 'No. It is said in the Book of History, "In presenting an offering to a superior, most depends on the demonstrations of respect. If those demonstrations are not equal

5. How Mencius regulated himself in differently acknowledging favours which he received. 1. 季任 and 季子 below, look much as if the former were the surname and name of the individual spoken of, yet Châo Ch'î's explanation of the terms, which is that followed in the translation, is no doubt correct. 任,—see chap. i. 以幣交,—see Bk. V. Pt. II. iv. 不報=不往報 平陸 —see Bk. II. Pt. II. vi. 1. 2. The two 之 here, and in the next paragraph = 往 之齊 'went to Ch'î,' i.e. to the capital of the State, as P'ing-lû was in Ch'î. 間,—*chien*, 3rd tone. 連 (Wû-lû's name) 得閒=連得其 間隙而間. 'I have got an opportunity' (literally, crevice), 'to ask.' 4. 書曰—see the Shû-ching, V. xii. 12, but in the classic the last clause 惟不役志于享 is not explanatory of the preceding, but is itself the first clause of a new sentence. See the Shû-

此乎孟子曰、居下位、不以
於上下、而去之仁者、固如
子在三卿之中名實未加
人也後名實者、自爲也、夫
淳于髡曰、先名實者、爲
平陸。
季子不得之鄒儲子得之
廬子悅或問之屋廬子曰、
志于享爲其不成享也屋
儀不及物曰不享惟不役

to the things offered, we say there is no offering, that is, there is no act of the will in presenting the offering."

5. '*This is* because the things so offered do not constitute an offering to a superior.'

6. Wû-lû was pleased, and when some one asked him *what Mencius meant*, he said, 'The younger of Zān could not go to Tsâu, but the minister Ch'û might have gone to P'ing-lû.'

CHAP. VI. 1. Shun-yü K'wän said, 'He who makes fame and meritorious services his first objects, acts with a regard to others. He who makes them only secondary objects, acts with a regard to himself. You, master, were ranked among the three chief ministers *of the State*, but before your fame and services had reached either to the prince or the people, you have left your place. Is this indeed the way of the benevolent?'

2. Mencius replied, 'There was Po-î;—he abode in an inferior

ching, *in loc.* 5. This is Mencius's explanation of the passage quoted. 6. The guardian of a State could not leave it to pay a visit in another. There was no reason, however, why Ch'û should not have paid his respects to Mencius in person.

6. How MENCIUS REPLIED TO THE INSINUATION OF SHUN-YÜ K'WÄN, CONDEMNING HIM FOR LEAVING OFFICE WITHOUT ACCOMPLISHING ANYTHING. 1. Shun-yü K'wän,—see Bk. IV Pt. I. xvii. That chapter and the notes should be read along with this. 名 and 實 are not here opposed to each other, as often,—'name' and 'reality.' The 'name' here is the fame of the 'reality.' 爲人, 'with a regard to others,' i.e. such a man's motive in public life is to benefit others.

自爲=爲已, 'with a regard to himself,' i.e. such a man's motive is to cultivate his own good and excellence. 上 refers to the prince; 下 refers to the people. 仁者,—it is assumed that the fact of Mencius's being among the high ministers of State took him out of the category of those who made themselves their aim in life, and the 仁者 therefore is a hit of the questioner. Throughout the chapter, 仁 has perhaps more the idea of perfect virtue, free from all selfishness, than of benevolence. 2. Po-î, &c., see Bk. V. Pt. II. i, with the other references there given. That I Yin went five

賢事不肖者伯夷也五就湯
五就桀者伊尹也不惡汙君、
不辭小官者柳下惠也三子
者、不同道其趨一也一者、何
也曰仁也君子亦仁而已矣、
何必同曰魯繆公之時公儀
子爲政子柳子思爲臣魯之
削也滋甚若是乎賢者之無
益於國也曰虞不用百里奚
而亡秦穆公用之而霸不用

situation, and would not, with his virtue, serve a degenerate prince. There was Î Yin ;—he five times went to T'ang, and five times went to Chieh. There was Hûi of Liû-hsiâ ;—he did not disdain to serve a vile prince, nor did he decline a small office. The courses pursued by those three worthies were different, but their aim was one. And what was their one aim? We must answer—"To be perfectly virtuous." And so it is simply after this that superior men strive. Why must they all *pursue* the same *course?*'

3. *K'wǎn* pursued, 'In the time of the duke Mû of Lû, the government was in the hands of Kung-î, while Tsze-liû and Tsze-sze were ministers. *And yet*, the dismemberment of Lû then increased exceedingly. Such was the case, a specimen how your men of virtue are of no advantage to a kingdom!'

4. *Mencius* said, '*The prince of* Yü did not use Pâi-lî Hsî, and thereby lost his State. The duke Mû of Chin used him, and became chief of all the princes. Ruin is the consequence of not employing

times to T'ang, and five times to Chieh is only mentioned here, however. He went to T'ang, it is said, in consequence of the pressing urgency of his solicitations, and then T'ang sent him to the tyrant to warn and advise him. Nothing could be farther at first from the wish of them both than to dethrone Chieh. 趨, 'to run,' used figuratively, 4th tone. 3. In this paragraph, K'wǎn advances in his condemnation of Mencius. At first he charged him with having left his office before he had

accomplished anything. Here he insinuates that though he had remained, he would not have served the State. Tsze-liû is the Hsieh Liû of Bk. II. Pt. II. xi; compare that chapter with this. Kung-î (named 休) was prime minister of Lû, a man of merit and principle. Mencius might have denied the fact alleged by K'wǎn, of the increased dismemberment of Lû under duke Mû. 4. Pâi-lî Hsî,—see Bk. V. Pt. I. ix. 用, 不用,—the 'using' means follow-

賢則亡削何可得與曰昔
者王豹處於淇而河西善
謳緜駒處於高唐而齊右
善歌華周杞梁之妻善哭
其夫而變國俗有諸內必
形諸外為其事而無其功
者髡未嘗覩之也是故無
賢者也有則髡必識之曰
孔子為魯司寇不用從而
祭燔肉不至不稅冕而行

men of virtue and talents;—how can it rest with dismemberment merely?'

5. *K'wăn* urged *again*, 'Formerly, when Wang P'âo dwelt on the Ch'î, the people on the west of the *Yellow* River all became skilful at singing in *his* abrupt manner. When Mien Ch'ü lived in Kâo-t'ang, the people in the parts of Ch'î on the west became skilful at singing in *his* prolonged manner. The wives of Hwa Châu and Ch'î Liang bewailed their husbands so skilfully, that they changed the manners of the State. When there is *the gift* within, it manifests itself without. I have never seen the man who could do the deeds *of a worthy*, and did not realize the work of one. Therefore there are *now* no men of talents and virtue. If there were, I should know them.'

6. *Mencius* answered, 'When Confucius was chief minister of Justice in Lû, the prince came not to follow *his counsels*. Soon after there was the *solstitial* sacrifice, and when a part of the flesh presented

ing the minister's counsels and plans. 削 | 郜而言, i.e. 'The Right of Ch'î denotes all about the western borders of the State.' Hwa (4th tone) Châu and Ch'î Liang were officers slain in battle, whose wives bewailed their loss in so pitiful a manner as to affect the whole State. Their cries, it is said, even rent the wall of the capital of Ch'î. See the 集證 and the 四書拓餘說, *in loc.*—The object of K'wăn is simply to insinuate that Mencius was a pretender, for that wherever ability was it was sure to come out. 6. Mencius shields himself behind Confucius, implying that he was beyond

何可得與 (and tone),—before 削 we must understand 求, 'If you seek for dismemberment merely, as the consequence,' &c. 5. The individuals named here all belonged to Ch'î, excepting the first, who was of Wei. 歌 is the general name for singing, and 謳 a particular style, said to be 短聲, 'short,' 'abrupt.' 齊右, it is said, 概指齊西

不知者以爲爲肉也其
知者以爲爲無禮也乃
孔子則欲以微罪行不
欲爲苟去君子之所爲
衆人固不識也。
孟子曰五霸者三王
之罪人也今之諸侯五
霸之罪人也今之大夫
今之諸侯之罪人也。天
子適諸侯曰巡狩諸侯

in sacrifice was not sent to him, he went away even without taking off his cap of ceremony. Those who did not know him supposed it was on account of the flesh. Those who knew him supposed that it was on account *of the neglect* of the usual ceremony. The fact was, that Confucius wanted to go away on occasion of some small offence, not wishing to do so without some apparent cause. All men cannot be expected to understand the conduct of a superior man.'

CHAP. VII. 1. Mencius said, 'The five chiefs of the princes were sinners against the three kings. The princes of the present day are sinners against the five chiefs. The Great officers of the present day are sinners against the princes.

2. 'The sovereign visited the princes, which was called "A tour of Inspection." The princes attended at the court of the sovereign,

the knowledge of K'wän.—The State of Ch'í, afraid of the influence of Confucius, who was acting as prime minister of Lŭ, sent to the duke a present of beautiful singing-girls and horses. The duke accepted them, and abandoned himself to dissipation. Confucius determined to leave the State, but not wishing to expose the bad conduct of his prince, looked about for some other reason which he might assign for going away, and found it in the matter mentioned. The 祭 is the 郊祭. 税 is used for 脱. 爲苟去, 'to do a disorderly going away.'

7. THE PROGRESS AND MANNER OF DEGENERACY FROM THE THREE KINGS TO THE FIVE CHIEFS OF THE PRINCES, AND FROM THE FIVE CHIEFS TO THE PRINCES AND OFFICERS OF MENCIUS'S TIME. 1. The 'three kings' are the founders of the three dynasties of Hsiá, Shang, and Châu. The 'five

chiefs of the princes' were the duke Hwan of Ch'í (B.C. 684-642), the duke Wăn of Tsin (636-629), the duke Mŭ of Ch'in (659-620), the duke Hsiang of Sung (651-636), and the king Chwang of Ch'ŭ (613-591). There are two enumerations of the 'five leading princes,' one called 三代之五伯, or chiefs of the three dynasties, and the other 春秋之五伯, or chiefs of the Ch'un-ch'iû. Only Hwan of Ch'í and Wăn of Tsin are common to the two. But Mencius is speaking only of those included in the second enumeration, and though there is some difference of opinion in regard to some of the individuals in it, the above list is probably that which he held. 'Sinners against,'—i.e. violating their principles and ways. 2. 天子…不給,—see Bk. I. Pt. II. iv. 5. 辟=闢; see

朝於天子曰述職春省耕而
補不足秋省斂而助不給入
其疆土地辟田野治養老尊
賢俊傑在位則有慶慶以地
入其疆土地荒蕪遺老失賢
掊克在位則有讓一不朝則
貶其爵再不朝則削其地三
不朝則六師移之是故天子
討而不伐諸侯伐而不討五
霸者摟諸侯以伐諸侯者也

which was called "Giving a report of office." It was a custom in the spring to examine the ploughing, and supply any deficiency *of seed;* and in autumn to examine the reaping, and assist where there was a deficiency of the crop. When *the sovereign* entered the boundaries of a State, if the *new* ground was being reclaimed, and the *old* fields well cultivated; if the old were nourished and the worthy honoured; and if men of distinguished talents were placed in office: then *the prince* was rewarded,—rewarded with an addition to his territory. *On the other hand,* if, on entering a State, the ground was found left wild or overrun with weeds; if the old were neglected and the worthy unhonoured; and if the offices were filled with hard tax-gatherers: then *the prince* was reprimanded. If *a prince* once omitted his attendance at court, he was punished by degradation of rank; if he did so a second time, he was deprived of a portion of his territory; if he did so a third time, the royal forces *were set in motion,* and he was removed *from his government.* Thus the sovereign commanded the punishment, but did not himself inflict it, while the princes inflicted the punishment, but did not command it. The five

Bk. I. Pt. I. vii. 16. 俊傑在位,—see | What follows belongs to 述職. 六師
Bk. II. Pt. I. v. 1. 慶=賞, 'to reward.' 掊 | (=軍),—see Analects, VII. x. 是故 = 'in
克=聚斂臣, 'impost-collecting minis- | harmony with these things,' all power being
ters;' literally, perhaps, 'grasping and able | lodged with the sovereign, and the princes
men.' Down to 讓 is explicatory of 巡狩. | being dependent on him. 討=治, 'to super-

故曰、五霸者三王之罪人
也。五霸桓公爲盛葵丘之
會諸侯束牲載書而不歃
血初命曰誅不孝無易樹
子無以妾爲妻再命曰尊
賢育才以彰有德三命曰
敬老慈幼無忘賓旅四命
曰士無世官官事無攝取
士必得無專殺大夫五命
曰無曲防無遏糴無有封

chiefs, *however*, dragged the princes to punish other princes, and hence I say that they were sinners against the three kings.

3. 'Of the five chiefs the most powerful was the duke Hwan. At the assembly of the princes in K'wei-ch'iû, he bound the victim and placed the writing upon it, but did not *slay it to* smear their mouths with the blood. The first injunction in their agreement was,—"Slay the unfilial; change not the son who has been appointed heir; exalt not a concubine to be the wife." The second was,—"Honour the worthy, and maintain the talented, to give distinction to the virtuous." The third was,—"Respect the old, and be kind to the young. Be not forgetful of strangers and travellers." The fourth was,—"Let not offices be hereditary, nor let officers be pluralists. In the selection of officers let the object be to get the proper men. Let not a *ruler* take it on himself to put to death a Great officer." The

intend, or order, punishment;' 伐 'to inflict the punishment.' 3. The duke Hwan nine times brought together an assembly of the princes, the chief gathering being at K'wei-ch'iû, B.C. 650. At these meetings, the usual custom was first to dig a square pit, over which the victim was slain. Its left ear was cut off, and its blood received in an ornamented vessel. The president then read the articles of agreement, with his face to the north, as in the presence of the spirits of the sun and moon, after which all the members of the meeting took the blood, and smeared the sides of their mouths with it. This was called 歃 (*shâ*) 血. The victim was then placed in the pit, the articles of agreement placed upon it, and the whole covered up. This was called 載書. See the 集證, *in loc.* On the occasion in the text, Hwan dispensed with some of those ceremonies. 命 was the term appropriated to the articles of agreement at such solemn assemblies, indicating that they were enjoined by the sovereign. 樹子, 'the son who has been tree-ed,' i.e. set up. 賓, 'guests,' officers from other States. 士無世官, 'officers no hereditary offices;' see Bk. I. Pt. II. 5. 3. 取士必得=必得其人. 無曲防, 'no crooked embankments.' 曲 has a

而不告、凡我同盟之人、
既盟之後、言歸于好。今之
諸侯皆犯此五禁、故曰今
之諸侯、五霸之罪人也。長
君之惡其罪小逢君之惡
其罪大今之大夫皆逢君
之惡故曰今之大夫今之
諸侯之罪人也。
魯欲使愼子爲將軍孟

fifth was,—"Follow no crooked policy in making embankments. Impose no restrictions on the sale of grain. Let there be no promotions without *first* announcing them *to the sovereign.*" It was *then* said, "All we who have united in this agreement shall hereafter maintain amicable relations." The princes of the present day all violate these five prohibitions, and therefore I say that the princes of the present day are sinners against the five chiefs.

4. 'The crime of him who connives at, and aids, the wickedness of his prince is small, but the crime of him who anticipates and excites that wickedness is great. The officers of the present day all go to meet their sovereigns' *wickedness,* and therefore I say that the Great officers of the present day are sinners against the princes.'

CHAP. VIII. 1. *The prince of* Lû wanted to make the minister Shăn commander of his army.

2. Mencius said, 'To employ an uninstructed people *in war* may

moral application. No embankments must be made selfishly to take the water from others, or to inundate them. 無遏糴, 'do not repress the sale of grain,' i.e. to other States in famine or distress. 封, 'appointments,' to territory or to office. 4. 長君之惡 'to lengthen the wickedness of the ruler,' i.e. to connive at and to aid it. 逢君之惡, 'to meet the wickedness of the ruler,' i.e. to anticipate and excite it.

8. MENCIUS'S OPPOSITION TO THE WARLIKE AMBITION OF THE PRINCE OF LÔ AND HIS MINISTER SHĂN KÚ-LÍ. 1. At this time Lû wanted to take advantage of difficulties in Ch'l, and get possession of Nan-yang. That was the name of the region on the south of mount T'âi, which had originally belonged to Lû. On the north of the mountain was the territory of Ch'l. Between the two States there had been frequent struggles for the district, which the duke P'ing of Lû (平公) now hoped to recover. Shăn, below, calls himself Kú-lí, but some say that that was the name of a Mohist under whom he had studied. His proper name was Tâo (到). He was a native of 趙, and not of Lû, but having a reputation for military skill, the duke of Lû wished to employ his services.

里太公之封於齊也亦爲方百
方百里也地非不足而儉於百
宗廟之典籍周公之封於魯爲
之地方百里不百里不足以守
里不千里不足以待諸侯諸侯
也曰吾明告子天子之地方千
勃然不悅曰此則滑釐所不識
勝齊遂有南陽然且不可愼子
殃民者不容於堯舜之世一戰
子曰不教民而用之謂之殃民

be said to be destroying the people. A destroyer of the people would not have been tolerated in the times of Yâo and Shun.

3. 'Though by a single battle you should subdue Ch'î, and get possession of Nan-yang, the thing ought not to be done.'

4. Shăn changed countenance, and said in displeasure, 'This is what I, Kû-lî, do not understand.'

5. *Mencius* said, 'I will lay the case plainly before you. The territory appropriated to the sovereign is 1,000 *lî* square. Without a thousand *lî*, he would not have sufficient for his entertainment of the princes. The territory appropriated to a Hâu is 100 *lî* square. Without 100 *lî*, he would not have sufficient wherewith to observe the statutes kept in his ancestral temple.

6. 'When Châu-kung was invested with *the principality of* Lû, it was a hundred *lî* square. The territory was indeed enough, but it was not more than 100 *lî*. When T'âi-kung was invested with the principality of Ch'î, it was 100 *lî* square. The territory was indeed enough, but it was not more than 100 *lî*.

將軍, now the common term for general, appears to have come into vogue about Mencius's time. In the text it = 'commander-in-chief.' 2. Compare Analects, XIII. xxx.—We may infer from this paragraph, that Shăn had himself been the adviser of the projected enterprise.

5 宗廟之典籍, 'the statute-records of the ancestral temple.' Those records prescribed everything to be observed in the public sacrifices, interviews with other princes, &c., and were kept in the temple. 6. Compare

良臣古之所謂民賊也君不鄉
爲君辟土地充府庫今之所謂
孟子曰今之事君者曰我能
仁而已。
事君也務引其君以當道志於
爲況於殺人以求之乎君子之
徒取諸彼以與此然且仁者不
者作則魯在所損乎在所益乎
今魯方百里者五子以爲有王
里也地非不足也而儉於百里。

7. 'Now Lû is five times 100 *lî* square. If a *true* royal ruler were to arise, whether do you think that Lû would be diminished or increased by him?

8. 'If it were merely taking the place from the one *State* to give it to the other, a benevolent man would not do it;—how much less will he do so, when the end is to be sought by the slaughter of men!

9. 'The way in which a superior man serves his prince contemplates simply the leading him in the right path, and directing his mind to benevolence.'

CHAP. IX. 1. Mencius said, 'Those who now-a-days serve their sovereigns say, "We can for our sovereign enlarge the limits of the cultivated ground, and fill his treasuries and arsenals." Such persons are now-a-days called "Good ministers," but anciently they were called "Robbers of the people." If a sovereign follows not

Analects, VI. xxii. 儉, 'sparingly,' = only. | AND POWER. 1. 辟 (=闢) 土地,—it is
8. 徒, 'merely,' i. e. if there were no struggle | to be understood that this was to be done at
andino slaughter in the matter. 9. 當道 | the expense of the people, taking their commons
here is different from the same phrase, 富路, | from them, and making them labour. Other-
in Bk. II. Pt. I. i. 1. | wise, it does not seem objectionable.—Châo

9. HOW THE MINISTERS OF MENCIUS'S TIME PAN- | Ch'î, however, gives the phrase another mean-
DERED TO THEIR SOVEREIGNS' THIRST FOR WEALTH | ing, making it=侵小國, 'appropriate
 | small States,' but this is contrary to analogous
 | passages, and confounds this paragraph with

一、何如孟子曰、子之道、貉
白圭曰、吾欲二十而取
一朝居也。
今之俗雖與之天下、不能
是輔桀也。由今之道、無變
不志於仁、而求爲之强戰、
之所謂民賊也。君不鄉道、
戰必克。今之所謂良臣、古
富桀也。我能爲君約與國、
道不志於仁而求富之、是

the right way, nor has his mind bent on benevolence, to seek to enrich him is to enrich a Chieh.

2. 'Or they will say, "We can for our sovereign form alliances with other States, so that our battles must be successful." Such persons are now-a-days called "Good ministers," but anciently they were called "Robbers of the people." If a sovereign follows not the right way, nor has his mind directed to benevolence, to seek to enrich him is to enrich a Chieh.

3. 'Although a prince, pursuing the path of the present day, and not changing its practices, were to have the throne given to him, he could not retain it for a single morning.'

CHAP. X. 1. Pâi Kwei said, 'I want to take a twentieth of the produce only as the tax. What do you think of it?'

2. Mencius said, 'Your way would be that of the Mo.

the next; compare Bk. IV. Pt. I. xiv. 2. 約 與 國, 'ally with other States.' Here Châo Ch'î differs again, making 約=期 'to determine beforehand,' 'undertake,' and joining 與 國 戰, 'undertake in fighting with hostile countries to conquer.' This also is an inferior construction. 3. 朝 居=朝 居 其 位, 'occupy the position for a morning.'

10. AN ORDERED STATE CAN ONLY SUBSIST WITH A PROPER SYSTEM OF TAXATION, AND THAT ORIGINATING WITH YÂO AND SHUN IS THE PROPER ONE FOR CHINA. 1. Pâi Kwei, styled Tan (see next chapter), was a man of Châu, ascetic in his own habits, and fond of innovations. Hence the suggestion in this chapter.—So, Châo Ch'î, and Chû Hsî has followed him. The author of the 四 書 拓 餘 說, however, contends that the Pâi Kwei described as above on the authority of the 'Historical Records,' 列 傳, lxix, was not the same here introduced. See that Work, in loc. 2. 貉 or 貊 was a common name for the barbarous tribes on the north. They were a pastoral people, and the climate of their country was cold. No doubt their civilization was inferior to that of

道也萬室之國、一人陶、則可
乎、曰、不可、器不足用也。曰、夫
貉五穀不生、惟黍生之、無城
郭宮室宗廟祭祀之禮、無諸
侯幣帛饔飧、無百官有司、故
二十取一而足也、今居中國、
去人倫無君子、如之何其可
也。陶以寡且不可以爲國況
無君子乎、欲輕之於堯舜之
道者大貉小貉也、欲重之於

3. 'In a country of ten thousand families, would it do to have *only* one potter?' *Kwei* replied, 'No. The vessels would not be enough to use.'

4. *Mencius* went on, 'In Mo *all* the five kinds of grain are not grown; it only produces the millet. There are no fortified cities, no edifices, no ancestral temples, no ceremonies of sacrifice; there are no princes requiring presents and entertainments; there is no system of officers with their various subordinates. On these accounts a tax of one-twentieth of the produce is sufficient *there*.

5. 'But now it is the Middle Kingdom that we live in. To banish the relationships of men, and have no superior men;—how can such a state of things be thought of?

6. 'With but few potters a kingdom cannot subsist;—how much less can it subsist without men of a higher rank than others?

7. 'If we wish to make the taxation lighter than the system of Yâo and Shun, we shall just have a great Mo and a small Mo.

China, but Mencius's account of them must be taken with allowance. 4. 城郭．—see Bk. II. Pt. II. i. 2. 宮室 go together as a general designation of edifices, called 宮, as 'four-walled and roofed,' and 室 (寶) as 'fur-nished.' So 祭祀 go together as synonymous, and also 幣帛, 'pieces of silk, given as presents.' 饔, 'the morning meal;' 飧, 'the evening meal;' together = 'entertainments.' 5, 6. 君子,—referring to the 百官 有 司. 7. The meaning is, that, under such systems, China would become in the one case a copy of the Mo, and in the other of its state under the tyrant Chieh.

堯舜之道者、大桀小桀也。

白圭曰、丹之治水也愈於

禹、孟子曰、子過矣、禹之治水、

水之道也、是故禹以四海為

壑、今吾子以鄰國為壑。水逆

行、謂之洚水、洚水者、洪水也、

仁人之所惡也、吾子過矣。

孟子曰、君子不亮惡乎執。

魯欲使樂正子為政、孟子

曰、吾聞之、喜而不寐。公孫

丑

If we wish to make it heavier, we shall just have the great Chieh and the small Chieh.'

CHAP. XI. 1. Pâi Kwei said, 'My management of the waters is superior to that of Yü.'

2. Mencius replied, 'You are wrong, Sir. Yü's regulation of the waters was according to the laws of water.

3. 'He therefore made the four seas their receptacle, while you make the neighbouring States their receptacle.

4. 'Water flowing out of its channels is called an inundation. Inundating waters are a vast *waste* of water, and what a benevolent man detests. You are wrong, my good Sir.'

CHAP. XII. Mencius said, 'If a scholar have not faith, how shall he take a firm hold *of things?*'

CHAP. XIII. 1. *The prince of* Lû wanting to commit the administration of his government to the disciple Yo-chăng, Mencius said, 'When I heard of it, I was so glad that I could not sleep.'

2. Kung-sun Ch'âu asked, 'Is Yo-chăng a man of vigour?' and

11. PÂI KWEI'S PRESUMPTUOUS IDEA THAT HE COULD REGULATE THE WATERS BETTER THAN YÜ DID. 1. There had been some partial inundations, where the services of Pâi Kwei were called in, and he had reduced them by turning the waters into other States, saving one at the expense of injuring others. 2. 水之道= 順 水 之 性. 4. See Bk. III. Pt. II.

ix. 3, but 洪 水 has there a particular application.

12. FAITH IN PRINCIPLES NECESSARY TO FIRMNESS IN ACTION. 亮 used as 諒. Chû Hsî explains it by 信.

13. OF WHAT IMPORTANCE TO A MINISTER—TO GOVERNMENT—IT IS TO LOVE WHAT IS GOOD. 1. 為 政, 'to administer the government,' as in

曰樂正子強乎。曰否。有知慮
乎。曰否。多聞識乎。曰否。然則
奚爲喜而不寐。曰其爲人也
好善。好善足乎。曰好善優於
天下。而況魯國乎。夫苟好善
則四海之內。皆將輕千里而
來告之以善。夫苟不好善。則
人將曰訑訑予既已知之矣
訑訑之聲音顏色距人於千
里之外。士止於千里之外。則

was answered, 'No.' 'Is he wise in council?' 'No.' 'Is he possessed of much information?' 'No.'

3. 'What then made you so glad that you could not sleep?'

4. 'He is a man who loves what is good.'

5. 'Is the love of what is good sufficient?'

6. 'The love of what is good is more than a sufficient qualification for the government of the kingdom;—how much more is it so for the State of Lû!

7. 'If *a minister* love what is good, all within the four seas will count 1,000 *lî* but a small distance, and will come and lay their good thoughts before him.

8. 'If he do not love what is good, men will say, "How self-conceited he looks? *He is saying to himself*, I know it." The language and looks of that self-conceit will keep men off at a distance of 1,000 *lî*. When good men stop 1,000 *lî* off, calumniators, flatterers, and sycophants will make their appearance. When a minister

chap. vi. 3. 2. 有知慮乎。一知 is in the 3rd tone; 'has he wisdom and deliberation?'—The three gifts mentioned here were those considered most important to government in that age, and Kung-sun Ch'âu knowing Yo-chăng to be deficient in them, put his questions accordingly. 4. On this paragraph it is said in the 日講:—'In the administration of government, the most excellent quality is with- out prejudice and dispassionately (虛中) to receive what is good. Now in regard to all good words and good actions, Yo-chăng in his heart sincerely loved them.' 5, 6. 足 is what is simply sufficient. 優 is what is sufficient and more. 8. 訑訑, as defined by Chû Hsî, is—自足其智。不嗜善言之

以雖衰行三則圖得諂讒
有未言其迎仕陳乎諂詔
禮行弗言之孟子　面面
則其行也致子曰　諛諛
就言也則敬曰古　之之
之也則就以所之　人人
禮迎去之有就君　居至
貌之之禮禮三子　國矣
衰致其貌言所何　欲與
則敬次未將去如　治讒
　　　　　　　　可

lives among calumniators, flatterers, and sycophants, though he may wish the State to be well governed, is it possible for it to be so?'

CHAP. XIV. 1. The disciple Ch'ăn said, 'What were the principles on which superior men of old took office?' Mencius replied, 'There were three cases in which they accepted office, and three in which they left it.

2. 'If received with the utmost respect and all polite observances, and they could say *to themselves* that the prince would carry their words into practice, then they took office with him. *Afterwards,* although there might be no remission in the polite demeanour of the prince, if their words were not carried into practice, they would leave him.

3. 'The second case was that in which, though *the prince could not be expected* at once to carry their words into practice, yet being received by him with the utmost respect, they took office with him. But afterwards, if there was a remission in his polite demeanour, they would leave him.

貌 'the appearance of being satisfied with one's own knowledge, and having no relish for good words.' 士＝善人.

14. GROUNDS OF TAKING AND LEAVING OFFICE. Compare Bk. V. Pt. II. iv. 7. The three cases mentioned here are respectively the 行可 之仕, the 際可, and the 公養, of that place. 1. This Ch'ăn is the Ch'ăn Tsin,

Bk. II. Pt. II. iii. 2. 迎 is simply＝接待, not 'to go out to meet.' 3. 雖未行其言 is to be understood as thought in the scholar's mind, corresponding to 言將行其言 in the preceding paragraph. In the 日講 indeed, the 言 there is made to be the language of the ruler, but see the gloss of the 備旨.

去之其下朝不食夕不食

饑餓不能出門戸君聞之

曰吾大者不能行其道又

不能從其言也使饑餓於

我土地吾恥之周之亦可

受也免死而已矣。

孟子曰舜發於畎畝之

中傅說舉於版築之間膠

鬲舉於魚鹽之中管夷吾

舉於士孫叔敖舉於海百

4. 'The last case was that of *the superior man* who had nothing to eat, either morning or evening, and was so famished that he could not move out of his door. If the prince, on hearing of his state, said, "I must fail in the great point,—that of carrying his doctrines into practice, neither am I able to follow his words, but I am ashamed to allow him to die of want in my country;" the assistance offered in such a case might be received, but not beyond what was sufficient to avert death.'

CHAP. XV. 1. Mencius said, 'Shun rose from among the channelled fields. Fû Yüeh was called to office from the midst of his building frames; Chiâo-ko from his fish and salt; Kwan Î-wû from the hands of his gaoler; Sun-shû Âo from *his hiding by* the sea-shore; and Pâi-li Hsî from the market-place.

in loc. 4. The assistance is in the shape of employment offered. If not, then 不可受 would not be a case of 就仕.

15. TRIALS AND HARDSHIPS THE WAY IN WHICH HEAVEN PREPARES MEN FOR GREAT SERVICES. 1. With Shun, Kwan Î-wû, and Pâi-li Hsî, the student must be familiar. Fû Yüeh,—see the Shû-ching, Pt. IV. Bk. VII, where it is related that the sovereign Kâo Tsung having 'dreamt that God gave him a good assistant,' caused a picture of the man he had seen in his dream to be made, and 'search made for him through the kingdom, when he was found dwelling in the wilderness of Fû-yen (傅巖之野). In the 'Historical Records,' it is said the surname was given in the dream as 傅, and the

name as 悅. Chiâo Ko is mentioned in Bk. II. Pt. I. i. 8, where it is said in the notes that his worth when living in retirement, was discovered by king Wăn. He was then selling fish and salt, and on Wăn's recommendation was raised to office by the last sovereign of Yin, to whose fortunes he continued faithful. Sun-shû Âo was prime minister to Chwang of Ch'û, the last of the five chiefs of the princes. So much is beyond dispute, but the circumstances of his elevation, and the family to which he belonged, are uncertain. See the 四書拓 餘說 *in loc.* 版築, 'planks and building.' Many of the houses in China are built of earth and mortar beaten together within a moveable frame, in which the walls are formed.

者家發心能以乏志任里
國拂於衡人動其於奚
恆士聲於恆心身是舉
亡出而慮過忍行人於
然則後而然性拂也市
後無喻後後曾亂必故
知敵入作能益其先天
生國則徵改其所苦將
於外無於困所為其降
憂患法色於不所心大

2. 'Thus, when Heaven is about to confer a great office on any man, it first exercises his mind with suffering, and his sinews and bones with toil. It exposes his body to hunger, and subjects him to extreme poverty. It confounds his undertakings. By all these methods it stimulates his mind, hardens his nature, and supplies his incompetencies.

3. 'Men for the most part err, and are afterwards able to reform. They are distressed in mind and perplexed in their thoughts, and then they arise to vigorous reformation. When things have been evidenced in men's looks, and set forth in their words, then they understand them.

4. 'If a prince have not about his court families attached to the laws and worthy counsellors, and if abroad there are not hostile States or other external calamities, his kingdom will generally come to ruin.

5. 'From these things we see how life springs from sorrow and calamity, and death from ease and pleasure.'

舉士,—士 is the officer who was in charge of him. 2. 餓其體膚, 'hungers his members and skin.' 空乏其身, 'empties his person.' 行佛, 云云, 'as to his doings, confounds what he is doing.' 行 is taken as 行事, and 為 as 心所謀為 曾,—used for 增. 3. The same thing holds true of ordinary men. They are improved by difficulties. 衡,—used for 橫. 徵於 色, 云云,—the meaning is, that, though most men are not quick of apprehension, yet when things are clearly before them, they can lay hold of them. 4. The same thing is true of a State. 法家, 'law families,' i.e. old families to whom the laws of the State are familiar and dear. 拂 is used for 弼 Such families and officers will stimulate the prince's mind by their lessons and remonstrances, and

矣。誨之而已
者是亦教
之教誨也
矣予不屑
教亦多術
孟子曰、
安樂也。
患而死於

CHAP. XVI. Mencius said, 'There are many arts in teaching. I refuse, as inconsistent with my character, to teach a man, but I am only thereby still teaching him.'

foreign danger will rouse him to carefulness and exertion.

16. How a refusal to teach may be teaching. The 亦 in 亦教 is not without its force, but we can hardly express it in a translation.

子不屑之教誨=子不屑教誨之. The 者 carries us on to the next clause for an explanation of what has been said.

BOOK VII.

TSIN SIN. PART I.

矣。則知其心曰、盡孟子
存知其性者、其章句上盡心
其天性也知其

CHAPTER I.   I. Mencius said, 'He who has exhausted all his mental constitution knows his nature. Knowing his nature, he knows Heaven.

TITLE OF THIS BOOK.—Like the previous Books, this is named from the commencing words— 盡心 'The exhausting of all the mental constitution.' It contains many more chapters than any of them, being, for the most part, brief enigmatical sentences, conveying Mencius's views of human nature. It is more abstruse also, and the student will have much difficulty in satisfying himself that he has really hit the exact meaning of the philosopher. The author of the 四書味根錄 says:—'This Book was made by Mencius in his old age. Its style is terse, and its meaning deep, and we cannot discover an order of subjects in its chapters. He had completed the previous six Books, and this grew up under his pencil, as his mind was

affected, and he was prompted to give expression to his thoughts. The first chapter may be regarded, however, as a compendium of the whole.'

1. By the study of ourselves we come to the knowledge of Heaven, and Heaven is served by our obeying our nature. 1. 盡其心 is, I conceive, to make one's self acquainted with all his mind, to arrest his consciousness, and ascertain what he is. This of course gives a man the knowledge of his nature, and as he is the creature of Heaven, its attributes must be corresponding. It is much to be wished that instead of the term Heaven, vague and indefinite, Mencius had simply said 'God.' I can get no other meaning from this paragraph. Chû Hsî, however, and all his school say that there

順受其正。　莫非命也。　三 孟子曰、　立 命也。　俟之所以　貳修身以　也。夭壽不　所以事天　心養其性、

2. ‘To preserve one’s mental constitution, and nourish one’s nature, is the way to serve Heaven.

3. ‘When neither a premature death nor long life causes a man any double-mindedness, but he waits in the cultivation of his personal character *for whatever issue;*—this is the way in which he establishes his *Heaven*-ordained being.’

CHAP. II. 1. Mencius said, ‘There is an appointment for everything. A man should receive submissively what may be correctly ascribed thereto.

is no work or labour in 盡 其 心; that it is the 知 至 of the Confucian chapter in the ‘Superior Learning,’ according to their view of it; that all the labour is in 知 其 性, which is the 物 格 of that chapter. If this be correct, we should translate:—‘He who completely develops his mental constitution, has known (come to know) his nature,’ but I cannot construe the words so. 2. The ‘preservation’ is the holding fast what we have from Heaven, and the ‘nourishing’ is the acting in harmony therewith, so that the ‘serving Heaven’ is just being and doing what It has intimated in our constitution to be Its will concerning us. 3. 命 is our nature, according to the opening words of the *Chung Yung*,—天命之謂性. 立 is to be taken as an active verb. 不 貳 不 疑, ‘causes no doubts,’ i.e. no doubts as to what is to be done. 俟之—之 referring to 夭 壽—It may be well to give the views of *Châo Ch‘î* on this chapter. On the first paragraph he says:—‘To the nature there belong the principles of benevolence, righteousness, propriety, and knowledge. The mind is designed to regulate them (心以制之); and having the distinction of being correct, a man can put forth all his mind to think of doing good, and then he may be said to know his nature. When he knows his nature, he knows that the way of Heaven considers what is good to be excellent.’ On the second paragraph he says:—‘When one is able to preserve his mind, and to nourish his correct nature, he may be called a man of perfect virtue (仁人) The way of Heaven loves life, and the perfect

man also loves life. The way of Heaven is without partiality, and only approves of the virtuous. Thus the acting *of the perfect man* agrees with Heaven, and hence it is said,—this is the way by which he serves Heaven.’ On the third paragraph he says:—‘The perfect man in his conduct is guided by one law. Although he sees that some who have gone before him have been short-lived, and some long-lived, he never has two minds, or changes his way. Let life be short as that of Yen Yüan, or long as that of the duke of Shâo, he refers either case equally to the appointment of Heaven, and cultivates and rectifies his own person to wait for that. It is in this way he establishes the root *of Heaven’s appointments* (此所以立命之本)’ These explanations do not throw light upon the text, but they show how that may be treated independently of the school of Chû Hsî. And the equal unsatisfactoriness of his interpretation may well lead the student—the foreign student especially—to put forth his strength on the study of the text more than on the commentaries.

2. MAN’S DUTY AS AFFECTED BY THE DECREES OR APPOINTMENTS OF HEAVEN. WHAT MAY BE CORRECTLY ASCRIBED THERETO AND WHAT NOT. Chû Hsî says this is a continuation of the last chapter, developing the meaning of the last paragraph. There is a connexion between the chapters, but 命 is here taken more widely, as extending not only to man’s nature, but all the events that befall him. 1. 正命, ‘the correct appointment,’ i.e. that which is directly the will of Heaven. No consequence flowing from evil or careless conduct is to be understood as being so. Chû Hsî’s definition is—莫之致而至者乃為正命, ‘that which comes without being brought on is the correct appointment.’—Châo Ch‘î says

是故知命者不立乎巖
牆之下盡其道而死者非
正命也桎梏死者非正
命也。
孟子曰求則得之舍
則失之是求有益於得
也求在我者也求之有
道得之有命是求無益
於得也求在外者也。
孟子曰萬物皆備於

2. 'Therefore, he who has the true idea of what is *Heaven's* appointment will not stand beneath a precipitous wall.

3. 'Death sustained in the discharge of one's duties may correctly be ascribed to the appointment *of Heaven*.

4. 'Death under handcuffs and fetters cannot correctly be so ascribed.'

CHAP. III. 1. Mencius said, 'When we get by our seeking and lose by our neglecting;—in that case seeking is of use to getting, and the things sought for are those which are in ourselves.

2. 'When the seeking is according to the proper course, and the getting is *only* as appointed;—in that case the seeking is of no use to getting, and the things sought are without ourselves.'

CHAP. IV. 1. Mencius said, 'All things are already complete in us.

there are three ways of speaking about the appointments or decrees of Heaven. Doing good and getting good is called 受命, 'receiving what is appointed.' Doing good and getting evil is called 遭命, 'encountering what is appointed.' Doing evil and getting evil is called 隨命, 'following after what is appointed.' It is only the first of these cases that is spoken of in the text. It must be borne in mind, however, that by 命 here Châo understands death, and that only, and we should acquiesce in this, if there did not seem to be a connexion between this chapter and the preceding. 2. 知命者,—he who knows, or has the true notion of, &c. 巖, 'precipitous'. and likely to fall. 4. The fetters are understood to

be those of an evil doer. 桎 are fetters for the hands, and 梏 those for the feet.

3. VIRTUE IS SURE TO BE GAINED BY SEEKING IT, BUT RICHES AND OTHER EXTERNAL THINGS NOT. This general sentiment is correct, but the exact truth is sacrificed to the point of the antithesis, when it is said in the second case that seeking is of no use to getting. The things 'in ourselves' are benevolence, righteousness, propriety, and knowledge, the endowments proper of our nature. The things 'without ourselves' are riches and dignities. The 'proper course' to seek these is that ascribed to Confucius, 'advancing according to propriety, and retiring according to righteousness,' but yet they are not at our command and control.

4. MAN IS FITTED FOR, AND HAPPY IN, DOING GOOD, AND MAY PERFECT HIMSELF THEREIN. 1. This paragraph is mystical. The all things are taken

我矣反身而誠樂莫大
焉彊恕而行求仁莫近
焉。
孟子曰行之而不著
焉習矣而不察焉終身
由之而不知其道者衆
也。
孟子曰人不可以無
恥無恥之恥無恥矣。
孟子曰恥之於人大

2. 'There is no greater delight than to be conscious of sincerity on self-examination.

3. 'If one acts with a vigorous effort at the law of reciprocity, when he seeks for *the realization of* perfect virtue, nothing can be closer than his approximation to it.'

CHAP. V. Mencius said, 'To act without understanding, and to do so habitually without examination, pursuing the proper path all the life without knowing its nature;—this is the way of multitudes.'

CHAP. VI. Mencius said, 'A man may not be without shame. When one is ashamed of having been without shame, he will *afterwards* not have *occasion* to be ashamed.'

CHAP. VII. 1. Mencius said, 'The sense of shame is to a man of great importance.

as the *principles* of all things, which all things moreover are chiefly the relations of society. When we extend them farther, we get embarrassed. 2. The 誠 here is that so largely treated of in the Chung Yung. 3. 恕 is the judging of others by ourselves, and acting accordingly. Compare the Doctrine of the Mean, xiii. 3.

5. How MANY ACT WITHOUT THOUGHT. Compare the Analects, VIII. ix. 行之、由之、—之 is to be understood of 道, but 其道 = 'its nature,' its propriety, which is the object of 著, and its grounds, which is the object of 察. Chû Hsî defines 著 as 知之明, 'knowing clearly,' and 察 as 識之精,

'knowing minutely and exactly.' 'There is much activity,' says 備旨, 'in the two verbs.' This use of 著 is not common.

6. THE VALUE OF THE FEELING OF SHAME. The last 恥 = shameful conduct.

7. THE SAME SUBJECT. The former chapter, it is said, was by way of exhortation (以勸); this is by way of warning (以戒). The second paragraph is aimed at the wandering scholars of Mencius's time, who were full of plots and schemes to unite and disunite the various princes. 機 'springs of motion,' 'machinery.' The third paragraph may also be translated, 'If a man be not ashamed at his being not like other men, in what will he be like them?'

G g 2

矣。爲機變之巧者、無所用恥
焉。不恥不若人、何若人有。
孟子曰、古之賢王、好善而
忘勢古之賢士、何獨不然樂
其道而忘人之勢故王公不
致敬盡禮、則不得亟見之見
且猶不得亟而況得而臣之
乎。
孟子謂宋句踐曰、子好遊

2. 'Those who form contrivances and versatile schemes distinguished for their artfulness, do not allow their sense of shame to come into action.

3. 'When one differs from other men in not having this sense of shame, what will he have in common with them?'

CHAP. VIII. Mencius said, 'The able and virtuous monarchs of antiquity loved virtue and forgot their power. And shall an exception be made of the able and virtuous scholars of antiquity, that they did not do the same? They delighted in their own principles, and were oblivious of the power of princes. Therefore, if kings and dukes did not show the utmost respect, and observe all forms of ceremony, they were not permitted to come frequently and visit them. If they thus found it not in their power to pay them frequent visits, how much less could they get to employ them as ministers?'

CHAP. IX. 1. Mencius said to Sung Kâu-ch'ien, 'Are you fond, Sir, of travelling *to the different courts?* I will tell you about such travelling.

8. How THE ANCIENT SCHOLARS MAINTAINED THE DIGNITY OF THEIR CHARACTER AND PRINCIPLES. 善 is not virtue in the abstract, but the good which they saw in others, in the scholars namely. 勢 is their own 'power.' As applied to the scholars, however, these things have to be reversed. They loved their own virtue (其道), and forgot the power of men, i.e. of the princes.

9. How A PROFESSIONAL ADVISER OF THE PRINCES MIGHT BE ALWAYS PERFECTLY SATISFIED. THE EXAMPLE OF ANTIQUITY. 1. Some make the party spoken to in this chapter to be Kâu (句 read as 鉤)-ch'ien of Sung. Nothing is known

身達則兼善天下。

志修身見於世窮則獨善其

古之人得志澤加於民不得

焉達不離道故民不失望焉。

不離道窮不失義故士得已

以囂囂矣故士窮不失義故士得達

人不知亦囂囂曰何如斯可

乎吾語子遊人知之亦囂囂

以囂囂矣曰尊德樂義則可

2. 'If a prince acknowledge you and follow your counsels, be perfectly satisfied. If no one do so, be the same.'

3. *Kâu-ch'ien* said, 'What is to be done to secure this perfect satisfaction?' Mencius replied, 'Honour virtue and delight in righteousness, and so you may *always* be perfectly satisfied.

4. 'Therefore, a scholar, though poor, does not let go *his* righteousness; though prosperous, he does not leave *his own* path.

5. 'Poor and not letting righteousness go;—it is thus that the scholar holds possession of himself. Prosperous and not leaving the *proper* path;—it is thus that the expectations of the people from him are not disappointed.

6. 'When the men of antiquity realized their wishes, benefits were conferred by them on the people. If they did not realize their wishes, they cultivated their personal character, and became illustrious in the world. If poor, they attended to their own virtue in solitude; if advanced to dignity, they made the whole kingdom virtuous as well.'

of him, but that he was one of the adventurers, who travelled about tendering their advice to the different princes. 2. To translate 知之 as I have done here, can hardly be called a paraphrase. Chû Hsî, after Châo Ch'î, explains 囂囂 as 'the appearance of self-possession and freedom from desire.' 'Perfectly satisfied,' conveys the idea of the phrase. 3. It is to be understood that the 'virtue' is that which the scholar has in himself, and the 'righteousness' is the course which he pursues. 4. 窮-人 不知之; 達 is the reverse. 5. 'Holds possession of himself,'—i.e. has what he chiefly loves and seeks. 6. 古之人-人-士.—Chû Hsî observes:—'This chapter shows how the scholar, attaching weight to what is internal, and holding what is external light, will approve himself good in all places and circumstances.'

孟子曰待文王而後
興者凡民也若夫豪傑
之士雖無文王猶興。

孟子曰附之以韓魏
之家如其自視欿然則
過人遠矣。

孟子曰以佚道使民
雖勞不怨以生道殺民
雖死不怨殺者。

孟子曰霸者之民驩

CHAP. X. Mencius said, 'The mass of men wait for a king Wăn, and then they will receive a rousing impulse. Scholars distinguished *from the mass*, without a king Wăn, rouse themselves.'

CHAP. XI. Mencius said, 'Add to a man the families of Han and Wei. If he then look upon himself without being elated, he is far beyond *the mass of* men.'

CHAP. XII. Mencius said, 'Let the people be employed in the way which is intended to secure their ease, and though they be toiled, they will not murmur. Let them be put to death in the way which is intended to preserve their lives, and though they die, they will not murmur at him who puts them to death.'

CHAP. XIII. 1. Mencius said, 'Under a chief, leading all the princes, the people look brisk and cheerful. Under a true sovereign, they have an air of deep contentment.

10. How PEOPLE SHOULD GET THEIR INSPIRATION TO GOOD IN THEMSELVES. 凡民, 'all the people,' i.e. ordinary people. 豪傑-俊傑, in Bk. II. Pt. I. v. 1. When a distinction is made between the characters, he who in wisdom is the first of 10,000 men, is called 英; the first of 1,000 is called 俊; the first of 100 is called 豪; the first of 10 is called 傑.

11. NOT TO BE ELATED BY RICHES IS A PROOF OF SUPERIORITY. Han and Wei,—see Bk. I. Pt. I. i. 1, notes; 'The families of Han and Wei,'—i.e. the wealth and power of those families. 附 used for 益, 'to increase,' indicates the externality of the additions. 欿然 is defined.

一不自滿足意, 'not being full of and satisfied with one's self.'

12. WHEN A RULER'S AIM IS EVIDENTLY THE PEOPLE'S GOOD, THEY WILL NOT MURMUR AT HIS HARSHEST MEASURES. The first part is explained rightly of toils in agriculture, road-making, bridge-making, &c., and the second of the administration of justice, where I should prefer to think that Mencius had the idea of a just war before him; compare Analects, XX. ii. 2. 佚道, 'a way of ease;' 生道, 'a way of life.'

13. THE DIFFERENT INFLUENCE EXERCISED BY A CHIEF AMONG THE PRINCES, AND BY A TRUE SOVEREIGN. 1. 虞 is explained in the dictionary, with reference to this passage, by 樂. It is the same as 娛 and 驩. 虞-歡娛. 皞皞 is 廣大自得之貌.

虞如也、王者之民皡皡
如也、殺之而不怨、利之
而不庸、民日遷善而不
知爲之者、夫君子所過
者化、所存者神、上下與
天地同流、豈曰小補之
哉。
孟子曰、仁言不如仁
聲之入人深也、善政不
如善教之得民也、善政

2. 'Though he slay them, they do not murmur. When he
benefits them, they do not think of his merit. From day to day
they make progress towards what is good, without knowing who
makes them do so.

3. 'Wherever the superior man passes through, transformation
follows; wherever he abides, his influence is of a spiritual nature.
It flows abroad, above and beneath, like that of Heaven and Earth.
How can it be said that he mends society but in a small way!'

CHAP. XIV 1. Mencius said, 'Kindly words do not enter so
deeply into men as a reputation for kindness.

2. 'Good government does not lay hold of the people so much
as good instructions.

3. 'Good government is feared by the people, while good instruc-

'the appearance of enlargement and self-possession.' In illustration of the condition of the
people under a true sovereign, commentators
generally quote a tradition of their state in the
golden age of Yâo, when 'entire harmony reigned
under heaven, and the lives of the people passed
easily away.' Then the old men smote the clods,
and sang, 日出而作 日入而息
鑿井而飲 耕田而食 帝力
於我何有哉, 'At sunrise we rise, and
at sunset we rest. We dig our wells and drink;
we cultivate our fields and eat.—What is the
strength of the Tî to us?' 2. 庸 is used in the
sense of 功, 'merit,' or meritorious work, and
the analogy of the other clauses determines the
meaning of 不庸, as in the translation.

3 君子 has reference to the 王者. par. 1.

It is used here in its highest application,—'the
sage.' 所過 所存,—the latter phrase is interpreted morally, being = 'when he has fixed his
mind to produce a result.' This is unnecessary.
神, 'spiritual,' 'mysterious:'—the effects are
sure and visible, but the operation is hidden. In
the influence of Shun in the time of his obscurity, when the ploughmen yielded the furrow,
and the potters made their vessels all sound, we
have an example, it is said, of the 所過者
化. In what it is presumed would have been
the influence of Confucius, had he been in the
position of a ruler, as described, Analects XIX.
xxv, we have an example of the 所存者
神. 補之, as an object for 之, I supply
'society.' It is understood that a leader of the
princes only helps the people in a small way.

14. THE VALUE TO A RULER OF REPUTATION AND
MORAL INFLUENCES. Kindly words are but brief.

民畏之善教民愛之善政
得民財善教得民心。
壹孟子曰人之所不學而
能者其良能也所不慮而
知者其良知也孩提之童
無不知愛其親也及其長
也無不知敬其兄也
仁也敬長義也無他達之
天下也。
夫孟子曰舜之居深山之

tions are loved by them. Good government gets the people's wealth, while good instructions get their hearts.'

CHAP. XV. 1. Mencius said, 'The ability possessed by men without having been acquired by learning is intuitive ability, and the knowledge possessed by them without the exercise of thought is their intuitive knowledge.

2. 'Children carried in the arms all know to love their parents, and when they are grown *a little*, they all know to love their elder brothers.

3. 'Filial affection for parents is *the working of* benevolence. Respect for elders is *the working of* righteousness. There is no other reason *for those feelings*;—they belong to all under heaven.'

CHAP. XVI. Mencius said, 'When Shun was living amid the deep retired mountains, dwelling with the trees and rocks, and

and on an occasion. A reputation for kindness must be the growth of time and of many evidences. With the whole chapter, compare Analects, II. iii.

15. BENEVOLENCE AND RIGHTEOUSNESS ARE NATURAL TO MAN, PARTS OF HIS CONSTITUTION. 1. I translate 良 by 'intuitive,' but it serves also to denote the 'goodness' of the nature of man. Chû Hsî so defines it:—良者本然之善也. 2. 孩 is defined in the dictionary by 小兒笑, 'an infant smiling.' When an infant has reached to this, then it is 人所提挈, 'taken by people in their arms.'

3. 達之天下 must be supplemented by 無不同, 'extend them (carry the inquiry about them) to all under heaven, and they are the same.' This is just laying down universality as a test that those feelings are intuitive to us. Châo Ch'î, however, explains differently:—'Those who wish to do good, have nothing else to do but to extend these ways of children to all under heaven.'

16. HOW WHAT SHUN WAS DISCOVERED ITSELF IN HIS GREATEST OBSCURITY. 決江河,—the 決 is the water itself bursting its banks; the agency of man in the matter is not to be supposed. So in the 備旨:—決江河謂

知者恆存乎疢疾獨孤臣　孟子曰人之有德慧術　矣。　無欲其所不欲如此而已　孟子曰、無爲其所不爲、　能禦也。　善行若決江河沛然莫之　幾希及其聞一善言見一　所以異於深山之野人者　中與木石居與鹿豕遊其

wandering among the deer and swine, the difference between him and the rude inhabitants of those remote hills appeared very small. But when he heard a single good word, or saw a single good action, he was like a stream or a river bursting its banks, and flowing out in an irresistible flood.'

CHAP. XVII. Mencius said, 'Let a man not do what *his own sense of righteousness tells him* not to do, and let him not desire what his *sense of righteousness tells him not* to desire ;—to act thus is all he has to do.'

CHAP. XVIII. 1. Mencius said, 'Men who are possessed of intelligent virtue and prudence in affairs will generally be found to have been in sickness and troubles.

2. 'They are the friendless minister and concubine's son, who keep their hearts under a sense of peril, and use deep precautions

江之決也、非人決之也。江 河 may be taken generally, or with special reference to the Yang-tsze and Yellow river. I prefer the former.

17. A MAN HAS BUT TO OBEY THE LAW IN HIM-SELF. The text is literally—' Not doing what he does not do,' &c. Much must be supplied to make it intelligible in a translation. Châo Ch'î interprets and supplies quite differently:—' Let a man not make another do what he does not do himself,' &c.

18. THE BENEFITS OF TROUBLE AND AFFLICTION.

1. Compare Bk. VI. Pt. II. xv. 德 and 慧 術 and 知 (4th tone) go together,—' intelligence of virtue, and wisdom of arts.' 存 retains its proper meaning of 在, ' to be in.' 疢 means properly ' fever,' ' any feverish disease,' but here 疢疾 = distresses generally. a 惟,—not joined with 孤, but qualifying the whole sentence. 獨 = 孤, ' fatherless,' friendless, not having favour with the sovereign. 孽子 is not the child of one who is a concubine merely, but a concubine in disgrace, or one of a very low rank. 孽 is often taken as if it were 櫱, the shooting forth of a tree after it has been cut down, moreover, the -辛- in it should be 屮.

孽子其操心也危其慮
患也深故達。

孟子曰有事君人者
事是君則爲容悅者也。

有安社稷臣者以安社
稷爲悅者也有天民者

達可行於天下、而後行
之者也、有大人者、正己

而物正者也。

孟子曰君子有三樂

against calamity. On this account they become distinguished for their intelligence.'

CHAP. XIX. 1. Mencius said, 'There are persons who serve the prince;—they serve the prince, that is, for the sake of his countenance and favour.

2. 'There are ministers who seek the tranquillity of the State, and find their pleasure in securing that tranquillity.

3. 'There are those who are the people of Heaven. They, *judging that*, if they were in office, they could carry out *their principles*, throughout the kingdom, proceed *so* to carry them out.

4. 'There are those who are great men. They rectify themselves and others are rectified.'

CHAP. XX. 1. Mencius said, 'The superior man has three

19. FOUR DIFFERENT CLASSES OF MINISTERS. 1. 有事君人者,—the 人 is joined with 有, and not to be taken with 君. Mencius speaks of 人, 'persons,' and not 臣, 'ministers,' to indicate his contempt. 爲容悅 is difficult. The common view is what I have given. 容是使君容我, 悅是使君悅我,—yung is to cause the prince to bear with—countenance—them;—yüeh is to cause the prince to be pleased with them.' In this case, 爲 should be read in 4th tone. It is said, however, to have 專務意, 'the idea of aiming at exclusively.' 2. 社稷臣, see Confucian Analects, XVI. i. 4.

悅, it will be seen, is not used here, as in the last paragraph. 3. 天民, 'Heaven's people,' those who seem dearer to Heaven and more favoured by it;—compare Bk. V. Pt. I. vii. 5. 4. 'The great men' are the sages, the highest style of men. 物 is to be understood of persons=君民, 'the sovereign and the people.' —The first class of ministers may be styled the mercenary; the second, the loyal; the third have no selfishness, and they embrace the whole kingdom in their regards, but they have their defined aims to be attained by systematic effort, while the fourth, unconsciously but surely, produce the grandest results.

20. THE THINGS WHICH THE SUPERIOR MAN DELIGHTS IN. TO OCCUPY THE THRONE IS NOT AMONG THEM. 1. 王天下 is to be taken as simply=有天下. The possession of the

而王天下不與存焉父母
俱存兄弟無故一樂也仰
不愧於天俯不怍於人二
樂也得天下英才而教育
之三樂也君子有三樂而
王天下不與存焉。
孟子曰廣土眾民君子
欲之所樂不存焉中天下
而立定四海之民君子樂
之所性不存焉君子所性

things in which he delights, and to be ruler over the kingdom is not one of them.

2. 'That his father and mother are both alive, and that the condition of his brothers affords no cause for anxiety ;—this is one delight.

3. 'That, when looking up, he has no occasion for shame before Heaven, and, below, he has no occasion to blush before men ;—this is a second delight.

4. 'That he can get from the whole kingdom the most talented individuals, and teach and nourish them ;—this is the third delight.

5. 'The superior man has three things in which he delights, and to be ruler over the kingdom is not one of them.'

CHAP. XXI. 1. Mencius said, 'Wide territory and a numerous people are desired by the superior man, but what he delights in is not here.

2. 'To stand in the centre of the kingdom, and tranquillize the people within the four seas ;—the superior man delights in this, but the highest enjoyment of his nature is not here.

3. 'What belongs by his nature to the superior man cannot be

sovereign sway is indicated, and not the carrying out of the true royal principles. 2. 兄弟無故 may be understood of every painful thing in the condition of his brothers, which would distress him. 3. We cannot but attach a personal meaning to ' Heaven ' here.

21. MAN'S OWN NATURE THE MOST IMPORTANT THING TO HIM, AND THE SOURCE OF HIS TRUE

ENJOYMENT. 1. This describes the condition of the prince of a large State, who has thereby many opportunities of doing good. 2. This advances on the meaning of the first paragraph. The individual indicated is the sovereign, who by his position can benefit the myriads of the people, and therein he feels delight. 所性 —what belongs to him by nature. 3. 君子

善養老者太公辟紂居　曰盍歸乎來吾聞西伯　北海之濱聞文王作興　孟子曰伯夷辟紂居　不言而喻。　益於背施於四體四體　其生色也睟然見於面　所性仁義禮智根於心　不損焉分定故也。君子　雖大行不加焉雖窮居

increased by the largeness of his sphere of action, nor diminished by his dwelling in poverty and retirement;—for this reason that it is determinately apportioned to him *by Heaven.*

4. 'What belongs by his nature to the superior man are benevolence, righteousness, propriety, and knowledge. These are rooted in his heart; their growth and manifestation are a mild harmony appearing in the countenance, a rich fullness in the back, and the character imparted to the four limbs. Those limbs understand *to arrange themselves,* without being told.'

CHAP. XXII. 1. Mencius said, 'Po-î, that he might avoid Châu, was dwelling on the coast of the northern sea when he heard of the rise of king Wăn. He roused himself and said, "Why should I not go and follow him? I have heard that the chief of the West knows well how to nourish the old." T'âi-kung, to avoid Châu, was dwelling on the coast of the eastern sea. When he heard of the rise of king

is not to be interpreted only of the prince of a State or the sovereign. Indeed in the two preceding paragraphs, though the individuals indicated are in those positions, the phrase, as well as here, has its moral significancy. 分 (4th tone) 定故也.—the nature is complete as given by Heaven. It can only be developed from within. Nothing can be added to it from without. This seems to be the idea. 4. 其生色也 extend over all the rest of the paragraph. 生 and 色 are in apposition; 色 is not to be taken as under the government of 生. The meaning is simply that moral and intellectual qualities indicate

themselves in the general appearance and bearing. 睟然 is explained as 清和潤澤之貌, 'the appearance of what is pure, harmonious, moistening, and rich,' and 盎 as 豐厚盈溢之意, 'meaning what is affluent, generous, full and overflowing.'—The whole description is rather strained.

22. THE GOVERNMENT OF KING WĂN BY WHICH THE AGED WERE NOURISHED. 1. Compare Bk. IV. Pt. I. xiii. 1. a. This is to be translated historically, as it describes king Wăn's government; compare Bk. I. Pt. I. iii. 4. 匹婦, corresponding to 匹夫, below;—'the private

東海之濱聞文王作興曰盍
歸乎來吾聞西伯善養老者、
天下有善養老、則仁人以爲
己歸矣。五畝之宅樹牆下以
桑匹婦蠶之、則老者足以衣
帛矣、五母雞二母彘無失其
時老者足以無失肉矣、百畝
之田匹夫耕之八口之家可
以無飢矣。所謂西伯善養老
者、制其田里教之樹畜導其

Wăn, he said, "Why should I not go and follow him? I have heard that the chief of the West knows well how to nourish the old." If there were a prince in the kingdom, who knew well how to nourish the old, all men of virtue would feel that he was the proper object for them to gather to.

2. 'Around the homestead with its five mâu, the space beneath the walls was planted with mulberry trees, with which the women nourished silkworms, and thus the old were able to have silk to wear. *Each family* had five brood hens and two brood sows, which were kept to their *breeding* seasons, and thus the old were able to have flesh to eat. The husbandmen cultivated their farms of 100 mâu, and thus their families of eight mouths were secured against want.

3. 'The expression, "The chief of the West knows well how to nourish the old," refers to his regulation of the fields and dwellings, his teaching them to plant *the mulberry* and nourish those animals, and his instructing the wives and children, so as to make them nourish

woman,' 'the private man.' 蠶之, silk-wormed them,' i.e. nourished silkworms with them. It is observed by 淮南子.—'The silkworm eats and does not drink, going through its transformations in twenty-seven days. The wife of the Yellow Tî (B.C. 2697–2597), whose surname was Hsî-ling (西陵氏), first taught the people to keep silkworms, and to manage their silk, in order to provide clothes. Future ages sacrifice to her as the 先蠶. Mencius has not mentioned before the number of brood sows and hens apportioned to a family. 3. 此之謂 responds to 所謂…者, at the beginning. The whole paragraph is the

妻子、使養其老、五十、非帛
不煖七十、非肉不飽不煖
不飽餒謂之凍餒文王之民
無凍餒之老者此之謂也。
二 孟子曰易其田疇薄其
稅斂民可使富也食之以
時用之以禮財不可勝用
也民非水火不生活昏暮
叩人之門戸求水火無弗

their aged. At fifty, warmth cannot be maintained without silks, and at seventy flesh is necessary to satisfy the appetite. Persons not kept warm nor supplied with food are said to be starved and famished, but among the people of king Wăn, there were no aged who were starved or famished. This is the meaning of the expression in question.'

CHAP. XXIII. 1. Mencius said, 'Let it be seen to that their fields of grain and hemp are well cultivated, and make the taxes on them light ;—so the people may be made rich.

2. 'Let it be seen to that the people use their resources of food seasonably, and expend their wealth only on the prescribed ceremonies :—so their wealth will be more than can be consumed.

3. 'The people cannot live without water and fire, yet if you knock at a man's door in the dusk of the evening, and ask for water and fire, there is no man who will not give them, such is the

explanation of that expression. 田里,一里 is the dwelling-place, the five mău allotted for buildings.

23. To PROMOTE THE VIRTUE OF THE PEOPLE, THE FIRST CARE OF A GOVERNMENT SHOULD BE TO CONSULT FOR THEIR BEING WELL OFF. 1. 易 i,— 4th tone, as in Bk. I. Pt. I. v. 3, et al. 田, 'grain fields.' 疇 'flax fields.' 易 and 薄 are both in the imperative, indicating the work of the ruler or government. So 食 and 用 in par. 2, where 之 may be referred to 財, or the

resources arising from the government just indicated 以時 may be best explained from Bk. I. Pt. I. iii. 3, 4. 以禮—the 禮 are the festive occasions of capping, marriage, &c., excepting on which a strict economy should be enforced. 3. Compare Bk. I. Pt. I. vii. 20-22. 昏 properly denotes half an hour after sunset, or thereabouts. 暮 is 日暮, 'the evening of the day.' The time of the request is inopportune, and the manner of it not according to propriety ;—and yet it is granted. 救 is the

不盈科不行君子之志於

光必照焉流水之爲物也、

術必觀其瀾日月有明容

人之門者難爲言觀水有

觀於海者難爲水遊於聖

小魯登太山而小天下故

孟子曰孔子登東山而

水火而民焉有不仁者乎。

使有菽粟如水火菽粟如

與者至足矣聖人治天下、

abundance of these things. A sage governs the kingdom so as to cause pulse and grain to be as abundant as water and fire. When pulse and grain are as abundant as water and fire, how shall the people be other than virtuous?'

CHAP. XXIV. 1. Mencius said, 'Confucius ascended the eastern hill, and Lû appeared to him small. He ascended the T'âi mountain, and all beneath the heavens appeared to him small. So he who has contemplated the sea, finds it difficult to think anything of *other* waters, and he who has wandered in the gate of the sage, finds it difficult to think anything of *others*.

2. 'There is an art in the contemplation of water.—It is necessary to look at it as foaming in waves. The sun and moon being possessed of brilliancy, their light admitted *even* through an orifice illuminates.

3. 'Flowing water is a thing which does not proceed till it has filled the hollows *in its course*. The student who has set his

general name for all kinds of peas and beans. 粟—as in Analects, XII. xi. 3.

24. HOW THE GREAT DOCTRINES OF THE SAGES DWARF ALL SMALLER DOCTRINES, AND YET ARE TO BE ADVANCED TO BY SUCCESSIVE STEPS. 1, 2. This paragraph illustrates the greatness of the sage's doctrines. The eastern hill was on the east of the capital of Lû. Some identify it with a small hill, called Fang (防), in the district of Ch'û-fau (曲阜), at the foot of which Confucius's parents were buried; others with a hill named Mâng (蒙), in the district of Pî, in the depart-

ment of Î-châu. The T'âi mountain is the chief of the five great mountains of China. It lay on the extreme east of Ch'î, in the present district of Tâi-an, in the department of the same name. In 難爲水, 爲 is used as in 爲衆, Bk. IV. Pt. I. vii. 5. After seeing the surging ocean, the streams are not worth being taken into account. And light penetrating every cranny assures us of its splendour in the great luminaries. 3. 君子 is here the aspiring student. 章, 'an elegant piece,' here for 'one lesson,' 'one truth.'

不爲也。墨子兼愛、摩　我拔一毛而利天下、　蓋孟子曰楊子取爲　與善之閒也。　舜與蹠之分無他利　利者、蹠之徒也。欲知　也鷄鳴而起、孳孳爲　孳孳爲善者舜之徒　蓋孟子曰鷄鳴而起、　道也不成章不達。

mind on the doctrines *of the sage*, does not advance to them but by completing one lesson after another.'

CHAP. XXV. 1. Mencius said, 'He who rises at cock-crowing, and addresses himself earnestly to the practice of virtue, is a disciple of Shun.

2. 'He who rises at cock-crowing, and addresses himself earnestly to the pursuit of gain, is a disciple of Chih.

3. 'If you want to know what separates Shun from Chih, it is simply this,—the interval between *the thought of* gain and *the thought of* virtue.'

CHAP. XXVI. 1. Mencius said, 'The principle of the philosopher Yang was—"Each one for himself." Though he might have benefited the whole kingdom by plucking out a single hair, he would not have done it.

2. 'The philosopher Mo loves all equally. If by rubbing *smooth*

25. THE DIFFERENT RESULTS TO WHICH THE LOVE OF GOOD AND THE LOVE OF GAIN LEAD. 1. 'A disciple of Shun,'—*i.e.* although such a man may not himself attain to be a sage, he is treading in the steps of one. 2. Chih (蹠 being used for 跖) is the robber Chih ; see Bk. III. Pt. II. 2. 3. 爲利—爲 is used here as in chap. xix. 1. I should prefer myself to read it in the 4th tone. It is observed by the scholar Ch'âng that 'by good and gain are intended the public mind and the selfish mind (公私而已).' 3. 利與善之閒 is intended to represent the slightness of the separation between them, in its initial principles, and I therefore supply 'the thought of.'

26. THE ERRORS OF YANG, MO, AND TSZE-MO. OBSTINATE ADHERENCE TO A COURSE WHICH WE MAY DEEM ABSTRACTLY RIGHT IS PERILOUS. 1. 'The philosopher Yang,'—see Bk. III. Pt. II. ix. 9,

10, 14. Chû Hsî says:—取者僅足之意, '取 conveys the idea of what is barely sufficient.' This is not correct. 楊子取 = 楊子所取, 'that which the philosopher Yang chose, was.' . . . . In the writings of the scholar Lieh (列子), Bk. VII, we find Yang Chû speaking of Po-ch'âng Tsze-kâo (伯成子高) that 'he would not pull out one of his hairs to benefit others,' and when questioned himself 'if he would pull out a hair to help an age,' declining to reply. 2. 'The philosopher Mo,'—see Bk. III. Pt. I v. 1 ; Pt. II. ix. 9, 10, 14. We are not to understand the rubbing the body smooth as an isolated act which somehow would benefit the kingdom. The smoothness would arise from labours undergone for the kingdom, like those of the great Yü, who wrought

亦口正者　孟執中莫頂
皆腹也甘　子一無執放
有有飢飲曰而權中踵
害飢渴是飢廢猶執利
人渴害未者百執中天
能之之得甘也一爲下
無害也飲食。也近爲
以人豈食渴　者所之
飢心惟之　爲惡子

his whole body from the crown to the heel, he could have benefited the kingdom, he would have done it.

3. 'Tsze-mo holds a medium *between these*. By holding that medium, he is nearer the right. But by holding it without leaving room for the exigency of circumstances, it becomes like their holding their one point.

4. 'The reason why I hate that holding to one point is the injury it does to the way *of right principle*. It takes up one point and disregards a hundred others.'

CHAP. XXVII. 1. Mencius said, 'The hungry think any food sweet, and the thirsty think the same of any drink, and thus they do not get the right taste of what they eat and drink. The hunger and thirst, in fact, injure *their palate*. And is it only the mouth and belly which are injured by hunger and thirst? Men's minds are also injured by them.

2. 'If a man can prevent the evils of hunger and thirst from

and waded till he had worn away all the hair on his legs. See the 集證, *in loc.* 3. Of Tsze-mo nothing seems to be known, but that he belonged to Lû. 執中 must be clearly understood as referring to a Mean between the selfishness of Yang Chû and the transcendentalism of Mo Tî. 近之-近道, the 道 mentioned in par. 4. The necessity of attending to the exigency of circumstances is illustrated by saying that a case may be conceived when it would be duty to deny a single hair to save the kingdom, and a case when it would be duty to rub the whole body smooth to do so. The orthodox way (道) of China is to do what is

right with reference to the whole circumstances of every case and time.

27. THE IMPORTANCE OF NOT ALLOWING THE MIND TO BE INJURED BY POVERTY AND A MEAN CONDITION. 1. 甘 perhaps is used adverbially, — 'readily;' compare Bk. II. Pt. I. I. 11. The two clauses 是未 and 飢渴 run parallel to each other, the latter being explanatory of the former. 害之-之-口腹. With reference to the mind, hunger and thirst stand for poverty and a mean condition. 2. 能無 以...爲='can prevent being.' 無 being

渴之害為心害則不

及人不為憂矣。

孟子曰柳下惠不

以三公易其介。

孟子曰有為者,辟

若掘井掘井九軔,而

不及泉猶為棄井也。

孟子曰堯舜性之

也湯武身之也五霸

假之也久假而不歸

being any evils to his mind, he need not have any sorrow about not being equal to other men.'

CHAP. XXVIII. Mencius said, 'Hûi of Liû-hsiâ would not for the three highest offices of State have changed his firm purpose of life.'

CHAP. XXIX. Mencius said, 'A man with definite aims to be accomplished may be compared to one digging a well. To dig the well to a depth of seventy-two cubits, *and stop* without reaching the spring, is after all throwing away the well.'

CHAP. XXX. 1. Mencius said, '*Benevolence and righteousness* were natural to Yâo and Shun. T'ang and Wû made them their own. The five chiefs of the princes feigned them.

2. 'Having borrowed them long and not returned them, how could it be known they did not own them?'

emphatic. 不及人,—人 refers to great men, sages, and worthies. Such a man has himself really advanced far in the path of greatness.

28. HÛI OF LIÛ-HSIÂ'S FIRMNESS. 'Hûi of Liû-hsiâ,'—see Bk. II. Pt. I. ix. 2, 3; Bk. V. Pt. II. i. 3, 5; Bk. VI. Pt. II. vi. 2. 和 'mildness,' 'friendly impressibility,' was a characteristic of Hûi, and Mencius, therefore, notices how it was associated with firmness of mind. The 'three kung' are the three highest officers about the royal court, each equal in dignity to the highest rank of nobility.

29. ONLY THAT LABOUR IS TO BE PRIZED WHICH ACCOMPLISHES ITS OBJECT. 辟—used for 譬. 軔—仞, 'eight cubits.' In the Analects, XIX. xxiii. 3, it is said, in the note, that the 仞 was seven cubits, while here its length is given as eight. Its exact length is a moot

point. See the 集證, *in loc.* 有為者, 'one who has that which he is doing.' The application may be very wide.

30. THE DIFFERENCE BETWEEN YÂO, SHUN, T'ANG, AND WÛ, ON THE ONE HAND, AND THE FIVE CHIEFS, ON THE OTHER, IN RELATION TO BENEVOLENCE AND RIGHTEOUSNESS. 1. 之 no doubt refers to 仁義 'benevolence and righteousness,' and a translation can hardly be made without supplying those terms. Though Yâo and Shun stood on a higher platform than T'ang and Wû, they agreed in sincerity, which is the common point of contrast between them and the chiefs. 身之, 'incorporated them' = made them their own. 2. Chû Hsî explains 歸 by 還, 'returned.' Admitting this, the meaning of 假 passes from 'feigning' to 'borrowing.' He seems to prefer viewing 惡知

惡知其非有也。

二 公孫丑曰伊尹曰予不
狎于不順放太甲于桐民
大悅太甲賢又反之民大
悅賢者之爲人臣也其君
不賢則固可放與孟子曰
有伊尹之志則可無伊尹
之志則篡也。

二 公孫丑曰詩曰不素餐

今君子之不耕而食何也

CHAP. XXXI. 1. Kung-sun Ch'âu said, 'Î Yin said, "I cannot be near *and see him* so disobedient *to reason*," and therewith he banished T'âi-chiâ to T'ung. The people were much pleased. When T'âi-chiâ became virtuous, he brought him back, and the people were *again* much pleased.

2. 'When worthies are ministers, may they indeed banish their sovereigns *in this way* when they are not virtuous?'

3. Mencius replied, 'If they have the same purpose as Î Yin, they may. If they have not the same purpose, it would be usurpation.'

CHAP. XXXII. Kung-sun Ch'âu said, 'It is said, in the Book of Poetry,

"He will not eat the bread of idleness!"

How is it that *we see* superior men eating without labouring?' Mencius replied, 'When a superior man resides in a country, if its

as = 'how could they themselves know?' but I much prefer the view in the translation.

31. THE END MAY JUSTIFY THE MEANS, BUT THE PRINCIPLE SHOULD NOT BE READILY APPLIED. 1. Compare Bk. V. Pt. I. vi. 5. 伊尹曰,—see the Shû-ching, Pt. IV. v. Bk. I. 9. The words are taken somewhat differently in the commentary on the *ching*, but I have followed what seems the most likely meaning of them. 9. 志 is the purpose, not suddenly formed on an emergency, but the determination and object of the whole life. It is said—志以其素定者言

32. THE SERVICES WHICH A SUPERIOR MAN RENDERS TO A COUNTRY ENTITLE HIM, WITHOUT HIS

DOING OFFICIAL DUTY, TO SUPPORT. This is an instance of the oft-repeated insinuation against Mencius, that he was content to be supported by the princes, while he would not take office; compare Bk. III. Pt. II. iv. 詩曰,—see the Shih-ching, I. ix. Ode VI. 素-空, 'empty,' without doing service. The old commentators and the new differ somewhat in their interpretations of the ode, but they agree in understanding its great lesson to be that people should not be receiving emolument, who do not actively serve their country. 耕 'ploughing,' labouring. This term is suggested from the ode,

孟子曰、君子居是國也、其君
用之、則安富尊榮、其子弟從
之、則孝悌忠信、不素餐兮、孰
大於是。
王子墊問曰、士何事、孟子
曰、尚志、何謂尚志、曰、仁義
而已矣、殺一無罪、非仁也、非
其有而取之、非義也、居惡在、
仁是也、路惡在、義是也、居仁
由義、大人之事備矣。

sovereign employ his counsels, he comes to tranquillity, wealth, honour, and glory. If the young in it follow his instructions, they become filial, obedient to their elders, true-hearted, and faithful.— What greater example can there be than this of not eating the bread of idleness?'

CHAP. XXXIII. 1. The king's son, Tien, asked *Mencius*, saying, 'What is the business of the *unemployed* scholar?'

2. Mencius replied, 'To exalt his aim.'

3. *Tien* asked *again*, 'What do you mean by exalting the aim?' The answer was, '*Setting it* simply on benevolence and righteousness. *He thinks* how to put a single innocent person to death is contrary to benevolence; how to take what one has not *a right to* is contrary to righteousness; that one's dwelling should be benevolence; and one's path should be righteousness. Where else should he dwell? What other path should he pursue? When benevolence is the dwelling-place *of the heart*, and righteousness the path *of the life*, the business of a great man is complete.'

where it occurs, 用之, 'use him,' i.e. his counsels, not as a minister.

33. HOW A SCHOLAR PREPARES HIMSELF FOR THE DUTIES TO WHICH HE ASPIRES. 1. Tien was the son of the king of Ch'i. His question probably had reference to the wandering scholars of the time, whose ways he disliked. They were no favourites with Mencius, but he prefers to reply to the prince according to his ideal of the scholar. 3. 仁 ... 義是也 represent the scholar's thoughts, his nursing his aim. We can hardly take 大人 as in chap. xix. 4, where it denotes the sages, the very highest style of man. Here it denotes rather the individuals in the various grades of official employment, to which 'the scholar' may attain.

孟子曰、仲子、不義與
之齊國而弗受人皆信
之、是舍簞食豆羹之義
也、人莫大焉亡親戚君
臣上下以其小者信其
大者奚可哉。
蠹桃應問曰、舜爲天子、
皐陶爲士瞽瞍殺人則
如之何孟子曰、執之而

CHAP. XXXIV. Mencius said, 'Supposing that the kingdom of Ch'î were offered, contrary to righteousness, to *Ch'ăn* Chung, he would not receive it, and all people believe in him, *as a man of the highest worth*. But this is *only* the righteousness which declines a dish of rice or a plate of soup. A man can have no greater *crimes* than to disown his parents and relatives, and the relations of sovereign and minister, superiors and inferiors. How can it be allowed to give a man credit for the great *excellences* because he possesses a small one?'

CHAP. XXXV. 1. T'âo Ying asked, saying, 'Shun being sovereign, and Kâo-yâo chief minister of justice, if Kû-sâu had murdered a man, what would have been done in the case?'

2. Mencius said, '*Kâo-yâo* would simply have apprehended him.

34. How MEN JUDGE WRONGLY OF CHARACTER, OVERLOOKING, IN THEIR ADMIRATION OF ONE STRIKING EXCELLENCE, GREAT FAILURES AND DEFICIENCIES. 仲子 is the Ch'ăn Chung of Bk. III. Pt. II. x, which see. I substitute the surname to avoid translating 子. In the translation of 人莫大焉, 焉 is taken as used for 乎, and what follows is under the regimen of 大, as if we were to complete the construction in this way:— 人之罪莫大乎亡親云云. Châo Ch'î interprets quite differently:—'But what a man should exalt is the greatest virtues, the propriety and righteousness in the great relations of life. He, however, denies them, &c.' Certainly the solecism of taking 焉 for 乎 is

better than this. 亡,—used for 無, but as a verb. Wang Yin-chih construes as I do, making the 焉=乎, =於, and construing 大 consequently in the comparative degree.

35. WHAT SHUN AND HIS MINISTER OF CRIME WOULD HAVE DONE, IF SHUN'S FATHER HAD COMMITTED A MURDER. 1. T'âo Ying was a disciple of Mencius. This is all that is known of him. 士 is not to be understood here as merely— 士師, Analects, XVIII. ii; XIX. xix. The 士師 of Shun's time was the same as the 大 司寇 of the Châu dynasty, the officer of Crime, under whom were the 士師, and others more subordinate. See the 集證 *in loc.* 2. We must understand Kâo-yâo as the

人之子與孟子曰王子宮
養移體大哉居乎夫非盡
王之子喟然歎曰居移氣
孟子自范之齊望見齊
訢然樂而忘天下。
負而逃遵海濱而處終身
視棄天下猶棄敝蹝也竊
之也然則舜如之何曰舜
舜惡得而禁之夫有所受
已矣然則舜不禁與曰夫

3. 'But would not Shun have forbidden such a thing?'

4. 'Indeed, how could Shun have forbidden it? *Kâo-yâo* had received *the law* from *a proper* source.'

5. 'In that case what would Shun have done?'

6. 'Shun would have regarded abandoning the kingdom as throwing away a worn-out sandal. He would privately have taken *his father* on his back, and retired into concealment, living somewhere along the sea-coast. There he would have been all his life, cheerful and happy, forgetting the kingdom.'

CHAP. XXXVI. 1. Mencius, going from Fan to Ch'î, saw the king of Ch'î's son at a distance, and said with a deep sigh, 'One's position alters the air, *just as* the nurture affects the body. Great is the influence of position! Are *we* not all men's sons *in this respect?*'

2. Mencius said, 'The residence, the carriages and horses, and

nominative to 執 之 must refer to Kû-sâu, though critics now understand 法 as the antecedent. No doubt the meaning is, 'He would simply have observed the law, and dealt with Kû-sâu accordingly.' 3 有所受之 —compare Bk. III. Pt. I. ii. 3. It is here implied that the law of death for murder was the will of Heaven, that being the source to which a reference is made. Kâo-yâo again must be understood as the nominative to 有. He, as minister of Crime, had to maintain Heaven's authority superior to the sovereign's will.

36. HOW ONE'S MATERIAL POSITION AFFECTS HIS AIR, AND MUCH MORE MAY MORAL CHARACTER BE EXPECTED TO DO SO. 1. Fan was a city of Ch'î, a considerable distance from the capital, to which we must understand Mencius was proceeding. It still gives its name to a district of Pû-châu (濮州), in the department of Ts'âo-châu (曹州). Châo Ch'î says that Fan was a city of Ch'î, the appanage of the king's sons by his concubines. On this view we should translate 王子 in the plural, but it proceeds from supposing that it was in Fan that Mencius saw the 王子, which the text does not at all necessitate. In 之齊, and 之宋 (p. 3), 之 = 往 養=奉養

室車馬衣服多與人同而
王子若彼者其居使之然
也況居天下之廣居者乎。
魯君之宋呼於垤澤之門、
守者曰此非吾君也何其
聲之似我君也此無他居
相似也。

三十七
孟子曰食而弗愛豕交
之也愛而不敬獸畜之也。
恭敬者幣之未將者也恭

the dress of the king's son, are mostly the same as those of other men. That he looks so is occasioned by his position. How much more *should* a *peculiar air distinguish* him whose position is in the wide house of the world!

3. 'When the prince of Lû went to Sung, he called out at the Tieh-châi gate, and the keeper said, "This is not our prince. How is it that his voice is so like that of our prince?" This was occasioned by nothing but the correspondence of their positions.'

CHAP. XXXVII. 1. Mencius said, 'To feed *a scholar* and not love him, is to treat him as a pig. To love him and not respect him, is to keep him as a domestic animal.

2. 'Honouring and respecting are what exist before any offering of gifts.

3. 'If there be honouring and respecting without the reality

'revenue or income.' 夫非盡人之子與.—some understand 王子 in the phrase between 夫 and 非, 'now, are not all kings' sons,' &c. But I prefer to understand with Châo Ch'î, 凡人與王子, and in English to supply *we* rather than *they*. 2. 孟子曰 seem here to be superfluous. 天下之廣居,—see Bk. III. Pt. II. iii. 2. 垤澤 'Ant-hill marsh,' was simply the name of a gate in the capital of Sung.

37. THAT HE BE RESPECTED IS ESSENTIAL TO A SCHOLAR'S ENGAGING IN THE SERVICE OF A PRINCE. 1. 豕交之, 'having pig intercourse with him.' 交=接 or 待 獸, as distinguished from 豕, leads us to think of dogs or horses, animals to which we entertain a sentiment higher than to those which we keep and fatten merely for our eating. 2. 恭敬者=所謂恭敬者. The paragraph is an explanation of what is meant by those terms. 將=奉, 'presented,' 'offered.' 3. 拘=留.

敬而無實、君子不可虛拘。

芸孟子曰、形色天性也。惟

聖人然後可以踐形。

芸齊宣王欲短喪。公孫丑

曰、爲朞之喪、猶愈於已乎。

孟子曰、是猶或紾其兄之

臂、子謂之姑徐徐云爾、亦

教之孝弟而已矣。王子有

其母死者、其傅爲之請數

月之喪。公孫丑曰、若此者

of them, a superior man may not be retained by such empty *demonstrations.'*

CHAP. XXXVIII. Mencius said, 'The bodily organs with their functions belong to our Heaven-conferred nature. But a man must be a sage before he can satisfy the design of his bodily organization.'

CHAP. XXXIX. 1. The king Hsüan of Ch'î wanted to shorten the period of mourning. Kung-sun Ch'âu said, 'To have one whole year's mourning is better than doing away with it altogether.'

2. Mencius said, 'That is just as if there were one twisting the arm of his elder brother, and you were merely to say to him— "Gently, gently, if you please." Your only course should be to teach such an one filial piety and fraternal duty.'

3. *At that time,* the mother of one of the king's sons had died, and his tutor asked for him that he might be allowed to observe

38. ONLY WITH A SAGE DOES THE BODY ACT ACCORDING TO ITS DESIGN. This is translated according to the consenting view of the modern commentators, but perhaps not correctly. 形 is taken for the bodily organs,—the ears, eyes, hands, feet, &c.; and 色 for their manifested operations,—hearing, seeing, handling, &c. 踐 is used as in the phrase 踐言, 'to tread upon the words,' that is, to fulfil them, to walk, act, according to them. The use of 色, in chap. xxi. 4. is analogous to this use of it here. One critic says :—形色天性、言形

色皆天性所在、非指形色 爲天性也, 'The bodily organs with their operations belong to our Heaven-conferred nature ; the meaning is that in these is our Heavenly nature, not that they are that nature.'

39. REPROOF OF KUNG-SUN CH'ÂU FOR ASSENTING TO THE PROPOSAL TO SHORTEN THE PERIOD OF MOURNING. Compare Analects, XVII. xxi. 1. The mourning is to be understood as that of three years for a parent. 3. The king's son here must have been a son by a concubine. Chû Hsî, after Châo Ch'î, supposes that he was not permitted to mourn the three years, through

何如也。曰、是欲終之而
不可得也、雖加一日愈
於已謂夫莫之禁而弗
爲者也。
十二孟子曰、君子之所以
教者五、有如時雨化之
者、有成德者、有達財者、
有答問者、有私淑艾
者、此五者、君子之所以教
也。

a few months' mourning. Kung-sun Ch'âu asked, 'What do you say of this?'

4. *Mencius* replied, 'This is a case where the party wishes to complete the whole period, but finds it impossible to do so. The addition of even a single day is better than not mourning at all. I spoke of the case where there was no hindrance, and the party neglected the thing itself.'

CHAP. XL. 1. Mencius said, 'There are five ways in which the superior man effects his teaching.

2. 'There are some on whom his influence descends like seasonable rain.

3. 'There are some whose virtue he perfects, and some of whose talents he assists the development.

4. 'There are some whose inquiries he answers.

5. 'There are some who privately cultivate and correct themselves.

6. 'These five ways are the methods in which the superior man effects his teaching.'

the jealous or other opposition of the full queen. In this case the son was anxious to prolong his mourning as much as he could. This explanation, bringing in the opposition of the full queen or wife, seems to be incorrect. See the 集證, *in loc.* While the father was alive, a son shortened the period of mourning for his mother. 4. 謂夫一夫 has a pronominal force.

40. HOW THE LESSONS OF THE SAGE REACH TO ALL DIFFERENT CLASSES. 1. The wish of the superior man is in all cases one and the same,—to teach. His methods are modified, however, by the different characters of men.

2. This class only want his influence, like plants which only need the dew of heaven. So was it, it is said, with Confucius and his disciples Yen Yûan and Tsâng Shin. 3. 成德者=成其德者 So a 其 is to be understood before 財(=材), and 間. So was it with Confucius and the disciples Yen and Min. 4. So was it with Mencius and Wan Chang. 5. This is a class, who never come into actual contact with their teacher, but hear of his doctrines, and learn them. His teachings, though not delivered by himself in person, do notwithstanding reach to them.

公孫丑曰道則高矣美
矣宜若登天然似不可及
也何不使彼爲可幾及而
日孳孳也孟子曰大匠不
爲拙工改廢繩墨羿不爲
拙射變其彀率君子引而
不發躍如也中道而立能
者從之。

孟子曰天下有道以道
殉身天下無道以身殉道。

CHAP. XLI. 1. Kung-sun Ch'âu said, 'Lofty are your principles and admirable, but *to learn them* may well be likened to ascending the heavens,—something which cannot be reached. Why not *adapt your teaching so as to* cause learners to consider them attainable, and so daily exert themselves!'

2. Mencius said, 'A great artificer does not, for the sake of a stupid workman, alter or do away with the marking-line. I did not, for the sake of a stupid archer, charge his rule for drawing the bow.

3. 'The superior man draws the bow, but does not discharge the arrow, having seemed to leap *with it to the mark;* and he there stands exactly in the middle of the path. Those who are able, follow him.'

CHAP. XLII. 1. Mencius said, 'When right principles prevail throughout the kingdom, one's principles must appear along with one's person. When right principles disappear from the kingdom, one's person must vanish along with one's principles.

41. THE TEACHER OF TRUTH MAY NOT LOWER HIS LESSONS TO SUIT HIS LEARNERS. 1. 何不 使彼—彼, 'those' refers to learners, which antecedent has been implied in the words, 宜若, 云云, 'it is right they should be considered,' &c. 爲可幾及— 爲=以爲, 'to consider,' 'regard.' 2. 繩 墨, 'string and ink,' a carpenter's marking-line. 彀率 (read lü), 'the limit to which a bow should be drawn.' 3 The difficulty here is with the words 躍如也, literally, 'leaping-like.' They belong, I think, to the superior man in all the action which is represented. No man can be taught how to hit. That is his own act. He is taught to shoot, and that in so lively a manner that the hitting also is, as it were, set forth before him. So with the teacher and learner of truth. As the learner tries to do as he is taught, he will be found laying hold of what he thought unapproachable.

42. ONE MUST LIVE OR DIE WITH HIS PRINCIPLES, ACTING FROM HIMSELF, NOT WITH REGARD TO OTHER MEN. 殉 means 'to bury along with the dead,' to associate with in death as in life.

未聞以道殉乎人者也。

公都子曰滕更之在門也、

若在所禮而不答何也。孟子

曰、挾貴而問、挾賢而問、挾長

而問、挾有勳勞而問、挾故而

問、皆所不答也。滕更有二焉。

孟子曰、於不可已而已者、

無所不已、於所厚者薄、無所

不薄也。其進銳者其退速。

2. 'I have not heard of one's principles being dependent for their manifestation on other men.'

CHAP. XLIII. 1. The disciple Kung-tû said, 'When Kăng of T'ăng made his appearance in your school, it seemed proper that a polite consideration should be paid to him, and yet you did not answer him. Why was that?'

2. Mencius replied, 'I do not answer him who questions me presuming on his nobility, nor him who presumes on his talents, nor him who presumes on his age, nor him who presumes on services performed to me, nor him who presumes on old acquaintance. Two of those things were chargeable on Kăng of T'ăng.'

CHAP. XLIV. 1. Mencius said, 'He who stops short where stopping is acknowledged to be not allowable, will stop short in everything. He who behaves shabbily to those whom he ought to treat well, will behave shabbily to all.

2. 'He who advances with precipitation will retire with speed.'

Another meaning is 以身從物, 'with the person to follow after things,'=to pursue. The first 道 is right principles in general.

The other 道 are those principles as held by individual men.

43. HOW MENCIUS REQUIRED THE SIMPLE PUR- SUIT OF TRUTH IN THOSE WHOM HE TAUGHT. Kăng was a younger brother of the prince of T'ăng. His rank made Kung-tû think that more than ordinary respect should have been shown to him, and yet it was no doubt one of the things which made Mencius jealously watch his spirit. Compare Bk. VI. Pt. II. ii. 6, 7.

44. FAILURES IN EVIDENT DUTY WILL BE ACCOM- PANIED BY FAILURE IN ALL DUTY. PRECIPITATE ADVANCES ARE FOLLOWED BY SPEEDY RETREATS. The first paragraph, it is said, has reference to errors of defect (不及者之弊), and the second to those of excess (有過).

舜之仁不徧愛人急親賢

知而不徧物急先務也堯

也急親賢之爲務堯舜之

當務之爲急仁者無不愛

四 孟子曰知者無不知也
六章

而愛物。

愛之而弗親親親而仁民仁民

四 孟子曰君子之於物也、
五章

CHAP. XLV. Mencius said, 'In regard to *inferior* creatures, the superior man is kind to them, but not loving. In regard to people generally, he is loving to them, but not affectionate. He is affectionate to his parents, and lovingly disposed to people *generally*. He is lovingly disposed to people *generally*, and kind to creatures.'

CHAP. XLVI. 1. Mencius said, 'The wise embrace all knowledge, but they are most earnest about what is of the greatest importance. The benevolent embrace all in their love, but what they consider of the greatest importance is to cultivate an earnest affection for the virtuous. Even the wisdom of Yâo and Shun did not extend to everything, but they attended earnestly to what was important. Their benevolence did not show itself in acts of kindness to every man, but they earnestly cultivated an affection for the virtuous.

45. THE SUPERIOR MAN IS KIND TO CREATURES, LOVING TO OTHER MEN, AND AFFECTIONATE TO HIS RELATIVES. This was intended, no doubt, against the Mohist doctrine of loving all equally. 物=animals. The second 親 is not to be understood only of parents. Compare 親親, D.M., xx. 12.

46. AGAINST THE PRINCES OF HIS TIME WHO OCCUPIED THEMSELVES WITH THE KNOWLEDGE OF, AND REGARD FOR, WHAT WAS OF LITTLE IMPORT-ANCE. 1. 無不知, 無不愛 are not our 'omniscient,' and 'all-loving,' but show the tendency and adaptation of the wise and the benevolent. The clauses that follow,— 富

務之爲急, 急親賢之爲務 show in what way truly great rulers come to an administration which appears to possess those characters. The use of th. 之 in those clauses is idiomatic. To reduce it to the ordinary usages of the particle, we must take the first as = 惟富務之事爲急, 'but only are they earnest about the things which it is most important *to know*,' and 惟急于 親賢之富務, 'but only are they earnest about what is most important, the cultivating affection for the virtuous.' The teaching of the chapter is substantially the same as that of Confucius, Analects, XII. xxii.

務。謂決是之不知　問無齒　流歠而　察放飯而　小功之總　喪而　三年之　也。不能

2. 'Not to be able to keep the three years' mourning, and to be very particular about that of three months, or that of five months; to eat immoderately and swill down the soup, and at the same time to inquire about *the precept* not to tear the meat with the teeth;—such things show what I call an ignorance of what is most important.'

2. 緦, 'coarse, unbleached, hempen cloth,' worn in mourning during the period of three months for distant relatives. 小功 is the name applied in the case of mourning which extends for five months. 放飯云云, see the Book of Rites, I. Sect. I. iii. 54, 55. 'These are cases adduced in illustration of what is insisted on in the previous paragraph;—the folly of attending to what is comparatively trivial, while overlooking what is important.

TSIN SIN. PART II.

不愛及其　者以其所　不愛及其所仁　愛及其所　者以其所　惠王也仁　不仁哉梁　孟子曰　章句下　盡心

CHAPTER I. 1. Mencius said, 'The opposite indeed of benevolent was the king Hûi of Liang! The benevolent, beginning with what they care for, proceed to what they do not care for. Those who are the opposite of benevolent, beginning with what they do not care for, proceed to what they care for.'

1. A STRONG CONDEMNATION OF KING HÛI OF LIANG, FOR SACRIFICING TO HIS AMBITION HIS PEOPLE AND EVEN HIS SON. Compare Bk. I. Pt. I. v, and other conversations with king Hûi. 1. 不仁 is more than 'unbenevolent' would mean, if we had such a term. It is nearly = 'cruel,' 'oppressive.' 仁者云 云,—compare Pt. I. xlv. Only 愛, being there opposed to 仁, is used with reference to animals, while here it expresses the feeling towards children and people and animals, and I have rendered it by 'to care for.' In the first case in the text, the progress is from one degree of love to another; in the second, from

伐善孟愛以不民惠所
下於子及殉能王愛
也此曰其之勝以公
敵則春所是故土孫
國有秋愛之驅地丑
不之無也謂其之曰
相矣義以所故何
征征戰其愛糜謂
也者彼所子爛也
上不弟其梁

2. Kung-sun Ch'âu said, 'What do you mean?' *Mencius answered*, 'The king Hûi of Liang, for the matter of territory, tore and destroyed his people, leading them to battle. Sustaining a great defeat, he would engage again, and afraid lest they should not be able to secure the victory, urged his son whom he loved till he sacrificed him with them. This is what I call—"beginning with what they do not care for, and proceeding to what they care for."'

CHAP. II. 1. Mencius said, 'In the "Spring and Autumn" there are no righteous wars. Instances indeed there are of one war better than another.

2. '"Correction" is when the supreme authority punishes its subjects by force of arms. Hostile States do not correct one another.'

one degree of infliction to another. 2. 糜, 'to boil rice till it is 糜爛, reduced to a pulpy mass.' So did Hûi seem to deal with the bodies of his subjects. 所愛子弟 refers to Hûi's eldest son (Bk. I. Pt. I. v. 1). He is called a 子弟 as being one of the youth of the kingdom. 殉之.—compare Pt. I. xlii.

2. HOW ALL THE FIGHTINGS RECORDED IN THE CH'UN-CH'IÛ WERE UNRIGHTEOUS:—A WARNING TO THE CONTENDING STATES OF MENCIUS'S TIME. 1. 無義戰,—'no righteous battles.' Both Châo Ch'î and Chû Hsî make 戰＝戰伐之事, 'the affairs of fighting and smiting,' i.e. all the operations of war detailed in the Ch'un-ch'iû. And rightly; for Mencius himself uses the term 伐 in the second paragraph. In the Ch'un-ch'iû itself there are mentioned of 'fightings' (戰) only 23, while the 'smitings' (伐) amount to 213. There are specified in it also 'invasions' (侵); 'sieges' (圍); 'carryings away' (遷); 'extinguishings' (滅); 'defeats' (敗); 'takings' (取); 'surprises' (襲); 'pursuits' (追); and 'defences' (戍); all of which may be comprehended under the term 戰. 2. Explains the assertion in the former paragraph. In the wars recorded by Confucius, one State or chief was said to 征 another, which could not be according to the meaning of the term. By

無敵焉。南面而征北
罪也。國君好仁、天下
善爲陳、我善爲戰、大
孟子曰、有人曰、我
血之流杵也。
仁伐至不仁、而何其
人無敵於天下、以至
取二三策而已矣。
不如無書。吾於武城、
孟子曰、盡信書、則

CHAP. III. 1. Mencius said, 'It would be better to be without the Book of History than to give entire credit to it.

2. 'In the "Completion of the War," I select two or three passages only, which I believe.

3. '"The benevolent man has no enemy under heaven. When *the prince* the most benevolent was engaged against him who was the most the opposite, how could the blood *of the people* have flowed till it floated the pestles of the mortars ?"'

CHAP. IV. 1. Mencius said, 'There are men who say—"I am skilful at marshalling troops, I am skilful at conducting a battle!"— They are great criminals.

2. 'If the ruler of a State love benevolence, he will have no enemy in the kingdom.

3. 'When *Tang* was executing his work of correction in the

上 is intended the sovereign ; by 下 the princes. Compare Bk. VI. Pt. II. vii. 2.

3. WITH WHAT RESERVATION MENCIUS READ THE SHÛ-CHING. This is a difficult chapter for Chinese commentators. Châo Ch'î takes 書 of the Shû-ching, which is the only fair interpretation. Others understand it of books in general. Thus Julien translates—'Si omnino fidem adhibeas libris.' Many say that Mencius had in view only the portion of the Shû-ching to which he refers in the next paragraph, but such a restriction of his language is entirely arbitrary. The strangest view is that of the author of the 四書拓餘說, whose judgments generally are sound and sensible. But he says here that Mencius is anticipating the attempts that would be made in after-ages to corrupt the classics, and testifying against them. We can see how the remarks were directed against the propensity to warfare which characterized his contemporaries. 2.

武成 is the title of the third Book in the fifth Part of the Shû-ching, professing to be an account by king Wû of his enterprise against the tyrant Châu. The words quoted in the next paragraph are found in par. 8. 3. For 杵 there are different readings ; see the 集澄 *in loc.* Doubtless there is much exaggeration in the language, but Mencius misinterprets the whole passage. The bloodshed was not done by the troops of king Wû, but by the forces of the tyrant turning against one another.

4. COUNSEL TO PRINCES NOT TO ALLOW THEMSELVES TO BE DECEIVED BY MEN WHO WOULD ADVISE THEM TO WAR. 1. Compare Bk. IV. Pt. I. xiv. 3. 2. Compare Bk. I. Pt. I. v. 6. 3. See Bk. I. Pt. II. xi, *et al.* 4. 革車, 'leathern carriages, or chariots,' said by some to be baggage-waggons, but, more probably, by others, chariots of war, each one of which had seventy-two foot-soldiers attached to it, so that Wû's army would

狄怨東面而征西夷怨曰

奚爲後我武王之伐殷也

革車三百兩虎賁三千人

王曰無畏寧爾也非敵百

姓也若崩厥角稽首征之

爲言正也各欲正已也焉

用戰。

孟子曰梓匠輪輿能與

人規矩不能使人巧。

孟子曰舜之飯糗茹草

south, the rude tribes on the north murmured. When he was executing it in the east, the rude tribes on the west murmured. Their cry was—"Why does he make us last?"

4. 'When king Wû punished Yin, he had *only* three hundred chariots of war; and three thousand life-guards.

5. 'The king said, "Do not fear. Let me give you repose. I am no enemy to the people!" *On this*, they bowed their heads to the earth, like the horns of animals falling off."

6. '"Royal correction" is but another word for rectifying. Each State wishing itself to be corrected, what need is there for fighting?'

CHAP. V. Mencius said, 'A carpenter or a carriage-maker may give a man the circle and square, but cannot make him skilful *in the use of them*.'

CHAP. VI. Mencius said, 'Shun's manner of eating *his* parched grain and herbs was as if he were to be doing so all his life. When

number 21,600, few as compared with the forces of his opponent. 兩 used for 輛, the 3rd tone, a numerative for carriages. 虎賁 (*pän*)—these appear to have been of the character of life-guards, named from their tiger-like courage and bearing. 5. See the Shû-ching, Pt. V. i. Sect. II. 9. But the text of the Classic is hardly recognisable in Mencius's version of it. The original is:—'Rouse ye, my heroes. Do not think that he is not to be feared, but rather hold that he cannot be withstood. The people are full of awe, as if their horns were falling from their heads.' 6. Perhaps it would

be well to retain the sound of 征 in the translation, and say, 'Now *chäng* means to rectify.' 各欲正已, 'each people wishes the *chäng-er* to correct itself.'

5. REAL ATTAINMENT MUST BE MADE BY THE LEARNER FOR HIMSELF. Compare Pt. I. xli. See also in Chwang-tsze, Bk. xiii. par. 10. 梓匠 輪輿 see Bk. III. Pt. II. iv. 3.

6. THE EQUANIMITY OF SHUN IN POVERTY AND AS SOVEREIGN. 草 must be taken as = 菜 茹 is a word used for 食, applied to eating

也若將終身焉、及其爲天子
也、被袗衣、鼓琴、二女果若固
有之。

七子曰吾今而後知殺人
親之重也殺人之父人亦殺
其父殺人之兄人亦殺其兄、
然則非自殺之也、一閒耳。

八孟子曰古之爲關也將以
禦暴今之爲關也將以爲暴。

he became sovereign, and had the embroidered robes to wear, the lute to play, and the two daughters *of Yáo* to wait on him, he was as if those things belonged to him as a matter of course.'

CHAP. VII. Mencius said, 'From this time forth I know the heavy consequences of killing a man's near relations. When a man kills another's father, that other will kill his father; when a man kills another's elder brother, that other will kill his elder brother. So he does not himself indeed do the act, but there is only an interval *between him and it.*'

CHAP. VIII. 1. Mencius said, 'Anciently, the establishment of the frontier-gates was to guard against violence.

2. 'Nowadays, it is to exercise violence.'

herba. 飯—食, 'to eat.' The 'embroidered robes' are the royal dress. On Shun's lute, see Bk. V. Pt. I. ii. 3. 果 used for 婐 (wǒ), 'a female attendant.'

7. HOW THE THOUGHT OF ITS CONSEQUENCES SHOULD MAKE MEN CAREFUL OF THEIR CONDUCT. Chû Hsî observes that this remark must have been made with some special reference,—吾 今而後 It is a maxim of Chinese teaching, that 'a man may not live under the same heaven with the slayer of his father, nor in the same State with the slayer of his elder brother;' but Mencius does not seem to think of that, but rather takes occasion from it to warn rulers to make their government firm in the attachment of their subjects, and not provoke their animosity by oppressive acts. —— 閒耳,—'there is only one interval;' that is, the death of a man's father or brother is the retribution for his previous conduct, the slayer or avenger only intervening.

8. THE BENEVOLENCE AND SELFISHNESS OF ANCIENT AND MODERN RULE CONTRASTED. Compare Bk. I. Pt. II. v. 3; Bk. II. Pt. I. vi. 2. But one does not see exactly how the ancient rule of examining the person, and not taking the goods, guarded against violence. Here, as elsewhere at times, Mencius is led away by his fondness for antithesis.

孟子曰身不行道不行
於妻子使人不以道不能
行於妻子。
孟子曰周于利者凶年
不能殺周于德者邪世不
能亂。
孟子曰好名之人能讓
千乘之國苟非其人簞食
豆羹見於色
孟子曰不信仁賢則國

CHAP. IX. Mencius said, 'If a man himself do not walk in the *right* path, it will not be walked in *even* by his wife and children. If he order men according to what is not the *right* way, he will not be able to get the obedience of *even* his wife and children.'

CHAP. X. Mencius said, 'A bad year cannot prove the cause of death to him whose stores of gain are large; an age of corruption cannot confound him whose equipment of virtue is complete.'

CHAP. XI. Mencius said, 'A man who loves fame may be able to decline a State of a thousand chariots; but if he be not *really* the man *to do such a thing*, it will appear in his countenance, in the matter of a dish of rice or a platter of soup.'

CHAP. XII. 1. Mencius said, 'If men of virtue and ability be not confided in, a State will become empty and void.

9. A MAN'S INFLUENCE DEPENDS ON HIS PERSONAL EXAMPLE AND CONDUCT. To the second 行 we are to suppose 道 as the nominative, while the third is like a verb in the *Hiphil* conjugation. The 人 is not so much as 他人, 'other men.' The whole 使人不以道 simply = 出令不當理, 'if his orders are not according to reason.'

10. CORRUPT TIMES ARE PROVIDED AGAINST BY ESTABLISHED VIRTUE. 不能殺, 不能亂, may be taken either actively or passively. 周于利者, 'he who is complete in gain,' i.e. he who has gained much, and laid much by. The 日講 expands this into 家有餘貨, 倉有餘粟.

11. A MAN'S TRUE DISPOSITION WILL OFTEN APPEAR IN SMALL MATTERS, WHEN A LOVE OF FAME MAY HAVE CARRIED HIM OVER GREAT DIFFICULTIES. Chû Hsî here expounds well:— 觀人不於其所勉, 而於其所忽, 然後可以見其所安之實, 'A man is seen not so much in things which require an effort, as in things which he might easily despise. By bearing this in mind when we observe him, we can see what he really rests in.'

12. THREE THINGS IMPORTANT IN THE ADMINISTRATION OF A STATE. 1. 不信, 'be not con-

是故得乎丘民而　社稷次之君爲輕。　孟子曰民爲貴、　有也。　仁而得天下未之　得國者有之矣、不　孟子曰不仁而　用不足。　下亂無政事、則財　空虛。無禮義則上

2. 'Without the rules of propriety and distinctions of right, the high and the low will be thrown into confusion.

3. 'Without *the great principles of* government and their various business, there will not be wealth sufficient for the expenditure.'

CHAP. XIII. Mencius said, 'There are instances of individuals without benevolence, who have got possession of a *single* State, but there has been no instance of the throne's being got by one without benevolence.'

CHAP. XIV. 1. Mencius said, 'The people are the most important element *in a nation;* the spirits of the land and grain are the next; the sovereign is the lightest.

2. 'Therefore to gain the peasantry is the way to become sovereign;

fided to;' perhaps rather 'confided *in.*' 'Will become empty and void.'—Châo Ch'î supplements thus:—'If the prince do not consort with and confide in the virtuous and able, then they will go away, and a country without such persons is said to be empty and void.' 2, 3. 'The high and the low,'—that is, the distinction of ranks. 禮義 may be considered a hendiadys, and so 政事 in the next paragraph. 義 is the right, or *rightness,* on which the rules of propriety are founded, and 事 is the various business that flows from the right principles of government.

13. ONLY BY BENEVOLENCE CAN THE THRONE BE GOT. Many commentators put 有之 in the potential mood, as if it were 或有之. This is not allowable. Facts may be alleged that seem to be in opposition to the concluding statement. The commentator Tsâu (鄒) says:— 'From the dynasty of Ch'in downwards, there have been cases, when the throne was got by men without benevolence, but in such cases it has been lost again after one or two reigns.'

14. THE DIFFERENT ELEMENTS OF A NATION—THE PEOPLE, TUTELARY SPIRITS, AND SOVEREIGN, IN RESPECT OF THEIR IMPORTANCE. 1. 社 is

properly the altar, or resting-place of the spirit or spirits of the ground, and then used for the sacrifice to that spirit or those spirits. 稷 —'pannicled millet,' and then generally the spirit or spirits presiding over grain. Together, the characters denote the 'tutelary spirits of a country,' on whom its prosperity depends, and to sacrifice to whom was the prerogative of its sovereign.—It is often said that the 社 was 'to sacrifice to the spirits of the five kinds of ground, and the 稷 to sacrifice to those of the five kinds of grain.' But this is merely one of the numerical fancies of which Chinese writers are fond. The five kinds of ground are mountains and forests (山林), rivers and marshes (川澤), mounds (丘陵), places of tombs (墳行), and plains (原濕). But it would be easy to make another division, just as we have six, eight, and other ways of speaking about the kinds of grain. The regular sacrifices to these tutelary spirits were three :—one in spring, to pray for a good harvest; one in autumn, to give thanks for the harvest; and a third in the first month of winter. 2. 丘民=田野之民, 'the people of

Ii 2

廉懦夫有立志聞柳下
故聞伯夷之風者頑夫
師也伯夷柳下惠是也、
孟子曰聖人百世之
置社稷。
時然而旱乾水溢則變
既成粢盛既潔祭祀以
侯危社稷則變置。犧牲
侯得乎諸侯為大夫。諸
為天子得乎天子為諸

to gain the sovereign is the way to become a prince of a State; to gain the prince of a State is the way to become a great officer.

3. 'When a prince endangers the altars of the spirits of the land and grain, he is changed, and another appointed in his place.

4. 'When the sacrificial victims have been perfect, the millet in its vessels all pure, and the sacrifices offered at their proper seasons, if yet there ensue drought, or the waters overflow, the spirits of the land and grain are changed, and others appointed in their place.'

CHAP. XV. Mencius said, 'A sage is the teacher of a hundred generations:—this is true of Po-î and Hûi of Liû-hsiâ. Therefore when men now hear the character of Po-î, the corrupt become pure, and the weak acquire determination. When they hear the character of Hûi of Liû-hsiâ, the mean become generous, and the

the fields and wilds,' the peasantry. According to the Châu Lî, nine husbandmen, heads of families, formed a *tsing* (井); four *tsing* formed a *yîh* (邑); and four *yîh* formed a *k'ew* (丘), which would thus contain 144 families. But the phrase 丘人, signifying the peasantry, is yet equivalent to 'the people.' Mencius uses it, his discourse being of the spirits of the land and grain. 3. The change of the 社稷 is taken by most commentators as merely a destroying of the altars and building others. This is Chû Hsî's interpretation:—土穀之神 不能為民禦災捍患則毀其 壇壝而更置之, 'when the spirits of

the ground and grain cannot ward off calamities and evils from the people, then their altars and fences are thrown down and others in different places erected.' Châo Ch'î is more brief. He simply says that in such a case 毀社稷而 更置之, which may mean that they destroyed the altars or displaced the spirits themselves. A changing of the altars merely does not supply a parallel to the removal of the princes in the preceding paragraph. And there are traces of deposing the spirits in such a case, and appointing others in their places. See the 四書拓餘說, in loc.

15. THAT PO-Î AND HÛI OF LIÛ-HSIÂ WERE SAGES PROVED BY THE PERMANENCE OF THEIR INFLUENCE. Compare Bk. V. Pt. II. i, et al. 'A hundred generations' is spoken generally. Between the

惠之風者、薄夫敦、鄙夫寬、奮
乎百世之上、百世之下、聞者
莫不興起也、非聖人而能若
是乎、而況於親炙之者乎。
孟子曰、仁也者、人也、合而
言之道也。
孟子曰、孔子之去魯曰、遲
遲吾行也、去父母國之道也、
去齊接淅而行、去他國之道
也。

niggardly become liberal. *Those two* made themselves distinguished a hundred generations ago, and after a hundred generations, those who hear of them, are all aroused *in this manner.* Could such effects be produced by them, if they had not been sages? And how much more did they affect those who were in contiguity with them, and felt their inspiring influence!'

CHAP. XVI. Mencius said, 'Benevolence is *the distinguishing characteristic of* man. As embodied in man's conduct, it is called the path *of duty.*'

CHAP. XVII. Mencius said, 'When Confucius was leaving Lû, he said, "I will set out by-and-by;"—this was the way in which to leave the State of his parents. When he was leaving Ch'î, he strained off with his hand the water in which his rice was being rinsed, *took the rice,* and went away;—this was the way in which to leave a strange State.'

two worthies themselves, several hundred years intervened.

16. THE RELATION OF BENEVOLENCE TO MAN. This chapter is quite enigmatic. 合 is taken as—合仁于人身, 'unite benevolence with man's person,' and 道 as the 率性之道 of the Chung-yung. The glossarist of Châo Ch'î refers to Analects, XV. xxviii, which is very good. Chû Hsî, however, mentions that in an edition of Mencius found in Corea, after 人也, there follow accounts of 'righteousness,' 'propriety,' and 'wisdom;—義也者宜也云云. If that was the original reading, the final clause would be:—'These, all united and named, are the path of reason.'

17. How CONFUCIUS'S LEAVING LÛ AND CH'Î WAS DIFFERENT. Compare Bk. V. Pt. II. i. 4.

厥
問
文
王
也。

不
殄
厥
慍
亦
不
隕

于
群
小
孔
子
也
肆

詩
云
憂
心
悄
悄
慍

傷
也
士
憎
茲
多
口。

理
於
口
孟
子
曰
無

六
貉
稽
曰
稽
大
不

上
下
之
交
也。

尼
於
陳
蔡
之
間
無

六
孟
子
曰、君
子
之

Chap. XVIII. Mencius said, 'The reason why the superior man was reduced to straits between Ch'ăn and Ts'âi was because neither the princes *of the time* nor their ministers *sympathized or communicated* with him.'

Chap. XIX. 1. Mo Ch'î said, 'Greatly am I from anything to depend upon from the mouths *of men*.'

2. Mencius observed, 'There is no harm in that. Scholars are more exposed than others to suffer from the mouths *of men*.

3. 'It is said, in the Book of Poetry,
    "My heart is disquieted and grieved,
       I am hated by the crowd of mean creatures."
This might have been said by Confucius. And again,
    "Though he did not remove their wrath,
       He did not let fall his own fame."
This might be said of king Wăn.'

18. The reason of Confucius's being in straits between Ch'ăn and Ts'âi. See Analects, XI. ii. The speaking of Confucius simply by the term 君子 is to be noted ;—compare Analects, X. vi 1, *et al.* Châo Ch'î observes that Confucius, in his exceeding modesty, said that he was not equal to the threefold way of the superior man (Analects, XIV. xxx), and therefore he might be spoken of as a superior man. It is difficult to see the point of this observation, nor does it meet the difficulty which arises from the use of the designation in the text. 上=君, 'the sovereigns,' and 下=臣, 'their ministers.' The princes did not honour him and seek his services. Their ministers did not honour him and recommend him to employment. This is the meaning of 無上下之交. The commentators, in their quest for profound meanings, make out the lesson to be that though a sage may be reduced to straits, the way of truth cannot be so reduced.

19. Mencius comforts Mo Ch'î under calumny by the reflection that it was the ordinary lot of distinguished men. 1. Of Mo Ch'î, nothing is known beyond what is here intimated. 理 is used in the sense of 賴, 'to depend on.' This is given to it in the dictionary, with a reference to this passage. The meaning is that not only did he not have a good word from men, but was spoken ill of by them. 2. 憎, it is concluded, from the comment of Châo Ch'î, is a mistake for 增, 'to increase,' and 茲 has substantially the same meaning. Retaining 憎, however, and taking 茲 in its sense of *this* or *these*, we get a tolerable meaning, 'The scholar hates those many mouths.' 3. For the first quotation, see the Shih-ching, I. vii. Ode I. st. 4, a description of her condition by the ill-used wife of one of the dukes of Wei (according to Chû Hsî), and which Mencius somewhat strangely would apply to Confucius. For the second, see III. i. Ode III. st. 8, descrip-

矣。今茅塞子之心矣。路、爲閒不用、則茅塞之之蹊閒、介然用之而成孟子謂高子曰山徑昏使人昭昭。昭使人昭昭、今以其昏孟子曰、賢者以其昭

之曰、以追蠡曰、是奚足王之聲。孟子曰、何以言高子曰、禹之聲尚文

CHAP. XX. Mencius said, 'Anciently, men of virtue and talents by means of their own enlightenment made others enlightened. Nowadays, it is tried, *while they are themselves in darkness*, and by means of that darkness, to make others enlightened.'

CHAP. XXI. Mencius said to the disciple Kâo, 'There are the footpaths along the hills;—if suddenly they be used, they become roads; and if, as suddenly they are not used, the wild grass fills them up. Now, the wild grass fills up your mind.'

CHAP. XXII. 1. The disciple Kâo said, 'The music of Yü was better than that of king Wăn.'

2. Mencius observed, 'On what ground do you say so?' and the other replied, 'Because at the pivot the knob of Yü's bells is nearly worn through.'

3. *Mencius* said, 'How can that be a sufficient proof? Are

tive of the king T'âi, though applied to Wăn. 聞 is in the sense of 聞, 'report,' 'reputation.'

20. HOW THE ANCIENTS LED ON MEN BY THEIR EXAMPLE, WHILE THE RULERS OF MENCIUS'S TIME TRIED TO URGE MEN CONTRARY TO THEIR EXAMPLE. In translating, I supply 古之 before 賢者, in contrast with the 今 below. To the two 使 a very different force is given. The former is the constraining influence of example; the latter is the application of pains and penalties.

21. THAT THE CULTIVATION OF THE MIND MAY NOT BE INTERMITTED. 蹊閒, 'spaces for the foot,' = footpaths; 山徑之蹊閒,—the 'footpaths of the hill-ways.' 介 (read *chiá*, as

夏, according to Chû Hsî, though the dictionary does not give such a sound to the character, nor do we find in it the meaning which suits this passage) 然, 'suddenly;' nearly = 爲閒 The Kâo here must have been a disciple of Mencius, different from the old Kâo, Bk. VI. Pt. II. iii. Châo Ch'î says that after studying with Mencius for some time, and before he fully understood his principles, he went off and addicted himself to some other teacher, and that the remark was made with reference to this course, and its consequences.

22. AN ABSURD REMARK OF THE DISCIPLE KÂO ABOUT THE MUSIC OF YÜ AND KING WĂN. 2. 追, —read *tui*, 'the knob, or loop, of a bell,' the part by which it is suspended. 蠡, 3rd tone,

哉城門之軌兩馬之
力與。
齊饑陳臻曰國人
皆以夫子將復爲發
棠殆不可復孟子曰
是爲馮婦也晉人有
馮婦者善搏虎卒爲
善士則之野有衆逐
虎虎負嵎莫之敢攖
望見馮婦趨而迎之

the ruts at the gate of a city made by a single two-horsed chariot?'

CHAP. XXIII. 1. When Ch'î was suffering from famine, Chǎn Tsin said *to Mencius*, 'The people are all thinking that you, Master, will again ask that the granary of T'ang be opened for them. I apprehend you will not do so a second time.'

2. *Mencius* said, 'To do it would be to act like Făng Fû. There was a man of that name in Tsin, famous for his skill in seizing tigers. Afterwards he became a scholar of reputation, and going once out to the wild country, he found the people all in pursuit of a tiger. The tiger took refuge in a corner of a hill, where no one dared to attack him, but when they saw Făng Fû, they ran and met him. Făng Fû *immediately* bared his arms, and descended

an insect that bores through wood; hence, metaphorically, anything having the appearance of being eaten or worn away. 3. The meaning is that what Kâo noticed was only the effect of time or long use, Yü being anterior to king Wăn, and did not necessarily imply any superiority of the music of the one over that of the other. The street contracts at the gate, and all the carriages that have been running over its breadth are obliged to run in the same ruts, which hence are deeper here than elsewhere.—There is much controversy about the phrase 兩馬之力. Châo Ch'î understands 兩馬 as meaning 'two kinds of horses;'— the 國馬, levied from the State, and employed on what we may call the postal service, and the 公馬, or 'public horses,' principally used in military service. On this view the meaning would be that the ruts *in question* were not made by these two kinds of carriages only. Chû Hsî, after the commentator Făng

(豐氏), taken the meaning as I have given, it in the translation. Another view takes 兩 in the sense of 車, taking it in the 4th tone, as in chap. iv. 4. See the 四書拓餘說 *in loc.*

23. HOW MENCIUS KNEW WHERE TO STOP AND MAINTAIN HIS OWN DIGNITY IN HIS INTERCOURSE WITH THE PRINCES. 1. At T'ang, whose name is still preserved in the village of Kan-t'ang, in the district of Chî-mo (郎墨), in the department of Lâi-châu, the princes of Ch'î, it would appear, kept grain in store, and on some previous occurrence of famine, Mencius had advised the king to open the granary. In the meantime, however, some difference had occurred between him and the prince. He intended leaving Ch'î, and would not expose himself to a repulse by making an application which might be rejected.

2. 善士, 'a good scholar,' or 'officer,' but 善 is to be taken only as='skilful.' 之

馮婦攘臂下車眾皆悅之、
其為士者笑之。
孟子曰、口之於味也、目
之於色也、耳之於聲也、鼻
之於臭也、四肢之於安佚
也、性也、有命焉、君子不謂
性也。仁之於父子也、義之
於君臣也、禮之於賓主也、
智之於賢者也、聖人之於

from the carriage. The multitude were pleased with him, but those who were scholars laughed at him.'

CHAP. XXIV. 1. Mencius said, 'For the mouth to desire *sweet* tastes, the eye to desire *beautiful* colours, the ear to desire *pleasant* sounds, the nose to desire *fragrant* odours, and the four limbs to desire ease and rest;—these things are natural. But there is the appointment *of Heaven in connexion with them*, and the superior man does not say *of his pursuit of them*, "It is my nature."

2. '*The exercise of* love between father and son, *the observance of* righteousness between sovereign and minister, the rules of ceremony between guest and host, *the display of* knowledge *in* recognising the talented, and *the fulfilling* the heavenly course by the sage;—these are the appointment *of Heaven*. But there is *an adaptation of our*

野-之-往 It did not belong to Fäng Fŭ, now an officer, to be fighting with tigers, playing the part of a bravo.

24. HOW THE SUPERIOR MAN SUBJECTS THE GRATIFICATION OF HIS NATURAL APPETITES TO THE WILL OF HEAVEN, AND PURSUES THE DOING OF GOOD WITHOUT THINKING THAT THE AMOUNT WHICH HE CAN DO MAY BE LIMITED BY THAT WILL. 1. 口 之於味, 'the mouth's relation to tastes;' that is, its constitution so as to be pleased with certain tastes. So, all the other clauses. 有 命焉, 'there is the appointment *of Heaven*,' i.e. every appetite naturally desires its unlimited gratification, but a limited amount or an entire denial may be the will of Heaven. 2. 智之

於賢者 is not 'the possession of knowledge by the talented,' but the exercise of wisdom in reference to them, recognising and appreciating their excellence. The sentiment is well illustrated by the case of Yen Ying, the minister of Ch'î, able and wise, and yet insensible to the superior excellence of Confucius and his principles.—Chû Hsî says well upon this chapter:— 'I have heard it observed by my master that the things mentioned in both of these paragraphs are in the constitution of our nature, and likewise ordained by Heaven. Mankind, however, consider that the first five are more especially natural, and, though they may be prevented from obtaining them, still desire them; and that the last five are more especially appointed by Heaven, so that if they do not come to them readily, they do not go on to put forth their strength to reach them. On this account,

不可知之之謂神樂正
大而化之之謂聖聖而
充實而有光輝之謂大。
己之謂信充實之謂美。
信曰可欲之謂善有諸
也信人也何謂善
子何人也孟子曰善人
蓋浩生不害問曰樂正
子不謂命也。
天道也命也有性焉君

nature *for them*. The superior man does not say, *in reference to them*, "It is the appointment of Heaven."'

CHAP. XXV. 1. Hâo-shăng Pû-hâi asked, saying, 'What sort of man is Yo-chăng?' Mencius replied, 'He is a good man, a real man.'

2. 'What do you mean by "A good man," "A real man?"'

3. The reply was, 'A man who commands our liking is what is called a good man.

4. 'He whose *goodness* is part of himself is what is called a real man.

5. 'He whose *goodness* has been filled up is what is called a beautiful man.

6. 'He whose completed goodness is brightly displayed is what is called a great man.

7. 'When this great man exercises a transforming influence, he is what is called a sage.

8. 'When the sage is beyond our knowledge, he is what is called a spirit-man.

9. 'Yo-chăng is between the two *first* characters, and below the four las .'

Mencius shows what is most important in each case, that he may induce a broader way of thinking in regard to the second class, and repress the way of thinking in regard to the first.'

25. THE CHARACTER OF THE DISCIPLE YO-CHĂNG. DIFFERENT DEGREES OF ATTAINMENT IN CHARACTER, WHICH ARE TO BE AIMED AT. 1. Châo Ch'î tells us that Hâo-shăng is the surname and Pû-hâi the name, and that the individual was a man of Ch'î. This is all we know of him. 3. It is assumed here that the general verdict of man-

kind will be on the side of goodness. Hence when a man is *desirable*, and commands universal liking, he must be a *good* man. 4. 有諸已, 'having in himself;' i. e. when a man has the goodness, without hypocrisy or pretence. Compare Bk. VI. Pt. II. xiii. Goodness is an attribute entering into all the others, and I have therefore thrice expressed it in the translation. 8. 聖而不可知之之謂神,—with this we may compare what is

子二之中四之下也。

孟子曰、逃墨必歸於楊、

逃楊必歸於儒歸斯受之

而已矣。今之與楊墨辯者、

如追放豚既入其苙又從

而招之。

孟子曰、有布縷之征、粟

米之征力役之征君子用

其一緩其二用其二而民

有殍用其三而父子離。

CHAP. XXVI. 1. Mencius said, 'Those who are fleeing from *the errors of* Mo naturally turn to Yang, and those who are fleeing from *the errors of* Yang naturally turn to orthodoxy. When they so turn, they should at once and simply be received.

2. 'Those who nowadays dispute with the followers of Yang and Mo do so as if they were pursuing a stray pig, the leg of which, after they have got it to enter the pen, they proceed to tie.'

CHAP. XXVII. Mencius said, 'There are the exactions of hempen-cloth and silk, of grain, and of personal service. The prince requires but one of these *at once*, deferring the other two. If he require two of them *at once*, then the people die of hunger. If he require the three *at once*, then fathers and sons are separated.'

said in the Doctrine of the Mean, 至誠如神, 'the individual possessed of the most complete sincerity is like a spirit.' In the critical remarks in the 四書合講, it is said, indeed, that the expression in the text is stronger than that there, but the two are substantially to the same effect. Some would translate 神 by 'divine,' a rendering which it never can admit of, and yet, in applying to man the term appropriate to the actings and influence of Him whose way is in the sea, and His judgments a great deep, Chinese writers derogate from the prerogatives of God.

26. RECOVERED HERETICS SHOULD BE RECEIVED WITHOUT CASTING THEIR OLD ERRORS IN THEIR TEETH. 1. 歸於儒 'they turn to the learned.' 'The learned' in Chinese phrase is equivalent to our 'the orthodox.' The name is still claimed in China by the followers of Confucius and other sages, in opposition to the Tâoists and Buddhists. 2. The disputations are with those who had been Yangists and Mohists. This sense of 招, 'to tie the legs,' is found in the dictionary with reference to this passage.

27. THE JUST EXACTIONS OF THE GOVERNMENT ARE TO BE MADE DISCRIMINATINGLY AND CONSIDERATELY. 布 is cloth, made from flax. 縷, 'silken fibres not spun;' but here, probably, silk, spun or unspun. 粟 'grain unthreshed;' 米, the same threshed:—here together, grain generally. The tax of cloth and silk was due in summer, that of grain after harvest, and personal service was for the leisure of winter. 君子=君. The prince might only require them, one at a time, and in their proper seasons.

孟子曰諸侯之寶三土地

人民政事寶珠玉者殃必及

身。

盆成括仕於齊孟子曰死

矣盆成括盆成括見殺門人

問曰夫子何以知其將見殺。

曰其為人也小有才未聞君

子之大道也則足以殺其軀

而已矣。

孟子之滕館於上宮有業

CHAP. XXVIII. Mencius said, 'The precious things of a prince are three;—the territory, the people, the government and its business. If one value as most precious pearls and jade, calamity is sure to befall him.'

CHAP. XXIX. P'an-ch'ǎng Kwo having obtained an official situation in Ch'ï, Mencius said, 'He is a dead man, that P'an-ch'ǎng Kwo!' P'an-ch'ǎng Kwo being put to death, the disciples asked, saying, 'How did you know, Master, that he would meet with death?' Mencius replied, 'He was a man, who had a little ability, but had not learned the great doctrines of the superior man.— He was just qualified to bring death upon himself, but for nothing more.'

CHAP. XXX. 1. When Mencius went to Tǎng, he was lodged in the Upper palace. A sandal in the process of making had been

28. THE PRECIOUS THINGS OF A PRINCE, AND THE DANGER OF OVERLOOKING THEM FOR OTHER THINGS. 土, 'the productive ground,' and 地, 'land generally.' 人 as distinguished from 民 = 'officers,' but the terms are not to be taken separately. So of 政事; see chap. xii.

29. How MENCIUS PREDICTED BEFOREHAND THE DEATH OF P'AN-CH'ǍNG KWO. Compare Confusius's prediction of Tsze-lû's death, Analects, XI. xii. Little is known of this Kwo. He is said to have begun learning with Mencius, but to

have soon gone away, disappointed by what he heard.

30. THE GENEROUS SPIRIT OF MENCIUS IN DEFENDING HIS INSTRUCTIONS. This, which is the lesson of the chapter, only comes out at the end, and has been commemorated, as being the remark of an individual act of extraordinary character, and at first disposed to find fault with Mencius's disciples. 1. 之 滕,—之-往. 上宮,—compare 雪宮, Bk. I. Pt. II. iv. This was evidently a palace appropriated by the duke of Tǎng for the lodging of honourable visitors. The first 館

屨於牖上、館人求之弗得。或問之曰、若是乎從者之廋也。曰子以是為竊屨來與。曰殆非也夫子之設科也、往者不追、來者不拒、苟以是心至、斯受之而已矣。

孟子曰人皆有所不忍、達之於其所忍仁也、人皆有所不為達之於其所為、義也。人能充無欲害人之

placed there in a window, and when the keeper of the place *came to* look for it, he could not find it.

2. *On this*, some one asked *Mencius*, saying, 'Is it thus that your followers pilfer?' Mencius replied, 'Do you think that they came here to pilfer the sandal?' The man said, 'I apprehend not. But you, Master, having arranged to give lessons, do not go back to inquire into the past, and you do not reject those who come to you. If they come with the mind to learn, you receive them without any more ado.'

CHAP. XXXI. 1. Mencius said, All men have some things which they cannot bear;—extend that feeling to what they can bear, and benevolence will be the result. All men have some things which they will not do;—extend that feeling to the things which they do, and righteousness will be the result.

2. 'If a man can give full development to the feeling which

is a verb, 'was lodged.' The second makes a compound noun with 人. 業屨,—the dictionary has, with reference to this passage, 事物已為而未成曰業 'things being done, but not completed, are said to be 業.' 2. Sáu (=廋), 'to hide,'= to steal and hide. 曰子以是=是 'these,' referring to 'followers.' 夫子之設科云云,—according to Chû Hsî, this is the observation of Mencius's questioner, suddenly awaking to an understanding of the philosopher. Anciently, 夫子 was read 夫子, 'now, I,' and Mencius was supposed to be himself the speaker. Chû Hsî is, no doubt, correct. 設科 is better than 設教科 conveying the idea of 'exercises' suited to different capacities. 是心一向道之心.

31. A MAN HAS ONLY TO GIVE DEVELOPMENT TO THE PRINCIPLES OF GOOD WHICH ARE IN HIM, AND SHOW THEMSELVES IN SOME THINGS, TO BE ENTIRELY GOOD AND CORRECT. This is a sentiment which we have found continually occurring in these analects. It supposes that man has more power over himself than he really has. 2. 穿=穿

心而仁不可勝用也人能
充無穿窬之心而義不可
勝用也人能充無受爾汝
之實無所往而不爲義也
士未可以言而言是以言
餂之也可以言而不言是
以不言餂之也是皆穿窬
之類也。
孟子曰言近而指遠者
善言也守約而施博者善

makes him shrink from injuring others, his benevolence will be more than can be called into practice. If he can give full development to the feeling which refuses to break through, or jump over, *a wall*, his righteousness will be more than can be called into practice.

3. 'If he can give full development to the real feeling of dislike with which he receives the salutation, "Thou," "Thou," he will act righteously in all places and circumstances.

4. 'When a scholar speaks what he ought not to speak, by *guile of* speech seeking to gain some end; and when he does not speak what he ought to speak, by *guile of* silence seeking to gain some end;—both these cases are of a piece with breaking through *a neighbour's wall.'

CHAP. XXXII. 1. Mencius said, 'Words which are simple, while their meaning is far-reaching, are good words. Principles which, as held, are compendious, while their application is extensive,

穴, 'to make a hole through.' 窬=窬墻 'to jump over a wall.' The two together are equivalent to 'to play the thief.' 3. 'Thou,' 'Thou,' is a style of address greatly at variance with Chinese notions of propriety. It can only be used to the very young and the very mean. A man will revolt from it as used to himself, and 'if he be careful to act so that men will not dare to speak to him in this style, he will go nowhere where he will not do righteousness.'— This is rather far-fetched. 4. 餂, 'to lick with the tongue;' = 'to inveigle.' To find an antecedent to the 之, we must understand the person who is spoken to, or before whom silence is kept; or, perhaps, 之 merely gives effect to the verb in the general sense of 'to gain some end.'

32. AGAINST AIMING AT WHAT IS REMOTE, AND NEGLECTING WHAT IS NEAR. WHAT ARE GOOD WORDS AND GOOD PRINCIPLES. 1. 不下帶— see the Book of Rites, Bk. I. Sect. II. iii. 15. The ancients did not look at a person below the girdle, so that all above that might be considered as near, beneath the eyes. The phrase 近言 = 'words which are near,' i.e. on

道也君子之言也不下帶、
而道存焉君子之守修其
身而天下平人病舍其田、
而芸人之田所求於人者
重而所以自任者輕。
孟子曰堯舜性者也湯
武反之也。動容周旋中禮
者盛德之至也哭死而哀、
非爲生者也經德不回、非
以干祿也言語必信非以

are good principles. The words of the superior man do not go below the girdle, but *great* principles are contained in them.

2. 'The principle which the superior man holds is that of personal cultivation, but the kingdom is thereby tranquillized.

3. 'The disease of men is this:—that they neglect their own fields, and go to weed the fields of others, and that what they require from others is great, while what they lay upon themselves is light.'

CHAP. XXXIII. 1. Mencius said, 'Yâo and Shun were what they were by nature; T'ang and Wû were so by returning *to natural virtue.*

2. 'When all the movements, in the countenance and every turn of *the body*, are exactly what is proper, that shows the extreme degree of the complete virtue. Weeping for the dead should be from *real* sorrow, and not because of the living. The regular path of virtue is to be pursued without any bend, and from no view to emolument. The words should all be necessarily sincere, not with any desire to do what is right.

common subjects, simple, plain. So, Chù Hsî; but the passage in the Lî Chî is not so general as his commentary. It gives the rule for looking by the sovereign. He is not to raise his eyes above a minister's collar, nor lower them below the girdle. Châo Ch'î tries to explain the expression without reference to the ancient rule for regulating the looking at men. According to him, 'words not below the girdle are all from near the heart.' 2. This is the explanation of 守約而施博; see Ana-

lects, VI. xxv. The paragraph is a good summary of the teaching of The Great Learning.

33. THE PERFECT VIRTUE OF THE HIGHEST SAGES, AND HOW OTHERS FOLLOW AFTER IT. 1. Compare Pt. I. xxx, but 之 has not here a special reference to certain virtues as there. 2. This is an exhibition of the highest style of virtue—that of Yâo and Shun, which does everything right, with no motive beyond the doing so. 'Weeping is from real sorrow, and not because of the living,' i.e. there is nothing of show in it, and no wish to make an impression on

正行也君子行法以俟命而
已矣。
孟子曰說大人則藐之勿
視其巍巍然堂高數仞榱題
數尺我得志弗爲也食前方
丈侍妾數百人我得志弗爲
也般樂飲酒驅騁田獵後車
千乘我得志弗爲也在彼者、
皆我所不爲也在我者皆古
之制也吾何畏彼哉。

3. 'The superior man performs the law *of right*, and thereby waits simply for what has been appointed.'

CHAP. XXXIV. 1. Mencius said, 'Those who give counsel to the great should despise them, and not look at their pomp and display.

2. 'Halls several times eight cubits high, with beams projecting several cubits;—these, if my wishes were to be realized, I would not have. Food spread before me over ten cubits square, and attendants and concubines to the amount of hundreds;—these, though my wishes were realized, I would not have. Pleasure and wine, and the dash of hunting, with thousands of chariots following after me;—these, though my wishes were realized, I would not have. What they esteem are what I would have nothing to do with; what I esteem are the rules of the ancients.—Why should I stand in awe of them?'

others. 3. Describes the virtue that is next in degree, equally observant of right, but by an intellectual constraint. 法＝天理之當然, 'the proper course indicated by Heavenly principles.'

34. HE WHO UNDERTAKES TO COUNSEL THE GREAT, SHOULD BE MORALLY ABOVE THEM. 1. 大人, 'great men.' The phrase is to be understood not of the truly great, as in ch. xxv. 6, *et al.*, but of the socially great, with an especial reference to the princes of the time, dignified by their position, but without corresponding moral qualities. 2. 堂高, 云云, and all the corresponding clauses, are under the government of some words like 彼大人有, 'those great men have,' to which 我弗爲, 'I would not do,' respond. 榱題,—these may be seen in the more important temples and public buildings throughout China, projecting all round, beneath the eaves. 般樂,—see Bk. II. Pt. I. iv. 4. 驅騁田獵, 'spurring and galloping in hunting.' 在彼

養心莫善於寡欲。
其為人也寡欲雖有不存焉
者寡矣。其為人也多欲雖有
存焉者寡矣。

曾晳嗜羊棗而曾子不忍
食羊棗。

公孫丑問曰、膾炙與羊
棗孰美。孟子曰、膾炙哉。公
孫丑曰、然則曾子何為食膾
炙而不食羊棗。曰、膾炙所同
也、羊棗所獨也。諱名不諱姓、姓
所同也、名所獨也。

CHAP. XXXV. Mencius said, 'To nourish the mind there is nothing better than to make the desires few. Here is a man whose desires are few:—in some things he may not be able to keep his heart, but they will be few. Here is a man whose desires are many:—in some things he may be able to keep his heart, but they will be few.'

CHAP. XXXVI. 1. Mencius said, 'Tsăng Hsî was fond of sheep-dates, and his son, the philosopher Tsăng, could not bear to eat sheep-dates.'

2. Kung-sun Ch'âu asked, saying, 'Which is best,—minced meat and broiled meat, or sheep-dates?' Mencius said, 'Mince and broiled meat, to be sure.' Kung-sun Ch'âu went on, 'Then why did the philosopher Tsăng eat mince and broiled meat, and would not eat sheep-dates?' Mencius answered, 'For mince and broiled meat

者, 'what are in them;' the thing which they commit to. 在我者 = the things which I possess.

35. THE REGULATION OF THE DESIRES IS ESSENTIAL TO THE NOURISHMENT OF THE MIND. 欲 must be taken in a bad, or at least an inferior sense—the appetites, while 心 is the heart naturally disposed to all virtue. 雖有不存焉, 'although there are' = virtues of the heart, that is,—'which are not preserved.'

36. THE SMALL FILIAL FEELING OF TSĂNG-TSZĔ IN HIS NOT EATING JUJUBES. 1. 羊棗, 'sheep-jujubes,' the small black northern fruit, so called from its resembling sheep's dirt. Such is Chû Hsî's account of the fruit. The writer of the 四書拓餘說 is for, however, seems to make out a case for 羊棗 being a kind of persimmon. Still, why call it a date, or jujube? See Bretschneider's Botanicon Sinicum, p. 118. o. Hsî must have eaten both the jujubes and the cooked meat, but his liking

思其次也敢問何如斯可謂
豈不欲中道哉不可必得故
進取獲者有所不爲也孔子
道而與之必也狂獲乎狂者
之狂士孟子曰孔子不得中
不忘其初孔子在陳何思魯
歸乎來吾黨之士狂簡進取
萬章問曰孔子在陳曰盍
姓所同也名所獨也。

there is a common liking, while that for sheep-dates was peculiar. We avoid the name, but do not avoid the surname. The surname is common; the name is peculiar.'

CHAP. XXXVII. 1. Wan Chang asked, saying, 'Confucius, when he was in Ch'ăn, said: "Let me return. The scholars of my school are ambitious, but hasty. They are for advancing and seizing their object, but cannot forget their early ways." Why did Confucius, when he was in Ch'ăn, think of the ambitious scholars of Lû?'

2. Mencius replied, 'Confucius not getting men pursuing the true medium, to whom he might communicate *his instructions*, determined to take the ardent and the cautiously-decided. The ardent would advance to seize their object; the cautiously-decided would keep themselves from certain things. It is not to be thought that Confucius did not wish to get men pursuing the true medium, but being unable to assure himself of finding such, he therefore thought of the next class.'

3. 'I venture to ask what sort of men they were who could be styled "The ambitious?"'

for the jujubes was peculiar, and therefore the sight of them brought him vividly up to his son, and he could not bear to eat them. But such points are not important to illustrate the meaning here.

37. TO CALL TO THE PURSUIT OF THE RIGHT MEDIUM WAS THE OBJECT OF CONFUCIUS AND

MENCIUS. VARIOUS CHARACTERS WHO FAIL TO PURSUE THIS, OR ARE OPPOSED TO IT. 1. See Analects, V. xxi. The differences between that text and what we have here will be noted. Perhaps Wan Chang was quoting from memory. 2. See Analects, XIII. xxi. As Mencius quotes that chapter, some think that there should be

狂矣。如琴張、曾皙、牧皮者、

孔子之所謂狂矣。何以謂之

狂也。曰其志嘐嘐然曰古之

人古之人。夷考其行而不掩

焉者也。狂者又不可得欲得

不屑不潔之士而與之是獧

也。是又其次也。孔子曰過我

門而不入我室。我不憾焉者、

其惟鄉原乎。鄉原德之賊也。

曰何如斯可謂之鄉原矣。曰

4. 'Such,' replied Mencius, 'as Ch'in Chang, Tsăng Hsî, and Mû P'ei, were those whom Confucius styled "ambitious?"'

5. 'Why were they styled "ambitious?"'

6. The reply was, 'Their aim led them to talk magniloquently, saying, "The ancients!" "The ancients!" But their actions, where we fairly compare them with *their words, did* not correspond with them.

7. 'When he found also that he could not get such as were *thus* ambitious, he wanted to get scholars who would consider anything impure as beneath them. Those were the cautiously-decided,—a class next to the former.'

8. *Chang pursued his questioning,* 'Confucius said, "They are only your good careful people of the villages at whom I feel no indignation, when they pass my door without entering my house. Your good careful people of the villages are the thieves of virtue." What sort of people were they who could be styled "Your good careful people of the villages?"'

a 曰 in the text after 孔子. 4. Ch'in Chang is the Lao mentioned, Analects, IX. vi. So, according to Chû Hsî, who quotes an instance from the Tâoist philosopher Chwang, of the waywardness of Lao, but Chwang's accounts of Confucius and his disciples are not to be trusted. The identification of the individual in the text with Lao, however, is no doubt correct, though Châo Ch'î makes him to be the Shih of the Analects, referring to XI. xvii. 3, 'Shih is specious,' and adding that he played well on the *ch'in*, and was therefore styled Ch'in. See the 四書拓餘說 *in loc.* Of Mû P'ei nothing is known. 6. 夷,—in the sense of 平, 'even.' 夷考, 'evenly examining.' 掩, 'to cover,'=to make good. 8. The first part of the saying here attributed to Confucius is not found in the Analects. For the second,

何以是嘐嘐也言不顧行行不
顧言則曰古之人古之人行何
爲踽踽涼涼生斯世也爲斯世
也善斯可矣閹然媚於世也者、
是鄉原也。萬章曰一鄉皆稱原
人焉無所往而不爲原人孔子
以爲德之賊何哉曰非之無舉
也剌之無剌也同乎流俗合乎
汙世居之似忠信行之似廉潔
眾皆悅之自以爲是而不可與

9. *Mencius* replied, 'They are those who say, "Why are they so
magniloquent? Their words have not respect to their actions, and
their actions have not respect to their words, but they say,—*The
ancients! The ancients!* Why do they act so peculiarly, and are
so cold and distant? Born in this age, we should be of this age, to
be good is all that is needed." Eunuch-like, flattering their generation;—such are your good careful men of the villages.'

10. Wan Chang said, 'Their whole village styles those men good
and careful. In all their conduct they are so. How was it that
Confucius considered them the thieves of virtue?'

11. *Mencius* replied, 'If you would blame them, you find nothing
to allege. If you would criticise them, you have nothing to criticise.
They agree with the current customs. They consent with an impure
age. Their principles have a semblance of right-heartedness and
truth. Their conduct has a semblance of disinterestedness and
purity. All men are pleased with them, and they think themselves
right, so that it is impossible to proceed with them to the principles

see XVII. xiii. 9. Before this paragraph we
must understand 孟子曰. The 曰 in
the text has for its subject 鄉原, or we may
take it in the infinitive, making the whole paragraph down to 也者 the antecedent subject

to the 是 that follows. 善斯可矣, 'to
be good is enough,' i.e. to be accounted good by
the age in which they live is enough for them.
踽踽 'the appearance of walking alone,' i.e.
acting peculiarly. 11. 流俗 is literally our

百有餘歲若禹皐陶則見而
孟子曰、由堯舜至於湯五
庶民興、斯無邪慝矣。
反經而已矣、經正則庶民興、
也、惡鄉原恐其亂德也、君子
恐其亂樂也、惡紫恐其亂朱
惡利口恐其亂信也、惡鄭聲、
其亂苗也、惡佞恐其亂義也、
孔子曰惡似而非者、惡莠恐
入堯舜之道、故曰、德之賊也。

of Yâo and Shun. On this account they are called "The thieves of virtue."

12. 'Confucius said, "I hate a semblance which is not the reality. I hate the darnel, lest it be confounded with the corn. I hate glib-tonguedness, lest it be confounded with righteousness. I hate sharpness of tongue, lest it be confounded with sincerity. I hate the music of Chăng, lest it be confounded with *the true* music. I hate the reddish blue, lest it be confounded with vermilion. I hate your good careful men of the villages, lest they be confounded with the *truly* virtuous."

13. 'The superior man seeks simply to bring back the unchanging standard; and, that being correct, the masses are roused to virtue. When they are so aroused, forthwith perversities and glossed wickedness disappear.'

CHAP. XXXVIII. 1. Mencius said, 'From Yâo and Shun down to T'ang were 500 years and more. As to Yu and Kâo Yâo, they

'current customs,' but 流, at the same time, stigmatizes the customs as bad. 居之-居 之於心者；行之-行之於身 者. 12. These are sayings of Confucius which are only found here. Such a string of them is not in the sage's style. 恐其亂苗, 'lest it confound the corn,'—be confounded with it. So in the other phrases. 鄭聲,—see Ana-

lects, XV. x. 紫—see Analects, X. vi. s. 13. This paragraph explains the rest of the chapter. The 經, or 'unchanging standard,' is the 中道, 'the right medium, which the sage himself pursues, and to which he seeks to recall others.

38. ON THE TRANSMISSION OF THE LINE OF DOCTRINE FROM YÂO TO MENCIUS'S OWN TIME. Compare Bk. II. Pt. II. xiii; Bk. III. Pt. II. x; et al. 1. From the commencement of Shun's

知之若湯、則聞而知之由湯至
於文王五百有餘歲若伊尹萊
朱則見而知之若文王則聞而
知之由文王至於孔子五百有
餘歲若太公望散宜生則見而
知之若孔子則聞而知之由孔
子而來至於今百有餘歲去聖
人之世若此其未遠也近聖人
之居若此其甚也然而無有乎
爾則亦無有乎爾。

saw *those earliest sages*, and' *so* knew their doctrines, while T'ang heard their doctrines *as transmitted*, and *so* knew them.

2. 'From T'ang to king Wăn were 500 years and more. As to Î Yin, and Lâi Chû, they saw *Tang* and knew his doctrines, while king Wăn heard them *as transmitted*, and so knew them.

3. 'From king Wăn to Confucius were 500 years and more. As to T'âi-kung Wang and San Î-shăng, they saw *Wăn*, and so knew his doctrines, while Confucius heard them *as transmitted*, and so knew them.

4. 'From Confucius downwards until now, there are *only* 100 years and *somewhat* more. The distance in time from the sage is so far from being remote, and so very near at hand was the sage's residence. In these circumstances, is there no one *to transmit his doctrines*? Yea, is there no one *to do so*?'

reign to that of T'ang's were 489 years, while from Tang to the rise of the Châu dynasty were 644 years. Here. as before, Bk. II. Pt. II. xiii, Mencius uses 500 as a round number. In 知之, the 之 refers to the doctrines of the sages. 2. Lâi Chû is not exactly identified. Most make him the same with T'ang's minister, Chung-hûi; see the Shû-ching, IV. ii. 3. T'âi-kung Wang,—see Bk. IV. Pt. I. xiii. Of San Î-shăng more can hardly be said to be known than that he was an able minister of king Wăn.

Chû Hsî seems to be wrong, however, in making San, instead of San-î, to be the surname. See the 四書拓餘說, *in loc.* 4. The concluding sentences here wonderfully vex commentators. In the 'Supplemental Commentary' (翼註) are found five different interpretations of them. But all agree that Mencius somehow takes upon himself the duty and responsibility of handing down the doctrines of the sage.

INDEXES.

INDEX I.

OF SUBJECTS.

The references to the Book, Part, Chapter, and Paragraph are marked thus—I. i. 1. 1. In the first edition, for Parts i and ii the characters 上 *and* 下 *were used in all the Indexes.*

Absurdity of a ruler not following wise counsellors, I. ii. 9.
Acknowledged favours, how Mencius, VI. ii. 5.
Action, faith necessary to firmness in, VI. ii. 12.
Adherence to one special course, against obstinacy, VII. i. 26.
Advantages, the greatest, of friendship, V. ii. 8.
Advice of Mencius with regard to mourning, III. i. 2.
Adviser of the princes might always be perfectly satisfied, how an, VII. i. 9.
Affliction, benefits of, VII. i. 18.
Aged, the, were nourished by the government of king Wăn, VII. i. 22.
Ages, different conduct of great men in different, reconcileable, IV. ii. 29.
Agreement of sages not affected by place or time, IV. ii. 1.
Agriculture, importance of a ruler attending to, III. i. 3 : a ruler should not labour at, with his own hands, III. i. 4.
Air, how one's material position affects his, VII. i. 36.
Ambition and avarice, evils of, I. ii. 11 : of king Hûi of Liang, VII. ii. 1.
Ambitious, who were the, VII. ii. 37.
Ancient(s), the, shared their pleasures with the people, I. i. 2 : surpassed other men in what, I. i. 7 : the music of the, I. ii. 1 : sovereigns, tours of inspection made by, I. ii. 4 : VI. ii. 7 : coffins used by the, II. ii. 7 : sages, how all men may become equal to the, III. i. 1 : kings practised benevolent government, III. ii. 5 : Mencius appeals to the example and maxims of the, III. ii. 7 : kings, the example and principles of, must be studied, IV. i. 1 ; 2 : the, exchanged sons, each one teaching the son of the other, IV. i. 18 : making friends of the, V. ii. 8 : the, cultivated the nobility that is of Heaven, VI. i. 16 : scholars maintained the dignity of their characters, how, VII. i. 8 : and modern rule contrasted, VII. ii. 8 : the, led men by their example, VII. ii. 20.
Animals, man how much different from, IV. ii. 19.
Antiquity, the example of, VII. i. 9.
Appetites, the superior man subjects his to the will of Heaven, VII. ii. 24.
Archer, he who would be benevolent is like an, II. i. 7.

Archery, learning, IV. ii. 24 : VI. i. 20.
Arrangement of dignities and emoluments according to the dynasty of Châu, V. ii. 2.
Association, influence of, III. ii. 6 : VI. i. 9 : with those of whom one does not approve, unavoidable, III. ii. 10.
Attainment, real, must be made by the learner for himself, VII. ii. 5.
Authority, punishment should be inflicted only by the proper, II. ii. 8.

Barbarians, influence of the Chinese on, III. i. 4 ; ii. 9.
Barley, illustration taken from, VI. i. 7.
Beauty, the love of, compatible with royal government, I. ii. 5 : only moral is truly excellent, IV. ii. 25.
Behaviour of Mencius with an unworthy associate, II. ii. 6.
Benefits of trouble and affliction, VII. i. 18.
Benevolence and righteousness, I. i. 1 : VI. ii. 4 : belongs naturally to man, II. i. 6 : IV. i. 10 : VI. i. 1 : VII. i. 15 ; ii. 16 : exhortation to, II. i. 7 : importance to all of exercising, IV. i. 2 : the only security of a prince, IV. i. 7 ; 8 : 9 : filial piety the richest fruit of, IV. i. 27 : the superior man preserves, IV. ii. 28 : and righteousness equally internal, VI. i. 4 ; 5 : it is necessary to practise with all one's might, VI. i. 18 : must be matured, VI. i. 19 : and righteousness, the difference between Yâo and Shun, T'ang and Wû, and the five Chiefs in relation to, VII. i. 30 : the throne can be got only by, VII. ii. 13.
Benevolent government, I. i. 5 ; 7 : III. i. 8 : IV. ii. 1 : safety and prosperity lie in, I. ii. 11 : affections of the people secured by, I. ii. 12 : glory the result of, II. i. 4 : the prince who sets about practising, has none to fear, III. ii. 5.
Bodily defects, how men are sensible of, VI. ii. 12 : organisation, only a sage can satisfy the design of his, VII. i. 38.
Book of Rites, quotations from, II. ii. 2 : III. ii. 3 : IV. i. 1.
Brilliant Palace, the, or Hall of Distinction, I. ii. 5.
Burial, Mencius's, of his mother, I. ii. 16 : II. ii. 7 : of Mo's parents, III. i. 5.

Calamity and happiness are men's own seeking,

II. i. 4 : the superior man is beyond the reach of calamity, IV. ii. 28.

Calumny, comfort under, VII. ii. 19.

Careful, the thought of consequences should make men, VII. ii. 7.

Cattle and sheep, illustration taken from feeding, II. ii. 4.

Character, how men judge wrongly of, VII. i. 34 : different degrees of attainment in, VII. ii. 25.

Charge of one's self the greatest of charges, IV. i. 19.

Chess-playing, illustration from, VI. i. 9.

Chief ministers, the duties of, V. ii. 9.

Chiefs of the princes, the five, VI. ii. 7.

Chieftain of the princes not a sovereign of the kingdom, II. i. 3 : influence of a, different from that of a true sovereign, VII. i. 13.

Childlike, the great man is, IV. ii. 12.

Common relations of life, importance of, to the prosperity of the kingdom, IV. i. 11.

Compass and square, use of the, IV. i. 2.

Concert, the character of Confucius a complete, V. ii. 1.

Condemnation of king Hûi of Liang, VII. ii. 1.

Confidence of the sovereign, how to obtain, IV. i. 12.

Consequences, the thought of, should make men careful, VII. ii. 7.

Conspicuous mound, monopolizing the, II. ii. 10.

Constitution, benevolence and righteousness part of man's, VII. i. 15.

Conviction, how Mencius brought home, II. ii. 4.

Cookery, Î Yin's knowledge of, V. i. 7.

Corn, assisting, to grow, II. i. 2.

Corrupt times are provided against by established virtue, VII. ii. 10.

Counselling princes from the ground of profit, danger of, VI. ii. 4.

Counsellors of great men should be morally above them, VII. ii. 34.

Counsels for the government of a kingdom, III. i. 3.

Courses, two, open to a prince pursued by his enemies, I. ii. 15 : of Yâo and Shun, open to all, VI. ii. 2.

Court, Mencius would not pay, to a favourite, IV. ii. 27.

Cultivation, men's disregard of self-, VI. i. 13 : men may become Yâos and Shuns by the, of their principles and ways, VI. ii. 2 : of the mind must not be intermitted, VII. ii. 21.

Death or flight, which should be chosen, I. ii. 15 : there are things which men dislike more than death, VI. i. 10 : how Mencius predicted the, of P'ân Ch'ang-kwo, VII. ii. 29.

Decencies may not be expected, where virtues are wanting, VII. i. 44.

Decrees of Heaven, man's duty as affected by the, VII. i. 2.

Deeds, not words or manners, prove mental qualities, IV. i. 16.

Defects, men are sensible of bodily, but not of mental or moral, VI. i. 12.

Defence, of Shun's conduct, V. i. 2 ; 3 : of Î Yin, V. i. 7 : of Confucius, V. i. 8 : of accepting presents from oppressors of the people, V. ii. 4.

Degeneracy, the progress of, from the three kings to the five chiefs of the princes, and from those princes to their ministers, VI. ii. 7.

Deluge, the Chinese, III. i. 4, note 7 ; ii. 9 ; IV. ii. 26 : VI. ii. 11.

Desires, the regulation of, essential, VII. ii. 35.

Developing their natural goodness may make men equal to the ancient sages, III. i. 1 : VII. ii. 31.

Dignities, arrangement of, in the Châu dynasty, V. ii. 2.

Dignity, how the ancient scholars maintained their, VII. i. 8 : how Mencius maintained his, with the princes, VII. ii. 23.

Disappointment of Mencius with the king Hsiang, I. i. 6.

Discrimination of what is right and wrong must precede vigorous right-doing, IV. ii. 8.

Disgraceful means which men take to seek wealth and honour, IV. ii. 33.

Disposition, a man's true, will often appear in small matters, VII. ii. 11.

Disputing, Mencius, not fond of, III. ii. 9.

Dissatisfaction with a parent, not necessarily unfilial, VI. ii. 3.

Division of labour, propriety of the, III. i. 4.

Doctrine, of the Mohists refuted, III. i. 5 : heretical, III. ii. 9 : of the Mean, quotation from the, IV. i. 12 : of the sages, to be advanced to by successive steps, VII. i. 24 : on the transmission of, from Yâo to Mencius's own time, VII. ii. 38.

Duties which the virtuous and talented owe to the young and ignorant, IV. ii. 7 : of different classes of chief ministers, V. ii. 9.

Duty, man's, how affected by the decrees of Heaven, VII. i. 2 : benevolence the path of, VII. ii. 16.

Dynasties, Hsiâ, Yin, and Châu, II. i. 1 : III. i. 3 : V. i. 6 : Châu, II. ii. 13 : V. ii. 2 : the three, III. i. 3 : IV. i. 3 ; ii. 20 : Hsiâ and Yin, IV. i. 2 : Shang or Yin and Châu, IV. i. 7.

Earth, advantages of situation afforded by the, II. ii. 1.

Earth-worm, an over-fastidious scholar compared to an, III. ii. 10.

Education, importance of a ruler attending to, III. i. 3.

Elated by riches, not to be, a proof of superiority, VII. i. 11.

Emoluments, arrangement of, in the Châu dynasty, V. ii. 2.

End, the, may justify the means, VII. i. 31.

Enjoyment, man's nature the source of his true, VII. i. 21.

Equanimity of Shun in poverty, and as sovereign, VII. ii. 6.

Error of a Mohist refuted, III. i. 5 ; ii. 9.

Errors of Yang, Mo, and Tsze-mo, VII. i. 26 ; ii. 26.

Evil, a warning to the violently, and the weakly, IV. i. 10 : speaking, brings with it evil consequences, IV. ii. 9.

Exactions just, should be made with discrimination, VII. ii. 27.

Example, influence of, III. ii. 6 : influence of a ruler's, IV. ii. 5 : the ancients led men by, VII. ii. 20.

Excellence, how a prince cannot subdue men merely by his, IV. ii. 16.

Excusing of errors, how Mencius beat down the, II. ii. 9.

Exhortation to benevolence, II. i. 7.

Explanation of friendly intercourse with

INDEX II.

OF PROPER NAMES

Tsze-chih, the minister of Tsze-k'wái of Yen, II. ii. 3.

Tsze-cho Zŭ, an archer of, IV. ii. 24.

Tsze-hsiá, a disciple of Confucius, II. i. 2 : III. i. 4.

Tsze-hsiang, a disciple of Tsäng-tsze, II. i. 2.

Tsze-kung, a disciple of Confucius, II. i. 2 : III. i. 4.

Tsze-k'wái, a king of Yen, II. ii. 3.

Tsze-liú, *Hsich Liú*, VI. ii. 6.

Tsze-lù, the designation of Chung Yú, a disciple of Confucius, II. i. 1 ; 8 : III. ii. 7 : V. i. 8.

Tsze-mo, a philosopher of Lû, VII. i. 26.

Tsze-shû I, a man who pushed himself into the service of government, II. ii. 10.

Tsze-sze, the grandson of Confucius, II. ii. 11 : IV. ii. 31 : V. ii. 3 ; 6 ; 7 : VI. ii. 6.

Tsze-tû, an officer of Chäng, remarkable for his beauty, VI. i. 7.

Tsze-yú, a disciple of Confucius, II. i. 2 ; 4.

Tung-kwo family, the, a branch of the family of duke Hwan of Ch'í, II. ii. 2.

Twan Kan-mû, a scholar of Wei, III. ii. 7.

Wái-ping, a son of the sovereign Tang, V. i. 6.

Wän, the king, I. i. 2 ; 7 ; ii. 2 ; 3 ; 5 ; 10 : II. i. 1 ; 3 : III. i. 1 ; 3 ; ii. 5 ; 9 : IV. i. 7 ; 13 ; ii. 1 ; 20 : VI. i. 6 ; ii. 2 : VII. i. 10 ; 22 ; ii. 19 ; 22 ; 38.

Wän, the duke of T'äng, I. ii. 13 ; 14 : III. i. 1 ; 3 ; 4.

Wän, the duke of Tsin, I. i. 7 : IV. ii. 21.

Wan Chang, a disciple of Mencius, III. ii. 5 : V. i. 1 ; 2 ; 3 ; 5-9 ; ii. 3 ; 4 ; 6 ; 8 : VII. ii. 37.

Wang Hwan, Tsze-áo, the governor of Ka in Ch'í, II. ii. 6.

Wang Liang, charioteer to Châo Chien, III. ii. 1.

Wang Pâo, a man of Wei, teacher of an abrupt style of singing, VI. ii. 6.

Wang Shun, an officer of the duke of Pt, V. ii.3.

Wei, the State of, IV. ii. 24 : V. i. 8 ; ii. 4.

Wei, one of the three families which ruled the State of Tsin, VII. i. 11.

Wei, a small State in what is now Shan-hsi, II. i. 1 : VI. i. 6.

Wei, a river in Châng, IV. ii. 2.

Wû, the State of, I. ii. 3 : IV. i. 7 ; 31.

Wû, son of king Wän, and joint founder of the Châu dynasty, I. ii. 3 ; 8 ; 10 : II. i. 1 ; ii. 7 : III. ii. 9 : IV. i. 9 ; ii. 20 : VI. i. 6 : VII. i. 30 ; ii. 4 ; 33.

Wû-ch'äng, a city in Lû, IV. ii. 31.

Wû Hwo, a man noted for his strength, VI. ii. 2.

Wû-ling, a wild place in what is now the department of Tsi-nan, III. ii. 10.

Wû-lû, a disciple of Mencius, VI. ii. 1 ; 5.

Wû-ting, a sovereign of the Shang dynasty, II. i. 1.

Yang Ch'äng, a city in what is now Ho-nan, V. i. 6.

Yang Chû, a heresiarch, probably between the times of Confucius and Mencius, III. ii. 9 : VII. i. 26 ; ii. 26.

Yang Hû, the chief minister of the Ch'í family in Lû, III. i. 3 ; ii. 7

Yâo, the Tî sovereign, II. i. 2 ; ii. 2 : III. i. 1 ; 4 ; ii. 4 ; 9 : IV. i. 1 ; 2 ; ii. 32 : V. i. 3-7 ; ii. 1 ; 6 : VI. i. 6 ; ii. 6 ; 8 ; 10 : VII. i. 30 ; 46 : ii. 6 ; 32 ; 37 ; 38.

Yellow River, the, VI. ii. 6.

Yen, the kingdom of, III. ii. 9.

Yen, the State of, I. ii. 10 ; 11 : II. ii. 8 ; 9.

Yen. chief minister of Ch'í, I. ii. 4 : II. i. 1. (Written also *Ngan* and *Gan*.)

Yen Ch'âu-yú, a worthy officer of Wei, V. i. 8.

Yen Húi, the favourite disciple of Confucius, IV. ii. 29.

Yen Pan, a son of Yen Húi above, V. ii. 3.

Yen Yûan, *i. q.* Yen Húi, II. i. 2 : III. i. 1.

Yî, a minister of Shun and of Yû, III. i. 4 : V. i. 6.

Yî-ya, the cook of duke Hwan of Ch'í, VI. i. 7.

Yin, State and dynasty of, II. i. 1 ; ii. 9 : III. i. 3 : IV. i. 2 ; 7 : V. ii. 4 : VII. ii. 4.

Yin-kung To, a famous archer, IV. ii. 24.

Yin Sze, a man of Ch'í, II. ii. 12.

Ying, a place between Ch'í and Lû, II. ii. 7.

Yo, a quarter in the capital of Ch'í, III. ii. 6.

Yo-châng, a disciple of Mencius, I. ii 16 : IV. i. 24 ; 25 : VI. ii. 13 : VII. ii. 25.

Yo-châng Ch'iû, a friend of Mäng Hsien, V. ii. 2.

Yû, a cruel sovereign of the Châu dynasty, VI. i. 6.

Yû-châu, a place somewhere about the north of the present Chih-li, V. i. 3.

Yû Zo, a disciple of Confucius, II. i. 2.

Yû, the Great, founder of the Hsiâ dynasty and of the feudal State, II. i. 8 : III. i. 4 ; 9 : IV. ii. 20 ; 26 ; 29 : V. i. 6 : VI. ii. 11 : VII. ii. 22 ; 35.

Yû, a small State adjoining Tsin, V. i. 9 : VI. ii. 6.

Yû, the mountain, V. i. 3.

Yû-kung Sze, an archer of Wei, IV. ii. 24.

Yûeh, the State of, IV. ii. 31 : VI. ii. 3.

Zän, a small State, VI. ii. 1 ; 5.

Zan Niú, a disciple of Confucius, II. i. 2.

Zan Yû, grand-tutor of the prince of T'äng, III. i. 2.

Zû, the name of a stream, III. i. 4.

INDEX III.

OF CHINESE CHARACTERS AND PHRASES;

INTENDED ALSO TO HELP TOWARDS THE FORMATION OF A DICTIONARY AND CONCORDANCE
FOR THE CLASSICS.

In the references, Books are separated by a colon; Parts of the same Book, and Chapters, by a semicolon.

THE 1st RADICAL, 一.

一
yĭ

(1) One; sometimes = a, L i. 7. 6, 10, 17; ii. 3. 5; 4. 5, *et alibi, saepe.* 一 民, every single individual of all the people, II. i. 1. 8. 一 國, any one State, and a whole State, IV. i. 6. 1. 一 心, all the heart, VII. ii. 37. 10. 一 鄉, VII. ii. 37. 10. 一 人, once with a reference to the sovereign, I. ii. 3. 7. 九 一, a ninth, 什 一, a tenth, 二 十 一, a twentieth, III. i. 3. 6, 15; ii. 5. 4; 8. 1: VI. ii. 10. 1, 4. 執 一, to hold to one point, be obstinate, VII. i. 26. 3, 4. (2) One and the same, exactly similar, VI. i. 14. 4; ii. 9. 3: VII. i. 20. 2, *et al.* (3) To unite, to be united, L i. 6. 2, 3, 4. (4) As an adverb and conjunction : once, once for all, as soon as, L i. 5. 1; ii. 3. 6, 8; 11. 2: III. ii. 1. 1; 2. 1: IV. i. 20, *et al.* (5) 一 ... 一, one ... another, now ... now, II. ii. 13. 2: III. ii. 9. 2.

丁
ting

太 丁, a son of the sovereign Tang, V. i. 6. 5. 武 丁, a sovereign of the Yin dynasty, II. i. 1. 8.

七
ch'i

Seven, L i. 3. 4; 7. 24; ii. 2. 1, 2; 11. 1, *et al.* May be used for the seventh, L i. 6. 6.

丈
chang

(1) Ten cubits, VII. ii. 34. 2. (2) 丈 夫, a man, III. i. 1. 4. 賤(小)丈 夫, II. ii. 10. 7; 12. 6. 大 丈 夫, III. ii. 2. 1, 2, 3. 丈 夫=a son, a man-child, III. ii. 3. 6.

三
san

(1) Three, I. ii. 12. 1; 16. 2: II. ii. 1. 2; 2. 6: III. i. 2. 2, 3, *et al., saepe.* 三 軍, the armies of a great State, II. i. 2. 5, *et al.* 三 代, the three dynasties of Hsiä, Shang, and Chäu, III. i. 3. 10, *et al.* 三 王, the founders of the three dynasties, IV. ii. 20. 5. 三 聖, the three sages,

Yü, Chäu-kung, and Confucius, III. ii. 9. 13. 三 子, the three worthies, Po-1, I Yin, and Hui of Liü-hsiä, VI. ii. 6. 2. 三 卿, the three highest officers of a State, VI. ii. 6. 1. 三 公, the three highest dignitaries at the sovereign's court, VII. i. 28. 三 樂, VII. i. 20. 三 寶, VII. ii. 28. May be used for the third, VI. ii. 7. 3, *et al.* (2) Adverbially, thrice, II. ii. 4. 1; 12. 1, 4, *et al.* (3) 三 子, my children, I. ii. 15. 1. (4) 三 苗, the name of a State, V. ii. 3. 2. 三 危, the name of a place, V. ii. 3. 2.

上
chang

(1) He, she, it, this, that, which is above, with the corresponding plurals,—spoken of place, time, and rank. *Passim.* 上 下, constantly appear as correlates, =superiors and inferiors; high and low; above and below. 上 者, 下 者, on the high grounds, on the low grounds, or they who were above, they who were below, III. ii. 9. 3. 上 世, the highest antiquity, III. i. 5. 4. 上 刑, the severest punishment, IV. i. 14. 3. 上 士, V. ii. 2. 3, 6, 7, 8. 上 農, V. ii. 2. 9. 上 位, V. ii. 6. 6. (2) A preposition, following the noun, sometimes with 之 between them, and the noun sometimes preceded by 於, and 乎, upon, above, by, I. i. 7. 4 : II. i. 6. 2: III. ii. 10. 1 : VII. ii. 15; 30. 1. (3) 上 帝, God, the most High God, L ii. 3. 7: IV. i. 7. 5; ii. 25. 2. (4) 上 宮, name of a palace, VII. ii. 30. 1.

上
shang

The 3rd tone. To ascend, L ii. 4. 7.

上
下
hsiä

Anciently, the 3rd tone. (1) He, she, it, this, that, which is below, with the corresponding plurals, spoken of place, time, and rank. *Passim.* On 上下, as correlates, see 上. 其下, the lowest case, VI. ii. 14. 4. Without 其, V. ii. 2. 9. 下士, V. ii. 2. 3, 6, 7, 8. (2) A preposition, used like 上 above. (3) 下帶, to go below the girdle, VII. ii. 32. 1. 爲下, to dig to a great depth, IV. i. 1. 6. (4) 天下, the world, = the kingdom, I. i. 3. 5; 5. 1; 6. 2, 6; V. 1. 3, 4; 3. 2; 4. 1, 3; 5. 1, 2, 5, 6, *et al., saepissime.* 普天之下, V. i. 4. 2. (5) In the name 柳下惠, II. i. 9. 2, 3, *et al.*

下
hsiá

A verb, to descend, IV. i. 3, 3, 4. 下雨, to rain, I. i. 6. 6. 下車, to descend from a carriage, VII. ii. 23. 2. So, 下木, III. i. 4. 15. ? 以下, III. i. 3. 16; and I. ii. 4. 7.

不
pú

(1) Not. *Passim.* With other negatives,—莫, 無, 非, 罔, it makes a strong affirmative. (2) 不勝, a name, III. ii. 6. 1. 不害, also a name, VII. ii. 25. 1.

丕
ch'áu

(1) The name of one of Mencius's disciples, Kung-sun Ch'áu, II. i. 1. 1; 2. 1; ii. 2. 2; 6. 2; 14. 1, *et al.* (2) The name of an officer of Ch'í, Ching Ch'áu, II. ii. 2. 4.

丙
ping

外丙, a son of the sovereign T'ang, said, according to the nterpretation of some, to have reigned two years, V. i. 6. 5.

且
ch'ieh

(1) And, and moreover, II. i. 1. 11; 2. 19; ii. 7. 4; 9. 2, 4, *et al., saepe.* 且夫, *ib.*, III. ii. 1. 3. (2) And, = and yet, and even if, carrying the mind on to anticipate a reply, which is often given by 況 or 而況, 平, L. i. 4. 5; II. ii. 9. 3; VI. ii. 10. 6. With this meaning, we find 且猶, II. i. i. 1. 7; ii. 2. 10; VII. i. 8. 然且, II. ii. 12. 1; VI. ii. 8. 3, 8. Observe 方且, III. i. 4. 16. (3) 且 = will, or let me, III. i. 5. 1, 2.

丕
p'ei

Great, III. ii. 9. 6.

世
shih

(1) An age, a generation; ages. May often be translated by—the world, I. i. 7. 2; ii. 14. 3; II. ii. 2. 6; IV. i. 1. 2; ii. 1. 3; 22. 1, *et al., saepe.* 世俗, the manners of the age, II. i. 1. 2, *et al.* 名世者, famous in their generation, II. ii. 13. 3; compare VII. i. 9. 6. 其世, = their character in their time, V. ii. 8. 2. (2) Hereditary; from age to age, I. ii. 5. 3; 7. 1; 15. 2; III. i. 3. 8; ii. 10. 5. 繼世

以有天下, to possess the throne by hereditary succession, V. i. 6. 4.

丘
ch'iû

(1) A hillock, 丘垤, II. i. 2. 28. 丘陵, III. ii. 1. 5. 丘民, the peasantry (but 丘 is there a territorial designation), VII. ii. 14. 2. (2) The name of Confucius, IV. ii. 21. 3. (3) 咸丘, a double surname, V. i. 4. 1, 2. (4) 靈丘, a city of Ch'í, II. ii. 5. 1. 石丘, a place in Sung, VI. ii. 4. 1, 2. 葵丘, the place of a famous meeting of princes, VI. ii. 7. 3.

Together, III. i. 4. 3. Also written 立立.

THE 2nd RADICAL, 丨.

中
chung

The middle. (1) Used as a preposition, after the noun, often with 於 or some other preposition before the noun. 之 also is often between the noun and 中, I. i. 2. 3; 11. 3; II. i. 10. 6; III. i. 4. 5; ii. 5. 5; 9. 4, *et al., saepe.* (2) 中心, in the heart's core, II. i. 3. 2; III. i. 5. 4. 中國 and 國中, in the middle of the kingdom, II. ii. 10. 3; III. i. 3. 15; 4. 17; IV. ii. 33. 1 (國 here only = city). 其中, the central one, III. i. 3. 19. 熱中, to burn at heart, V. i. 1. 5. 中士, an officer of the middle class, V. ii. 2. In the same chapter, 中 simply, of the middle quality. (3) A mean, average, III. i. 3. 7. (4) The Mean, IV. ii. 20. 2. To keep the Mean, IV. ii. 7. (5) 中天下而立, to stand in the centre of the nation, VII. i. 21. 2; compare 41. 3; 26. 3; ii. 37. 2. (6) 中國, the Middle Kingdom, III. i. 4. 7, 12; ii. 9. 3; VI. ii. 10. 5.

中
chung

The 4th tone. To hit the mark, II. i. 7. 5; V. ii. 1. 7. 中禮, VII. ii. 33. 2.

THE 3rd RADICAL, 丶.

丹
tan

(1) 丹朱, the name of Yâo's son, V. i. 6. 2. (2) The name of 白圭, VI. ii. 11. 1.

主
chú

(1) To count—be counted—as the principal thing, II. ii. 2. 4. (2) To preside over, V. i. 8. 6. (3) Being a host, V. ii. 3. 5; VII. ii. 24. 2. (4) To make one's host, i.e. to lodge with, V. i. 8. 1, 2. Observe para. 3, 4; 其所爲主 and 其所主.

THE 4th RADICAL, 丿.

乃
nái

(1) To be, I. i. 7. 8, 9; ii. 4. 6; V. i. 4. 1. (2) An initial particle, of varying power,—seeing this, but, now, &c., I. ii. 15. 1; II.

i. 2. 22: IV. ii. 28. 7: VI. i. 6. 5; ii. 6. 6. Observe 乃 ... 乃, VI. i. 6. 5.

久 *chiú*

A long time, for a long time; to be a long time, II. i. 1. 3, 8; 2. 22; ii. 14. 3: III. ii. 9. 2: V. i. 6. 2; ii. 1. 4: VII. i. 30. 2.

之 *ch.h*

(1) Of, = the sign of the possessive case. But it would often be very harsh to translate it by *of*, I. i. 1. 4; 3. 1, 3. 4, *et al, saepissime*. The regent follows the 之, and the regimen precedes it. They may be respectively a noun, a phrase, or a larger clause. 之 followed by 於 is very common in Mencius; e.g. VII. i. 24. (2) Him, her, it, them. *Passim.* (3) It is often difficult to determine the antecedent to 之. It has to be gathered from the context; and sometimes 之 merges in the verb, making it an emphatic neuter, or = a passive; e.g. I. i. 3. 2; 6. 6; 7. 4: IV. ii. 14; 15: VII. i. 3. 1; 5; 13. 3; 30. 1. (4) 有 and 有之, as in (2), but also impersonally, = there is ..., I. ii. 3. 1; 8. 1, *et saepe*. So, the negative 未之有, where the 未 attracts the 之 to itself. The same is to be observed of 莫. (5) We have 作之君, I. ii. 3. 7; 爲之辭, II. ii. 9. 4; 與之處, III. i. 4. 1; and other similar expressions, where we may suppose two objectives, the 之 being = to, for, &c., him, it, them. Observe especially 莫之死, I. ii. 12. 1, and 與之示之, V. i 5. (6) 之謂, is called, or is what is called. 此之謂, I. i. 4. 6. We might reduce this to (1), ... is the *saying of* this. But this cannot be done where 謂 is followed by an adjective or other words, e.g. VII. ii. 25. 謂之 comes under (2), compare 名之, IV. i. 2. 4; 何服之有, IV. ii. 3. 4; 何卿之間, V. ii. 9. 1; and 是之取爾, IV. ii. 18. 2. (7) 如之何, how, I. ii. 6. 1; 14. 1, *et saepe*. (8) Observe 草尚之風, III. i. 2. 4. (9) In names, 之奇, V. i. 9. 2; 之師 and 之他, IV. ii. 24. 2; 盈之, III. ii. 8. 1; 子之, II. ii. 8. 1; and 夷之, III. i. 5. 1, 2. (10) As a verb. To go, or come, to, V. i. 5. 7; 6. 1; 9. 3, *et al, saepe*.

乍 *chá*

Suddenly. II. i. 6. 3.

乎 *hú*

(1) A particle of interrogation. Found alone; preceded by another interrogation, as 焉, 惡, 惡乎, by 不亦, and by 況, I. i. 1. 2; 2. 1: II. ii. 9. 2: III. i. 2. 2: IV. ii. 27. 3: V. i. 7. 7; ii. 5. 3: VI. ii. 1. 3, 8, *et al, saepe*. Also in indirect interrogation, II. ii. 2. 3: IV. ii. 32. 1. (2) A particle of exclamation, I. i. 7. 7; ii. 5. 4: III. i. 4. 11, *et al.* Preceded by 哉, VII. i. 36. 1; followed by 哉, I. ii. 8. 4; preceded by 何 and followed by 哉, II. ii. 2. 6. (3) Partly interrogative and partly exclamatory. Alone; preceded by 其 固, and 必也, I. ii. 1. 1, 3; 2. 2: III. ii. 9. 3: VI. ii. 6. 1: VII. ii. 37. 2, 7, *et al.* Immediately preceded by 矣, II. i. 2. 18, 19. ? by 也, III. ii. 10. 6. (4) A preposition, — after verbs, and adjectives, = in, of, to, from, &c., I. ii. 12. 2; 15. 1: II. i. 1. 3, 10; 2. 28; ii. 11. 3; 3. 3, 7, *et al, saepe*. Observe 在乎, VI. i. 19. 1. (5) Than, in comparisons, II. ii. 2. 4; i. 8. 5. (6) Observe 有時乎, V. ii. 5. 1; 云乎, V. ii. 7. 4; 盍歸乎來, IV. i. 13. 1; 有乎爾, VII. ii. 38. 4.

乏 *fá*

Needy. 窮乏者, VI. i. 10. 7, 8. 空乏, to impoverish, VI. ii. 15. 2.

乘 *shăng*

To mount upon, III. i. 3. 2. To take advantage of, II. i. 1. 9.

乘 *shàng*

In 3rd tone. (1) A carriage, I. ii. 16. 1. 萬乘千乘百乘之國, the kingdom, a great State, the possessions of the chief of a large clan, I. i. 1. 4, *et al.* The classifier of carriages, III. ii. 4. 1: IV. ii. 2. 1: VII. ii. 34. 2. (2) To drive a carriage, III. ii. 1. 4. (3) A team of four horses, V. i. 9. 2. (4) A set of four arrows, IV. ii. 24. 2. (5) Name of a Book, IV. ii. 21. 2. (6) 乘田, name of Confucius's office, when in charge of the public fields, V. ii. 5. 4.

THE 5TH RADICAL, 乙.

九 *chiú*

Nine, VII. i. 29: VI. ii. 2. 2, *et al.* 九 —, a ninth, I. ii. 5. 3. But in III. i. 3. 15, 九 — refers to a mode of territorial division.

乞 *ch'í*

To beg, IV. ii. 33. 1. 乞人, a beggar, VI. i. 10. 6.

也 *yĕ*

(1) A final particle, used both at the end of sentences, and of clauses, or separate members of a sentence. Sometimes we miss it, where it might be; and sometimes it might be dispensed with, I. i. 2. 2, 3; 3. 1, 2, 3, 4; *et passim.* (2) After the adverb 今; after proper names (though

rarely in Mencius), and very often after a clause in the first member of a sentence: it = *quod*, now, or may often be left untranslated. In these cases, it is often, but far from always, followed by other particles, I. i. 3. 1; 7. 8, 21, 22: IV. i. 14. 1, *et passim*. (3) As correlate of 者, concluding the explanation of the character or sentiment which precedes 者. The 者, however, is often wanting, I. ii. 4. 2, 3; 10. 2; 11. 1: II. i. 2. 9: III. i. 3. 6, 10, *et saepe*. (4) 者也 is found at the end of sentences, sometimes preceded by 者 and sometimes not. 者, however, may generally be explained independent of the 也, I. i. 1. 5; ii. 8. 2, 5, *et saepe*. (5) 也者 in the first member of a sentence resumes a word or subject, and the explanation or account of it follows, II. i. 9. 1: VII. ii. 37. 9, *et al.* We find 也者, however, at the commencement of a chapter, where no discourse is resumed, VII. ii. 16. Observe VI. I. 8. 2. (6) It is often interrogative, following 何, 惡, 在, &c., I. i. 3. 1; 4. 5; ii. 1. 6, 7; 4. 4, *et saepe*.

乾 kan
亂 luan

旱乾, dry, drought, VII. ii. 14. 4.

To confound, III. i. 4. 18: VI. ii. 15. 2: VII. ii. 10. 亂 = to be confounded with, VII. ii. 37. 12. Rebellious, III. ii. 9. 11. To be in confusion; a state of confusion, II. i. 2. 22: III. ii. 9. 2, 5: IV. ii. 29. 2: V. ii. 1. 1, 2: VII. ii. 12. 2.

THE 6TH RADICAL, 丨.

子 yü

I, me, we, my, I. i. 2. 4; 7. 9; ii. 16. 3: II. i. 1. 3; 2. 16, 26; 4. 3, *et al.*, *saepe*.

事 shih

(1) Affairs; doings, achievements; business, I. i. 7. 1, 2: VII. i. 33. 1, 3; ii. 28. 1, *et al.*, *saepe*. 無非事者,... were for real business, I. ii. 4. 5. 必有事焉, there must be the practice of . . ., II. i. 2. 16. 無事, without doing service, III. ii. 4. 2; without difficulty, IV. ii. 26. 2. 以為...事, to make—one's business, V. i. 8. 1. 好事者, one who is fond of strange things, V. i. 8. 1; 9. 1. Compare 事 and 功 in III. ii. 4. 3, and VI. i. 6. 5. (2) To serve—parents, a sovereign, a teacher, a greater State, &c., I. i. 5. 3; 7. 21, 22, *et al.*, *saepe*. 以大事小, I. ii. 3. 1, 2.

THE 7TH RADICAL, 二.

二 r

(1) Two; the second, III. i. 3. 17; 5. 3, *et al.* (2) 二三子, see 三, (3). But 二三策 = two or three passages, VII. ii. 3. 2.

于 yü

(1) A preposition = by, to, in, on, for, *saepe*. It occurs commonly in quotations from the older classics. Mencius himself prefers 於, though he does also use 于. (2) In the double surname, 淳于, IV. i. 17. 1: VI. ii. 6. 1, 5.

云 yün

(1) Says. In a quotation, V. i. 4. 1. Observe V. ii. 3. 4. (2) 云爾, closing a sentence, or the member of a sentence. It is difficult to translate, and Wang Yin-chih regards it simply as a final particle, II. ii. 2. 4: III. ii. 6. 7: IV. ii. 24. 1: VII. i. 39. 2. So 云乎, V. ii. 7. 4.

五 wu

Five. *Saepe.* 五 = the fifth, IV. ii. 30. 2. Adverbially, = five times, VI. ii. 6. 2.

井 ching

(1) A well, II. i. 6. 3: III. i. 5. 3: V. i. 2. 3: VII. i. 29. 市井之臣, a scholar living unemployed in a city or market-place, V. ii. 7. 1. (2) A system of dividing the ground on a plan of nine squares, III. i. 3. 13, 18, 19.

亟 chi
亟 ch'i

In haste, quickly; to be in haste, I. i. 2. 3: II. i. 8. 2.

The 2nd tone. Frequently, IV. ii. 18. 1: V. ii. 6. 4, 5; 7. 4: VII. i. 8. 1.

THE 8TH RADICAL, 亠.

亡 wang

(1) To expire, die, I. i. 2. 4: VI. ii. 6. 4. 死亡, I. i. 7. 21, 22: IV. i. 8. 4; 9. 5. To be utterly lost; to perish, I. ii. 4. 6, 7, 8: IV. i. 2. 4; 3. 2; 7. 1; 8. 1; ii. 21. 1: V. i. 9. 3: VI. i. 8. 4; 16. 3; 18. 2; ii. 15. 4. 亡 = not to be found, gone away, I. ii. 7. 1. (2) To cause to die or perish, VI. i. 8. 2. (3) Not at home, III. ii. 7. 3.

亡 wu

Used for 無, not being, not having, IV. i. 19. 3; ii. 28. 7. Used actively, and = to disown, VII. i. 34.

交 chiao

(1) Intercourse; to have intercourse with, I. ii. 3. 1: V. ii. 4. 3, 4: VI. i. 15. 2; ii. 5. 1: VII. ii. 18. 交 = mutually, I. i. 1. 4. 交易, to deal with and exchange, III. i. 4. 5. 交際, intercourse, and its expression by presents, V. ii. 4. 1. To be intermingled, to cross one another, III. i. 4. 7. 內交於..., to seek the favour of ..., II. i. 6. 3. 交 = to treat as, VII. i. 37. 1. (2) A man's name, VI. ii. 2. 1, 2, 6.

亦
yī

Also. *Saepe.* It is difficult sometimes, and doubtful whether we ought, to bring out the *also* in another language;—as in I. i. 1. 2, 3; 7. 17; II. ii. 10. 6, *et al.* 不亦…乎, 亦…而已 are common phraseologies, I. ii. 2. 2; II. ii. 9. 3; VI. ii. 6. 2; VII. i. 39. 2. Observe 抑亦, II. ii. 4. 3; III. ii. 10. 3. 亦不, where 亦=still, III. ii. 6. 1; VII. ii. 19. 3; and 則亦=yea, VII. ii. 38. 4.

亥
hái

A surname, V. ii. 3. 4.

享
hsiang

(1) To present an offering; an offering, VI. ii. 5. 4, 5. (2) To accept an offering—as a sacrifice, V. i. 5. 6.

京
ching

A capital, IV. i. 7. 5.

亮
liang

To have faith, VI. ii. 12.

毫
po

The name of T'ang's capital, referred to the present department of Kwei-têh in Ho-nan, III. ii. 5. 2: V. i. 6. 5; 7. 9.

亶
t'an

The name of king T'ai, one of the ancestors of king Wân, I. ii. 5. 5.

THE 9TH RADICAL, 人.

人
jên or
zăn

(1) A man, men; other men. *Passim.* 人=humanity, man's nature, VI. i. 1. 2; 2. 3; VII. ii. 16. 人人, all men, or each man, IV. i. 11; ii. 2. 4, *et al.* (2) It indicates officers and rulers, in distinction from 民, the people, I. i. 2. 3; II. i. 1. 13, *et al.* So, perhaps, VII. ii. 28. 人, with reference to the sovereign, I. ii. 3. 7. (3) Following names of States it = native, natives, people. So 齊人, 魯人, &c. &c. But 殷人 and 周人, III. i. 3. 6, are different, meaning the founders of the Yin and Châu dynasties. So 國人, the people of the State, or merely a common man, I. ii. 7. 4, 5: II. ii. 8. 2; 10. 3: IV. i. 11; ii. 8. 3; 24. 2, *et al.* (4) With other characters, it forms concrete substantives, especially nouns expressing office or profession. We have 匠人 and 玉人, I. ii. 9; 矢人 and 函人, II. i. 7; 廩人, V. ii. 6. 5; 虞人, V. ii. 7. 7; 館人, VII. ii. 30; 校人, V. i. 2. 4. (5) Observe also 罪人; 狄人; 嬖人; 竆人; 鄉人; 族人; 野人, which means both country people, and uncultivated

people; 良人 =husband, IV. ii. 38. 1: 侍人, V. i. 8. 1; 聖人, II. i. 2. 17, 20, 22, 25, 28; ii. 9. 3: III. i. 4. 2, 8, 13; ii. 9, 5, 10, 14: IV. i. 1. 5; 2. 1: V. i. 7. 7: VI. i. 7. 3. 8: VII. i. 23. 3; 24; 88; ii. 15; 24. 2; 38. 4; 寡人, the humble 'I' of the prince of a State, I. i. 8. 1: 5. 1; 7. 4, *et al.*; 夫人, the wife of a prince, III. ii. 3. 3; 大人, III. i. 4. 6: IV. i. 20; ii. 6; 11; 12: VII. i. 19. 4; 33. 3; ii. 34. 1; 小人, II. ii. 12. 7: III. i. 2. 4; 4. 6, *et al.*; 庶人, the masses, the people, I. i. 1. 4: II. i. 7. 2: V. ii. 2. 6, 7, 8, *et al.*; 門人, disciples, III. i. 4. 13: VII. ii. 29; 人牧, 人君, 人臣, 人子, 人弟, but the characters here are possibly not in apposition, but in regimen. (6) 為人, VII. ii. 35.

什
shih

什一, a tenth part, a tithe, III. i. 3. 6, 15; ii. 8. 1.

仁
zăn

Benevolence, benevolent, to be benevolent. *Passim.* Mencius does not use the term for 'perfect virtue,' as Confucius does, though it may sometimes have that meaning. In VII. i. 24. 2, *love* seems the proper rendering.

仇
ch'óu

To show oneself an enemy to, III. ii. 5. 2.

今
chin

Now, the present, modern time: also, in the same way as our logical use of *now*, in discoursing. *Passim.* We find 今也 and 今夫; 今日, 今時, 富今之時, and 富今之世. 今而後, from this time forth, I. ii. 12. 2, *et al.*

介
chieh

(1) Firm purpose, VII. i. 28. (2) Used for 芥, a stalk of the mustard plant, a straw, V. i. 7. 2.

介
chieh

In the 4th tone. 介然, suddenly, VII. i. 21.

仕
shih

To take—be in—office, II. i. 2. 22; ii. 14. 1: III. ii. 3. 1, 5, 6, *et al.* Observe 當仕, V. ii. 7. 9. 仕者, officers, I. i. 7. 18; ii. 5. 3. So 仕 alone, II. ii. 8. 1.

他
t'a

(1) Other, another, I. i. 7. 9: V. i. 3. 2; ii. 4. 3: VII. ii. 17. 他日, another day, other days. It may mean formerly, next day, and afterwards, I. ii. 1. 2; 16. 1: II. ii. 4. 4; 10. 3: III. i. 2. 4; 4. 13; 5. 2, 4: ii. 10. 5: IV. i. 14. 1: VI. ii. 5. 2. 無他, nothing else, for no other reason, I. i. 7. 12; ii. 1. 6, 7: II. ii. 2. 9: VI. i. 11. 4; ii. 3. 2: VII. i. 15. 3; 25. 3; 36. 3. So, 豈有

他 哉, I. ii. 10. 4 : VI. i. 14. 1. 言 他,
spoke of something else, I. ii. 6. 3.
他, went elsewhere, IV. ii. 33. 1. (2) Read
t'o, a name, IV. ii. 24. 2.

仞
zân

A measure of eight cubits, VII. ii. 84. 2.

代
tài

(1) Alternate, one after another, III. ii.
9. 5. For, instead of, V. ii. 2. 6, 7, 8. (2)
三 代, the three dynasties ;—Hsiâ,
Shang, and Châu, III. i. 2. 2 ; 3. 10 : IV.
i. 3. 1. (3) A name, 陳 代, III. ii. 1. 1.

令
ling

To employ, 使 令, to be employed,
I. i. 7. 16.

令
ling

The 4th tone. (1) An order ; to order,
I. ii. 11. 4 : IV. i. 7. 2. (2) Good, VI. i. 17. 3.

以
i

(1) To take, to use. But our idiom
requires, for the most part, that it be
translated as a preposition,—by, at, with,
because of, according to, &c. It precedes the
principal verb of the sentence, as in I. i.
2. 3, 文 王 以 民 力 爲 臺 'king
Wăn used the people's strength to make
his tower,' or 'made his tower with the
people's strength ;' or in V. i. 5. 1, 堯 以
天 下 與 舜 'Yâo took the king-
dom and gave it to Shun ;' or simply, 'Yâo
gave the kingdom to Shun.' It follows
the principal verb, and then its prepo-
sitional force is more apparent, e.g. I. i.
4. 2, 殺 人 以 梃, 'to kill a man with
a stick.' We might indeed translate, ' to
kill a man, using a stick.' Its regimen
sometimes precedes it, e.g. V. i. 7. 2, —
介 不 以 與 人, 一 介 不 以
取 諸 人, 'one straw he would not
have taken and given to men, or taken and
received from men,' or simply, 'he would
neither have given nor taken a single
straw.' This position of the regimen is
for the sake of emphasis. Examples, of
the first two usages especially, occur
very frequently. Julien argues (see the
'Treatise on Four Chinese Characters,'
appended to his Translation of Mencius)
that in many cases it is merely = a sign
of the accusative case. And it is difficult
sometimes to give any other force to the
以, as in II. i. 1. 5 : III. i. 4. 10 : IV. ii.
28, et al., yet a peculiar significancy may
be traced in it. Observe 所 以, that
by, for, from, which, — a force sometimes
sustained by 以 alone ; 是 以, hence ;
and 何 以, whereby, or wherefore. 以
is found without any regimen, joined to
告, I. i. 12. 2, et al., sæpe. 有 以 and
無 以 are abbreviations for 有 所

以, 無 所 以, I. i. 5. 2, 3, et al. In
a sentence which has no accessory, 以
= to use, to act, according to, &c., e.g. V.
ii. 1. 3. 以 爲, and often with a regimen
of 以 intervening, frequently means to
take to be, to consider, to be considered.
But by no means always. Sometimes also
the 以 is omitted. (2) It often = the
conjunction because, II. i. 2. 15, et al. (3)
To, so as to ;—often forming, with a verb
following, our infinitive. Sometimes the
以 = 'wherewith to,' 'and thereby,' I. i.
1. 2 ; 7. 12, 15, 16, 21, 22, et al., sæpe. To
this belong 以 來, 以 下, and 以
至. (4) It is often used after 可, forming
our potential mood, and = the to, which is
suppressed after our auxiliaries. Passim.
(5) Used as = 已, 'to stop,' I. i. 7. 2. (6)
Observe 明 以 教 我, I. i. 7. 19 ; 樂
以 天 下, I. ii. 4. 3 ; 以 羑 然, II.
ii. 7. 1 ; 以 寸, IV. ii. 7 ; and some other
sporadic cases.

仲
chung

The second of brothers. It is used in
designations, V. i. 6. 5. 仲 尼, the
designation of Confucius, I. i. 4. 6 ; 7. 2,
et al. It follows the surname, or what
is equivalent to it, without any other
character, and then may be taken as =
the name, II. ii. 2. 3 :—II. i. i. 8 :—II. i. i.
1, 2, 3, 4, 5 ; ii. 2. 8, 10 :—V. ii. 3. 2 :—III.
ii. 10. 1, 2, 3, 5, 6 : VII. i. 24.

仰
yang

To look up to, II. i. 5. 6 ; ii. 9. 4 : IV.
ii. 20. 5. 仰 望, IV. ii. 33. Used adverbially with the correlate 俯, = above,
below, I. i. 7. 21 : VII. i. 20. 3.

任
zăn

(1) A charge, office, VI. ii. 15. 2. 任
business, purpose, L. ii. 9. 1. A burden,
VI. ii. 2. 3. (2) As a verb. To charge,
to burden, V. i. 7. 6 ; ii. 1. 2. Observe
IV. i. 14. 3, and 聖 之 任 者, V. ii.
1. 5-

任
zăn

The 2nd tone. (1) A burden, = baggage, III. i. 4. 13. (2) The name of a
small State, VI. ii. 1. 1 ; 5. 季 任, the
younger brother of the chief of Zăn. VI.
ii. 5. 1.

伊
i

A surname. 伊 尹, the minister of
T'ang, II. i. 2. 22, 23 ; ii. 2. 8, 10, et al.
伊 訓, the name of a Book in the Shû-
ching, V. i. 7. 9.

伋
ch'î

The name of Confucius's grandson, IV.
ii. 31. 2 : V. ii. 6. 4.

伍
sòu

Five men in rank or file. 伍 = ranks,
II. ii. 4. 1, 2.

伏
fŭ

To be lying down, I. i. 2. 3.

伐
fá

(1) To smite, to attack; 伐 = to punish, I. ii. 8. 1; 10. 1, 4; 11. r: II. ii. 8. 1, 2: III. ii 5. 1, 6; 9. 6: IV. i. 8. 4: V. i. 7. 6; 9. 2: VII. ii. 2. 2; 3. 3; 4. 4. 討而不伐, VI. ii. 7. 2. (2) To hew down, to lop,—applied to trees, and to the mind, VI. i. 8. 1, 2.

休
hsiŭ

(1) Happiness; to be happy, I. ii. 4. 5: III. ii. 6. 5. (2) The name of a place, II. ii. 14. 1.

伯
po or păi

(1) The eldest of brothers, 伯兄 VI. i. 5. 3. (2) A title of nobility, V. ii. 2. 3, 4. So 西伯, IV. i. 13. 1: VII. i. 22. 1, 3. (3) In the designation 伯夷, II. i. 2. 22, 23; 9. 1, 3, *et al., saepe.* (4) Must be used for 佰, a hundred, III. i. 4. 18.

似
sze and shih

As; to be like to, I. i. 6. 2: II. i. 2. 6: VII. i. 26. 3; 41. 1; ii. 37. 11. 相似, like one another, similar, II. ii. 2. 5: VI. i. 7. 3, 4, 5, 6. To be like what is right, II. ii. 5. 1. 似者, a semblance, VII. ii. 37. 12.

位
wei

(1) Position, status, i.e. of dignity, IV. i. 1. 7; iv. 1. 5. 7; ii. 2. 3, *et al., saepe.* 在位 is frequent. 正位, the correct place, i.e. propriety, III. ii. 2. 3. 天位, all *legitimate* dignities, V. ii. 3. 4. 易位 = to dethrone, V. ii. 9. 1. (2) Position, place, III. i. 2. 4: IV. ii. 27. 1, 3.

佑
yŭ

To assist, III. ii. 9. 6.

何
ho

(1) What, why, what kind of, I. i. 1. 3, 6, *et al., saepe.* 何也, 何與, 何哉, at the beginning or end of sentences, generally = why is this? how is it? I. i. 3. 1; 7. 10; ii. 16. 1. But sometimes 何也 simply = is or was what? VI. i. 7. 8; ii. 6. 2, *et al.* In VI. i. 9. 2, 何哉 = is of what avail? Other characters sometimes come between 何 and the particles, and with the same difference of usage. 何以, whereby, what to, I. i. 1. 4, *et al., saepe.* 何由, what from? how? I. i. 7. 4. 何爲, what do? why? I. ii. 5. 4: VII. ii. 36. 2. But observe 何爲也哉, V. ii. 7. 3. 何之, where are you going? VI. ii. 4. 2. (2) 如何, generally with 之 between, = what, what is to be done? Difficulty, surprise, or indignation is generally implied, but not always. The phrase 如之何則可, = how is the exigency to be met? is common, I. i. 4. 6; 5. 1; ii. 6. 1, 2, 3: V. ii. 2. 1, *et al., saepe.* Other words are found also between 如 and 何, and then the phrase = what has . . . to do with— ? I. ii. 14. 3, *et al.* (3) 何如, what sort of? of what nature? in what manner? At the end of a sentence, 何如 = what do you think of? What shall be said? I. i. 3. 2; 7. 3: VII. ii. 37. 3, 8, *et al., saepe.* (4) 何有, what difficulty is there? I. ii. 5. 5: VI. ii. 1. 4, *et al.*

余
yŭ

Me, III. ii. 9. 3.

佚
yi

(1) Ease, enjoyment, VII. i. 12; ii. 24. (2) To be without office, in obscurity, 遺佚, II. i. 9. 2: V. ii. 1. 3.

作
tso

(1) To rise up, arise, II. i. 1. 8, 11: III. ii. 9. 5, 7, 9, 10, *et al.* To be aroused to rise, to act, VI. ii. 15. 3. 我疾作, I have become ill, IV. ii. 24. 2. (2) To make, to form; to cause to be, I. i. 4. 6; ii. 3. 7; 4. 6, 10: II. i. 4. 6: IV. i. 8. 5. To be made, IV. ii. 21. 1.

佞
ning

Glib-tonguedness, VII. ii. 37. 12.

使
shih

(1) To cause, to make to; to make to be, I. i. 3. 3; 4. 6; 5. 3, 4; 7. 18, 21, *et al., saepe.* Observe 行或使之, I. ii. 16. 3. 使 = to send (once, we have the addition of 來), II. ii. 2. 1; 6. 1, *et al., saepe.* (2) To employ, to command; no other verb following, II. i. 2. 22; 5. 1, *et al.* (3) 如使 = if, supposing that, II. ii. 10. 5: V. ii. 6. 5: VI. i. 7. 5. Without the 如, VI. i. 9. 3; ii. 14. 4.

使'
shih

The 4th tone. To be commissioned, ? I. i. 7. 16. 使者, a messenger, V. ii. 6. 4.

來
lâi

(1) To come, I. i. 1. 2; 2. 3, *et al., saepe.* 以來 and 而來, downwards, II. i. 2. 23, 27, 28; 5. 6; ii. 18. 4: VII. ii. 38. 4. Observe 盍歸乎來, IV. i. 13. 1, *et al.* (2) The coming, next, III. ii. 8. 1; 2, 3.

來'
lâi

The 4th tone. To lead on, III. i. 4. 8.

侈
ch'ih

Extravagance, wild license, I. i. 7. 20.

侍
shih

To be by, in attendance on, II. ii. 10. 2. 侍人, an attendant, with a bad meaning, V. i. 8. 1, 2. 侍妾, attendant girls, concubines, VII. ii. 34. 6.

供
kung

To supply, to furnish, I. i. 7. 16 : III. ii. 3. 3 ; 5. 2 : V. ii. 4. 6.

侮
wü

To despise, insult, II. i. 4. 4 : IV. i. 8. 4 ; 16.

侯
hau

(1) A title of nobility, V. ii. 2. 3, 4. A prince,—following the name of the State, I. ii. 16. 3 : V. i. 8. 3 諸 侯, the princes of the kingdom. *Saepe.* It often = one of the princes, a prince, II. i. 2. 4 : III. i. 2, *et al.* Observe I. ii. 4. 6, where the 'Daily Readings' has 小 國 諸 侯

(2) An introductory particle, i. q. 惟, IV. i. 7. 5.

侵
ch'in

To make incursions on ; to attack stealthily, I. ii. 14. 2 ; 15. 1 : III. ii. 5. 6 : IV. ii. 24. 2.

便
p'ien

便 嬖, attendants and favourites, I. i. 7. 16.

係
hsi

To bind, 係 累, I. ii. 11. 3.

俊
tsun

A man of distinction, 俊 傑, II. i. 5. 1 : VI. ii. 7. 2.

俑
yung

Wooden images of the dead, I. i. 4. 6.

俗
sü

Manners, practices, customs, II. i. 1.8 : VI. ii. 6. 5 ; 9. 3. 流 俗, current customs (with a bad meaning), VII. ii. 37. 11. 世 俗, the manners of the age, I. ii. 1. 2 : IV. ii. 30. 2.

保
pao

(1) To protect and love, I. i. 7. 3, 4, 10, 12 ; ii. 3. 2, 3 : II. i. 6. 7 : III. i. 5. 3. (2) To preserve, IV. i. 3. 3.

俟
tse

To wait for, II. ii. 2. 5 : V. ii. 7. 9 : VII. i. 1. 3 ; ii. 33. 3.

信
hsin

(1) Truthfulness, fidelity, I. i. 5. 3 : III. i. 4. 8 : VI. i. 16. 1 : VII. i. 27. 11, 12. True, real, V. i. 9. 1 : VII. ii. 25. 1, 2, 4 ; 33. 2. (2) To believe ; to have confidence in (it may be to obey or follow, as principles ; or to employ, as officers), I. ii. 11. 2 : IV. i. 1. 8 : V. i. 2. 4 : VII. i. 34 ; ii. 3. 1 ; 12. 1. To be believed ; to obtain the confidence of, IV. i. 12. 1 ; ii. 11. (3) As an adverb, really, truly, II. i. 5. 6 : III. i. 5. 3 : V. i. 2. 1 ; 4. 2 : VI. i. 2. 2.

信
shun

In 1st tone. To stretch out straight, to straighten, VI. i. 12. 1.

脩
siu

See 脩

俯
fu

To stoop, used adverbially, with the correlate 仰, = below, I. i. 7. 21, 22 : VII. i. 20. 3.

俱
chü

Together ; = both, VI. i. 9. 3 : VII. i. 20. 2.

倉
ts'ang

A granary ; a storehouse for grain generally. Commonly found along with 廩, a granary for rice, I. ii. 12. 2 : III.

i. 4. 3 : V. i. 1. 3 ; 2. 3 ; ii. 6. 6. Used as a verb, I. ii. 5. 4. (2) A name, 藏 倉, I. ii. 16. 1, 3.

倍
pei

(1) To rebel against, revolt from, III. i. 4. 12, 14. (2) Double, as much again as, I. ii. 11. 3 : III. i. 4. 18 : IV. i. 14. 1 : V. ii. 2. 6, 7, 8 : VI. ii. 6. 7. In this second sense, the character is aspirated, and in the 2nd tone, in the Canton dialect.

倒
tao

Inverted, upside down, II. i. 1. 13.

倦
ch'üan

To be tired, weary, II. i. 2. 19 : VI. i. 16. 1.

倪
yi

Children and youths, I. ii. 11. 4.

倫
lun

Always used with reference to 人 倫, the relationships of human society, II. ii. 2. 4 : III. i. 3. 10 ; 4. 8 : IV. i. 2. 1 ; ii. 19. 2 : V. i. 2. 1 : VI. ii. 10. 5.

偃
yen

To bend, III. i. 2. 4.

假
chiü

(1) To feign, pretend to, II. i. 3. 1 : VII. i. 30. 1. (2) To borrow, V. i. 9. 2 : VI. ii. 2. 6 : VII. i. 30. 1.

偕
chieh

Together with, I. i. 2. 3, 4. As a verb, II. i. 9. 2.

偪
pi

To press upon, III. i. 4. 7.

側
ch'ai

Side, the side, II. i. 9. 2 ; ii. 9. 3 : V. ii. 1. 3.

傑
chieh

A heroic character, 俊 傑, II. i. 5. 1 : VI. ii. 7. 2. 豪 傑, III. i. 4. 12 : VII. i. 10. 1.

傅
fu

(1) A tutor (an official title), VII. i. 39. 3. To act as tutor, to teach, III. ii. 6. 1. (2) 傅 說, an ancient statesman, VI. ii. 15. 1.

備
pei

All-complete ; to be prepared, ready, III. i. 4. 6 ; ii. 3. 3 : V. i. 1. 3, ii. 6. 6 : VII. i. 4. 1 ; 33. 3.

傳
ch'uan

(1) To transmit, hand down (used both actively and passively), I. i. 7. 2 : IV. i. 28. 7 : V. i. 6. 1 ; 9. 3. (2) To communicate, deliver, as an order, a pledge, II. i. 12 : V. ii. 7. 1.

傳
chuan

The 4th tone. Records, a Record, I. ii. 2. 1 ; 8. 1 : III. ii. 3. 1. Observe 以 傳 食 於 諸 侯, III. ii. 4. 1. The dictionary defines this use of 傳 by 續

傷
shang

To hurt, wound, II. i. 7. 1 : IV. ii. 31. 1. Wounded, IV. ii. 20. 3. 傷 = to be contrary to, IV. ii. 28. 無 傷, there is no harm, it does not matter, I. i. 7. 8 : VII. ii. 19. 2. So, 何 傷 哉, III. ii. 10. 4.

僕
p'o

(1) A charioteer, driver, IV. ii. 24. 2.
(2) 僕僕爾, an adverb, in a troubled manner, V. ii. 6. 5.

偽
wei

Deceit; deceitfully, III. i. 4. 17, 18: V. i. 2. 4.

儀
i

(1) Ceremonies, demonstrations of respect, VI. ii. 5. 4. (2) A name, 張儀 III. ii. 2. 1. 公明儀, III. i. 1. 4; ii 3. 1; 9. 9: IV. ii. 24. 1. (3) 公儀, a double surname, VI. ii. 6. 3.

億
yi

A hundred thousand, IV. i. 7. 5.

儉
chien

Economical, III. i. 3. 4: IV. i. 16. Niggardly to, II. ii. 7. 5. To be limited to, only to amount to, VI. ii. 8. 6.

鄦
wû

朝鄦, the name of a place, I. ii. 4. 4.

儒
zû

儒 and 儒者, the learned, the followers of Confucius, the orthodox, III. i. 5. 3: VII. ii. 26. 1.

優
yû

More than sufficient, VI. ii. 18. 6.

儵
ch'û

The surname of a minister of Ch'î, IV. ii. 32: VI. ii. 5. 1, 2, 3. 6.

THE 10TH RADICAL, 儿.

元
yüan

(1) Used for the head, III. ii. 2. 2: V. ii. 7. 5. 元士, head officers, a name appropriate to scholars of the first class in the royal domain, V. ii. 2. 5. (2) A name, 曾元, IV. i. 19. 3.

允
yün

To believe, accord with, V. i. 4. 4.

兄
hsiung

An elder brother, II. ii. 9. 3: III. i. 5. 3, *et al., saepe.* 伯兄, the eldest brother, VI. i. 5. 3. 父兄, fathers and elder brothers; elder relatives, I. i. 5. 3; ii. 11. 3, *et al., saepe.* 兄弟, brothers, I. i. 7. 12; ii. 1. 6, *et al., saepe.* Embracing cousins, V. ii. 3. 1 兄 = sisters, V. i. 5. 2.

充
ch'ung

(1) To fill, to fill up, develop, carry out, II. i. 6. 7: III. ii. 10. 6: V. ii. 4. 5: VI. ii. 9. 1 · VII. ii. 25. 5, 6; 31. 2, 3. 充塞, to stop up, III. ii. 9. 9. Full, I. ii. 12. 2. The filling up, II. i. 2. 9. (2) A surname, II. ii. 7. 1; 18. 1.

兆
chào

A prognostic, = a trial, V. ii. 4. 6.

先
hsien

(1) First (adverb and adjective); before (preposition); former, V. i. 9. 3; ii. 4. 6: VI. i. 5. 3; 7. 5, 8; 15. 2; ii. 16. 2: VII. i. 46. 1: II. i. 2. 2. 先君, former princes, III. i. 2. 3 先王, the former (ancient)

sovereigns, I. ii. 1. 2; 4. 4, 8, *et al.* 先生, our master, you, master, IV. i. 24. 2; ii. 31. 1: VI. ii. 4. 2, 4, 5, 6. 先子, my grandfather, II. i. 1. 3 先知, first knowing; 先覺, first apprehending, V. i. 7. 5; ii. 1. 2. 先聖, the former sages, III. ii. 9. 10. (2) To make first or chief, I. i. 1. 4, *et al.;* 先後 generally appears as correlate. To take the initiative, I. ii. 16. 1 : III. ii. 7. 3: IV. ii. 8. 3. (3) 先之, to set the example, III. i. 2. 4. 之先 = to excel him, III. i. 4. 12. Perhaps these examples, and those also under (2), should be read 先, the 4th tone.

先
hsien

The 4th tone. To precede, VI. ii. 2. 4.

光
kwang

Light, VII. i. 24. 2. 光 = glory, glorious. III. ii. 5. 6; VII. ii. 25. 6. Observe 用 光, I. ii. 5. 4.

克
k'o

(1) To conquer, VI. ii. 9. 2. 掊克 = grasping able ministers, VI. ii. 7. 2. (2) The name of 樂正克, I. ii. 16. 3: IV. ii. 24. 3.

免
mien

To escape from, avoid. Followed by 於, I. i. 4. 5; 7. 21, 22. Used absolutely, or actively, I. ii. 15. 1: IV. ii. 28. 7: VI. ii. 14. 4.

兔
t'û

A rabbit, a hare, I. ii. 2. 2. 兔者, harecatchers, I. ii. 2. 2.

堯
tâ

驩兜, a minister of Shun, banished by him, V. i. 3. 2.

THE 11TH RADICAL, 入.

入
zû

To enter, I. i. 3. 3; ii. 2. 3; 16. 2, *et al., saepe.* Used metaphorically, 入道, to go in and on to principles, VII. ii. 37. 11. Used in correlation with 出, = at home, at court, and abroad, I. i. 5. 3: III. ii. 4. 3: VI. ii. 15. 4. But in III. i. 3. 18, 入 = going out and coming in; and in VI. i. 8. 4 they are spoken of the mind.

內
nèi

(1) Within. A preposition, following the noun, I. i. 3. 3. (河內); 7. 17. When the noun has an adjective joined to it, a 之 precedes 內, I. ii. 2. 3; 6. 3: III. ii. 5. 3, 7, *et al.* (2) With 外 as correlate. The seclusion of the house, the harem, I. ii. 5. 5. The family, generally, II. ii. 2. 4. Internal, what is internal, within, VI. i. 4. 1, 2, 4; 5. 1, 2, 3, 5; ii. 6. 5.

內
nâ

Used for 納 (1) To receive, III. ii. 7. 2. 內 = to force, V. i. 7. 6; ii. 1. 2.

(2) 内 交, to form a friendship with, gain the favour of, II. i. 6. 3.

全
ch'üan

兩
liang

兩
liang

To be complete, perfect, IV. i. 21.

Two, a pair of, VII. ii. 22. 3.

The 4th tone. A numerative for carriages, VII. ii. 4. 1.

THE 12TH RADICAL, 八.

八
pā

Eight, I. i. 7. 17, 24, *et al., saepe.* The eighth, I. i. 6. 6: IV. ii. 18. 3.

公
kung

(1) Public, III. i. 3. 9. 公 養 之 仕, to take office sustained by the State, V. i. 4. 7. (2) A title of nobility, translated by *duke*, V. ii. 2. 3, 4; 3. 4; 6. 6, *et al.* 三 公, the three highest officers at the royal court, VII. i. 28.—It often follows the names of States, and honorary titles of the dukes. 周 公, II. i. 1. 7, *et al., saepe.*—齊 景 公, I. ii. 4. 4, 10, *et al.*— 桓 公, II. i. 2. 8, 10. *et al.*—晉 平 公, V. ii. 3. 4.—秦 穆 公, V. i. 9. 1, 3, *et al.*—得 平 公, I. ii. 16. 1.—滕 定 公, III. i. 2. 1.— 滕 文 公, I. ii. 12. 1. *et al.*—穆 公, I. ii. 12. 1.—衞 靈 公, V. ii. 4. 7.— 衞 孝 公, V. ii. 3. 3.—費 惠 公, V. ii. 3. 3.—虞 公, V. i. 9. 3. (3) Used in double surnames, 公 明, V. i. 1. 2.— III. i. 1. 4, *et al.* 公 孫, II. i. 1. 1, *et al.* —III. ii. 2. 1. 公 都, II. ii. 5. 4: III. ii. 9. 1, *et al.* 公 儀, VI. ii. 6. 3. 公 輸, IV. i. 1. 1. 公 行, IV. ii. 27. 1. Compare 庾 公, and 尹 公, IV. ii. 24. 2. (4) 公 劉, and 古 公 亶 父, ancestors of the Châu family, I. ii. 5. 3. 太 公 and 太 公 望, a minister of the kings Wân and Wû, IV. i. 13. 1: VI. ii. 8. 6: VII. i. 22. 1; ii. 38. 3.

六
liù

Six, II. i. 1. 8. 六 律, the pitch-tubes, IV. i. 1. 1, 5. 六 等, the six degrees of dignity, V. ii. 2. 3. 六 師, the royal forces, VI. ii. 7. 2.

兮
hsi

A particle, much used in poetry, IV. i. 8. 2: VII. i. 32. 1,

共
kung

To have in common, III. i. 2. 2; 3. 10. To share, V. ii. 3. 4.

共
kung

The 1st tone. (1) 共 爲, to perform, discharge, V. i. 1. 2. (2) 共 工, a name of office;—the superintendent of Works, V. i. 3. 2.

兵
ping

Sharp weapons of war, I. i. 3. 2, 5; 5. 3; 7. 14; ii. 11. 3: II. ii. 1. 3, 4; 3. 4: IV. i. 1. 9: VI. ii. 4. 3.

其
ch'i

The third personal pronoun; the possessive pronoun of the third person; the, that. Both singular and plural. *Passim.*

具
chü

Completely provided with, II. i. 2. 20.

典
tien

(1) A rule, a statute, 典 刑, V. i. 6. 5. 典 籍, VI. ii. 8. 5. (2) A canon, 堯 典, name of a Book of the Shû-ching, V. i. 4. 1.

兼
chien

To unite, comprehend, embrace together; together, II. i. 2. 18: IV. ii. 20. 5: VI. i. 10. 1; 14. 1; VII. i. 9. 6. Observe III. ii. 9. 11. 兼 金, 'fine silver,' II. ii. 3. 1. 兼 愛, Mo's principle of loving all equally, III. i. 9. 9: VII. i. 26. 2.

THE 13TH RADICAL, 冂.

冉
zan

A surname. 冉 牛, a disciple of Confucius, II. i. 2. 18, 20.

再
tsäi

Twice, again, V. ii. 6. 4, 5: VI. ii. 7. 2, 3.

冕
mien

A cap of full dress or ceremony, VI. ii. 6. 6.

THE 14TH RADICAL, 冖.

冠
kwan

A cap, a bonnet, II. i. 9. 1: IV. ii. 29. 6, 7: V. ii. 1. 1. To wear a cap, III. i. 4. 4.

冠
kwan

The 4th tone. To cap; the ceremony of capping, III. ii. 2. 2.

冢
ch'ung

冢 宰, a prime minister, III. i. 3. 4.

THE 15TH RADICAL, 冫.

冬
tung

Winter, VI. i. 5. 5.

況
hwang

More properly 況. How much more, —in the concluding member of a sentence, IV. i. 14. 2. It is generally followed by 乎 at the end of the clause, V. i. 7. 7: VII. i. 36. 2. 況 is sometimes immediately preceded by 而, and in the previous clause we have the particles 且 猶, 猶, 然 且, and 且, II. ii. 2. 10; 9. 2: V. ii. 4. 5; 7. 3, 4 (與 for 乎) 8 (況 乎 … 乎): VI. ii. 8. 8; 10. 6: VII. ii. 16.

冶
yě

To melt, fuse, 冶—a founder, III. i. 4. 5.

凍 *tung* To freeze. 凍 = to suffer from cold, I. i. 5. 4; ii. 6. 1: VII. i. 22. 3.

THE 16TH RADICAL, 几.

几 *chi* A stool, II. ii. 11. 2.

凡 *fan* All,—preceding the noun or clause to which it belongs, II. i. 6. 7: V. ii. 2. 3 (*bis*); 4. 4; VI. i. 7. 3; 10. 3; ii. 7. 3; VII. i. 10.

凰 *hwang* The female of the phœnix. 鳳凰, the phœnix, II. i. 2. 28.

凱 *k'ai* 凱風, the name of an ode, VI. ii. 3. 3. 4.

THE 17TH RADICAL, 凵.

凶 *hsiung* Bad, calamitous. Spoken of seasons, and joined to 年 or 歲, I. i. 7. 21, 22; ii. 12. 2: II. ii. 4. 2: III. i. 3. 7: VI. i. 7. 1: VII. ii. 10. Without 年 or 歲, I. i. 3. 1.

出 *ch'u* (1) To go, or come, out, I. i. 6. 2; ji. 4. 10; 16. 1, *et al., saepe.* 出乎, and 出於, to come out from, I. ii. 12. 2: II. i. 2. 28; but 出於 = to travel on, I. i. 7. 18, *et al.* (2) To send out, to issue, I. ii. 11. 4: IV. i. 24. 2. 出 = to put away, to divorce, IV. ii. 30. 5. (3) To quit, leave, II. ii. 12. 1, 4, 5, *et al.* (4) As correlate with 入, abroad, in opposition to at home, I. i. 5. 3: III. ii. 4. 3; in opposition to at court, VI. ii. 15. 4. See 入.

函 *han* A cuirass, defensive armour, II. i. 7. 1.

THE 18TH RADICAL, 刀.

刃 *zan* A sharp weapon, I. i. 3. 2; 4. 2, 3.

分 *fan* (1) To divide, III. i. 3. 13. 分 = to divide, impart to, III. i. 4. 10. (2) To distinguish. 無分於, indifferent to, VI. i. 2. 1, 2. Difference, VII. i. 25. 3.

分 *fan* The 4th tone. The lot, apportionment, VII. i. 21. 3.

刑 *hsing* (1) To punish; punishments, I. i. 5. 3; 7. 20; III. i. 8. 3; IV. i. 14. 3. Penal laws, II. i. 4. 2: IV. i. 1. 8: V. i. 6. 5. (2) To give an example to, I. i. 7. 12.

初 *ch'u* First, VI. ii. 7. 3. Early ways, VII. ii. 37. 1.

別 *pieh* The 4th tone. To distinguish, III. i. 3. 19. 有別, to have separate functions, III. i. 4. 8.

利 *li* (1) Sharp, I. i. 5. 3. 利口, sharpness of tongue, VII. ii. 37. 12. (2) Gain, profit; to profit, I. i. 1. 2, 3, 4, 6, *et al., saepe.* 利

達, advancement, IV. ii. 33. 2. 地利, advantages of situation, II. ii. I. 1, 2, 3. 4. To count profitable, IV. i. 8. 1. (3) Naturalness, being unconstrained, IV. ii. 26. 1.

制 *chih* To make; to regulate, I. i. 5. 3; 7. 21, 22: III. i. 3. 13: VII. i. 22. 3. Regulations, rules, VII. ii. 34. 2. 有制, to keep within certain rules, III. i. 3. 4. 制 = an allotment, V. ii. 2. 4.

刺 *ts'ze* To stab, II. i. 2. 4. To criticise, VII. ii. 37. 11. In I. i. 3. 5, where it means to *wound*, it is said to be read *ts'i*, in the 4th tone.

削 *hsiao* To cut, to pare, = to dismember; to deprive of territory, IV. i. 2. 4: VI. ii. 6. 3. 4; 7. 2.

前 *ch'ien* (1) Before, in front of. 食前, food spread before me, VII. ii. 34. 2. 於前, before you, I. i. 7. 16. 於王前, before your Majesty, II. ii. 2. 4. (2) Former, I. ii. 16. 1, 2. 前日, formerly, II. ii. 3. 1; 7. 1; 10. 2; 13. 1.

則 *tsê* (1) Then; denoting either a logical sequence or a sequence of time, but generally the former. The sequence is often in the course of the thought, and we find it difficult to translate the character in English. *Passim.* 然則, well then so then, is very common. So is 如之何 (or 如何) 則可. (2) A rule, a pattern; an example, V. i. 4. 3: VI. i. 6. 8. (3) To make a pattern of, to correspond to, III. i. 4. 11. These two usages are in quotations from the older classics. In Mencius himself, 則 is simply the particle.

剛 *kang* Strong, II. i. 2. 13.

割 *ko* To cut 割烹 = cookery, V. i. 7. 1, 8.

創 *ch'wang* To begin, to found, I. ii. 14. 3.

劍 *chien* A sword, I. ii. 3. 5: III. i. 2. 4.

劉 *liu* 公劉, an ancestor of the kings of the Châu dynasty, I. ii. 5. 4.

THE 19TH RADICAL, 力.

力 *li* Strength, force; vigorously, I. i. 2. 3; 7. 10: III. i. 3. 12, *et al.* 竭力, to do one's utmost, I. ii. 15. 1: V. i. 1. 2. 心力, I. i. 7. 17. 目力, IV. i. 1. 5. 勞力, to labour with the strength, = the sweat of the brow, III. i. 4. 6. 力役

THE 24TH RADICAL, 十.

十
shih
Ten, tens, I. i. 3. 2, 4, *et al.*, *saepe*. 十 一月十二月, the eleventh month, the twelfth month, IV. ii. 2. 3.

千
ch'ien
A thousand, I. i. 1. 2, 4; 7. 18, *et al.*, *saepe*.

半
pan
Half, II. i. 1. 13: III. ii. 10. 1.

卑
pei
Low, mean, I. ii. 7. 3: II. i. 1. 3: III. ii. 6. 2: V. ii. 5. 2, 3. 5.   To consider mean, II. i. 9. 2.

卒
tsŭ
(1) To die, IV. ii. 1. 1, 2.   (2) At last, IV. ii. 33. 1: VII. ii. 23. 2 (afterwards). So, 於卒也, V. ii. 6. 4.

卒
ts'ŭ
卒然, abruptly, I. i. 6. 2.

南
nan
(1) South, southern, II. i. 3. 2: V. i. 5. 7.   南 = in the south, I. i. 5. 1.   南 = to go southwards, I. ii. 4. 4.   南面, the royal position, with the face to the south, V. i. 4. 1.   But I. ii. 11. 2: III. ii. 5. 4: and VII. ii. 4. 3, are different.   (2) 南陽, the name of a place, VI. ii. 8. 3.   南蠻, a barbarian of the south, III. i. 4. 14.

博
po
(1) Extensive; extensively, IV. ii. 15: VII. ii. 32. 1.   Applied to the wide loose garments of poverty, II. i. 2. 4, 7.   (2) To gamble, IV. ii. 30. 2.

THE 26TH RADICAL, 卩.

危
wei
(1) To be in peril, I. i. 1. 4: IV. i. 2. 4.   To endanger, I. i. 7. 14: IV. ii. 30. 2.   Perils, IV. i. 8. 1.   危 = is under a sense of peril, VII. i. 18. 2.   (2) 三危, the name of a place, V. i. 3. 2.

卽
chi
(1) A particle, = that is, indeed, I. i. 7. 6.   (2) To approach, go to, III. i. 2. 4.

郤
ch'io
To refuse, decline, V. ii. 4. 2, 3.

卿
ch'ing
A noble; a high dignitary or chief minister, II. i. 2. 1; ii. 6. 1, 2; 10. 6: III. i. 3. 16: IV. i. 3. 3: V. i. 8. 2; ii. 2. 3, 5, 6, 7; 9. 1, 2, 4: VI. i. 16. 1; ii. 6. 1.

THE 27TH RADICAL, 厂.

厚
hâu
Thick.   厚 = liberally, sumptuously, III. i. 5. 2.   所厚者, where one should treat well, VII. i. 44. 1.

原
yüan
An origin; a fountain.   Seems to be used for 源, II. ii. 14. 1; 18. 2.

原
yüan
The 4th tone, i. q. 愿.   Your good, careful people, VII. ii. 37. 8, 9, 10.

厥
chüeh
His, their.   It occurs only in quotations from the Shih-ching and Shû-ching. I. ii. 3. 7; 5. 5: III. i. 1. 5; ii. 5. 5. VII. ii. 4. 5; 19. 3.

厲
li
(1) To oppress, III. i. 4. 3, 5.   (2) The title of an unworthy sovereign, VI. i. 6. 2.   厲 = 'The Cruel,' IV. i. 2. 4.

厭
yen
To be satiated, II. i. 2. 19.

厭
yen
The 1st tone, i. q. 厭.   But the meaning seems to be the same as above,—to be satisfied, I. ii. 4. 7.

THE 28TH RADICAL, 厶.

去
ch'ü
(1) To go away from; to leave.   Both active and neuter, I. ii. 11. 4; 13. 2; 14. 2; 15. 1, 2, *et al.*, *saepe*.   (2) To be distant from, II. i. 1. 8: IV. ii. 1. 3; 7: V. i. 6. 2: VII. ii. 38. 4.

去
ch'ü
The 3rd tone.   To put away; to remove, I. ii. 7. 4: II. ii. 4. 1: III. ii. 8. 1, *et al.*

THE 29TH RADICAL, 又.

又
yu
Moreover, further;—continuing a narrative by the addition of further particulars, I. ii. 11. 3: II. i. 1. 8; 2. 8, 10, 16, *et al.*, *saepe*.   又 = and still, III. ii. 5. 2.

及
chi
(1) To come to; to reach to; to attain to, I. ii. 13. 2: II. ii. 11. 4: III. i. 3. 9: VI. ii. 5. 4: VII. i. 27. 2; 29; ii. 1. 1, 2; 28. 1.   及 = to wait for, V. i. 8. 3.   以及, so as to reach to, I. i. 7. 10, 12.   及, I. ii. 11. 4: II. ii. 2. 6: VII. i. 41. 1.   (2) At the commencement of clauses, a conjunction, = and when, I. i. 5. 1; 7. 20: II. i. 4. 2, 4; ii. 9. 4: III. i. 2. 5; 3. 3; ii. 9. 5: VII. i. 15. 2; 16; ii. 6.   (3) As a preposition or conjunction, = and, I. i. 2. 4; along with, IV. i. 9. 6.

友
yu
(1) A friend, friends, I. ii. 6. 1: II. i. 9. 1, *et al.*   Joined with 朋, II. i. 6. 3: III. i. 4. 8: IV. ii. 30. 4.   (2) Maintaining friendship with; to be friendly, II. i. 9. 1: III. i. 3. 18: V. ii. 3. 1, 3, 5; 7. 4.   (3) A name, 然友, III. i. 2.

反
fan
(1) To return (neuter), I. ii. 4. 7; 12. 2, *et al.*   Active; sometimes = to recall, I. ii. 11. 4: II. ii. 4. 3; 12. 4, *et al.*   反命 to report the execution of a commission, III. i. 2. 5; ii. 1. 4, *et al.*   (2) To turn back to, I. i. 7. 17, 23, *et al.* ? VII. ii. 33. 1; 37. 13.   (3) To turn the thoughts inwards, I. i. 7. 9.   Compare 自反, self-examination, II. i. 2. 7: IV. ii. 28. 4, 5, 6.   反身, IV. i. 12. 1: VII. i. 4. 1.   反其仁, &c., IV. i. 4.   (4) To turn round, II. i. 1. 6.   (5) On the contrary, yet, II. i. 2. 10.   Contrary to what should be, IV. i.

18. 2; ii. 24. 2. (6) 反覆, to repeat, again and again, V. ii. 9. 1, 4: VI. i. 7. 2. Observe II. ii. 6. 1, 2.

叔 shú   (1) 叔父, a father's younger brother, an uncle, VI. i. 5. 4, 5. (2) 管叔, an elder brother of Châu-kung, II. ii. 9. 2, 3. (3) In surnames, VI. ii. 15. 1.—II. ii. 10. 6.

取 ch'ü   To take, I. ii. 10. 2, 3; 11. 1; 14. 2, et al., saepe. To obtain, receive, I. i. 1. 4. To find; choose; approve of, III. i. 5. 3: IV. i. 8. 3; 18. 1, 2; 21. 3; 24. 2, et al. To seize, III. ii. 5. 5, 6, et al.

受 shòu   To receive, II. i. 2. 4: 9. 1; ii. 3. 1, 3, 4: V. ii. 4. 2, 3; 5. 4, 5, et al., saepe. To accept, V. i. 5. 5, 6. 其所受教, those whose instructions they might receive, II. ii. 2. 9. 有所受之, it was received from a proper source, VII. i. 35. 4.

叟 sàu   Venerable Sir, I. i. 1. 2; 5. 1. 高叟, that old Kâo, VI. ii. 3. 2.

叢 ts'ung   A thicket, IV. i. 9. 2.

THE 30TH RADICAL, 口.

口 k'âu   (1) The mouth, I. i. 7. 16: VI. i. 7. 5, 8 (口 = the tongue, tongues, VII. ii. 19. 2); 24. 1; 37. 12. 口體 the mouth and body,=the body, IV. i. 19. 3. 口腹, VI. i. 14. 6: VII. i. 27. 1. (2) 口 = individuals, a sort of numerative, I. i 3. 4; 7. 24: VII. i. 22. 2.

召 chào   To call, to summon, I. ii. 4. 10: II. ii. 2. 5, 7, 10: V. ii. 7. —, 3, 4, 9.

叩 k'âu   To knock at, VII. i. 23. 3.

古 kü   Antiquity, ancient, I. ii. 1. 3: II. i. 2. 22, et al., saepe. Of frequent occurrence, sometimes meaning the ancients generally, but often the ancient kings and worthies, I. i. 2. 3; 7. 12: II. ii. I. 13, et al. 古者, the ancients, anciently, II. ii. 7. 2: IV. i. 18. 3: III. ii. 7. 1. 古公, the ancient duke, the title of 亶父, an ancestor of the Châu family, I. ii. 5. 5.

可 k'o   May. Passim. Like may in English, 可 may represent possibility, liberty, or ability. 可以 is very frequent, = may. The 以 may sometimes be explained by thereby, therewith, but not always. 可 is not always an auxiliary, but often conveys a complete meaning. Observe 可 and 不可 in III. ii. 1. 4, &c. &c.

句 kau   The 1st tone. In the name 句踐, I. ii. 8. 1.—VII. i. 9. 1.

史 shih   History; historical, IV. ii. 21. 3.

右 yu   (1) The right, 左右, to—on the right and left, I. ii. 6. 3: II. ii. 10. 7: IV. ii. 14. (齊右, the right = the west—of Ch'î, VI. ii. 6. 5. 右 = attendants, I. ii. 7. 4, 5: ? disciples, IV. ii. 31. 1. (2) 右師, the title of a high officer at the courts of the princes, IV. ii. 27. 1, 2.

司 sze   To preside over. The phrase 有司 = 'the officers,' generally those of inferior rank, I. ii. 12. 1, 2; 16. 1: III. i. 2. 4: VI. ii. 10. 4. 有司者, II. ii. 10. 7. 司徒, the minister of instruction, III. i. 4. 8. 司寇, the minister of justice, VI. ii. 6. 6. 司城, the city-master, V. i. 8. 3. 司馬, the master of the horse, V. i. 8. 3.

各 ko   Each, every, VII. i. 4. 6.

合 ho   (1) To agree with, I. i. 7. 9: IV. ii. 20. 5. VII. ii. 37. 11. (2) To unite, IV. ii. 1. 3. Observe VII. ii. 16. 1.

同 t'ung   (1) The same, I. ii. 16. 2: II. i. 2. 22: III. i. 4. 17, et al., saepe. Often = to be the same, to agree, in or with. 有同與, are there points in which they agree? II. i. 2. 24. To make the same, III. i. 4. 18. To consider as common, II. i. 8. 3. 同乎, agreeing with, VII. ii. 37. 11. 同朝 = all in my court, II. ii. 10. 2. Adverbially,—together, in common, III. i. 3. 19: VII. i. 13. 3. (2) To share, I. ii. 1. 6, 7; 2. 2; 4. 2, et al. (3) A name, II. ii. 8. 1, 2.

后 hàu   (1) A prince, a ruler, I. ii. 11. 2: III. ii. 5. 4. (2) 夏后氏 and 夏后 = the great Yü, the founder of the Hsiâ dynasty. Sometimes = the Hsiâ dynasty, or its founder, II. i. 1. 10: III. i. 3. 6: IV. i. 2. 5: V. i. 6. 7. (3) 后稷, the title of Shun's minister of agriculture, Tsî (Chî), III. i. 4. 8: IV. ii. 29. 1, 2, 3, 4.

名 ming   (1) The name, VII. ii. 36. 2. To name, III. i. 4. 11: IV. i. 2. 4. 無名之指, the fourth finger, VI. i. 12. 1. (2) Fame, VI. ii. 6. 1: VII. ii. 11. 名世者, illustrious men, II. ii. 13. 3.

吏 lì   An officer, a minister, III. i. 3. 13: V. i. 8. 3. 委吏, the office first held by Confucius, V. ii. 5. 4. 天吏, II. i. 5. 6; ii. 8. 2.

君 chün   A prince, a ruler. Passim. It very often occurs in correlation with 臣, a minister.

君子, the superior man, a designation of the individual high in talents and virtue. Sometimes indicates station. 人君, see on 人. 都君, a designation of Shun, V. i. 2. 3.

吠 *fei*

To bark, II. i. 1. 10.

否 *fâu*

(1) No, I. i. 7. 10, 15, 16; ii. 16. 2, *et al., saepe.* (2) Or not, II. i. 2. 1; ii. 2. 3; 4. 1.

吳 *wú*

The name of a State, I. ii. 3. 1: IV. i. 7. 2.

告 *kâo*

To tell, inform, announce to, I. ii. 1. 6, 7; 12. 2; 15. 1; 16. 2, 3, *et al., saepe.* 無告 者, the helpless, those who have none to whom they can tell their wants, I. ii. 5. 3.

To announce respectfully and request, IV. i. 26. 2: V. i. 2. 1, 2.

吾 *wú*

(1) *Passim.* I, my. (2) In the name 皆夷吾, VI. ii. 15. 1.

周 *châu*

(1) Complete, VII. ii. 10. (2) 周旋, turning or wheeling about, VII. ii. 33. 2. (3) i.q. 賙, to help, give alms to, VII. i. 6. 2; 2: VI. ii. 14. 4. (4) Name of the Châu dynasty, or its original seat, I. ii. 3. 6: II. i. 1. 10; ii. 13. 4, *et al., saepe.* 周 人, the founders of the Châu dynasty, III. i. 3. 6. 周公, the famous duke of Châu, II. i. 1. 7, *et al., saepe.* 周道, V. ii. 7. 8. (5) A name, VI. ii. 6. 5.—V. i. 8. 3. (6) A surname, III. ii. 3. 1.

味 *wei*

Taste, flavours, VI. i. 7. 5, 8; 17. 3: VII. ii. 2a. 1.

呼 *hû*

To call out, VII. i. 36. 3.

命 *ming*

(1) To charge, admonish; orders, III. ii. 2. 2; 3. 6: IV. i. 7. 2; 3: V. i. 2. 4, *et al.* To appoint. Applied very frequently to the ordinances of a sovereign or ruler, I. ii. 4. 6; 16. 1, *et al., saepe.* Applied also to the ordinances or appointments of Heaven or God, II. i. 4. 6: III. i. 4. 6; *et al.* 命 = the Heaven-ordained, meaning our nature, VII. i. 1. 3. Observe II. ii. 14. 3 反命 to return—i. e. report the execution of a commission, is common. (2) To instruct; instructions, III. i. 5. 5: V. i. 1. 2; 2. 2: VI. ii. 7. 3. (3) 辭命, speeches, II. i. 2. 18; 9. 1. (4) In a double surname V. i. 1. 1.

和 *ho*

Harmony, accord; harmonious, accommodating, II. ii. 1. 1, 3: V. ii. 1. 5.

咸 *hsien*

(1) All, III. ii. 9. 6: V. i. 2. 3; 3. 2. (2) 咸丘, a double surname V. i. 4. 1, 2.

哅 *hsü*

To chatter and clamour about. III. ii. 6. 1.

咽 *yen*

The 4th tone. To swallow, take a mouthful, III. ii. 10. 1.

哀 *âi*

Sorrow; to lament, III. i. 2. 4, 5: VII. ii. 33. 2. Alas for! I. ii. 5. 3. 哀哉 alas!—at the end of the sentence, IV. i. 10. 3: VI. i. 11. 2.

哇 *wâ*

To vomit, III. ii. 10. 5.

哉 *tsâi*

A particle of exclamation, indicating admiration or surprise. The most common use of it in Mencius is at the close of interrogative sentences. It is then preceded by 豈, 豈...也. 可... 乎, 何, 奚, 惡, 焉, and perhaps other characters, I. i. 2. 4; 7. 4, 7, 16, 17, 2a, *et al., saepe.* 何哉 is frequent, I. ii. 16. 1, 2: V. ii. 4. 2, *et al.* Observe 何為也哉, V. ii. 7. 3. It is used at the end of sentences, V. i. 2. 4, *et al.* and at the end of commencing clauses, the subject exclaimed about following, and the sentence often closing with 矣, 也, 乎, or some other particle, I. ii. 3. 4; 4. 5; 5. 5, *et al., saepe.* 哀哉 alas! VI. i. 11. 2, *et al.*

員 *yüan*

Things round, circles, IV. i. 1. 1, 5; 2. 1.

哭 *k'û*

To wail; to bewail, III. i. 2. 4, 5; 4. 13: VI. i. 6. 5: VII. ii. 33. 2.

哿 *ko*

May. 哿矣 = may get through, I. ii. 5. 3.

唐 *t'ang*

(1) A name of Yâo, V. i. 6. 7. (2) A name, V. ii. 3. 4. (3) 高唐, a place, VI. ii. 6. 5.

商 *shang*

(1) Traders, travelling merchants, I. i. 7. 18 (商賈): II. i. 5. 2; ii. 10. 7. (2) The Shang dynasty, IV. i. 7. 5.

問 *wun*

(1) To ask; to ask about; a question. *Passim.* 問 is often followed by 於, to ask of or about; once, by 乎, II. i. 1. 3. (2) 學問 = to study; learning, III. i. 2. 4: VI. i. 11. 4. (3) To send to inquire for, V. ii. 6. 4. 問疾, II. ii. 2. 3. (4) Fame, VII. ii. 19. 3.

啟 *ch'i*

(1) To commence, I. ii. 5. 4. (2) To instruct, III. ii. 9. 6. (3) The name of Yü's son, V. i. 6. 1;—of the count of Wei, VI. i. 6. 3.

啜 *chüh*

To taste, to sip, 餔啜, IV. i. 25.

善 *shen*

(1) Good, virtuous; what is good; excellent, I. i. 7. 21; ii. 4. 5; 5. 4: II. i. 8; 8. 2, 3, 5, *et al., saepe.* (2) Skilful; to

喜 *hsi*

喟 *wei* 喟然, the sound of sighing, VII. i. 36. 1.

喻 *yü* (1) To illustrate, I. i. 3. 2. (2) To understand, VIII. ii. 15. 3 : VII. i. 21. 4.

喪 *sang* To mourn for, I. i. 3. 3, et al. The period of, and all pertaining to, mourning, I. ii. 16. 1, 2 : VII. i. 39. 1, 3, et al.

喪 *sang* The 4th tone. (1) To die, expire; ruin, I. i. 2. 4 : IV. i. 1. 9. (2) To lose, I. i. 5. 1 : III. ii. 1. 2 : V. ii. 7. 5 : VI. i. 10. 5.

喬 *ch'iao* Lofty. 喬木, I. ii. 7. 1 : III. i. 4. 15.

嗜 *shih* To find pleasure in; to relish, I. i. 6. 4, 6 : VII. ii. 36. 1.

嘐 *hsiao* 嘐嘐, magniloquent, VII. ii. 37. 6, 9.

嘑 *hu* 嘑爾, with an insulting voice, VI. i. 10. 6.

嘗 *ch'ang* (1) To try, 嘗試, I. i. 7. 19. (2) Forming the past tense, I. ii. 1. 2 : II. i. 2. 7, 15 ; ii. 6. 1, 2, et al., saepe. The combination 未嘗 is frequent.

噲 *k'uai* In the designation 子噲, II. ii. 8. 1.

嚽 *chuai* To bite, gnaw, III. i. 5. 4.

器 *ch'i* Vessels; implements, I. ii. 11. 3, 4 : V. ii. 4. 6 : VII. ii. 10. 3. 械器, III. i. 4. 5. 器皿, III. ii. 3. 3

嚮 *hsiang* Over against. 相嚮, towards one another, III. i. 4. 13.

嚴 *yen* (1) To dread, II. i. 2. 4. (2) Pressed by urgency of affairs, II. ii. 7. 1.

囂 *hsiao* 囂囂, indifferent and self-satisfied, V. i. 7. 3 : VII. i. 9. 2, 3.

囊 *nang* A sack, I. ii. 5. 4.

THE 31st RADICAL, 口.

四 *ssu* Four. Saepe. 四海 and 四海之內, a name for all subject to the royal rule, I. i. 7. 12 : III. ii. 5. 3, 7, et al., saepe. Observe IV. ii. 18. 2 : VI. ii. 11. 3. 四方 and 四境, the four quarters of the kingdom or a State, I. ii. 3. 7; 6. 3 : II. i. 1. 10, et al. 四體 四支, and

四肢, tho four limbs, II. i. 6. 6 : IV. ii. 30. 2 : VII. i. 21. 4 : ii. 24. 1. 四端, the four virtuous principles of our nature, II. i. 6. 6, 7. 四罪, four criminals, V. i. 3. 2. 四夷, all the barbarous tribes about the Middle Kingdom, I. i. 7. 16.

回 *hui* The name of Confucius's favourite disciple, IV. ii. 29. 2, 3.

因 *yin* (1) Then, therefore, I. i. 7. 20. (2) By means of, taking advantage of, II. ii. 10. 4 : III. i. 5. 1. (3) To accord with, IV. i. 1. 6.

困 *k'un* To be distressed, VI. ii. 15. 3.

固 *ku* (1) Firm; to be made strong, II. i. 1. 4. (2) Stupid, VI. ii. 3. 2. (3) As an adverb, —certainly, indeed, as a matter of course, I. i. 7. 5, 17; ii. 11. 3 : VII. ii. 6. 1, et al., saepe.

囿 *yü* A park, I. ii. 2. 1, 2, 3 : III. ii. 9. 5. 靈囿, the name of king Wăn's park, I. i. 2. 3.

圉圉 *yü* 圉圉, the appearance of being embarrassed, V. i. 2. 4.

國 *kwo* A State. Passim. 萬乘之國, the royal kingdom. 千乘之國, the State of a Adu, I. i. 1. 4; but such a State is called 萬乘之國, I. ii. 10. 4 : II. i. 1. 13. 國人 = the people, I. ii. 7. 4, 5 : VII. ii. 23; but also = a common man, IV. ii. 3. 1. 國家, a State, with its component great families, I. ii. 9. 2, et al., saepe. 中國, the Middle Kingdom, I. i. 7. 16, et al.; but = in the middle of the State, II. ii. 10. 3. 國 = city, IV. ii. 33. 1 : VII. ii. 4. 4. Used for 君, V. ii. 7. 4. 爲國, to administer a State, III. i. 3. 1

園 *yüan* A garden, III. ii. 9. 5.

THE 32nd RADICAL, 土.

土 *tu* The ground, soil, II. ii. 7. 4 : IV. ii. 8. 1 : V. i. 4. 2. Territory, VI. ii. 7. 2;—but for this meaning 土地 is commonly used, meaning also newly-cultivated ground, I. i. 7. 16; ii. 15. 1 : IV. i. 14. 2, 3 : VI. ii. 9. 1; 14. 4, et al. 平土, plains, III. ii. 9. 4.

土 *tu* The 4th tone. Bark about the roots of the mulberry tree, II. ii. 4. 3.

在 *tsai* To be in; to be on; to depend on;—the where, wherein, and whereon following. Passim. As a preposition,—in, on, I. i. 7. 20 : III. i. 3. 3; in the case of, V. i. 3. 2.

惡在, where is, how is, L. i. 4. 5 : III. i. 3. 7 : VII. i. 33. 3. Observe 惟我在, I. ii. 3. 7; 惟義所在, IV. ii. 11. 1; also III. ii. 1. 2 : VI. i. 2. 3 : VII. i. 48. 1.

圭 kwei / **地** tí

(1) 圭田 the holy field, III. i. 3. 16. (2) A name, VI. ii. 10; 11. 1.

(1) The earth in correlation with heaven, II. i. 2. 13; VII. i. 18. 3. 地= position, II. ii. 1. 1, 2, 3: VI. i. 7. 2. (2) The ground; territory, I. i. 5. 1, 2: II. i. 1. 8: V. ii. 2. 4, 5, 6, 7, 8, et al., saep. =lands, III. i. 3. 7. Observe 井地 III. i. 3. 13. 土地 is common in this sense. See 土壤地 also occurs, III. i. 3. 14. (3) 地=place, L. i. 7. 4, 7: IV. ii. 31. 3. 地=regions, IV. ii. 1. 3.

均 chūn

Equal, III. i. 3. 13.

坐 tso

To sit, L. i. 7. 4 : II. i. 9. 1; ii. 11. 2, 3, et al.

垂 ch'ui

(1) To hand down, I. ii. 14. 3. (2) 垂涕 to shed tears, VI. ii. 3. 2. (3) 垂棘 the name of a place, V. i. 9. 2.

垣 yüan / **埕** t'ieh

A wall, III. i. 7. 2.

(1) An anthill, II. i. 2. 28. So Chū Hsī explains it, but in the dictionary its sound with that meaning is chih. (2) 垤澤 the name of a gate, VII. i. 36. 3.

城 ch'ang

(1) City walls, I. ii. 13. 2 : VII. ii. 22. 3. 城郭 inner and outer or suburban walls, II. i. 1. 2, 3: IV. i. 1. 9: VI. ii. 10. 4. (2) A city, cities, IV. i. 14. 2. 司城 V. i. 8. 3. (3) 武城 the name of a city, IV. ii. 31. 1. 陽城 id., V. i. 6. 1.

城 ni

A boundary; to bound in, II. ii. 1. 4.

執 chih

To lay hold of, to hold; to apprehend, IV. i. 7. 6; ii. 3. 4; 20. 2; 24. 2: VI. ii. 12. 1 : VII. i. 36. 2. 執中 to hold a medium; 執一 to hold to one point, VII. i. 26. 3, 4.

基 chi

鎡基 a hoe, II. i. 1. 9.

堂 t'ang

The hall or principal apartment in a house, L. i. 7. 4 : VII. ii. 34. 2. (2) 明堂 the Brilliant palace, built for the purpose of Audience, I. ii. 5. 1, 2.

堅 chien

Strong, I. i. 5. 3 : II. ii. 1. 3.

堪 k'an

To endure, IV. ii. 29. 2.

堯 yáo

The name of the ancient sovereign, II. i. 2. 26 ; ii. 2. 4, et al., saepissime.

報 páo

To acknowledge, to reply to, VI. ii. 5. 1.

場 ch'ang

(1) An open area or arena, III. i. 4. 13. (2) 場師 a plantation keeper, VI. i. 14. 3.

塗 t'u

(1) Mire, mud, II. i. 9. 1 : V. ii. 1. 1 (塗炭). (2) Roads, I. i. 3. 5; 7. 18.

塞 sái

To fill up, II. i. 2. 13. 充塞 to fill up and stop, III. ii. 9. 9. So 茅塞 VII. ii. 21. 1.

塡 t'ien

塡然, the sound of the drum, I. i. 3. 2.

墁 man

Ornaments on walls, = to disfigure, III. ii. 4. 5.

境 ching

A border, a boundary, I. ii. 2. 3. 四境之內, 四境 I. ii. 6. 3: II. i. 1. 10. Name of a prince of Ch'i, VII. i. 33. 1.

墊 tien / **墨** mo

(1) Ink. 繩墨, a carpenter's marking line, VII. i. 41. 2. (2) Black, III. i. 2. 4. (3) Surname of a heresiarch. 墨者, a Mohist, III. i. 5. 1, 2: VII. ii. 26. 1, 2. 墨氏, III. ii. 9. 9. 墨翟, III. ii. 9. 10, 14.

Tombs, IV. ii. 33. 1.

播 fan / **壑** ho

A channel for water; a ditch, III. i. 5. 4 : VI. ii. 11. 3. In other cases, always in combination with 溝 I. ii. 12. 2 : II. ii. 4. 2: III. i. 3. 7; ii. 1. 2 : V. ii. 7. 5.

壙 k'uang

A tract beyond cultivation, IV. i. 9. 2.

壤 zang

(1) Mould, III. ii. 10. 3. (2) 壤地 territory, III. i. 3. 14.

壞 huái

To pull down, III. ii. 9. 5.

THE 33RD RADICAL, 士.

士 shih

(1) A scholar, a man of education and ability. Passim. (2) An officer, I. i. 1. 4, et saepe. This and the preceding meaning run into each other. 上士, 中士, 下士, 元士, V. ii. 2. 3, 5, 6, 7, 8.

壬 zǎn

仲壬 a son of the sovereign Tang, V. i. 6. 5.

壯 *chwang* Strong, V. ii. 5. 4. 壯 = in vigorous manhood, I. i. 5. 3; ii. 9. 1; 12. 2: II. ii. 4. 2.

壹 *yi* Solely employed, exclusively active, II. i. 2. 1.

壺 *hú* A goblet, or jug; a vessel for liquids, I. i. 10. 4; 11. 3: III. ii. 5. 5. Always in the phrase 壺漿.

壽 *shóu* Long life, VII. i. 1. 3.

THE 35TH RADICAL, 夊.

夏 *hsià* (1) Summer, III. ii. 7. 4: VI. i. 5. 5. (2) Great;—a name for China, III. i. 4. 12. (3) The name of a dynasty, I. ii. 4. 5: III. i. 3. 10: V. i. 6. 6; 7. 6; ii. 4. 4. 夏后氏, the great Yü, the founder of the Hsiá dynasty, III. i. 3. 6. 夏后, a sovereign, sovereigns, of the Hsiá, II. i. 1. 10: IV. i. 2. 5 (?): V. i. 6. 7. (4) 子夏, the designation of one of Confucius's disciples, II. i. 2. 6, 20: III. i. 4. 13. (5) 頁夏, the name of a place, IV. ii. 1. 1.

夔 *kwei* Repeated, = the appearance of being reverential, V. i. 4. 4.

THE 36TH RADICAL, 夕.

夕 *hsì* The evening, VI. ii. 14. 4.

外 *wái* The outside; outside; without, III. i. 4. 7; i. 9. 1; 10. 5: V. ii. 4. 4; 6. 4: VI. i. 6. 7; ii. 6. 5: VII. i. 3. 2. (2) External; what is external, VI. i. 4. 1, 2, 4; 5; 5. 3, 5; ii. 15. 4. To make to be external, II. i. 2 15. (3) 三年之外, after three years; 於...外 at a distance of ..., V. ii. 1. 7; VI. ii. 18. 8. (4) In correlation with 內, abroad, L. ii. 5. 5: II. ii. 2. 4. (5) 外丙, a son of the sovereign Tang, V. i. 6. 5.

夜 *yè* Night, IV. ii. 18. 2; 20. 5: VI. i. 8. 1, 2.

多 *to* Many; much, I. i. 1. 4; iii. 1, 2, *et al.*, *saepe.* To become many, III. ii. 9. 5. In other cases it contains the copula in the same way. Many times, II. ii. 4. 2. Mostly, VII. i. 36. 2. 多聞 and 多聞識, extensive information, V. ii. 7. 3: VI. ii. 18. 2.

THE 37TH RADICAL, 大.

大 *tá* Great, large; greatly. *Passim.* To make great, I. ii. 8. 5. 大 = if the result were great, III. ii. 1. 1. 大體, the nobler

part of our nature, VI. i. 15. 1, 2. 大匠, a master-workman, VI. i. 20. 2: VII. i. 41. 2. 大夫, see 夫. 大人, see 人.

太 *tái* 太甲, the name of a Book in the Shú-ching, II. i. 4. 6, *et al.* III. ii. 5. 6; V. i. 6. 8. 太誓, *id.*, 太丁, a son of the sovereign Tang, V. i. 6. 5. 太王, an ancestor of the House of Châu, I. ii. 3. 1; 5. 5; 14. 2; 15. 1. 太師, the Grand music-master, I. ii. 4. 10. 太公 and 太公望, a minister of Wăn and Wû, IV. i. 13. 1: VI. ii. 8. 6: VII. i. 22. 1; ii. 38. 3. 太山, the T'ai mountain in Shantung, I. i. 7. 11: II. i. 2. 28: VII. i. 24. 1.

天 *tien* (1) Heaven;—the material heaven: the heavens, the sky, I. i. 6. 6: II. i. 2. 13; 4. 3: IV. ii. 26. 3: V. i. 4. 1, 2: VII. i. 41. (2) Its more common use is for the supreme, governing Power, with more or less of personality indicated, I. i. 8. 2, 3, 7; 10. 2; 14. 3; 16. 3: II. i. 4. 6; 5. 6; 7. 2; ii. 1. 1, 2; 8. 2; 13. 1, 5: III. i. 5. 3: IV. i. 1. 10; 7. 1, 5; 8. 5; 12. 2: V. i. 5. 2, 3, 4; 5, 6, 7; 6. 1, 2, 4; 7. 5, 9; ii. 1. 2; 3. 4: VI. i. 6. 8; 7. 1; 15. 2; 16. 1, 2, 3; ii. 15. 2: VII. i. 1. 1, 2; 19. 3; 20. 3; 38. 1; ii. 24. 2: ?V. i. 1. 1, 2. (3) 天子, the highest designation of the sovereign, I. ii. 4. 5: II. ii. 7. 2, *et al.*, *saepe*. 天下, see 下.

夫 *fú* (1) A male, males, I. ii. 5. 5: III. i. 8. 17. A husband, I. ii. 5. 3. 夫 = a fellow, I. ii. 8. 3. So, when joined with 褐, II. i. 2. 4; with 頑, V. ii. 1. 1; with 鄙, V. ii. 1. 3; with 薄, VII. ii. 15. 夫婦, 夫妻, III. i. 4. 8: IV. ii. 30. 5. 匹夫, see 匹. 丈夫, see 丈. 農夫, a husbandman, III. i. 4. 5, 9, *et al.* Observe 夫...布, II. i. 5. 5. (2) 大夫, a general name for the officers of a court, below the chief minister. *Saepe.* See especially V. ii. 2. 3. (3) 夫子 = our master—used in conversation. Applied to Mencius. *Passim.* Applied to Confucius. *Saepe.* 夫 = your husband, III. ii. 2. 2. Observe IV. i. 18. 2, meaning, my master; and so generally, IV. ii. 24. 3. (4) 夫人, the wife of a prince, III. ii. 3. 3.

夫 *fú* The 2nd tone. (1) An initial particle, which may generally be rendered by *now*. Sometimes, however, we must use *then* or *but*; and sometimes it will hardly admit

of being rendered in English. *Passim.*
(2) A final particle, with exclamatory force, IV. ii. 24. 2: VI. i. 1. 2; ii. 7. 2. (3) Intermediate in sentences, with a demonstrative force, I. i. 6. 6: II. ii. 2. 6: VII. i. 39. 4. To this are to be referred 今夫, 若夫, and 且夫, the two former of which are common.

失
shih

To lose, II. i. 1. 8; ii. 1. 4; 4. 1, 2, *et al.*, *saepe.* To lose,—not to get, I. i. 3. 4; 7. 24, *et al.* To fail of or in, III. ii. 1. 4: VI. ii. 7. 2, *et al.* 自失, to lose one's self, II. i. 9. 2: compare IV. i. 19 1.

夷
i

(1) Even; evenly. In the phrase 夷考, VII. ii. 37. 6. (2) To wound, = to be offended, IV. i. 18. 2. (3) Used for 彝, the invariable rules of virtue, VI. i. 6. 8. (4) Barbarous tribes;—properly those on the east, as in 夷狄, III. i. 9. 11. But used generally, III. i. 4. 12. We have also 昆夷, I. ii. 3. 1; 四夷, I. i. 7. 16; 東夷, IV. ii. 1. 1; and 西夷, I. ii. 11. 2, *et al.* (5) A surname, III. ii. 1. 5. (6) In the honorary epithet, 伯夷, II. i. 2. 22, 23, *et al.*, *saepe.* Also in the name, 替夷吾, VI. ii. 15. 1.

奄
yen

The name of a State, III. ii. 9. 6.

奉
fung

Services, VI. i. 10. 7, 8.

奇
ch'i

In a name. 宮之奇, V. i. 9. 2.

契
hsieh

Shun's minister of Instruction, III. i. 4. 8.

奚
hsi

(1) An interrogative particle, = how, why, what, I. i. 7. 22; ii. 11. 2: III. ii. 1. 2; 5. 4: IV. ii. 28. 4. 6: V. i. 2. 3. 4; 3. 2; ii. 4. 6; 7. 4, 5: VI. ii. 1. 7; 2. 3: VII. i. 34; ii. 4. 3; 22. 3. 奚為, I. ii. 16. 2: VI. ii. 13. 3. In names, 百里奚, V. i. 9. 1, 2: VI. ii. 6. 4; 16. 1. 嬖奚, III. ii. 1. 4.

奪
to

To snatch, take by force; to rob, I. i. 1. 4; 3. 4; 5. 4; 7. 23: III. ii. 5. 2: IV. i. 16. 1: VI. ii. 1. 8. Observe VI. i. 15. 2.

奮
fun

To press forward; to make himself distinguished, VII. ii. 15.

THE 38TH RADICAL, 女.

女
nü

A woman, a female; a daughter, I. ii. 5. 5: III. ii. 4. 3; 5. 5: IV. i. 17. 1: V. i. 1. 3. 4; 2. 1; ii. 6. 6: VII. ii. 6. 女子, a daughter, III. ii. 2. 2; 3. 6.

女
zü

The 3rd tone. For 汝, you, your, I. i. 2. 4; ii. 9. 1, 2: III. ii. 1. 4; 2. 2.

女
nü

The 4th tone. To give a daughter to one in marriage, IV. i. 7. 2: V. ii. 6. 6.

好
hâo

The 4th tone. To love, be fond of. *Saepe.* 好事, to be fond of strange things, V. i. 8. 1; 9. 1. 歸于好, to become friendly, VI. ii. 7. 3. Mencius never uses 好 as an adjective in the 3rd tone, 好 = good, fine, unless in V. i. 1. 4.

如
jú or zü

(1) As. *Saepe.* We often find 如是 and 如此, thus, such, so. (2) As = if, though, since, I. i. 3. 2; 5. 3; ii. 5. 4; 5, *et al.*, *saepe.* So 如使, VI. i. 7. 5; 10. 3, *et al.* (3) 如何, 如之何, 何如, see on 何, but observe the difference between 何如 at the beginning and at the end of a sentence. Observe also I. ii. 14. 3. (4) After adjectives, it = our termination *ly*, VII. i. 13; 12. 2, *et al.* (5) 如 = to wish, II. ii. 2. 1.

妃
fei

A consort, a wife. The dictionary says that the most honourable inmate of the harem next to the queen was called 妃, but it seems to have the highest meaning in I. ii. 5. 5.

妄
wang

Irregular, utterly lost, IV. ii. 28. 6.

妁
chiâo

媒妁, a go-between, a matchmaker, III. ii. 3. 6.

妣
pi

A deceased mother. In 考妣, V. i. 4. 1.

妻
ch'i

A wife, I. i. 5. 4, *et al.*, *saepe.* 妻子, wife and child, wives and children. *Saepe.*

妻
ch'i

The 4th tone. To give to one to wife, V. i. 2. 2. To have to wife, V. i. 1. 4.

妾
ch'ieh

A concubine, IV. ii. 33. 1, 2: VI. ii. 10. 7, 8; ii. 7. 3. In VII. ii. 34. 2, 侍妾 = 'attendants and concubines.' 姜婦 = women, III. ii. 2. 2.

始
shih

To begin; beginning; first, I. i. 2. 3; 3. 3; 4. 6; ii. 6. 3; 4. 9; II. 2: II. i. 6. 7; ii. 10. 7: III. i. 3. 2 (N.B.), 13; 5. 3; ii. 5. 4: V. i. 2. 4; ii. 1. 6.

姑
ku

(1) For the present, if you please, I. ii. 9. 1, 2: II. i. 2. 21: VII. i. 39. 2. (2) In III. i. 5. 4, the meaning is undetermined.

姓
hsing

A, or the, surname, V. ii. 9. 1, 4: VII. ii. 36. 2. 百姓, the people, I. i. 7. 5, 6, 7, 10, 12, *et al.*, *saepe.*

委
wei

To give up; to cast away, II. ii. 1. 3: III. i. 5. 4.

委 *tsei*
The 4th tone. Public stores of grain, &c. 委吏, the first office held by Confucius, V. ii. 5. 4.

姜 *chiang*
姜女, the wife of king Tʻai. 姜 is the surname, I. ii. 5. 5.

姣 *chiáo*
Beauty, VI. i. 7. 7.

威 *wei*
Majesty, dread, I. ii. 3. 3: III. ii. 2. 3. To overawe, II. ii. 1. 4.

娶 *chʻü*
To marry (on the part of the man), IV. i. 26. 2: V. i. 2. 1, 2; ii. 5. 1.

婦 *fú*
(1) A married woman, a wife, III. i. 4. 8; ii. 2. 2. 匹婦, III. ii. 5. 3: V. i. 7. 6; ii. 1. 2: VII. i. 22. 2. See 匹. (2) A name, 馮婦, VII. ii. 23. 2.

媒 *mei*
媒妁, a matchmaker, III. ii. 3. 6.

婆 *láu*
A name. 離婁, IV. i. 1. 1.

媚 *mei*
To flatter, VII. ii. 37. 9.

嫁 *chiá*
To be married (on the part of the woman), III. ii. 2. 2.

嫂 *aio*
An elder brother's wife, IV. i. 17. 1, 3: V. i. 2. 3.

嬖 *pi*
A favourite (in a bad sense), and 嬖人, I. i. 7. 16; ii. 16. 1, 3: III. i. 1. 4.

嬴 *ying*
The name of a place, II. ii. 7. 1.

THE 39TH RADICAL, 子.

子 *tsze*
(1) A son. *Passim.* But often it is equivalent to *child, children;*—especially in the frequently recurring phrase 妻子. So, in 赤子, an infant, III. i. 5. 3. 女子, a daughter, III. ii. 3. 6. 處子, a virgin daughter, VI. ii. 1. 8. (2) A general appellation for virtuous men, which may be translated by *gentleman, disciple, philosopher,* &c. *Saepe.* In this sense it is often used in conversation, and is equivalent to *You, Sir.* Observe 吾子, II. ii. 1. 3, and 二三子, my friends, my disciples, I. ii. 15. 1. In this sense it is very common after surnames and honorary epithets. We have 孔子, 孟子, 告子, &c. &c. It is used also after the surname and name or epithet together, as in 孟獻子, *et al.* (3) A title of nobility, V. ii. 2. 3, 4, 5. So, in 微子, II. i. 1. 8: VI. i. 6. 3, and 箕子, II. i. 1. 8. (4) It enters

often into designations, as in 子路, 子思, &c. &c. Into names also, as in 西子, IV. ii. 25. 1, and perhaps 羈子, IV. ii. 24. 2 and 子椒, II. i. 10. 6, and 子濯, IV. ii. 24. 2, seem to be equivalent to surnames. (5) Phrases formed with 子 are—天子, the highest name for the sovereign. *Saepe.* 子弟, sons and younger brothers= youths, I. ii. 11. 3: II. i. 5. 6, *et al.*; 弟子, disciples, II. i. 1. 7; ii. 10. 3; II. 3: IV. i. 7. 3; 子孫 descendants, I. ii. 14. 3, *et al.* Observe IV. i. 7. 3; 先子, see 先: 世子, the crown prince, III. i. 1. 1, *et al.*; 眸子, the pupil of the eye, IV. i. 15. 1, 2; 樹子, the designated heir, VI. ii. 7. 3; 夫子, see 夫; 小子, little children, said to the disciples by Confucius, IV. i. 8. 3; 14. 1; 羈子, a boy, II. i. 6. 3: IV. i. 8. 2; 童子, *id.*, III. ii. 5. 2, 3; and 君子, see 君.

Half-an-one, V. i. 4. 2.

子 *chieh*

孔 *kʻung*
A surname. That of Confucius. *Passim.* 孔距心, II. ii. 4. 2, 4

存 *tsʻun*
(1) To be in, IV. i. 15. 1, *et al.* 存—to abide, VII. i. 18. 3. (2) To be preserved, II. i. 1. 8, *et al.*, saepe. 存=to be alive, VII. i. 20. 2. To preserve, IV. ii. 19. 1, *et al.* Observe 存心, IV. ii. 28.

孝 *hsiáo*
(1) Filial piety; filial; to be filial, I. i. 8. 4; 5. 3; 7. 24, *et al.*, saepe. (2) The honorary epithet of a duke of Wei, V. ii. 4. 7.

季 *chi*
(1) In a name, VI. i. 5. 1, 5. (2) A surname, V. i. 14. 1.—V. ii. 4. 7. 季孫 II. ii. 10. 6. Observe 季子 and 季任, VI. ii. 5.

孟 *mäng*
(1) The great, chief, 趙孟, VI. i. 17. 2. (2) A surname. That of Mencius. *Passim.* 孟仲子, II. ii. 2. 3—孟季子, VI. i. 5. 1, 5—孟獻子, V. ii. 3. 2—孟施舍 and 孟賁, II. i. 2. 2, 5, 6, 8.

孤 *kú*
Young and fatherless, I. ii. 5. 3. 孤—friendless, VII. i. 18. 2.

孥 *nú*
Children. Said by Chû Hsî to mean wives and children, I. ii. 5. 3.

孩
hái

An infant, able to smile. 孩提之童, VII. i. 15. 2.

孫
sun

(1) A grandson, IV. i. 2. 4. 子孫 descendants, I. ii. 14. 3. Observe 孫子, IV. i. 7. 5. (2) In double surnames, II. i. 1. 1, *et al.*—II. ii. 10. 6.—VI. ii. 15. 1.

孰
shú

Who, which:—interrogative, I. i. 6. 3, 5, 6; 7. 17, 18; ii. 1. 4: IV. i. 19. 1, 2, *et al.*

孳
tsze

孳孳, to be earnest and careful in, VII. i. 25. 1, 2; 41. 1.

學
hsiáo
or *hsio*

(1) To learn; learning, I. ii. 9. 1, 2: II. i. 2. 19, 22, *et al., saepe.* 學問, to study, III. i. 2. 4: VI. i. 11. 4. (2) A school, or college, of a higher order, III. i. 8. 10.

孺
zu

(1) 孺子, a boy, II. i. 6. 3; IV. i. 8. (2) In a name, IV. ii. 24. 2.

孽
nieh

(1) The sons of concubines, VII. i. 18. 2. (2) 孽 = calamities, II. i. 4. 6: IV. i. 8. 5.

THE 40TH RADICAL, 宀.

宇
yü

The sides of a house, below the eaves. 宇 = a settlement, I. ii. 5. 5.

宅
chái

A homestead, a dwelling, I. i. 3. 4; 7. 24: II. i. 7. 2: IV. i. 10. 2, 3: VII. i. 22. 2.

守
sháu

To guard, have the charge of; to observe, but with the idea of guarding, I. ii. 4. 5; 13. 2; 15. 2: II. i. 2. 6, 8; ii. 5. 5: III. i. 8. 18; ii. 4. 3: IV. i. 8; 19. 1, 2; ii. 31. 2: VI. ii. 5. 1: 7. 5: VII. ii. 32. 1, 2. 守者, a keeper, VII. i. 36. 3.

安
an

(1) Ease, quiet, VI. ii. 15. 5: VII. ii. 24. 1. (2) Tranquil; to be in repose; to repose in, II. i. 7. 2; 12. 5: IV. i. 10. 2, 3; 8. 1: V. i. 5. 6: VII. i. 32. 2. (3) To give repose to, I. ii. 3. 6, 7, 8: II. ii. 11. 3: VII. i. 19. 2. (4) Quietly, in tranquillity, I. i. 4. 1: III. ii. 2. 1: IV. ii. 14. 1.

宋
sung

(1) The name of a State, II. i. 2. 16; ii. 3. 1, 3: III. i. 1. 1; 2. 1; 4. 3, *et al.* (2) A surname, VI. ii. 4. 1.—VII. i. 9. 1.

完
wan

Complete; to complete, IV. i. 1. 9: V. i. 2. 3.

宗
tsung

Pertaining to one's ancestors. In the phrase 宗廟, the ancestral temple, I. ii. 11. 3: IV. i. 8. 3: VI. ii. 8. 5; 10. 4. 宗國, the State which we honour, III. i. 2. 3.

官
kwan

An officer. 百官, all the officers, III. i. 2. 3, 4, 5, *et al.* An office, V. ii. 2. 6, 7, 8, 9, *et al.* In some cases it is hard to say to which of these meanings we should assign the character. Applied to the senses and the mind, VI. i. 15. 2.

定
ting

(1) To settle, compose; to be settled, I. i. 6. 2: III. i. 2. 3; 3. 13; ii. 9. 3 (N.B.): IV. i. 20; 24. 2; 28. 2: V. ii. 9. 4: VII. i. 21. 2, 3. (2) An honorary epithet, III. i. 2. 1.

宜
í

(1) To be right, reasonable; to seem to be; ought, ought to be, I. i. 7. 7; ii. 2. 2, 3: II. ii. 2. 5; 9. 3: III. ii. 1. 1: IV. i. 1. 7; 24. 2; ii. 24. 1; 28. 4: V. i. 2. 1; ii. 5. 3: VII. i. 41. 1. (2) In a name, VII. ii. 33. 3.

客
k'o

A visitor, a stranger, II. ii. 11. 3.

室
shih

(1) A house, I. ii. 9. 1: II. ii. 10. 3, *et al., saepe.* 宮室, houses, edifices, III. ii. 9. 5: IV. i. 10. 7; ii. 10. 4: VII. i. 26. 1. 室 = a palace, V. ii. 3. 5. 室 = a family, a house, IV. i. 6. 1: V. ii. 2. 1: VI. ii. 10. 3. 處室者, IV. ii. 33. 1. (2) 室 = a wife. 有室, III. ii. 3. 6. 男女居室, male and female dwell together, V. i. 2. 1.

宣
hsüan

An honorary epithet. 齊宣王, I. i. 7. 1, *et al., saepe.*

宮
kung

(1) A palace, V. i. 2. 3; 5. 7; 7. 9. 宮 = a house, an establishment, III. i. 4. 5. 宮室, see 室. (2) A surname, V. i. 9. 2. In the double surname 北宮, II. i. 2. 4, 6.—V. ii. 2. 1. (3) 上宮 and 雪宮 are the names of two palaces, VII. ii. 30. 1: I. ii. 4. 1.

害
hái

(1) To injure; to be injured; injury, I. i. 15. 1: II. i. 2. 13, 16, *et al., saepe.* It is often followed by 於, III. i. 4. 4, *et al.* (2) In a name, 浩生不害, VII. ii. 25. 1.
What, why, I. ii. 2. 4. Chû Hsî, however, explains it here by *when.*

宴
ao

To be at ease, to feel happy, III. ii. 3. 3.

宵
hsiáo

At night, III. i. 3. 2.

宰
tsái

(1) A chief officer, IV. i. 14. 1. 冢宰, see 冢. (2) A surname, II. i. 2. 18, 25, 26.

家
chiá

(1) A house, a home, III. ii. 2. 2. (2) A family, families, I. i. 8. 4; 7. 24: III. i. 3. 19: VII. i. 22. 2. (3) A family, a clan,—the possessions of a great officer. *Passim.* This is the most common use of the term in Mencius. The combination 國家 is frequent, see 國. Sometimes it = the chief of such a family, I. i. 1. 4: V. ii. 3. 2, 3. (4) A husband, 有家, III. ii. 3. 6. Observe 家那, I. i. 7. 12; and 東家, VI. ii. 1. 8.

容
yung

(1) Countenance, deportment, V. i. 4. 1; VII. ii. 33. 2. (2) To be tolerated, VI. ii. 8. 2. To get the countenance of, VII. i. 19. 1. (3) To be admitted (as light), VII. i. 24. 2. (4) 罪不容於死, death is not enough for the crime, IV. i. 14. 2.

宿
hsŭ

(1) To stop over night, II. ii. 2. 4; 11. 1, 3 (N.B.); 12. 1, 4, 6. (2) 宿 = to cherish, V. i. 3. 2.

密
_mi_

遏密, to hush, V. i. 4. 1.

寇
_k'ou_

(1) A robber, plunderers, IV. ii. 3. 1, 4; 31. 1, 2. (2) 司寇, chief minister of Justice, VI. ii. 6. 6.

富
_fu_

(1) Riches; rich; to become rich, I. ii. 5. 3; 16. 2: II. ii. 2. 6; 10. 5, _et al._, _saepe_. Often in the phrase 富貴, 富 = abundant, good, VI. i. 7. 1. (2) To make rich, IV. i. 14. 2: VI. ii. 9. 1. To desire the riches of, III. ii. 5. 3.

寐
mei

To sleep, VI. ii. 13. 1, 3.

寒
han

To suffer from cold, I. i. 3. 4; 7. 24. 寒疾, a cold, II. ii. 2. 1. To subject to the influence of cold, VI. i. 9. 2.

察
_ch'a_

To examine, to observe closely, I. i. 3. 1; 7. 10; II. i. 7. 4, 5: IV. ii. 19. 2: VII. i. 5. 察 = to be extremely particular, VII. i. 46. 2 (observe the idioms).

寓
_yü_

To lodge (active), IV. ii. 31. 1.

寡
kwá

(1) Few, little, generally in correlation to 多 or 衆, I. i. 7. 17; II. i. 2. 16, _et al._ (2) Old and husbandless, widowed, I. ii. 5. 3. (3) 寡人, the humble designation of themselves by the princes,—the opposite of our We, I. i. 3. 1; 4. 1; 5. 1; 7. 4, _et al._ (4) 寡 = equal,—in the phrase 寡妻, which is explained by 嫡,—such a wife as seldom is to be found, I. i. 7. 12. Compare 寡小君 in Analects, XVI. xiv.

實
shih

(1) To be full; to fill, I. ii. 12. 2: III. ii. 5. 5 (實 = to put). Joined with 充, VII. ii. 25. 5, 6; 31. 3. (2) Sincerity, VII. i. 37. 3. 其實, in reality, III. i. 3. 6. 實 = meritorious services, VI. ii. 6. 1. (3) Fruit, III. ii. 10. 1. Metaphorically, IV. i. 27. 1, 2.

寧
ning

To enjoy repose; to give repose to, III. ii. 9. 11: VII. ii. 4. 5.

寬
k'wan

(1) Wide and loose, II. i. 2. 4, 7. (2) Generous, V. ii. 1. 3: VII. ii. 15.

寶
páo

Precious things, VII. ii. 28.

寵
ch'ung

To distinguish, to exalt, I. ii. 3. 7.

寸
_ts'un_

An inch, inches, II. ii. 7. 2: IV. ii. 7 (N.B.): VI. i. 1. 5; 2. 2. Observe 尺寸, VI. i. 14. 1, 6.

封
fäng

(1) Dykes 封疆, the border-divisions of a State, II. ii. 1. 4. (2) To appoint, —to territory or office, V. i. 8. 1, 2: VI. ii. 7. 3; 8. 6.

射
shih

To shoot with an arrow and string; to shoot, VI. i. 9. 3; ii. 2. 3.

射
shê

To shoot; archery, V. ii. 1. 7: VI. i. 20. 1. 射者, an archer, II. i. 7. 5: III. ii. 1. 5. So, sometimes, 射 alone.

將
chiang

(1) Shall, will, should, would; to be going to, to be about to. _Passim._ It expresses a purpose, and often, especially in questions, puts it delicately. Will be, III. i. 1. 5. (2) To offer, present, V. ii. 6. 5. (3) ? To assist, IV. i. 7. 5. (5) 將軍, a general, VI. ii. 8. 1.

專
chiuan

Entirely, exclusively, II. i. 1. 3. 專心, with exclusive attention, VI. i. 9. 3. To presume, take on oneself, VI. ii. 7. 3.

尊
tsun

To honour, II. i. 4. 2; 5. 1, _et al._, _saepe_. Honour; to be honoured, VII. i. 33. 1. Honourable, II. i. 7. 2: III. ii. 6. 2. An honourable situation, V. ii. 5. 2, 3. Honourable things, II. ii. 2. 6.

尋
hsin

A measure of eight cubits, III. ii. 1. 1, 3.

對
tui

To reply. _Saepe._ Used properly of the reply of an inferior to a superior.

導
táo

To lead, conduct, IV. ii. 3. 3. To lead on, influence, VII. i. 23. 3.

小
hsiáo

Small, little; a little (adverb). _Saepe._ 小 = mean creatures, VII. ii. 19. 3. To consider small, VII. i. 24. 1. To make small, I. ii. 9. 1. Of phrases with 小 we have—小子, see 子; 小人, the opposite of 君子 and 大人, _saepe_; 小體, the meaner part of our constitution, VI. i. 15. 1, 2 (compare 14. 2, 3); 小民, the inferior people, III. i. 3. 10; 小勇, mean, small valour of a bravo, I. ii. 3. 5; 小丈夫, a small man, II. ii. 12. 6; 小功, the name of the five months' period of mourning, VII. i. 46. 2; 小弁, name of an ode, VI. ii. 3. 1, 4,

少
sháo

(1) Few, I. ii. 1. 4: V. i. 6. 2. 加少, to decrease, I. i. 3. 1. (2) In a little, V. i. 2. 4.

少
sháo

The 4th tone. Young, V. i. i. 5.

尚
shang

(1) Still (adv.), III. i. 5. 1; ii. 10. 6. (2) To exalt, VII. i. 38. 2, 3. (3) To surpass, II. ii. 2. 9: VII. ii. 22. 1. (4) 尚 = to go up to court, V. ii. 3. 5. To ascend, V. ii. 8. 2. (5) To add to, be added to. 不可尚 已, III. i. 4. 13. Observe 草尚之 風, the grass, when the wind is on it . . ., III. i. 2. 4.

THE 43RD RADICAL, 尢.

尤
yú

(1) A fault, I. ii. 4. 9. (2) To grudge against, to blame, I. ii. 12. 2: II. ii. 13. 1.

就
chiú

To go to, to approach, I. i. 6. 2, 7; 7. 4, 6, 7, *et al., saepe.*

THE 44TH RADICAL, 尸.

尸
shih

To personate the dead at sacrifices, being a resting-place for their spirits, VI. i. 5. 4.

尺
ch'ih

A cubit, II. i. 1. 8; III. i. 4. 17; ii. 1. 1, 3: VI. i. 14. 1, 6: ii. 2. 2: VII. ii. 34. 2.

尼
ni

The 4th tone. To stop, I. ii. 16. 3.

尼
ni

仲尼, the designation of Confucius, I. i. 4. 6; 7. 2, *et al.*

尹
yin

(1) 伊尹, the chief minister of the sovereign Tang, II. i. 2. 22, 23, *et al., saepe.* (2) A surname, II. ii. 12. 1, 3, 7. 尹公, apparently a double surname, IV. ii. 24. 2.

居
chü

(1) To dwell, reside, in,—generally applied to places, but sometimes to official positions; residence, seat. *Passim.* It is applied metaphorically also to virtues, and their opposites, as in II. i. 4. 1: III. ii. 2. 1, 3: III. i. 10. 1, 3; compare II. ii. 2. 19. In VII. ii. 37. 11, 居之 = their principles; compare IV. ii. 14. 居一, to choose an alternative, II. ii. 3. 1. In VII. i. 36. 1, 2, 3; 居 = status, position. In VI. ii. 9. 3, = to retain. 居者, those who stayed at home, I. ii. 5. 4. (2) In a name, III. ii. 6. 2.

屋
wu

(1) A house, III. i. 3. 2: IV. ii. 31. 1 (*N.B.*). (2) 屋廬, a double surname, VI. ii. 1. 1.

屈
ch'ü

(1) To bend (act.), III. ii. 2. 3. To be bent, VI. i. 12. 1. (2) The name of a place in Tsin, V. i. 9. 2.

屑
hsieh

Always in the phrase 不屑, = not to consider pure, not to condescend or

stoop to, II. i. 9. 1, 3: VI. i. 10. 6; ii. 16. 1: VII. ii. 37. 7.

屏
ping

The 3rd tone. To drive away, IV. ii. 30. 5.

屨
chü

Shoes or sandals, made of woven materials, III. i. 4. 1, 17, 18; ii. 10. 4: VI. i. 7. 4: VII. ii. 30. 1, 2.

履
lü

To tread, V. ii. 7. 8.

屬
shú

Belongings, = relationships, IV. ii. 30. 5.

屬
chü

To collect, I. ii. 15. 1.

THE 46TH RADICAL, 山.

山
shan

Hills, a mountain, II. ii. 1. 4: III. i. 4. 7: VI. i. 2. 3; 8. 1. 山 = wooded hills, I. i. 8. 3. 山徑, hill-paths, VII. ii. 21. 東山, VII. i. 24; 太山, I. i. 7. 11: II. i. 2. 28: VII. i. 24; 梁山, I. ii. 15. 1; 崇山, V. i. 3. 2; 羽山, V. i. 3. 2; 箕山, V. i. 6. 1; 牛山, VI. i. 8. 1; and 岐山, I. ii. 14. 2; 15. 1,—are all names of mountains.

岌
ko

岌岌, dangerous, unsettled, V. i. 4. 1.

岐
ch'i

A mountain, by which was the original seat of the Chau family, giving also its name to the adjacent country, I. ii. 3, 5. 岐周, IV. ii. 1. 2. 岐山, see 山.

岑
chin

A small high hill. 岑樓, VI. ii. 1. 5.

崇
ch'ung

(1) The name of a place in Ch'i, II. ii. 14. 2. (2) 崇山, see 山.

崩
pang

To die,—spoken of a sovereign, II. i. 1. 7: V. i. 5. 7; 6. 1, 5. 崩角, the horns lowered to the ground, as when two bulls are fighting, VII. i. 4. 5.

喁
yü

A corner or bend of a hill, VII. ii. 38. 2.

嶽
yo

A neighbourhood in the capital of Ch'i, III. ii. 6. 1.

巍
wei

巍巍, majestic, III. i. 4. 11: VII. ii. 34. 1.

巖
yen

Precipitous, VII. i. 2. 2.

THE 47TH RADICAL, 巛.

川
ch'uan

A stream, IV. i. 1. 1.

巡
hsün

To perambulate. 巡狩, to make a tour of inspection—spoken of the ancient sovereigns, I. ii. 4. 5: VI. ii. 7. 2.

巢 *ch'āo* Nests, = shelter-huts, III. ii. 9. 3.

州 *chāu* (1) 幽州, the name of a place, V. i. 3. 2. (2) In a name, III. ii. 6. 2.

THE 48TH RADICAL, 工.

工 *kung* (1) A workman, VII. i. 41. 2. 百工, the various workmen, III. i. 4. 5, 6. 工 = a charioteer, III. ii. 1. 4. 工師, the master of the workmen, I. ii. 9. 1. (2) In opposition to 朝, = officers, IV. i. 1. 8. (3) 共工, the title of an ancient high officer, V. i. 3. 3.

左 *tso* The left. 左右, to—on—the left and right, I. ii. 6. 3: II. ii. 10. 7: IV. ii. 14. 1. 左 = attendants, I. ii. 7. 4, 5. ? disciples, IV. ii. 21. 1.

巧 *ch'iáo* Skill; skilful; to be skilful, IV. i. 1. 1: V. ii. 1. 7: VII. i. 7. 2; ii. 6.

巨 *chü* Large, great, I. ii. 9. 1: III. i. 4. 18: IV. i. 6. 巨擘, the thumb, III. ii. 10. 2.

巫 *wū* A witch,—one who prays and makes incantations on behalf of others, II. i. 7. 1.

差 *ts'ee* An order; a difference, III. i. 6. 3: V. ii. 2. 8.

THE 49TH RADICAL, 己.

己 *chī* Self. Myself. Himself, yourself,—and the plurals. *Passim.* 自己, the same, II. i. 4. 5. Observe III. ii. 10. 5: VI. ii. 8. 2: VII. i. 9. 5.

已 *i* (1) To stop, end, I. ii. 6. 1: III. ii. 8. 1, 2, 3, *et al., saepe.* 無已, if I may not stop, I. ii. 13. 2. Its most common use is at the end of sentences in the phrase 而已矣, and there stop,— and nothing more. *Passim.* So 而已, alone, VI. ii. 2. 2. Also without the 而, IV. ii. 30. 5. 不得已, not to be able to stop, what is the result of necessity, is also frequent, I. ii. 7. 3; 14. 2, *et al., saepe.* 已, alone, at the end of clauses and sentences, gives strong emphasis to the previous assertion, I. i. 7. 16, 20: II. i. 9. 1, 2, *et saepe.* (2) 已, = to decline, VI. i. 10. 8; to avoid, IV. i. 9. 4; to dismiss, I. ii. 6. 2. (3) Indicates the past tense. Must be translated sometimes by *was, were,* I. ii. 16. 1: IV. ii. 10. 1: VI. ii. 13. 8.

巷 *hsiang* A lane, IV. ii. 29. 2.

THE 50TH RADICAL, 巾.

市 *shih* A market-place, markets, I. i. 7. 18; ii. 5. 3; 11. 2; 15. 1, *et al.* 市井之臣, V. ii. 7. 1. In II. ii. 10. 7, 爲市者 is probably—'those who established markets,' rather than 'market-dealers.' Observe II. i. 5. 2.

布 *pū* Cloth,—of flax, III. i. 4. 17; ii. 4. 3: VII. ii. 27: ? II. i. 5. 5.

希 *hsī* Always in the phrase 幾希, 'little,' few, IV. ii. 19. 1; 33. 2: VI. i. 8. 2: VII. i. 16.

帛 *pái* Cloth,—of silk, I. i. 8. 4; 7. 24: III. i. 4. 17: VII. i. 22. 2, 3. 幣帛, VI. ii. 10. 4; see 幣.

帝 *ti* (1) A ruler, or sovereign, the ruler;— used of Yâo and Shun, II. i. 8. 9: V. i. 1. 3, 4; 2. 2; ii. 3. 5. (2) 上帝, God, the most High God, I. ii. 3. 7: IV. i. 7. 5; ii. 25. 2.

帥 *shuái* A leader, II. i. 2. 9.

帥 *shū* Formerly in the entering tone. To lead, V. i. 4. 1.

師 *shih* (1) A military host, I. ii. 4. 6; 10. 4; 11. 3: VI. ii. 4. 5, 6. 六師, the royal armies, VI. ii. 7. 2. (2) A teacher, master, III. i. 1. 4; 3. 11; 4. 12, 14, *et al.* So, 先師, IV. i. 7. 3. (3) To make one's master, to follow, IV. i. 7. 4. (4) 場師, a plantation-keeper, VI. i. 14. 3. 工師, the master of the workmen, I. ii. 9. 1. 太師, the Grand music-master, I. ii. 4. 10. So, 師 alone, IV. i. 1. 1: VI. i. 7. 6. 士師, the chief criminal judge, I. ii. 6. 2: II. ii. 5. 1. 右師, title of a high officer, IV. ii. 27. 1, 2. ? II. ii. 14. 3.

席 *hsi* A mat, mats, III. i. 4. 1.

帶 *tái* A girdle, a sash, VII. ii. 32. 1.

常 *ch'ang* Regular, V. ii. 6. 2, 4. Constant, unchanging, IV. i. 7. 5. 常 = an average, III. i. 3. 7. 常常, constantly, V. i. 3. 3.

幣 *pi* 幣帛, pieces of silk given as gifts or presents, VI. ii. 10. 4. So, 幣 alone, V. i. 7. 3: VI. ii. 5. 1: VII. i. 37. 2.

幡 *fan* Lq. 翻. 幡然, changing-like, suddenly, V. i. 7. 4.

THE 51st RADICAL, 干.

干
kan

(1) A shield, I. ii. 5. 4: V. i. 2. 3. (2) To seek for, II. ii. 12. 1: VII. ii. 33. 2. (3) In names. 比干, the uncle of the tyrant Châu, II. i. 1. 8: VI. i. 6. 3. 一段干木, III. ii. 7. 2.

平
p'ing

(1) To be brought to a state of perfect order. Spoken of the physical condition of the country, III. i. 4. 7; of its government, III. ii. 9. 11: IV. ii. 29. 1: VII. ii. 32. 2. 平治, II. ii. 13. 5: IV. i. 1. 1. 平政, to make government even, to dispense equal justice, IV. ii. 2. 4. Compare III. i. 2. 13. (2) Even, level, IV. i. 1. 5: III. ii. 9. 4. 平旦, the day-break, the time evenly between night and day, VI. i. 3. 2. (3) An honorary epithet, V. ii. 8. 5.—I. ii. 16. 1. (4) 平陸, the name of a place, II. ii. 4. 1: VI. ii. 5. 1, 2, 6.

年
nien

A year, years. Saepe.

幸
hsing

Fortunate, lucky; fortunately, III. i. 2. 1: IV. i. 1. 8. Observe the idiom of 幸 followed by 而, II. ii. 2. 1: IV. ii. 20. 5.

THE 52nd RADICAL, 幺.

幼
yu

Young, to treat as the young; the young, I. i. 7. 12; ii. 6. 3; 9. 1: III. i. 4. 8; ii. 6. 2: VI. ii. 7. 3.

幽
yu

(1) Dark, III. i. 4. 15. (2) An honorary or rather dishonouring epithet of a sovereign, IV. i. 2. 4: VI. i. 6. 2. (3) 幽州, the name of a place, V. i. 3. 2.

幾
chi

The 1st tone. (1) To hope, VII. i. 41. 1. (2) In the phrase 幾希, little, few, IV. ii. 19. 1; 33. 2: VI. i. 8. 2: VII. i. 16. (3) In the phrase 庶幾, near to, or expressive of a wish, I. ii. 1. 1, 3, 7: II. ii. 12, 4, 5.

幾
chi

Several, I. ii. 12. 2: II. ii. 4. 2. ? how many, IV. i. 24. 2.

THE 53rd RADICAL, 广.

序
hsü

(1) A kind of school, I. ii. 3. 4; 7. 24: III. i. 3. 10. (2) A due order, III. i. 4. 8.

底
ti

(1) I. q. 砥, a whetstone, V. ii. 7. 8. (2) 底 = to come to, IV. i. 28. 2.

庖
p'âu

A kitchen; shambles, I. i. 4. 4; 7. 8: III. ii. 9. 2. 庖, the master of the kitchen, ? purveyor, V. ii. 6. 6.

府
fu

A treasury. 府庫, I. ii. 12. 2: III. i. 4. 3: VI. ii. 9. 1.

庠
hsiang

A kind of school, I. i. 3. 4; 7. 24: III. i. 8. 10.

庭
t'ing

The court below and before the hall or principal apartment of a house, IV. ii. 33. 1.

度
tü

(1) A measure for determining the length, I. i. 7. 13. (2) A model, rules, I. ii. 4. 5: II. ii. 7. 2: IV. i. 1. 8.

度
to

To measure, I. i. 7. 9, 13.

庫
fu

An arsenal, 府庫, see 府.

庫
pi

有庫, the name of a State, V. i. 3. 2, 3.

庶
shu

(1) Numerous, 庶物, the multitude of things, IV. ii. 19. 2. 庶民, the masses of the common people, I. i. 2. 3: IV. ii. 19. 1; VII. ii. 37. 13. 庶人, the common people, I. i. 1. 4: II. ii. 7. 2, et al., saepe. (2) In the phrase 庶幾, see 幾.

康
K'ang

康誥, the name of a Book in the Shû-ching, V. ii. 4. 4.

庾
yü

庾公, appears to be a surname, IV. ii. 24. 2.

庾
shu

To pilfer and hide, VII. ii. 30. 3. Not well made; see the dictionary. I. q. 廋 below, and in Analects, II. 10. 4, 5.

庸
yung

(1) Ordinary, VI. i. 5. 4. (2) Merit; to think of one's merit, VII. i. 13. 3. (3) 附庸, a name of certain small principalities, V. ii. 2. 4.

廉
lien

Pure, disinterested; purity, moderation, III. ii. 10. 1, 2: IV. ii. 23: V. ii. 1. 1: VII. ii. 15; 37. 11. (2) 飛廉, a supporter of the tyrant Châu, III. ii. 9. 6.

廋
shu

To hide, be concealed, IV. i. 15. 2.

廄
chiu

A stable, I. i. 4. 4: III. ii. 9. 9. But this is a vulgar form of the character in the first text.

廚
ch'u

A kitchen, I. i. 7. 8.

廛
ch'an

(1) A house, a dwelling-place, III. i. 4. 1. (2) A stance for a shop or booth, II. i. 5. 5. To levy a ground-rent on such stance, II. i. 5. 2.

廟
miâo

A shrine or temple. Always in the phrase 宗廟; see 宗.

廢
fei

To put aside, disregard; to make void, I. i. 7. 4: IV. ii. 24. 2: V. i. 2. 1; 6. 4: VII. i. 26. 4; 41. 2. To decay;—spoken of States, IV. i. 3. 2.

廣
kuang

Wide, III. ii. 2. 3: VII. i. 21. 1; 36. 2. 廣譽, wide-reaching praise, VI. i. 17. 3.

廩
lin

A granary. Always in connexion with 倉, L. ii. 12. 2: III. i. 4. 3: V. i. 1. 3; 2. 3; ii. 6. 6. 廩人, the store-keeper, V. ii. 6. 5.

廬
lü

(1) The shed tenanted by a prince mourning for his father, III. i. 2. 5. (2) 屋盧, see 屋.

THE 54TH RADICAL, 廴.

廷
t'ing

A courtyard. In the phrase 朝廷, the court, II. ii. 2. 6: IV. ii. 27. 3.

THE 55TH RADICAL, 廾.

弁
p'an

小弁, the name of an ode in the Shih-ching, VI. ii. 3. 1, 2, 4.

弈
yi

Chess-playing, IV. ii. 30. 2: VI. i. 9. 3. 弈秋, a name or nickname, VI. i. 9. 3.

THE 56TH RADICAL, 弋.

式
shih

To make a model, to imitate, II. ii. 10. 3.

弑
shih

To murder; to be murdered.—Spoken with reference to killing a sovereign, I. i. 1. 4; ii. 8. 2: III. ii. 9. 7: IV. i. 2. 4.

THE 57TH RADICAL, 弓.

弓
kung

A bow, I. ii. 5. 4: IV. ii. 24. 2: VI. i. 9. 3; ii. 3. 2. 弓人, a bow-maker, II. i. 7. 3.

弟
ti

(1) A younger brother, II. ii. 9. 3: III. i. 4. 2, et al., saepe. Found often along with 兄. But sometimes 兄弟 = relatives, V. i. 8. 1; and in V. i. 8. 2, it = sisters. 子之兄弟 you and your brother, III. i. 4. 12. 子弟, sons and younger brothers = youths. Saepe. In II. i. 5. 6, it seems to = children; and in VII. ii. 1. 2, a son. (2) Used for 悌, fraternal duty, VII. i. 39. 2. (3) 弟子, disciples, II. i. 1. 7: II. ii. 10. 3; 11. 3 (= I, your disciple): IV. i. 7. 3.

弔
tiao

(1) To condole with,—on occasions of death and mourning, II. ii. 2. 2; 6. 1: III. i. 2. 5; ii. 3. 1, 2, 3: IV. ii. 27. 1. (2) To console, L. ii. 11. 2: III. ii. 5. 4.

引
yin

To draw; to lead on; to lead away, VI. i. 15. 2; ii. 8. 9: VII. i. 41. 3. 引 = to take, III. ii. 6. 1. 引領, to stretch out the neck, I. i. 6. 6.

弗
fu

Not. Passim.

弨
ch'ao

A bow,—the name of that belonging to Shun, V. i. 2. 3.

弱
jio or zao

Weak, the weak, I. i. 7. 17; ii. 12. 2: III. ii. 5. 2: IV. i. 7. 1.

張
chang

(1) To draw a bow. 張 = to display, to be displayed, I. ii. 5. 4: III. ii. 5. 6. (2) 子張, one of Confucius's disciples, II. i. 2. 20: III. i. 4. 13. 琴張, also one of Confucius's disciples, VII. ii. 37. 4. (3) A surname, 張儀, III. ii. 2. 1.

強
ch'iang

Strong, vigorous, I. i. 5. 1: IV. i. 7. 1: VI. ii. 13. 2.

強
ch'iang

The 3rd tone. To make one's self strong to, IV. i. 3. 4; 14. 2: VI. ii. 9. 2.

彊
ch'iang

Strong: strength, I. i. 7. 17; ii. 11. 3.

彊
chiang

To act vigorously at, I. ii. 14. 3: VII. i. 4. 3. To force, III. i. 4. 13. 彊 = by dint of pressing, III. i. 1. 4.

彌
mi

A surname, V. i. 8. 2.

彀
kou

To draw a bow to the full, VI. i. 20. 1: VII. i. 41. 2.

THE 58TH RADICAL, 彐.

彘
chih

A sow, swine, I. i. 3. 4, 5; 7. 24: VII. i. 22. 2.

THE 59TH RADICAL, 彡.

形
hsing

(1) The bodily organs, VII. i. 38 (N. B.). (2) To manifest, be manifested, VI. i. 6. 5. Appearance, representation, I. i. 7. 11.

彫
tiao

To cut, carve, 彫琢, I. ii. 9. 2.

彰
chang

To display, give distinction to, VI. ii. 7. 3.

彭
p'ang

A surname, III. ii. 4. 1.

THE 60TH RADICAL, 彳.

役
yi

To serve, perform service, IV. i. 7. 1: V. ii. 7. 2. 力役, personal service, VII. ii. 27. A servant, II. ii. 7. 3. 役志 to make the will to serve, VI. ii. 5. 4.

往
wang

(1) To go to. Passim. 無所往而不..., in all places and circumstances..., VII. ii. 31. 3; 37. 10. (2) 往者, the past, VII. ii. 30. 2.

征
ch'ing

(1) To exact duties; exactions, I. ii. 5. 3: II. i. 5. 2, 3; ii. 10. 7: III. ii. 8. 1: VII. ii. 27. 1. (2) To take, 征利, I. i. 1. 4. (3) To punish, to execute royal justice, I. i. 5. 5; ii. 11. 2, 3: III. ii. 5. 3, 4, 5: VII. ii. 2. 2; 4. 3.

徂
tsu

(1) To go to; to march, I. ii. 3. 6, but the meaning is doubtful. (2) Seems to be used for 殂, and 徂落 = to decease, V. i. 4. 1.

待 *tái* (1) To wait, to wait for. May sometimes be translated by *until*, II. i. 1. 9; 3. 1; ii. 4. 1, *et al., saepe.* (2) To treat, behave to, entertain, IV. ii. 28. 4; 31. 1: V. ii. 4. 4. In I. ii. 11. 1, the two meanings seem to come together.

很 *han* To be refractory and quarrelsome, IV. ii. 30. 2. Is often written 狠.

律 *lü* Pitch-tubes, for determining the upper musical accords, 六律, IV. i. 1. 1, 5.

後 *háu* That which is after. (1) As a noun. Posterity, I. i. 4. 6; IV. i. 26. 2. An after period, II. i. 2. 27. Futurity: here 後之 may be considered = an adjective, future, III. ii. 4. 3. (2) As an adjective. Future, coming after, I. ii. 14. 3; 16. 1, *et al., saepe.* (3) As a verb. To make an after consideration, I. i. 1. 4; ii. 11. 2: VII. ii. 4. 3, *et al.* To follow, keep behind, VI. ii. 2. 4. To follow after, succeed to (neuter), IV. ii. 1. 3. (4) As an adverb. Afterwards. *Passim.* Especially when preceded by 然 or 而 其 後, meaning *afterwards*, occurs once. (5) As a conjunction and preposition, after words and clauses, generally preceded by 之 = after, VI. ii. 7. 3, *et al.*

彼 *pi* That, those. *Saepe.* It may be sometimes rendered conveniently by the third personal pronoun.

徐 *hsü* (1) Slowly, VI. i. 39. 2. 徐徐, gently, VI. i. 39. 2. (2) A surname, III. i. 5. 1, 3, 5: IV. ii. 18. 1.

徑 *ching* A footpath, VII. ii. 21.

徒 *tú* (1) Foot (adjective), IV. ii. 2. 3. (2) Merely, only, II. i. 2. 16; ii. 9. 4; 13. 5: IV. i. 1. 3; 25: VI. ii. 8. 8. (3) A disciple, disciples, I. i. 7. 2: III. i. 4. 1; ii. 9. 14: IV. ii. 22. 2: VII. i. 25. 1, 2.

得 *tu* (1) To get, to be got; both with and without an objective following. *Passim.* When there is no objective, the sense of the 得 must often be supplied from what precedes. 得乎 and 得於, to gain, to get the regard of, I. ii. 4. 2: IV. i. 28. 1: VII. ii. 14. 2. 必得, must get the proper men, VI. ii. 7. 3. 得我, see 已. 不得已, see 已. (2) The auxiliary *can, could*, 而 comes frequently between 得 and the verb.

徙 *hsi* To remove, III. i. 3. 18: IV. ii. 4. 1.

從 *ts'ung* To follow—both physically, and = to act according to, I. i. 7. 21; ii. 9. 1, 2: IV. ii. 30. 2, *et al., saepe.* 從於, to follow, be in the train of, IV. i. 24. 1; 25. 1. 從 followed by 而 means *to follow up*, = thereupon, thereafter, I. i. 7. 20: II. ii. 10. 2, *et al.*, but each character has its proper meaning. 從 = from, VI. i. 4. 2.

從 *tsung* The 4th tone. 從者, followers in immediate attendance, III. ii. 4. 1: IV. ii. 31. 1: VII. ii. 30. 2.

御 *yü* 御者, a charioteer, III. ii. 1. 5.

御 *yü* I. i. 7. 12. The meaning is doubtful.

徧 *p'ien* All round, the whole of, IV. ii. 33. 1: VII. i. 46. 1.

復 *fú* (1) To report, I. i. 7. 10. (2) To repay, 復讐, to avenge, III. ii. 5. 3.

復 *fáu* The 4th tone. Again, II. i. 1. 1; 2. 17; ii. 11. 3: III. i. 1. 3; 2. 4; ii. 9. 10: IV. i. 19. 3: VI. i. 6. 5: VII. ii. 28. 1. As a verb, to repeat, to try again, III. ii. 1. 4: VII. ii. 1. 2.

微 *wei* (1) Small, slight; in small degree, II. i. 2. 20: III. ii. 9. 7: IV. ii. 31. 3: VI. ii. 6. 6. 微服, the dress of a common man, V. i. 8. 3. The sentence to which this belongs has been omitted in the translation.—微服而過宋, 'He assumed, however, a private dress, and passed by Sung.' (2) The name of a State, II. i. 1. 8: VI. i. 6. 3.

俟 *hsi* To wait for, I. ii. 11. 2: III. ii. 5. 4.

徵 *chǎng* To be evidenced, VI. ii. 15. 3.

徵 *chih* 徵招, the name of a piece of music, I. ii. 4. 9.

徹 *ch'eh* (1) To put away, II. i. 4. 3. (2) To remove,—as the materials of a meal, IV. i. 19. 3. (3) The share-system on which the Chau dynasty divided the lands, III. i. 3. 6.

德 *tě* Virtue, virtuous. *Passim.* Used for conduct in a bad sense, IV. i. 4. 1. 振德之, to stimulate and do them good, III. i. 4. 8.

THE 61ST RADICAL, 心.

心 *hsin* (1) The heart; the mind :—denotes the mental constitution generally. *Saepe.* See note on II. i. 2. (2) In a name, 孔距心, II. ii. 4. 2, 3, 4.

必 *pi* Must, used as an auxiliary, and to assert also what is necessary. Often = what will certainly, would certainly; to be sure to. *Passim.* 必也 only occurs once, VII. ii. 37. 2.

忍 *jăn or zĭn* — (1) To bear, to endure, V. ii. 1. 1, 3, *et al.* 忍人之心 a heart that cannot bear the sufferings of others. So 忍人之政, II. i. 2. 3; IV. ii. i. 5. (2) To harden, to make enduring, VI. ii. 15. 2.

忖 *ts'un* — To reflect, consider. 忖度, to measure by reflection, I. i. 7. 9.

志 *chih* — (1) The will; aim, purpose. *Passim.* In II. i. 2. 9, 10, it appears to be used synonymously with 心. In V. i. 4. 2, it = the aim or scope of a writer. 心志 VI. ii. 15. 2. 志於, the will bent on or directed to, is common. We have the phrases—得志, III. ii. 2. 3, *et al.*; 立志, VII. ii. 16, *et al.*; 尚志, VII. i. 33. 2, 3; 役志, VI. ii. 5. 4; 致志, VI. i. 9. 3; 志士, a determined scholar, III. ii. 1. 2: V. ii. 7. 5. (2) A Record, a History, III. i. 2. 3; ii. 1. 1.

忘 *wang* — To forget; to be forgetful of, I. ii. 4. 7: II. i. 2. 16: III. i. 2. 1; ii. 1. 2: IV. i. 1. 4; ii. 20. 4: V. i. 1. 2; ii. 3. 2; 7. 5: VII. i. 8. 1; 35. 6; ii. 37. 1.

忠 *chung* — True-hearted; true-heartedness, sincerity, I. i. 5. 3: III. i. 4. 10: IV. ii. 28. 5, 6: 31. 1: VI. i. 16. 1: VII. i. 32; ii. 37. 11.

快 *k'wái* — To be cheerful, to find pleasure, I. i. 7. 14; 15.

忸 *ne* — 忸怩 to be and look ashamed, V. i. 2. 3.

怍 *tso* — To blush, VII. i. 20. 3.

怒 *nŭ* — To be angry; anger, I. ii. 3. 6. 7, 8; 9. 1: II. ii. 12. 6: III. ii. 2. 1: IV. i. 18. 2: V. i. 3. 2.

思 *sze* — (1) To think; to think of, I. ii. 5. 4: II. i. 2. 4; 3. 2; 9. 1: III. i. 5. 2: IV. i. 12. 2, *et al.*, *saepe.* Thinking, thoughts, IV. i. 1. 5: V. i. 2. 3. (2) 子思, the designation of Confucius's grandson, II. ii. 11. 3, 4: IV. ii. 31. 2, 3: V. ii. 3. 3; 6. 4; 7. 4: VI. ii. 6. 3.

息 *hsi* — 息敖, indolent and indifferent, II. i. 4. 4.

急 *chi* — Urgent, earnest, III. ii. 3. 2, 6: IV. ii. 29. 4: VII. i. 46. 1 (*N.B.*)

性 *hsing* — The nature,—generally used of that of man, III. i. 1. 2, and especially in the 6th Book, Part I. Applied generally, or away from man, IV. ii. 26. 1: VI. i. 2. 3; 8. 1. To be natural; to possess, to enjoy by nature, VII. i. 21. 2, 3, 4; 30. 1; ii. 24. 1, 2; 33. 1.

怨 *yüan* — To murmur, I. ii. 11. 2: VI. ii. 3. 1, 2, 3, 4, *et al.*, *saepe.* 自怨, to murmur against himself, to become contrite, V. i. 6. 5. 怨天, II. ii. 13. 1 ; compare II. i. 7. 5. 怨 = to be dissatisfied, V. i. 1. 1; compare I. ii. 5. 5. Resentment, I. i. 7. 14: V. i. 3. 2.

怩 *ni* — 忸怩, see 忸.

怵 *ch'ü* — 怵惕 to be alarmed, II. i. 6. 3.

恆 *hăng* — Constant, fixed; constantly, generally, I. i. 7. 20: III. i. 3. 3: IV. i. 5. 1; ii. 28. 3: VI. ii. 15. 3, 4: VII. i. 18.

恐 *k'ung* — To fear, be afraid; sometimes = our *lest*, I. i. 7. 22; ii. 3. 8; 14. 1: II. i. 7. 1: III. i. 2. 4: IV. i. 16. 1: VII. ii. 1. 2; 37. 12. The 3rd tone. To feel pleased, II. ii. 7. 4.

恕 *shü* — The principle of reciprocity, making our own feelings the rule for our conduct to others, VII. i. 4. 3.

恝 *chieh* — The appearance of being without sorrow, V. i. 1. 2.

恣 *tsze* — License. 放恣, III. ii. 9. 9.

恥 *ch'ih* — The sense of shame; to feel ashamed of; shameful, I. i. 5. 1; ii. 8. 7: II. i. 7. 3, 4: IV. i. 7. 3, 4; ii. 18. 3: V. ii. 5. 5: VI. ii. 14. 4: VII. i. 6; 7. 1, 2, 3.

恩 *ăn* — Kindness, I. i. 7. 10, 12: II. ii. 2. 4: IV. ii. 30. 4.

恭 *kung* — To respect, honour, IV. i. 1. 13; 16: V. ii. 4. 1; 6. 3. 恭敬, VI. i. 6. 7: VII. i. 37. 2, 3. 恭 = gravely complaisant, III. i. 8. 4. 不恭, wanting in self-respect, II. i. 9. 3.

息 *hsi* — (1) To stop (active and neuter), III. ii. 9. 9, 13. To rest from toil, I. ii. 4. 6. 安息, to rest in quiet, III. ii. 9. 5. (2) To grow, applied to trees and to the mind, VI. i. 8. 1, 2. (3) A name, V. i. 1. 2; ii. 3. 3.

悄 *ch'iáo* — 悄悄, to be disquieted and grieved, VII. ii. 19. 3.

悌 *ti* — Brotherly duty; to be obedient as a younger brother, I. i. 3. 4; 5. 3; 7. 24: III. ii. 4. 3.

悅 *yüeh* — (1) To be pleased; to be pleased with, I. ii. 10. 3; 11. 2: II. i. 1. 3, 13; 3. 2; 5. 1, 2, 3, 4, 5, *et al.*, *saepe.* Is sometimes followed by 於, V. i. 8. 3: VI. ii. 4. 5, 6. (2) To please, give pleasure to, IV. i. 12. 1; ii. 2. 5: VI. i. 7. 8.—Observe 爲容悅, VII. i. 19. 1; 以爲悅 II. ii. 7. 3: VII. i. 19. 2; and 以我爲悅 VI. i. 4. 4.

悔 *hui*
To repent of, V. i. 6. 5.

患 *hwan*
Calamities; what causes sorrow and grief, IV. i. 23; ii. 9. 1; 28. 7: VI. i. 2. 3; 15. 4, 5: VII. i. 18. 2. What will endanger life, VI. i. 10. 2, 3, 4. To be grieved, I. ii. 11. 1: II. ii. 9. 2.

悴 *tsui*
憔悴, famished, to be distressed. II. i. 1. 11.

悻 *hang*
悻悻然, angry-like, II. ii. 12. 6.

情 *ch'ing*
(1) The feelings proper to humanity, VI. i. 6. 5; 8. 2. (2) 情 = the truth, or reality, IV. ii. 18. 3. (3) 情 = the quality or proper nature, III. i. 4. 18.

惑 *hwo*
To be deluded, perplexed, II. i. 1. 7: VI. i. 16. 3. To be in error, IV. ii. 29. 7.

惕 *t'i*
怵惕 see 怵

惟 *wei*
A particle, both initial and medial. *Passim.* It almost always means only. Observe its use in quotations from the older classics.

惠 *hui*
(1) To be kind; kindness, III. i. 4. 10: IV. ii. 2; 28. (2) An honorary epithet, 梁惠王, I. i. 1. 1; 2. 1, et al.—柳下惠, II. i. 9. 2, 3, et al.—費惠公, V. ii. 3. 3.

惡 *o*
Wicked, bad; wickedness, II. i. 2. 4; 9. 1: VI. i. 1. 7; 15. 1; 18. 2; ii. 25. 2: V. ii. 1. 1: VI. ii. 7. 4.

惡 *wu*
To dislike, detest, hate, I. i. 4. 5: II. i. 4. 1, 2; 9. 1, et al., saepe. 羞惡之心 II. i. 6. 4, 5: VI. i. 6. 7.

惡 *wu*
The 1st tone. (1) How, I. i. 7. 7; ii. 3. 5, et al., saepe. It is sometimes followed by 乎, adding an exclamatory force to it, I. i. 6. 2: II. i. 2. 11: V. ii. 5. 3: VI. ii. 12. 1. 惡在, where, how does it consist with, I. i. 4. 5: III. i. 3. 7: VI. i. 5. 4: VII. i. 33. 3. 惡在 is both initial and final. (2) An exclamation, Oh! II. i. 2. 19; ii. 2. 4; 9. 2.

惰 *to*
To be lazy, IV. ii. 30. 2.

惴 *chui*
To have mental anxiety, to be afraid, II. i. 2. 7.

惻 *ts'i*
To commiserate, 惻隱之心 II. i. 6. 3, 4; 5: VI. i. 6. 7.

愚 *kwân*
Unintelligent, stupid, I. i. 7. 19.

愆 *ch'ien*
Transgression, error, IV. i. 1. 4.

愈 *yu*
(1) To be better,—spoken of disease, II. ii. 2. 2, 3: III. i. 5. 1. (2) To surpass, IV. ii. 24. 1. Followed by 於, VI. ii. 11. 1: VII. i. 39. 1, 4. (3) To increase, VI. ii. 3. 4.

意 *i*
To think, IV. i. 25. 1. One's own ideas, V. i. 4. 2.

愛 *ai*
To love; to care for, I. ii. 5. 5: III. i. 5. 3; ii. 9. 9: IV. i. 4. 1; ii. 28. 2, 3: V. i. 1. 2; 2. 4; 3. 2: VI. i. 4. 4; 13; 14. 1: VII. i. 14. 3; 15. 2; 26. 2; 37. 1; 45; 46. 1: ii. 1. 1, 2. 愛 = to grudge, I. i. 7. 5, 6, 7.

惡 *wân*
To be hated, VII. ii. 19. 3.

愧 *k'wei*
To be ashamed, VII. i. 20. 3.

愬 *su*
To complain, announce their wrongs, I. i. 7. 18.

慎 *shin*
(1) To be careful, to be cautious, I. ii. 7. 3: II. i. 7. 1. (2) A surname, VI. ii. 8. 1, 4.

慈 *ts'e*
To be kind to; affectionate, IV. i. 2. 4: VI. ii. 7. 3.

慊 *ch'ien*
(1) To be dissatisfied, II. i. 2. 4. (2) To be satisfied (also read *ch'ieh*), II. i. 2. 15.

慕 *mu*
To desire, to affect, IV. i. 6. 1. To desire with affectionate longing, V. i. 1. 1, 5: VI. ii. 3. 5.

慚 *ts'an*
To feel ashamed, II. ii. 9. 1.

慝 *t'é*
Wickedness; hidden wickedness, I. ii. 4. 6: VII. ii. 37. 13.

慢 *man*
To despise; to neglect, I. ii. 12. 2: II. ii. 2. 6: III. i. 3. 13.

慧 *hui*
Intelligence, discernment, II. i. 1. 9: VII. i. 18. 1.

慮 *lü*
To think anxiously; to be anxious about, II. i. 2. 5; ii. 11. 4: VII. i. 15. 1; 18. 2. Anxious thoughts, VI. ii. 15. 3. 知慮, VI. ii. 18. 2.

慶 *ch'ing*
Congratulation; to be rewarded, VI. ii. 7. 2.

憂 *yu*
To be sorrowful; to grieve for; sorrow, cause of distress, I. ii. 4. 6: III. i. 4. 7, 8, 9: IV. i. 9. 5; ii. 28. 7; 29. 2: V. i. 1. 4; ii. 3: VI. ii. 15. 5: VII. i. 27. 2; ii. 19. 3. 采薪之憂 = 'a little sickness,' II. ii. 2. 3. Observe 憂民之憂, I. ii. 4. 3.

憎 *tsäng*
To hate. But the text is doubtful, VII. ii. 19. 2.

憔 *ch'iáo*
憔悴, see 悴.

憚 *tan*
To dread, to shrink from, III. i. 4. 5.

憫 *min*
憮 *wŭ*
憾 *han*
應 *ying*
應 *ying*
懟 *tui*
懲 *ch'ăng*
懿 *i*
懦 *zŭ*
懷 *hwai*
懸 *hsuan*
懼 *chü*

To sorrow, II. i. 9. 2 : V. ii. i. 3.

憮然, the appearance of being surprised, thoughtful-like, III. i. 5. 5.

To feel indignant, vexed, I. i. 3. 3 : VII. ii. 37. 8.

A name, VII. i. 35. 1.

The 4th tone. To answer, II. ii. 8. 2; ii. 2 : VI. ii. 1. 8.

To incur the resentment of, V. i. 2. 1.

To repress; to punish, III. i. 4. 16; ii. 9. 12.

Admirable, VI. i. 6. 8.

Weak, timid, V. ii. 1. 1 : VII. ii. 15.

To cherish in the thoughts, VI. ii. 4. 5, 6.

To be suspended. 倒懸, hung up by the heels, II. i. 1. 13.

To fear, be alarmed, II. i. 2 5 : III. ii. 2. 1 ; 9. 8, 10, 11.

THE 62ND RADICAL, 戈.

戈 *ko*
戎 *zung*
成 *ch'ăng*

A spear, I. ii. 5. 4.

The wild tribes of the West, III. i. 4. 16; ii. 9. 12.

(1) To perfect, complete, I. i. 2. 3 : IV. i. 1. 1 : V. i. 9. 3 : VI. ii. 5. 5 : VII. i. 40. 3. Observe 成功, I. ii. 14. 3; and 成章, VII. i. 24. 3. To be perfect, III. ii. 3. 3 : VII. i. 14. 4. To become completed, IV. ii. 2. 3 : VII. ii. 21. (2) Spoken with reference to music. Confucius is called 集大成, a complete concert, V. ii. i. 6. (3) A surname, III. i. 1. 4. In a double surname, VII. ii. 29. (4) 武成, the name of a book in the Shū-ching, VII. ii. 3. 2.

我 *wo*

(1) I, we, me, us; my, our. *Passim.* Observe 為我 in III. ii. 9. 9 : VII. i. 26. 1; and 於我 and 得我 in VI. i. 4. 4; 10. 7. (2) 宰我, one of Confucius's disciples, II. i. 2. 18, 25, 26.

戒 *chieh*

(1) To caution; a caution, III. i. 2. 5; ii. 2. 2. 戒之, beware, I. ii. 12 2. Cautious, using precautions, II. ii. 3. 4. (2) 齊戒 = to fast, IV. ii. 25. 2. According to the dictionary, this meaning may be reduced to the preceding. (3) To issue a proclamation, I. ii. 4. 9.

戕 *ch'iang*

To do violence to, VI. i. 1. 2. This character has several other pronunciations.

或 *hwo*

(1) Some (both singular and plural), I. i. 3. 2; ii. 10. 2; 15. 2; 16. 2, *et al., saepe.* (2) Perhaps, II. ii. 2. 6. 或者, II. ii. 2. 2. This meaning and the other are connected, and the dictionary gives them together, saying that 或 is a word of uncertainty. Observe I. ii. 16. 3 : II. i. 4. 3; ii. 6. 2 : III. i. 4. 12, 17, 18 : V. i. 7. 7 : VI. i. 6. 7. (3) Used for 惑, VI. i. 9. 1.

戚 *ch'i*

(1) A kind of axe, I. ii. 5. 5. (2) Relatives by affinity, I. ii. 7. 3 : II. ii. 4, 4, 5 : V. ii. 9. 1 : VII. i. 34. 1. Used as a verb, 戚之, to consider him as a relative, VI. ii. 3. 2. (3) Sorrow, grief, III. i. 2. 5. 戚戚, the appearance of being sorrowful, I. i. 7. 9.

戟 *chi*

A kind of spear, II. ii. 4. 1.

戢 *chi*

To collect, I. ii. 5. 4.

戮 *lu*

(1) To put to death, to slaughter, III. ii. 9. 6 : IV. ii. 4. (2) Disgrace, IV. ii. 30. 2.

戰 *chan*

(1) To fight, to conduct battles; fightings, wars, I. i. 3. 2; 7. 17 : II. ii. 1. 5 : IV. i. 14. 2; 2 : VI. ii. 8. 3; 9. 2 : VII. ii. 2. 1 ; 4. 1, 6. 戰之, making them fight, leading them to battle, VII. ii. 1. 2. (2) A name, III. i. 3. 13.

戴 *tai*

(1) To carry on the head, I. i. 3. 4 ; 7. 24. (2) A surname, III. i. 6. 1.—III. ii. 8. 1. (3) A name, III. ii. 10. 5.

THE 63RD RADICAL, 戶.

戶 *hu*
房 *fang*
所 *so*

A door,—properly an inner door, II. i. 4. 3 : IV. ii. 29. 7. 門戶, VI. ii. 14. 4 : VII. i. 23. 3.

To be distressed, reduced to straits, VII. ii. 18.

(1) A place, III. ii. 6. 2 : V. i. 2. 4. (2) The compound relative what, = that which, those which. *Passim.* Sometimes it is simply the relative, the antecedent, if we may so call it, being expressed, as in 所居之室. The idea of place as the antecedent often enters into the phrase where it is thus used. 無所 and 無所不, 有所 and 有所不 are to be marked, VII. i. 7. 2; ii. 1. 2; 31. 1, 3; 37. 2, 10, *et al., saepe.* 所以, whereby, the whereby, is very common; and 所, alone, has sometimes the same

force. Observe 在所禮, VII. i. 43. 1 (compare IV. ii. 28. 7); 有所受之, III. i. 2. 3; VII. i. 35. 4; 所過, 所存, VII. i. 18. 3; 所就, 所去, VI. ii. 14. 1; 兼所愛, VI. i. 14. 1; 未有所終…, V. ii. 4. 6; 所爲, 所主, V. i. 8. 4; 惟義所在, IV. ii. 11. 1; 所敎, 所受敎, II. ii. 2. 9; 所安, II. ii. 2. 20; 所之, I. ii. 16. 1; 惟君所行, I. ii. 4. 9.

戾
li

In the phrase 狠戾, III. i. 3. 7.

手
shŏu

THE 64TH RADICAL, 手.

The hand, hands, II. i. 1. 6: IV. i. 17. 1, 3; 27. 2 (N.B.); ii. 3. 1.

才
ts'ái

The natural powers; abilities, I. ii. 7. 2; VI. i. 6. 6, 7; 7. 1; 8. 2; VII. ii. 29. In the concrete, = men of good talents, IV. ii. 7: VI. ii. 7. 3: VII. i. 20. 4.

扣
k'áu

To rap, knock against, IV. ii. 24. 2.

扶
fú

扶持, to support, sustain, III. i. 3. 18.

承
ch'áng

(1) To receive, I. i. 4. 1.   (2) To receive and carry out, III. i. 9. 6, 13. 承繼 V. i. 6. 2. A passage here has been omitted in the text:— 啓賢, 能敬承繼禹之道, 益之相禹也, 歷年少, 施澤於民未久.— ' that Ch'i was a wise and worthy prince, able reverently to receive and carry on the principles of Yü, and that Yih assisted Yü only for a few years, conferring benefits on the people for a short time.'   (3) To resist, III. ii. 9. 12.   This is the meaning assigned by Chû Hsi.

把
pá

To grasp,—with one hand. 拱把, VI. i. 13.

抑
yi

(1) An initial particle, = come now, I. i. 7. 14.   (2) Or, I. i. 7. 16.   Followed by 亦, II. ii. 4. 3: III. ii. 10. 3.   (3) To repress, III. ii. 9. 11.

折
cheh

To break off, I. i. 7. 11.

抽
ch'áu

To take out, IV. ii. 24. 2.

拂
fú

To shake off, 拂亂, to confound, VI. ii. 15. 2.   Read pi, i. q. 弼, to assist; able, VI. ii. 15. 4.

抱
páo

To embrace, encircle, 抱關, to go round the gates, i.e. to guard them, V. ii. 5. 3; 6. 3.

拒
chü

To resist, to reject, VII. ii. 30. 3.

拔
pá

(1) To pull out, VII. i. 26. 1.   (2) To rise high, II. i. 2. 28.   In this meaning it should probably be read p'o; see the dictionary.

拘
chü

To detain, VII. ii. 35. 3.

拙
chüeh

Stupid, VII. i. 41. 2.

招
cháo

(1) To call, to summon, III. ii. 1. c: V. ii. 7. 5, 6, 7.   (2) To tie the legs, VII. ii. 26. 2.

招
sháo

Used for 韶, the name of Shun's music. 微招, 角招, two pieces of music, I. ii. 4. 9.

拜
pái

To make an obeisance ; to pay one's respects, II. i. 8. 2: III. ii. 7. 3: V. ii. 6. 4; 5.

拯
ch'áng

To deliver, rescue, I. ii. 11. 3.

拱
kung

To grasp with the two hands, VI. i. 13.

持
ch'ih

To hold, to grasp, II. ii. 4. 1.   Applied to the will,—to maintain, II. i. 2. 9, 10. 扶持 see 扶.

指
chih

A finger, VI. i. 12. 1, 2; 14. 4.   To point out, = meaning, scope, VI. i. 4. 4: VII. ii. 32. 1.

挫
ts'o

To push.   A push, II. i. 2. 4.

振
chán

(1) To stimulate, III. i. 4. 8.   (2) To bring to a close, to wind up,—in music, V. ii. 1. 6.

挾
chiá

(1) To take under the arm, I. i. 7. 11.   (2) To presume on, V. ii. 3. 1: VII. i. 43. 2.

括
kwo

A name, VII. ii. 29. 1.

捆
k'wǎn

To beat and hammer. 捆屨, to make sandals, III. i. 4. 1.

捐
chüan

To remove, V. i. 2. 3.

授
shǎu

To give,—properly with the hand, IV. i. 17. 1.   Generally, to give, II. ii. 10. 3. To give up, surrender, III. i. 5. 2.

掊
p'áu

To collect imposts. 掊克, = exacting, able ministers, VI. ii. 7. 2.

掌
chang

(1) The palm, I. i. 7. 12: II. i. 1. 8; 6. 2. 熊掌, bears'-paws, VI. i. 10. 1.   (2) To manage, direct, III. i. 4. 7; ii. 1. 4.

排 p'ái
To arrange, = to regulate the course of, III. i. 4. 7.

掘 ch'ueh
To dig, III. ii. 9. 4 : VII. i. 29. 1.

接 chieh
To come into contact; to have intercourse with. (1) To receive, admit to one's presence, V. i. 3. 3. (2) 相接 to have intercourse with, VI. ii. 4. 5, 6. But in I. i. 3. 2, 既接 = being crossed, spoken of weapons. (3) 接淅, to let the water of rice strain off through the hand, V. ii. 1. 4 : VII. ii. 17. (4) Used of the manner in which a present is offered, V. ii. 4. 3.

推 t'ui
(1) To push, V. i. 7. 6 ; ii. 1. 2. (2) To push out, carry out, I. i. 7. 12. To consider, prosecute the study of, II. i. 9. 1. In these two cases, we should read the character ch'ui.

掩 yen
To cover. Applied to the bodies of the dead, III. i. 5. 4 ; to the nose, IV. ii. 25. 1; to wickedness, IV. i. 15. 1. To cover = to make good, to come up to, VII. i. 37. 6.

揲 k'wei
To examine, to calculate, IV. i. 1. 8; ii. 1. 4.

提 t'i
To lift with the hand, to carry, 孩 提之童, children carried in the arms, VII. i. 15. 2.

揖 yi
To salute, with the hands joined before the breast, = to bow to, III. i. 4. 13 : IV. ii. 27. 3.

揚 yang
(1) To display, be displayed, put forth, III. ii. 5. 6. (2) A kind of battle-axe, I. ii. 5. 4.

揜 yen
Used for 掩, to cover up, V. i. 2. 3.

揠 yá
To pull up, II. i. 2. 16.

揣 ch'ui
To feel with the hand, = to adjust, VI. ii. 1. 5.

援 yüan
(1) To draw,—spoken of a bow, VI. i. 9. 3. 援, to press, to hold fast, II. i. 9. 2. (2) To draw out, to rescue, IV. i. 17. 1, 2, 3.

搆 kóu
搆兵, to be fighting together, VI. ii. 4. 3.

損 sun
To diminish, to be diminished, III. ii. 8. 2 : VII. i. 21. 3.

搏 po
(1) To seize, IV. ii. 3. 4 : VII. ii. 23. 2. (2) To strike with the hand, VI. i. 2. 3.

攎 láu
To drag, to drag away, VI. ii. 1. 8; 7. 2.

摩 mo
To rub, i.e. to rub smooth, VII. i. 26. 2.

標 p'iao
To beckon, to motion to, V. ii. 6. 4.

撓 náo
To bend, 膚撓, to flinch from strokes at the body, II. i. 2. 4.

撫 fú
(1) To tranquillize, = to subdue, I. i. 7. 16. (2) To hold, to grasp, I. ii. 8. 5.

播 po
To sow; to disseminate, III. i. 3. 2 : IV. i. 1. 7 : VI. i. 7. 2.

撻 tá
To beat, II. i. 2. 4 : III. ii. 6. 1. 撻 = to oppose, I. i. 5. 3.

擇 chái
To choose, I. ii. 14. 2 ; 15. 2 : II. i. 7. 2: III. i. 3. 13 : IV. ii. 28. 6. 牛羊何擇, what was there to choose between an ox and a sheep? I. i. 7. 7.

擊 chi
To beat, strike, 擊柝, V. ii. 5. 3 ; 6. 3.

操 ts'áo
To hold fast,—spoken of the mind, VI. i. 8. 4 : VII. i. 18. 2. 操 = principles, III. ii. 10. 2, 6. In this meaning it should be the 4th tone, according to the dictionary.

擘 pi
巨擘, the thumb, III. ii. 10. 2.

擴 k'wo
To stretch out and expand, 擴而充之, II. i. 6. 7.

攖 ying
To encounter, to press near to, VII. ii. 23. 2.

攘 zang
(1) To steal,—upon occasion offered, III. ii. 8. 2. (2) To bare, VII. ii. 23. 2.

攝 shêh
To act for, undertake one's duties, V. i. 4. 1. 攝 = a plurality of offices, VI. ii. 7. 3.

THE 65TH RADICAL, 支.

支 chih
Used for 肢 四支, the four limbs, IV. ii. 30. 2.

THE 66TH RADICAL, 攴.

收 shâu
To take back, IV. ii. 3. 3, 4.

攸 yû
(1) I.q. 所 有攸, some, III. ii. 5. 5. (2) Appears to be a mere expletive, I. i. 2. 3. (3) 攸然 the appearance of a fish let go in the water, V. i. 2. 4.

改 kâi
To alter, change (active and neuter); to reform, II. i. 9. 4 : IV. i. 2. 4; 14. 1 (改於); ii. 29. 1 : V. ii. 4. 5 : VI. ii. 15. 3 : VII. i. 41. 2. Observe 改之 and 改諸, II. ii. 12 4, 5. 改曰, 'spake with an altered mind,' V. i. 7. 4. In II. i. 1. 10, 不改 = does not need more.

攻 kung
(1) To attack, II. i. 5. 6; ii. 1. 2, 5: V. i. 7. 9. 攻 = to expose one's errors, IV. i. 14. 1. (2) To undertake, to proceed to do, I. i. 2. 3.

放 *fang* — (1) To banish,—spoken of men, animals, and doctrines, I. ii. 8. 1: III. ii. 9. 4, 10, 13: V. i. 3. 1. 2, 3; 6. 5: VII. i. 31. 1, 2. (2) To lose, let stray; stray, lost, VI. i. 8. 2; 11. 2, 3, 4: VII. ii. 26. 2. (3) Dissolute, self-abandoned, I. i. 7. 20: III. i. 3. 3; ii. 5. 2. So 放恣, III. i. 9. 9. (4) 放飯, to eat immoderately; but other meanings are given to the phrase, VII. i. 46. 2.

放 *fang* — The 3rd tone. (1) To, going on to, I. ii. 4. 4: IV. ii. 18. 2: VII. ii. 26. 2. (2) 放勳, a designation of Yáo or (? possibly) of Shun, III. i. 4. 8: V. i. 4. 1.

政 *chǎng* — Government. *Passim.* 政事, the principles and business of government, VII. ii. 12. 3; 28. So 政刑, II. i. 4. 2. 爲政, the administration of government, is very common; but it = to give law to, in I. ii. 11. 1: IV. i. 7. 4. 聽政, IV. ii. 2. 1. 行政, to practise a government, is common. 施政 is also found. Observe 以政, V. i. 3. 3.

故 *kù* — The cause or reason of a thing. (1) 有故, 無故, there being a cause, there being no cause, IV. ii. 3. 3, 4: VII. i. 20. 2 (*N.B.*) Observe 故 alone, III. i. 5. 3. At the end of a clause, 故 = because, VI. i. 5. 4: VII. i. 21. 3. Observe 以 … 之故, VII. ii. 1. 2. (2) 故 and 是故, in continuation of a subject, —therefore, thus. *Passim.* (3) Facts, phenomena, IV. ii. 26. 1, 2. (4) Ancient, old, I. ii. 7. 1: II. i. 1. 8. 故 = old acquaintance, VII. i. 43. 2.

效 *hsiào* — 效死 = to be prepared to die, to strive to death, I. ii. 13. 2; 15. 2.

教 *chiào* — To teach. *Saepe.* Instructions; lessons, I. i. 3. 4; 7. 24: IV. i. 14. 2, 3. Observe II. i. 2. 19; and V. ii. 4. 4. Pronounced in the 1st tone, it = to call in, to employ, I. ii. 9. 2.

敏 *min* — Alert, intelligent, and active, I. i. 7. 19: IV. i. 7. 5.

救 *chiù* — To save, I. ii. 11. 1; 12. 1: III. ii. 5. 5: V. i. 7. 6. 救 = to put out, to save from fire, VI. i. 18. 1. 救 = to part, to stop from fighting, IV. ii. 29. 6, 7. 救死, to save themselves from death, I. i. 7. 22.

敖 *do* — (1) 怠敖, indolent indifference, idle sauntering, II. i. 4. 4. (2) A name, VI. ii. 15. 1. (3) 予敖, a designation, IV. i. 24. 1; 25. 1; ii. 27. 3.

敗 *pái* — To ruin, IV. i. 8. 1. To be defeated, I. i. 5. 1: VII. ii. 1. 2.

敝 *pí* — Worn-out, VII. i. 35. 6.

敢 *kan* — To venture, dare, presume. *Saepe.* 敢問, 'I venture to ask,' is a common way of asking a question. Observe 請勿復敢見, II. ii. 11. 3.

散 *san* — (1) To be scattered, I. ii. 5. 4; ii. 1. 6; 12. 2: II. ii. 4. 2. (2) A surname, VII. ii. 38. 3.

敦 *tun* — (1) Generous, V. ii. 1. 3: VII. ii. 15. (2) To manage; but this meaning is not found in the dictionary, II. ii. 7. 1.

敬 *chǎng* — To respect, revere; the feeling of reverence; reverential, II. ii. 2. 4: III. ii. 2. 2: IV. i. 2. 2; 4. 1, *et al.*, *saepe.* 恭敬 VI. i. 5. 2, 3, *et al.* On the difference between the terms, see IV. i. 1. 13.

敷 *fū* — To set forth, 敷治, III. i. 4. 7.

數 *shú* — (1) Number, II. ii. 13. 4. Several, I. i. 3. 4: II. ii. 2. 3; 5. 1, *et al.*, *saepe.* ? a few, VII. i. 39. 3. (2) 數 = an art, VI. i. 9. 3.

數 *ts'ú* — Close, close-meshed, I. i. 8. 3.

敵 *tí* — An enemy, I. i. 5. 5, 6: II. i. 2. 5; 5. 6: III. ii. 5. 4: IV. i. 7. 5, 6: VII. ii. 3. 3; 4. 2. Hostile, VI. ii. 15. 4: VII. ii. 2. 3. To be an enemy to, to oppose, I. i. 7. 17; ii. 3. 5: VII. ii. 4. 5.

毆 *ch'ú* — I.q. 驅. To drive, chase, IV. i. 9. 3. 4.

整 *chǎng* — To marshal, I. ii. 3. 6.

斂 *lien* — To ingather. The ingathering,—spoken of the harvest, I. ii. 4. 5: VI. ii. 7. 2. 稅斂, all taxes and imposts, I. i. 5. 3: VII. i. 23. 1.

THE 67TH RADICAL, 文.

文 *wǎn* — (1) A character, as delineated, = a word, V. i. 4. 2. (2) Style, method of composition, IV. ii. 21. 3. (3) Elegant, adorned, VI. i. 17. 3. To adorn, 節文, IV. i. 27. 2. (4) An honorary epithet, 文王, I. i. 2. 3, *et al.*, *saepissime.* 晉文, II. i. 7. 1, 2: IV. ii. 21. 3. 滕文公, I. i. 13, *et al.*

THE 69TH RADICAL, 斤.

斤 *chǐn* — A bill,—a general name of all crooked knives, 斧斤, I. i. 3. 3: VI. i. 8. 1, 2. An axe, 斧斤, see above.

斬
chan
斯
szu

To cut in two, = to terminate, IV. ii. 22. 1.

(1) This, these, I. i. 4. 6; 7. 12; ii. 5. 3. 4, *et al.*, *saepe*. (2) As a conjunction, forthwith, then, thereupon, &c., I. i. 3. 5; II. i. 6. 2: III. ii. 7. 2; 8. 3: VII. ii. 37. 3, 8, 13. In several cases we can hardly tell whether to take the character as a conjunction, or as the demonstrative, following its antecedent, to give emphasis to the sentence. Observe also I. ii. 8. 6, and 5. 4, where it seems a mere expletive. (3) 斯須, i. q. 須臾, an instant, VI. i. 5. 4. (4) In a name, IV. ii. 24. 2.

新
hsin
斷
cho
斷
tuan

New, III. i. 3. 12.

To cut, how, I. ii. 9. 1.

In the phrase, 龍斷, a conspicuous mound, II. ii. 10. 6, 7.

THE 70TH RADICAL, 方.

方
fang

(1) That which is square, IV. i. 1. 1, 5; 2. 1. Square, the adjective,—followed by the dimension, I. i. 5. 2; 7. 17, *et al.*, *saepe*. Observe the note on V. ii. 2. (2) A quarter, region, direction, III. 4. 1: VI. i. 2. 1. The phrase 四方 is common. 無方, without reference to their where-from, IV. ii. 20. 2. (3) 方 = class, a resemblance, V. i. 2. 4. (4) To neglect, violate, I. ii. 4. 6. (5) As a conjunction, 方且, III. i. 4. 16; 爰方, I. ii. 5. 4.

於
yü

Passim. (1) A preposition, in, at, on. But after many verbs and adjectives we must translate it variously,—by to, from, &c. &c., and often it need not be translated at all. 至於, down to, coming to, &c., is common. After the possessive 之於 = in relation to, and so, sometimes, when not preceded by 之. 於 = compared with, II. i. 2. 23. After 志 it is common, and what may be called composite verbs, such as 得罪, 有功, &c. (2) Than, forming the comparative degree of preceding adjectives. *Saepe.* But observe II. i. 2. 28, at the end.

於
wu

(1) How! I. i. 2. 3. (2) 於陵, the name of a place, III. ii. 10. 1, 5, 6.

施
shih

To give, to dispense; to be given to, to be shown, I. i. 5. 3; 7. 18; ii. 5. 3: IV. i. 9. 1: V. i. 6. 2: VI. i. 17. 3: VII. i. 21 (?); ii. 32. 1. (2) In the name, 孟施舍, II. i. 2. 5, 6, 8.

施
shih

The 1st tone. 施施, complacently, IV. ii. 33. 1.

施
i
旅
ch'i
旜
chan
旄
mào

Dodgingly, = secretly, IV. ii. 33. 1.

A flag, with dragons emblazoned, and bells attached, V. ii. 7. 6.

A flag,—of silk, unemblazoned, V. ii. 7. 6.

(1) A white cow's tail,—used to make signals with. 旄 = streamers, I. ii. 1. 6, 7. (2) I. q. 耄, very old persons, I. ii. 11. 4.

旅
lü

(1) Hosts. Properly, 500 men make a 旅, I. ii. 3. 6. (2) A stranger, a traveller, I. i. 7. 18: II. i. 5. 3: VI. ii. 7. 3.

旋
hsüan

周旋, going round, the turnings of the body, VII. ii. 33. 2.

旌
ching

A flag,—made of feathers suspended from the top of the staff, III. ii. 1. 2: V. ii. 7. 5, 6.

族
tsú

The head of an arrow, III. i. 2. 5.

THE 71ST RADICAL, 无.

既
chi

A particle of past time. May often be translated by have, having, having been, I. i. 3. 2: II. i. 2. 10 (N.B.), 18, 19; ii. 5. 1 (N.B.); 6. 2 (N.B.): III. i. 3, 13; ii. 9. 4, 5, *et al.*, *saepe*. Observe 既而, V. i. 7. 4; 既 ... 而, VI. i. 16. 3; and 既已, VI. ii. 13. 8. In these and similar instances there should be a comma after 既. It does not form an adverb with the character that follows.

THE 72ND RADICAL, 日.

日
zih

(1) The sun, I. i. 2. 4: II. ii. 2. 4: V. i. 4. 1: VII. i. 24. 2. (2) A day, days, the day, II. ii. 4. 1: III. i. 2. 10. 1: IV. i. 24. 2; ii. 2. 5; 3. 4; 20. 5, *et al.* 他日, see 他. 今日, to-day, II. i. 2. 16, *et al.* 明日, to-morrow, II. ii. 2. 2, *et al.* 前日, formerly, II. ii. 7. 1, *et al.* 終日, all the day, III. i. 1. 4. 無日, in no time, I. i. 2. 3: IV. i. 9. 日至, the solstice, IV. ii. 26. 3: but VI. i. 7. 2 is different. 冬日, in winter, VI. i. 5. 5. 暇日, leisure days, I. i. 5. 3. 竭日之力, to exert the strength the whole day, II. ii. 12. 6. 日 alone = daily, from day to day, II. ii. 12. 5: III. ii. 6. 1; 8. 2: V. i. 3. 1, *et al.*

旦
tan

The morning, IV. ii. 20. 5. 旦旦, from morning to morning, i. q. from day to day, VI. i. 8. 2. 平旦, the day-break, also VI. i. 8. 2.

暮
mu

The evening, II. ii. 6. 1. 昌暮, the dusk of the evening, VII. i. 23. 3.

暴
p'u

(1) Violence, oppression, cruelty, VI. i. 6. 2; VII. ii. 8. 1. Oppressive, III. i. 3. 13; ii. 9. 5. 7. To oppress, IV. i. 2. 4; V. i. 3. 3. Applied to the mind, II. i. 2. 9, 10. 自暴, to do violence to one's nature, IV. i. 10. 1. So 暴 alone, VI. i. 7. 1. (2) A name, I. ii. 1. 1.

暴
p'u

(1) To dry or bleach in the sun, III. i. 4. 13. 暴 = to warm genially, VI. i. 9. 2.

(2) To exhibit, V. i. 5. 5, 6.

曠
k'wang

Empty; to leave empty, IV. i. 10. 3. 曠 = unmarried, I. ii. 5. 5.

THE 73RD RADICAL, 曰.

曰
yueh

To say. *Passim.* Often the nominative is not expressed, and must be supplied from the context. In this case, 曰 sometimes = it is said. It is also used in descriptive accounts, and = is called, means.

曲
ch'u

Crooked. Observe 無曲防, VI. ii. 7. 3.

曳
i

To trail after one, I. i. 3. 2.

更
käng

(1) To change = to reform, II. ii. 9. 4. It was originally made from 丙 and 攴.
(2) A name, III. ii. 4. 1.—VII. i. 43. 1, 2.

書
shu

(1) A writing,—of a covenant, VI. ii. 7. 3. Writings, books, V. ii. 8. 2. (2) The Shû-ching, I. ii. 3. 7; 11. 1: III. i. 1. 5; ii. 5. 2, 4; 9. 3, 6: V. i. 4. 4: VI. ii. 5. 4. Observe VII. ii. 3. 1.

曾
tsäng

A surname, 曾子, I. ii. 12. 2: II. i. 2. 6, 7, 8, *et al., saepe.* 曾晳, see 晳,—曾元, IV. i. 19. 3.—曾西, II. i. 1. 3, 4.

曾
tsäng

A particle, indicating the present complete tense, II. i. 1. 3: V. i. 9. 3.

會
hui

To assemble; the assembly of, VI. ii. 7. 3. To meet, = to engage in battle, II. i. 2. 2.

會
kuei

To calculate, enter accounts, V. ii. 5. 4.

曹
ts'ao

The name of an ancient principality, used as a surname, VI. ii. 2, 1.

THE 74TH RADICAL, 月.

月
yueh

(1) The moon, II. ii. 9. 4: VII. i. 24. 2. (2) A month, months, I. i. 6. 6: II. ii. 5. 1, *et al.* 月 = every month, III. ii. 8. 2.

有
yü

(1) To have, possess. *Passim.* (2) The impersonal substantive verb, there is, there was. Also *passim.* It is often diffi-

cult to determine to which of these meanings we shall refer particular examples. 有之, and 未之有, at the end of sentences, are to be noted, I. i. 3. 4; 7. 5, 24, *et al., saepe.* 有為, to have doing, to be capable of achievement, II. ii. 2. 7: III. i. 1. 4: IV. ii. 8. 1: V. i. 3. 3: VII. i. 29. 有餘 = and more, VII. ii. 38. 1, 2, 3, 4, *et al.* 有司, see 司. Observe V. i. 7. 2. (3) The surname of one of Confucius's disciples, II. i. 2. 25, 28: III. i. 4. 13. (4) 有庳, the principality of Shun's brother, V. i. 3. 2, 3.

有
yü

The 4th tone. And; again, III. ii. 9. 7: V. i. 4. 1; 5. 7; 6. 1.

朋
p'äng

朋友, friends, II. i. 6. 3: III. i. 4. 8: IV. ii. 30. 4.

服
fü

(1) Clothes, V. i. 8. 3: VI. ii. 2. 5. 衣服, III. ii. 3. 3: VI. ii. 36. 2. (2) To wear, V. ii. 2. 5. To wear mourning, IV. ii. 3. 2, 3, 4. (3) To subdue, I. i. 7. 17: II. i. 3. 2: IV. ii. 16. 1. (4) To submit, IV. i. 7. 5: V. i. 3. 2. (5) To be obnoxious to, IV. i. 14. 3.

朕
chän

I (not yet the imperial *we*), V. i. 2. 3 (N. B.); 7. 9.

望
wang

(1) To look to from a distance; to look for, to hope; expectation, example, what is looked for or to, I. i. 3. 2; 6. 2, 6; ii. 11. 2: II. ii. 12. 5: III. ii. 5. 4, 7: IV. ii. 20. 3; 31. 1: VII. i. 9. 5. 望見, VII. i. 36. 1; ii. 23. 2. 仰望, IV. ii. 33. 1. 守望, III. i. 3. 18. (2) 望望然, = with a high air, II. i. 9. 1. (3) 太公望, a counsellor of Wän and Wû, VII. ii. 38.

朝
chäo

The morning; in the morning, I. ii. 5. 5: II. ii. 2. 1; 6. 1: III. ii. 1. 4: IV. ii. 28. 7: VI. ii. 9. 3; 14. 3.

朝
ch'áo

(1) A sovereign's court, I. i. 7. 18, *et al.* (2) To appear in court, to do homage to, I. ii. 4. 5: II. ii. 2. 1, 5: V. i. 4. 1: VI. ii. 7. 2. 朝覲, V. i. 5. 7. To make to appear at court, to give audience to, I. i. 7. 16: II. i. 1. 8; 2. 24. (3) Court (adjective), II. i. 9. 1: V. ii. 1. 1. (4). 朝鮮, the name of a place, I. ii. 4. 4.

朞
chi

A round year, VII. i. 39. 1.

期
ch'i

期 = to model one's self on, VI. i. 7. 5, 6.

THE 75TH RADICAL, 木.

木
mü

(1) A tree, trees, I. i. 7. 16, 17; ii. 7. 1; 9. 1, *et al.* Wood, a piece of wood, II. ii. 7. 1: VI. ii. 1. 5. 材木, supplies of wood, I. i. 3. 3. (2) In a name, III. ii. 7. 2.

未
wei
Not yet. *Passim.*

末
mo
The extremity; the point, the top, I. i. 7. 10: VI. ii. 1. 5.

本
pan
(1) The root. The lower end, VI. ii. 1. 5. 本＝a spring, IV. ii. 18. 2, 3. Source, origin, III. i. 5. 3: IV. i. 5. 1; 19. 2. What is radical, essential, IV. ii. 26. 1. Observe 反其本, I. i. 7. 17, 23. (2) Proper, VI. i. 10. 3: V. ii. 5. 5 (*N.B.*).

朱
chu
(1) Vermilion colour, VII. ii. 37. 12. (2) In names, 朱桑, VII. ii. 38. 2.— 丹朱, V. i. 6. 2—楊朱 III. ii. 9. 9.

杌
wei
檮杌 the name under which the annals of Ch'ü were composed, IV. ii. 21. 2.

李
li
A plum-tree, III. ii. 10. 1.

材
ts'ai
Fine trees, VI. i. 8. 8. 材木, supplies of wood, I. i. 8. 3.

杞
ch'i
(1) A species of willow, VI. i. 1. 1. (2) A surname, VI. ii. 6. 5.

束
su
To bind, VI. ii. 7. 3.

杠
chiang
A small bridge, IV. ii. 2. 3.

杯
pei
A cup, VI. i. 18. 1.

杵
ch'u
A wooden pestle, VII. ii. 3. 3.

東
tung
The east, on the east; eastern, I. i. 3. 1; 6. 1; ii. 11. 2: II. i. 8. 2: III. ii. 5. 4; 5: IV. ii. 33. 1: V. i. 4. 1: VI. i. 2. 1, 2; ii. 1. 8 (*N.B.*): VII. ii. 4. 3. 東山, VII. i. 24. 1. 東海, IV. i. 13. 1: VII. i. 22. 東夷, IV. ii. 1. 1. Observe 東郭氏, II. ii. 2. 2.

枉
wang
To bend, make crooked, III. ii. 1. 1, 3, 5: V. i. 7. 7.

林
lin
A forest, I. i. 3. 3.

果
kwo
(1) Certainly, really, indeed, IV. ii. 33: VI. i. 5. 3, 5. (2) To carry into effect; resolute to execute, I. ii. 16. 3: II. ii. 2. 5: IV. ii. 11.

婐
wo
Used for 婐, a female attendant, VII. ii. 6.

枝
chih
A branch of a tree, I. i. 7. 11.

柝
t'o
A watchman's rattle, V. ii. 5. 3; 6. 3.

柳
liu
(1) A willow-tree, VI. i. 1. 1, 2. (2) In designations, 柳下惠, II. i. 9. 2, 3. *et al.*—泄柳 and 子柳, II. ii. 11. 3: III. ii. 7. 2: VI. ii. 6. 3.

校
hsiao
(1) A kind of seminary, III. i. 8. 10. (2) 校人, a pond-keeper, V. i. 2. 4.

校
chiao
To compare, III. i. 8. 7.

栗
li
齊栗, full of awe, V. i. 4. 4.

格
ko
To correct, IV. i. 20.

根
kun
To be rooted, VII. i. 21. 4.

桃
t'ao
A surname, VII. i. 35. 1.

桀
chieh
The last sovereign of the Hsiâ dynasty; is sometimes＝a tyrant, I. ii. 8. 1: VI. i. 9. 1, 3: V. i. 6. 4: VI. ii. 2. 5; 6. 2; 9. 4; 10. 7.

桎
chih
桎梏, handcuffs and fetters, VII. i. 2. 4.

桐
t'ung
(1) A species of tree, probably belonging to the *euphorbiae*, VI. i. 13. 1, Bretschneider, *Paulownia*. (2) The name of the place where Tang's grave was, V. i. 6. 5: VII. i. 31.

桑
sang
The mulberry-tree, I. i. 3. 4; 7. 24: III. i. 4. 3: VII. i. 22. 2.

桓
hwan
(1) An honorary epithet, 齊桓 and 桓公, I. i. 7. 1, 2: II. ii. 2. 8, 10: IV. ii. 21. 3: VI. ii. 7. 3.—季桓子, V. ii. 4. 7. (2) A surname, 桓司馬, V. i. 8. 3.

桮
pei
I. q. 杯, a cup, VI. i. 1. 1, 2.

梁
liang
(1) A bridge,—of a large size, IV. ii. 2. 3. (2) A weir, I. ii. 5. 3. (3) The name of a State, I. i. 1. 1; 2. 1, *et al.* (4) A name, VI. ii. 6. 5. (5) 梁山, the name of a mountain, I. ii. 15. 1.

梃
t'ing
A stick, a staff, I. i. 4. 3; 5. 3.

梏
ku
(1) Handcuffs, 桎梏, see 桎. (2) To fetter, VI. i. 8. 2. Châo Ch'î explains it here by 亂.

梧
wu
The same as the 桐 above, VI. i. 14. 3.

梓
tsze
(1) A species of tree, the wood of which is most valuable, VI. i. 13. 1 (Bretschneider, *Catalpa*). (2) A carpenter, who makes articles of furniture, III. ii. 4. 3, 4: VII. ii. 5.

條
(tiáo)

(1) 條理, 'discriminated and regulated,'—spoken of a concert, and = 'the blended harmony,' V. ii. 1. 6. (2) 鳴條, the name of a place, IV. ii. 1. 1.

械
裡
棄
(hsie)

械器, various utensils, III. i. 4. 5.

A spade, or shovel, III. i. 5. 4.

To abandon, throw away, spurn, I. i. 3. 2; ii. 6. 1: VII. i. 29; 35. 6, *et al.* To be rejected, IV. i. 14. 2. 棄田, to throw fields out of cultivation, III. ii. 9. 5. 自棄, to throw one's self away, abandon one's self to work wickedness, IV. i. 10. 1.

棗
(tsǎo)

The date, 羊棗, VII. ii. 36. 1, 2, now commonly called from the appearance of the fruit 羊矢棗

棘
(chí)

(1) 棘棘, a sour date-tree, VI. i. 14. 3. (2) 垂棘, the name of a place in Tsin, V. i. 9. 2.

棠
(t'ang)

The name of a place, where the princes of Ch'i kept a granary, VII. ii. 23. 1.

棬
(ch'üan)

A wooden bowl, VI. i. 1. 1, 2.

樓
(lèu)

A bed, a couch, V. i. 2. 3.

棺
(kuan)

An inner coffin, 棺槨, I. ii. 16. 2: II. ii. 7. 4.

槨
(ko)

An outer coffin, 棺槨, see above.

楊
(yang)

The surname of the heresiarch 楊朱, III. ii. 9. 9, 10, 14: VII. i. 26. 楊 = Yangism and Yangists, VII. ii. 26. 1, 2.

楚
(ch'ù)

The name of a State, I. i. 5. 1, 3; 7. 16, 17; ii. 6. 1; 13. 1, *et al.*, *saepe.* 楚人, I. i. 7. 17: III. ii. 6. 1: VI. i. 4. 4.

業
(yè)

(1) An inheritance, the foundation of an inheritance, I. ii. 14. 3. (2) 業 = instruction. 受業於門, VI. ii. 2. 6. (3) Partly finished, VII. ii. 30. 1.

極
(chí)

An extremity (in a painful sense), I. ii. 1. 6. To push to extremities, IV. ii. 3. 4.

榮
(yung)

Glory, II. i. 4. 1 : VII. i. 32.

榱
(ts'ui)

榱題, the projecting ornaments round the eaves of great buildings, VII. ii. 34. 2.

構
(kèu)

構怨, to excite resentment, I. i. 7. 14.

槁
(kǎo)

Dry; withered, I. i. 6. 6 : II. i. 2. 16: III. ii. 10. 3.

樓
(lèu)

A high gallery, 岑樓, the pointed peak of a high building, VI. ii. 1. 5. See note *in loc.*

樂
(lì)

A sour date-tree, VI. i. 14. 3.

(1) To be happy, to rejoice; to delight in, I. i. 2. 1, 2, 3, 4; ii. 1. 4, 6, 7, 8: IV. i. 3. 4; 8. 1, *et al.*, *saepe.* A delight, VII. i. 20. 1, 2, 3, 4, 5, *et al.* Pleasure, in a bad sense, I. ii. 4. 8: II. i. 4. 4, *et al.* (2) 樂歲, good years, I. i. 7. 21, 22 : III. i. 3. 7.

樂
(yo)

(1) Music, I. ii. 1. 1, 2, 3, 4, 5, 6, 7; 4. 10: II. i. 2. 27: IV. i. 27. 2: VII. ii. 37. 12. (2) 樂正, a double surname, I. ii. 16. 2, 3, *et al.*—V. ii. 3. 2.

樹
(shù)

(1) To plant,—of trees, I. i. 3. 4 ; 7. 24: VII. i. 22. 2, 3. To sow,—of grain, III. ii. 10. 3 : VI. i. 7. 2. 樹藝, III. i. 4. 8. (2) Appointed, legitimate, VI. ii. 7. 3. The tone with these meanings was different anciently from that of the character in its common acceptation of *trees.*

機
(chi)

A spring, a contrivance, VII. i. 7. 2.

橐
(t'o)

A sack open at both ends, I. ii. 5. 4.

橫
(hèng)

Perverse, lawless; unreasonable; unreasonably, lawlessly, III. i. 4. 7; ii. 9. 9: V. ii. 1. 1. 橫逆, perversity and unreasonableness, IV. ii. 28. 4, 5, 6.

檟
(chiǎ)

The name of a tree, supposed to be the same as the 梓, but not yet fully identified, VI. i. 14. 3.

To regulate, to restrict, I. i. 3. 5.

檢
(chien)

檀杭, see 杭, IV. ii. 21. 2.

檮
(t'áo)

Sprouts, VI. i. 8. 1.

檿
(nieh)

權
(ch'üan)

(1) The weight of a steel-yard. 權 = to weigh, I. i. 7. 13. (2) The exigency of circumstances, IV. i. 17. 1: VII. i. 26. 3.

THE 76TH RADICAL, 欠.

次
(ts'ǔ)

Next,—in order or degree, V. ii. 2. 7, 9: VI. ii. 14. 3: VII. ii. 37. 2, 7. To be next, to come next to, II. i. 2. 9, 10: IV. i. 14. 3: VII. ii. 14. 1.

欣
(hsin)

欣欣然, smiling-like, I. ii. 1. 7.

欲
(yù)

To desire, like, wish, I. i. 2. 4 ; 7. 15, 16, 17, 18, 23, *et al.*, *saepissime.* Desires, IV. ii. 30. 2 : VII. ii. 35.

欺 *ch'i*

To impose on; to be imposed on, III. i. 4. 17: V. i. 2. 4.

歆 *k'an*

歆然, without elation, VII. i. 11.

歃 *shā*

歃血, to smear the sides of the mouth with blood, VI. ii. 7. 3.

歌 *ko*

To sing, IV. i. 8. 2: VI. ii. 6. 5 (indicating singing in some peculiar style). Used actively, 謳歌, V. i. 5. 7; 6. 1.

歎 *t'an*

To sigh, VII. i. 36. 1.

歠 *chüeh*

To drink, to sip, III. i. 2. 4. 流歠 to swill down, VII. i. 46. 2.

歡 *hwan*

Pleased. 歡樂, to rejoice in, I. i. 2. 3.

THE 77TH RADICAL, 止.

止 *chih*

(1) To stop, desist,—spoken of walking, retiring from office, &c., I. i. 3. 2; ii. 16. 3: II. i. 2. 22: III. ii. 5. 4: VI. ii. 15. 8. To stay, reside; to remain, I. ii. 1. 2: II. ii. 7. 1: V. ii. 1. 1. (2) Active, to stop, I. ii. 11. 4: II. i. 9. 2.

正 *chëng*

(1) To correct, rectify; to be rectified; correct; what is correct, II. i. 7. 5; 9. 1: III. i. 3. 13; ii. 2. 2, 3; 9. 6. 13, *et al., saepe.* To make straight, V. i. 7. 7. What may be correctly ascribed to, VII. i. 2. 1; 3. 4. (2) To have a purpose in the mind, II. i. 2. 16: VII. ii. 33. 2. (3) 樂正 a double surname;—see 樂.

此 *ts'ze*

This, these. *Passim.* 如此, and 若 此, thus, so, such, are common.

步 *pù*

A pace, I. i. 3. 2: V. ii. 1. 7.

武 *wû*

(1) Firmness, martial vigour. 威武, III. ii. 2. 3. (2) 武王, the first sovereign of the Châu dynasty, I. ii. 3. 6; 8. 1; 10. 3, *et al., saepe.* (3) 武丁, a sovereign of the Shang dynasty, II. i. 1. 8. (4) 武 城, name of a place, IV. ii. 31. 1. (5) 武 成, a Book of the Shû-ching, VII. ii. 3. 2.

歲 *sui*

A year, the years; the character of a year as good or bad, I. i. 3. 5: II. ii. 18. 4: VII. ii. 38. 1, a, 3, 4. 樂歲, I. i. 7. 21, 22: III. i. 3. 7: VI. i. 7. 1 (富歲) 饑歲, I. ii. 12. 2: II. ii. 4. 2.

歷 *li*

To pass over, = to change, IV. ii. 27. 3. 歷—for a period of, V. i. 6. 2.

歸 *kwei*

To return, II. i. 2. 16; ii. 10. 1, 2; 12. 5, *et al., saepe.* Used actively, = to repay, VII. i. 30. 2. To turn to, come to, I. i. 6. 6; ii. 11. 2; 15. 1: III. ii. 5. 4; 9. 9, *et al., saepe.*

THE 78TH RADICAL, 歹.

死 *sze*

To die; death; the dead, I. i. 3. 5; 4. 6; 7. 4, 6, 7, 8, *et al., saepe.* To die for, I. ii. 12. 3. 死亡, I. i. 7. 21, 22: IV. i. 3. 4; 9. 5.

殀 *yâo*

To die at an early age, VII. i. 1. 3.

殃 *yang*

Calamities, I. ii. 10. 2: VII. ii. 27. 1. To bring calamities on, to destroy, VI. ii. 8. 2.

殄 *t'ien*

To exhaust, extirpate. 殄 = to remove, VII. ii. 19. 3.

殆 *tâi*

(1) Perilous, in a dangerous condition, V. i. 4. 1. (2) A particle, I apprehend, is near to, I. i. 7. 17: VII. ii. 23. 1; 30. 2. Followed by 於, IV. ii. 31. 1.

殉 *hsün*

To bury along with the dead, to sacrifice, VII. ii. 1. 2. 殉 = to accompany, VII. i. 42. 1, 2.

殊 *shû*

To be different, VI. i. 7. 1, 5.

殍 *p'iâo*

To die of hunger, VII. ii. 27. 1.

殖 *chih*

繁殖, to swarm, III. i. 4. 7.

殘 *ts'an*

To oppress, treat cruelly, I. ii. 12. 2. 殘 = a ruffian, an oppressor, oppressors, I. ii. 8. 3: III. ii. 5. 5, 6.

殛 *chi*

According to Chû Hsî, to cut off. ? to imprison, V. i. 3. 2.

THE 79TH RADICAL, 殳.

殷 *yin*

The dynasty so called, II. i. 1. 8, 10, *et al., saepe.* 殷人, the founder of the Yin dynasty, III. i. 3. 6.

段 *twan*

A surname, III. ii. 7. 2.

殺 *shā*

To kill, put to death, I. i. 3. 5; 4. 2; 6. 4, 6, *et al., saepissime.* Observe III. ii. 3, and VII. ii. 10.

毀 *hûi*

(1) To pull down; to break, I. ii. 5. 1, 2; 11. 3: III. i. 4. 5: IV. i. 8. 4; ii. 31. 1. (2) To blame, reproach, IV. i. 21.

THE 80TH RADICAL, 毋.

毋 *mû*

A mother; 父母, parents, I. i. 5. 4; 7. 21, 22, *et al., saepe.* 民父母, the parent of the people,—spoken of a ruler, I. i. 4. 5; ii. 7. 6: III. i. 3. 7. 母鷄, 母 彘, brood hens, brood sows, VII. i. 22. 2.

每 *mei*

Every, IV. ii. 2. 5.

THE 81st RADICAL, 比.

比
pi

(1) To compare, II. i. 1. 3: VI. ii. 1. *1.* 比 於, to be compared with, I. ii. 4. 4. (2) 比 干, an uncle of the tyrant Châu, II. i. 1. 8: VI. i. 6. 3.

比
pi

The 4th tone. (1) For, on behalf of, I. i. 5. 1: II. ii. 7. 4. (2) And when ..., I. ii. 6. 1. (3) To classify, III. i. 4. 18. (4) To bend to the will of, act as a partizan, III. ii. 1. 5. (5) To join together, to collect, V. ii. 4. 5.

THE 82nd RADICAL, 毛.

毛
mâu

Hair, VII. i. 26. 1.

毫
hâo

Fine hair, 秋 毫, = what is very small, I. i. 7. 10. 一 毫, = the least, one thread of ten filaments of silk being called a 毫, II. i. 2 4.

THE 83rd RADICAL, 氏.

氏
shih

Family, I. ii. 16. 3. 夏 氏 后, the sovereigns of the Hsia dynasty, the family, i.e. of the great Yü, the prince of Hsia. 季 氏, IV. i. 14. 1. 景 丑 氏, II. ii. 2. 4. 東 郭 氏, II. ii. 2. 2. 楊 氏, 墨 氏, III. ii. 9. 9.

民
min

The people, — usually in distinction from rulers and superior men. *Passim.* Observe the phrases— 丘 民, VII. ii. 14. 2; 天 民, VII. i. 19. 3; 凡 民, VII. i. 10. 1: V. ii. 4. 4; 蒸 民, VI. i. 6. 8; 庶 民, I. i. 2. 3: VII. ii. 37. 13; 黎 民, I. i. 8. 4; 7. 24. 民 = mankind, II. i. 2. 23, 27, 28.

氓
mâng

People, — settling in a State from other States, II. i. 5. 5: III. i. 4. 1, 2: V. ii. 6. 2.

THE 84th RADICAL, 气.

氣
ch'i

(1) The air, breath, VI. i. 8. 2. (2) Air, = carriage, VII. i. 36. 1. (3) Specially deserving of notice is its use in II. i. 2. 8, 9, 10, 11, 12, 13, 14, = energy, the passion-nature.

THE 85th RADICAL, 水.

水
shui

Water, waters, I. ii. 5. 5; 10. 4; 11. 3; *et al., saepe.* 水 = cold water, VI. i. 5. 5.

永
yung

Perpetually, always, II. i. 4. 6: IV. i. 4. 3: V. i. 4. 3.

氾
faa

Water overflowing. 氾 濫 於, to inundate, III. i. 4. 7; ii. 9. 3.

求
ch'iû

(1) To seek for; to ask for; to seek, I. i. 7. 9, 15, 16, 17; ii. 9. 1, *et al., saepissime.* (2) The name of one of Confucius's disciples, IV. i. 14. 1.

汙
wû

(1) Impure, vile, mean, II. i. 9. 2: III. i. 3. 13: V. i. 9. 3; ii. 1. 3: VI. i. 6. 2: VII. ii. 37. 11. (2) A pool, 汙 池, III. ii. 9. 5.

汙
wâi

Low. To rank one's self low, II. i. 2. 25. Perhaps some of the instances under 汙, *wû*, should be read as *wâi*, particularly III. ii. 9. 5, VII. i. 37. 11, and one or two others.

汝
zû

(1) You, thou, IV. ii. 31. 1: V. i. 2. 3: VII. ii. 31. 3. (2) Name of a stream, III. i. 4. 7.

江
chiang

The river by eminence, — the Yang-tzse, III. i. 4. 7, 13; ii. 9. 4. ? VII. i. 16. 1.

池
ch'ih

A pond, I. i. 2. 4; 3. 3: III. ii. 9. 5: V. i. 2. 4. A moat, I. ii. 13. 2: II. ii. 1. 3.

決
chüeh

(1) To lead forth a stream, III. i. 4. 7: VI. i. 2. 1. The waters of a stream overflowing, VII. i. 16. (2) To bite things through with the teeth, VII. i. 46. 2.

沐
mû

Properly, to wash the hair; 沐 浴, to bathe, IV. ii. 25. 2.

沒
mei

To die, pass away, III. i. 4. 13; ii. 9. 5.

沈
shân

A surname, II. ii. 8. 1, 2. 沈 猶 a double surname, IV. ii. 31. 1.

沓
t'â

沓 沓, dilatory, IV. i. 1. 11, 12.

沛
p'ei

(1) A thick marshy jungle, III. ii. 9. 5. (2) 沛 然, vehemently, overwhelmingly, like the sudden fall of rain, or overflow of water, I. i. 6. 6: IV. i. 6. 1: VII. i. 16.

沮
chü

The 3rd tone. To stop, I. ii. 16. 3.

河
ho

(1) The Yellow river, III. ii. 9. 4. 河 東 and 河 內, I. i. 3. 1; 河 西, VI. ii. 6. 5. (2) 九 河, the nine branches of the 河, which Yü regulated, III. i. 4. 7. 南 河, the most southern of these, V. i. 5. 7. (3) May be used for a river generally, II. i. 2. 28: VII. i. 16.

油
yû

油 然, the appearance of thick clouds, I. i. 6. 6.

沼
châo

A pond, I. i. 2. 1, 3. 靈 沼, the name given to king Wân's pond, I. i. 2. 3.

治
ch'ih

To govern, regulate; to manage; to attend to, I. i. 7. 22; ii. 5. 3; 6. 2; 9. 2: II. i. 4. 3; 6. 2; ii. 10. 7; 13. 5 (平 治), *et al., saepe.*

治
chih

The 4th tone. To be well governed; where management and regulation take their effect, I. ii. 6. 3: II. i. 2. 22; III. i. 4. 7; ii. 9. 2: IV. i. 4. 1: V. i. 5. 6; ii. 1. 1, 2: VI. ii. 7. 2; 13. 8.

泄
i

泄 泄, to be at one's ease, IV. i. 10, 11.

泄
hsieh

(1) To slight, neglect, IV. ii. 20. 4. (2) A surname, II. ii. 11. 3: III. ii. 7. 2.

泉
ch'üan

A spring of water, II. i. 6. 7: III. ii. 10. 3: VII. i. 29. 泉原, IV. ii. 18. 2.

法
fa

(1) Laws, IV. i. 1. 3, 4, 8. 法=the law of right, VII. ii. 33. 3. 法 = to enforce the laws, = to tax, II. i. 5. 2. 法家 families attached to the laws or constitution VI. ii. 15. 4. (2) An example; to serve as an example, be imitated, II. i. 1. 7: III. i. 3 11: IV. i. 2. 2; ii. 23. 7.

泗
sze

The name of a stream, a tributary of the Hwái, III. i. 4. 7.

泚
ch'i

The perspiration starting, III. i. 5. 4.

泣
ch'i

To weep; the silent shedding of tears, III. i. 2. 5: IV. ii. 33. 1, 2: V. i. 1. 1, 2: VI. ii. 3. 2.

注
chú

To lead, conduct, III. i. 4. 7; ii. 9. 4.

泰
t'ai

Extravagant, III. ii. 4. 1.

洋
yang

洋 洋, = at ease, or in the abundant water, V. i. 2. 4.

洒
hsi

To wipe away, I. i. 5. 1.

洚
chiang

Waters flowing out of their course, 洚水, spoken of the great inundation, III. ii. 9. 3: VI. ii. 11. 4.

洪
hung

Overflowing; vast. 洪水, used like the above, III. i. 4. 7; ii. 9. 3. 11: VI. ii. 11. 4.

活
huo

To live, II. i. 4. 6: IV. i. 8. 5: VII. i. 23. 3.

洽
hsiá

To permeate, imbue. Followed by 於, II. i. 1. 7.

洿
wū

A pool, I. i. 3. 3.

流
liú

(1) To flow, II. i. 1. 12: III. i. 4. 7: VI. i. 2. 1: VII. i. 13. 3; 24. 3. 流俗 current customs, — in a bad sense, VII. ii. 37. 11; but not so 流風, II. i. 1. 8. Observe I. ii. 4. 6, 7, 8. (2) To float, VII. i. 46. 2. (3) To banish, V. i. 3. 2. (4) 流歠, see 歠, VII. ii. 3. 3.

浚
hsün

To dig, to deepen, V. i. 2. 3.

淳
pú

淳然, rapidly; the appearance of springing up, I. i. 6 6: VI. i. 7. 2.

浩
hào

(1) The appearance of vast waters. 浩然, resolutely, II. ii. 12. 5. 浩然之氣, the vast flowing passion-nature, II. i. 2. 11, 12. (2) 浩生, a double surname, VII. ii. 25. 1.

滄
lang

滄浪, the name of a stream, IV. i. 8. 2.

浴
yū

沐浴, to bathe, IV. ii. 25. 2.

海
hái

The sea; seas, II. i. 2. 28: III. i. 4. 7, et al. 海 = the sea-shore, I. ii. 4. 4: VI. ii. 15. 1. 四海 and 四海之內 are expressions for the kingdom, III. ii. 5. 3, 7: IV. i. 3. 3; 6. 1: V. i. 4. 1: VI. ii. 13. 7: VII. i. 21. 2. So 海內, without the 四, I. i. 7. 17. 東海, IV. i. 13. 1: VII. i. 22. 1. 北海 I. i. 7. 11: IV. i. 13. 1; V. ii. 1. 1: VII. i. 22. 1.

洧
wei

The name of a stream, IV. ii. 2. 1.

浼
mei

To defile, be defiled, II. i. 9. 1, 2: V. ii. 1. 3.

消
hsiao

To diminish, to decay away, III. ii. 9. 4: VI. i. 8. 3.

涉
shih

To wade, IV. ii. 2. 3.

涕
t'i

Tears, IV. i. 7. 2: VI. ii. 3. 2.

涸
k'ö

To be dried up, IV. ii. 18. 3.

涼
liang

涼涼, cold and distant, VII. ii. 37. 9.

淅
hsi

The water in which rice is being washed, V. ii. 1. 4: VII. ii. 17.

淇
ch'i

The name of a stream, a tributary of the Yellow river, VI. ii. 6. 5.

淑
shu

Virtuous. Used actively, to make virtuous, to improve, IV. i. 9. 6; ii. 22. 2: VII. i. 40. 5.

淫
yin

Licentious, unregulated, II. i. 2. 17: III. ii. 9. 10, 13. To make dissipated, III. ii. 2. 3.

深
shñn

Deep (both literally and metaphorically); deeply, I. i. 5. 3; ii. 10. 4: II. ii. 1. 3: III. i. 2. 4: IV. ii. 14. 1: VII. i. 14. 1; 16. 1; 18. 2.

淮
huái

The name of a river, which flows through Ho-nan and An-húi, III. i. 4. 7; ii. 9. 4.

淳
shún

淳于, a double surname, IV. i. 17. 1: VI. ii. 6. 1.

淵 (1) A gulf, an abyss, IV. i. 9. 3. (2) The designation of Confucius's favourite disciple, II. i. 2. 18, 20: III. i. 1. 4.

混 I.q. 滾 混混, the appearance of water flowing freely from a spring, IV. ii. 18. 2.

清 Clear, pure; purifying, IV. i. 8. 2, 3: V. ii. 1. 1, 5.

淹 To reside long, V. ii. 4. 6.

渴 To be thirsty, to suffer from thirst, II. i. 1. 11: VII. i. 27. 1, 2.

湍 湍水, water whirling round, VI. i. 2. 1.

游 子游, the designation of one of Confucius's disciples, II. i. 2. 20: III. i. 4. 1, 3.

湯 (1) Warm water, things hot, VI. i. 5. 5. (2) The founder of the Yin dynasty, I. i. 2. 4; ii. 3. 1; 8. 1; 11. 1, 2, et al., saepe.

源 源源, incessantly, V. i. 3. 3.

準 Level. The instrument,—the level, IV. i. 1. 5.

溝 A ditch,—made in dividing the fields, 4 feet wide, and the same depth, V. i. 7. 6; ii. 1. 2. 溝壑, L. ii. 12. 2: II. ii. 4. 2; III. i. 3. 7; ii. 1. 2: V. ii. 7. 5. 溝澮, IV. ii. 18. 3.

溢 To overflow, VII. ii. 14. 4. To spread forth,—spoken of instruction, IV. i. 6. 1.

溱 The name of a stream, IV. ii. 2. 1.

滄 滄浪, see 浪, IV. i. 8. 2.

溺 To drown, to be drowned, I. i. 6. 5: IV. ii. 29. 4: VI. i. 7. 1. To go to ruin, IV. i. 9. 6. To be drowning, IV. i. 17. 1, 2, 3.

滅 To extinguish; extinguished, III. ii. 9. 6.

滋 To increase, II. i. 1. 7: VI. ii. 6. 3.

滑 滑釐, a name, VI. ii. 8. 4.

滕 The name of a State, I. ii. 13. 1; 14. 1; 15. 1: II. ii. 6. 1, 2, et al.—滕文公 I. ii. 13. 1; 14. 1; 15. 1: III. i. 1. 1; 8. 1. 4. 1.—滕定公, III. i. 2. 1.—滕更, VII. i. 43. 1, 2.

滯 Congealed, impeded, 需滯 dilatory, II. ii. 12. 1.

滸 Banks, I. ii. 5. 5.

漯 The name of a stream, III. i. 4. 7.

漁 To be a fisherman, to catch fish, II. i. 3. 4.

漢 The name of a river, a large branch of the Yang-tsze, in Hü-pei, III. i. 4. 7, 13; ii. 9. 4. 雲漢, the Milky Way, V. i. 4. 2.

潔 To be clean, pure; what is clean, III. ii. 3. 3: IV. ii. 25. 1: VII. ii. 14. 4; 37. 7, 11. To keep pure, V. i. 7. 7.

漿 Congee. ? any beverage, I. ii. 10. 4; 11. 3: III. ii. 5. 5.

潤 To moisten and nourish, VI. i. 8. 1. 潤澤 = to modify and adjust, III. i. 3. 20.

潦 行潦, rain-pools, II. i. 2. 28.

澤 (1) A marsh; marshy thickets, III. i. 4. 7; ii. 9. 5: IV. i. 1. 6. 澤=a pond, I. ii. 5. 3. (2) Favours, benefits; beneficial influence, II. ii. 12. 1: IV. i. 1. 6; ii. 3. 3, 4; 22. 1: V. i. 6. 2; 7. 6; ii. 1. 2: VII. i. 9. 6. (3) 垤澤 the name of a gate, VII. i. 36. 3.

澮 A small ditch, tributary to a 溝, IV. ii. 18. 3.

激 To dam up, VI. i. 2. 3.

濁 Muddy, IV. i. 8. 2, 3.

濕 I.q. the character in the text of II. i. 4. 1, = what is low and wet.

濟 With the 3rd tone. The name of a stream, III. i. 4. 7.

濟 In the 3rd tone. (1) To ferry, convey across, II. ii. 12. 1, 4. (2) To succeed, II. i. 5. 6.

濡 Impeded, 濡滯, see 滯 II. ii. 12. 1.

濫 氾濫, to overflow, inundate, III. i. 4. 7; ii. 9. 3.

濯 (1) To wash, III. i. 4. 13: IV. i. 8. 2, 3. Observe IV. i. 7. 6. (2) 濯濯, sleek and fat, I. i. 2. 3. But the same phrase is used for the denuded appearance of a bare mountain, in VI. i. 8. 1. (3) 子濯 is used as if it were a surname in IV. ii. 24. 2.

濱 The brink of water, a coast, IV. i. 18. 1: V. ii. 1. 1: VII. i. 22. 1; 35. 6. Observe 率土之濱 V. i. 4. 2.

瀹 To clear the course of rivers, III. i. 4. 7.

爲 (1) — *Passim* (1) To be, I. i. 1. 4; 7. 20; ii. 2. 3; 3. 1; 4. 5, 6, *et al.*, *saepissime*. At the beginning of clauses, 爲 continuing what precedes, often = *who is, who was*. Before nouns of relation and proper names, it = *to play, to be in the position*, I. ii. 4. 2: II. i. 1. 4; ii. 2. 10, *et al.*, *saepe*. So in the phrase 其爲人也, 以爲, with and without intermediate words, often = to take to be, to regard, to consider, I. i. 7. 5, 7; ii. 2. 2; II. 3, *et saepe*. Often, however, 以 爲 simply = to be, or to use to make. (2) To make; to do; to be done, I. i. 2. 3; 7. 10, 11, 12, 13, 16, 17, *et saepissime*. 何 爲 and 奚 爲 = why, I. ii. 5. 4; II. 2, *et al*. 有 爲, see 有, 爲 = to exercise, to administer, to govern, II. ii. 4. 4: III. i. 3. 1. The phrase 爲 政, to administer government, and sometimes to give law to the kingdom, is frequent, I. i. 11. 1; II. i. 10. 6: IV. i. 1. 3; 6; 7. 4, *et al.* 爲 = to establish, II. ii. 10. 7. So 定 爲, III. i. 2. 3; and 設 爲, III. i. 3. 10. 爲 = to seek to be, III. i. 3. 5.— Observe 爲 食, 爲 飮, II. i. 1. 11; 爲 陳, 爲 戰, VII. ii. 4. 1; 爲 設 辭, II. i. 2. 18; 民 之 爲 道, III. i. 3. 3, but 人 之 有 道 in 4. 8 is to be understood differently, through the force of the 有; 爲 神 農 之 言, III. i. 4. 1; 爲 閒, III. i. 5. 5: VII. ii. 21; 不 可 爲 衆, IV. i. 7. 5; 我 何 以 … 爲 哉, V. i. 7. 3; 其 所 爲 主, V. i. 8. 4; 爲 詩, VI. ii. 3. 2; 難 爲 水, 爲 言, VII. i. 24. 1; 爲 之 氓, 爲 之 辭, 爲 之 兆, II. i. 5. 5; ii. 9. 4: V. ii. 4. 6.

爲 (2) — The 4th tone. For, in behalf of. Before clauses, it is most conveniently taken as a conjunction, *because*, I. i. 4. 6; 7. 10, 11, 16, *et al.*, *saepissime*. 爲 我, for self, the principle of Yang Chû, III. ii. 9. 9: VII. i. 26. 1. Observe 自 爲, VI. ii. 6. 1, and 何 爲, V. ii. 7. 3. But should not 何 爲 and 奚 爲 always have the 爲 in the 3rd tone? 爲 = consequently, I. ii. 16. 3.

爵 *chio* (1) Nobility, noble rank, II. i. 7. 2; ii. 2. 6; 8. 1: V. ii. 2. 1 (*N.B.*): VI. i. 16. 1, 2, 3; ii. 7. 2. (2) The name of a bird, or birds in general, IV. i. 9. 3.

THE 88TH RADICAL, 父.

父 *fu* (1) A father. *Passim.* The combinations 父 子, 父 母, and 父 兄 are common. 父 母 may denote the ruler, as the parent of the people, I. i. 4. 5; ii. 7. 6. 父 兄 may denote all elder relatives, III. i. 2. 3, 4. (2) 亶 父 (3rd tone), the name of one of the remotest ancestors of the Châu dynasty, I. ii. 5. 5.

THE 89TH RADICAL, 爻.

爾 *r* (1) You, your, I. ii. 12. 2; II. i. 1. 3; 9. 2: V. i. 1. 2; ii. 1. 3. 7: VII. ii. 4. 5; 31. 3. (2) After adjectives, makes adverbs, i. q. 然, VI. i. 10. 6. (3) A final particle, synonymous with 耳, = simply, just so, III. i. 5. 3: IV. i. 9. 1; ii. 18. 2: V. i. 2. 3: VII. ii. 38. 4. 云 爾, II. i. 2. 4: III. ii. 5. 7: IV. ii. 24. 1: VII. i. 39. 2. (4) Thus, VI. i. 7. 1 — ? III. i. 3. 2, where perhaps 爾 = you. (5) I. q. 邇, what is near, IV. i. 11.

THE 90TH RADICAL, 爿.

牀 *ch'wang* A couch, V. i. 2. 3.

牆 *ch'iang* A wall, III. ii. 3. 6: IV. ii. 31. 1 (牆 屋): VI. ii. 1. 8: VII. i. 2. 2; 22. 2.

THE 91ST RADICAL, 片.

版 *pan* 版 築, building-frames, VI. ii. 15. 1.

牖 *yu* A window, VII. ii. 30. 1. 牖 戶, spoken of a nest, II. i. 4. 3.

THE 92ND RADICAL, 牙.

牙 *ya* 易 牙, a famous cook of antiquity, VI. i. 7. 5.

THE 93RD RADICAL, 牛.

牛 *niu* (1) A cow, an ox; cattle, I. i. 7. 4, 6, 7, 8: II. ii. 4. 3: III. ii. 5. 2, *et al.* (2) 牛 山, the name of a hill, VI. i. 8. 1. (3) 冉 牛, one of Confucius's disciples, II. i. 2. 18, 20. Full, II. i. 2. 3.

牧 *mû* (1) To feed, to tend, II. ii. 4. 3. (2) To browse on, VI. i. 8. 1. (3) Pasture, II. ii. 4. 3. (4) 人 牧, a shepherd of men, a ruler, I. i. 6. 6. (5) 牧 宮, name of a palace, V. i. 7. 9. (6) A surname, V. ii. 3. 2.—VII. ii. 37. 4.

物 *wü* (1) Things, substances. I. i. 7. 13: III. i. 4. 18; 5. 3: IV. ii. 19. 2; 28. 4: VI. i. 4. 5; 8. 3; 9. 2; 15. 2; ii. 5. 4 (articles): VII.

i. 4. 1 ; 24. 3 ; 46. 1. (2) The inferior creatures (this meaning is included in some of the above examples), VII. i. 46. 1. (3) 物 = others, IV. i. 7. 2 : VII. i. 19. 4.— Observe 有物, 有則, VI. i. 6. 8.

牲 *shēng* (1) Cattle—embracing oxen, sheep, and pigs, and sometimes more kinds, V. i. 9. 1. (2) Cattle set apart for sacrifice, victims, VI. ii. 7. 3. Generally in connexion with 犧, which see.

牼 *k'ēng* A name, VI. ii. 4. 1.

牽 *ch'ien* To lead forward, to drag, I. i. 7. 4.

犀 *hsi* The rhinoceros, III. ii. 9. 6.

犧 *hsi* A victim, called 犧 as being 'spotless,' 犧牲, III. ii. 3. 3 ; 5. 2 : VII. ii. 14. 4.

THE 94TH RADICAL, 犬.

犬 *ch'üan* A dog, dogs, I. ii. 15. 1 : IV. ii. 8. 1 : V. ii. 6. 4 : VI. i. 3. 3 ; 7. 5 ; 11. 3.

犯 *fan* To violate, IV. i. 1. 8 : VI. ii. 7. 3.

狂 *k'wang* Ambitious, ardent, VII. ii. 37. 1, 2, 3, 4, 5, 7.

狄 *ti* The wild tribes on the North, I. ii. 14. 2 ; 15. 1 : III. i. 4. 16 (戎狄) ; ii. 9. 11 (夷狄), 12 (戎狄) 北狄, I. ii. 11. 2 : III. ii. 6. 4 : VII. ii. 4. 3.

狎 *hsiá* To be near to, VII. i. 31. 1.

狐 *hú* The fox, III. i. 5. 4.

狗 *kiu* A dog, dogs, I. i. 3. 4, 5 ; 7. 24 : II. i. 1. 10.

狩 *shiu* 巡狩, a sovereign's tour of inspection, I. ii. 4. 5 : VI. ii. 7. 2. 狩 is explained by 守, and = the fiefs.

狸 *lí* Joined with 狐. ? the wild cat, III. i. 5. 4.

狼 *lang* (1) A wolf, IV. i. 17. 1 : VI. i. 14. 4. (2) 狼戾 = to lie about in abundance, III. i. 3. 7.

猛 *mêng* Fierce, III. i. 9. 11.

猶 *iú* (1) As ; to be as, I. i. 7. 16 : II. i. 1. 8, 13 ; 4. 1 ; 6. 6, *et al., saepissime.* (2) Still, yet, I. ii. 2. 2 ; 11. 4 : II. i. 1. 5, 7, *et al., saepe.* Observe 且猶 ... 而況, II. ii. 2. 10 ; 7. 4. (3) In a double surname, IV. ii. 31. 1.

獄 *yü* 訟獄者, litigants, V. i. 5. 7 ; 6. 1. Cautiously-decided, VII. ii. 37. 2, 7.

猿 *ch'üan* —

獨 *tú* Only ; alone, I. i. 2. 4 ; 7. 10, 12 ; ii. 1. 4 : II. ii. 7. 3, 4, *et al., saepe.* Old and childless, solitary, I. ii. 5. 2 In solitude, retirement, VII. i. 9. 6, *et al.* Peculiar, VII. ii. 36. 2.

玁 *hsien* 玁狁, a tribe of northern barbarians. I. ii. 3. 1.

獲 *huo* (1) To get, obtain ; catch, III. ii. 1. 4 : V. ii. 2. 9. 獲於 —to get the confidence of, IV. i. 12. 1. (2) A name, VI. ii. 2. 3.

獵 *lieh* To hunt, 田獵, I. ii. 1. 6, 7 : VII. ii. 34. 2. ? 獵較, V. ii. 4. 5, 6.

獸 *shòu* A brute animal ; a wild animal, I. i. 4. 5 ; ii. 4. 7 : III. i. 4. 7 ; ii. 9. 11 : IV. i. 9. 2. 獸畜, to nourish as a dog or a horse, VII. i. 37. 1. 禽獸, birds and beasts, irrational animals, is common, I. i. 7. 8, 10, 12 : III. i. 4. 7, 8, *et al.*, 鳥獸, I. i. 2. 4 : III. ii. 9. 4. 走獸, quadrupeds, II. i. 2. 28. An otter, IV. i. 9. 3.

獻 *hsien* An honorary epithet, V. ii. 3. 2.

THE 95TH RADICAL, 玄.

玄 *hsüan* Sky-colour. 玄 = dark silks, III. ii. 6. 5.

率 *hsü and shuái* (1) To follow ; following, along, I. ii. 5. 5 ; IV. i. 1. 4 (率由) : V. i. 4. 2. (2) To lead (*shuái*), I. i. 4. 4, 5 : II. i. 5. 6 : III. i. 4. 6, 18 ; ii. 5. 2 ; 9. 9 : IV. ii. 14. 2 : VI. i. 1. 2.

彀 *kü* 彀率, the limit to which a bow should be drawn, VII. i. 41. 2.

THE 96TH RADICAL, 玉.

玉 *yü* A gem, a precious stone, jade, I. ii. 9. 2 ; 15. 1 : VI. i. 3. 2 : VII. ii. 28. 1. Used for the 'musical stone,' V. ii. 1. 6.

王 *wang* (1) A king, kings. *Passim.* 三王, the l unders of the three ancient dynasties, VI. ii. 7. 1, 3, *et al.* 王者, one who is a true king. I. ii. 5. 2 ; 14. 2 : II. i. 1. 11, *et al., saepe.* 王政, true royal government, I. ii. 5. 3 : III. ii. 5. 7. So, 王道, I. i. 3. 3. On the meaning of 王, see II. i. 3. 1. It follows the names of States and honorary epithets. (2) A surname, V. ii. 3. 3.—III. ii. 1. 4.—VI. ii. 6. 5.— II. ii. 6. 1.

王
wang

The 4th tone. To exercise the royal authority (active and neuter), I. i. 8. 4; 5. 2; 7. 2, 3; 5, 9, 10, 11, 24; ii. 1. 8; 4. 3; 5. 4, 5; II. i. 1. 6, 7, 10; 2. 1; 5. 6; ii. 2. 8; III. ii. 1. 1; IV. i. 9. 4, 5; ii. 10. 1; V. i. 6. 5; VI. ii. 4. 6; VII. i. 20. 1, 5.

珠
chû

A pearl, I. i. 15. 1; VII. ii. 28.

班
pan

To distribute, arrange, V. ii. 2. 1; Order, rank, II. i. 2. 23.

理
lî

(1) 條理, see 條, V. ii. 1. 6.   (2) The mental constitution, VI. i. 7. 8.   (3) To depend on, VII. ii. 19. 1.

琢
cho

To cut and polish a gem, I. ii. 9. 2.

琅
lang

琅邪, the name of a place, I. ii. 4. 4.

琴
ch'ín

(1) The harpsichord or lute, V. i. 2. 3; VII. ii. 6.   (2) A surname, VII. ii. 87. 4.

璞
p'o

A gem unwrought, I. ii. 9. 2.

璧
pî

An auspicious gem, which was fashioned round, V. i. 9. 2.

環
hwan

(1) To surround, II. ii. 1. 2.   (2) A name, V. i. 8. 1, 2, 4.

THE 97TH RADICAL, 瓜.

瓢
p'iáo

A gourd; a gourd dish, IV. ii. 29. 2.

THE 98TH RADICAL, 瓦.

瓦
wǎ

A tile, III. ii. 4. 5.

甑
tsăng

An earthenware pot or pan, used for steaming, III. i. 4. 4.

THE 99TH RADICAL, 甘.

甘
kan

Sweet. 甘＝sweet food, I. i. 7. 16. 甘, to count sweet, or readily, VII. i. 27. 1.

甚
shǎn

Excessive; an exceeding degree; exceedingly, I. i. 7. 17; ii. 1. 1, 3; 14. 1, et al., saepe. 甚於 . . . more, in a greater degree, than . . . , II. i. 1. 11; VI. i. 10. 2, 3, 5. 已甚者 extraordinary things, IV. ii. 10. Observe I. i. 7. 13.

THE 100TH RADICAL, 生.

生
shǎng

(1) To produce; to be produced,—spoken of men and things, II. i. 2. 15, 17, 23, 27, 28; 5. 6: III. i. 5. 3; ii. 9. 2, et al., saepe. (2) Life; to live; to grow; living, I. i. 3. 3: IV. ii. 24. 2: V. i. 2. 4: VI. i. 8. 1, 2; 10. 1, 2, 3, 4, 5, 6: VII. i. 21. 4; 23. 3, et al., a way of life, i. e. 生道 calculated to foster life and happiness, VII. i. 12. 1.   (3) To be born, to be born in, III. ii. 3. 6: IV. ii. 1. 1, 2: VII. ii.

87. 9. 先生, master, a respectful way of speaking to or of an individual, IV. i. 24. 2; ii. 31. 1: VI. ii. 4. 2, 4, 5, 6.   (4) In a double surname, VII. ii. 25. 1.   (5) In a name, VII. ii. 38. 3.

產
ch'ǎn

(1) Livelihood, I. i. 7. 20, 21, 22: III. i. 4. 12. (2) A native, III. i. 8. 3. 產-breed, V. i. 9. 2. (3) 子產, a designation, IV. ii. 2. 1: V. i. 2. 4.

甥
shǎng

A son-in-law, V. ii. 3. 5.

THE 101ST RADICAL, 用.

用
yung

(1) To use; to be used, I. i. 3. 1, 3; 4. 6; 7. 10, et al., saepissime. (2) Used for 以 Initial, ＝for, on the part of, V. ii. 8. 6; 用＝thereby, I. ii. 5. 4: III. ii. 5. 6.

THE 102ND RADICAL, 田.

田
t'ien

(1) A field, fields, I. i. 3. 4; 7. 24: III. i. 3 (N.B.). 7, 9, 13, 18, 19, et al., saepe. 圭田＝the holy field, III. i. 3. 16. 田疇, VII. i. 23. 1. 田野, IV. i. 1. 9: VI. ii. 7. 2. 田里, IV. ii. 3, 4: VII. i. 22. 3. 乘田, the office held by Confucius in charge of the public fields, V. ii. 5. 4. (2) 田 and 田獵, to hunt, I. ii. 1. 6, 7: III. ii. 1. 2: V. ii. 7. 5: VII. ii. 84. 2.

由
yû

(1) From, proceeding from, I. i. 7. 4; ii. 16. 1: II. i. 1. 8; 2. 1, 27; 6. 4; 9. 3, et al., saepissime. (2) By, to proceed by, to walk in, III. ii. 2. 3; 3. 6; 9. 4, et al., saepe. (3) Used for 猶, in both its meanings of as and still, I. i. 6. 6; 7. 3; ii. 1. 3: II. i. 1. 6; ii. 12. 5, et al. (4) 由由然, at his ease, II. i. 9. 2: V. ii. 1. 3. (5) The name of 子路, III. ii. 7. 4.—In the name 譬由, V. i. 8. 2.

甲
chiǎ

(1) A coat of mail; ＝defensive armour, I. i. 3. 2; 5. 3; 7. 14: IV. i. 1. 9. (2) 太甲, the name of a Book in the Shû-ching, II. i. 4. 6: IV. i. 8. 5: V. i. 6. 4: VII. i. 31. 1.

申
shǎn

(1) To inculcate especially, repeatedly, I. i. 3. 4; 7. 24. (2) A surname, II. ii. 11. 3.

男
nan

(1) A male, IV. i. 17. 1: V. i. 1. 3; 2. 1; ii. 6. 6. (2) A title of nobility, V. ii. 2. 3, 4, 5.

界
chieh

A border, boundaries, II. ii. 1. 4: III. i. 3. 13.

畏
wei

To fear, to dread, I. i. 6. 2; ii. 3. 2, 3; 11. 1, 3: II. i. 1. 3; 2. 5; 4. 2: III. i. 1. 4; ii. 5. 7: V. ii. 4. 4: VII. i. 14. 3; ii. 4. 5; 34. 2.

畎
chüen

A small channel of water. 畎畝 channelled fields, V. i. 1. 3; 7. 3, 4; ii. 6. 6: VI. ii. 15. 1.

畔
pan

To rebel, to rebel against, II. ii. 1. 4, 5; 9. 1, 2, 3.

畜
ch'ü

(1) To stop, restrain, I. ii. 4. 9. (2) To keep in store, have laid up, IV. i. 9. 5. (3) Read *hsiü*, to keep, to nourish, I. i. 3. 4; 7. 21, 22, 24: V. i. 2. 4; ii. 6. 4: VII. i. 22. 3; 37. 1.

畝
mŭ

An acre. Its size has varied at different times. Now 6.61 *mŭ* = an English acre, I. i. 3. 4; 7. 24; III. i. 3. 6, 16, 17, 19; 4. 9: V. ii. 2. 8: VII. i. 22. 2. 畎畝, see 畎.

畢
pi

(1) To be finished, III. i. 3. 19: V. i. 5. 7; 6. 1. (2) A surname, III. i. 3. 13.— IV. ii. 1. 2.

略
lo

A general summary, an outline, III. i. 3. 20: V. ii. 2. 1.

畦
hui

A field of fifty *mŭ*. Used for fields generally, III. ii. 7. 4.

畫
hua

To draw figures on, III. ii. 4. 5.

異
i

(1) Different, to be different. Followed by 於, from, I. i. 3. 5; 4. 2, 3; 7. 11, 17, *et al.*, *saepe*. (2) Strange; to think it strange, to be offended, I. i. 7. 7: II. i. 2. 1; ii. 10. 6: IV. ii. 27. 3: V. ii. 9. 3.

留
liú

(1) To detain, II. ii. 11. 2. (2) To remain, VI. ii. 2. 6. The character is often, but improperly, written 留.

當
tang

(1) To sustain, be equal to, correspond to, IV. ii. 12. 17. To be matched, II. i. 1. 7. (2) To oppose, withstand. The meaning is associate with the above, I. ii. 3. 5. (3) In, at; to be in,—applied to time and circumstances, I. ii. 5. 5; II. i. 1. 1 (*N.B.*), 13; ii. 3. 3, 4; 13. 5, *et al.*, *saepe*. (4) Ought, IV. ii. 9: VII. 46. 1. What ought to be, right, VI. ii. 8. 9.

當
tang

The 4th tone. To be correct, V. i. 5. 4.

疆
chiang

Borders, boundaries, II. ii. 1. 4; III. ii. 3. 1, 4, 5; 5. 6: IV. ii. 3. 3: VI. ii. 7. 2.

疇
ch'ü

A flax field, 田疇 see 田.

THE 103RD RADICAL, 疋.

疏
shü

(1) Distant, distance, II. i. 1. 11. Spoken of relationship. I. ii. 7. 3: VI. ii. 3. 4; with verbal force, VI. ii. 3. 3. (2) Coarse, III. i. 2. 2: V. ii. 3. 4. (3) To separate, III. i. 4. 7.

疑
i

(1) To doubt, I. i. 5. 6: III. i. 1. 3: VI. i. 7. 3. (2) A name, II. ii. 10. 6.

THE 104TH RADICAL, 疒.

疢
ch'ün

Any feverish distemper. But 疢疾 = sickness and distress generally, VII. i. 18. 1.

疾
chi

(1) Sickness; aching, painful, I. ii. 1. 6, 7: II. ii. 2. 1, 2, 3: III. i. 1. 5: IV. ii. 24. 2. 疾痛 VI. i. 12. 1. 疾病 I. ii. 1. 7: III. i. 3. 13. 疢疾, see above. (2) A moral infirmity, II. i. 3. 4, 5. (2) Quickly; hurried, VI. i. 14. 4; ii. 2. 4. (3) To be aggrieved with, I. i. 7. 18. Angrily, I. ii. 12. 1.

疕
ch'ü

An old ulcer. 癰疕 = an ulcer-doctor, or perhaps a name, V. i. 8. 1, 2. 4.

病
ping

(1) A disease; to be unwell, II. ii. 2. 2, 3: III. i. 5. 1: IV. i. 9. 5. 疾病 I. ii. 1. 7: III. i. 3. 13. Understood in a moral sense, = infirmity, VI. ii. 2. 7: VII. ii. 33. 3. (2) To be troubled with, distressed by, III. ii. 7. 4: IV. ii. 2. 2. 病 = tired, II. i. 2. 16.

痛
t'ung

To be pained. 疾痛, see 疾.

瘳
chi

A surname, V. i. 8. 1, 2, 4.

瘳
ch'üu

To be cured, III. i. 1. 5.

癰
yung

癰疕, see 疕.

THE 105TH RADICAL, 癶.

登
tăng

To ascend, II. ii. 10. 7: VII. i. 24. 1; 41. 1. 登 = to be made to grow, III. i. 4. 7.

發
fa

(1) To send forth,—as in discharging arrows, II. i. 7. 5: IV. ii. 24. 2: VII. i. 41. 3; or in exercising government, I. i. 7. 18; ii. 5. 3. To be sent forth, manifested, II. i. 2. 17: VI. ii. 15. 3. (2) To rise, come forth, VI. ii. 15. 1. (3) To open a granary, to cause it to open,—to send forth the stores, I. i. 3. 5; ii. 4. 9: VII. ii. 23. 1.

THE 106TH RADICAL, 白.

白
pái

(1) White; to pronounce to be white, I. i. 2. 3: VI. i. 3. 2; 4. 2, 3. 頒白者 grey-haired, I. i. 3. 4; 7. 24. (2) A surname, VI. ii. 10; 11.

百
pái

(1) A hundred. *Passim.* It is used as a round number, signifying all of a class. We have 百世, II. i. 2. 27, *et al.*; 百官 III. i. 2. 3, 4, 5, *et al.*; 百神, V. i. 5. 6; 百姓, V. i. 5. 6, *et al.*; 百工, III. i. 4. 5, 6; 百穀, III. i. 3. 2. (2) 百里, a double surname, V. i. 9. 1, 2: VI. ii. 6. 4; 15. 1.

皇
hwang

皇皇如, anxious-like, III. ii. 3. 1.

皆
chieh

Passim. All. At the commencement of clauses, with reference to preceding statements. If it have a noun with it, the

THE 108th RADICAL, 皿.

A vessel, 器皿, III. ii. 2. 3.

(1) To fill; full, III. ii. 9. 9; IV. i. 14. 2; ii.13. 2. 3; VII. i.24. 3. (2) In a name, III. ii. 8. 1.
盈 成, a double surname, VII. ii. 20. 1.

(1) To add to; more, I. ii. 10. 4; VI. ii. 8. 7; 16. 2. (2) Of advantage, profitable, II. ii. 2. 16; VI. ii. 8. 3; VII. i. 8. 1, 2; (3) A minister of Shun and Yü, III. i. 4. 7; VI. i. 6. 1, 2, 4, 6.

Why not; would it not be better to..., I. ii. 7. 23; II. ii. 10. 3; IV. i. 13. 2; ii. 31. 4, 5; VII. i. 22. 1; ii. 37. 1.
An appearance of fullness, VII. i. 21. 4.

Complete, grant; flourishing state, II. i. 1. 10; 2. obi; V. i. 4. 1; VI. ii. 7. 3; VII. ii. 33. 2.

The 1st tone. A vessel full, III. ii. 8. 3; 5. 2; VII. ii. 14. 4.

A robber, III. ii. 10. 3; V. ii. 4. 5.

To covenant solemnly, VI. ii. 7. 3.

To oversee, II. ii. 9. 2, 3.

(1) To exhaust, to carry out to the utmost degree, in the way of doing or thinking, I. i. 5. 1; 7. 17; II. ii. 9. 2; III. i. 2. 4; V. ii. 4. 5; VII. i. 2. 0; 7. 1; 2. 8; 8. Observe 自盡, III. i. 2. a, and 盡 於人心, II. ii. 7. a. (2) All, IV. ii. 33. 1; VII. i. 35. 1. Entirely, III. i. 4. 3; VII. ii. 3. 1.

THE 109th RADICAL, 目.

The eye, I. i. 7. 16; II. i. 2. 4; III. i. 6. 4; II. ii. 10. 1; IV. i. 1. 5; ii. 32. 3; V. ii. 1. 1; VI. i. 7. 7, 8; 10. 3; VII. ii. 24. 1.
(1) Straight; to be straight; to make straight, III. ii. 1. 1, 3, 5; IV. i. 1. 6; V. ii. 7. 8. Metaphorically, to correct; rectitude, II. i. 2. 13; III. i. 4. 8; 5. 2. (2) Only, I. i. 3. 2; 4. 1. 2; II. ii. 7. a.

Dull, to be dull, IV. i. 15. 1.

眼眩, see 眩, III. i. 1. 5.

眸子, the pupil of the eye, IV. i. 15. 1, 2.

Many, numerous; a multitude; the multitude, I. i. 7. 17; II. i. 4; 11. 4; ii. 4; sage.

睟然 mild-like, VII. i. 21. 4.

To be harmonious, III. i. 9. 18.

To look aside, III. i. 6. 4.

眩眩, to throw into a state of confusion.—medicine in its beneficial operation, yet causing distress, III. i. 1. 5.

睊睊 with eyes askance, I. ii. 4. 6.

To be clear, IV. i. 15. 1.

瞽瞍, the name of Shun's father, IV. i. 28. 2; V. i. 2. 3; 4. 1, 2, 4; VI. i. 6. 3; VII. i. 35.

See above.

To watch, to spy, IV. ii. 52; 33. 1.

To watch, III. ii. 7. 3.

THE 110th RADICAL, 矛.

To reverence, 矜式, II. ii. 10. 3.

THE 111th RADICAL, 矢.

An arrow, I. ii. 5. 4; II. i. 7. 2. 3; III. ii. 1. 4; IV. ii. 24. 2; V. i. 7. 8.
A final particle, found passim. It gives definiteness and decision to statements. Where the last clause of a sentence or paragraph is introduced by 則 斯 or

亦 it generally ends with 矣. After
而已 it may be looked for. After single adjectives and other words its force is both decisive and exclamatory.

知
chih   To know, to understand. *Passim.* 知 = to acknowledge, i.e. to know and employ, VII. i. 9. 2.

知'
chih   The 4th tone. Used for 智, to be wise; wise; wisdom. 知 者, VII. i. 46. 1.
知 慮, VI. ii. 13. 2. 術 知, VII. i. 18. 1.

矩
chü   A square,—the carpenter's instrument so called, IV. i. 1. 1, 5; 2. 1; VI. i. 20. 2; VII. ii. 5.

短
toan   Short, I. i. 7. 13; III. i. 1. 5 (N. B.); 4. 17. To shorten, VII. i. 39. 1.

THE 112TH RADICAL, 石.

石
shih   (1) A stone, a rock, VII. i. 16. (2) 石 丘, the name of a place, VI. ii. 4. 1.

破
p'o   To break, to split. Used for the blows of an axe, strong and well aimed, III. ii. 1. 4.

磽
ch'iao   Stony ground; poor in soil, VI. i. 7. 2.

磯
chi   Stones in a river, interrupting and fretting the current, VI. ii. 8. 4; there 不可磯 = what will admit of no contradiction.

THE 113TH RADICAL, 示.

示
shih   To show, indicate, V. i. 5. 4. 5.

社
shê   The spirits of the land, or their altars. Always in the phrase 社 稷, the tutelary spirits of a country, and may be used for the country itself, IV. i. 3. 3; VII. i. 19. 2; ii. 14. 1, 3, 4.

祀
sze   To sacrifice; to sacrifice to, III. ii. 5. 2; IV. ii. 25. 2. 祭 祀, sacrifices, VI. ii. 10. 4; VII. ii. 14. 4.

祜
hü   Happiness, prosperity, I. ii. 3. 6.

祇
chih   Reverent, reverently, V. i. 4. 4.

祖
tsü   先 祖, ancestors, III. i. 2. 3.

神
shan   (1) A spirit. 百 神, all spiritual beings who are sacrificed to, V. i. 5. 6. Spiritual,—mysterious, VII. i. 13. 3; ii. 25. 8. (2) 神 農, one of the most ancient sovereigns, III. i. 4. 1.

祥
hs'iang   Auspicious, IV. i. 18. 4; ii. 17.

祭
chi   To sacrifice or make offerings to; sacrifices; sacrificial, III. i. 2. 2, 3; ii. 3. 3; IV. ii. 33. 1; V. i. 5. 6; ii. 4. 6; VI. ii. 6. 6 (N.B.).
祭 祀, see 祀.

祼
kuan   I. q. 灌. To pour out a libation, IV. i. 7. 5.

祿
lü   Emolument, revenue, salary, I. ii. 5. 2; II. ii. 8. 1; 14. 1; III. i. 8. 8, 13; ii. 10. 3; V. ii. 2. 1, 6, 7, 8, 9; 3. 5; VII. ii. 33. 2. To grant to, to endow, V. i. 7. 2.

禁
chin   To forbid, prohibit; prohibitions, I. ii. 2. 3; 5. 3; VI. ii. 7. 3; VII. i. 35. 3, 4; 39. 4.

禍
huo   Calamity, II. i. 4. 4, 5. 禍 = an outbreak, attack, IV. ii. 31. 1. Used as a verb, VI. i. 1. 2.

福
fu   Happiness, II. i. 4. 5, 6; IV. i. 4. 3.

禦
yü   To withstand, oppose; to hinder; to ward off, I. i. 6. 6; 7. 3, 18; II. i. 1. 10; 7. 2; VII. i. 16; ii. 8. 1. To stop and rob, V. ii. 4. 4, 5.

釋
shan   To resign, give over to another, V. i. 6. 7.

禮
li   (1) What is proper; the principle of propriety; the rules of ceremony and politeness in accordance therewith, I. i. 7. 22; ii. 16. 1; II. i. 2. 27; 6. 5; 7. 3, *et al., saepissime.* To be polite to, III. i. 3. 1; VII. i. 43. 1, *et al.* 禮 貌, a polite demeanour, VI. ii. 14. 3. The same, used as a verb, IV. ii. 30. 1. (2) The Book of Rites, II. ii. 2. 5; III. ii. 3. 3. The Ritual Usages, III. ii. 2. 2.

THE 114TH RADICAL, 内.

禹
yü   The great Yü, the founder of the Hsia dynasty, II. i. 8. 2; III. i. 4. 7, 9; ii. 9. 4, 11, *et al., saepe.*

禽
ch'in   Birds, III. ii. 1. 4. In the phrase 禽 獸, birds and beasts, irrational animals, sometimes applied metaphorically to men, I. i. 7. 8, 10, 12; III. i. 4. 7, 8; ii. 1. 5; 9. 5, 9; IV. ii. 19. 1; 38. 6; VI. i. 8. 2.

THE 115TH RADICAL, 禾.

私
sze   Private; privately, III. i. 3. 9, 19; IV. ii. 22. 2 (N.B.); VII. i. 40. 5. 以 其 私, II. ii. 8. 1. As a verb, to be selfishly attached to, to monopolize, II. ii. 10. 5; IV. ii. 30. 2.

秉
ping   To grasp, maintain. 秉 夷, VI. i. 6. 8.

秋
ch'iü   (1) The autumn; in the autumn; autumnal, I. i. 7. 10; ii. 4. 5; III. i. 4. 13; VI. ii. 7. 2. (2) 春 秋, a historical Work, compiled by Confucius, III. ii. 9. 8, 11; IV. ii. 21. 1, 2; VII. ii. 2. 1. (3) A name, VI. i. 9. 3.

taxes, I. i. 5, 3; VII. i. 23, 1. 頁稅 =revenues, V. i. 8, 3.

L., 脫. To lasso, put off, VI. ii. 6. 6.

A kind of spurious grain, 稊莠 VI. i. 19.

The young, III. i. 3, 7.

To sow, III. i. 4, 4.

The 3rd tone. Seed, VI. i. 7, 2; 19.

(1) To style, to pronounce, to speak of, III. ii. 9, 1; VII. ii. 30, 1; VII. i. 10. (2) To praise, III. i. 1, 2; IV. ii. 18, 1. (3) To lift up, — to proceed to, III. i. 3, 9.

The 4th tone. To correspond, to be equal to, II. ii. 7, 2.

(1) The spirits presiding over the grain or agriculture of a country. 社稷, too 社 (2) 后稷, the title of Shun's minister of agriculture, III. i. 4, 8. The 后 is dropped, and 稷 becomes a proper name, IV. ii. 29, 2, 3, 5; 4.

Paddy, III. ii. 3, 2.

To sow, II. i. 8, 4; III. i. 4, 8.

(1) To bow down, 稽首, to bow the head to the ground, V. ii. 6. 4, 5; VII. ii. 3. (2) A name, VII. ii. 19, 1.

A general name for grain, I. i. 3, 3; generally spoken of as 五穀 the five kinds of grain, III. i. 4, 7, 9, 11; VI. i. 19; ii. 10, 4. But we have also 百穀 III. i. 3, 2. 穀祿 the grain available for salaries, III. i. 3, 18.

An honorary epithet, I. ii. 12, 1. —V. i. 9, 1, 3; VI. ii. 6, 4;

Stores of straw, grain, &c., in the open air; ricks, I. ii. 3, 4.

To reap, III. i. 4, 8.

fully excavated, III. ii. 9, 3.

To leap over, — as if it were 踰 VII. ii. 31, 2, 4. The dictionary explains it differently, however, and makes it = 'an opening in the wall.'

To peep, to steal a sight, III. ii. 3, 6.

(1) Poor, in poverty and distress I. ii. b, 3; V. i. 1, 3; VII. i. 9, 4, 5, 6; 21, 2. 窮乏, VI. i. 10, 7, 8. 阨窮, II. i. 9, 2; V. ii. 1, 3. (2) To exhaust, II. ii. 12, 6. See 力. (3) To be at one's wit's end, II. i. 2, 17.

(1) To steal, VII. ii. 30, 2. (2) Privately, VII. i. 35, 6. (3) Joined with other verbs so as to qualify them deferentially, II. i. 2, 20; ii. 7, 1; IV. ii. 21, 3.

THE 117th RADICAL, 立.

(1) To stand; to stand erect, I. i. 3, 1; 7, 18; II. i. 5, 1; ii. 1; III. ii. 2, 3; IV. ii. 33, 1; V. i. 4, 1; i. 5, 3; VII. i. 2, 2; 21, 2; ii. 3. 立 而..., — quickly, IV. ii. 19, 3; = with indifference, II. ii. 1, 3. To stand fast, to be established, VI. i. 16, 2. (2) To set up; to appoint; to establish; to be set up, appointed, V. i. 5, 2; 6, 5; ii. 1, 1; VII. i. 1, 5; ii. 18, 1.

(1) Anything definite and complete, a lesson, a piece, VII. i. 24, 3. (2) 憲章 = rule, canons, IV. i. 1, 2. (3) A name, 萬章 III. ii. 5, 2; V. i. 1, 1, 2, 3 et al., supra. —匡章 III. ii. 10, 2; IV. ii. 30, 1. 章子, IV. ii. 30, 2, 3, 5, is peculiar; see on par. 1.

Boys under fifteen. A child, VII. i. 16, 2. A lad, III. i. 4, 17. So 童子, III. ii. 5, 2, 9.

To exhaust, to carry to the utmost, I. ii. 16, 1; IV. i. 1, 5; V. i. 1, 2.

(1) A principle, principles, II. i. 6, 5; 6, 7. (2) Correct, upright, IV. ii. 24, 2.

THE 118th RADICAL, 竹.

To laugh, to smile; smiling, I. i. 7, 7; 10; III. ii. 7, 4; IV. i. 10, 1; VI. ii. 3, 2; VII. ii. 23, 2. To laugh at, I. i. 1, 2; VII. ii. 23, 2.

符 *fú*
A check, or token. 符節, the two halves of such a token, the fitting of which was an evidence of the holder's authority, IV. ii. 1. 3.

等 *tăng*
A degree, a class, III. i. 5. 3: V. ii. 2. 2. To graduate, to arrange according to merit, II. i. 2. 27.

筋 *chin*
A sinew, a muscle, VI. ii. 15. 2.

答 *tá*
To answer, VI. i. 5. 4; ii. 1. 4: VII. i. 40. 1; 43. 1, 2. To respond to,—in conduct, IV. i. 4. 1.

策 *ts'è*
A slip of bamboo containing writing. 策 = a passage, a piece, VII. ii. 3. 2.

算 *suan*
To reckon. 無算, incalculable, VI. i. 6, 7.

箕 *chi*
(1) The name of a State, 箕子, II. i. 1. 7. (2) 箕山, the name of a hill, V. i. 6. 1.

管 *kuan*
(1) A fife or flute, I. ii. 1. 6, 7. (2) An honorary epithet in 管叔, II. ii. 9. 2, 3. A surname in 管仲, and 管夷吾, II. i. 1. 1, 2, 3, 4, 5; ii. 2. 8, 10: VI. ii. 15. 1.

節 *chieh*
(1) To regulate, to order according to the proper divisions, IV. i. 27. 2. (2) 符節, see 符.

範 *fan*
A law, a rule. Used as a verb, III. ii. 1. 4.

築 *chu*
To beat, as in forming mud walls. 築 = to build, I. ii. 13. 2: III. i. 4. 13; ii. 10. 3. 築 = to fortify, I. ii. 14. 1. 板築, see 板.

篡 *ts'uan*
To usurp; usurpation, V. i. 5. 7: VII. i. 31. 3.

篤 *tú*
To consolidate, I. ii. 3. 6.

簞 *tan*
A small basket or dish for holding rice. Always in the phrase 簞食, I. ii. 10. 4; 11. 3: III. ii. 4. 1; 5. 5: IV. ii. 29. 2: VI. i. 10. 6: VII. i. 34; ii. 11.

簡 *chien*
(1) To slight, IV. ii. 27. 2, 3. (2) Hasty, VII. ii. 37. 1. (3) An honorary epithet, III. ii. 1. 4.

簿 *pú*
A register, V. ii. 4. 6.

籍 *chi*
A record, V. ii. 2. 2: VI. ii. 8. 5.

籥 *yo*
A musical instrument, pipes, I. ii. 1. 6, 7.

THE 119TH RADICAL, 米.

米 *mí*
Rice hulled, II. ii. 1. 3: III. i. 3. 7: VII. ii. 27. 1. See 粟.

粒 *li*
Grains of rice, III. i. 3. 7.

粟 *hsü*
Rice in the husk. 米粟, II. ii. 1. 3. 粟米, VII. ii. 27. 1. 粟 alone, I. i. 3. 1: III. i. 4. 4, 5; ii. 4. 3; 10. 3: IV. i. 14. 1: V. ii. 6. 2, 5: VI. ii. 2. 2: VII. i. 23. 3. Medhurst translates it as above, and apparently after K'ang-hsi's dictionary; still the 本草綱目 says that anciently 粟 was the general name for all glumaceous grain. It is now commonly spoken of millet. I have translated it sometimes by 'grain,' and sometimes by 'millet.'
Barbadoes millet, VI. i. 17. 3.

粱 *liang*
A kind of millet. Always in the phrase 粱肉, III. ii. 3. 3; 5. 2: VII. ii. 14. 1.

粥 *chü*
Congee, III. i. 2. 2, 4.

糗 *ch'iu*
Parched grain, rice or wheat, VII. ii. 6.

糜 *mi*
To boil rice to a mass. 糜爛 = to tear and destroy, VII. ii. 1. 2.

糞 *fün*
To manure; the manuring, III. i. 3. 7: V. ii. 2. 9. The rendering of the sentence in the first of these instances is in accordance with the commentaries, but it may be doubted.

糧 *liang*
Provisions of grain, I. ii. 1. 6; 5. 4.

糴 *ti*
To purchase grain, VI. ii. 7. 3. All the commentaries explain here as if it meant 'to sell grain.' The meaning is—'Do not prevent our sale and *their* purchase.'

THE 120TH RADICAL, 糸.

紂 *chău*
Epithet of the last sovereign of the Yin dynasty, I. ii. 8. 1, 3: VII. i. 22. 1, *et al*, *sæpe*.

約 *yo*
(1) To form alliances, VI. ii. 9. 2. (2) What is most important, II. i. 2. 6. 8. (3) Compendious, VII. ii. 32. 1.—In IV. ii. 15, the term combines the ideas of condensation and importance.
To pay over, V. i. 8. 3.

納 *ná*
紛紛然, confusedly, III. i. 4. 5.

素 *sù*
(1) Of white, undyed, silk, III. i. 4. 4. (2) For nothing, without doing service, VII. i. 32. 1.

索 *so*
Ropes of grass, III. i. 3. 2.

紫 *tsze*
Reddish blue, VII. ii. 37. 12.

累 *lei*
I. q. 縲 係累, to put in confinement, I. ii. 11. 3.

(3) Perpetual, the whole.

... the day, III. ii. 1. 9.

... 終 不, never, III. i. 2. 1. 終 身, all the life, IV. i. 9. 5; ii. 28. 9; 30. 5; V. i. 1. 5; VII. i. 5; 35. 6; ii. 3. Observe this phrase in I. i. 7. 21, 22, and IV. ii. 33. 1.

絕 chüeh. To cut short, III. i. 1. 5. To cut, to stop intercourse with, II. ii. 11. 4: IV. i. 7. 2.

給 chi. To supply. 不 給, a deficiency in the crop, I. ii. 4. 5: VI. ii. 7. 2.

絮 hsü. Rejected floss-silk. 縷 絮, III. i. 4. 17.

統 t'ung. A thread of connexion. 統 = a beginning, I. ii. 14. 3.

絲 sz. Silk from the silkworm. See 絲.

綏 sui. To give tranquillity to, III. ii. 6. 5.

經 ching. (1) To define, to plan, I. i. 2. 3: III. i. 3. 13. (2) The unchanging standard, VII. ii. 37. 13.

緩 hwan. To delay; not to be urgent about, III. i. 3. 2: VII. ii. 27.

綢 ch'âu. 綢 繆, to intertwine, weave together, II. i. 4. 3.

維 wei. A particle,—used as the copula, III. i. 3. 12: V. i. 1. 3.

綯 t'âo. To twist. 索 綯, III. i. 3. 2.

綽 ch'o. 綽 綽 然, freely, at ease, II. ii. 5. 5.

緡 A surname, VI. ii. 6. 5.

緣 From. 緣 木 = to climb a tree, or on a tree, I. i. 7. 16, 17.

緦 The mourning worn for three months, VII. i. 46. 2.

縮 縮 = upright, II. i. 2. 7.

縷 Threads. 麻 縷, III. i. 4. 17. 布 縷, VII. ii. 27. 1. Here it probably means cloth of silk.

績 Merit, doing, V. i. 2. 3.

繡 hsiu. Embroidered garments, VI. i. 17. 3.

繩 shăng. A line, string,—used with reference to a carpenter's line, IV. i. 1. 5: VII. i. 41. 2.

縶 To bind. 縶 = to yoke, V. i. 7. 2.

繳 cho. To adjust a string to an arrow, to draw it back after it has been discharged, VI. i. 9. 3.

繼 chi. To continue; to be continued, I. ii. 14. 3: II. i. 1. 7: IV. i. 1. 5; 15. 2; ii. 20. 5: V. i. 6. 2, 4 (繼 世), 1; ii. 3. 4, 5. 繼 此, after this, II. ii. 10. 2. 繼 而 . . . , immediately after, II. ii. 14. 3.

纓 ying. Strings to tie on a cap, IV. i. 8. 2, 3. To tie on, IV. ii. 29. 6, 7.

纑 lû. Hempen threads, III. ii. 10. 4.

THE 121st RADICAL, 缶.

缺 ch'üeh. To be wanting, III. ii. 9. 6.

THE 122nd RADICAL, 网.

罔 wang. (1) To catch in a net, II. ii. 10. 4. To entrap, I. i. 7. 20: III. i. 3, 3: V. i. 2. 4. (2) None, not. 罔 不, V. ii. 4. 4.

罕 han. Seldom, VI. i. 9. 2.

罟 kû. A net for catching fish, I. i. 3. 3.

罪 tsui. (1) A crime, offence; a fault, I. i. 7. 4, 6, 7, 20; ii. 3. 13: II. ii. 4. 3, 4, et al., saepe. 罪 人, and sometimes 罪 alone, sinners, criminals, I. ii. 5. 3; 6. 3: V. i. 3. 2: VI. ii. 7. 1, 2, 3. 4. 得 罪 於 . . . , to offend against, IV. i. 6; ii. 30. 5. (2) To condemn, I. i. 3. 5: III. ii. 9. 8.

置 chih. (1) To place, III. ii. 6. 1. To appoint, I. ii. 11. 4. 變 置, to displace and appoint others, VII. ii. 14. 3, 4. (2) A stage, a post station, 置 郵, II. i. 1. 12.

罰 fâ. Punishment, III. ii. 6. 4. 刑 罰, I. i. 5. 3: 罰 = penalties, fines.

罷 *pá*
To make to cease, to stop, VI. ii. 4. 3,
5, 6.

THE 123RD RADICAL, 羊.

羊 *yang*
The sheep or goat, I. i. 7. 4, 6, 7, 8: II.
ii. 4. 3: III. ii. 5. 2: V. i. 1. 3; 2. 3; 9. 1;
ii. 5. 4; 6. 6: VI. i. 8. 1. 羊棗, sheep-
dates, a kind of persimmon, VII. ii. 36.
1, 2.

美 *mei*
(1) Good, admirable; beautiful; beauty,
I. ii. 1. 6, 7; 16. 2: II. i. 7. 2; ii. 2. 4; 7. 1
(美然, too good), 2: VI. i. 7. 8; 8. 1, 2;
10. 7; 19. 1: VII. i. 41. 1; ii. 25. 5; 36. 2.

羞 *hsiu*
To be ashamed; the feeling of shame,
II. i. 6. 4, 5; 9. 2: III. ii. 1. 5: IV. ii. 33. 2:
V. ii. 1. 3: VI. i. 6. 7.

羣 *ch'ün*
A flock, a company, VII. ii. 19. 3.

羨 *hsien*
An overplus, III. ii. 4. 3.

義 *i*
Righteousness; our consciousness of
what is righteous, and the determinations
thereof; what is right. *Passim.* The combinations of 仁義, and 禮義, are
very common.

羹 *kāng*
Soup, V. ii. 3. 4; 豆羹, VI. i. 10. 6:
VII. i. 34; ii. 11.

羸 *léi*
Meagre, feeble, II. ii. 4. 2.

THE 124TH RADICAL, 羽.

羽 *yü*
(1) Feathers, a feather, I. i. 7. 10; ii. 1.
6, 7: VI. i. 8. 2; ii. 1. 6. (2) 羽山, the
name of a mountain, V. i. 8. 2.

羿 *i*
A famous archer of antiquity, IV. ii.
24. 1: VI. i. 20. 1: VII. i. 41. 2.

翅 *shih*
Only, VI. ii. 1. 7.

習 *hsi*
To practise, do habitually, VII. i. 5.

翟 *ti*
The name of the heresiarch Mo, III. ii.
9. 9, 10, 14.

翼 *yi*
Wings. Used as a verb, to give wings
to, to assist, III. i. 4. 8.

THE 125TH RADICAL, 老.

老 *lao*
To be old; old; the old, L. i. 7. 12, 24;
ii. 5. 3; 12. 2; 16. 1: II. ii. 4. 2: III. i. 3.
7; ii. 6. 2: IV. i. 18. 1, 2: V. i. 4. 1: VI.
i. 7. 2, 3: VII. i. 22. 1, 2, 3.

考 *k'ao*
(1) A deceased father, V. i. 4. 1. (2) To
examine, II. ii. 13. 4: VI. i. 14. 1: VII. ii.
37. 6 (夷考).

者 *chä*
Passim. (1) He (or they) who; this (or
that), these (or those) who (or which).
It is put after the words (verbs, adjectives,
nouns), and clauses to which it belongs,

I. i. 1. 4; 8. 1, 4: 4. 6; 5. 1, 3. 6. *et al.,*
saepissime. Observe 賢者, I. i. 2. 1, 2:
ii. 4. 1; 16. 1, *et al.*; 使者, V. ii. 6 :
墨者, III. i. 5. 1. 2, *et similia.* (2) After
若 with intervening words, phrases
where a numeral is used, and many
other cases, 者 is equivalent to *one, this,*
these. E. g. 若寡人者, 'such an
one as I,' I. i. 7. 4; 誠有百姓者,
ibid. 6: 變人有臧倉者, there
was one Tsang Ts'ang, I. ii. 16. 3: 二
聖者, III. ii. 9. 13; 二者, IV. i. 2.
2.—This seems to be the proper force of
the character, so that it is an emphatic
demonstrative by which the mind is made
to pause on what has just been said. (3)
It stands at the end of the first member
of a clause or sentence, when the next
gives a description or explanation of the
subject of the other, terminated generally
by the particle 也, but not always, L. i.
7. 9, 12; ii. 4. 2, 3: III. i. 3. 6, 7, *et passim.*
(4) 也者, at the end of the first member
of a sentence, resume a previous word or
statement, and lead on to an explanation
or account of it. E. g. II. i. 9. 1. Observe
VII. ii. 16.—This case and the preceding
may easily be brought under (2). (5)
者也, occur continually at the end of
sentences, preceded generally in a previous clause by 者, and for the most part
the force of 者 in (1) is apparent, I. i. 1.
5; ii. 8. 2: II. i. 1. 10, 11, *et passim.* (6)
It forms adverbs with 昔 and 古, I. ii.
4. 4: II. ii. 7. 2, *et al., saepe.*

Old, aged, I. ii. 15. 1.

耆 *ch'i*
耆 *shih*
The 4th tone. To relish; a relish, VI.
i. 4. 5; 7. 5. 8.

THE 126TH RADICAL, 而.

而 *r*
Passim. A conjunction, meaning *and,*
and yet, which latter signification is often
nearly or altogether = *but.* Its use, however, is very idiomatic, and it cannot
always be literally translated into
English. 而已, and 而已矣,
are very common. So is 然而, - 'so,
and yet.'... Observe 繼而, II. ii. 14.
3; 既而, V. i. 7. 4; 從而, VI. i. 8. 1,
et sim.; also 由 ... 而來, II. ii. 13. 4,
et al.; 而誰, V. i. 7. 5. Its use after
得 is to be noted. E. g. IV. ii. 2. 4: V. i.
4. 1, 4.

THE 127TH RADICAL, 耒.

耒
lei

A plough-handle, 耒耜, III. i. 4. 2;
ii. 3. 5.

耕
kăng

To plough; to cultivate the ground. I.
i. 5. 3, 4; ii. 4. 5: III. i. 4. 3, 4, 5, 6, 7, 8,
11, *et al., saepe*. 耕者 = husbandmen,
I. i. 7. 18; ii. 5. 3; II. 2: II. i. 5. 4. 耕
= to labour, to do work, VII. i. 32. 1.

耘
yun

To weed, II. i. 2. 16.

耜
tsze

A ploughshare. 耒耜, see 耒.

耡
nău

To weed, I. i. 5. 3, 4.

耰
yü

A harrow. 耰 = to cover the seed, VI.
i. 7. 2.

THE 128TH RADICAL, 耳.

耳
r

(1) The ear, I. i. 7. 16: III. ii. 10. 1:
IV. i. 1. 5: V. ii. 1. 1: VI. i. 7. 6, 8; ii. 2:
VII. ii. 24. 1.   (2) A final particle, simply,
only, just, I. i. 8. 2; ii. 1. 2: II. ii. 10. 2,
7: III. i. 4. 11: IV. i. 22; ii. 30. 2: VI. i.
6. 7; 10. 5; 17. 1; ii. 2, 3, 7: VII. ii. 7.
耳 = indeed, I. i. 8. 1 (?).

聘
p'ing

To invite or call forth men of worth by
presents, V. i. 7. 3, 4.

聖
shing

Sage (= 'great and capable of transforming'), VII. ii. 25. 7; sageness; a
sage, II. i. 1. 8; 2. 18, 19: III. ii. 9. 9, 10,
13: IV. ii. 1. 4: V. ii. 1. 5, 6, 7: VII. ii.
25. 7, 8. 聖人, II. i. 2. 17, 20, 22, 25,
28, *et al., saepe*.

聚
chü

To collect, to be collected, II. i. 1. 1: IV.
i. 1. 9; 9. 1.

聞
win

To hear; to become acquainted with
by report, I. i. 7. 1, 2, 4, 8, 16, 17; ii. 1.
4. 6. 7, *et al., saepissime*; information, I. i.
4. 6. 7, *et al., saepissime*. 多聞, extensive
information, V. ii. 7. 3. 多聞識, *id.*,
VI. ii. 13. 2.

聞
wăn

The 4th tone.   Reputation, notoriety,
IV. i. 1. 2; ii. 18. 3: VI. i. 17. 3.

聰
ts'ung

Acuteness of hearing, IV. i. 1. 1.

聲
shing

A sound; a voice, I. i. 7. 8; ii. 1. 6, 7:
II. i. 2. 4: III. i. 4. 13: V. ii. 1. 6: VI. i.
7. 6, 8; ii. 15. 3: VII. i. 14. 1; 36. 3.
聲音, I. i. 7. 16: VII. ii. 18. 8 (= language).
聲 = music, VII. ii. 22. 1; 37. 12. Reputation, II. i. 6. 3: IV. ii. 18. 3 (聲聞):
VII. i. 14. 1.

職
chih

An office; the duties of office, I. ii. 4. 5:
II. i. 4. 2; ii. 5. 5 (N.B.): V. i. 1. 2; ii. 3.
4: 6. 3; 7. 9 (N.B.): VI. ii. 7. 2.

聽
t'ing

To hear, to listen to; to hear and follow,
I. i. 7. 16; ii. 7. 4, 5: II. i. 11. 3: IV. i. 8.
3; 15. 2; ii. 3. 3, 4, *et al*. 聽政, to administer the government, IV. ii. 2. 1. Compare III. i. 2. 4.

THE 129TH RADICAL, 聿.

聿
yü

So,—a continuative particle, I. ii. 5. 5.
The dictionary, however, explains the
character here by 自, himself.

肆
sze

And so, though, VII. ii. 19. 3.

THE 130TH RADICAL, 肉.

肉
zău

Flesh, meat, I. i. 3. 4; 4. 4: 7. 8, 24:
III. ii. 5. 2; 9. 9; 10. 5: IV. i. 14. 2; 19.
3; ii. 33. 1: V. ii. 6. 4, 5: VI. ii. 6. 6: VII.
i. 22. 2, 3.

肖
hsiáo

不肖, not equal to, degenerate; incompetency, II. ii. 7. 1: IV. ii. 7. 1: V. i.
6. 2: VI. ii. 6. 2.

肢
chih

A limb. 四肢, VII. ii. 24. 1.

肥
fei

Fat (adj.), I. i. 4. 4: III. ii. 9. 9.   Rich
food, I. i. 7. 16. Rich, spoken of soil, VI.
i. 7. 2.

肩
chien

The shoulders, III. ii. 7. 4: VI. i. 14. 4.

育
yü

To cherish and train, VI. i. 7. 3: VII.
i. 20. 4. To be maintained and nourished,
III. i. 4. 8.

背
pei

The back, VI. i. 14. 4: VII. i. 21. 4.

脊
hsü

Mutually, I. ii. 4. 6; 5. 5: IV. i. 9. 6:
V. i. 1. 3 (N.B.)

胡
hú

A surname, I. i. 7. 4.

胷
hsiung

I. q. 胸.   The breast, IV. i. 15. 1.

脅
hsieh

The ribs. 脅 = to shrug up, III. ii. 7. 4.

脩
hsiū

I. q. 修, to cultivate, improve, I. i. 5.
3: VI. i. 16. 2, 3: VII. i. 1. 3; 9. 6; ii. 32.
1.   To repair, IV. ii. 31. 1. 脩 = to do,
I. ii. 4. 4.

能
năng

To be able; can.   As the auxiliary,
passim; but it is often used absolutely,
e.g. I. i. 7. 10, 11; ii. 16. 3: V. i. 9. 3, *et al.,
saepe*. 能 alone, and 能者, men of
ability, II. i. 4. 3; 5. 1.   Ability, VII. i.
15. 1. 能 = to amount to, V. ii. 2. 4.

腹
fú

The belly, IV. ii. 3. 1: VI. i. 14. 6: VII.
i. 27. 1.

膏
kāo

膏 = fat meat, VI. i. 17. 2. 膏澤,
rich favours, IV. ii. 3. 3, 4.

膚
fu

膚
ying

膾
kwti

膠
chiáo

臂
pei

(1) The skin, VI. i. 14. 1, 6. 體膚 and 膚 alone, = the body, II. i. 4 ; ii. 7. 4 : VI. ii. 15. 2. (2) Admirable, IV. i. 7. 5.

To smite, III. i. 4. 16 ; ii. 9. 12.

Minced meat, VII. ii. 36. 2.

A surname, II. i. 1. 8 : VI. ii. 15. 1.

The arm, the lower arm, VI. ii. 1. 8 ; VII. i. 39. 2 ; ii. 23. 2.

THE 131st RADICAL, 臣.

臣
ch'ên

臥
wo

臧
tsang

A minister, an officer of a court, I. i. 7. 14, 16 ; ii. 4. 10 ; 6. 1 ; 7. 1 ; 8. 2, *et al.*, *saepissime.* 君臣 in correlation often occur. In the first person, ‘ I, your minister,’ I. i. 7. 2, 4, 5, *et al.* In a wider sense, subjects, II. i. 1. 8 : III. ii. 5. 5. To employ as a minister, II. ii. 2. 8, 9, *et al.*

To rest, to sleep, II. ii. 11. 2, 3.

A surname, I. ii. 16. 1, 3.

THE 132nd RADICAL, 自.

自
tsze

臭
ch'ou

皋
kāo

(1) From, as a preposition, I. ii. 11. 2 : II. i. 2. 23, 27 ; 8. 2, *et al.* *saepissime.* According as, V. i. 5. 8. (2) Self, of all persons. Generally joined with verbs in a reflex sense. We have 自反自失, 自怨自艾, &c. &c., II. i. 2. 7 ; 4. 4, 5, 6 ; 6. 6 ; 9. 2, *et al., saepissime.* Observe 自爲, II. ii. 5. 3 : VI. ii. 6. 1.

Smells, odours, VII. ii. 24. 1.

皋陶, a minister of Shun, III. i. 4. 9, *et al.*

THE 133rd RADICAL, 至.

至
chih

致
chih

臺
t'ai

(1) To come, to arrive at ; sometimes = to, till, I. i. 3. 5 ; 7. 12 ; ii. 1. 6 : II. ii. 2. 4 ; 9. 1, *et al., saepissime.* 至於, to come to, as to, is very common ; e.g. I. ii. 2. 3 ; 9. 2 ; 10. 2 : VII. ii. 38. 1, 2, 3, 4, *et al.* (2) Most, forming the superlative degree ; the utmost degree, II. i. 2. 13 : IV. i. 2. 1 ; 12. 3, *et al.* Chief, II. i. 2. 9. (3) 日至, the solstice, IV. ii. 26. 3.

(1) To carry to the utmost degree, VI. ii. 14. 2, 3 : VII. i. 8. 1. 致志, VI. i. 9. 3. (2) To bring about by effort, V. i. 6. 2. 致 = to calculate, IV. ii. 26. 3. (3) To resign, II. ii. 5. 2 ; 10. 1.

(1) A tower, I. i. 2. 3, 4. 靈臺, the name of king Wan's tower, *ibid.* (2)

The designation of a low officer, a servant. V. ii. 6. 4.

A name, II. ii. 3. 1 ; VII. ii. 23. 1.

臻
chên

THE 134th RADICAL, 臼.

與
yü

與
yü

與
yü

興
hsing

(1) With, along with. *Passim.* E.g. I. i. 2. 3 ; ii. 1. 4, 6, 7, 8 : II. i. 9. 1, 2 ; ii. 2. 4, 5, 7 : VII. i. 13. 3 ; ii. 26. 2. Another preposition, as *from* or *to*, is sometimes required in our idiom. Observe 約與 國, VI. ii. 9. 2 ; and 與禽獸奚 擇哉, IV. ii. 28. 6. (2) And, I. i. 3. 3 ; 4. 2, 3 ; 7. 11, *et al., saepissime.* Sometimes it is better to translate by or, II. i. 1. 2 : VI. ii. 1. 1, 2, 6, 7, *et al.* (3) For, III. ii. 1. 4 : IV. i. 9. 1. (4) To give, to give to. I. i. 6. 5, 6 : V. i. 5. 1, 2, 3, 4, 5, 6, *et al., saepe.* (5) To help, II. i. 7. 5. (6) Than, V. i. 7. 4.

The 4th tone. To share in ; to be concerned about, III. i. 4. 11 : IV. ii. 31. 1 : V. ii. 1. 2 : VII. i. 20. 1, 5. VI. i. 18. 1 is marked with this tone, but Chū Hsī explains by 助, ‘ to assist,’ as in (5) above.

The 2nd tone. *Passim.* A final particle, interrogative, and also with exclamatory force. It implies generally that the speaker has a well-formed idea on the subject of the question in his own mind, and that he wishes to express his own surprise, or to involve an opponent in difficulty, I. i. 7. 4, 10, 12, 14, 16, 17 ; ii. 1. 4, 7 ; 5. 3 ; 7. 3 ; 16. 1, *et al., saepissime.*

(1) To arise, II. ii. 13. 3 : IV. i. 1. 9 : VI. i. 6. 2. (2) To rouse one's self, to be aroused, IV. i. 13. 1 : VII. i. 10 ; 22. 1 ; ii. 15 ; 37. 13. 興之, to raise itself—spoken of grain, I. i. 6. 6. (3) To raise, I. i. 7. 14. 興發, to open the granaries, I. ii. 4. 9. (4) To flourish, IV. i. 8. 6.

舉
chü

(1) To lift, to raise, I. i. 7. 10 : III. i. 5. 4 ; ii. 5. 7 : VI. ii. 2. 3. 舉 = to promote ; to be lifted up, promoted, III. i. 4. 7 : V. i. 9. 3 ; ii. 6. 4, 6 : VI. ii. 15. 1. 舉 = to allege, insist on, VII. i. 26. 4 ; ii. 37. 11. 舉 = to take, I. i. 7. 12. 舉 = to complete, I. ii. 10. 2. (2) All, I. ii. 1. 6, 7 : II. ii. 12. 5 : VI. i. 7. 3.

舊
chiü

Old, ancient, III. i. 3. 12 : IV. i. 1. 4. 舊 = former, IV. ii. 3. 2.

THE 135th RADICAL, 舌.

The tongue, III. i. 4. 14.

舌
shê

舍
shê

(1) To lodge in a booth, I. ii. 4. 9. 舍 館, a lodging house, IV. i. 24. 2. (2) Only, III. i. 4. 2 (? *N.B.*) (3) A name, II. i. 2. 5, 6, 8.

舍
shè

(1) To neglect, pass over, I. ii. 7. 2; 9. 1, 2: II. i. 2. 16, 21; 13. 5 (= besides). 舍己, to give up his own views, II. i. 8. 3. To give over, to cease, IV. ii. 18. 2. (2) To let go, I. i. 7. 4: V. i. 2. 4. (3) To discharge, as arrows, III. ii. 1. 4. The dictionary gives this instance under the 3rd tone.

The name of a State, III. i. 4.16; ii.9.12.

舒
shū

THE 136TH RADICAL, 舛.

舜
shun

The ancient emperor, so called, II. i. 2. 26; 8. 3; ii. 2. 4, _et passim._

舞
_wu_

To make postures, 手之舞之, IV. i. 27. 2.

THE 137TH RADICAL, 舟.

般
_p'an_

To be abandoned to pleasure, 般樂, II. i. 4. 4: VII. ii. 34. 2. Read without the aspirate, it is the name of Yen Hûi's son, V. ii. 3. 3.

THE 138TH RADICAL, 艮.

良
liang

(1) Good, III. ii. 1. 4: IV. i. 15. 1: VI. i. 8. 3 (良心, the good natural heart); 17. 1; ii. 9. 1, 2. 良 = intuitive, VI. i. 15. 1. (2) 良人, the goodman, a husband, IV. ii. 33. 1. (3) A name, III. ii. 1. 4.

THE 139TH RADICAL, 色.

色
_sè_

(1) The countenance, the looks, I. i. 4. 4; ii. 1. 2, 7: III. ii. 7. 4; 9. 9: V. ii. 2, 4: VI. ii. 15. 3: VII. ii. 11. 像色, II. ii. 13. 1; 顔色, VI. ii. 13. 8. (2) Colour, colours; sights, I. i. 7. 16: VI. i. 1. 1: VI. i. 4. 1; 7. 8: VII. ii. 24. 1. (3) The appetite of sex, VI. ii.1. 2, 7. Beautiful women—a euphemism, I. ii. 6. 5: V. i. 4, 5. Observe VII. i. 21. 4, where 色 = manifestations; and 38, where it functions.

艴
_po_

艴然, flushed-like, II. i. 1. 3.

THE 140TH RADICAL, 艸.

艾
_ai_

(1) The mugwort, or moxa, IV. i. 9. 5. (2) Beautiful, 少艾, beautiful young women, V. i. 1. 5. (3) To rule, to correct, V. i. 6. 5: VII. i. 11. 5. In this sense, it is interchanged with 乂, and should be read i.

芥
chieh

The mustard plant. But it is used as simply = grass, IV. i. 28. 1; ii. 8. 1.

芒
mang

芒芒然, tired-like. ? Stupid-like, II. i. 2. 16.

芸
yün

I.q. 耘. To weed, VII. ii. 32. 3.

芻
_ch'ü_

(1) Grass, pasturage, II. i. 4. 3. 芻者, grass-cutters, I. ii. 2. 2. 負芻, grass-carriers, IV. ii. 31. 1. (2) The flesh of grass-fed animals, VI. i. 7. 8.

苗
miáo

(1) Growing corn, I. i. 6. 6: II. i. 2. 16: VII. ii. 37. 12. (2) 三苗, the name of an ancient State, near the Tung-t'ing lake, V. i. 3. 2.

A pig-pen, VII. ii. 26. 2.

苟
_li_
kóu

(1) If, I. i. 1. 4; 7. 20; ii. 14. _et al., saepe._ (2) Improper, without some apparent cause, VI. i. 10. 2; ii. 6. 6.

若
_zo_

(1) As, such as; to be as (i. e. like, and sometimes equal to), I. i. 7. 4, 16, 17, 18, _et passim._ As if; seeming to be, I. i. 7. 6: II. i. 9. 1; ii. 2. 5, _et al., saepe_ 宜若...然, 'may rightly be deemed to be so,' occurs several times. As to, I. i. 7. 20; ii. 14. 3; II. i. 8. 5: VII. ii. 38. 1, 2, 3, _et al., passim._ 乃若, IV. ii. 28. 7: VI. i. 6. 5. 不若, 莫若, 豈若...哉, all = is it not the better plan to..., I. ii. 1. 4: IV. i. 7. 4: V. i. 7. 3, 4. 相若, III. i. 4. 17. 辟若, VII. i. 29. (2) If, I. i. 7. 7; ii. 11. 3, _et al., saepe._ (3) = to conform to virtue, V. i. 4. 4. (4) The name of one of Confucius's disciples, II. i. 2. 25, 28, _et al._

To embitter, to be embittered, I. i. 7. 22: VI. ii. 15. 2.

苦
_k'u_

Surpassing, the first among a thousand, VII. i. 20. 4.

英
ying

Vigorous-looking, V. ii. 5. 4.

苗
chü

暢茂, luxuriant, III. i. 4. 7.

茂
màu

The name of a city of Ch'i, VII. i. 36. 1.

范
fan

Coarse, wild grass, III. i. 8. 2: VII. ii. 21. 1 (_N. B._)

茅
miáu

This, these, II. ii. 12. 1: III. ii. 8. 1 (今兹): VII. ii. 19. 2

兹
tsze

To eat, VII. ii. 6.

茹
_ju_

The name of a rude tribe or State, III. i. 4. 16; ii. 9. 12.

荆
ching

Grass, III. i. 2. 4. 草木 = vegetation, III. i. 4. 7. 草萊, see 萊. 草芥, IV. i. 28. 1. 草莽, see 莽. 草木 = herbs, VII. ii. 6.

草
_ts'áo_

A kind of spurious grain. 黄稊, VI. i. 19.

黄
_ti_

荒
huang
(1) 荒蕪, overgrown with grass and weeds, VI. ii. 7. 2. (2) Wild, ruinously addicted to hunting, I. ii. 4. 6, 7, 8.

荏
li
To come forth and descend to. 荏 = to govern. I. i. 7. 16.

莊
chwang
(1) A surname, I. ii. 1. 1, 2. (2) The name of a street in the capital of Ch'í, III. ii. 6. 1.

莒
chü
The name of an ancient State, I. ii. 3. 6.

莘
hsin
An ancient name for the territory of 虢 in the time of Châu, V. i. 7. 2.

莠
yü
A useless plant growing amid corn, and like it. ? Darnel, VII. ii. 37. 12.

莩
p'iào
I. q. 殍. To die. 餓莩, I. i. 3. 5; 4. 4; III. ii. 4. 9.

莫
mo
(1) Not; not to be, not to have, i.q. 無, I. i. 5. 1; ii. 12. 1; II. i. 8. 5; ii. 2. 4, 9, *et al., saepissime.* Often it = no one, and in this case it generally attracts the object of the following verb to itself, I. i. 7. 3; ii. 12. 2: II. i. 1. 10; 2. 27; 7. 2: III. i. 3. 14; 4. 17, *et al., saepe.* 莫不 and 莫非 are strong affirmations, = there is nothing (or none) but..., I. i. 6. 6: II. i. 1. 8: IV. i. 20; ii. 5, *et al.* 莫若, see 若. So 莫如, II. i. 4. 2; 7. 4, *et al.* (2) 子莫, a worthy and thinker of Lû, VII. i. 26. 3.

莽
mang
莽 = grass, plants, V. ii. 7. 1.

菑
tsái
I.q. 災. Calamities, IV. i. 8. 1.

菜
ts'ái
Vegetables, V. ii. 3. 4.

菹
tsü
Grassy marshes. ? Bogs, III. ii. 9. 4.

菽
shû
Pulse, VII. i. 23. 3.

萃
ts'ui
A grassy level, II. i. 2. 28.

萊
lái
(1) Fields lying fallow; commons, IV. i. 14. 3. (2) A surname, VII. ii. 38. 2.

萌
mǎng
Buds; to bud, VI. i. 8. 1; 9. 2.

華
hwá
The 4th tone. A surname, VI. ii. 6. 5.

萬
wan
(1) Ten thousand, I. i. 1. 4; ii. 9. 2; 10. 2, 4: II. i. 1. 13; 2. 4. 7; ii. 10. 3, 5: III. i. 4. 18; ii. 10. 5: VI. i. 10. 7; ii. 10. 3. In several of these examples, the phrase is 萬乘之國, applicable properly only to the royal domain, but used pre-tentiously of the great fiefs. 萬 = all, VII. i. 4. 1. (2) A surname. 萬章, III. ii. 5. 1 : V. i. 1. 1, 2, *et al., saepe.*

落
lo
To descend, 徂落 = to decease, V. i. 4. 1.

著
chú
(1) To be manifested, III. ii. 9. 9. (2) To know clearly, VII. i. 5.

葛
ko
The name of an ancient State. 葛 and 葛伯, I. ii. 3. 1; II. 2: III. ii. 5. 2, 4.

葵
k'wei
葵丘, the name of a place, VI. ii. 7. 3.

葬
tsang
To bury, inter, II. ii. 7. 1: III. i. 5. 2; 5. 2, 4.

蒙
mèng
(1) To wear on the head, IV. ii. 25. 1. (2) A name. 逢蒙, IV. ii. 24. 1; 咸丘蒙, V. i. 4. 1, 2.

蒸
chêng
(1) All, 蒸民, VI. i. 6. 8. (2) I.q. 烝, to steam, III. ii. 7. 2.

蓋
kái
(1) To cover, V. i. 2. 3. (2) A particle, continuative and sometimes illative, I. i. 7. 17; ii. 4. 9: III. i. 5. 4: V. ii. 3. 4; 6. 4.

蓋
kái
The name of a place, II. ii. 6. 1: III. ii. 10. 5.

蓰
hsi
Five times, fivefold, III. i. 4. 18: VI. i. 6. 7.

蔡
ts'âi
The name of a State, VII. ii. 18.

蔽
pi
To obscure, cloud over, keep in the shade, II. i. 2. 17: VI. i. 15. 2.

蕘
záo
蕘者, fuel-gatherers, I. ii. 2. 2.

蕢
k'wei
A straw-basket, VI. i. 7. 4.

蕩
t'ang
Great, 蕩蕩乎, how vast! III. i. 4. 11.

蕪
wú
Overgrown with woods. 荒蕪, see 荒.

薄
po
Thin. 薄 = mean, shabby, V. ii. 1. 3: VII. i. 44. 1; ii. 15. 1. 薄 = slight, IV. ii. 24. 1. 薄 = a spare simplicity, III. i. 5. 2. 薄 = to make light, I. i. 5. 3: VII. i. 23. 1.

薛
Hsieh
(1) The name of a State, I. ii. 14. 1 : II. ii. 3. 1, 4. (2) A surname, III. ii. 6. 2.

廩
chien
To present, to introduce, V. i. 5. 5, 6; 6. 1, 2.

薪
hsin
(1) Firewood, I. i. 7. 10: VI. i. 18. 1. 采薪之憂 = 'a little sickness,' II. ii. 2. 3. (2) Grass, plants, IV. ii. 31. 1.

薨
hwang
The death of a prince, III. i. 2. 1, 4.

藉
tsǐ

藉 =mutual dependence, a borrowing of services, III. i. 3. 6.

藏
tsang

To lay up, to deposit, I. i. 7. 18: II. i. 5. 2: V. i. 3. 2.

菠
miǎo

To despise, VII. ii. 34. 1.

藝
i

I.q. 蓻 樹藝, to cultivate, III. i. 4. 18.

藥
yo

Physic, III. i. 1. 5.

蘇
sū

To revive, I. ii. 11. 2.

藍
lo

A kind of basket, III. i. 5. 4.

THE 141st RADICAL, 虍.

虎
hǔ

(1) A tiger, III. ii. 9. 6 : VII. ii. 23. 2. 虎賁 =life-guards, VII. ii. 4. 4. (2) A name, III. i. 3. 5.

虐
nio

To oppress, tyrannize over ; oppressive, I. ii. 4. 6 ; II. 3 : II. i. 1. 11 : III. i. 3. 7.

處
ch'u

The 3rd tone, a verb. (1) To reside in, to dwell, III. ii. 10. 5 : V. i. 7. 3. 4; ii. 1. 1, 3 : VI. ii. 6. 5 : VII. i. 35. 6. Observe 處守, VI. ii. 5. 1. 處室, IV. ii. 33. 1. 處仁, to dwell in love, V. i. 6. 5 ; but the same in II. i. 7. 2 is different. (2) To live in retirement ; unemployed, III. ii. 9. 9 : V. ii. 1. 4. (3) 處子, an unmarried daughter, VI. ii. 1. 8. (4) To manage as business, an occasion for, II. ii. 3. 5.—In, III. i. 4. 1, 與之處 'gave him a place to reside in,' perhaps 處 is the 3rd tone.

虛
hsü

Empty, VII. ii. 12. 1. Used adverbially, VII. i. 37. 3.

虞
yü

(1) 驩虞如, joyful and pleasant-like, VII. i. 13. 1. (2) To measure, to reckon. 不虞, unexpected, that cannot be reckoned on, IV. i. 21. (3) 虞人, a forester, III. ii. 1. 2 : V. ii. 7. 5, 6, 7. (4) 虞 =Shun,—said in the dictionary to be the surname that arose from him, V. i. 6. 7. (5) The name of a State, V. i. 9. 2 : VI. ii. 6. 4. 虞公, V. i. 9. 3. (6) A name, II. ii. 7. 1 ; 13. 1.

號
hao

A name or mark. 號 =argument, VI. ii. 4. 4.

號
hao

The 1st tone. To cry out. 號泣, V. i. 1. 1, 2.

號
ho

The name of a State, V. i. 9. 2.

THE 142nd RADICAL, 虫.

蚋
zui

蚋 =蜹 abbreviated. A gnat, III. i. 5. 4.

蚓
yin

An earthworm, III. ii. 10. 2, 3, 6.

蚤
tsǎo

Interchanged with 早. Early in the morning, IV. ii. 33. 1.

蛇
shé

A snake, III. ii. 9. 3, 4.

蚳
ch'ih

A surname, II. ii. 5. 1, 2, 3. But the dictionary does not mention the character as such.

螬
ts'ao

Dung-worms, III. ii. 10. 1.

蠅
ying

A fly, III. i. 5. 4.

蠹
tù

An insect that eats through wood. 蠹 =the appearance of being worn away, VII. ii. 22. 2.

蠶
tsan

The silkworm. To keep silkworms, III. ii. 3. 3. To nourish silkworms on, VII. i. 22. 2.

蠻
man

The wild tribes of the South, III. i. 4. 14.

THE 143rd RADICAL, 血.

血
hsiéh

Blood, VI. ii. 7. 3 : VII. ii. 3. 3.

THE 144th RADICAL, 行.

行
hsing

(1) To go ; to set out ; to proceed, I. ii. 4. 6 : II. i. 1. 12, et al., sæpe. To make to go, to lead, VI. i. 2. 3 ; ii. 14. 2. To advance, in contrast with 止, 'to stop,' I. ii. 16. 3. 行潦, rain-pools, II. i. 2. 28. 補行, to assist on the journey, or expedition, II. ii. 6. 1. (2) To do, perform ; to carry out, to practise ; to be practised, carried out, I. i. 4. 5; 7. 9, 23; ii. 5. 2, 4; 9. 1, et al., sæpe. This meaning is kindred to the above, and derived from it. The way regulates the conduct. 行道, 'to carry out principles,' often occurs, but 行道之人, VI. i. 10. 6, is literally 'a tramper.' Observe the two meanings in IV. ii. 19. 2 —Observe also 行, 佛, VI. ii. 16. 2; 行乎, IV. ii. 1. 3, and II. i. 1. 3; 與有行, V. i. 9. 3; 足以行矣, 而不不行, and 行可, V. ii. 4. 6, 7. (3) A name, III. i. 4. 1, 3.— IV. ii. 31. 1.

行
hsing

The 4th tone. Actions, conduct ;— always as a noun, I. ii. 4. 8 : II. i. 2, 18 : III. ii. 9. 5, 7, 13 : IV. ii. 11 : V. i. 5. 4, 5; 7. 7 : VI. ii. 2. 5 : VII. i. 16. 1 ; ii. 33. 2 ; 37. 6, 9. Medhurst, Williams, and Wade give the pronunciation as here represented; but according to K'ang-hsi's dictionary, it should be expressed by *hâng.*

行 hang — The 2nd tone. 公行, a double surname, IV. ii. 27. 1.

衍 yen — A name, III. ii. 3. 1.

術 shü — An art, a contrivance, L. i. 7. 8 : VI. ii. 16 : VII. i. 18. 1 ; 24. 2. 術 =a profession, II. i. 7. 1.

衞 wei — The name of a State, IV. ii. 24. 2 ; 31. 2 ; V. i. 8. 1, 2, 3. 衞靈公, and 孝公, V. ii. 4. 7.

衡 hâng — L.q. 橫. Crosswise. 衡=disorderly ; perplexed, I. ii. 3. 7 : VI. ii. 15. 3.

THE 145TH RADICAL, 衣.

衣 i — Clothes ; robes, II. i. 9. 1 : III. i. 4. 8 ; ii. 9. 5 : V. ii. 1. 1 ; VII. ii. 6. 衣服, III. ii. 3. 3 : VII. i. 36. 2. 衣=grave-clothes, I. ii. 16. 2.

衣 i — The 4th tone. To wear. I. i. 3. 4 ; 7. 24 : III. i. 4. 1, 4 : VII. i. 22. 2.

襄 shuai — To decay, become small and feeble, III. ii. 9. 5, 7 : V. i. 6. 1 : VI. ii. 14. 2, 3.

衾 ch'in — A shroud, I. ii. 16. 2.

袒 t'an — To strip up the sleeve, to bare the arm, 袒裼, II. i. 9. 2 : V. ii. 1. 3.

袗 ch'ên — Embroidered robes, VII. ii. 6.

被 p'i — The 4th tone. To be covered with. 被 = to be affected by, to receive, IV. i. 1. 2 : V. i. 7. 6 ; ii. 1. 2. 被 = to wear, to have to wear, VII. ii. 6.

被 p'i — The 2nd tone. L.q. 披. 被髮, the hair dishevelled, unbound, IV. ii. 20. 5, 6.

裳 ch'ia — A name, V. ii. 3. 2.

裎 ch'êng — Naked. 裸裎, II. i. 9. 2 : V. ii. 1. 3.—There must be a difference in the meaning of the two terms, but I have not found it indicated.

裕 yü — Abundance of clothes ; abundance generally. 有餘裕='yea, and more,' II. ii. 5. 5.

補 pu — To mend clothes. To mend or repair generally ; to supply ; to assist, I. i. 4. 5, 10 : III. i. 1. 5 ; ii. 4. 3 : VI. i. 7. 2 : VII. i. 18. 3 (*N.B.*)

裸 lo — Naked. 裸裎, see 裎.

襄 kuo — To tie or wrap up, I. ii. 5. 4.

裼 hsi — To put off the upper garment. 袒 裼 see 袒.

褊 pien — Narrow. 褊小, I. i. 7. 6 : III. i. 3. 14.

褐 ho — Cloth of hair ; coarse cloth, II. i. 2. 4, 7 : III. i. 4. 1, 4.

襄 hsiang — (1) An honorary epithet. 梁襄 王, I. i. 6. 1. (2) 子襄, the designation of a disciple of Tsäng Shän, II. i. 2. 7.

襲 hsi — To take by surprise, II. i. 2. 15 (*N.B.*)

THE 146TH RADICAL, 西.

西 hsi — (1) The west ; on the west ; western, I. i. 5. 1 ; ii. 5. 5 ; II. i. 3. 2 : VI. i. 2, 1, 3 : ii. 6. 5. 西伯, the chief of the West-king Wän, IV. i. 13. 1 : VII. i. 22. 1, 3. 西夷, I. ii. 11. 2 : III. ii. 5. 4 ; IV. ii. 1. 2 : VII. ii. 4. 3. (2) 西子, a famous beauty, IV. ii. 25. 1. (3) Part of the designation of the grandson of Tsäng Shän, II. i. 1. 3, 4.

要 yäo — The 1st tone. (1) To seek for, II. ii. 6. 3 : VI. i. 16. 3. 要=to seek an introduction to, V. i. 7. 1, 8 ; 9. 1. (2) 要=to intercept, II. ii. 2. 3 : III. ii. 5. 2 : V. i. 8. 3.

覆 fü — (1) 反覆, repeatedly ; to repeat. V. ii. 9. 1, 4 : VI. i. 8. 2. (2) 顛覆, to overturn, VI. i. 6. 5.

覆 füu — To cover, overspread, III. i. 1. 5.

THE 147TH RADICAL, 見.

見 chien — To see. *Passim.* 望見, to see from a distance, VII. i. 36. 1 ; ii. 23. 2. Very often it=to visit, e.g. I. i. 1. 1 : II. ii. 10. 2 : III. ii. 7. 1, 2, 3. 見於..., to have an interview with—spoken of a ruler. V. ii. 7. 4. It forms the passive voice, III. ii. 5. 5 : VII. ii. 29.

見 hsien — (1) To appear, to be seen, II. ii. 12. 6 : III. i. 5. 2 : VII. i. 21. 4 ; 2. 11. (2) To become illustrious, VII. i. 9. 6. (3) To have an interview with, an audience of ..., I. ii. 1. 1, 2 ; 16. 2 : II. ii. 4. 4 ; 6. 1 : V. i. 4. 4 (*N.B.*)

規 k'wei — A compass, the instrument so called. IV. i. 1. 1, 5 ; 2. 1 : VI. i. 20. 2 : VII. ii. 5. 1.

視 shih — To regard, to look at,—often=to consider, II. i. 2, 4, 5 : IV. ii. 3. 1 ; 20. 3, et al. To see, I. ii. 3. 5 ; 12. 1 : V. ii. 1. 1 ; 7. 8, et al. 視朝, to hold a court, to give audience, II. ii. 2. 1. 視=equal to, V. ii. 2. 5.

覘 ti — To see, VI. ii. 6. 5.

親
ch'in

(1) To love, show affection to, I. ii. 12. 3: III. i. 5. 3: IV. i. 11. 1, *et al.*, *saepe.* Mutual affection, III. i. 2. 2; 8. 18 (親睦); 4. 8. To be loved, IV. i. 4. 1. (2) To be near, to approach, II. ii. 7. 4: VII. ii. 15. To touch one another, IV. i. 12. 1. Intimate, I. ii. 7. 1. (3) In person, personally, V. i. 7. 4: VI. ii. 1. 3. (4) Relatives. Very often it is used of *parents*, I. i. 1. 5: II. ii. 7. 5: IV. i. 11; 12. 1; 19. 1, 2, 4, *et al.* But it is also used more widely, VII. i. 34; 45; ii. 7. 親戚, II. i. 1. 4, 5.

覲
chin

To wait on a superior, to appear at court, 朝覲, V. i. 5. 1; 6. 1.

覘
chien

A name, III. i. 1. 4.

覺
chiao

To understand, apprehend; to make to understand, to instruct, V. i. 7. 5; ii. 1. 2.

觀
kuan

To view, contemplate; to discern, II. i. 2. 26; 6. 4; ii. 7. 2: III. i. 2. 5; 8. 9; ii. 7. 4: IV. i. 14. 2; 15. 2; ii. 33. 2: V. i. 8. 4: VII. i. 24. 1, 2. To make a visit of inspection, I. ii. 4. 4.

THE 148TH RADICAL, 角.

角
chiao

(1) A horn, VII. ii. 4. 5. (2) 角招, the name of a piece of music, I. ii. 4. 10.

解
chieh

To remove, II. ii. 9. 2 (N.B.): V. i. 1. 4. To relieve, to unloose, II. i. 1. 13.

觫
su

觳觫, the appearance of fearing death, I. i. 7. 4, 6.

觳
hu

See above.

THE 149TH RADICAL, 言.

言
yen

A word, words; a saying, I. ii. 3. 4; 5. 4, *et passim.* To speak, say; to speak of, I. i. 7. 9, 16; ii. 1. 5; 6. 3, *et saepissime.* 言語, VII. ii. 33. 2. 言 = to mean, meaning, I. i. 6. 12: VI. i. 17. 3. 爲言 = means, VII. ii. 4. 6; but in VII. i. 24. 1 the same phrase = to think anything of the words of others. 言 = to cherish, think of, II. ii. 4. 1, *et al.* This usage is only found in some quotations from the Shih-ching. 有言, to have a saying, or to say, *saepe.* But in IV. i. 10. 1 it = to have speech.

計
chi

To calculate, V. ii. 5. 4.

討
t'ao

To punish; to order to be punished, VI. ii. 7. 2. To put to death, III. ii. 9. 6.

訕
(i)

訕訕, the appearance of being self-conceited, VI. ii. 18. 8.

訓
hsün

(1) To instruct, V. i. 6. 5. (2) 伊訓, the name of a Book in the Shû-ching, V. i. 7. 9.

訕
shan

To revile, IV. ii. 33. 1.

託
t'o

To entrust, I. ii. 6. 1. 託 = to accept a stated support from, V. ii. 6. 1.

訟
sung

To contend, wrangle. 訟獄者, litigants, V. i. 5. 7; 6. 1.

訢
yin

訢然, cheerfully, VII. i. 85. 6.

設
shê

To establish, 設爲, III. i. 8. 10. 設科, to institute instruction, VII. ii. 30. 2. 設心, to settle in one's mind, IV. ii. 30. 5.

許
hsü

(1) To allow, to accede to, I. i. 7. 10. To promise, II. i. 1. 1. (2) A surname, III. i. 4. 1, 3, 4, 5, 17, 18.

詖
pi

One-sided, only half the truth, II. i. 2. 17: III. ii. 9. 13.

試
shih

To try. 嘗試, to try to follow, I. i. 7. 19. 試劍, sword-exercise, III. i. 2. 4.

詩
shih

A piece of poetry; an ode. Generally, with reference to some piece of the Shih-ching, I. ii. 4. 10: II. i. 4. 3: IV. ii. 21. 1: V. i. 4. 2; ii. 8. 2: VII. i. 6. 8; ii. 3. 1, 2. 詩云 and 詩曰 are the forms of quotation from the Shih-ching. *Passim.*

詭
kuei

Deceitful; deceitfully, III. ii. 1. 4.

詳
hsiang

(1) Particulars, V. ii. 2. 2: VI. ii. 4. 4. Minutely, IV. ii. 15. 1. (2) A name, II. ii. 11. 3.

誅
chu

To cut off, to put to death, I. ii. 8. 3; 12. 1: III. ii. 9. 6: V. i. 3. 2; 7. 9; ii. 4, 5: VI. ii. 7. 3.

誓
shih

湯誓 and 太誓 are the names of Books in the Shû-ching, I. i. 2. 4. — III. ii. 5. 6: V. i. 5. 8.

語
yü

言語, words, VII. ii. 33. 2. A saying, V. i. 4. 1. 語 = speech, language, III. ii. 6. 1.

語
yü

To tell, speak to about . . . , I. i. 6. 2; 7. 11; ii. 1, 2: II. ii. 11. 3; 12. 1: VII. i. 9. 1.

誣
wu

To delude, III. ii. 9. 9.

誦
sung

To repeat, croon over, VI. ii. 2. 5. To relate, II. ii. 4. 4.

誨
hui

To instruct, to teach, VI. i. 9. 3; 20. 2; ii. 16 (教誨).

誠
ch'êng

(1) To be sincere; sincerity, IV. i. 12. 1, 2 (N.B.), 3: VII. i. 4. 2. (2) Really, truly, indeed, I. i. 6. 6; 7. 6, 7, 11: II. i. 1. 2; 8. 2; ii. 12. 7: III. i. 2. 5; 4. 3; 5. 4: V. i. 2. 4; 4. 1.

說 *shwo*
To speak of, discuss, III. ii. 9. 10 (說者): IV. ii. 15. 說辭, II. i. 2. 18. To explain, explanation, V. i. 4. 2; ii. 4. 5. Speakings, =doctrines, III. ii. 9. 5, 7, 9, 13.

說 *shúi*
To counsel, V. i. 7. 6: VI. i. 4. 3, 4, 5, 6: VII. ii. 34. 1.

說 *yüeh*
Lq. 悅 To be pleased, I. i. 7. 9; ii. 4. 10 (傳說, see 傳)

誰 *shûi*
Who, whom, I. i. 5. 5; 6. 6: II. i. 4. 3; ii. 13. 5: III. ii. 6. 2, et al.

諂 *ch'an*
Abbreviated for 讇. To flatter; flatteringly, III. ii. 7. 4: VI. i. 13. 8.

諄 *chun*
諄諄然, repeatedly and specifically, V. i. 5. 3.

談 *t'an*
To talk with, converse, IV. ii. 33. 1: VI. ii. 3. 2.

論 *lun*
To discuss, to consider, V. ii. 8. 2.

請 *ch'ing*
To request, to beg; to beg leave. Sometimes, especially in the first person, it is merely a polite way of expressing a purpose, I. i. 3. 2; 5. 6; 7. 13, 19; ii. 1. 5; 3. 5; 15. 3; 16. 1, et al., saepe. Observe II. ii. 10. 2; 11. 3: V. ii. 4. 3.

諛 *yü*
To flatter, 面諛之人, sycophants, VI. ii. 13. 8.

諫 *ch'ien*
To reprove, to remonstrate; admonitions. It is often followed by 於, II. ii. 6. 2; 12. 6: IV. ii. 3. 3, 4: V. i. 9. 2, 3; ii. 9. 1, 4.

諱 *hûi*
To avoid, to conceal, VII. ii. 36. 2.

諺 *yen*
A common saying, I. ii. 4. 5.

諾 *no*
A reply, affirmative and immediate, I. ii. 16. 1: II. ii. 2. 5.

諸 *chû*
(1) Not merely one; all, I. i. 7. 16; ii. 7. 4, 5: II. ii. 10. 3. (2) A preposition. In, from, on, to, &c., I. i. 7. 12; ii. 7. 5, et al., saepissime. (3) As an interrogative, generally, 諸=之乎. Yet once we have the 乎 expressed, V. i. 8. 1; and 諸 remains=之, which it is in II. ii. 12. 4, where there is no interrogation, I. i. 7. 4; ii. 1. 2. 1; 5. 1 (N.B.); 8. 1, et al., saepissime. (4) 諸侯, see 侯 (5) 諸馮, the name of a place, IV. ii. 1. 1.

謀 *mâu*
To consult, take counsel, I. ii. 11. 1, 4. A counsel, a plan, I. ii. 13. 2. Counselling, II. ii. 2. 7.

謂 *wei*
(1) To address, to say to, I. ii. 5. 1; 6. 1; 10. 2: II. i. 2. 7, 16; ii. 4. 1; 5. 1; 10. 3, et al., saepissime. To tell to, to inform, III. ii. 1. 4. (2) To say; to speak of, I. i. 6. 17: II. i. 6. 3, 6, et al., saepe. 謂 = to suppose, III. ii. 6. 2. (3) To call; to be called, I. i. 2. 3; ii. 4. 7; 8. 3: VII. ii. 37. 3, 4, 5, 8, et passim. Observe 之謂 which occurs continually, e.g. I. i. 7. 9: II. i. 3. 2; 4. 6: VII. ii. 25, 2, 3, 4, 5, 6, 7, 8. Sometimes, where 之謂, followed by a particle, terminates the sentence, we can explain the characters without insisting on a peculiar idiom. At other times we can explain them by understanding 所 before 謂; but in a multitude of cases we have simply to accept the idiom. 謂之, which also is frequent. is different. 謂=to mean, meaning, II. ii. 2. 6: VI. i. 7. 8, et al. 何謂, what do you mean, what is meant, II. i. 2. 17: III. i. 5. 3: IV. i. 24. 2, et al.—Observe I. ii. 7. 1: VI. i. 1. 6.

To plan; plans, III. ii. 9. 6: V. i. 2. 3.

謨 *mû* / 謳 *du*
To sing,—in some peculiar, abrupt manner, VI. ii. 6. 5. 謳歌, to sing (active and neuter), V. i. 5. 6; 6. 1.

謹 *chin*
To give careful attention to, I. i. 3. 4; 7. 24.

譈 *túi*
To detest, V. ii. 4. 4.

譏 *chi*
To inspect. 譏而不征, I. ii. 5. 3: II. i. 5. 3.

識 *shih*
To know, I. i. 7. 4; ii. 7. 2: II. ii. 2. 1, 3; 10. 2; 12. 1: V. i. 2. 3; 4. 1; ii. 6. 4: VI. i. 4. 3; 10. 7, 8; ii. 6. 5, 6. To understand, VI. ii. 8. 4. 多聞識, of much information, VI. ii. 13. 2.

警 *ching*
To warn, III. ii. 9. 3.

譬 *p'i*
To compare, 譬則..., V. ii. 1. 7.

議 *i*
To discuss, indulge in discussions, III. ii. 9. 9.

譽 *yü*
Praise, IV. i. 21: VI. i. 17. 3.

讀 *tû*
To read, V. ii. 8. 2.

變 *pien*
To change; to be changed, I. ii. 1. 2; II. i. 11. 1. 8; ii. 14. 2: III. i. 4. 12, 16; ii. 5. 4: V. ii. 9. 2: VI. ii. 6. 5; 9. 3: VII. i. 7. 2 (=versatile); 41. 2; ii. 14. 3, 4.

讒 *ch'an*
To calumniate, VI. ii. 13. 8. To revile, I. ii. 4. 6.

讐 *ch'au*
(1) An enemy, IV. ii. 8. 1, 4. (2) 復讐, to avenge, III. ii. 5. 3. (3) In a name, V. i. 8. 2.—The character is also written 讎

賜
ts'ze

To give, present a gift; a gift, III. ii. 7. 3: V. ii. 4, 2, 5. 賜 = to give pay, and 賜於 . . ., to receive pay, V. ii. 6. 3.

賢
hsien

(1) Admirable, possessed of talents and virtue; to be talented and virtuous; the possession of talents and virtue. *Passim*, E. g. I. ii. 7. 3, 4; 16. 1: II. i. 4, 2; 5. 1; 9. 2. As a verb, = to praise, IV. ii. 29. 1. (2) To surpass, be superior, II. i. 1. 3; 2. 6, 26.

賤
chien

Mean; a mean condition, III. ii. 2. 3 (貧賤): VI. i. 14. 2, 3. 賤 = bad, the worst, III. ii. 1. 4. As a verb, to consider mean; to make mean, II. ii. 10. 7: III. i. 5. 2; ii. 3. 6: VI. i. 14. 5; 17. 2.

賦
fu

To exact, IV. i. 14. 1. To pay a tax, III. i. 3. 15.

質
chi

A pledge, an introductory present, III. ii. 3. 1, 4: V. ii. 7. 1.

賴
lai

To depend on, = be good, VI. i. 7. 1.

贍
sham

To avail for, be adequate to, I. i. 7. 22: II. i. 8. 2.

贐
chin

A gift to a traveller for the expenses of his journey, II. ii. 3. 3.

THE 155TH RADICAL, 赤.

赤
ch'ih

赤子, an infant, III. i. 5. 3. 赤子之心, the child-heart, IV. ii. 12.

赧
nan

赧赧然, red and blushingly, III. ii. 7. 4.

赫
hè

To blaze with anger, I. ii. 3. 6.

THE 156TH RADICAL, 走.

走
tsau

To run; to run to, I. i. 3. 2: IV. i. 9. 2. To gallop, I. ii. 5. 5. 走獸, quadrupeds, II. i. 2. 28.

赴
fu

To come, I. i. 7. 18.

起
ch'i

To arise; to rise, II. i. 2. 17: III. i. 3. 11; ii. 9. 10: IV. ii. 33. 1: VII. i. 25. 1, 2. To begin with, II. i. i. 8. 與起, to be aroused, VII. ii. 15.

超
chāo

To leap over, I. i. 7. 11.

越
yüeh

(1) To go beyond, exceed with, I. ii. 3. 7. (2) 越 = to roll over (顚越), V. ii. 4. 4. (3) The name of a State, IV. ii. 31. 1. 越人, VI. ii. 3. 2.

趙
chāo

The name of a part of Tsin, and the clan name of its chief, VI. i. 17. 2. In III. ii. 1. 4, 趙簡子 is, perhaps, 'the officer Chien of Chāo.'

趨
ch'ü

To run, to hasten, II. i. 2. 10, 16; ii. 2 3: VII. ii. 23. 2. 其趨, their aim, VI. ii. 6. 2.

THE 157TH RADICAL, 足.

足
tsü

(1) The foot, IV. i. 8. 2, 3; ii. 3. 1: VI. i. 7. 4. (2) To be sufficient; enough, I. i. 7. 5, 10, 12, 16, 21, 22; *et passim*. May sometimes be conveniently translated by 'to be able,' e. g. VII. i. 22. 2. 足 = abundant, VII. i. 23. 3. 饜足, to satisfy one's self, IV. ii. 33. 1. As a verb, 不我足, do not count me sufficient to . . ., III. i. 2. 4.

跖
chih

The name of a famous robber, 次跖 III. ii. 10. 3.

距
ch'ü

To resist, to keep at, or banish to, a distance, III. ii. 9. 10. 13, 14; VI. ii. 13. 8. In a name, II. ii. 4. 2, 4.

跡
chi

Foot-prints, III. i. 4. 7.

路
lù

(1) A road, a path, I. i. 3. 4; 7. 24: II. i. 5. 3; ii. 2. 3; 6. 1, 2, *et al.*, *saepe*. On the way, II. i. 13. 1. As a verb, . . . 而路, and run about on the roads, III. i 4. 6. 當路 = to obtain the management of the government, II. i. 1. 1. (2) 子路, a disciple of Confucius, II. i. 1. 3; 8. 1, *et al.*

踐
chien

(1) To tread upon. 踐 = to fulfil, satisfy the design of, VII. i. 38. 1. 踐位, to occupy the throne, V. i. 5. 7. (2) 句踐 the name of a famous prince of Yüeh, I. ii. 3. 1, and of an adventurer of Mencius's time, VII. i. 9. 1.

踰
yü

To cross over; to leap over, I. ii. 15. 1: III. ii. 3. 6; 7. 2: IV. ii. 27. 3: VI. ii. 1. 8. To overstep, to exceed, I. ii. 7. 3; 16. 1, 2.

踵
chung

(1) The heel, VII. i. 26. 2. (2) To come to, III. i. 4. 1.

踽
ch'ü

踽踽, the appearance of walking alone, i.e. of acting peculiarly; unsociable, VII. ii. 37. 8.

蹄
t'i

The foot-prints of animals, III. i. 4. 7.

蹈
t'ao

蹈 = to dance, 足之蹈之, IV. i. 27. 2.

蹊
hsi

蹊間, foot-paths, VII. ii. 21. 1.

蹙
ts'ih

Urged, embarrassed, I. ii. 1. 6: V. i. 4. 1.

蹝
hsi

A shoe or sandal of straw, VII. i. 35. 6.

蹠
chih

I.q. 跖, VII. i. 25. 2, 3.

蹴 *tsü*
To tread on. 蹴爾 (adverb) = having trampled on, VI. ii. 10. 6.

就 *tsü*
Followed by 然 = uneasy-like, II. i. 1. 3. The uneasiness would be indicated by some motions of the feet.

蹶 *chüeh*
(1) To stumble, II. i. 2. 10. (2) To overturn, IV. i. 1. 10. In the tonal notes on this latter passage, we are told to read the character *kwei*; but in the dictionary the meaning, 'to overturn,' is given under the other pronunciation.

躍 *yüo*
To leap, I. i. 2. 3 ; VII. i. 41. 3. To make to leap, VI. i. 2. 3.

THE 158TH RADICAL, 身.

身 *shin*
(1) The body, VI. i. 10. 8 ; 14. 1 ; ii. 15. 2. (2) One's person, one's self, I. i. 1. 4 ; 5. 1 ; ii. 15. 2 ; 16. 1 : III. i. 2. 3 ; 4. 6 ; ii. 9. 5 ; 10. 4, *et al.*, *saepissime*. 修身, to cultivate one's person ; 反身, self-examination ; and 守身, to keep one's self ; e.g. IV. i. 12. 1 ; 19. 1, 2 : VII. i. 1. 3 ; 4 ; 9. 6. 身之 = to acquire by effort, be virtuous by endeavour, VII. i. 30. 1. (3) 終身, all the life. See 終.

軀 *ch'ü*
The body, VII. ii. 29. 1.

THE 159TH RADICAL, 車.

車 *chü or ch'ü*
A carriage, I. ii. 1. 6, 7 : III. ii. 4. 1 : VII. i. 36. 2 ; ii. 4. 5 (革車, 'chariots of war') ; 34. 2. Read *ch'ê*, with nearly the same meaning. A waggon-load, VI. i. 18. 1.

軌 *kwei*
Wheel-ruts, VII. ii. 22. 3.

軍 *chün*
(1) A host, 三軍, the armies of a great State, II. i. 2. 5 : VI. ii. 4. 5, 6. (2) 將軍, a general, a commander-in-chief, VI. ii. 8. 1.

軔 *zin*
I.q. 仞. Eight cubits, VII. i. 29.

軻 *k'o*
The name of Mencius, I. ii. 16. 2 : V. ii. 2. 1 : VI. ii. 4. 4.

較 *chüao*
To struggle. 獵較, V. ii. 4. 5, 6. But the meaning is not well understood.

載 *tsai*
(1) To carry with one in the same carriage, III. ii. 8. 1, 4. (2) To begin, III. ii. 5. : V. i. 7. 9. (3) A particle, = 則, IV. i. 9. 6. (4) To serve, perform duties to, V. i. 4. 4. (5) 載書, to write articles of agreement, and place them on the victim of the covenant, VI. ii. 7. 3.

載 *tsai*
The 3rd tone. A year, V. i. 4. 1 ; 5. 7.

輔 *fü*
To support, to aid, I. i. 7. 19 : II. i. 1. 8 (輔相) ; ii. 2. 6 ; 6. 1 (*N.B.*) : III. i. 4. 8 : VI. ii. 9. 2.

輕 *ch'ing*
(1) Light, I. i. 7. 13 : III. i. 4. 17 : VI. ii. 1. 7. 輕 = small, VII. ii. 32. 3. 輕 = least important, VII. ii. 14. 輕 = light clothing, I. i. 7. 16. 輕 = readily, easily, I. i. 7. 21. (2) As a verb. To consider small, VII. ii. 13. 7. To lighten, III. ii. 8. 1 : VI. ii. 10. 7. To make light of, to slight, III. ii. 4. 3. 輕身, to undervalue one's self, I. ii. 16. 1.

輝 *hui*
Bright. 光輝, brightly displayed, VII. ii. 25. 6.

輪 *lun*
(1) The wheel of a carriage, VI. ii. 24. 2. (2) A wheelwright. 輪輿, carriage-wrights, III. ii. 4. 3, 4 : VII. ii. 5. 1.

輸 *shü*
公輸, a double surname, IV. i. 1. 1.

輿 *yü*
(1) Properly, the bottom or frame of a carriage or waggon. A carriage ; a waggon-load, I. i. 7. 10 ; ii. 16. 1 : VI. ii. 1. 6. (2) A carriage-wright ; see 輪.

轉 *chüan*
(1) To turn over. In the phrase 轉於 (or 乎) 溝壑, I. ii. 12. 2 : II. ii. 4. 2 : III. i. 3. 7. (2) 轉附, the name of a place, I. ii. 4. 4.

THE 160TH RADICAL, 辛.

辛 *hsin*
A name, III. i. 4. 2.

辜 *kü*
A transgression. 不辜, innocent, II. i. 2. 24.

僻 *p'i*
(1) I.q. 僻. Depraved ; moral deflection, I. i. 7. 20 : III. i. 3. 3. (2) I.q. 闢. To open up, to bring under cultivation, I. i. 7. 16 : II. i. 1. 10 : IV. i. 1. 9 ; 14. 3 : VI. ii. 7. 2 ; 9. 1. (3) To remove from the way, IV. ii. 2. 4. (4) A name, III. i. 5. 1.

辟 *pi*
To twist, III. ii. 10. 4. The pronunciation and meaning are taken from the tonal notes and Chû Hsî. The dictionary does not give them.

辟 *pi*
I.q. 避. To avoid, III. ii. 7. 2 ; 10. 5 : IV. i. 13. 1 : VI. i. 10. 2, 3, 4 : VII. i. 22. 1.

辟 *p'i*
I.q. 譬. 辟若, may be compared to, VI. i. 20.

辨 *pien*
To discriminate, VI. i. 10. 7.

辭 *ts'ü*
(1) Language, words, II. i. 2. 17 : III. ii. 9. 10, 13. 辭 = a sentence, V. i. 4. 2. 以辭, in express words, V. ii. 4. 3. The

遊 *yú*
To wander; to travel, associate with, I. ii. 6. 1: IV. ii. 36. 1: VII. i. 9. 1; 16. An imperial tour, I. ii. 4. 5. 遊=to be a student of, VII. i. 24.

運 *yün*
To make to go round, = accomplish easily, I. i. 7. 12: II. i. 1. 8; 6. 2. To go round, make a revolution, I. ii. 10. 4.

過 *kwo*
The 3rd tone. (1) To go beyond; to exceed; more than, I. i. 7. 12: II. i. 1. 10; 2. 2; ii. 13. 4: III. ii. 10. 1: IV. ii. 18. 3: ? VI. i. 2. 3: VII. i. 11. (2) To err; faults, transgressions, II. i. 8. 1; ii. 9. 3, 4: III. ii. 1. 5: IV. i. 1. 4: V. i. 6. 5; ii. 9. 1, 4: III. ii. 3. 4; 11. 2, 4; 15. 3.

過 *kwo*
The 1st tone. To pass by, I. i. 7. 4: III. i. 1. 1; 4. 7; 5. 4: IV. ii. 25. 1; 29. 1: V. i. 8. 3: VII. i. 13. 3; ii. 38. 7.

遏 *o*
To stop, to restrict, I. ii. 8. 6: V. i. 4. 1: VI. ii. 7. 3.

達 *tá*
(1) To reach to, II. i. 1. 10; ii. 7. 2: III. i. 2. 2; 5. 4: V. ii. 2. 4: VII. i. 24. 3. To carry out, to extend, VII. i. 15. 3; 40. 3; ii. 31. (2) To obtain advancement; to be in office, IV. ii. 33. 2: VII. i. 9. 4, 5, 6; 19. 3. To find vent, I. i. 6. 7. (3) To be intelligent, VII. i. 18. 2. (4) Universally acknowledged, II. ii. 2. 6.

道 *tào*
(1) A road, a path, I. i. 3. 4; 7. 24: III. i. 4. 7: IV. i. 8. 5: V. i. 9. 11: VI. i. 8. 2: VII. i. 41. 3. It occurs everywhere with a moral application, meaning the way or course to be pursued, the path of reason, of principle, of truth, &c. E.g. I. ii. 3. 1: II. i. 2, 3, 14; 4. 3; ii. 1. 4; 2. 4, 6, 7; 14. 1. (2) Doctrines, principles, teachings. Also *passim*. E.g. III. i. 4. 3, 12, 14, 18; ii. 1. 5; 2 3; 4. 4; 9. 5, 7, 9, 10.—This usage and the preceding run into each other. The *principles* underlie the *course*, and the *course* follows from the *principles*. (3) To speak about, discourse, I. i. 7. 2: III. i. 1. 2; 4. 3: VI. ii. 3. 2.

違 *wéi*
(1) To oppose, go contrary to, I. i. 3. 3: III. ii. 2. 2. (2) To avoid, escape from, II. i. 4. 5: IV. i. 8. 5. To escape notice, II. i. 2. 27. (3) To be distant from, VI. i. 8. 2.

遠 *yüan*
To be distant; distant, far, II. i. 2. 2, 26; ii. 3. 3: III. i. 4. 1; ii. 9. 4, *et al.* To keep at a distance, V. i. 7. 7. 遠臣 ministers from a distance, V. i. 8. 4. To consider far, I. i. 1. 2: VI. i. 12. 1.

遠 *yüan*
The 4th tone. To put away to a distance; to keep away from, I. i. 7. 8: III. ii. 9. 6.

適 *shih*
(1) To go to, I. ii. 4. 5: III. i. 4. 17: VI. ii. 7. 2. (2) Only, merely, VI. i. 14. 6.

適 *chih*
Lq. 讁 To blame, remonstrate with, IV. i. 20. 1.

遭 *tsáo*
To meet with, V. i. 8. 3.

遲 *ch'íh*
遲遲, slowly, by-and-by, V. ii. 1. 4: VII. ii. 17.

遵 *tsun*
To follow, IV. i. 1. 4. To follow the line or course of, I. ii. 4. 4: VII. i. 35. 6.

遷 *ch'ien*
To remove, I. ii. 11. 3. To remove to, III. i. 4. 15: IV. ii. 1. 1 (followed by 於) To transfer to, V. i. 1. 3. Applied morally; —to move towards, V. i. 6. 5: VII. i. 18. 2.

選 *hsüan*
To choose. 選擇, III. i. 3. 13.

遺 *wéi*
It is also pronounced í. (1) To neglect, I. i. 1. 5: VII. ii. 7. 2. To be neglected, 遺佚, II. i. 9. 2: V. ii. 1. 3. (2) To be left; remaining, II. i. 1. 8: V. i. 4. 2.

遺 *wéi*
The 4th tone. To make a present, to present, III. ii. 5. 2.

避 *pí*
To withdraw from, V. i. 5. 7; 6. 1. To avoid, escape from, I. ii. 10. 4.

邇 *r*
What is near; the near, IV. ii. 20. 4.

THE 163RD RADICAL. 邑.

邑 *yí*
A city or town, III. ii. 5. 5. To build a town, I. ii. 15. 1.

邠 *pin*
The name of the ancient seat of the family of Châu, I. ii. 14. 2; 15. 1.

邦 *pang*
A State, a country, III. i. 8. 12. Observe 家邦, I. i. 7. 12.

邪 *hsieh*
(1) Corrupt, depraved; what is not correct, perversity, I. i. 2. 20: II. i. 2. 17: III. i. 8. 3; ii. 9. 5, 7, 9, 10, 13: IV. i. 1. 13: VII. ii. 10. 1; 37. 13. (2) Read yâ. 琅邪, the name of a place, I. ii. 4. 4.

郊 *chiâo*
The borders of a country; to be situated in the borders, I. ii. 2. 3; 4. 10: VI. i. 8. 1.

郭 *kwo*
(1) An outer wall of fortification. 郭, see 城. 郭 alone, IV. ii. 33. 1. (2) 東郭 = a double surname, II. ii. 2. 2.

郢 *ying*
畢郢, the name of a place, IV. ii. 1. 2.

郵 *yú*
A post-station. 置郵, II. i. 1. 12.

都 *tú*
(1) A capital, but used for any principal city, II. ii. 4. 4. (2) 都君, a name given to Shun, V. i. 2. 3. (3) 于都, the designation of an ancient officer, distinguished for his beauty, VI. i. 7. 7. (4) 公都, a double surname, belonging to a disciple of Mencius, II. ii. 5. 4: III. ii. 9. 1, *et al.*

P p 2

鄒
tséu

The name of the State of which Mencius was a native, I. i. 7. 17; ii. 12. 1 : III. i. 2. 2, 4 : VI. ii. 1. 4; I. i, 2, 6. 鄒人, I. i. 7. 17. 鄒君, VI. ii. 2. 6.

鄉
hsiang

A village, a neighbourhood. III. i. 3. 18: IV. ii. 29. 7, *et al.* 鄉人, a villager, II. i. 9. 1 : IV. ii. 28. 7 : V. ii. 1. 1, 3. *et al.* 鄉黨, II. i. 6. 3; ii. 2. 6, *et al.* 鄉原, your good people of the villages, VII. ii. 37. 12. 鄉 = place, VI. i. 8. 4—In this last instance ought we not to read the character in the 4th tone?

鄉
hsiang

The 4th tone. I. q 嚮 (1) Towards; to be directed to, VI. ii. 9. 1, 2. 2) Formerly, in the former case, VI. i. 10. 8.

鄙
p'i

Mean, niggardly. 鄙夫, V. ii. 1. 3: VII. ii. 15.

鄭
chàng

The name of a State, IV. ii. 2. 1 : V. i. 2. 4 : VII. ii. 37. 12. 鄭人, IV. ii. 21. 2.

鄰
lin

A neighbour, III. i. 5. 3; ii. 8. 2. Neighbouring, III. ii. 5. 2. 鄰國, I. i. 3. 1, 2; ii. 3. 1 : II. i. 6. 6 : VI. ii. 11. 3. A neighbourhood, 鄰鄰, IV. ii. 29. 7. It is also written 隣.

THE 164TH RADICAL, 酉.

酌
cho

To pour out wine into the cup, VI. i. 5. 3.

配
p'ei

To agree, be in harmony, with, II. i. 4. 6 : IV. i. 4. 3. To be the mate of, II. i. 2. 14.

酒
chíu

Wine, spirits, I. ii. 4. 7 : III. ii. 5. 2 : IV. i. 8. 4 (強酒); 19. 3, *et al.*

醉
tsúi

To be drunk, IV. i. 3. 4. To be filled, exhilarated, VI. i. 17. 3.

醜
ch'óu

Fellows. 醜 = of equal extent, II. ii. 2. 9.

醫
A physician, II. ii. 2. 3.

釁
hsin

To consecrate by smearing with blood, I. i. 7. 4.

THE 165TH RADICAL, 釆.

采
ts'ái

(1) 采色, variegated colours, I. i. 7. 16. (2) To gather. Observe 采薪之憂, II. ii. 2. 3.

THE 166TH RADICAL, 里.

里
li

(1) A neighbourhood ; a hamlet, II. i. 5. 5 ; 7. 2. (2) In the phrase 田里, 里 = a residence, IV. ii. 3. 3, 4 : VII. i. 22.

3. (3) A measure of length. At present it is a little more than one-third of an English mile. 方里 is a square *li*, III. i. 3. 19 ; but square *lis* are often meant, where the 方 is omitted, I. i. 3. 2 ; 5. 1, 2 ; 7. 17; II. ii. 1, 2, 3 ; 11. 1, *et al.*, *saepe.* (4) 百里, a double surname, V. i. 9. 1, 2 : VI. ii. 6. 4 ; 15. 1.

重
chúng

Heavy, I. i. 7. 13 : III. i. 4. 17 : VI. ii. 1. 6. Applied metaphorically ;—heavy consequences, VII. ii. 7. Heavy charge, V. i. 7. 6 ; ii. 1. 2. Great, important : precious, I. ii. 11. 3, 4 : VI. ii. 1. 1, 2, 6, 7 : VII. ii. 32. 3. As a verb,—to make heavy, VI. ii. 10. 7.

野
yé

Wild country, wilds; the country as opposed to the town, the fields, I. i. 4. 4; 7. 18 : II. i. 5. 4 : III. ii. 9. 9 : IV. i. 14. 2 : V. i. 7. 2 ; ii. 7. 1 : VII. ii. 23. 2. 田野, IV. i. 1. 9 : VI. ii. 7. 2. 野人, countrymen, men rude and uncultivated, III. i. 3. 14, 19 : V. i. 4. 1 : VII. i. 16. 1.

量
liang

To measure, II. i. 2. 5.

釐
li

In a name, VI. ii. 8. 4.

THE 167TH RADICAL, 金.

金
chin

Metal, metallic, V. ii. 1. 6. In VI. ii. 1. 6 金 = gold. In IV. ii. 24. 2 金 = steel. In II. ii. 3. 1 I have translated by silver, but many contend that *gold* is meant.

釜
fù

An iron boiler, without feet, III. i. 4. 4.

鈞
chün

(1) A weight of thirty catties, I. i. 7. 10 : VI. ii. 2. 3. (2) I. q. 均, all equally, VI. i. 15. 1, 2.

鉤
káu

A hook or clasp, VI. ii. 1. 6. In the text it is printed 釣, which, though used, is not correct.

銳
rúi

Vigorously, with precipitation, VII. i. 44. 2.

鍾
chúng

The name of a measure, containing sixty-four *kún* (斗), or nearly seven hundredweight according to present measures, II. ii. 10. 3 : III. ii. 10. 5 : VI. i. 10. 7.—See a note on the Life of Mencius.

鎡
tsze

鎡基, a hoe, II. i. 1. 9.

鏑
i

A name, V. ii. 2. 1.

鎰
yi

A weight, variously estimated at twenty, twenty-four, and thirty *taels*, or Chinese ounces, I. ii. 9. 2 : II. ii. 3. 1.

鐘 *chung* — A bell, I. i. 7. 4 ; ii. 1. 6, 7.

鐵 *t'ieh* — Iron. 鐵 = an iron share, III. i. 4. 4.

鑒 *chien* — 鑒 = a mirror ; or a beacon, IV. i. 2. 5. It is more commonly written 鑑.

鑠 *shúo* — To melt. 鑠 = to infuse, VI. i. 6. 7.

鑽 *tsuan* — To bore, III. ii. 3. 6.

鑿 *tso* — To chisel, or bore. 鑿 = to dig, I. ii. 13. 2. Used metaphorically, IV. ii. 26. 2.

THE 168TH RADICAL, 長.

長 *ch'ang* — 2nd tone. (1) Long ; length, I. i. 7. 13 : III. i. 1. 5 ; 4. 17. Tall, VI. ii. 2. 2. (2) To excel, II. i. 2. 11. (3) A surname, V. i. 2 ; ii. 3. 3.

長 *chang* — 3rd tone. (1) To be grown up, age ; old ; elders, III. i. 4. 8 ; ii. 6. 2 : IV. i. 11. 1 : V. ii. 3. 1 : VI. i. 4. 2, 3, 4 ; ii. 2. 1 : VII. i. 15. 2, 3 ; 43. 2. Eldest, I. i. 5. 1. 長於 older than, VI. i. 5. 3. As a verb, to give the honour due to age, IV. i. 11 : VI. i. 4. 2, 3, 4. 長者 an elder, I. i. 7. 3. It is twice used by Mencius for himself, II. ii. 11. 4 : IV. i. 24. 2. (2) To grow, II. i. 2. 16 : VI. i. 8. 3. Well grown, superior, V. ii. 5. 4. (3) To preside over, II. ii. 2. 6. Superiors, officers, I. i. 7. 11 ; ii. 12. 1, 3. (4) To make long. 長 = to connive at and aid, VI. ii. 7. 4.

THE 169TH RADICAL, 門.

門 *mǎn* — A door ; a gate, III. i. 4. 1, 7 ; ii. 2. 2 ; 7. 2, 3, et al., *saepe.* 門戶, VI. ii. 14. 4. 門 = school, VI. ii. 2. 6 : VII. i. 24. 1 : 43. 1. 門人, disciples, III. i. 4. 13 : VII. ii. 29. 1.

閉 *pi* — To shut, III. ii. 7. 2 : IV. ii. 29. 7 : V. ii. 7. 8. To repress, IV. i. 1. 13.

閔 *min* — (1) To be grieved, II. i. 2. 16. (2) Appears in a quotation from the Shū-ching for 暋 violent, reckless, V. ii. 4. 4. (3) The surname of one of Confucius's disciples, II. i. 2. 18, 20.

閑 *hsien* — 閑 = to defend, III. ii. 9. 10.

閒 *hsien* — 閒暇, to be at leisure, II. i. 4. 2, 4.

閒 *hsien* — A space, an interval, II. ii. 13. 3 : IV. ii. 7. 1 : VII. ii. 21. ... 之閒, the space between, I. i. 6. 6 : III. ii. 6. 1 : IV. i. 18. 4 ; ii. 18. 3 : VII. i. 25. 3. So 於(or 于) ... 之閒, II. i. 2. 13 : VI. ii. 15. 1 :

VII. i. 18. Among, IV. ii. 33. 1. 為閒, in a little, III. i. 5. 5 : VII. ii. 21. But in some editions, 閒 in these two instances is put in the third tone. The K'ang-hsi dictionary simply says that 閒 is the vulgar form of 間:

閒 *chien* — 3rd tone. (1) To occupy the space between, I. ii. 13. 1. (2) To blame, IV. i. 20. (3) 一 閒, one interval, VII. ii. 7. (4) 得閒, to find an opportunity, VI. ii. 5. 2 — It is more correct to write 閒, and not 間.

閹 *yen* — 閹然 eunuch-like, VII. ii. 37. 8.

關 *kwan* — A frontier gate ; a pass, I. ii. 2. 3 ; 5. 3 : II. i. 5. 3 : III. ii. 8. 1 : V. ii. 5. 3 ; 6. 3 : VII. ii. 8. 1. To bend a bow, VI. ii. 3. 2.

THE 170TH RADICAL, 阜.

阨 *i* — Straits ; to be in circumstances of distress, V. i. 8. 3. 阨窮, II. i. 9. 2 : V. ii. 1. 3.

阱 *ching* — A pit-fall, I. ii. 2. 3.

防 *fang* — A raised dyke, an embankment, VI. ii. 7. 3.

阻 *chu* — An obstruction, a difficult pass. 險阻, III. ii. 9. 4.

阿 *o* — To flatter, II. i. 2. 25.

附 *fu* — (1) To be attached to. 附庸, the name of certain small principalities, V. ii. 2. 4. To join one's self to, III. ii. 5. 5. To add to, VII. i. 11. (2) 轉附, the name of a place, I. ii. 4. 4.

陋 *láu* — Mean and low, IV. ii. 29. 2.

降 *chiang* — (1) To send down, to confer,—spoken of Heaven, VI. i. 7. 1 ; ii. 15. 2. To produce, I. ii. 3. 7. (2) To descend, come down, I. ii. 11. 2 : III. ii. 5. 4.

陰 *yin* — (1) To be dark and cloudy, II. i. 4. 3. (2) 陰 = the north side, V. i. 6. 1.

陵 *ling* — (1) A high mound, a height, 丘陵 III. ii. 1. 5 : IV. i. 1. 6. (2) 於陵, the name of a place, III. ii. 10. 1, 5, 6.

陳 *ch'ǐn* — (1) To set forth, II. ii. 2. 4 : IV. i. 1. 13. (2) A surname, II. ii. 3. 1 ; 10. 4 : VI. ii. 14. 1 : VII. ii. 23. 1.—III. ii. 1. 1.—II. ii. 9. 2.—III. ii. 10. 1, 2, 3, 5, 6 : VII. i. 34. 1.—III. ii. 4. 2, 3. 12. (3) The name of a State, VII. ii. 18 ; 37. 1 : V. i. 8. 3.

陳
ch'in

The marshalling of an army, VII. ii. 4. 1.

陶
t'áo

(1) To make pottery, II. i. 8. 4 : VI. ii. 10. 3, 6. A potter, III. i. 4. 5. (2) 鬱陶, anxiously, V. i. 2. 3.

陶
yáo

皋陶, a minister of Shun, III. i. 4. 9 : VII. i. 35. 1 ; ii. 38. 1.

陷
hsien

To fall into a pit. 陷 = to be involved, to be sunk, I. i. 7. 20 : II. i. 2. 17 : III. i. 3. 3 : IV. i. 9. 5. Used actively,—陷溺, I. i. 6. 5 : VI. i. 7. 1.

陸
lü

平陸, the name of a place, II. ii. 4. 1 : VI. ii. 5. 1, 2, 6.

陽
yang

(1) The sun, III. i. 4. 13. (2) A surname, III. i. 3. 5 ; ii. 7. 3. (3) 南陽, the name of a place, VI. ii. 8. 3.

隅
yü

A corner, III. ii. 9. 6.

階
chieh

Steps, or stairs, leading up to a hall, IV. ii. 27. 3. A ladder, V. i. 2. 3.

隕
yün

To fall down ; to let fall, VII. ii. 19. 3.

隘
ai

Narrow-minded, II. i. 9. 3.

隙
chi

A crevice, 穴隙, III. ii. 3. 6.

際
chi

交際 and 體際 gifts of princes to secure friendship, or procure intercourse, V. ii. 4. 1, 5. 際可, a proper reception, V. ii. 4. 7.

險
hsien

Difficult and dangerous positions, II. ii. 1. 4 : III. ii. 9. 4.

隱
yün

(1) To conceal, II. i. 9. 2 : V. ii. 1. 3. (2) To be pained by, sympathize with, I. i. 7. 7. 惻隱之心, the feeling of commiseration, II. i. 6. 3, 4, 5 : VI. i. 6. 7. (3) To lean upon, II. ii. 11. 2. In this meaning, it ought to be read in the 3rd tone.

THE 172ND RADICAL, 隹.

集
chi

To collect ; to be collected, II. i. 2. 15 : IV. ii. 18. 3. Altogether, I. i. 7. 17. 集大成, a complete concert, V. ii. 1. 6.

雉
chih

Pheasants. 雉者 pheasant-catchers, I. ii. 2. 2.

雖
sui

Though. *Passim*. Sometimes, especially when no verb is expressed, we may translate conveniently by *even*, *even in the case of*. E.g. II. i. 2. 7 ; 4. 2 : III. i. 3. 9.

雛
ch'u

A chicken. But —— 匹雛 is understood of a duckling, VI. i. 2. 3.

雞
chi

Fowls, I. i. 3. 4 ; 7. 24 : III. ii. 8. 2 : VI. i. 11. 3 : VII. i. 22. 2 (母雞, 'brood hens'). 雞鳴, cocks crow, II. i. 1. 10 ; but 雞 = at cock-crowing, VII. i. 25. 1, 2.

離
li

(1) To be separated, I. i. 5. 4 ; ii. 1. 6 : VII. ii. 27. 1. 離 = to be alienated, IV. i. 18. 4. (2) To leave, forsake, II. ii. 2. 17 : VII. i. 9. 4, 5. (3) A surname, IV. i. 1. 1.

離
li

To go away from, III. ii. 4. 5. But the character may be read in the same tone as above.

難
nan

To be difficult ; to find it difficult ; what is difficult, II. i. 1. 8 ; 2. 2, 12 : III. i. 4. 10 ; ii. 3. 6 : IV. i. 1. 13 ; 6 ; 11 : V. i. 2. 4 : VI. ii. 2. 7 : VII. i. 24. 1.

難
nan

The 4th tone. To dispute, IV. ii. 28. 6.

THE 173RD RADICAL, 雨.

雨
yü

Rain, I. i. 6. 6 ; ii. 11. 2 : II. i. 4. 3 : III. ii. 5. 4 : IV. i. 18. 3 : VI. i. 7. 2 ; 8. 1 : VII. i. 40. 2.

雨
yü

The 4th tone. To rain upon, III. i. 8. 9.

雪
hsüeh

(1) Snow, VI. i. 3. 2. (2) 雪宮, the name of a palace, I. ii. 4. 1.

雲
yün

(1) Clouds, I. i. 6. 6 ; ii. 11. 2. (2) 雲漢, 'The Milky Way,' the name of an ode in the Shih-ching, V. i. 4. 2.

霓
i

A rainbow, I. ii. 11. 2.

霄
hsiao

A name, III. ii. 3. 1.

露
lu

Dew. 雨露, VI. i. 7. 2 ; 8. 1.

霸
pa

To become chief and arbiter among the princes, II. i. 3. 1 : VI. ii. 6. 4. To raise to become such, II. i. 1. 5 ; 2. 1 : III. ii. 1. 1. 霸者, such a chief, VII. i. 13. 1. 五霸, VI. ii. 7. 1, 2, 3 : VII. i. 30. 1.

靈
ling

(1) 靈丘, the name of a place, II. ii. 5. 1. (2) 靈臺 靈沼 靈囿, the names of king Wăn's tower, pond, and park, I. i. 2. 3. The 靈 may be variously translated. (3) An honorary epithet, V. ii. 4. 7.

THE 175TH RADICAL, 非.

非
fei

Passim. (1) No ; not ; not to be. Very often it = it is not, it is not that ; if not, if there be not. E.g. I. i. 3. 5 ; 7. 7, 10, 11 ; ii. 1. 2 ; 7. 1 ; 13. 2 ; 14. 2 ; 15. 2 ; 16. 2 : II. i. 2. 15, 16, 22 ; ii. 2. 4. 莫非 非不 無非 are all strong affirma-

tions. E.g. I. ii. 4. 5: II. i. 1. 8; 8. 4:
VI. ii. 8. 6: VII. i. 2. 1. (2) To be contrary to; what is contrary to. E.g. IV.
ii. 6. 1; 28. 7: V. i. 2. 4. (3) To be wrong;
what is wrong. E.g I. ii. 4. 2: II. i. 3. 1:
IV. i. 20. (4) To blame; to disown, I. ii.
4. 1, 2: III. i. 4. 14: IV. i. 1. 12; 10. 1:
VII. ii. 37. 11. 是非之心, II. i. 6.
5: VI. i. 6. 7. Observe II. i. 2. 22: V. ii.
1. 2; and VII. ii. 37. 11.

靡
mi

Not, IV. i. 7. 5: V. i. 4. 2.

THE 176TH RADICAL, 面.

面
mien

The face, II. i. 12. 6: III. i. 2. 4; 5. 4,
et al. 面諛之人, sycophants, VI.
ii. 13. 8. 南面, on, or towards, the
south, I. ii. 11. 2: III. ii. 6. 1: VII. ii.
3. So 東面; but 南面, in V. i. 4.
1, is the face to the south, the position of
a sovereign giving audience. 北面,
V. i. 4. 1; ii. 6. 4, is the position of a
minister.

THE 177TH RADICAL, 革.

革
ko

Skins freed from the hair, but not
tanned. Still it is used as = leather.
革車, chariots of war, VII. ii. 4. 4.
The buff-coat, helmet, and other armour
of defence, 兵革 II. ii. 1. 3, 4.

THE 178TH RADICAL, 韋.

韓
han

The name of a powerful family in Tsin,
VII. i. 11.

THE 180TH RADICAL, 音.

音
yin

A note in music. 五音, IV. i. 1. 1, 5.
The sound or notes of musical instruments, I. ii. 1. 6, 7. 八音, V. i. 4. 1.
聲音,—spoken of instruments and
the voice, I. i. 7. 16: VI. ii. 13. 8.

THE 181ST RADICAL, 頁.

頂
ting

The top of the head, VII. i. 26. 2.

順
shun

(1) To obey; to accord with; obedience;
agreeably to reason, submissively, II. ii.
1. 4, 5: III. ii. 2. 2: IV. i. 7. 1; 16: VI.
i. 1. 2: VII. i. 2. 1; 31. 1. To persist in,
II. ii. 9. 4. Observe IV. i. 28. 1, and V.
i. 1. 3, 4. (2) A name, V. ii. 3. 3.

須
hsü

斯須, a brief season, VI. i. 5. 4.

頌
sung

(1) Interchanged with 誦. To repeat,
croon over, V. ii. 8. 2. (2) 魯頌, the
name of a Book of the Shih-ching, III. i.
4. 16.

頒
pan

頒白者, gray-haired people, I. i.
3. 4; 7. 24. See the dictionary on the
usage.

頑
wan

Obstinate. It seems, however, to be
used in the sense of *corrupt*, V. ii. 1. 1:
VII. ii. 15.

領
ling

The neck, I. ii. 6. 6.

頞
o

The root of the nose. 蹙頞 = to knit
the brows, I. ii. 1. 6.

頮
p'an

Used for 盼. 頮顏 means to turn
up the nose, and generally to look dissatisfied, III. ii. 10. 5.

頗
ri

榱題, the ornamental wood-work
under the eaves of public buildings, VII.
ii. 34. 2.

願
yüan

To wish, desire, I. i. 4. 1; 5. 1; 7. 19:
II. i. 1. 4; 2. 22; 5. 1, 2, 3, 4, 5; ii. 7. 1;
10. 2: III. i. 4. 1, 2; 5. 1: ii. 3. 6: VI. i.
17. 3; ii. 2. 6; 4. 4.

顏
yen

(1) 顏色, the countenance, III. i.
2. 5: VI. ii. 13. 8. (2) A surname, II. i.
2. 18, 20: III. i. 1. 4: IV. ii. 29. 2, 3, 5.
—V. i. 8. 2.—V. ii. 3. 3.

顙
sang

The forehead, III. i. 5. 4: VI. i. 2. 3.

顛
tien

顛覆, to overturn, V. i. 6. 5.

類
lei

A class, sort; kinds, I. i. 7. 11: II. i. 2.
28: III. ii. 3. 6; 10. 6: V. ii. 4. 5: VI. i.
7. 3, 5; 12. 2: VII. ii. 31. 4.

顣
tsü

I.q. 蹙. 顣顩, see 頞.

顧
ku

To look round, I. i. 2. 1; ii. 6. 3: IV.
ii. 33. 1. To regard, think of, have reference to, IV. ii. 30. 2: V. i. 7. 2: VII. ii.
37. 9.

顯
hsien

To be distinguished, III. ii. 9. 6: IV. ii.
33. 1. To make illustrious, II. i. 1. 5: V.
i. 9. 3.

THE 182ND RADICAL, 風.

風
fêng

(1) The wind, III. i. 2. 4. To expose
one's self to the wind, II. ii. 2. 1. (2)
Manners; character,—with the idea of
influence implied, II. i. 1. 8: V. ii. 1. 1, 3:
VII. i. 15. (3) 凱風, the name of an
ode in the Shih-ching, VI. ii. 3. 3, 4.

THE 183RD RADICAL, 飛.

飛
fei

(1) To fly. 飛鳥, birds, II. i. 28.
(2) 飛廉, a supporter of the tyrant
Châu, III. ii. 9. 6.

THE 184TH RADICAL, 食.

食
shih

(1) To eat; to consume, devour; to be
consumed, I. i. 3. 3, 4, 5; 4. 4, 5; 7. 8, 24,
et passim. 以爲食, to be a living,

III. i. 4. 1. 食 not unfrequently has this meaning, = to get a living, to support life. (2) Viands, food to eat, III. ii. 4. 4, 5 ; 9. 5 : V. ii. 4. 6 (N.B.): VII. ii. 34. 2. (3) An eclipse, II. ii. 9. 4.

食
tsze
(1) Rice cooked; food generally, I. i. 3. 5 ; ii. 10. 4 ; 11. 3, *et al.* (2) To feed, to support; 食於 . . ., to be supported by, III. i. 4. 6; ii. 4. 4, *et al., saepe.* To feed cattle, V. i. 9. 1, 3.

飢
chi
Interchanged with 饑. To be hungry, to suffer from hunger, I. i. 3. 4 ; 4. 4, 6 ; 7. 24 ; ii. 4. 6, *et al., saepe.*

飦
chien
A kind of thick congee. 飦粥, III. i. 2. 2.

飧
sun
The evening meal. 饔飧, III. i. 4. 3 : VI. ii. 10. 4. In the first instance the characters have a verbal force.

飲
yin
To drink; drink, I. ii. 4. 6 : II. i. 1. 11: III. ii. 10. 3, *et al., saepe.*

飯
fan
To eat, VII. ii. 6. 放飯, to eat immoderately, VII. i. 46. 2.

飽
pao
To eat to the full, to be filled; to the full, I. i. 7. 21 : III. i. 4. 8 : V. ii. 3. 4 : VII. i. 22. 3. ? Actively, VI. i. 17. 3.

餂
tien
To gain some end with, VII. ii. 31. 4. In the dictionary it is explained by 'to take with a hook,' = to beguile.

餉
hsiang
To carry provisions to the labourers in the fields; provision-carriers, III. ii. 5. 2.

養
yang
To nourish,—spoken generally of persons, the body, the mind, &c. *Passim.* To keep cattle, V. i. 9. 1. Nurture, VII. i. 36. 1.

養
yang
The 4th tone. To support,—used with reference to the support of parents, scholars, and superiors generally, I. i. 5. 4 : III. i. 3. 7, 14, 19 ; 4. 3 (?), *et al., saepe.*

餐
ts'an
To swallow, to eat and drink. 素餐 to eat the bread of idleness, VII. i. 32. 1.

餒
nei
To be famished, II. i. 2. 14, 15. 凍餒, I. ii. 5. 1 (used actively): VII. i. 22. 3.

餓
o
To be hungry, to suffer from hunger, VI. ii. 14. 4. 饑餓, I. ii. 5. 4. 餓莩 (or 殍), I. i. 3. 5 ; 4. 4 : III. ii. 9. 9. To expose to hunger, VI. ii. 15. 2.

餔
pu
To eat. 餔啜, IV. i. 25.

餘
yü
That which is over; a remnant, the remains, IV. i. 19. 3; ii. 33. 1 : V. i. 4. 2. Supernumerary, III. i. 8. 17. 有餘, to have enough and to spare; and more, II. ii. 5. 2; 13. 4 : III. ii. 4. 3 : VI. ii. 2. 7 : VII. ii. 38. 1, 2, 3, 4.

館
kwan
A lodging-house, IV. i. 24. 2 : VI. ii. 2. 6 ; VII. ii. 30. 1. To lodge (active); to be lodged, IV. i. 24. 2 : VII. ii. 30. 1.

餱
hou
Dried provisions, I. ii. 5. 4.

餽
kwei
To present or send as a gift, II. ii. 3. 1 3. 4, 5 : V. ii. 4. 4 ; 6. 2, 4.

饋
k'wei
To offer as a gift, i. q. 餽, III. ii. 5. 2 7. 3 ; 10. 5 : V. i. 2. 4.

饑
chi
To suffer from famine ;—interchange also with 飢, I. ii. 12. 2 : II. ii. 4. 2 : VI i. 22. 2 (飢); ii. 23. 1.

饔
yung
The morning meal. 饔飧, see 飧

饗
hsiang
Generally, to entertain. But = to l entertained by, V. ii. 3. 5.

饜
yen
To get satiated, to partake plentiful of, IV. ii. 33. 1. To be satisfied, I. i. 1.

THE 185TH RADICAL, 首.

首
shau
The head, I. ii. 1. 6 : III. ii. 5. 7 : V. 6. 4, 5 : VII. ii. 4. 5.

THE 187TH RADICAL, 馬.

馬
ma
(1) A horse, horses, I. i. 4. 4 ; ii. 1. 7 ; 5. 5 ; 15. 1. 犬馬畜, to nouris as a dog or a horse, V. ii. 6. 4. (2) 司馬 the master of the horse, but used as a so of surname, V. i. 8. 3.

馮
fang
(1) A surname, VII. ii. 23. 2. (2) 嘗 馮, the name of a place, IV. ii. 1. 1.

馳
ch'i
To gallop. 馳馬 = horsemanshi III. i. 2. 4. 馳驅, III. ii. 1. 4.

駟
sze
A team of four horses, V. i. 7. 2.

駕
chia
The yoking of a carriage, I. ii. 16. 1 : ii. 2. 5 : V. ii. 7. 9.

駒
chü
A name, VI. ii. 6. 5.

驅
ch'ü
(1) To drive away, III. ii. 9. 4, 6, (2) To urge, I. i. 7. 21 : VII. ii. 1. 2. To urge on a horse, 馳驅, III. ii. 1. 驅騁, VII. ii. 34. 2.

驕
chiao
To carry one's self proudly to, IV. 33. 1.

驩
huan
(1) I. q. 歡. 驩虞如, cheerfu like, VII. i. 13. 1. (2) 驩兜, a crimina banished by Shun, V. i. 3. 2. (3) A name II. ii. 6. 1 : IV. ii. 27. 2.

騁
ch'ang
To gallop. 驅騁, see 驅.

THE 188TH RADICAL, 骨.

骨
kú

The bones, VI. ii. 15. 2.

體
t'i

The body, I. i. 7. 16; II. i. 2. 9: IV. i. 19. 3: VII. i. 36. 1. 四體, the four limbs, II. i. 6. 6: IV. i. 3. 3: VII. i. 21. 4. 大體, 小體, VI. i. 14. 2; 15. 1, 2. 一體, one member; 具體, all the members, II. i. 2. 20.

THE 189TH RADICAL, 高.

高
kāo

(1) High, lofty, II. ii. 1. 3: IV. i. 1. 6, 7; ii. 26. 3: V. ii. 5. 5: VI. ii. 1. 5: VII. i. 41. 1; ii. 34. 2. (2) A surname, II. ii. 12. 2: VII. ii. 21; 22.—VI. ii. 3. 1, 2. (3) A name, V. i. 1. 2. (4) 高唐, the name of a place, VI. ii. 6. 5.

THE 190TH RADICAL, 髟.

髡
'uān

More correctly written 髮. A name, IV. i. 17. 1: VI. ii. 6. 1, 5.

髮
fā

The hair, IV. i. 29. 6, 7.

THE 191ST RADICAL, 鬥.

鬨
hung

To fight, to have a brush, I. ii. 12. 1.

鬩
t'âu

To quarrel, IV. ii. 29. 5, 6. 鬩狼, IV. ii. 30. 2.

THE 192ND RADICAL, 鬯.

鬱
yü

鬱陶, anxiously, V. i. 2. 3.

THE 193RD RADICAL, 鬲.

鬲
m

膠鬲, a distinguished minister at the close of the Yin dynasty, II. i. 1. 8: VI. ii. 15. 1.

鬻
yü

(1) To sell, V. i. 9. 1, 3. (2) 獯鬻, the name of a barbarous tribe, I. ii. 3. 1.

THE 194TH RADICAL, 鬼.

魏
wei

The name of a great family in Tsin, VII. i. 11.

THE 195TH RADICAL, 魚.

魚
yü

A fish, fish, I. i. 2. 3; 3. 3; 7. 16, 17: IV. i. 9. 3: V. i. 2. 4; VI. i. 10. 1; ii. 15. 1.

魯
lü

(1) The name of a State, I. ii. 12. 1; 16. 1, 3, et al., sæpe. 魯人, V. ii. 4. 5. 魯繆公, VI. ii. 6. 3, et al. 繆公 occurs in three other places, but without

the 魯. 魯平公, I. ii. 16. 1. (2) 魯頌, the name of a Book in the Shih-ching, III. i. 4. 16.

鯀
kwǎn

The father of the great Yü, V. i. 3. 2.

鰥
kwan

A widower, I. ii. 5. 3.

THE 196TH RADICAL, 鳥.

鳥
niǎo

Birds, I. i. 2. 3, 4: II. i. 2. 28: III. i 4. 7; ii. 9. 4.

鳳
fông

鳳凰, a sort of Chinese phœnix, II. i. 2. 28.

鳴
ming

(1) The sound of a bird. 雞鳴, see 雞. To beat, cause to sound, IV. i. 14. 1. (2) 鳴條, the name of a place, IV. ii. 1. 1.

鴃
chüeh

The shrike or butcher-bird, III. i. 4. 14.

鴈
yen

A wild goose, I. i. 2. 1.

鴻
hung

Large. Joined with 鴈 and 鵠, I. i. 2. 1: VI. i. 9. 3.

鵝
o

A goose, III. ii. 10. 5.

鵠
hú

The swan, VI. i. 9. 3.

鵙
pí

The cackling of a goose. 鵙鵙者, III. ii. 10. 5.

鶴
ho

鶴鶴 = glistening, I. i. 2. 3.

鸇
chan

A kind of hawk, IV. i. 9. 3.

THE 197TH RADICAL, 鹵.

鹹
yen

Salt, VI. ii. 15. 1.

THE 198TH RADICAL, 鹿.

鹿
lü

The deer, I. i. 2. 1, 3; ii. 2. 3: VII. i. 16.

麀
yü

The female deer, a doe. 麀鹿, I. i. 2. 3.

麋
mi

A species of deer, distinguished for its size and strength, and that sheds its horns in winter, 麋鹿, I. i. 2. 1; ii. 2. 3.

麒
ch'i

The male of the Ch'i-lin, a fabulous animal, the chief of all quadrupeds, II. i. 2. 2, 8.

麗
li

Number, IV. i. 7. 5.

麟
lin

The female of the Ch'i-lin. See 麒

THE 199th RADICAL, 麥.

麥
mái

Wheat; all bearded grain. 麰麥, see 麰

麰
máu

麰麥, barley, VI. i. 7. 2.

THE 200th RADICAL, 麻.

麻
má

Hemp, II. i. 4. 17.

THE 201st RADICAL, 黃.

黃
hwang

Yellow, III. ii. 19. 3.   黃 = yellow silks, III. ii. 5. 5.

THE 202nd RADICAL, 黍.

黍
shú

Millet, III. ii. 5. 2: VI. ii. 10. 4.

黎
li

Black. 黎民, the black-haired people, V. i. 4. 2.

THE 203rd RADICAL, 黑.

黝
yú
黨
tang

A name, II. i. 2. 4, 6.

(1) Properly, a village of 500 families. 鄉黨, a neighbourhood; neighbours, II. i. 6. 3; ii. 2. 6: V. i. 9. 3. (2) A party, a school. VII. ii. 37. 1.

THE 205th RADICAL, 黽.

黿
tcú
鼈
pieh

A name, II. ii. 5. 1, 2, 3.

The turtle, I. i. 2. 3; 3. 3.

THE 206th RADICAL, 鼎.

鼎
ting

A tripod, a boiler with three feet and two ears, I. ii. 16. 2. 鼎肉, flesh from the pot, V. ii. 6. 4, 5.

THE 207th RADICAL, 鼓.

鼓
kú

(1) A drum, I. i. 8. 2; ii. 1. 6, 7: IV. i. 14. 1. (2) To strike, to play on, VII. ii. 6. In this sense the character should have 攴, and not 支, on the right.

THE 209th RADICAL, 鼻.

鼻
pi

The nose, IV. ii. 25. 1: VII. ii. 24. 1.

THE 210th RADICAL, 齊.

齊
ch'i

(1) On a level, equal, II. ii. 2. 9: III. 4. 18: VI. i. 7. 2. To adjust evenly, V. ii. 1. 5. (2) The name of a State, I. i. 1; 7. 6, 17, et al., saepe. 齊人, I. ii. 1; 14. 1, et al. 齊王, VII. i. 36. 1. 齊 宣王, I. i. 7. 1, et al., saepe. 齊 公, I. ii. 4. 4, 10, et al. 齊桓, I. i. 1, 2: IV. ii. 21. 3.

齊
chái

To adjust one's thoughts,—in connexion with fasting, II. ii. 11. 3: IV. 25. 2. 齊栗, the appearance of aspect and dread, V. i. 4. 4.

齊
tzze

The lower edge of a mourning garment not hemmed, but even and not frayed III. i. 2. 2.

THE 211th RADICAL, 齒.

齒
ch'ih
齕
kih

(1) The front teeth. 齒 = with teeth, VII. i. 46. 2. (2) Age, II. ii. 2. A name, I. i. 7. 4.

THE 212th RADICAL, 龍.

龍
lung
龍
lung

(1) The dragon, III. ii. 9. 3, 4. (2) surname, III. i. 8. 7: VI. i. 7. 4.

The 3rd tone, used for 壟, a mound 龍斷, II. ii. 10. 6, 7.

NOTE.

According to the calculation of Châo Ch'i, the Seven Books of Mencius contain in all 261 ipteis and 34,685 characters. Tsâo Hsün, a scholar of the present dynasty, gives, as the result a careful reckoning, 258 chapters and 35,226 characters. (See 焦孝廉孟子正義, Châo Ch'i's Introduction.)

If there be no omissions in the above Index, the different characters used by Mencius unting a character for each variation of tone) amount to 2,022, or thereabouts.

In the Analects, the Great Learning, and the Doctrine of the Mean, there are 1,648 different racters.

Altogether the different characters in the Four Books amount to about 2,500, certainly not 500.

END OF VOL. II.

Made in the USA
Las Vegas, NV
03 August 2023

75589927R00350